W0036142

PRINCIPLES OF MANAGEMENT

Competencies, Processes, and Practices

SECOND EDITION

Anil Bhat

Professor and Head
Department of Management
BITS, Pilani

Arya Kumar

Dean – Alumni Relations and
Professor – Economics and Finance
BITS Pilani

OXFORD
UNIVERSITY PRESS

OXFORD
UNIVERSITY PRESS

Oxford University Press is a department of the University of Oxford.
It furthers the University's objective of excellence in research, scholarship,
and education by publishing worldwide. Oxford is a registered trade mark of
Oxford University Press in the UK and in certain other countries.

Published in India by
Oxford University Press
22 Workspace, 2nd Floor, 1/22 Asaf Ali Road, New Delhi 110 002

© Oxford University Press 2008, 2016

The moral rights of the author/s have been asserted.

First Edition published in 2008
Second Edition published in 2016
Fourth impression 2023

All rights reserved. No part of this publication may be reproduced, stored in
a retrieval system, or transmitted, in any form or by any means, without the
prior permission in writing of Oxford University Press, or as expressly permitted
by law, by licence, or under terms agreed with the appropriate reprographics
rights organization. Enquiries concerning reproduction outside the scope of the
above should be sent to the Rights Department, Oxford University Press, at the
address above.

You must not circulate this work in any other form
and you must impose this same condition on any acquirer.

ISBN-13: 978-0-19-945758-8
ISBN-10: 0-19-945758-1

Typeset in Baskerville
by Ideal Publishing Solutions, Delhi
Printed in India by Nutech Print Services India

For product information and current price, please visit www.india.oup.com

Third-party website addresses mentioned in this book are provided
by Oxford University Press in good faith and for information only.
Oxford University Press disclaims any responsibility for the material contained therein.

Dedicated to
all those management thinkers, teachers, learners, and practitioners
who make a difference to the way organizations
create value for the society at large

Features of

5

Management Control Systems

INTRODUCTION

After taking steps to plan and organize, to achieve the desired goals, an organization needs to put in place a control mechanism to ensure success with a greater degree of certainty. Therefore, apart from planning, organizing, and leading, the fourth key function of management is controlling, which is most crucial. This function ensures that due mechanism has been put in place to monitor the progress vis-à-vis predetermined milestones and take necessary corrective measures for deviations, if any.

Learning Objectives

After studying this chapter, you will be able to:
- Understand the importance of control as a management function
- Understand how control is an essential function for achieving goals
- Learn about important features and characteristics of controlling
- Understand about steps involved

Learning Objectives Each chapter begins with learning objectives that focus learning and the knowledge you should acquire by the end of the chapter.

Coca-Cola

Coca-Cola's operations in India have come under intense scrutiny as many communities are experiencing extreme water shortage, and contamination in the groundwater and soil as a result of its bottling plant operations. It has also been alleged that due to the amount of water required to produce Coca-Cola, ground water is drying up, forcing farmers to relocate. A public movement is emerging to hold the company accountable for wrong actions. The state of Kerala had imposed a ban on its products and the matter is pending in the Supreme Court. One of the largest Coca-Cola plants located in Plachimada has remained shut for 17 months because the village council refused that the water used to produce Coke may contain unhealthy pesticides and other chemicals beyond permissible limits. In 2003, the Centre for Science and Environment (CSE), a non-governmental organization in New Delhi, claimed that aerated waters produced by soft drink manufacturers in India, including multinational giants PepsiCo and Coca-Cola, contains toxins including lindane, DDT, etc., that can cause cancer and a breakdown of the immune system. The CSE found that PepsiCo's Indian-produced soft drink products had 36 times and Coca-Cola's 30 times the level of pesticide residues permitted under European Union regulations.

Exhibits The chapters contain exhibits that help in understanding the application of the theory discussed in the chapter.

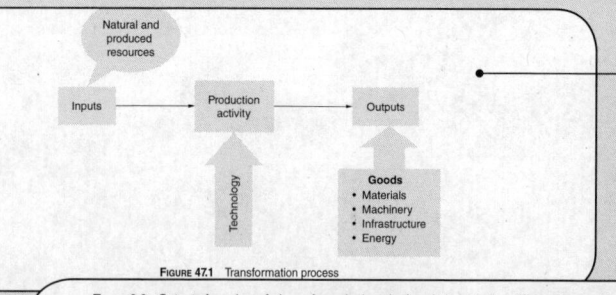

FIGURE 47.1 Transformation process

Figures and Tables All chapters contain figures and tables to illustrate the topics discussed in the chapter.

TABLE 9.2 Output of number of pieces for a single unit of capital employing different levels of labour per day

Capital	Number of labourers	Capital labour ratio	Total product (TP_L) number of job pieces	Average product of labour (AP_L)	Marginal product of labour (MP_L)	Production stages
1	1	1	5	5.00	5	
1	2	1:2	14	7.00	9	Stage I
1	3	1:3	27	9.00	13	
1	4	1:4	36	9.00	9	
1	5	1:5	41	8.20	5	Stage II
1	6	1:6	45	7.50	4	
1	7	1:7	47	6.71	2	

the Book

Summary The summary at the end of each chapter draws together the main concepts discussed within the chapter. This will help you reflect and evaluate important concepts.

SUMMARY

A market is any suitable arrangement in which the buyers and sellers could closely interact (physically or otherwise) to arrive at exchange decisions. Markets are classified broadly depending upon the importance of an individual firm in relation to the entire market and whether products placed in the market are homogenous or not.

Pure competition is a market model in which there are a large number of firms having homogenous or standardized product. They can enter or exit easily and have perfect knowledge about the markets. Pure monopoly exists when a single firm is the sole producer of a product for which there are no close substitutes. In an oligopoly market situation, there are a few sellers and the decision of one affects the other because of their small size. In a pure oligopoly market, firms produce homogeneous products, whereas in a differentiated oligopoly market, firms produce and sell differentiated products. Monopolistic competition is a market situation in which there are many sellers of a particular product that are differentiated in some way or the other. In this market, firms may enjoy economic profits, that is, over and above normal profits. However, in case of free entry (as in pure competition), economic profits will be zero in the long run.

A clear understanding of the market in which a firm operates helps in taking objective decisions to optimize the firm's objectives such as maximization of profit, maximization of output at least cost, and minimization of cost of production for a given level of output. The strategies of pricing and output that need to be adopted vary with market conditions.

KEYWORDS

Differentiated oligopoly An oligopoly market situation wherein firms produce and sell differentiated products.

Economic profit Profits over and above normal profit, that is, revenue less the opportunity cost of inputs.

Market Any suitable arrangement in which the buyers and sellers can closely interact to arrive at exchange decisions.

Market price A price where demand and supply curve intersect with each other indicating a match between what consumers and sellers are willing to do.

Market structure It refers to the relationship between buyers and sellers and the special features of a market that affect the demand and supply forces.

Monopolistic competition A market situation having many sellers of a particular product that are differentiated in some way or the other.

Normal profit Profits that are sufficient to sustain and induce a seller in the industry.

Oligopoly A market situation having few sellers and having interdependency as the decision of one affects the other because of their small size.

Price discrimination The act of charging different prices to different buyers for the same product.

Pure competition A market model in which there are a large number of firms having a homogenous product. These firms can enter or exit easily and have perfect knowledge about the markets.

Pure monopoly It exists when a single firm is the sole producer of a product for which there are no close substitutes.

Pure oligopoly In an oligopoly market situation firms produce homogeneous products.

Keywords All technical terms have been explained at the end of each chapter as keywords. This will help you retain all the new terms that you have learnt in the chapter.

Exercises A series of concept review questions, critical thinking exercises as well as project assignments highlight the major topics covered in the chapter. The questions enhance learning and can be used for review and classroom discussion.

EXERCISES

Concept Review Questions

1. How does economic activity at national or global level affect a business entity?
2. Define macroeconomics. What are the variables with which macroeconomics deals with?
3. Define gross domestic product (GDP). What are the two approaches by which GDP is measured? What precautions need to be used while measuring GDP?
4. Define investment. Differentiate between gross investment and net investment. In what way does investment contribute to growth in GDP?
5. Define the relationship between gross national product (GNP), net national product (NNP), national income, and disposable income.
6. In what way does inflation affect the working of a business entity?

Critical Thinking Question

Economic growth directly affects business prospects. Comment critically.

Project Assignments

1. The service sector in the Indian economy is growing at an accelerated rate. Collect data on the share of primary, secondary, and service sectors in the total GDP for the last five years. Interpret it and estimate which sector is going to have bright prospects in the coming years and why?
2. Indian economy has been gaining a lot by export earnings through the software industry. What are the strengths of the Indian IT industry? Collect details of foreign exchange earnings by the export of IT products during the last 10 years. Analyse the same to comment on the future prospects of IT industry in India.

Companion Online Resources

Visit india.oup.com/orcs/9780199457588 to access both teaching and learning solutions online.

Online Resources

The following resources are available to support the faculty using this text:

For Faculty

- PowerPoint Slides
- Multiple Choice Questions

For Students

- Flashcard Glossary

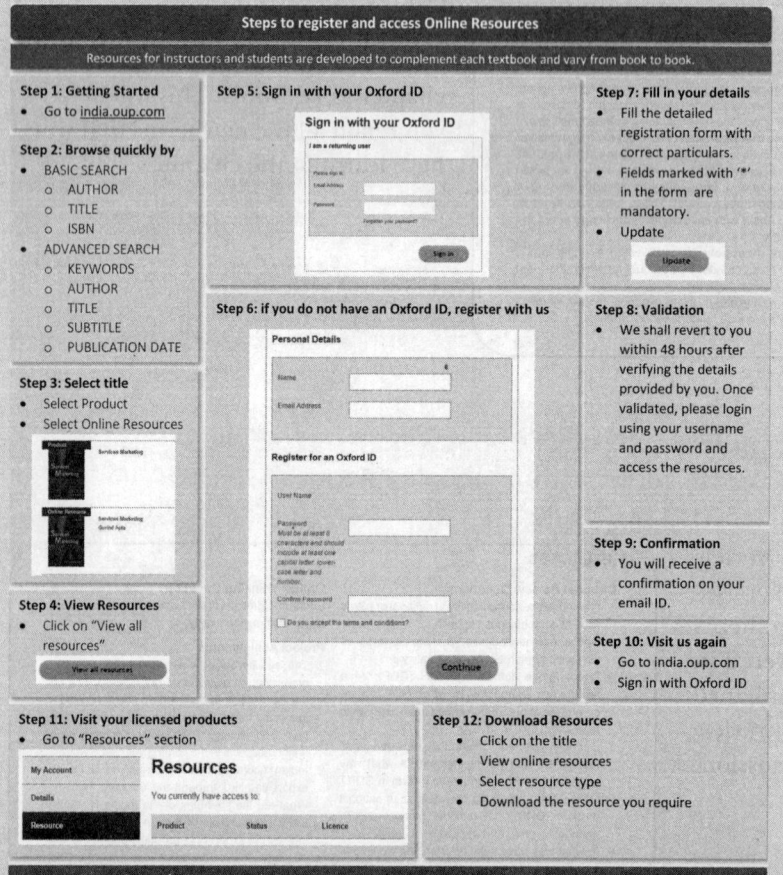

Steps to register and access Online Resources

Resources for instructors and students are developed to complement each textbook and vary from book to book.

Step 1: Getting Started
- Go to india.oup.com

Step 2: Browse quickly by
- BASIC SEARCH
  - AUTHOR
  - TITLE
  - ISBN
- ADVANCED SEARCH
  - KEYWORDS
  - AUTHOR
  - TITLE
  - SUBTITLE
  - PUBLICATION DATE

Step 3: Select title
- Select Product
- Select Online Resources

Step 4: View Resources
- Click on "View all resources"

Step 5: Sign in with your Oxford ID

Step 6: if you do not have an Oxford ID, register with us

Step 7: Fill in your details
- Fill the detailed registration form with correct particulars.
- Fields marked with '*' in the form are mandatory.
- Update

Step 8: Validation
- We shall revert to you within 48 hours after verifying the details provided by you. Once validated, please login using your username and password and access the resources.

Step 9: Confirmation
- You will receive a confirmation on your email ID.

Step 10: Visit us again
- Go to india.oup.com
- Sign in with Oxford ID

Step 11: Visit your licensed products
- Go to "Resources" section

Step 12: Download Resources
- Click on the title
- View online resources
- Select resource type
- Download the resource you require

For any further queries, please write to us at HEMarketing.in@oup.com with your mobile number.

Preface to the Second Edition

There are many authors who have contributed books that deal with 'principles' of management. Our motivation to write *Principles of Management: Competencies, Processes, and Practices* was to use an approach that emphasized the importance of both managerial and organizational functions in business. The book continues to provide a lucid coverage of the important aspects of management such as planning, organizing, leading, and controlling as well as organizational functions, such as finance, marketing, operations management, management information systems, strategy, and human resources.

The second edition of the book has been updated and enriched with five new chapters. Part I now includes a new chapter on Management Control Systems; Part II has a new chapter on Security Analysis and Portfolio Management; Part IV has a chapter on Organizational Change and Development; and Part VII includes two new chapters on Online Social Media and Project Management, respectively. We have made an effort to keep the same approachable style of writing in these new chapters that characterized writing of the first edition of the book. We hope this edition will help the readers develop critical and evidence-based perspective about various principles, processes, and practices of management.

We received encouraging feedback from students and instructors who appreciated our efforts and confided in us that they consulted this book in their 'hour of need'. The book was also accepted well by engineering students who were interested in having an overview of management.

Key Features

- Describes several managerial and economic analytical tools
- Provides chapter-end exercises to facilitate experiential learning, information gathering, and analysis
- Provides caselets and examples to explain the concepts
- Includes detailed sections on managerial competencies with separate chapters on motivation, team effectiveness, communication, conflict management, leadership, decision-making, emotional intelligence, stress management, and creativity and entrepreneurship
- Contains critical thinking questions to enable students to apply concepts to real-life situations and sharpen their learning

Online Resource Centre

For Instructors

- PowerPoint Slides
- Multiple Choice Questions for Assessment

For Students

- Flashcard Glossary

Coverage and Structure

The first section on *Management Functions and Business Environment* distills management thought from various schools of management and discusses management functions in the context of business environment and society. The concept of planning and controlling as tools for effective management and organizational effectiveness is also elaborated in this section.

The second section focuses on *Economic and Financial Analysis.* These two sections set the tone for the rest of the chapters. The chapters in the second section cover business and economic fundamentals, principles of production, markets, national income accounting, goals and functions of finance, financial statements, financial ratio analysis, and security analysis and portfolio management. The third section, *Excelling through People,* includes chapters on human resource management, job design, recruitment and selection, and training and development.

In the fourth section *Managerial Competencies,* topics such as motivation, team effectiveness, communication, conflict management, leadership, decision-making, emotional intelligence, stress management, and creativity and entrepreneurship have been discussed. This new edition includes a new chapter on organizational change and development.

The fifth section on *Creating and Delivering Customer Value* deals with the marketing function. It starts with a chapter on marketing research and goes on to describe marketing planning, designing marketing-mix, customer relationship management (CRM), advertising management, and brand management.

The sixth section *Quantitative Methods* covers various quantitative tools such as statistical inference, forecasting and time series analysis, regression analysis, index numbers, and statistical quality control.

The seventh section *Operations and Technology Management* is covered through chapters on production and operations management, supply chain management, Kaizen, Six Sigma, Japanese 5S practice, total quality management and technology management, information systems, and international management. This section now includes two new, topical, and therefore, important chapters on social media and project management.

Given our experience in both academic and corporate world, we have emphasized a perspective that balances theory with practice. It is, therefore, hoped that the book will provide students with an inspirational approach to understand and appreciate the basic principles of management while sufficiently exposing them to the actual practices and processes.

We appreciate feedback from instructors and students in order to improvise the contents and structure of the book further. We gratefully acknowledge the constant help and suggestions that our family members, colleagues and students, and publisher Oxford University Press (OUP) provided during the course of getting this book to its second edition.

Every effort has been made to determine and contact copyright holders. In case of any omissions, the publisher will be pleased to make suitable acknowledgment in future editions.

ANIL BHAT
ARYA KUMAR

Preface to the First Edition

Management deals with getting things done for, with, and through people. It is an applied discipline and is practised like medicine, engineering, law, etc. Management is both an art as well as a science. It is the art of making people more effective than they would have been without a manager. Dealing with people is far from easy; nevertheless, it is the management's responsibility to achieve and maintain an organization's effectiveness. We have to remember that management, like any other skill, can be improved with proper understanding and practice.

Although the term 'management' originated sometime in the sixteenth century, as per the *Oxford English Dictionary*, it is only since the last two centuries that the discipline of management has been progressively enriched by insights of practitioners, engineers, philosophers, and academicians. The recent proliferation of management literature, self-help books, educational courses, and the iconic status of some business leaders in public consciousness indicates the current popularity of this discipline.

For most students, a postgraduate degree in management has become an aspiration after graduation. It is estimated that both in India as well as in the United States the number of annually graduating MBA students is in hundreds of thousands. This is not just a reflection of a passing infatuation with management, but the ground reality that modern societies cannot do without organizations and modern organizations cannot do without effective and efficient management.

The first management education programme was started at Harvard in 1908 and was followed by one at Massachusetts Institute of Technology (MIT) in 1925. These pioneering institutes used different pedagogies predominantly consisting of case methodology and quantitative analysis respectively. The American Assembly of Collegiate Schools of Business (AACSB) and the European Foundation for Management Development (EFMD) conducted a comprehensive review of management education and published a report titled *Managers for the XXI Century*. This report advocated the need for a more integrated management education incorporating a number of functional, quantitative, non-quantitative, and analytical fields including humanities and sciences. As per Mintzberg (2004), a foremost thought leader of management education, synthesis and not analysis is the essence of management.

Most of the popular textbooks on management essentials have been using an approach that emphasized managerial functions without relating these to organizational functions in sufficient detail. The combination of managerial, organizational, and interpersonal skills is extremely essential for a manager. It is our firm belief that the first course on management should not only excite students towards this discipline, the practice of which is going to play such an important role in their career, but it should also make them reflect and internalize certain skills and competencies by relating the concepts and techniques to their contemporary environment. Also, the first course should act both as a guide map for other core courses in a management programme, or even if it is to be a stand-alone course in an engineering programme, it should provide sufficient coverage to different functional areas of management.

The All India Council for Technical Education's (AICTE) management education review committee in the year 2003 suggested that there was a need to emphasize context specificity in the management curriculum in India. Thus, keeping in view the AICTE's recommendations and the various aspects of management education discussed earlier, we have designed the textbook to break new ground by doing away with the singular approach that characterized many popular textbooks on the first course on management. We think as the textbook gives equal importance to rigour and relevance, it will meet the exacting requirements of management teachers and will be useful to practising managers as well.

About the Book

The structure, content, and the multi-perspective approach of *Management—Principles, Processes, and Practices* makes it distinctly unique. The content is balanced with a due focus on concepts and theory, and tools and applications. The contents are subordinated to the purpose of the book, which is to balance the treatment of the subject between its breadth and depth. An integrated approach that is comprehensive and jargon free has been adopted in the book.

The book discusses managerial functions, such as planning, organizing, leading, and controlling as well as organizational functions, such as finance, marketing, operations management, MIS, strategy, and human resources in detail. The whole exposition is divided into seven sections as under:

- Management functions and business environment
- Economic and financial analysis
- Excelling through people
- Managerial competencies
- Creating and delivering customer value
- Quantitative methods
- Operations and technology management

Such a classification will help students to integrate and assimilate various areas as they relate to each other. Even a student undergoing a single, short-term course on management will be able to learn and appreciate various aspects of managerial functions in different organizational areas. The book has a section dealing with managerial competencies that includes chapters on motivation, team effectiveness, communication, conflict management, leadership, decision making, emotional intelligence, stress management, and creativity and entrepreneurship.

The coverage of different management theories includes not only contemporary approaches, such as TQM, learning organization, and chaos theory, but also Indian and Japanese management approaches. The first section titled 'Management Functions and Business Environment' is written with a view to give students an excellent exposition of managerial functions in the context of an organization's internal environment as well as the external business environment. It focuses on the generic nature of managerial functions and the universal appeal of management as a discipline. This section has chapters on planning and organizational effectiveness as well because of their added importance.

Pedagogical Features

The various pedagogical features of the text are:

- Learning objectives before each chapter highlight major learning insights.
- End-chapter exercises such as critical review questions will enable the students to reflect on various issues.

- Special care has been taken to streamline the flow of the content.
- Caselets and examples provided in the chapters have an Indian context to make the subject matter interesting and relevant.
- Each chapter has a project assignment for the student that will facilitate experiential learning, information gathering, and analysis.
- The book gives a description of many managerial and economic analytical tools.
- The key terms introduced in a chapter are provided after the summary section of each chapter.
- References are provided in each chapter for an advanced learner.

Given our experience in both the academic as well as corporate world, we have emphasized a perspective that balances theory with practice. It is, therefore, hoped that the book will provide students with a refreshing approach to the basic principles of management while sufficiently exposing them to the actual practices and processes.

Acknowledgements

It is not possible to acknowledge by name all the individuals who have contributed to this book directly or indirectly. Our foremost debt goes to writings of eminent management thinkers, and, in particular, to Henri Fayol, Peter Drucker, and Sumantra Ghosal whose approach towards management has been a source of inspiration and guidance in this endeavour.

We are grateful to the Birla Institute of Technology and Science (BITS), Pilani where a culture of excellence and intellectual freedom breeds a spirit of enquiry. Our colleagues have been a source of many memorable interactions on different aspects of management. One of the unique features of BITS programmes of studies is that all students across the institute, irrespective of their disciplines, have to take a course titled 'Principles of Management'. The administration of this course as a multi-section second year course for around 800 students is itself an exercise in management. We are thankful for being given an opportunity to teach this course and have enjoyed many insightful interactions with students both inside and outside the class.

Our interactions with fellow academicians reinforced our belief about the need for adopting a holistic approach in management teaching that has both rigour and relevance for which we are immensely grateful. We would also like to put on record our appreciation for the passion and commitment of academically inclined and entrepreneurially accomplished BITS alumni who spent countless hours in sharing with us many complexities of the business world. Many of the insights in the book about management practice are a result of these interactions.

Our involvement with the Center for Entrepreneurial Leadership (CEL) at BITS, Pilani and with National Entrepreneurship Network (NEN), founded by Wadhawani Foundation, gave us an opportunity to experience first-hand challenges and problems faced by start-up companies. This motivated us to reflect deeper into the complexity of management issues as well as relevance of management principles for their effectiveness and organizational growth. We would like to thank both CEL and NEN team members.

The entire editorial team from Oxford University Press deserves our thanks for their professionalism and for bearing with our constantly overshooting deadlines. We also owe our gratitude to the anonymous peer reviewers whose valuable feedback enabled us to improve the text. We would gratefully acknowledge any suggestions regarding the contents, presentation of the text, or any mistakes that might have crept in.

We would like to express our special indebtedness to respected Mr Shambhu Dassji for cheerfully ensuring that our thoughts get expressed in a clear and unambiguous language. We thank him for his contribution in the first editing of the text, which was done by him as a special labour of love. Whatever ambiguity may have remained is solely due to us. His suggestions have enabled us to bring in qualitative improvement in the whole text. The first author also wishes to convey his gratitude to his guru, late Pt J.N. Fotedar, for his immense *gurukripa*.

We would like to thank our parents—Mrs Sheila Fotedar Bhat and Dr J.N. Bhat, and Mrs Dhanwanti Devi and Mr Shambhu Dass respectively—for inculcating and nurturing the spirit of enquiry in us and teaching us the importance of values in life. Our special thanks to our spouses and children for their encouragement and support. We also extend our gratitude to our brothers and sisters, and their families for their support.

ANIL BHAT

ARYA KUMAR

Brief Contents

Detailed Contents

Part II   Economic and Financial Analysis

Part III   Excelling through People

Part IV   Managerial Competencies

Part VII   Operations and Technology Management

Part I
Management Functions and Business Environment

Part 1

1

Essentials of Management

INTRODUCTION

Modern human is an organization's person. He expects organizations to fulfil his needs, provide employment, and even looks towards them for personal fulfilment, status, and achievement. The socio-economic landscape of modern societies is dominated by various types of organizations—both business enterprises and non-profit institutions. Herbert Simon (1991), the famous Nobel laureate, once questioned the use of the term 'market economy' and suggested that ubiquity of organizations demanded that term to be more appropriately replaced by 'organizational economy'. Ghoshal and Moran (2005) gave an empirical support for the positive association between prosperity of an economy and the role of companies operating in that economy by plotting the number of *Fortune 500* companies per 100 million working population and gross domestic product (GDP) per capita for different countries. According to him, companies are able to engender resource combination and exchange, that is, *value creation* in a manner that markets alone cannot. In addition, companies have some distinct advantage over markets in terms of their capacity for creating value through sharing, transferring, synthesizing, and creating knowledge, the most valuable of all resources.

It follows then that organizations are specific organs of our modern society whose purpose is to create value and thus enrich the quality of life of people. From this perspective, they are almost indispensable. Various kinds of organizations are engaged in delivering goods and services to billions of people around the world. They work in different sectors such as education, health, transport,

Learning Objectives

After studying this chapter, you will be able to:

- Appreciate role of organizations for quality of life in modern societies
- Comprehend the generic functions of management
- Understand what is meant by policies, procedures, methods, and strategies
- Understand different dimensions of organizational structure
- Understand the function of leading
- Understand controlling function
- Understand managerial roles and competencies

communication, and consumer goods. These organizations have become very large with a few generating revenues larger than the GDP of certain countries. In this era of globalization many of these organizations are actually transnational corporations. They have also grown very complex in terms of their tasks and processes as well as number of employees with different skills, expertise, and diverse cultural backgrounds. These conglomerates not only have varied employees, but their other stakeholders such as customers, shareholders, communities, suppliers, and strategic partners too are spread across the globe. Such a scale demands compliance with different regulatory regimes in different countries. Hence, these organizations need a greater level of coordination to attain their organizational goals in an effective and efficient manner. As the famous management guru Peter Drucker (1974) puts it, *efficiency* refers to 'doing things right' and *effectiveness* refers to 'doing the right thing'. Effectiveness is the key to an organization's success and this is achieved by setting right organizational goals. No amount of efficiency can make up for lack of effectiveness. Efficiency is concerned with getting the most output out of least input of scarce resources of the organization, whether it is capital, human resource, plant and machinery, or information resources.

ESSENCE OF MANAGEMENT

What is that process that drives an organization towards its performance? What is that specific organ of an organization that has the responsibility for delivering the results consistently? Who has the authority to plan, organize, lead, and control different organizational activities so that the organization attains it goals? And lastly, what is that discipline, that body of organized knowledge, which deals with getting things done for, with and through people? It is *management*. Unfortunately, the word management is used interchangeably for all the aforementioned purposes. Additionally, as management is an applied discipline and is practised like other disciplines such as medicine, engineering, and law, it is also a profession or a career.

The term management is of sixteenth century vintage as per the *Oxford English Dictionary*, but mankind has been using the knowledge of getting projects (wars, irrigation projects, roads and buildings, etc.) accomplished since historical times. It is only for the last two centuries that the discipline of management has been progressively enriched by insights of practitioners, engineers, philosophers, and academicians. The recent deluge of advertising in public media, proliferation of management literature, self-help books, educational courses, and pop books on management as well as iconic status of some of the business leaders in public consciousness indicates its current popularity. For most students, a post graduate degree in management has become an aspirational degree after graduation. It is estimated that both in India as well as in the United States the number of annually graduating MBA students is more than the combined strength of students who finish their engineering, medicine, and law degrees. This does not reflect just a passing infatuation with management but the ground reality that modern societies cannot do without organizations and modern organizations cannot do without effective and efficient management. It also hints at the universality of management. The next section seeks to explore and capture the generic functions of management.

What is management? What do managers do? The American Management Association defines management as 'the process of getting work done through people'. L.F. Urwick (1970) writes that knowledge about managing must break down into two categories—knowledge about work; and knowledge about employees.

He further states that knowledge about work breaks down into essentially— (1) knowledge about the tasks that individuals are asked to perform; and (2) knowledge about the relationships between the tasks that members of a group perform. Similarly, knowledge about people can be divided into—(1) knowledge about the behaviour of individuals; and (2) knowledge about the behaviour of individual persons as influenced by their membership of groups of all kinds and the degree of impact of that membership on individuals.

This categorization explains as to why management is both an art as well as a science. It is the art of making people more effective than they would have been without a manager. The science is in how a manager does this. Use of statistically validated theories and techniques already available constitutes the scientific aspect of management. However, humans are very complex and situations and contexts change. Science has not figured it all out, nor will it ever be able to. Wise managers combine the best previously developed theories or techniques with their own moment-to-moment study of the specifics of the personalities that they actually have to deal with in their management situations. That is the art aspect of management. Management, like medicine, is an applied art and its successful practice depends on applying to specific cases the knowledge derived from a whole series of underlying disciplines, ranging from operations research to psychology to cultural anthropology. As the underlying disciplines are at varying degree of sophistication in their development as sciences, management can never aspire to be completely a science. Dealing with people is far from easy. Nevertheless, it is the management's responsibility to achieve and maintain a business organization's effectiveness. However, if done successfully, it can be a very rewarding experience. We have to remember that management, like any other skill, is something that one can improve at with study and practice.

GENERIC FUNCTIONS OF MANAGEMENT

Traditionally, management includes the following generic functions—planning, organizing, leading, and controlling. These classical management functions were first stated by a French industrialist Henri Fayol (1967) at the beginning of the last century and were later elaborated by British management consultant Lyndall Urwick (1970). However, there has been a controversy about this universalistic approach, the best known critic being Henri Mintzberg (1975), a professor at McGill University, who has described the functions of Fayol and others as 'folklore' as these formulations are not supported by the evidence of research. He has proposed a role theory of managerial work as an alternative to the work of the classical writers. Mintzberg's theory was largely developed from his study of five chief executive officers and, as some researchers contend, was developed on the basis of the questionable practice of not going beyond the observable activities themselves.

Harold Koontz (1980) from University of California, whose textbook first popularized the managerial functions approach, thinks that the question of what managers do day-by-day is secondary to what will be more useful for classification of management knowledge. He states that functional approach permits us to look at the basic aspects of management, which have a high degree of universality across different contexts. Typically, managerial jobs are characterized by variety, fragmentation, and brevity, and oral communication with a wide variety of people both inside and outside the organization. Managerial work is largely cerebral and may not be directly observable. As will be clear from the matrix in Fig. 1.1, these managerial functions are differentiated from the different organizational functions or organizational areas, namely marketing, finance, operations, human resource, strategy, management information systems, etc. This matrix provides the framework of management fabric whose pigeon holes can be used to categorize managerial knowledge about managerial concepts, theories, levels, roles, tasks, activities, techniques, methodologies, skills, and competencies.

We will now discuss generic managerial functions of planning, organizing, leading, and controlling in some detail before turning our attention to the description of managerial roles as described by Mintzberg. Further, to carry out these roles productively, managers must possess certain skills, traits, and competencies. A detailed exploration of these concepts will be carried out in the later chapters.

Organization functions → Management functions ↓	Operations	Marketing	Finance	Human resources	Strategy	Management information systems (MIS)
Planning						
Organizing						
Leading						
Controlling						

FIGURE 1.1 Managerial functions' matrix

Planning

It has become a cliché that good management starts with good planning. The process of planning includes identification of organizational objectives and selection of policies, procedures, and methods designed to lead to the attainment of these objectives. Essentially it is about selecting goals and objectives and also the means of accomplishing them. A manager will never succeed without a plan. If a manager happens to make it to the goal, it will have been by luck or chance and the results will not be replicable. Such managers will never have a track record of accomplishments.

The first step in planning is setting organizational objectives. This process has been studied by both economists and management theorists in some detail in terms of a firm as a whole as well as from the perspective of groups of people interested in the performance of the firm. It stands to reason that people associate themselves with an organization to satisfy their own objectives. These groups can be categorized as internal groups comprising owners, managers, and employees and external groups comprising suppliers, customers, and the government. If only the economic objectives of the inside groups are considered, then the objectives of the owners, managers, and employees would be profits, salaries, and wages, respectively. Similarly suppliers are interested in the organization's sales revenue, customers look to the firm as a source of value-laden quality goods and services, and the government is interested in tax revenue and employment generation.

All of these groups though have to contribute to the firm in return of the benefits received from the firm. Owners contribute capital, employees their services, and suppliers raw material. Further, each of these groups may view itself competing with other groups for the economic gains generated by the firm's activities. Therefore, employees may feel that owners gain more profits at the cost of their wages or suppliers may feel that their bills are cleared after much delay though the firm may be cash-rich. Hence, one of the most important tasks of the management is to allocate resources in such a way that the competing interests of these stakeholders are properly taken care of. Otherwise, the effectiveness of the firm may be jeopardized. Apart from considering the interests of these competing stakeholders, there should be an organizational objective that would provide an overall direction for the firm's activities in the long run. Considering profit as the universal objective of organizations, though convenient, has two principal disadvantages—one that we may be confusing the primary goal of all organizations with the goals of a specific group that of owners; and the second that the profit objective cannot be readily applied to non-profit institutions. Certain management thinkers have instead focused on organizational survival and growth as the primary objective of organizations.

This perspective, that all organizations have the common objective of survival and growth, may not be applicable to a firm functioning as a sole proprietorship or partnership as the firm legally ceases to exist with the death of the owner or co-owner. Management guru Peter Drucker (1955) has suggested that every firm or organization exists to create something of economic value. This value is created from the perspective of the customer as he is the one who provides the funds used to finance the activities of the organization as well as to pay all the stakeholders. Hence, the ultimate objective of a firm may be considered as the production of goods and/or services.

Flowing from this perspective of ultimate objective of a firm, management by objectives (MBO) a management system first put forth by Peter Drucker (1974) envisages the need to create a hierarchy of compatible objectives within an organization. These objectives then identify the economic contribution of each part of the organization in measurable terms. The divisions, units, or departments of a firm do not produce completed products or services in isolation; instead, all of them contribute towards producing economic value. The philosophy of MBO requires that for several organizational levels, a hierarchy of objectives be identified and these objectives be specified in the form of measurable goals.

It should be borne in mind that the ultimate objective of an organization as an entity is the creation of economic value in the form of products and services and the MBO perspective is a structured and coordinated way of achieving the same. The MBO rests on four elements—goal specificity, participative decision-making, an explicit time period, and performance feedback. The empirical evidence available suggests that this system helps increase productivity but only in times of stability and it runs into rough weather when the environment is dynamic. In addition, if MBO is viewed as a casual annual exercise of paperwork then obviously it is not worth the effort because the spirit of this management system is missed. As personal commitment to the goals of an operating unit makes it more likely that goals of the unit will be accomplished, participation of employees in defining these goals is typically encouraged. The employees are rewarded to the extent these objectives have been objectively accomplished than on some other subjective criterion such as traits or personality types.

After the organizational objectives have been identified, planning is concerned with the appropriate policies, procedures, and methods necessary to achieve overall organizational objectives. *Policies* are general statements that serve as guidelines by which these objectives are to be attained. These may be basic or general or these may govern any specific organizational functional area such as human resource, and marketing. *Procedures* are more specific and structured as these enumerate the chronological sequence of steps to be taken in order to accomplish an objective while a *method* specifies how one step of the procedure is to be performed. For example, a broad recruitment policy may specify an annual recruitment of students from top management institutions to replenish managerial assets of a company while a recruitment procedure will specify the steps for such a process—from applying to interviewing to selection. The method of interviewing the potential management trainee may also be specified.

Decision-making is a part of the planning process and is concerned with selecting a course of action from a set of alternatives, obviously using some criterion. Some authors consider decision-making as the essence of management. Generating alternatives or courses of action is a creative and non-linear process while evaluating these alternatives is relatively straightforward, given that a criterion exists.

Environmental factors

Planning is done under the constraints of environmental factors, namely politico-legal, economic, sociocultural, and technological (PEST). A *strategy* is a plan or a specific course of action that can be taken to achieve an organization's goal in the context of competitive environment. It usually signifies a long-term plan as the allocation of resources cannot be reversed easily during short-term planning. Strategic plans provide a wider scope to retain flexibility while the operational plans are often stated in finer detail. Chandler (1962) defines strategy as the determination of the basic long-term goals and objectives of an enterprise, and the adoption of courses of action and the allocation of resources necessary for carrying out these goals. Strategic plans are distinguished whether these are made at corporate-level, business-unit level, or at functional level. Michael Porter (1980), a highly respected author and professor of corporate strategy at Harvard business school, thinks that organizations may pursue one of the three generic strategies at business level—(1) differentiation strategy that seeks to differentiate organization's goods and services from competitors; (2) leadership strategy that attempts to reduce costs of the organization below the costs of the competing firms; and (3) focus strategy that tries to concentrate the organization's focus on a specific target segment or specific market. At the corporate level integration, diversification and merger/acquisition strategies are possible for a growth oriented firm. SWOT analysis explains how through an analysis, strategies may be crafted to exploit an organization's *strengths* (internal core competencies) and avoiding *weaknesses* (internal) vis-à-vis *opportunities* and *threats* (in the environment).

In a nutshell, managers need to figure out their goals. Next, they should figure out the best way to get there. What resources does one have? What can one get? They need to compare strengths and weaknesses of individuals and other resources. Will putting five workers on a task that takes fifteen hours cost less than renting a machine that can do the same task with one worker in six hours? If the manager changes the early shift by an hour, can they handle the early evening rush and eliminate the need to hire an extra person for the second shift? All the probable scenarios should be evaluated and planned for. The worst possible scenario should also be figured out and planned for. After evaluating different plans managers should use their best judgement to select a plan that will work. One of the management planning tools, which is most often overlooked but is very effective, is employee feedback.

Organizing

The relatively abstract exercise of planning must next be translated into reality by specifying tasks and jobs, by grouping people into units or departments, by deciding where decisions will be made, and by specifying the reporting structure. This is the managerial function known as organizing. Organizing as per Koontz (1972) is about designing an intentional structure of roles for people to fill. An organizational role should incorporate major responsibility and tasks as well as necessary authority for achieving the objectives.

Like the term management, there is some ambivalence in using the term organization. A search for its definition on the Internet turns up some interesting semantic variations, namely an arrangement, a group, well-organized systems, administration, result of distributing persons, consisting of an act of forming something, and the act of organizing a business. This ambiguity has been seen to cause considerable confusion in the development of management theory as per Koontz (1961) in his now famous classic article, 'The Management Theory Jungle'. Urwick (1970) thinks that the term organization is used to mean the structure of positions or posts into which the total activities necessary to any human system of collaboration are subdivided as well as, when preceded by an article (an, or, the), it is used to mean a system of human collaboration regarded as a whole. March and Simon (1958) even refused to define the exact term organization and instead took it as an empirical phenomenon, which like many phenomena of the world defy neat categorization. Some organization theorists have defined organizations as the patterned activities of individual members. Katz and Kahn (1966) contend that these activities are the organization, for in their absence, the organization ceases to exist. This sounds like a very abstract concept of an organization.

A formal organization structure is important from the perspective of effecting a change, as changing attitudes, motives, or goals of people is relatively difficult. *Organizational structure* is the pattern of relationships that exists between various positions. A description of relationship between and among different levels in an organization is referred to as the *scalar process*. The most frequent structure is the hierarchical structure, which consists of a vertical dimension of differentiated levels of authority and responsibility and a horizontal dimension of differentiated units (termed as departmentation). An *organigram* is the pictorial representation of this hierarchy.

Departmentation   It can be defined as grouping of activities at any level. Several different bases for grouping of activities can be used. Departmentation based on numbers is useful for undifferentiated manpower but the complexity of organizations in modern times necessitates the use of specialized manpower. Hence, departmentation on the basis of function is more appropriate (whether finance, marketing, production, etc.). Departmentation can be also on the basis of product line, territory, customer type, or process depending upon the appropriateness to achieve results productively. Grouping of activities into different groups makes intra-group coordination possible, though at the expense of inter-group coordination.

Peter Drucker (1974) states that in designing the building blocks of an organization the following four questions have to be answered by the organizer:

1. What should the units of the organization be?
2. What components should join together, and what components should be kept apart?

3. What size and shape pertain to different components?

4. What is the appropriate placement and relationship of different units?

Further he states that organizing is not just assembling of activities and functions, as that would be just a mechanical exercise, which is contrary to the required attribute of that of adaptation (i.e., organic nature). While organizing, the desired results should always be kept in mind. Drucker feels that key activities and values should play a major role in the design of an organization's structure. He concurs with Chandler (1962) that strategy should determine structure and not vice-versa, and thinks that a business should always review its organization structure when its strategy changes. The management guru then gives a prescription that while designing the structure of an organization, it should be kept in mind that key activities should not be subordinated to non-key activities, revenue-producing activities should never be subordinated to non-revenue producing activities, and finally, support activities should not be mixed with revenue-producing and result-contributory activities.

Span of control   After departmentation, the concept of 'span of control' is important for understanding organizational structure. Span of control refers to the number of subordinates a manager supervises. The number of subordinates that a manager can effectively supervise is not a constant but varies as per their abilities, complexity of tasks, and the kind of interaction required. Larger span of control generally reduces the number of hierarchical levels in an organization thus, producing a flatter organization.

Line and staff relationships   Another element of organization structure is line and staff relationships. Line refers to chain of command or line of authority that extends from top to bottom of an organization. As modern organizations are complex entities, the line is augmented by advisory or staff departments. In a manufacturing concern, production, marketing, and finance are typically considered to be line activities, whereas design, purchase, or personnel are examples of staff activities. Line activities in an organization are directly concerned with attaining the goals of the organization, whereas the function of staff activities is to facilitate and help attain objectives through improved productivity of line activities.

Authority flows down the vertical hierarchy and is not actually vested in people but in organizational positions. As per Bernard (1962), a manager has authority only if subordinates chose to follow his commands. The other side of authority is responsibility and in fact, managers are given authority in consonance with their responsibility. Many managers confuse authority with power. Managers may sometimes delegate their authority to subordinates for carrying out their responsibilities effectively. The greatest barrier to delegation is the fear that the subordinate will not do the job properly.

Centralization is the concentration of authority at the top, whereas *decentralization* is delegation of authority to the lower level. What prompts an organization to centralize or decentralize its structure? Centralized organizations encourage close supervision of subordinates at every level in order to ensure compliance of established policies, procedures, and methods, whereas in decentralized organizations operating decisions are pushed down to the lowest level possible in order to empower employees, train and motivate them, and increase the span of control. Increase in the span of control leads to a flatter organization. Delegation of decision-making power down the chain of command is termed as vertical decentralization, whereas shift of power from line managers to staff managers is termed as horizontal decentralization. Centralization and decentralization should not be treated as absolutes but rather as two ends of a continuum.

Contingency view   Another view, the contingency view of organization design, considers an optimal organization design to be an outcome of four situational factors, namely technology, size, environment, and organizational life cycle. Virtual organizations, learning organizations, transnational organizations, and team organizations are some of the emerging organizational forms that have attracted attention in modern times. In a nutshell, after finalizing the plan, the next stage is the implementation of that plan.

Leading

After the management has made plans, organized work, created a structure, and hired the right people, the role of leading becomes important. Leading is motivating the members of an organization towards attaining organizational goals. It is like conducting an orchestra. Although all players (workers) in the orchestra have the music sheet (the plan) in front of them and they know which section (department) is playing which piece and when, it is the conductor (manager–leader) who indicates cues for each section to make the music happen. Undeniably, leadership is a very critical part of the overall managerial process. Effective leadership is about influencing an individual, group, or team so that organizational objectives are met successfully. Managers lead in an attempt to persuade others to join them in pursuit of organizational goals that emerge from planning and organizing steps. Leading involves mastery over various skills, namely motivation, leadership, teamwork, communication, negotiation, and conflict resolution.

Motivation   It is a driver of human behaviour. The managerial process of motivating uses knowledge from different motivation theories in an attempt to influence employees. Motivation theories differ in what they emphasize (in substance or content). Need theory and equity theory deal with people's various needs and whether they are satisfied or dissatisfied in terms of the fulfilment of these needs in organizational context. Reinforcement theory deals with how the consequences of a specific behaviour affect its repetitive occurrence. Expectancy theory details the process by which people choose from among alternative actions based on their expectation of what do they gain from each of their behaviours. Goal-setting theory focuses on the process of setting goals and how the goals themselves affect motivation.

Leadership approaches   Leadership has been studied extensively under three approaches. The *trait theory* of leadership examined leaders and identified few common traits of empathy, intelligence, self-confidence, and a vast domain of traits that are not universal. The *behavioural approach* focused on leadership styles and their efficacy, the styles being task-oriented or person-oriented. The *contingency approach* sought to identify appropriate leadership styles on the basis of the situation. Basically all the approaches to leadership described earlier are transactional theories of leadership, that is, about leaders who motivate their followers in the direction of established goals by clarifying role and task requirements. However, there is another type of leader who inspires followers to transcend their own self-interest for the good of the organization—the transformational leader. The latest approaches have focused on these transformational, visionary, and charismatic leaders.

Work teams are groups whose members possess complementary skills and work synergistically towards a specific common goal. The group behaviour is influenced by factors such as roles, norms, conformity, size, and cohesiveness. The teams could be problem-solving, self-managing, cross-functional, or even virtual. Effective leaders need to lead the teams while they go through forming, storming, norming, performing, and adjourning stages through their communication, negotiation, and conflict resolution skills.

During norming stage there will be conflict about who will control the group, but at the completion of this stage the leadership hierarchy will be clear within the group. From the norming stage the group moves to the performing stage when it gets down to perform the task at hand. In the adjourning stage the group prepares for its disbandment by wrapping up the activities after having completed its mandate.

Controlling

Controlling is the last of the managerial functions that helps managers to keep track of the progress and monitor the effectiveness of planning, organizing, and leading. A manager needs to supervise whether everything is going according to the plan. When it is not going according to the plan, the manager needs to step in and adjust the plan, just as the orchestra conductor will adjust the tempo. This is an iterative process. When something is out of sync, a manager needs to plan a fix, organize the resources to make it work, lead the people who will make it happen, and continue to monitor the effect of the change. A properly designed control system can help managers anticipate, monitor, and respond to the changing environment.

Controlling provides the critical link back to planning and is an ongoing process, which has three steps—(1) measurement of actual performance; (2) comparing actual performance against the standard; and (3) taking managerial action to correct any deviations. What is sought to be controlled is the performance of people, processes, or organization. This is accomplished through feed-forward, concurrent, or feed-back controls depending upon whether the managers implement the controls before, during, or after the activity has been completed, respectively. Traditional financial controls are based on liquidity, leverage, activity, and profitability ratios. Managers are now increasingly using economic value added (EVA) and market value added (MVA) methods that are based on economic value created. A new approach by the nomenclature of 'balance scorecard' methodology has been developed that measures customer, internal process, and people/innovation/growth assets along with financial performance. Organizations are also using benchmarks (i.e., best practices of superior performing companies) as standards of excellence against which to measure and compare. Sometimes the standard itself may require to be changed.

MANAGEMENT ROLES

To meet the many demands placed on managers as they carry out managerial functions described earlier and interact with workers and the external environment, managers take on numerous roles, that is, an organized set of behaviours belonging to an organizational position. The manager's universe includes pleasing customers by meeting or exceeding customers' needs and expectations, providing leadership, acting ethically, valuing diversity in his employees, and coping with global challenges. Henri Mintzberg (1975) categorized all the activities of managers after these were empirically captured, into three basic behaviours—interpersonal contact, information processing, and decision-making. Ten roles in all were chosen to describe all the activities observed by him during the study. In handling interpersonal relationships, managers adopt the three interpersonal roles of figurehead, leader, and liaison. In handling information, managers assume the three informational roles of monitor,

Exhibit 1.1   Managerial roles and skills

Interpersonal Roles

- Figurehead role means acting as a symbolic head at ceremonies as well as receiving visitors.
- Leader role indicates all those activities that are directed at subordinates to influence them and motivate them.
- Liaison role means establishing a network of contacts both within and with outsiders.

Informational Roles

- Monitor role is about collecting inside and outside information.
- Disseminator role is about transmitting the relevant information to subordinates.
- Spokesperson role is transmitting information to outsiders.

Decisional Roles

- Entrepreneur role is about initiating new projects.

- Disturbance handler role is the role of making short-term and long-term adjustments to maintain organizational equilibrium.
- Resource allocator role is controlling allocation of resources.
- Negotiator role is negotiating with outsiders.

Management Skills

To perform management functions and assume multiple roles, managers must master three kinds of skills:

Technical skills: Managers must be able to use the processes, practices, techniques, and tools of a specialty area.

Conceptual skills: Managers must possess the capacity to develop ideas, understand abstract relationships, and solve problems.

Human skills: Managers must display the ability to interact and communicate with people to gain cooperation.

disseminator, and spokesperson. In handling decisions, managers take on the four decisional roles of entrepreneur, disturbance handler, resource allocator, and negotiator. A few studies such as by McCall and Segrist (1980) attempted to test validity of Mintzberg's classification of roles in actual operating situations and found that activities in certain roles overlapped too much to be considered separate (for example, figurehead, disseminator, disturbance handler, and negotiator roles). We have to also bear in mind that managerial work is cerebral and is not, to a large extent, directly observable. Managers rarely reflect on the demands of their jobs as a neatly organized set of roles but more so as a chaotic, fragmented, and time-pressed flow of activities. Exhibit 1.1 illustrates managerial roles and skills.

LEVELS OF MANAGEMENT

Managers can be described by the functional areas in which they perform and the level at which they perform. Although all managers perform the same basic functions, the extent to which they perform these universal activities varies with levels in the management hierarchy. Top management, consisting of the chief executive officer and the vice-presidents, is responsible for the overall management of the organization and directs its relations with the external environment. These managers need conceptual skills the most. Top managers spend most of their day (over 75 per cent) planning and leading. Middle management consists of all managers below vice-presidents but above supervisors. Middle managers are responsible for setting objectives that are in line with top management's goals and further translate them into plans for first-line managers to implement. These managers need a blend of all three skill sets. First line management consists of supervisors, team leaders, team facilitators, supervisors, and directs the actual work of the organization at the operating level. These managers need technical skills the most. Functional managers can also be identified by the areas or functions of the organization for which they are responsible, such as marketing, finance, operations, and human resources.

SUMMARY

Managers allocate and monitor the use of organizational resources in the form of information, material, money, and people. Managers collectively constitute an organization's management team that sets and achieves goals through the management functions of planning, staffing, leading, and controlling.

Managers have two main jobs—running a business and building an organization. Managers have different roles to perform and require a mix of conceptual skills, technical skills, and human skills for different level positions.

Organizations are created by managers to meet stated goals. Managers make sure that everyone shares and delivers a common set of values. Organizations exist everywhere as a means for individuals, groups, and societies to meet their needs. Managers transform organizations into viable entities through leadership.

All managers perform the same basic management functions—planning, organizing, leading, and controlling.

KEYWORDS

Controlling It is the process of checking results against plans and taking corrective action as needed to reduce deviations from previously set guidelines.

Effectiveness It means 'doing the right thing' and is measured in terms of goal attainment.

Efficiency It means 'doing things right' and is measured as a ratio of output to input.

Generic managerial functions These are the universal functions of planning, organizing, leading, and controlling.

Leading The process of guiding and stimulating individuals and groups to achieve organizational goals within a supportive environment.

Managerial roles The roles assumed by managers to perform management functions.

Managerial skills The skills managers must master to perform different managerial functions. These can be categorized as technical, human, and conceptual skills.

Organizational functions The specialized functions that are grouped in organizations such as finance, production, and marketing.

Organizing It is the process of creating structure, establishing relationships, and allocating resources to accomplish goals.

Planning The process of identifying goals and ways of achieving them in order to prepare the organization for the future.

EXERCISES

Concept Review Questions

1. What is meant by managerial functions? Contrast these with organizational functions.
2. What are the criticisms levelled against Mintzberg's managerial roles theory?
3. What is the essence of managerial work?

Critical Thinking Questions

1. What is the major difference between authority and power? Can a manager delegate his responsibilities?

2. Are good leaders born or made? Do you subscribe to the contingency theory of leadership? Why and why not?

Project Assignment

Keep a log of your activities throughout a week and categorize the activities into the generic managerial functions of planning, organizing, leading, and controlling. Does this evidence support the universality of management?

REFERENCES

Barnard, Chester I. (1938), *The Functions of the Executive*, Harvard University Press, Cambridge, Massachusetts.

Bernard, Chester I. (1962), *The Functions of the Executive*, Cambridge, MA, Harvard University Press.

Brodie, M.B. (1967), *Fayol on Administration*, Lyon Grant and Green, London.

Chandler, Alfred D. (1962), *Strategy and Structure*, M.I.T Press, London.

Drucker, Peter F. (1955), *The Practice of Management*, William Heinemann Ltd, London.

Drucker, Peter F. (1974), *Management: Tasks, Responsibilities, Practices*, William Heinemann Ltd, London.

Ghoshal, Sumantra and Peter Moran (2005), 'Towards a Good Theory of Management', (ed.) Julian Birkinshaw and Gita Piramal, *Sumantra Ghoshal on Management*, Pearson Education Ltd, UK.

Katz, D. and R.L. Kahn (1966), *The Social Psychology of Organizations*, John Wiley, New York.

Koontz, Harold (1961), 'The Management Theory Jungle', *Academy of Management Journal*, vol. 4, no. 3, December, pp. 174–88.

Koontz, Harold (1980), 'The Management Theory Jungle Revisited', *Academy of Management Review*, vol. 5, no. 2, pp. 175–87.

Koontz, Harold and Cyril O'Donnell (1972), *Principles of Management: An Analysis of Managerial functions*, 5th edition, McGraw-Hill Book Company, New York.

Koontz, Harold and Heinz Weihrich (1990), *Essentials of Management*, 5th edition, McGraw-Hill Book Company, New York.

March, James G. and Herbert A. Simon (1958), *Organizations*, John Wiley and Sons Inc., USA.

McCall, M.W and C.A. Segrist (1980), *In Pursuit of the Manager's Job–Building on Mintzberg*, Greensboro, NC Center for Creative Leadership, USA.

Mintzberg, Henri (1975), 'The Manager's Job: Folklore and Fact', *Harvard Business Review*, vol. 53.

Porter, Michael E. (1980), *Competitive Strategy*, The Free Press, New York.

Simon, Herbert A. (1991), 'Organization and Markets', *Journal of Economic Perspectives*, vol. 5, no. 2, pp. 25–44.

Urwick, L.F. (1970), 'Papers in the Science of Administration', *Academy of Management Journal*, December, pp. 361–71.

2

Evolution of Management Theory

Learning Objectives

After studying this chapter, you will be able to:

- Appreciate evolution of management discipline and management theory
- Comprehend different schools of management thought
- Critically understand their strengths and weaknesses and modern day relevance
- Know the contribution of pioneers of management thought
- Become aware of contemporary approaches to management
- Become acquainted with 'Eastern' management thought

INTRODUCTION

According to Webster's _Third International Dictionary_, theory refers to a coherent group of general propositions used as principles of explanation. A study of the development of management theory is indispensable to the study of management as a discipline. In relation to other disciplines, management is relatively new, though generalizations on military strategy, military logistics, motivation, compensation, roles, money-making, occupational specialization, and superior–subordinate relations have been in existence since ancient times. These generalizations were about organizing and making effective organizational activities.

Since early times, people have had a notion of value of division of labour, specialization, and mass production. In China and Rome, imperial governments operated vast territories through bureaucratic setups that occurred in second century BC. These territories were probably ruled according to the concepts of specialization and division of labour. Chinese philosopher Menicus (third century BC) discussed division of labour and Greek philosopher Plato (fourth century BC) observed that specialization can increase productivity. At the height of its power, the Roman army standardized its fighting techniques. Archeological remains testify to the use of mass production techniques for glass-blowing and pottery-making as early as 500 BC. To truly understand current management thought, it is necessary to examine work of management pioneers, as also the contextual and environmental factors that formed the basis of their theories.

Adam Smith with his philosophy of free market and laissez-faire economic prescription and James Watt with his steam engine (built with Matthew Boulton in 1765), perhaps share the credit of nudging the world toward industrialization. Smith's *The Wealth of Nations* (1937) rejects the importance of land as a factor of production; instead, it emphasizes that labour was paramount, and that division of labour would effect a great increase in production. To illustrate his viewpoint, he used the example of pin-making. One worker could probably make only 20 pins per day. However, if 10 people divided up the 18 steps required to make a pin, they could make a combined amount of 48,000 pins in one day.

Smith had argued that market and competition were the best regulators of economic activity. Work specialization and division of labour provided managers with the greatest opportunity for increased productivity. The use of steam power lowered production costs and prices, and expanded markets. Advances in technology and the need to supervise larger number of workers under one roof created the factory system. The factory system in time became complex and brought in its wake its own problems for owners, managers, and society though contributing greatly in generating economic wealth.

Industrial Revolution brought about the emergence of large-scale business and its need for professional managers. Four management pioneers—Robert Owens, Charles Babbage, Andrew Ure, and Charles Dupin proposed different solutions for coping with the pressures of the new large-scale industrial organizations. Robert Owens (1771–1858), a successful Scottish entrepreneur and a utopian socialist, sowed the first seeds of concern for the workers, criticizing his fellow factory owners for treating their equipment better than they treated their workers. Owen deplored the monotony engendered by division of labour and believed each man should do a number of different jobs switching easily from one job to another. Charles Babbage (1792–1871) is known as the progenitor of concepts of operations research/management science and the concepts behind the present day computer. He invented a mechanical calculator (a 'difference engine'), a versatile computer (an 'analytical engine'), and a punch-card machine. Babbage analysed the manufacturing processes and the skills used, and suggested improved practices. He also wrote about the economic principles of manufacturing.

Andrew Ure (1778–1857) and Charles Dupin (1784–1873) were early industrial educators. Ure believed workers must recognize the benefits of mechanization and saw little merit in their resistance to its introduction, while Dupin's concepts such as time study, the need for workers to receive concise instructions, and the need to discover and publish the best way to perform work with the least amount of worker's energy seem to have influenced many management philosophers. Needless to say, modern managers use many of the practices, principles, and techniques developed from earlier concepts and experiences.

In his book, *Theories of Management: Implications for Organizational Behavior and Development* (1975), Raymond E. Miles elucidated a useful model of the evolution of management theory, which included the classical, human relations, and human resources management.

Claude S. George, Jr. in his book *The History of Management Thought* (1974) describes four schools of management thought—traditional school, behavioural school, management process school, and quantitative school. Harold Koontz in his famous *Academy of Management* article 'The Management Theory Jungle' (1961) classifies the major schools of management theory into six main schools—management process, empirical, human behaviour, social systems, decision theory, and mathematical. He returned to re-examine the issue and wrote in his article 'The Management Theory Jungle Revisited' (1980) that the 'jungle' appears to have become even more dense and impenetrable and in place of earlier six there seemed to be now eleven approaches—empirical, inter-personnel behaviour, group behaviour, the cooperative social systems, socio-technical systems, decision theory, systems, management science, contingency, managerial roles, and operational theory.

The next section discusses the management schools that are considered important from the vantage point of historical evolution of management as a discipline as well as for their continued relevance in some form or the other.

MAJOR SCHOOLS OF MANAGEMENT THEORY

Academicians and practitioners from different eras focused on and wrote about what they believed to be relevant aspects of good management practice. Over a period of time, management thinkers have sought to organize and classify this voluminous information about management. These attempts at classification have resulted in the identification of different management schools though some disagreement exists as to the exact number of management schools identified—as few as three and as many as twelve. To some degree, the relatively large numbers of management schools-of-thought reflect a lack of consensus among management scholars about the basic questions of theory and practice of their relatively young discipline. In this section, we discuss the major schools of management theory—classical, behavioural, quantitative, systems, contingency, and other approaches.

CLASSICAL SCHOOL

The classical school is the oldest formal school of management thought, which began around 1900 and continued into the 1920s. This school is mainly concerned with increasing the efficiency of workers and organizations based on management practices, which were an outcome of careful observation. It includes bureaucratic, scientific, and administrative management. Bureaucratic management relies on guidelines for structuring with formalization of rules, procedures, and a clear division of labour. Scientific management focuses on the 'one best way' to do a job. Administrative management focuses on the manager and basic managerial functions.

Scientific Management

In the late 19th century, management decisions were often arbitrary and workers had a vested interest in working at a slow pace. There was no systematic management, and workers and management were often in conflict. Scientific management sought to create a revolution in the workplace by a systematic study of work methods in order to improve efficiency. Frederick W. Taylor was its main proponent. Other major contributors were Frank Gilbreth, Lillian Gilbreth, and Henry Gantt.

The American Society of Mechanical Engineers (ASME) was founded in 1880 and was one of the first to be active in the area of scientific management. Associations of engineers wrote about management problems, as management relied heavily on engineers in the new factories. In 1866, Henry Towne, President of the Yale and Towne Manufacturing Company wrote a paper, *The Engineer as an Economist* that suggested that ASME become a clearing house for information on managerial practices, as no management association was in existence at that time.

Probably the most famous management pioneer is Frederick W. Taylor (1856–1915), the father of scientific management. Taylor rose from a common labourer to become a chief engineer in just six years. Taylor began a scientific study of what workers ought to be able to produce. This study led to the beginnings of scientific management. Taylor used time studies to break tasks down into elementary movements and designed complementary piece-rate incentive systems. Taylor believed that the management's responsibility was in knowing what it wanted workers to do and then seeing that they do it in the best and cheapest way. Many of Taylor's definitive studies were performed at the Bethlehem Steel Company in Pittsburgh. To improve productivity, Taylor examined the time and motion details of a job, developed a better method for performing that job, and trained workers. One of his famous experiments involved the study of workers loading pig iron to a rail car. Taylor broke the job down into its smallest constituent movements, timing each one with a stopwatch. The job was redesigned with a reduced number of motions as well as effort and the risk of error. Rest periods of specific interval and duration were used to improve the output. Furthermore, Taylor offered a piece rate that increased as workers produced more. With scientific management, Taylor increased the workers' output from 12 to 47 tons per day. Taylor's method gave rise to dramatic increases in productivity. He wrote *Shop Management* in 1903, became the President of the ASME in 1906, and lectured a lot, including at Harvard from 1909 to 1914.

In 1911, Frederick Taylor published *Principles of Scientific Management* in which he proposed work methods designed to increase worker productivity. Its contents became widely accepted by managers worldwide. The book described the theory of scientific management. Scientific management was defined as methods aimed at determining the one best way for a job to be done. During the same period, organized labour waged an all-out war on Taylorism resulting in a congressional investigation; however, the findings of the committee reported no evidence to support worker abuse. In fact, Taylor did not neglect the human side of work, as often suggested. He simply emphasized on the individual worker not the group. Taylor called for a revolution to fuse the interests of labour and management into a mutually rewarding whole. He developed many new concepts such as functional authority. In other words, Taylor proposed that all authority was based on knowledge, not position.

Taylor's disciple, Henry Gantt (1861–1919) known for developing charts used for planning and controlling, worked with Taylor at the Midvale Steel Company. Gantt strongly felt that it is the foreman's job to teach the workers to be hardworking and cooperative which, in turn, would lead to their becoming knowledgeable about their job. Gantt focused on the importance of the qualities of leadership and management skills in building effective industrial organizations. Just like Taylor, Gantt called for the scientific study of working conditions, tasks, and worker cooperation. Other Taylor associates Frank Gilbreth (1868–1924) and Lillian Gilbreth (1878–1972) was a husband–wife team that brought many significant contributions to scientific management. Frank began as an apprentice bricklayer, and later became a chief superintendent and independent contractor. Frank's early work parallels Taylor's and, in later years, Frank formed his own management consulting company, which was closely associated with scientific management methods. Frank Gilbreth published a series of books describing the best way of laying bricks, handling materials, training apprentices, and improving methods while lowering costs and paying higher wages. In 1907, Frank Gilbreth met Frederick Taylor and soon became one of Taylor's most ardent advocates. Frank focused his attention on motion study (similar to Taylor's time study). He made use of motion picture cameras, lights, and clocks calibrated in fractions of minutes to create 'micromotion' study and developed a list of 17 basic motions he termed 'therbligs' (Gilbreth spelled backwards) to help analyse any worker movement. Dr Lillian Gilbreth's thesis turned book, *The Psychology of Management*, showed concern for the worker and attempted to show how scientific management would benefit the individual worker and the organization.

Critics of scientific management contend that Taylor regarded poor workers as automatons whose sole motivation came in the form of piecework rate. According to them, he negated the role of workers as thinking human beings. They were told clearly what to do and how to do and the orders had to be carried out for better or worse. It has to be borne in mind that Taylorism may no longer be appropriate in present times of knowledge workers but it was well adapted to the spirit and conditions of that time. It was a first serious attempt to create a science of management. Henry Ford applied scientific management as a basis for mass production of cars. Scientific approach intruded for the first time in the domain, which was reserved for experience and intuition alone. The modern avatar of this school is the neoclassical school so aptly represented by Peter Drucker who brought fresh air by applying common sense to the analysis of challenges of management in modern times.

Together with engineers, who were concerned with mechanical efficiency, industrial psychologists studied human efficiency for improving productivity. The father of industrial psychology was Hugo Munsterberg (1863–1916) who established his psychological laboratory at Harvard and published *Psychology and Industrial Efficiency* (1913), which mentioned theories related to Taylor's scientific management. This book discussed the demands jobs made on people, and the importance of finding people whose mental capabilities made them well matched for the work; the psychological conditions under which the greatest output might be obtained from every worker; and the necessity of creating the influences on human needs that were desirable for the interests of business. Munsterberg's recommendations were based on empirical studies. In brief, the main principles of scientific management are as follows:

1. Scientific methods should be applied to work in order to determine the best method for accomplishing each task.
2. Workers should be scientifically selected based on their qualifications and trained to perform their jobs in the optimal manner.
3. Cooperation between workers and management is to be based on mutual self-interest.
4. Management is to take complete responsibility for planning the work and that workers' primary responsibility should be implementing management's plans.
5. Scientific development of performance standards and the implementation of a pay-for-performance incentive plan are based on work standards.

Scientific management focuses on worker and machine relationships. Organizational productivity can be increased by increasing the efficiency of production processes. The efficiency perspective is concerned with creating jobs that economize on time, human energy, and other productive resources. Jobs are designed so that each worker has a specified, well-controlled task that can be performed as instructed. Specific procedures and methods for each job must be followed with no exceptions.

Administrative Management

In contrast to scientific management, which deals largely with jobs and work at the individual level, administrative management provides a more general theory of management. Administrative management focuses on the processes and principles of management. Administrative management emphasizes the role of the manager and the functions of management. Henri Fayol is the major contributor to this school of management thought.

Henri Fayol (1841–1925), known as the father of modern management, was a French industrialist who developed a framework for studying management. He wrote *General and Industrial Management* in 1967. Fayol was a management practitioner who brought his experience to bear on the subject of management functions and principles. He argued that management was a universal process consisting of planning, organizing, commanding, coordinating, and controlling functions. Fayol believed that all managers performed these functions. These functions distinguished management as a separate discipline of study apart from accounting, finance, and production. His 14 principles of management included division of work, authority and responsibility, discipline, unity of command, unity of direction, subordination of individual interests to general interests, remuneration of personnel, centralization, scalar chain, order, equity, stability of tenure of personnel, initiative, and esprit de corps (union is strength). In many aspects Henri Fayol was probably the first management thinker who focused on the role of management as well as on how best a company could be organized. His functional model of organizing is still the most dominant way of structuring organizations though there is a whiff of change in terms of an exhortation to override functional mindsets.

Although administrative management has been criticized as being rigid and inflexible, many of Fayol's principles of management, when applied with the flexibility that he advocated, are still considered relevant.

Bureaucratic Management

Max Weber (1864–1920), known as the father of modern sociology, considered bureaucracy as the most logical and rational structure for large organizations. Organizations formalize behaviour to reduce its variability and ultimately that makes it easy to predict and control it. The work of Max Weber runs chronologically parallel to that of Fayol and Taylor. He was a professor, editor, government consultant, and author. Weber used the concept of 'bureaucracy' as an ideal organizational arrangement for the administration of large-scale organizations. Weber's concept of the best administrative system was actually similar to Taylor's. Some of Weber's essential elements included division of labour and chain of command. He also believed that selection should be based on technical qualifications, officials'/managers' appointments should be based on qualifications, managers should not be owners, and impersonal and uniform rules should be applied.

Organic structure is a contrast to the *mechanistic structure* of a bureaucracy founded on legal or rational authority comprising laws, procedures, rules, etc. Positional authority of a superior over a subordinate stems from legal authority. Charismatic authority stems from the personal qualities of an individual. Efficiency in bureaucracies comes from—clearly defined and specialized functions; use of legal authority; hierarchical form; written rules and procedures; technically trained bureaucrats; appointment to positions based on technical expertise; promotions based on competence; and clearly defined career paths.

Bureaucratic management focuses on the ideal form of organization. Max Weber was the major contributor to bureaucratic management. Weber's observations led him to conclude that many of the earlier organizations were inefficiently managed, with decisions based on personal relationships and loyalty. He proposed that a form of organization, called a bureaucracy, characterized by division of labour, hierarchy, formalized rules, impersonality, and the selection and promotion of employees based on ability, would lead to a more efficient management. Weber also contended that managers' authority in an organization should not be based on tradition or charisma but on the position held by managers in the organizational hierarchy.

Bureaucracy has come to stand for inflexibility and waste, but Weber did not advocate or favour the excesses found in many bureaucratic organizations of today. Weber's ideas formed the basis for modern organization theory and are still descriptive of some organizations.

Some dysfunctions of a bureaucratic structure are that it has an inherent propensity to impersonalize workplace, reject innovative ideas, result in high employee turnover, and lead to poor customer service. In the tradition of classical school gurus, Peter Drucker, the neoclassical writer and perhaps the most respected and prolific management writer of modern times, made an enduring contribution to understanding the role of manager in a business society. Drucker (1955) developed three broader managerial functions—(1) managing a business; (2) managing managers; and (3) managing workers and work. He proposed that the manager must put economic considerations first in every decision. Drucker recognized that there may be other non-economic consequences of managerial decisions, but that the emphasis should still be placed on economic performance.

BEHAVIOURAL SCHOOL

The behavioural school of management thought developed, in part, because of naïve and over-simplified theories of classicists and failure of their application to group behaviour and the discoveries and advances in psychological theory known as behaviourism. The classical school emphasized efficiency, process, and principles. This emphasis seemed to disregard important aspects of organizational life, particularly related to human behaviour. Therefore, the behavioural school focused on trying to understand the factors that affect human behaviour at work. The behavioural school of management thought began late in the scientific management era, but achieved large-scale recognition in 1930s. The real catalyst for the emergence of the behavioural school was a series of experiments conducted at the Hawthorne plant of Western Electric between 1924 and 1932, inspired by Elton Mayo and Fritz J. Roethlisberger. This research became known as the Hawthorne experiments.

Elton Mayo (1880–1949), as part of the Harvard research group, was asked to work with Western Electric to continue the Hawthorne studies. Mayo was intrigued by the initial results of the early illumination studies, which showed that output had increased upon changes in illumination either way—either more or less. The explanation was that the increased output came from a change in mental attitude in the group, as the workers developed into a social unit. From other similar experiments the Mayoists came to the conclusion that employees have social needs along with their physical needs, and managers need skills that include human relations skills.

Another contributor to the behavioural school of thought was Mary Parker Follett who described concepts of the universal goal, the universal principle, and the law of the situation. The universal goal of organizations is an integration of individual effort into a synergistic whole. The universal principle is a circular or reciprocal response emphasizing feedback to the sender (the concept of two-way communication). Law of the situation emphasizes that there is no one best way to do anything, but that it all depends on the situation. Follett is a more advanced thinker as she pre-empted certain principles, which were to later come from systems and contingency approach schools. She believed the primary leadership task was to define the purpose of the organization and integrate that purpose with individual and group purposes. In other words, she thought that organizations should be based on a group ethic rather than individualism. Therefore, managers and employees should view themselves as partners rather than adversaries. She stressed the involvement of workers in solving problems and believed that management is a continuous and dynamic process.

Another contributor to this school was Chester Barnard (1886–1961), a self-made scholar who studied economics at Harvard and joined the AT&T Systems in 1909 and became the President of New Jersey Bell in 1927. In Barnard's best known work, *The Functions of the Executive* (1938) he described a theory of organizations in order to stimulate others to examine the nature of cooperative systems. Looking at the disparity between personal and organizational motives, Barnard described an 'effective–efficient' dichotomy. According to Barnard, effectiveness deals with goal achievement, and efficiency is the degree to which individual motives are satisfied. He viewed formal organizations as integrated social systems where cooperation, common purpose, and communication are universal elements, whereas the informal organization provides communication, cohesiveness, and maintenance of feelings of self-worth. Barnard proposed the 'acceptance theory of authority' based on his idea that employees have free wills and can thus choose whether or not to follow management's orders. Bosses have authority only if subordinates accept that authority.

Human Relations

Behavioural or human relations management emerged in the 1920s and dealt with the human aspects of organizations. Hawthrone experiments conducted by Elton Mayo, Roethlisberger, Homans, and others culminated in certain insightful conclusions:

1. There was no direct cause–effect relationship between working conditions and productivity. Worker attitude was found to be important.
2. Whenever employees are given special attention, productivity is likely to change irrespective of working conditions.
3. An employee's complaint frequently is a symptom of some underlying problem on the job, at home, or in the person's past.
4. The workplace is a social system and informal group influence could exert a powerful effect on individual behaviour.

Barnard developed the concepts of strategic planning and the acceptance theory of authority. Strategic planning is the formulation of major plans or strategies, which guide an organization in pursuit of its major objectives. According to Barnard, the three top functions of the executive were to—(1) establish and maintain an effective communication system; (2) hire and retain effective personnel; and (3) motivate those personnel.

His acceptance theory of authority suggests that authority flows downward but depends on acceptance by the subordinate. The acceptance of authority depends on four conditions—(1) employees must understand what the manager wants them to do; (2) employees must be able to comply with the directive; (3) employees must think that the directive is in keeping with organizational objectives; and (4) employees must think that the directive is not contrary to their personal goals.

Barnard believed that there exists a zone of indifference or a range within each individual in which he would willingly accept orders without consciously questioning authority. It was up to the organization to provide sufficient incentives to broaden each employee's zone of indifference so that the manager's orders would be obeyed.

Human Resources School

Beginning in the early 1950s, the human resources school represented a substantial progression from human relations. The behavioural approach did not always increase productivity. Therefore, motivation and leadership techniques became a topic of great interest. The human resources school understands that employees are very creative and competent, and that much of their talent is largely untapped by their employers. Employees want to do meaningful work, contribute, and participate in decision-making and leadership functions.

According to the human resources school, the manager should possess skills for diagnosing the causes of human behaviour at work, interpersonal communication, and motivating and leading the workers. The focus became satisfying worker needs. If workers' needs were satisfied, the workers would in turn be more productive. Therefore, the human resources school focuses on issues of communication, leadership, motivation, and group behaviour. The individuals who contributed to the school are too numerous to mention, but some of the best-known contributors include Mary Parker Follett, Chester Barnard, Abraham Maslow, Kurt Lewin, Renais Likert, and Douglas McGregor. The human resources school of thought still influences management theory and practice, as contemporary management focuses attention on human resource management, organizational behaviour, and applied psychology in the workplace.

Behavioural Science

Behavioural science and the study of organizational behaviour emerged in the 1950s and 1960s. The behavioural science school was a natural progression of the human relations movement. It focused on applying conceptual and analytical tools to the problem of understanding and predicting behaviour in the workplace. However, the study of behavioural science and organizational behaviour was also a result of criticism of the human relations approach as being simplistic and manipulative in its assumptions about the relationship between worker attitudes and productivity. The behavioural science school has contributed to the study of management through its focus on personality, attitudes, values, motivation, group behaviour, leadership, communication, and conflict, among other issues. Some of the major contributors to this school include Douglas McGregor, Chris Argyris, Frederick Herzberg, and Renais Likert among others.

QUANTITATIVE SCHOOL

The quantitative school focuses on improving decision-making via the application of mathematical and statistical models in management. Its roots can be traced back to scientific management.

Management Science and MIS

Management science, also known as operations research (OR), uses mathematical and statistical approaches to solve management problems. It developed during World War II as military strategists tried to apply scientific knowledge and methods to the complex problems of war. Organizations began to apply management science after the war. George Dantzig (1963) developed linear programming, an algebraic method to determine the optimal allocation of scarce resources. Other tools used in industry include inventory control theory, goal programming, queuing models, game theory, and simulation. The computers made many management science tools and concepts more accessible for industry. There are several factors that make up the OR approach:

- a system-wide orientation;
- specific identification and quantification of system goal/goals;
- specific identification and quantification of all variables that affect (constraint) the attainment of goal/goals;
- Construction of a mathematical model to represent the situation being studied;
- appropriate technique to derive feasible optimal solution; and
- implementation of solution.

Increasingly, management science and management information systems (MIS) are intertwined. Management information systems focus on providing needed information to managers in a useful format and at the proper time. Decision support systems (DSS) attempt to integrate decision models, data, and the decision-maker into a system that supports better management decisions. Presently, enterprise resource planning (ERP) software, acting as a backbone for the entire processes of an enterprise, is being adopted increasingly by business enterprises. It utilizes the potential of not only an organization-wide integration but reaches out to partners in the supply value chain. Managers have also become aware of the potential of knowledge management for their organizations.

Production and Operations Management

This school focuses on the operation and control of the production process that transforms resources into finished goods and services. It has its roots in scientific management but became an identifiable area of management study after World War II. It uses many of the tools of management science.

Operations management emphasizes productivity and quality of both manufacturing and service organizations. W. Edwards Deming (1986) exerted a tremendous influence in shaping modern ideas about improving productivity and quality. Major areas of study within operations management include capacity planning, facilities location, facilities layout, materials requirement planning, scheduling, purchasing and inventory control, quality control, computer integrated manufacturing, Just-In-Time (JIT) inventory systems, and flexible manufacturing systems.

SYSTEMS SCHOOL

Systems theory and a contingency view can help integrate the theories of management. Appropriate managerial techniques can be applied as required by environmental conditions. A broad perspective is valuable to managers when overseeing one unit or the total integration of all subunits.

Systems Theory

During the 1940s and World War II, systems analysis theory emerged. This viewpoint uses systems concepts and quantitative approaches from mathematics, statistics, engineering, and other related fields to solve problems. Managers find optimal solutions to management problems by using scientific analysis, which is closely associated with the systems approach to management. A system is an interrelated and interdependent set of elements functioning as a whole. It is an open system that interacts with its environment. It is composed of inputs from the environment (material or human resources), transformation processes of inputs to finished goods (technological and managerial processes), outputs of those finished goods into the environment (products or services), and feedback (reactions from the environment).

Subsystems are systems within a broader system. Interdependent subsystems (such as production, finance, and human resources) work towards synergy in an attempt to accomplish an organizational goal that could not otherwise be accomplished by a single subsystem. Systems develop synergy.

This is a condition in which the combined and coordinated actions of the parts of a system achieve more than all the parts could have achieved acting independently. Entropy is the process that eventually leads to the decline of a system.

The systems school focuses on understanding the organization as an open system that transforms inputs into outputs. This school is based on the work of a biologist,

Ludwig von Bertalanffy (1968), who believed that a general systems model could be used to unite science. Early contributors to this school included Kenneth Boulding and James Rosenzweig.

The systems school began to have a strong impact on management thought in the 1960s as a way of thinking about management techniques that would allow managers to relate different specialties and parts of the company to one another, as well as to external environmental factors. The systems school focuses on the organization as a whole, its interaction with the environment, and its need to achieve equilibrium. General systems theory received a great deal of attention in the 1960s, but its influence on management thought has now somewhat diminished. It has been criticized as too abstract and too complex. However, many of the ideas inherent in the systems school formed the basis for the contingency school of management.

CONTINGENCY SCHOOL

In the mid-1960s the contingency view of management or situational approach emerged. This view emphasizes the fit between organizational processes and the characteristics of the situation. It calls for fitting the structure of the organization to various possible or chance events. It questions the use of universal management practices and advocates using traditional, behavioural, and systems viewpoints independently or in combination to deal with various circumstances. The contingency approach assumes that managerial behaviour is dependent on a wide variety of elements. Thus, it provides a framework for integrating the knowledge of management thought.

The contingency school focuses on applying management principles and processes as dictated by the unique characteristics of each situation. It emphasizes that there is no one best way to manage and that it depends on various situational factors, such as the external environment, technology, organizational characteristics, characteristics of the manager, and characteristics of the subordinates. Contingency theorists often implicitly or explicitly criticize the classical school for its emphasis on the universality of management principles; however, most classical writers recognized the need to consider aspects of the situation when applying management principles.

The contingency school originated in the 1960s. It has been applied primarily to management issues such as organizational design, job design, motivation, and leadership style. For example, optimal organizational structure has been theorized to depend upon organizational size, technology, and environmental uncertainty; optimal leadership style, meanwhile, has been theorized to depend upon a variety of factors, including task structure, position power, characteristics of the work group, characteristics of individual subordinates, quality requirements, and problem structure, to name a few. A few of the major contributors to this school of management thought include Joan Woodward, Paul Lawrence, Jay Lorsch, and Fred Fiedler, among many others.

CONTEMPORARY AND OTHER APPROACHES

Management research and practice continues to evolve and new approaches to the study of management continue to be advanced. New management viewpoints are emerging. This section briefly describes some contemporary approaches such as total quality management (TQM), learning organization, organizational excellence approach and chaos theory approach, and two Eastern approaches (in contrast to Western management approaches)—Indian and Japanese management approaches. While neither of these management approaches offers a complete theory of management, they do offer additional insights into the field of management. Quality management emphasizes on achieving customer satisfaction by providing high quality goods and services.

Total Quality Management

A quality revolution swept through the world of business during the latter part of the twentieth century. The universal term used to describe this phenomenon was total quality management (TQM). This revolution was led by a small group of quality gurus, the most well-known being W. Edwards Deming and Joseph Juran. Deming, an American, is considered to be the father of quality control in Japan. In fact, Deming (1986) suggested that most quality problems are not the fault of employees, but the system. He emphasized the importance of improving quality by suggesting a five-step chain reaction. This theory proposes that when quality is improved—(1) costs decrease because of less rework, fewer mistakes, fewer delays, and better use of time and materials; (2) productivity improves; (3) market share increases with better quality and prices; (4) the company increases profitability and stays in business; and (5) the number of jobs increases. Deming developed a 14-point plan to summarize his teachings on quality improvement. These fourteen points are listed in Exhibit 2.1.

Joseph Juran's (1962) experience led him to conclude that more than 80 per cent of all quality defects are caused by factors within the management's control. He referred to this as the 'Pareto principle'. From this theory, he developed a management trilogy that included quality planning, quality control, and quality improvement. Juran suggested that an area be selected, which has experienced chronic quality problems. It should be analysed, and then a solution generated and finally implemented. The quality work of Juran and Deming changed the way people looked at business.

Total quality management is a philosophy or approach to management that focuses on managing the entire organization to deliver quality goods and services to customers. This approach to management was implemented in Japan after World War II and was a major factor in their economic renaissance. TQM has been implemented by many companies worldwide and appears to have fostered performance improvements in many organizations. It has at least four major elements:

Exhibit 2.1   Deming's 14 points

1. Create consistency of purpose towards the improvement of product and service, and communicate this goal to all employees.
2. Adopt the new philosophy of quality throughout all levels with the organization.
3. Cease dependence on inspection to achieve quality; understand that quality comes from improving processes.
4. No longer select suppliers based solely on price. Move towards developing a long-term relationship with a single supplier.
5. Processes, products, and services should be improved constantly, reducing waste.
6. Institute extensive on-the-job training.
7. Improve supervision.

8. Drive out fear of expressing ideas and concerns.
9. Break down barriers between departments. People should be encouraged to work together as a team.
10. Eliminate slogans and targets for the workforce.
11. Eliminate work quotas on the factory floor.
12. Remove barriers that rob workers of their right to pride of workmanship.
13. Institute a programme of education and self-improvement.
14. Make sure to put everyone in the company to work to accomplish the transformation.

1. Employee involvement is essential in preventing quality problems before they occur.
2. A customer focus means that the organization must attempt to determine customer needs and wants and deliver products and services that address them.
3. Benchmarking means that the organization is always seeking out other organizations that perform a function or process more effectively and using them as a standard or benchmark to judge their own performance. The organization will also attempt to adapt or improve the processes used by other companies.
4. Finally, a philosophy of continuous improvement means that the organization is committed to incremental changes and improvements over time in all areas of the organization.

The quality advocates taught managers about the strategic importance of high-quality goods and services. Shewhart (1931) pioneered the use of statistics for quality control. Japan's Ishikawa (1990) emphasized prevention of defects in quality and drew managements' attention to internal as well as external customers. Deming sparked the Japanese quality revolution with calls for continuous improvement of the entire production process. Juran trained many US managers to improve quality through teamwork, partnerships with suppliers, and Pareto analysis (the 80/20 rule). Feigenbaum (2004) developed the concept of total quality control, thus involving all business functions in the quest for quality. He believed that the customer determined quality. Crosby (1979), a champion of zero defects, emphasized how costly poor-quality products could be.

Learning Organization

The contemporary organization faces unprecedented environmental and technological change. Therefore, one of the biggest challenges for organizations is to continuously change in a way that meets the demands of this turbulent competitive environment. The learning organization can be defined as one in which all employees are involved in identifying and solving problems, and which allows the organization to continually increase its ability to grow, learn, and achieve its purpose. The organizing principle of the learning organization is not efficiency, but problem-solving. Three key aspects of the learning organization are—a team-based structure, empowered employees, and open information. Peter Senge (1990) is one of the best-known experts on learning organizations.

Excellence Approach

This approach was proposed by Peters and Watermans (1982) in their best-selling book, *In Search of Excellence*. It challenged managers to take a fresh, unconventional look at managing. The authors isolated eight attributes of excellence after studying many of the best-managed and most successful companies in America. Generally, the excellent companies were found to be relatively decentralized and value-driven organizations dedicated to innovation, experimentation, customer satisfaction, and humane treatment of employees. Critics of the excellence approach caution managers to avoid the quick-fix mentality, in which organizational problems and solutions are oversimplified.

Chaos Theory

This theory has been used to model the corporation as a complex adaptive system that interacts and evolves with its surroundings. Many seemingly random movements in nature exhibit structured patterns. Living systems operate at their most robust and efficient level in the narrow space between stability and disorder—poised at 'the edge of chaos'. It is here that the agents within a system conduct the fullest range of productive interactions and exchange the greatest amount of useful information.

Indian Management Style

It is a distinctive way of dealing with and handling of a situation pertaining to the management of an organization. It deals with various functions and methods of management to deal with managerial issues and challenges. India has an invaluable treasure by way of contributions by *rishis* in the form of Vedas, Upanishads, and epics such as Ramanayana and Mahabharata. Integrating management with India's psycho-spiritual heritage has been the main thrust of the Indian philosophy of management. It stresses value-based management, emphasizing upon going into the root cause of a problem, so as to come out with long-term sustainable solutions that lead to desirable personal and organizational gains. It lays greatest emphasis on understanding the human mind and its management for improving personal and professional effectiveness. The uniqueness of Indian approach to management lies in simultaneous growth of the company and its employees by identifying the dormant potentialities of the employees to benefit them and the company. Indian wisdom aims at enlightened management of man, mind, and material. Therefore, the philosophy of Indian management attempts to integrate spirituality with professional pursuits. The value-based approaches to management coupled with insights of Indian epics and texts add a new dimension to the diagnosis and response to managerial problems. It is this aspect that has been gaining more and more acceptance in the field of management. Even Mahatma Gandhi, one of India's greatest leaders, is quoted to have said 'Bhagavad Geeta, one of the key Indian scriptures, could be viewed as an executive's primer on how to achieve true greatness as a leader.' For example, Geeta's verse 2.47 basically focuses on non-attachment to results—'You have a right to perform your prescribed duty, but you are not entitled to the fruits of action. Never consider yourself the cause of the results of your activities, and never be attached to not doing your duty.' It is the over concern and attachment to the results that create anxiety and, in turn, lack of total involvement and concentration while performing the task or duty. The essence of the verse is to develop an attitude of detachment. What is important is to manifest larger 'I' by overcoming selfish 'I'. Swami Ranganathananda has rightly stated that when this little 'I' expands, it becomes the ripe ego, which alone can experience its oneness with everybody else. We should learn to say 'We' instead of 'I'.

It is an attitude of detachment to the outcome and focused concentration on the work in hand that paves the way for success. While responding to a challenge, the whole energy has to be organized and unified with single-pointed determination. What is important is to shed our personal attachments and sense of ownership. Geeta teaches us to develop a visionary perspective in whatever work we do with a sense of larger vision for the common good.

Management of mind is the most crucial ingredient for achieving success, which requires equipping oneself with qualities such as detachment, unbiasedness, equanimity, and wisdom. It is only a peaceful, vigilant, and alert mind that makes one an effective manager. Such a manager is capable of achieving success on personal, professional, and spiritual planes.

Some of the pioneering contributions have been made in the field of Indian management thought by S. Chakraborty in his books, *Human Response in Organisations* (1985), *Foundations of Managerial Work* (1989), *Management by Values: Towards Cultural Congruence* (1998), *Ethics in Management: Vedantic Perspectives* (1995), and *Values and Ethics in Management: Theory and Practice* (1999). The common theme and thread running through his works is the assertion that our own heritage and culture provide the much needed foundations for building an indigenous management philosophy that could provide long-term and sustainable solutions to ever emerging complex managerial issues and challenges.

In *Ethics in Management*, Chakraborty (1998) has emphasized on Vedantic philosophy as rediscovered by Mahatma Gandhi, Gurudev Tagore, Swami Vivekananda, and Sri Aurobindo. The relevance of Indian management is evident from the lives of our greatest rulers and leaders who were simultaneously seers and kings, *raja–rishis* such as Janaka, Ashoka, and Milinda. Ancient texts have demonstrated that profound wisdom could be achieved not only by world-renouncing hermits, but also by householders such as Vashishtha–Arundhati, Agastya–Lopamudra, Yajnavalkya–Maitreyi, Vidura, Krishna and, though many would dispute this, Bhishma.

Therefore, Indian management has made a valuable contribution to the existing management philosophies by highlighting 'value-based management' as inherited from Indian heritage and culture that has perennial relevance for finding long-term solutions to managerial issues and challenges.

Japanese-style Management

Also known as 'nihonteki keiei', it has become a popular phrase in the West. This refers to basically the difference between Japanese management techniques and those widely practised in the West. The basic differences that are often highlighted are—participative management, shared decision-making, lifetime employment, job rotation, promotion-based seniority, group consensus, JIT, quality circles, Kaizen, TQM, and the suggestion system. These are the aspects of management around which Japanese management philosophy revolves. Japanese management culture emphasizes cohesion and long-term continuity, as visible in the traditional expectation of lifetime employment. A family bond amongst employees within the organization is the hallmark of organizational culture. This has resulted in building trust between managers and their subordinates in Japanese organizations.

Participative style of management assumes that irrespective of position in the organization, every individual has a potential to contribute and this needs to be channelized in an organized way through participative approach to management. Toyota Motor's Chairman, Eiji Toyota had said that 'One of the features of the Japanese workers is that they use their brains as well as their hands. Our workers provide 1.5 million suggestions a year, and 95 per cent of them are put to practical use. There is an almost tangible concern for improvement in the air at Toyota' (Masaaki 1986).

The Japanese success during the post-war economic growth is basically the result of participation of all members within the organization to focus on development and continuous improvement of efficiency and quality management systems to improve operational productivity and product quality. It is a participative approach to management that brings in involvement and commitment of employees of the organization to contribute their best to organizational goals.

SUMMARY

Management is an interdisciplinary and international field that has evolved in bits and pieces over the years. The six approaches to management theory discussed in this chapter are—(1) classical approach; (2) behavioural approach; (3) quantitative approach; (4) systems approach; (5) contingency approach; and (6) other approaches.

Classical school constitutes approaches such as scientific management, administrative management, and bureaucratic management. Useful lessons have been learned from each approach. Dedicated to promoting production efficiency and reducing waste, Frederick W. Taylor, the father of scientific management, and his followers revolutionized industrial management through the use of standardization, time-and-motion study, selection and training, and pay incentives. Henri Fayol's universal approach assumes that all organizations, regardless of purpose or size, require the same management process. Furthermore, it assumes that this rational process can be reduced to separate functions and principles of management.

Management has turned to the human factor in the human relations movement and organizational behaviour approach. Emerging from such influences as unionization, the Hawthorne studies, and the philosophy of industrial humanism, the human relations movement began as a concerted effort to make employees' needs a high management priority. Today, organizational behaviour theory tries to identify the multiple determinants of job performance.

Quantitative approach consists of management science, also known as operations research (OR), and uses mathematical and statistical approaches to solve management problems.

Advocates of the systems approach recommend that modern organizations be viewed as open systems. Open systems depend on the outside environment for survival, whereas closed systems do not. Chester I. Barnard stirred early interest in systems thinking in 1938 by suggesting that organizations are cooperative systems energized by communication. General systems theory, an interdisciplinary field based on the assumption that everything is systematically related, has identified a hierarchy of systems and has differentiated between closed and open systems.

A comparatively new approach to management thought is the contingency approach, which stresses situational appropriateness rather than universal principles. The contingency approach is characterized by an open-system perspective, a practical research orientation, and a multivariate approach to research. Contingency thinking is a practical extension of more abstract systems thinking.

Along with TQM, excellence approach, chaos theory, and the two Eastern approaches form the basis of other approaches discussed in the chapter. The Indian management approach stresses detachment to the outcome and focuses on the work in hand. The Japanese management approach stresses a participative approach to management, which brings in involvement and commitment of employees.

KEYWORDS

Bureaucracy An organization that is formally designed and highly structured.

Contingency approach This approach stresses situational appropriateness rather than universal principles for managerial decision-making.

Indian management It is an attitude of detachment to the outcome and focused concentration on the work in hand that paves the way for success.

Japanese management It is a participative approach to management that brings in involvement and commitment of employees of the organization to contribute their best to organizational goals.

Learning organization It can be defined as one in which all employees are involved in identifying and solving problems, which allows the organization to continually increase its ability to grow, learn, and achieve its purpose.

Management science Also known as operations research (OR), it uses mathematical and statistical approaches to solve management problems.

Scientific management A sub-school of classical school of management that believed in application of methods of science—observation, measurement, and experiment to problems of management. The objective of this approach was to increase industrial productivity.

Systems theory This approach views organizations as open systems interacting constantly with their environment.

Total quality management (TQM)   It is a philosophy or approach to management that focuses on managing the entire organization to deliver quality goods and services to customers.

EXERCISES

Concept Review Questions
1. What is scientific in scientific management?
2. What is the major difference between classical and behavioural schools of management thought?
3. What are the criticisms leveled against mathematical school especially against management science approach?

Critical Thinking Questions
1. Why would Indian management thought have had to wait so long for its recognition and why is there no mention of it in most of the books on management?

2. How in your opinion will technology affect and change management practice in future and what will remain unchanged?

Project Assignment
Go through the original writings of any one of the management pioneers such as Taylor, Henri Fayol, Chester Bernard, Elton Mayo, and Homans. Prepare a presentation before your class defending your author for his pioneering contribution and continuing relevance for the modern workplace.

REFERENCES

Barnard, Chester I. (1938), *The Functions of the Executive*, Harvard University Press, Cambridge, Massachusetts.

Chakraborty, S.K. (1993), *Management by Values: Towards Cultural Congruence*, Oxford University Press, USA.

Crosby, Philip (1979), *Quality is Free*, McGraw-Hill, New York.

Dantzig, George (1963), *Linear Programming and Extensions*, Princeton University Press, Princeton, New Jersey.

Deming, W. Edwards (1986), *Out of Crisis*, MIT Press, Cambridge, Massachusetts.

Drucker, Peter F. (1955), *The Practice of Management*, William Heinemann Ltd, London.

Fayol, Henri (1967), *General and Industrial Management*, Pitman, London.

Feigenbaum, A.V. (2004), *Total Quality Control*, McGraw-Hill Professional, New York.

George, Jr. Claude S. (1974), *The History of Management Thought,* Prentice Hall of India Pvt. Ltd, New Delhi, India.

Gilbreth, Lilian (1914), *The Psychology of Management: The Function of the Mind in Determining,* *Teaching and Installing Methods of Least Waste,* www.gutenberg.org/text/16256, accessed on 15 January 2008.

Ishikawa, Kaoru (1990), *Introduction to Quality Control*, translated by J.H. Loftus, Chapman and Hill, London.

Juran, Joseph M. (ed.) (1962), *Quality Control Handbook*, 2nd edition, McGraw-Hill Book Company, New York.

Koontz, Harold (1980), 'The Management Theory Jungle Revisited', *Academy of Management Review*, vol. 5, no. 2, pp. 175–87.

Miles, Raymond E. (1975), *Theories of Management: Implications for Organization Behavior and Development*, McGraw-Hill, New York.

Peters, T.L. and R.H. Watermans Jr. (1982), *In Search of Excellence; Lessons from America's best-run companies*, Harper and Row, New York.

Shewart, Walter A. (1931), *Economic Control of Quality of Manufactured Product*, D. Van Nostrand Company, New York.

Smith, Adam (1937), *The Wealth of Nations*, Modern Library, New York.

3

Business Environment and Society

Learning Objectives

After studying this chapter, you will be able to:

- Learn and appreciate the significance of business environment and society in management
- Understand difference between old and emerging economies
- Understand the application of Michael Porter's model in diagnosing the competitive business environment
- Gain knowledge on the significance of corporate social responsibility in today's business environment
- Assess the importance of social audit
- Evaluate the difference between business ethics and ethics in business
- Comprehend the steps involved in ethical decision-making
- Define what is meant by corporate governance and its relevance to ethical standards

INTRODUCTION

The result of managerial actions as reflected in the organizational performance is the outcome of synchronization of internal systems to respond effectively to the external environment. Organizations in today's fast changing environment face intense competition, economic fluctuations, changing profile of developing and developed economies, technological breakthroughs and developments, changing social values, demographic profiles, legal systems, regulatory mechanisms, government policies, cultural profiles, etc. Organizations have to keep adjusting, adopting, and adapting by developing inbuilt response mechanisms. The test of success of managerial decisions lies in achieving customer satisfaction by developing competitive edge in providing organizational products and services that meets customer needs and requirements at the right time and the right place. Successful organizations not only focus their efforts on satisfaction of customers and other stakeholders but also on society in general. They attempt to contribute for the well-being of the society in and around their operations. The real challenge for the organizations in the present context is to achieve results by being sensitive to the social environment on one hand and having ethical approach to management on the other. Long-term sustainable growth necessarily requires ethical and value-based approach to achieve organizational goals on a continuing basis.

In this chapter, we will discuss about the importance and relevance of organizational environment for strategic management as also the need for social concern and value-based management.

EXTERNAL ENVIRONMENT

All organizations, irrespective of their goals, operate amidst changing external environment that affects and influences their strategic decisions. Management particularly at the senior and top levels must consider external factors for effective decision-making. Macro-environment that affects working of all or most organizations includes economic systems, economic conditions, political system, demographics, cultural background, technology, and legal framework (Fig. 3.1).

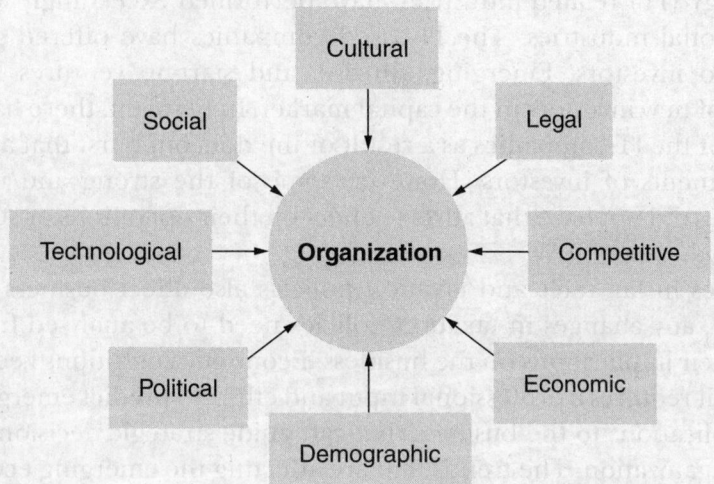

FIGURE 3.1   Macro-environment affecting organization

All the macro-environment factors—technological, demographic, economic, political, competitive, legal, cultural, and social—need to be continuously monitored and their implications on the operations of the organization need to be precisely identified. It is the systematic approach to environmental scanning that enables managers to identify important events and trends outside their organizations. It is the understanding of these factors that helps top management in its task of charting the company's future course of action.

Emerging Economy

Economics deals with optimum resource allocation so as to fulfil, to the maximum possible extent, human wants and needs. Its main focus is on understanding how people and nations produce, distribute, and consume goods and services. The vital issues concerning economic development are inflation, taxes—individual and corporate, employment of and wages paid to labour, cost of production, production processes, prices of goods and services, competitive forces, technological developments and their implications to the cost of production, and organized labour and their collective bargaining position. These issues directly affect business decisions. Any change in interest rates affect cost of capital and, in turn, cost of production. It may lead to change in consumer preferences in favour of or against savings. Inflation too affects demand for goods and services as well as cost of production. Unemployment and availability of labour affect wage rates. Corporate entities depend on raising finances from capital markets and, therefore, the effect of economic forces on operations of capital markets and general sentiments of investors affect corporate decisions pertaining to raising funds from the public. Investors seek companies that are likely to yield better returns on their investments. During the past decade, technology-based industries, in particular information technology (IT) related industries, have performed exceedingly well as compared to traditional industries. The IT-based companies have offered good investment returns to investors. Emerging, sunrise, and start-up ventures have attracted a number of new investors in the capital market. In between, there has been a setback to some of the IT companies as a result of the dot.com burst that adversely affected the sentiments of investors. However, some of the strong and well-managed IT companies did not have that adverse effect on their operations or stock price during that period.

Changes in tax rates and taxation policies also affect business operations and, therefore, any changes in taxation policies need to be analysed from the point of view of their implications on the business. Economic conditions keep changing over time and it requires a professional input and effort to predict emerging changes and their implications to the business that can guide strategic decision-making process for the organization. The trends that are affecting the emerging economies that are growing are given in Table 3.1.

From the aforesaid profile of changes, it is evident that the whole complexion of business and non-business entities has been undergoing a revolutionary change. It is this change that has vital implications to the future growth of these entities under the changed context in which information, knowledge, and global operations have been playing dominant roles.

TABLE 3.1 Trends affecting emerging economies

Old economies	Emerging economies
• Dominance of agriculture and manufacturing	• Dominance of service sector
• Local and national markets	• Global markets
• Customer behaviour—loyalty	• Customer behaviour—highly fluid
• Competitive forces—tolerable	• Competitive forces—intense
• Regulated economic regime	• Deregulated regime
• Emphasis on physical assets land, machines, and equipment	• Emphasis on human assets knowledge and information
• Physical barriers for growth	• Physical barriers—far less important

Demographics

Demographic characteristics of the population reflect the details on parameters, such as age profiles, gender profile, family as a unit and size of families, income levels, education pattern in the society and the target group, and occupation pattern. The understanding of these parameters helps in defining the characteristics of people comprising groups or other social units to comprehend the social dynamics having direct implications and bearing on the organizational strategies to achieve its goals. Population growth directly affects availability and composition of labour force. Age profile of the population affects the dynamics as regards average age in the organization and its implications on absorption of new technology, ideas, and knowledge. Organizations are required to analyse workforce demographics and their implications on availability and formulation of their human resource plans.

A diverse and young workforce provides a number of advantages in terms of flexibility, adaptation to change, etc. in an organization. Management should have policies so as to provide equality to women and minorities in employment opportunities, future growth prospects, compensation, etc. Organizations are required to make strategic plans in the backdrop of demographic data to recruit, retain, train, develop, motivate, and productively utilize people of varied demographic backgrounds, so as to achieve their goals. Managers need to prepare themselves to effectively respond to ever increasing pressure and challenges resulting from a diverse workforce.

Technological Environment

In the present context, companies cannot grow and develop without incorporating existing and emerging technologies in their strategic plans. Introduction of new technologies in an area leads to new products and services, advancement in production techniques resulting in cost advantages, and better ways to manage by way of improved communication systems and decision-making processes. Further, emergence of any new technology results in bringing about a complete change in the dynamics of that industry by developing new markets and different niches. New technologies also give rise to emergence of new techniques of production that may have greater automation on one hand and lesser dependency on human input, having direct implications on the human aspect of management. New technologies are also providing new ways to manage and communicate.

Management information systems backed up by computers have started facilitating quick decision-making processes by providing information when it is needed. Technology has been creating ever new options resulting in creation of new business opportunities of which business and non-business organizations need to be aware. Some of the options that have recently emerged as a result of IT are explained here.

Computer-aided designs and computer-controlled machines have enabled improvement in efficiency of operations, precision in quality of production, wide ranging flexibility in coming out with alternate designs to meet customer requirements as compared to traditional manufacturing machines. Internet shopping and selling have resulted in overcoming physical barriers to tap markets. Real time online financial and production systems enable companies to develop effective control mechanism and enable executives to take their decisions based on the latest information. This has also enabled development of decision support systems that are based on online flow of data that gets instantly processed.

Technology has been playing a vital role in manufacturing systems and distribution networks. Thus, the operation of for-profit and non-profit organizations is fast changing due to changes in technology. Managers need to be alert to technological changes and their implications to their companies, so as to effectively tackle and manage their operations.

Social Environment

Societal trends and preferences as reflected in the way people think and behave have a bearing on the issues related to management of human resources, social corporate actions, and strategic decisions pertaining to products and services that a company produces and offers. Smoking had become a fashion at one point of time. However, there is lot of publicity against smoking because of its health hazards. In India a joint family used to be a matter of pride, while in the present context multiplicity of family units has become a norm resulting in consequential effect on demand for products and services. Similarly, environmental issues have become prominent in the present context. These issues have direct implications on industries to prevent environmental pollution and to work for the protection of natural environment. Thus, changes in the social norms and values need to be taken into account by the management of organizations, as they have direct bearing on their operations.

Cultural Environment

Culture relates to the shared characteristics—language, religion, heritage, and values that differentiate the members of one group of people from those of another or from one nation of people from that of another. Values relate to basic beliefs of individuals and considerable importance and meaning is attached to them. Managers need to be conscious and careful about culture and values of their stakeholders, so as to develop and make their strategies and actions compatible to them. Values of individuals greatly affect operations of the organization, particularly to develop interpersonal relationships with the stakeholders. The approach to identify the problem, possible alternative solutions to the problem, clarity about ethical and non-ethical behaviour, and approaches to lead and control employees largely depend upon careful analysis about cultural practices and values of people. Thus, a careful diagnosis of culture and value system helps a great deal in understanding the expectations of customers, employees, and other stakeholders. This helps to develop appropriate response systems to manage effectively.

Competitive Environment

Each organization operates in the context of its immediate competitive environment consisting of the competitors operating in the same product or service industry. This mainly consists of specific organizations with which company directly or indirectly interacts and gets affected so far as its decisions are concerned. The competitive environment mainly constitutes forces that operate on the organization consisting of rivalry amongst existing competitors, threat of new entrants, threat of substitutes, power of suppliers, and power of customers.

Michael Porter's model—competitive diagnosis

Michael Porter, a Harvard professor, first developed the model constituting competitive forces, as shown in Fig. 3.2. A scientific diagnosis of these operating forces enables an organization to identify its competitive advantages and disadvantages so as to work out strategies to adapt to the competitive environment in order to influence the competitive environment to create favourable conditions for its operations.

The first step to understand the position and standing of an organization is to identify its competitors that may include local companies, regional, national, and global organizations operating in the same product/service line; domestic and global companies affecting its business; small domestic companies encroaching on its market share; and above all, elements, such as Internet shopping. After identifying its competitors, the organization needs to analyse the tactics used by them. The tactics for driving competitive advantage may include price reduction, product development, advertising, packaging, sales force incentives, supply chain management, and incentives offered to retailers, wholesalers, etc. It is important to understand that high technology and growth industries offer greater opportunities for growth as well as profits. However, when the industry reaches a maturity stage, its growth slows down and profits as well as profit margins decline. Ultimately, weaker companies are forced to quit the market and only the stronger companies survive.

New entrants' threat The barriers to entry may result from factors, such as government policies, huge capital investment, cost disadvantage as compared to established players in the market, disadvantage because of lack of distribution network, etc. In case such factors exist, the threat to established players in the market becomes less serious an issue. However, in case the industry does not have such barriers, the threat of

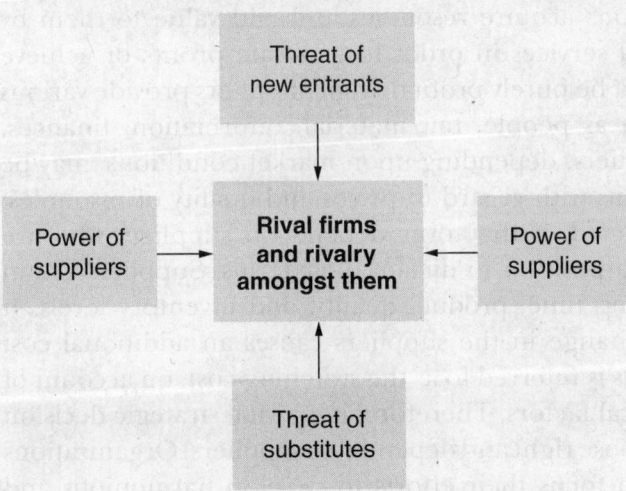

Figure 3.2 Michael Porter's model—competitive diagnosis

Emerging Indian economy

Various changes have happened in Indian economy ever since the process of liberalization and globalization was initiated in the early 1990s. The visible changes in the social transformation, such as proportionately far higher increase in the younger population, which is becoming financially independent at much younger age; accelerated increase in nuclear families; and increased media exposure, have contributed a great deal in increased consumption level of goods and services. It is estimated that presently more than half of the Indian population is part of the workforce. The fast growing services sector coupled with accelerated industrial growth is going to open up much needed opportunities for employment. Partha Duttagupta, CEO of Barista has stated 'Indian consumers were traditionally quite thrifty. A closed economy with limited opportunities for employment and, hence, the threat of an uncertain future as well as high interest rates pushed consumers towards higher savings.' The present generation has both multiple employments as also abundant entrepreneurial opportunities. With increased income potential, credit culture for spending is taking deeper roots. The economy is poised for high growth. All these changes are likely to give further boost to the culture of consumerism.

new entrants becomes a matter of serious concern. The company should formulate strategies to counter the moves of new entrants to safeguard its growth.

Threat of substitutes　Technological developments and innovations in the industry result in substitute products/services. Companies should not only understand and analyse the threat to their business from existing substitutes but also from potential substitutes. Therefore, companies are required to continuously work out the implications to their operations arising from existing and potential substitutes and create strategies to counter their effects on their business.

Power of suppliers　Organizations acquire resources and add value to them by converting them into goods and services in order to generate profits or achieve their other objectives that may not be purely profit driven. Suppliers provide various resources to organizations, such as people, raw material, information, finances, machines, and equipment. Suppliers, depending upon market conditions, may be in a position to dictate their terms with regard to prices and quality of resources. Organizations get adversely affected, if they over depend on suppliers who are powerful and are, therefore, in a position to dictate their terms. Suppliers are in a position to affect manufacturing time, product quality, and inventory levels. It is important to learn that any change in the suppliers causes an additional cost incurred by the organization. This is referred to as the switching cost, on account of economical as well as psychological factors. Therefore, it is a vital strategic decision on the part of organizations to choose right and dependable suppliers. Organizations in today's environment ought to focus their efforts to develop harmonious and trustworthy relationships with their suppliers.

Power of customers The ultimate test of success of an organization lies in winning the goodwill of existing and prospective customers. A company cannot exist if it does not have adequate customers to support its infrastructure, capital, manpower, etc. Customers add value to the existence of an organization. When a person buys a pair of shoes from a store, he/she acts as a final customer of the company. However, when a car manufacturer buys steel from steel manufacturers or clutches from clutch manufacturers, it acts as an intermediate consumer, and sells the cars to its dealers who in turn sell the same to final consumers. Similarly, when retailers purchase the products from wholesalers, they act as intermediate consumers.

Customer service means providing customers what they want, the way they want, and at a place and time they want. The quality of customer service depends on the speed and dependability with which an organization delivers its products and services. Organizations need to keep on developing strategies and take actions that lead to providing good customer service resulting in customer satisfaction, which is a source of competitive advantage. Overdependence on a few high-worth and prominent customers results in competitive disadvantage. High-worth customers are powerful and there is a possibility that they may switch over to other suppliers. Large customers having alternatives to get the product or service are able to use their power to negotiate better terms. Customer bargaining power is likely to be strong in case he/she purchases relatively large share of the supplier's output. High-worth customers spend a large proportion of their budget on the product/service and are in a position to have enough capital to go in for production on their own by integrating backwards.

All the above factors need to be appropriately diagnosed by the managers to identify their competitive advantages and disadvantages, so as to chalk out strategies that can enable them to achieve their corporate goals and objectives by responding effectively to various environmental forces.

Legal and Political Environment

The working of organizations in any society gets affected by political and legal framework and the system within which they have to operate. The policy thrust given to different industries keeps changing with the change in political regime. The clear policy thrust along with the massive investment that was made in telecom sector by the Indian government has changed the whole complexion of the communication industry in India. It was mainly an outcome of the initiative taken by the government in response to political will during the 1990s. Different industrial associations attempt to influence government decisions by providing facts and figures backed up by research outcomes and their likely adverse effects on the industry. Some of these prominent associations are Federation of Indian Chambers of Commerce and Industry (FICCI), Confederation of Indian Industry (CII), Bharat Chamber of Commerce and Industry (BCCI), Sports Industries Federation (SIF), Builders Association of India (BAI), Organization of Pharmaceutical Producers of India (OPPI), Chemical & Alkali Merchants' Association (CAMA), The Textile Association India (TAI), National Association of Software and Service Companies

Lucas–TVS Ltd

Lucas–TVS Limited, a joint venture between Lucas Varity Plc, UK and T V Sundaram Iyengar & Sons, India, manufactures automotive components and reaches out to all segments of the automotive industry, such as passenger cars, commercial vehicles, tractors, jeeps, two-wheelers, and off-highway vehicles. In 1985, the top management of Lucas–TVS had initiated a journey to make their firm a world-class manufacturing organization and took a series of steps for the same. The company's oldest plant at Padi, Chennai, acted as a test bed for several of their initiatives.

In 1983, Lucas–TVS understood that the entry of Maruti Udyog Ltd changed the Indian auto market. The top management realized the need for this paradigm shift in order to remain competitive vis-à-vis the new entrants from the global arena. A task force that was set up to work out the adaptability of the change process recommended that Lucas–TVS should focus initially on maximizing the potential of human resources, on improving the layout to facilitate smooth flow of work, and on developing clear priorities for investing in new technology and automation. After ensuring a due support of workforce for the proposed initiatives, the company had modified the layout from a process layout to a product-based layout. It also identified concrete areas where operators were given intensive training to upgrade their skills.

In 1991–92, there was severe recession in the Indian economy and Lucas–TVS's sales growth was far below the management's expectations. With liberalization, the economy was opened up to foreign competitors and investors. Steep rise in product variety increased the need for manufacturing complexities and focus on quality emerged as an important requirement for competing successfully in the new market.

In response to these new pressures, both internal and external, the company implemented simplified material flow by introducing cellular manufacturing, creating team structure, providing cross-training to work force, and introducing world-class product introduction system through in-house design. At this stage, the company initiated a low-price strategy that required tight cost control, detailed reporting, highly-structured system, and quantitative targets. To respond to emerging challenges, the company initiated various moves including process re-engineering and low-cost distribution. Considerable attention was also devoted to streamlining quality assurance systems resulting in the award of ISO 9001 in 1993.

From 1995, the company has been focusing on developing capabilities and flexibility to implement single piece flow within the plant, while simultaneously achieving just-in-time (JIT) deliveries to customers. In 1995, the company faced external pressures especially from the original equipment manufacturers (OEMs) who demanded quick responses, JIT deliveries in small lots, and reduction in prices. The implications of these developments were that Lucas–TVS needed to—(1) maintain sufficient finished goods inventories in their warehouse in New Delhi; and (2) reduce inventory levels to cut costs. By late 1998, the company had streamlined the distribution system and was following a bi-weekly shipment schedule from the Padi plant to the warehouse in New Delhi.

At the company strategy meeting in January 1999, Balaji, the Chief Executive and MD of Lucas–TVS while acknowledging the accomplishments that his managers and workers had achieved in the last 12 years, addressed issues, such as tremendous proliferation of parts and products due to the increase in the number of OEMs, the inability of around 90 per cent of their suppliers in matching their requirements, and venturing into IT-based systems as challenges ahead for them.

Source: Based on information from www.lucas-tvs.com/tvsgroup.html; www.lucas-tvs.com/, accessed on 15 July 2007.

(NASSCOM), etc. Each of these associations works for the common cause of its members who belong to the industry. Lobbying for the interests of its members becomes one of the main purposes behind the formation of such associations.

An alliance is an effort jointly put in by two or more than two organizations, groups, or individuals for achievement of common goals and objectives. An alliance broadens managerial power when the achievement of goals becomes an impossible task for an individual. Similarly, it also limits managerial power, as alliance requires certain decisions to be taken jointly.

A joint venture involves the entry of two or more firms to form a separate entity. Each firm gains from the other's competence, which in turn enables timely and efficient achievement of combined goals. Success of joint ventures mainly depends on complementary capabilities, such as distribution channels, technology, or finance available with the partners. Joint ventures are becoming an increasingly common way for firms to form strategic alliances to gain from each other's expertise and competence. Joint ventures require certain legal procedures to comply with, such as memorandum of understanding (MoU), joint venture agreement, ancillary agreement, regulatory approvals, etc.

Managers need to ensure compliance with the statutory provisions pertaining to companies in the country of their operations. In case of any conflict or dispute, they should also know how to take recourse to legal measures to safeguard their interests. Above all, the political set-up governs governmental priorities that have a direct bearing on the operations of the companies.

CORPORATE SOCIAL RESPONSIBILITY

Over the years the social involvement of corporate sector has been increasing. Earlier corporate entities were mainly focused on their economic objectives—profit, profitability, cost of production, margins, etc. However, nowadays corporate entities are posed with the challenge pertaining to the social responsibility of business. Earlier social responsibility was mainly the concern of universities, non-governmental organizations, non-profit organizations, charitable trusts, churches, etc. As such the idea of social responsibility of business is not new. Prominent business houses, such as Tatas, Birlas, and the Bajaj group, had ingrained contribution to society as a separate mission in their philosophy of business. All these groups have been contributing to the society in the areas of education, health, rural development, drinking water, etc. through specially formed trusts. The idea of social responsibility of business is getting more and more ingrained in recent years. It was given an impetus particularly with the publication of the book *Social Responsibilities of the Businessman* by Howard R. Bowen (1953), who suggested that businesses should consider the social implications of their decisions. Although there is no firm agreement on the definition of corporate social responsibility (CSR), the widely accepted definition focuses on need for seriously considering the impact of the company's actions on society. Another concept similar to CSR is social responsiveness, which refers to the extent to which a company's policies and programmes are geared to the social environment, so that it turns out to be beneficial to both the society and the company. The responsiveness focuses on actions that result in ways and means of a firm's responses to social concerns as against responsibility that focuses more on 'need' and 'should' for corporate sustained growth.

Here it is important to understand that responsiveness to social environment does not mean that managers should just be reactive to the social concerns as and when required. Corporate entities should anticipate and prepare themselves in advance to meet and respond to the emerging challenges and situations by being proactive in the area of social responsibility.

The CSR basically refers to the obligation towards the society voluntarily assumed by the business. The philosophy of business as highlighted by Keith Davis and Robert Blomstrom (1975) states 'social responsibility is the obligation of decision-makers to take actions which protect and improve the welfare of society as a whole along with their own interests'. This implies that business has to be viewed more than a money-making proposition and it provides a great opportunity to serve society. A business entity should focus its efforts on protecting the welfare of the society by creating positive benefits for the society. Different organizations have integrated CSR at different levels in terms of intensity of contribution to the other stakeholders, such as social interest groups, environmental groups, local community groups, media, consumer groups, and the society at large (Fig. 3.3). The first level is *economic responsibility*. It implies that profit is the basic foundation for all other activities. Every business entity should fulfil *legal responsibilities* by following rules and regulations of the game by obeying laws that determine what is right and what is wrong in the society. After fulfilling economic and legal responsibilities, the organization has to gear up its operations to fulfil *ethical responsibilities*. It implies taking actions and doing things that are right, just, and fair for the society, and do not cause any harm to people in general. The highest level of CSR relates to *voluntary responsibilities*, implying contributing resources for the well-being of the community and society, so as to improve the overall quality of life. Organizations that have integrated CSR in their philosophy of business contribute a great deal for the welfare of the society.

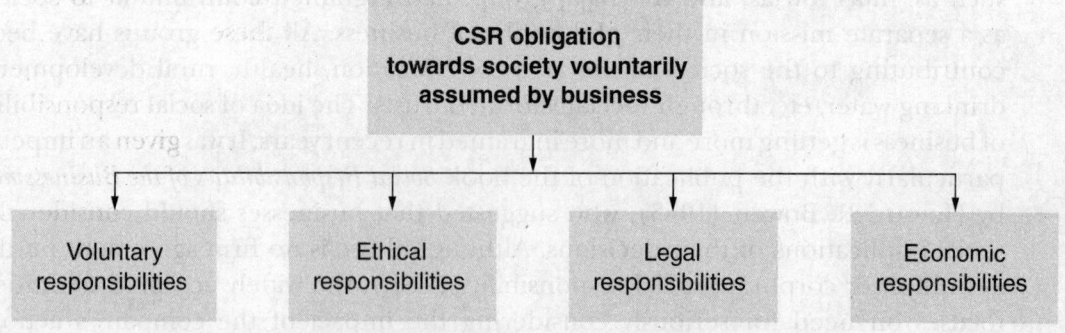

FIGURE 3.3   CSR: Different dimensions

CSR initiatives of Indian companies

Infosys Technologies Infosys Foundation, run by Sudha Murthy 'networks with the underprivileged people to lift them up. The foundation has identified five areas of operations—aged people/destitute/handicapped, rural upliftment, academically brilliant but economically backward students, education (books, schools, libraries), and health services to the underprivileged'.

Reliance The company has made a big difference in the lives of people living near its offices and plants by contributing in the areas of health, environment, and empowerment of women.

Tata Group Sir Dorabji Tata and the Sir Ratan Tata Trusts (1932) are the trusts formed by Tatas and have contributed to the founding and development of the following premier institutions, such as Tata Memorial Hospital (cancer prevention), Tata Institute of Fundamental Research (1945), Tata Institute of Social Sciences (1936), National Centre for Performing Arts (1966), Tata Theatre, and Piramal Gallery.

Tata Steel has defined its group purpose pertaining to CSR, as it will constantly strive to improve the quality of life of the communities it serves through excellence in all facets of its activities. Tata Steel is the only Indian company to have pledged to translate the Global Compact principles on human rights, labour, and environment into practice and was conferred the Global Business Coalition Award for Business Excellence in the Community for HIV/AIDS.

NTPC National Thermal Power Corporation (NTPC) has been contributing for the resettlement and rehabilitation programme for people affected directly or indirectly in the wake of the projects undertaken by NTPC.

Kamat Hotels (India) Ltd The Kamat Group had a humble and modest beginning. A clear vision along with determination and hard work, have gone a long way in helping the group to success. They have laid the strong foundation for a successful restaurant chain in India. The brand Kamat has been able to gain a strong foothold in the hospitality industry. Today customers treat Kamats as synonymous with value for money. The belief system inculcated in each and every employee focuses on the philosophy of best food and service at affordable prices. The Orchid (Kamat Hotels India) Ltd became Asia's first hotel to win the ECOTEL certification shortly after opening in May 1997 and today is the only hotel in the world to win over 50 international/national awards in eight years since inception. Under the management of Orchid owner, Vithal Kamat and Director, Param Kannampilly, the hotel has earned more environmental accolades than any other hotel in the world. It has become one of only six hotels in the world to maintain top-level, 'five-globe', ECOTEL certified status as well as ISO 14001.

The eco-friendly attitude ingrained in their philosophy of business is not merely lip service, as evident from several activities that the group undertakes for creating greater awareness about adopting friendly practices by the society at large. In one of their hotels, households from housing societies are invited. The ways and means to conserve water by using rainwater harvesting techniques are demonstrated. Employees are prepared to work for the cause of ecological issues, by devoting certain number of hours towards this cause.

The group is also focusing its efforts to be culture-sensitive by setting up heritage hotels.

Source: Based on www.orchidhotel.com/mumbai_hotels/balance.pdf; invesing.businessweek.com/research/stocks/snapshot/snapshot.asp on Kamat Hotels (India) Ltd, accessed on 10 August 2007.

This of course also provides them indirect goodwill, brand image, and even business gains. Some of the examples from Indian corporate world contributing for the CSR as part and parcel of their business have been provided in this chapter.

Advantages of CSR

Organizations that integrate CSR as part and parcel of their philosophy of growth, derive various advantages, such as improved financial performance, cost reduction, enhanced brand image and reputation, increased customer satisfaction, enhanced productivity, quality, increased market share, more engaged investors, environmental sustainability, and above all, competitive edge in the market.

Social Audit

The CSR has posed a basic question as to the criterion and process to measure social performance. This has given rise to the concept of 'social audit', which was first proposed by Bowen in the 1950s.

The social audit has been defined by Fenn and Bauer (1973) as 'a commitment to systematic assessment of and reporting on some meaningful, definable domains of the company's activities that have social impact'. Social audit provides an assessment of the impact of an organization's non-financial objectives through systematically and regularly monitoring its performance and the views of its stakeholders. Social audit can be categorized into two broad categories, namely (1) mandatory as required by government involving pollution check, employment standards, labour amenities to be provided as per the Factory Act, minimum wages to be provided, stipulated reservation to backward classes as applicable, if any, etc.; and (2) evaluation of variety of voluntary social programmes undertaken by companies (Fig. 3.4).

For effectively undertaking social audit, a corporate entity has to be clear about its organizational objectives—both internal and external. It should evaluate—(1) its action plans, that is, how is it going to work for achievement of objectives; and (2) indicators to measure the performance.

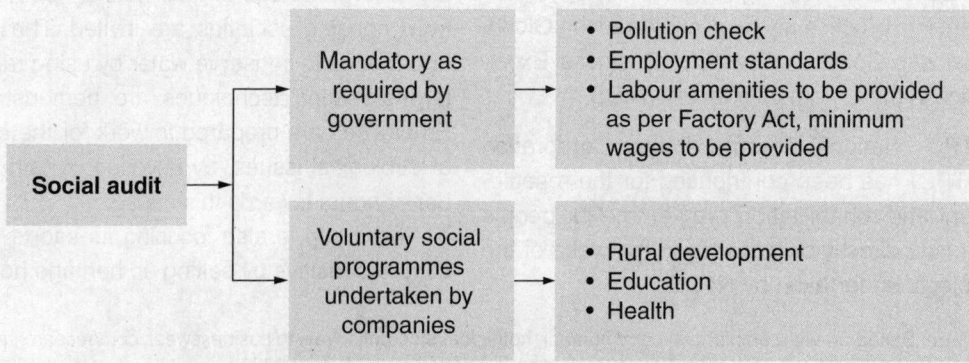

FIGURE 3.4 Social audit: Mandatory vs voluntary audit

Once indicators are in place, the organization can develop simple procedures to find out what is going on vis-à-vis the targets and to take action to bridge the gaps, if any.

ETHICS

All individuals, irrespective of their vocation, are concerned with ethics. Ethics refer to the principles of right and wrong, and moral duty and obligation that are accepted by an individual or a social group. Personal ethics relate to the rules and values that individuals follow to live and lead their life. Accounting ethics relate to code of accepted accounting practices and rules that are to be adhered to in case of company accounts.

Since ethics emanate from philosophy and not science, there is no singular correct answer to the question 'is this ethical?'. As such there are different views of ethics that can be applied to evaluate whether a particular decision or behaviour is ethically acceptable or not.

Managers while performing their roles in pursuit of achievement of corporate goals have to compete for getting information and resources, and influence employees and other stakeholders. What matters the most is the criteria and principles governing morality and acceptable conduct of business.

Normative Ethics

There are three types of moral theories pertaining to normative ethics—utilitarian theory, theory based on rights, and theory of justice. Utilitarian theory suggests that plans and actions of managers should give rise to greatest benefit and good to the largest number of people. Theory of rights emphasize that all people have rights while working in an organized group, or governmental body by law or tradition or nature. As per the Constitution of India, people have fundamental rights to equality, right to particular freedom, cultural and educational rights, right to freedom of religion, right against exploitation, and right to constitutional remedies. The theory of justice emphasizes that decision-makers' approach to problem-solving should be based on and guided by fairness, equity, and objectivity (Fig. 3.5).

Utilitarian view

The utilitarian view focuses on the welfare of the greatest number of people. It implies the greatest good for the greatest number as a criterion for weighing and evaluating decisions. Therefore, the decision that benefits the greatest number of people would be the decision of choice. This decision can be viewed as ethical as per utilitarian view, even if few people are adversely or negatively affected by it.

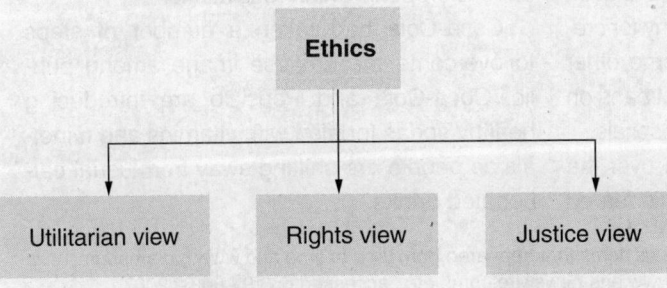

FIGURE 3.5   Ethics: Different viewpoints

Rights view

The rights view focuses on the premise that individuals have basic rights that must be protected, irrespective of associated cost to the society or to the organization. The protection of individual's rights is the main concern as per the rights view.

Justice view

The justice view is grounded in the idea that rules of organizational or societal existence must be imposed equitably to all. The focus is making a decision that is objective, without prejudice to emotions, and fair to everyone involved.

Business Ethics

Business ethics relate to true and honest practices that are adhered to in the conduct of business in various areas of operation, such as advertising, competition, public relations, social responsibilities, consumer liberty and independence, and behavioural attributes of a corporate entity in its operations in home country and abroad. Unethical practices leading to temporary business gains are becoming more and more prominent in the present context. Business houses attempt to gain competitive advantage to improve their profits by taking recourse to unethical acts,

Coca-Cola

Coca-Cola's operations in India have come under intense scrutiny as many communities are experiencing extreme water shortage, and contamination in the groundwater and soil as a result of its bottling plant operations. It has also been alleged that due to the amount of water required to produce Coca-Cola, ground water is drying up, forcing farmers to relocate. A public movement is emerging to hold the company accountable for wrong actions. The state of Kerala had imposed a ban on its products and the matter is pending in the Supreme Court. One of the largest Coca-Cola plants located in Plachimada has remained shut for 17 months because the village council refused to renew its license, blaming the company for creating pollution and water shortage. Some other state governments have imposed partial bans on the product in schools, colleges, and hospitals.

There exists a widespread concern over the process of producing the soft drink. It is feared that the water used to produce Coke may contain unhealthy pesticides and other chemicals beyond permissible limits. In 2003, the Centre for Science and Environment (CSE), a non-governmental organization in New Delhi, claimed that aerated waters produced by soft drink manufacturers in India, including multinational giants PepsiCo and Coca-Cola, contains toxins including lindane, DDT, etc., that can cause cancer and a breakdown of the immune system. The CSE found that PepsiCo's Indian-produced soft drink products had 36 times and Coca-Cola's 30 times the level of pesticide residues permitted under European Union regulations.

Coca-Cola had taken a number of steps to overcome the adverse image among public. Coca-Cola and PepsiCo are introducing healthy sodas fortified with vitamins and minerals as people are shifting away from usual carbonated drinks.

Source: Developed on the basis of various news items that appeared from time to time and www.indiaresource.org/campaigns/coke/2004/cokemehdiganj.html, www.ens-newswire.com/, etc., accessed on 19 August 2007.

such as insider trading, bribery, unethical accounting practices by providing incorrect information to customers and investors, and using wrong means to influence people in power. Managers by being dishonest to customers and colleagues try to take advantage of the situation. Enron, WorldCom, and Tyco International are some of the recent cases from the corporate world where the management manipulated company data for personal gains, thus leading to the collapse of these companies. As a result, investors who had put in their hard-earned money lost all they had invested. These incidents have created a greater debate in favour of business ethics. The need for profits through values and long-term sustained growth requiring adherence to ethical business practices is being realized more and more by managers. 'There are two big driving forces behind the growth of the ethics industry: Sarbanes–Oxley Act 2002 and the USA sentencing guidelines. The debate has shifted from whether to be ethical to how to be ethical. Five years ago, the debate was theoretical. Now, corporate governance is an important part of the analysis on Wall Street', says Michael Connor, publisher of the magazine *Business Ethics*. An example of Coca-Cola, the way it reacted and responded to the challenges posed by public movement, is given here.

Ethical climate
Ethical climate of an organization refers to the ways and means by which decisions are evaluated and made keeping in view what is right and wrong. The ethical criteria used to judge the decisions in an organization create a climate and culture in the organization. Ethical climate in the organization should help in explicitly defining its corporate standards and expectations from its employees. Employees need to dovetail their personal ethical codes with that of organizational standards and expectations so as to contribute their best to the achievement of organizational goals.

Ethical decision-making
An organization should develop policies that ensure ethical inputs in the process of decision-making. Further, certain checks and balances as defined through operational guidelines may help in avoiding non-adherence to ethical standards and code of conduct. The steps that can help in ethical decision-making are as follows:

1. Define the problem and issue clearly and explicitly.
2. Jot down the values relevant to the situation for the issue under consideration from the short- and long-term perspective.
3. Analyse the issue vis-à-vis conflicting values and choose an alternative that takes care of most crucial values.
4. Implement the decision.

Code of ethics
Every profession and organization should have well-defined code of ethics. A code means a statement of policies, principles, and rules that define the boundaries within which an individual should behave in the organization. Code of ethics is required for all organizations, business or otherwise, and for all professions. For example,

Wipro Limited's emphasis on code of conduct and values in management has been the secret of its success.

CORPORATE GOVERNANCE AND ETHICAL STANDARDS

'Corporate governance, which can be defined narrowly as the relationship of a company to its shareholders or, more broadly, as its relationship to society...', according to an article in *Financial Times* (1997). 'Corporate governance is about promoting corporate fairness, transparency and accountability' according to J. Wolfensohn, President of the World Bank, as quoted in an article in *Financial Times* (21 June 1999). Figure 3.6 illustrates the various steps in ethical decision-making.

Since liberalization, India's economic scenario has undergone rapid changes. The process of globalization has significantly increased business risks and has compelled Indian companies to adopt international norms of transparency and good governance. In the emerging global competitive scenario, the freedom of executive management and its ability to respond to the dynamics of a fast-changing business environment will be the key input to the success of the organization. Professionally managed corporates have started defining their corporate governance practices to provide all required information to the shareholders and other stakeholders, in order to win their confidence.

ITC defines corporate governance as a systemic process by which companies are directed and controlled to enhance their wealth-generating capacity. Since large corporations employ vast quantum of societal resources, the company believes that the governance process should ensure that these companies are managed in a manner that meets stakeholders' aspirations and societal expectations.

HDFC, within its web of relationships with its borrowers, depositors, agents, shareholders, and other stakeholders has always maintained its fundamental principles of corporate governance—integrity, transparency, and fairness. For HDFC, corporate governance is a continuous journey, seeking to provide an enabling environment to harmonize the goals of maximizing shareholder value and maintaining a customer-centric focus.

Organizations that follow corporate governance practices move continuously towards raising their ethical standards. Professional approach to management ensures greater and greater public disclosure and publicity, and an increased concern about the well-informed public. To ensure strict adherence to ethical codes,

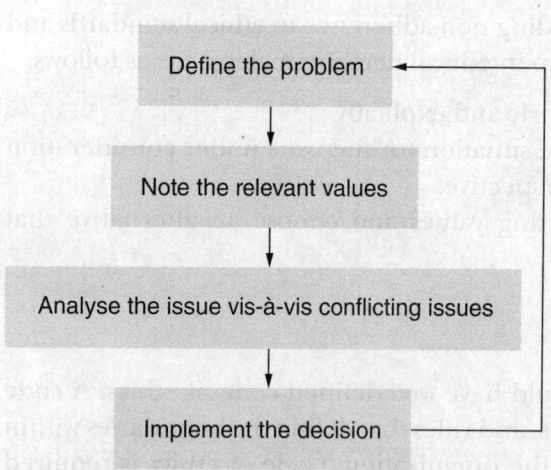

FIGURE 3.6 Steps in ethical decision-making

Ethical dilemma

My mother is serving as a senior manager in a multinational bank. Therefore, it is difficult for her to single-handedly manage the house along with her career. We have been always depending upon a trustworthy and reliable servant. Sushmita has been serving as servant in our house for the past 10 years. Her husband was an alcoholic and had died long back without leaving a penny behind. Sushmita had a small child of seven years old to take care of. Suddenly, she was diagnosed with a critical disease that demanded complete bed rest for a year along with medication. She did not seek any monetary help from my mother. However, she requested my mother to employ her young son.

We tried to convince her about the importance of education and, in particular, elementary education that would play a critical role in shaping his future. However, her helplessness made her adamant to stick to her decision of seeking an employment for the child. Sushmita represents numerous other people all over the country who live hand-to-mouth to make both ends meet and, therefore, are not able to appreciate the importance of education. This leads to a perpetual cycle of poverty.

My mother did not mind substituting Sushmita with her son. She thought that by doing so she will get a trustworthy servant and at the same time could provide a livelihood to their family. However, my father felt that it is the moral responsibility of every educated person to advocate and contribute to the promotion of education, so as to dispel the darkness of ignorance and poverty. This led to dilemma and conflict in the family.

Wipro Limited—Code of business conduct and ethics

Azim Premji, the Chairman of Wipro Limited, leads by example. He practises what he preaches. According to him, there has to be no scope for the slightest deviation when it comes to upholding basic ethical values. Wipro managers felt pensive when they heard that their Chairman was flying down to Bangalore for a meeting. It was obvious to them that something crucial was in the offing. Premji came straight to the point. A senior general manager of the company had been given marching orders because he had inflated a travel bill. The man's contribution to the company was significant; the bill's amount was not. Yet, he had to go for this seemingly minor lapse. It was, Premji stressed, a matter of principle.

Wipro's code of conduct for employees says it all, 'Don't do anything that you're unwilling to have published in tomorrow's newspapers with your photograph next to it'.

Wipro, in its code of conduct and business ethics, has highlighted its promise as 'With utmost respect to human values, we promise to serve our customer with integrity, through innovative, value-for-money solutions, by applying thought, day after day.'

Premji has stressed the basic ethics of the company in these words, 'We believe that all of you have the maturity and integrity to take a call when faced with major choices and dilemmas. To make your job easier we have tried to define some guidelines in critical areas like conflict of interest, confidentiality, intellectual property, insider trading, sexual harassment, etc.'

(contd)

Exhibit (*Contd*)

The company has clearly stated that it will only obtain and conduct business legally and ethically. There has to be utmost concern about quality of products and the efficiency of services at the most competitive prices.

On the issue of situations involving 'conflict of interest' where the interests or benefits of one person or entity conflict with the interests or benefits of the company, the code of conduct emphatically states that employees are expected to devote their full attention to the business interests of the company.

It is this clarity in business and values that Wipro has imbibed in its culture and that has taken it to great heights in achieving extraordinary results year after year.

Source: Based on information from www.wipro.com/pdf_files/code_of_business_conduct_Dec04.pdf, accessed on 9 September 2007, and Life Positive, accessed in January 2001, www.lifepositive.com/Mind/worls/corporate-manmanagement-premji.asp, accessed on 9 September 2007.

organizations make due provisions to ensure their effective implementation and enforcement. In such organizations, unethical managers are duly punished by withholding their privileges and benefits. Great emphasis is also now being laid to teaching of ethics and values as part and parcel of course curriculum in business schools as also in university system, so as to raise ethical standards in business dealings.

SUMMARY

All organizations, irrespective of their goals, operate amidst changing social, cultural, legal, competitive, political, economic, and technological environment. These factors affect and influence their strategic decisions. Technology has been instrumental in the creation of new business opportunities. Organizations have to develop inbuilt response mechanisms to keep adjusting, adopting, and adapting to rapid environmental changes.

Earlier corporate entities were mainly focusing on their economic objectives—profit, profitability, cost of production, margins, etc. However, now corporate entities are posed with the challenge pertaining to social responsibility of business. Earlier social responsibility was mainly the concern of universities, non-governmental organizations, non-profit organizations, charitable trusts, churches, etc. Now different organizations have integrated CSR at different levels in terms of intensity of contribution to the other stakeholders, such as social interest groups, environmental groups, local community groups, media, consumer groups, and the society at large.

The ethical criteria used to judge the decisions in an organization create a climate and culture in the organization. Ethical climate in the organization should help in explicitly defining its corporate standards and expectations from its employees. An organization should develop policies that ensure ethical inputs in the process of decision-making. Every profession and organization should have well-defined code of ethics, corporate governance practices, and ethical standards.

It is the implementation of well-defined code of ethics and good corporate governance practices in an organization that helps in long-term sustainable growth.

KEYWORDS

Alliances It refers to an effort jointly put in by two or more than two organizations, groups, or individuals for the achievement of common goals and objectives.

Business environment Micro and macro forces within which a business operates is called a business environment.

Business ethics It refers to true and honest practices to be adhered to in the conduct of business.

Code of ethics A statement of policies, principles, and rules that define the boundaries within which an individual should behave in the organization.

Corporate governance It is about promoting corporate fairness, transparency, and accountability.

Corporate social responsibility (CSR) The obligation of a business entity towards the society. It is about the way companies manage the business processes to produce a positive impact on society.

Economic responsibilities It is about maximizing profits and value for shareholders by producing goods and services that satisfy customer needs and wants.

Emerging economy Economies that are undergoing fast transformation leading to accelerated growth under the changed context in which information, knowledge, and global operations play a critical and dominant role.

Ethical decision-making Policies that ensure ethical inputs in the process of decision-making.

Ethical responsibilities It refers to taking actions and doing things that are right, just, and fair for the society and do not cause any harm to people in general.

Ethics in business It refers to principles of right and wrong, moral duty, and obligation that are accepted by an individual or a social group.

Joint venture Involves two or more firms entering into a partnership to form a separate entity.

Legal responsibilities A company's obligations to comply with various laws that regulate day-to-day business activities and operations.

Michael Porter's model A scientific diagnosis of competitive operating forces that enables an organization to identify its competitive advantages and disadvantages.

Social audit A commitment of an organization towards systematic assessment and reporting on some meaningful, definable domain of the company's activities that have social impact.

EXERCISES

Concept Review Questions

1. What is the real challenge for organizations in this fast changing business environment? Discuss.
2. What are the characteristics of an emerging economy?
3. Define the five forces that operate on an organization as per Michael Porter's model. What is the purpose of diagnosing these competitive forces?
4. Define corporate social responsibility. What are the different levels at which organization can respond to the challenge of CSR? Which level is said to be the best way for long-term sustainable growth of the organization and why?
5. What are the three types of moral theories pertaining to normative ethics? What is their relevance to business decision-making?
6. What are the steps involved in ethical decision-making?
7. How are corporate governance and ethical standards related?

Critical Thinking Question

'Ethics and business ethics are two different concepts.' Comment critically.

Project Assignments

1. Take four companies from a particular industry and go through their websites particularly from the point of view of policies and practices followed in the area of CSR. Compare their policies and practices vis-à-vis their corporate financial performance. Comment on the relevance of CSR

practices and their effect on corporate performance.

2. Consider a particular industry and take a specific company within the industry and analyse relevance, magnitude, and intensity of Porter's five forces operating on it. Based on the analysis of these forces, work out competitive advantage in favour of the company and the strategy that would be most relevant for the company to strengthen its competitive advantage.

REFERENCES

Bowen, Howard R. (1953), *Social Responsibilities of the Businessman*, Harper Brothers, New York.

Fenn, Dan H., Jr and Raymond A. Bauer (1973), 'What is a Corporate Social Audit?', *Harvard Business Review*, January–February, p. 38.

Census India (2010), 'Age Structure and Marital Status', Census India, http://censusindia. gov.in/Census_And_You/age_structure_and_ marital_status.aspx, accessed on 30 June 2014.

4

Planning—A Tool for Effective Management

INTRODUCTION

Effective planning is essential for the success of any organization. Successful conceptualization and implementation of projects require the coordination of a wide array of activities, information, and expertise. Since business opportunities are time bound, organizations need to act quickly to effectively avail them. Once acquired, projects need to be implemented efficiently and quickly. These challenging developments in the business environment have heightened the need for effective planning and control. Thus, achieving any goal at corporate or individual level requires a systematic and well-planned process of decision-making. Early efforts at diagnosing a problem helps in identifying remedies and in tackling the problem with least input of resources such as time, money, capital, and personnel. Those organizations that successfully grow, develop, and diversify are usually found to be the ones that have put in place a meticulous system of planning as a prerequisite before entering into the action phase. The concept of planning is equally applicable to individuals and organizations for its effectiveness.

PLANNING

Planning refers to a systematic approach towards making decisions about goals and objectives and the associated activities that need to be carried out along with various resource requirements (Fig. 4.1). It is not an informal

Learning Objectives

After studying this chapter, you will be able to:

- Understand the importance of planning
- Know what plan and planning mean
- Learn about the steps involved in planning
- Learn about different types and levels of planning
- Understand SWOT analysis as a tool for business strategies development
- Understand the use of BCG matrix in categorization of businesses
- Understand the concept of MBO and its relevance to planning

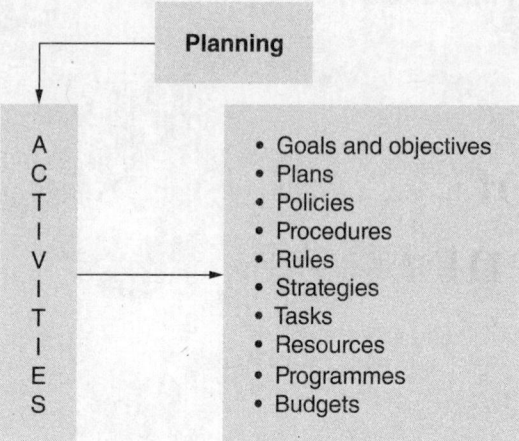

Planning

A
C
T
I
V
I
T
I
E
S

- Goals and objectives
- Plans
- Policies
- Procedures
- Rules
- Strategies
- Tasks
- Resources
- Programmes
- Budgets

FIGURE 4.1   Planning and its various facets

or unorganized response to a situation. Rather, it is a conscious, purposive, directed, and controlled effort put in by managers to achieve predetermined objectives. It provides a clear direction to individuals, groups, and departments to carry on their activities along with the provision to modify their actions depending upon the changing conditions. The need and importance of a formal and organized planning process has been growing with the ever-increasing complexity of the working environment.

Planning is the first and foremost step to be taken before undertaking any activity in the field of management. It helps in setting the direction for the achievement of goals. It is essential to customize the planning process to meet the needs and nature of the organization. Some common terms that would be used to understand the concept of planning are—goals and objectives, plans, policies, procedures, rules, strategy, task, resources, programme, and budget.

Goals and objectives   Goals refer to specific objectives that an organization aspires to accomplish in total, or in some combination, in order to achieve its mission. It represents the end point of planning. It is the end towards which organizing, staffing, leading, and controlling functions are geared up. Objectives are clear and verifiable yardsticks against which performance can be measured. The accomplishment of various functional and departmental objectives leads to the achievement of goals. Goals are ends that the managers aspire to achieve. They should be specific, clear, challenging, and realistic. The definition of goals may vary from organization to organization. In case of corporate entities, they may be defined in terms of profit, return on investment, return on assets, market share, and product diversification. Larger organizations develop a hierarchy of goals at top, middle, and lower levels. Corporate goals are set by top management—board of directors chief executive officer, and the top layer of executives. The degree of participation and involvement in the process of setting goals at the top differs from one organization to another. The setting of sub-goals at subsequent levels in the organization has to be in tune and harmony with top-level goals. This helps managers at subsequent levels to visualize their roles in contribution to the accomplishment of corporate goals.

Plans   Plans are the actions or means that a manager proposes to use for achieving predetermined goals. This step enables a manager to define a set of actions that may realize organizational goals, resources required for the same, and the obstacles that may come in the way. A plan indicates what the management wants to achieve. It specifies the steps that are to be taken towards the achievement of goals.

Policies   Policies refer to a broad statement and/or a set of guidelines that direct decision-making. It is a plan of action adopted by an individual or an organization. They define the framework within which managers are expected to make decisions leading to the achievement of objectives. However, all policies may not be in the written form. Certain repeated actions or precedents set by senior level managers may also be considered as policies for the organization. Thus, a policy is a standing plan that provides broad guidelines within which executives need to take actions consistent with achievement of organizational objectives. 'Our organization will only sanction loans to companies having excellent rating' can be a policy for sanction of loans adopted by a bank. Similarly, a company may specify its policy as 'procurement of quality raw materials from leading suppliers' or a policy 'to recruit only graduates and postgraduates who have obtained distinction from universities recognized by the University Grants Commission'.

Procedures   Procedures are plans that set out the required methods and processes to handle future activities. A process may be defined as a series of acts especially of a practical or mechanical nature involved in a particular form of work. Procedures in an organization cut across departments and thereby bring in uniform practices.

Rules   Rules refer to principles or conditions that govern behaviour. They define specific required actions and inactions in given circumstances. They do not provide for discretion or deviation in making decisions. They are a guide to conduct or action that the organization is required to follow in order to achieve its goals.

Strategies   Strategies are an elaborate and systematic plan of action. These are the methods or processes required in total, or in some combination, to achieve goals. It is a pattern of actions duly backed-up by resource allocations.

New priorities and policies   New priorities relate to any material change in product and or service profile from the current business activity. This change means introduction of additional products or services having funding implications to the organization. Although major increases in costs due to continuation of current levels of products and service are technically not new priorities, if significant, for the sake of simplicity and clarity they should be included in this category.

All new priorities should be brought forward, irrespective of their source of funding. This helps in communicating changes in business practice and service levels both horizontally and vertically within business and finance. No priority in an organization is considered approved unless the approval is communicated in writing by an appropriate sanctioning authority. Usually a company's policies specifically prohibit the undertaking and the implementation of new priorities solely on the basis that the unit does not need financial support, as it has funding capacity. All new priorities will require a sound business case before being considered by the appropriate authority. Proper justification for new priorities should include the following:

1. What will be the benefits of this priority to the 'customers'?
2. Is it possible to discontinue old programmes so as to shift resources internally to fund the priority?

3. What are the implications if the priority is not approved?

4. All new priorities proposed to be undertaken should be prioritized on the following criteria—mandatory, due to external regulations; critical, for improvement; and important, for operational efficiency.

Objectives   Objectives are specific targets that must be accomplished in total, or in some combination to achieve the predetermined goals in the plan. They are 'milestones' along the way of implementing the strategies.

Tasks   A piece of work that is undertaken to contribute towards the achievement of objectives is referred to as a task. Particularly in small organizations, people are assigned various tasks required to implement the plan. When the scope of the plan is very limited, tasks and activities are often essentially the same.

Resources   Resources include the people, materials, machines, technologies, money, etc. required to implement the strategies or processes. The costs of these resources are often depicted in the form of a budget.

Programmes   A programme is a combination of goals, policies, procedures, rules, set of activities to be undertaken, resources to be deployed, and other interrelated actions required to be undertaken for accomplishment of a purpose. Programmes are normally required to be backed up and supported by budgets.

Budgets   A budget is a statement of expected provisions or results expressed in numerical terms. It can be for inputs as well as outputs. When we refer to the budget pertaining to inputs, it relates to resources while budget pertaining to outputs relates to goals and objectives. Budget can be expressed in various units such as physical units—number of labour/machine hours and financial terms—profit in rupees, salaries in rupees, etc. A budget is also used as an effective instrument of control. Any deviations from the budget, positive or negative, have to be duly analysed, and corrective action taken.

Steps Involved in the Planning Process

The steps involved in the planning process involves situational analysis; formulating desired goals, objectives, and result; goal and plan evaluation; establishing goals and plans; chalking out strategies to reach goals; and acknowledging completion.

Situational analysis

The contingency approach to planning begins with situational analysis (Fig. 4.2). Keeping in view the time and resource constraints, a planner should collect, process, analyse, and interpret all relevant data pertaining to the objectives under consideration. Scanning the internal environment helps in identifying the forces that operate within the system and their implication on the organizational goals. An in-depth situational analysis enables understanding of past events, examination of current situations, and working out alternative future scenarios. 'Taking stock' is a basic prerequisite to any planning process, whether done consciously or unconsciously. For strategic planning, it is important to conduct an internal as well

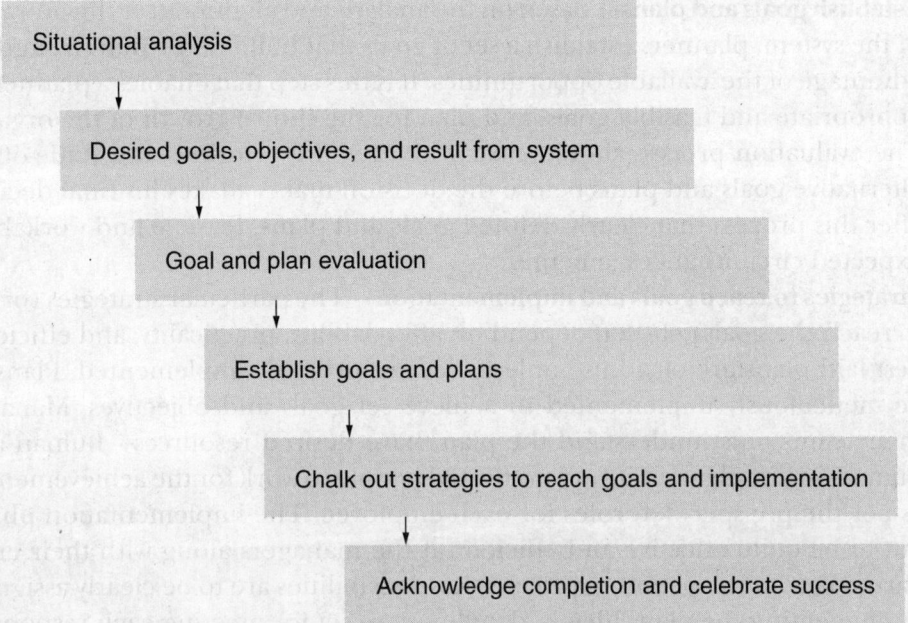

FIGURE 4.2   Various steps involved in planning

as external scanning of environment. This scan usually involves considering various driving forces or major influences that are likely to have implications on the future working of the organization. For example, during strategic planning, planners often conduct a 'SWOT analysis'. SWOT is an acronym for the strengths, weaknesses, opportunities, and threats faced by the organization. During this analysis, planners can also use a variety of assessments or methods to 'measure' the health of a system.

Desired goals, objectives, and results   During planning, planners (consciously or unconsciously) have in mind an overall outcome. For example, during strategic planning, it is critical to keep in mind the mission, or overall purpose, of the organization. As an outcome of situational analysis, the planning process sets alternative goals that the organization plans to pursue and the ways and means to achieve the same. This step unfolds creativity in the organization, resulting in multiple solutions to the issue under consideration. Any evaluation of the alternatives should only be thought of after generating all possible alternative solutions to the problem.

Goal and plan evaluation   After having identified various alternatives to resolve the issue, decision-makers have to evaluate the advantages and disadvantages, and potential implications of each alternative goal and plan. These alternatives have to be evaluated in the light of organizational capabilities and competencies, existing or proposed, to be developed. At this stage, the decision-maker has to prioritize various goals and eliminate those that do not agree with the organization's existing potential and capacity. He also needs to consider the implications of various other plans designed to achieve high-priority goals.

Establish goals and plans   Based on the analysis and alignment to the overall mission of the system, planners establish a set of goals that build on proven strengths to take advantage of the available opportunities. It is this step that enables a planner to select appropriate and feasible goals, and plan for the future growth of the organization. The evaluation process should clearly identify the priorities and trade-offs among alternative goals and plans before the decision-maker makes his final decision. It is after this process that clearly defined goals and plans, feasible and workable within expected circumstances, emerge.

Strategies to reach goals and implementation   The particular strategies (or methods to reach the goals) chosen depend on affordability, practicality, and efficiency. The best laid plans are of no use unless they are properly implemented. Plans need to be meticulously implemented to achieve set goals and objectives. Managers and their teams must understand the plan, have desired resources—human and non-human—to implement it, and motivated people to work for the achievement of goals as per the pre-specified roles for each employee. The implementation phase turns out to be quite effective and efficient, if the managers along with their employees participate, in the planning process. Responsibilities are to be clearly assigned while implementing the plan. Ideally, deadlines are set for meeting each responsibility.

Acknowledge completion and celebrate success   This critical step is often ignored, eventually undermining the success of many future organizational planning efforts. The purpose of a plan is to address a current problem situation or pursue a developmental goal. It is important for the leader to acknowledge the team effort and celebrate after the problem has been solved or the goal met. However, this step is often ignored in the planning process at times due to the unnecessary hurry to solve the next problem. Skipping this step results in apathy, scepticism, and cynicism amongst the employees. It is very important to celebrate success to boost the morale of employees and encourage them for performing better in their future tasks and roles.

TYPES AND LEVELS OF PLANNING

It is also important to know that planning is undertaken in cycles within a particular time frame (Fig. 4.3). Businesses prepare the following types of plans in order to meet their stated objectives:

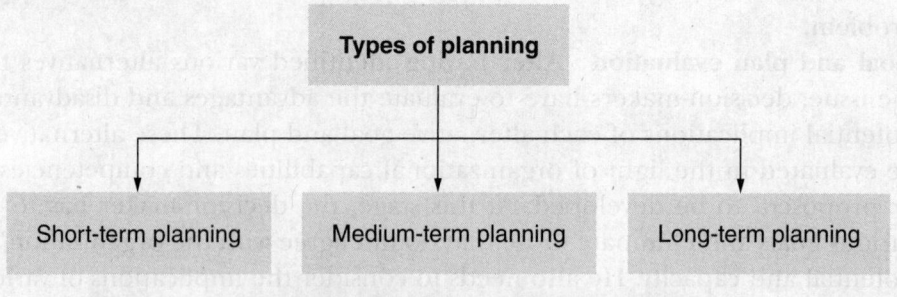

FIGURE 4.3   Types of planning

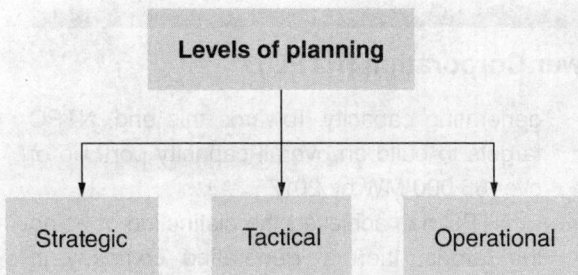

FIGURE 4.4   Levels of planning

Short-term plan: Designed to solve immediate, pressing problems. It is normally for a period of less than six months.

Medium-term plan: Designed to address problems, issues, and challenges with a six-month to three-year time horizon.

Long-term plan: Designed to set long-term, strategic objectives for the company with a time horizon of three to five years.

Levels of planning in an organization correspond with the levels of managers (Fig. 4.4). The three vital levels of managers and associated planning levels are top-level, middle-level, and frontline-level. The top-level is involved in strategic planning, the middle-level with tactical planning, and the frontline with operational planning.

Strategic planning

Business managers are often so engrossed in immediate issues that they lose track of their ultimate goals. That is the reason why a strategic plan and its review become essential for the success of an organization. Strategic planning may not necessarily lead to success, but without it a business is much more likely to fail. A strategic plan should include:
- framework for decision-making and for securing support/approval;
- basis for more detailed planning;
- an insight about the business to others in order to inform, motivate, and involve;
- mechanism for benchmarking and performance monitoring; and
- long-term direction for the business.

Strategic planning is undertaken by the top-level management. It deals with decision-making about the organization's long-term goals and strategies. Strategic plans have a dominant external environment orientation and input. Strategic goals are the end results that a company aspires to achieve for its long-term survival and growth. They have to emphasize on both effectiveness and efficiency issues pertaining to organizational growth. Strategic goals should be visionary, conceptual, and directional, in contrast to an operational plan, which is likely to be of short-term, tactical, focused, implementable, and measurable. As an example, compare the process of planning a vacation (where, when, duration, budget, who goes, how to travel—are all strategic issues) with the final preparations (tasks, deadlines, funding, weather, packing, transport, and so on are all operational matters). It should be realistic and attainable so as to allow managers to think strategically. Some of the vital strategic goals include return on equity, return on assets, quantity, and quality of outputs.

National Thermal Power Corporation (NTPC)

The vision of National Thermal Power Corporation (NTPC) is to be 'A world class integrated power major, powering India's growth, with increasing global presence'. Its mission is to 'develop and provide reliable power, related products and services at competitive prices, integrating multiple energy sources with innovative and eco-friendly technologies and contribution to society.' Over the last three decades, NTPC has spearheaded development of thermal power generation in the Indian power sector. In this process, it has built a strong portfolio of coal and gas/liquid fuel based generation capacities. The company has made initial forays in the area of hydropower development and plans to have a significant share of hydro power in its future generation portfolio. Although NTPC is also offering technical services, both in domestic and international markets, through its consultancy wing, the generation business continues to be the single largest revenue generator for NTPC.

Developing and operating world-class power stations is NTPC's core competence. Its scale of operation, financial strength, and large experience serve to provide an advantage over competitors. To meet the objective of making available reliable and quality power at competitive prices, NTPC continues to speedily implement projects and introduce state-of-the-art technologies. India's power generation capacity can be expected to grow from the current levels of 120 GW (approx.) to about 225–250 GW (approx.) by 2017. NTPC currently accounts for about 20 per cent of the country's installed capacity and almost 60 per cent of the total installed capacity in the central sector in the country. Going forward, in its target to remain the largest generating utility of India, NTPC endeavours to maintain or improve its share of India's generating capacity. Towards this end, NTPC targets to build an overall capacity portfolio of over 66,000 MW by 2017.

NTPC has achieved the distinction of being the largest thermal generating company in India. In the past, this focus was adequate as the industry was highly regulated with limited diversification opportunities. However, over the last few years, the country has been facing acute shortages, both in coal and gas, severely affecting optimum utilization of its power stations. These shortages are likely to continue in future as well. This is in spite of the fact that India is one of the largest producers of coal in the world. To safeguard its competitive advantage in power generation business, NTPC has moved ahead in diversifying its portfolio to emerge as an integrated power major, with a presence across the entire energy value chain. In fact, to symbolize this change, NTPC has taken on a new identity and a new name 'NTPC Limited'. NTPC has recently diversified into coal mining business primarily to secure its fuel requirements and support its aggressive capacity addition programme. In addition, NTPC is also emphasizing on diversification in the areas of power trading and distribution. Diversification would also allow NTPC to offer new growth opportunities to its employees while leveraging their skills to capitalize on new opportunities in the sector.

By the year 2017, NTPC would have successfully diversified its generation mix, diversified across the power value chain and entered overseas markets. As a result, NTPC would have altered its profile significantly. Elements of the revised profile that NTPC seeks to achieve are:

- Placed among the top five market capitalization corporations in the Indian market

(Contd)

Exhibit *(Contd)*

- An Indian MNC with presence in many countries
- Diversified utility with multiple businesses
- Setting benchmarks in project construction and plant availability and efficiency
- Preferred employer

- Have a strong research and technology base
- Loyal customer base in both bulk and retail supply
- A leading corporate citizen with a keen focus on executing its social responsibility

Source: Based on information from http://www.ntpc.co.in/growthplans/growth.shtml. Accessed on 10 June 2007.

Tactical and operational planning

Strategic plans of the organizations give rise to goals that become the basis for planning among the middle- and the frontline-level managers. Goals and objectives become far more specific and short-term as planning process moves from strategic to tactical and then to operational.

Tactical planning deals primarily with the specific goals and plans pertaining to functional areas—production, marketing, human resources management, etc. It deals with major actions pertaining to the implementation phase of the planning process. Some of the salient features of a tactical plan are that it:

- turns strategy into reality;
- usually has medium term, that is, one- to two-year time span;
- derives input from the strategic plan and usually gets integrated with the annual budget process; and
- focuses on project plans and project budgets.

Operational planning deals with specific systems, procedures, and processes required to implement the tactical plan at the level of the operational or frontline manager. The operational plans have a very short time span say daily, weekly, or monthly and focus mainly on routine tasks such as daily production planning and control, sales, delivery schedules, and personnel management aspects. It is important to understand that there should be one to one coordination between strategic, tactical, and operational plans. All the three should support each other mutually. The guiding force behind operational plans should emanate from tactical plans and for tactical plans from strategic plans. Operational plans help project managers to organize tasks and monitor progress.

SWOT ANALYSIS

SWOT analysis is used for developing business strategies. It evaluates the strengths and weaknesses within the organization and the opportunities and threats present in the external environment (Fig. 4.5).

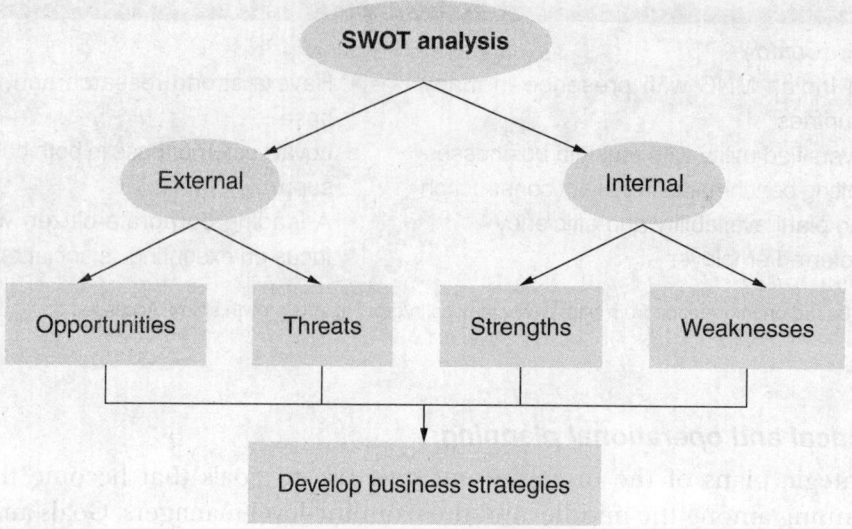

FIGURE 4.5   SWOT analysis

Threats and opportunities

A systematic and successful strategic management largely depends upon rigorous and thorough analysis of external environment relevant to the organization. The various components of external environment as highlighted in the earlier chapter are—economic, social, cultural, technological, legal, and competitive. The external environment analysis begins with industry analysis in the light of overall economic development. Stakeholders' analysis relates to all those individuals/groups that affect and get affected by the organization's mission, goals, and objectives. They include customers, employees, suppliers, government, competitors, unions, regulatory bodies, etc. Environmental analysis also examines other vital forces such as macroeconomic conditions, technological factors, and sociocultural influences. The purpose of environmental analysis is to come out with future trends relevant to the organization.

Thus, by conducting an external environmental analysis, organizations attempt to identify external threats and opportunities that are presented before it. These can be found in the industry the firm operates in, the market place, competition, and technology.

The organization's own industry may undergo structural changes in terms of size and segmentation, growth patterns in a particular stage in the life cycle of the industry, established patterns and relationships, and international scenario. The marketplace may undergo changes due to economic or social factors such as customers, distribution channels, economic factors, social/demographic profiles, political set-up, and environmental factors.

Competition can be a source of threats or opportunities to the organization. It may create new identities, performance criteria, dynamics about market shares, new product and service developments, aggressiveness, strengths, and weaknesses.

New developments in technology may cause fundamental changes in products, processes, and service delivery mechanisms. Technological developments lead to the emergence of substitute products, alternative solutions, cost savings, and qualitative improvements.

Strengths and weaknesses

Strengths and weaknesses are essentially internal to the organization and pertain to its resources. These relate to human and non-human resources, processes, and programs in key areas. Resources are the inputs that enhance the performance of an organization. Resources can be divided into two broad categories—tangible and intangible, and human and non-human. Tangible resources are assets such as machines, raw materials, building, and real estate. Intangible resources are the assets that are abstract in nature such as goodwill, culture, human capabilities, and culture.

Resources provide the competitive edge to the organization if they are of special customer value and are rare and difficult to copy. The organization should be able to organize resources in order to derive the greatest competitive advantage out of them. Every organization has to identify its major strengths and weaknesses that contribute positively or negatively to its organizational goals. A proper diagnosis of internal strengths and weaknesses helps in the proper allocation of resources according to the objective of either maximizing profit or minimizing losses. It also enables to identify the need for those resources that need to be acquired, so as to overcome certain weaknesses or to minimize the adverse effect emanating from the weaknesses of the organization. Internal resource diagnosis includes the following areas:

- Sales—marketing—distribution—promotion—support
- Management—systems—expertise—resources
- Operations—efficiency—capacity—processes
- Products—services—quality—pricing—features—range—competitiveness
- Finances—sources—cost of capital—profit—performance
- R&D—competence—effort—direction—resources
- Costs—productivity—purchasing
- Systems—organization—structures

It is the quantity and quality of resources that gives rise to core competencies in an organization. For start-up ventures, the strengths and weaknesses are related mainly to the promoter(s)—their experience, expertise, management abilities, and financial resourcefulness—rather than to the project.

Tata Steel

The global steel demand in the twentieth century has evolved in phases as a result of a series of global events. The early years from 1900–14 recorded a compound annual growth rate (CAGR) of 5 per cent in the steel demand. The first surge in steel demand was witnessed

(Contd)

Exhibit (*Contd*)

around 1942 (CAGR of 7 per cent). There is a strong demand for growth and move for consolidation through mergers and acquisitions in the global steel industry. The great visionary Jamshedji Nusserwanji Tata (J.N. Tata) founded Tata Steel in 1907. The range and magnitude of problems that confronted the company by the early nineties when the economy was liberalized included global competition, product quality issues, and poor compliance in meeting delivery commitments, an outdated plant, and an oversized workforce. The top management had set up two task forces—one to examine realization-related issues and the other to examine cost-related issues. The company began to harness its unutilized deposits of iron ore at Joda in Orissa. Historically, the mining of ore was done leaving areas of the blue dust as raw material for its sinter plant. This change resulted in uniform mining operations.

By benchmarking with the best plants in the world such as Nippon Steel, CST, and POSCO, the production of the sinter plant was increased by 60 per cent which was as good as having one sinter plan free. A programme was launched to use the company's poor quality coal for making good quality coke. The new technology reduced the use of imported coal for coke to a large extent. This has given the company significant sustainable cost advantage because Indian coal is relatively low cost.

The company took aggressive steps to maximize usage of its blast furnaces. It took several measures to become self-sufficient in its fuel needs. The company set a record for reducing manpower while maintaining the human touch. Its employee separation scheme (ESS) has become a benchmark for its humane approach

to management. Simultaneously, the modernization of the facilities became an important focus area.

More than the use of tools and techniques, Tata Steel's journey towards international competitiveness had much to do with the personal commitment and change oriented leadership of its top management with an intense focus on the 3Cs: change, costs, and customers. In 1996, the company systematically embarked on the quest for excellence for the organization as a whole through the JRD Tata Quality Value (JRDQV) Award.

The willingness of the top management to create total transparency and subject its performance to discipline and scrutiny of the entire organization helped greatly in bringing about a mental transformation in the entire workforce. Tata Steel had made significant strides to address the challenges that confronted it consequent to the changed economic policies of the country during the nineties. Tata Steel can go in for inorganic growth aggressively through mergers and acquisitions at a global level. The cyclical nature of the steel industry makes Tata Steel vulnerable to demand and financial risks. There is likely to be a huge over-capacity in steel production worldwide leading to stiff global competition

Tata Steel's production in volume terms has grown at the CAGR of 5.99 per cent during 1990–91 to 2005–06, with the production level of 4.55 million tonnes in 2005–06. The revenue has grown at CAGR of 14.33 per cent in the corresponding period, as a result of enriched product mix and branding. The company continues to be one of the major producers of low cost steel in the world.

Source: Based on the data from www.tatasteel.com/, accessed on 10 July 2007; and other published sources.

Objective

The SWOT objective is to build up a clearer picture about the outstanding good and bad points, achievements, and failures and other critical features within the company. The key objective of SWOT analysis is to identify and prioritize the key aspects of strengths, weaknesses, opportunities, and threats of the organization.

Develop business strategies

Once the SWOT analysis is complete, the future strategy may be relatively easy to formulate. Corporate strategy enables the organization to identify markets and businesses in which it competes. Resource allocation to those businesses is done according to well-defined priorities. SWOT analysis helps in identification of possible strategies based on the following criteria:

- build and develop on strengths;
- resolve and overcome weaknesses;
- exploit and avail opportunities; and
- avoid or minimize the effect of threats.

BCG MATRIX

Boston Consulting Group (BCG) has introduced a growth/share matrix in response to the requirements of senior executives to manage complex and fast-changing modern organizations (Fig. 4.6). This tool enables the mapping of all the organization's businesses based on the criteria of market growth and relative competitive position vis-à-vis competitors. This analysis categorizes the organization's businesses into four major categories—stars, dogs, cash cows, and question marks as shown in Fig. 4.6.

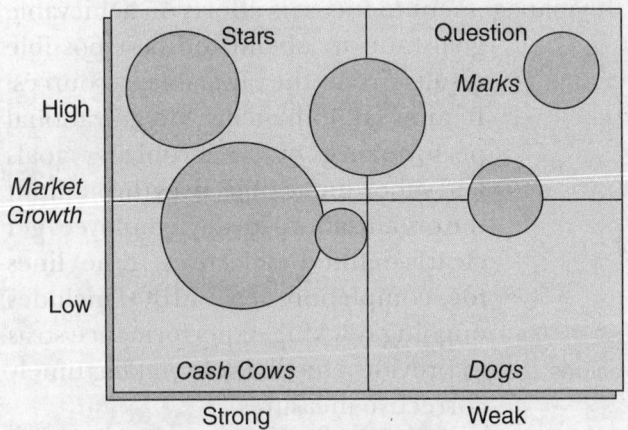

FIGURE 4.6   BCG matrix

Stars are the businesses having high growth as well as a strong competitive position. Low growth and weak competitive position businesses are called *dogs*. *Cash cow* businesses have low growth but have strong competitive position and *question marks* are the businesses that have high growth but weak competitive position.

MANAGEMENT BY OBJECTIVES (MBO)

Peter Drucker (1955) first outlined the concept of management by objectives (MBO) in his book *The Practice of Management*. However, in the nineties, Drucker himself undermined the significance of this concept when he said: 'It's just another tool.

It is not the great cure for management inefficiency. Management by objectives works if you know the objectives. Ninety per cent of the time you don't.' It was defined by Dale McConkey (1983) as 'a systems approach to managing an organization'. Brenneman (1975), writing in a book devoted to higher education management, defined MBO as 'a dynamic process, designed to enable institutions and people to operate in terms of results'. Mali (1986), defined it as 'a participative system of managing in which managers look ahead for improvements, think strategically, set performance, stretch objectives at the beginning of a time period, develop action and supporting plans, and ensure accountability for results at the end of the time period.' James Harvey (1974), in a text specifically concerned with MBO in post-secondary programmes, defined it as 'both a broad concept and a system' (Christ Frank 1997).

MBO is presently used as a vital concept to manage situations in companies the world over. It is defined as an integrated managerial system that is systematically and consciously directed towards achievement of organizational and individual objectives (Fig. 4.7). It is a system in which specific performance objectives are determined through participative approach. Progress towards objectives is periodically reviewed and rewards determined accordingly. MBO is a management system that is goal driven and success oriented. It is used in a variety of areas such as performance appraisal, strategic planning, production planning and control and other managerial subsystems such as human resource planning and management, budgeting, financial management, etc. Thus, it is a systematic and organized approach that enables the management to focus its efforts on achievable goals and to obtain the best possible results from the available resources. It aims at enhancing organizational performance by synchronizing goals and subordinate objectives throughout the organization. Ideally, employees get clearly-defined objectives, time lines for completion, etc. MBO includes ongoing tracking of performance so as to provide a feedback for taking timely corrective measures.

The salient features of MBO as presented in Fig. 4.8 are—cascading of organizational goals and objectives; specific objectives for each team/group and member; participative decision-making process; explicit time period deadlines; and performance evaluation and feedback.

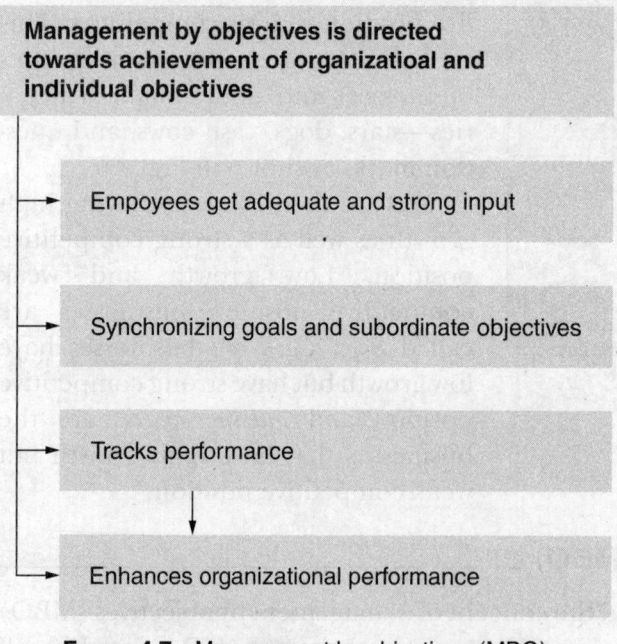

Management by objectives is directed towards achievement of organizatioal and individual objectives

Empoyees get adequate and strong input

Synchronizing goals and subordinate objectives

Tracks performance

Enhances organizational performance

FIGURE 4.7 Management by objectives (MBO)

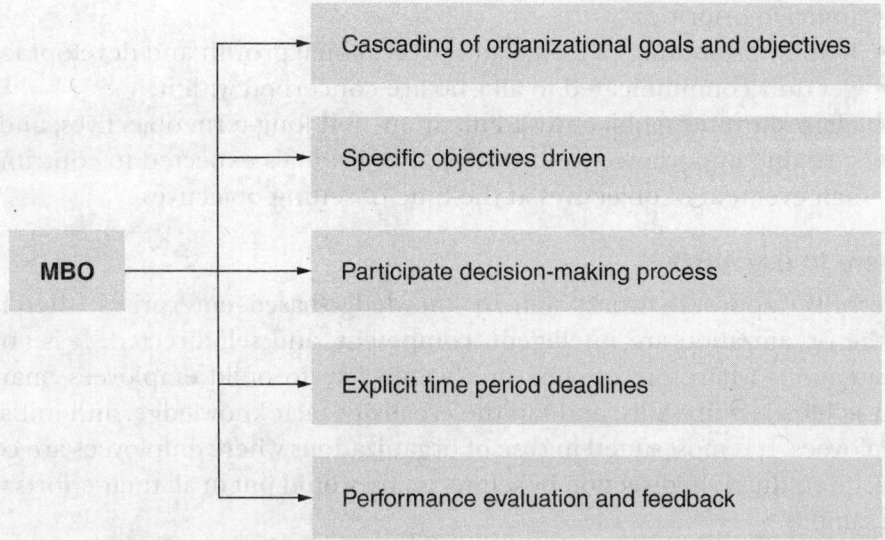

FIGURE 4.8   Salient features of MBO

Setting objectives

Effective management requires the setting of clear objectives. Without having a clear objective no group or individual can perform effectively or efficiently. One of the major criteria to set clear objectives is the scope of measuring it. Therefore, objectives should be set in such a way that they provide a clear direction to the people who have to contribute and perform for achievement of the same. It is always desirable to have a participatory approach to set objectives. However, management aspirations and expectations should be kept in view while adopting a participatory approach to set objectives. Objectives are both quantitative and qualitative in nature. Quantitative objectives are measurable and verifiable at the end of the period. However, at times, it becomes difficult to come out with verifiable objectives, particularly while dealing with personnel matters or research and development efforts. However, efforts should be made to give a verifiable meaning to even qualitative objectives, so that performance can be assessed.

Setting precise, measurable, and well-defined objectives is indeed a difficult task. It requires an intelligent input from superiors and practice and team effort on the part of subordinates. Objectives should:
- cover the main features of the job;
- be verifiable;
- indicate the time frame within which they are to be achieved;
- indicate associated cost involved;
- indicate quantity and quality aspects of the expected achievements;
- have an element of challenge;

- indicate priorities;
- help in promoting personal and professional growth and development;
- get duly communicated to all who are concerned with it;
- align short-term objectives to medium- and long-term objectives; and
- give due importance to the views of individuals expected to contribute in the achievement of objectives at the time of setting objectives.

Where to use MBO

The MBO approach works well in knowledge-based enterprises wherein people in the organization are intelligent, competent, and self-directed. It is appropriate in situations where the organization would like to build employees' management and self-leadership skills, and tap the creativity, tacit knowledge, and initiative of its employees. It is most suited in case of organizations where employees are competent and, given the right direction by setting goals, would put in all their efforts to achieve the same.

Benefits of MBO

An MBO approach to management provides clear goals and in turn helps in motivating people who are involved in the process. This approach to management provides the following benefits:

- ensures personal commitment to organizational goals;
- provides goal and role clarity in the organization and in turn helps in devising organizational structure conducive for improving efficiency and effectiveness;
- ensures result-oriented planning;
- develops effective control mechanism leading to timely corrective actions;
- less supervision of subordinates and increased motivational level as a result of each employee's clear definition of responsibilities;
- increase in employees' accountability; and
- improves managerial effectiveness and efficiency resulting in greater satisfaction level to the employees.

Disadvantages of MBO

The MBO approach to management can fail if the managers, particularly at the top level, lack the conviction and commitment in its implementation. Shortcomings in its implementation lead to lack of achievement. Some of the commonly found weaknesses in implementation of MBO are as:

- failure to teach the philosophy of MBO across the organization;
- lack of guidelines to goal setters;
- difficulty in setting verifiable objectives;
- over-emphasis on short-term achievements at the cost of long-term growth and development;
- lack of flexibility to attune changes with changing environmental forces;
- over-emphasis on quantitative goals, even where it may not be applicable;

- it turns out to be paper passing buck, especially in organizations wherein well set mechanisms to monitor and evaluate the performance does get laid down; and
- it is time consuming to imbibe the philosophy of MBO in the organization.

SUMMARY

An important factor for achieving success in any organization is effective planning. The planning processes have to be customized to meet the needs and nature of the organizations. Policy is a plan of action adopted by an individual or an organization. Strategies are an elaborate and systematic plan of action. Resources include the people, materials, machines, technologies, money, etc., required to implement the strategies or processes. As an outcome of situational analysis, the planning process sets alternative goals that the organization plans to pursue and the alternative ways and means to achieve the same. Plans need to be meticulously implemented to achieve set goals and objectives.

Strengths and weaknesses are essentially internal to the organization pertaining to resources. These relate to resources in key areas. Resources are the inputs that enhance performance of an organization. Every organization has to identify its major strengths and weaknesses that contribute positively or negatively to organizational goals. Corporate strategy enables the organization to identify markets and businesses in which it competes and allocates resources to those businesses as per well-defined priorities.

Management by objectives works if the objectives are known. McConkey defined it as a systems approach to managing an organization. It aims to enhance organizational performance by synchronizing goals and subordinate objectives throughout the organization. Management by objectives ensures personal commitment to organizational goals and result-oriented planning.

KEYWORDS

BCG matrix   It enables mapping of all businesses of the organization based on the criteria of market growth and relative competitive position vis-à-vis competitors.

Budget   A statement of expected provisions/results expressed in numerical terms.

Goals and objectives   Goals are specific objectives that an organization aspires to accomplish in total, or in some combination, in order to achieve some larger purpose.

Levels of planning   It goes with levels of managers—top level, middle level, and frontline level.

Planning   It is a systematic approach to making decisions about goals and objectives and the associated activities that need to be carried out along with various resource requirements.

Plans   Actions or means that a manager proposes to use for achieving predetermined goals.

Policies   Broad statements and guidelines that govern the thought process in decision-making.

Procedures   Plans that set out the required methods and processes to handle future activities.

Programme   A combination of goals, policies, procedures, rules, and set of activities undertaken for the accomplishment of a purpose.

Resources   Inputs required to implement strategies or processes.

Rules   They specifically define required actions and inactions in given circumstances.

Situational analysis   It is used to collect, process, analyse, and interpret all relevant data pertaining to the planning issue under consideration.

Strategy   An elaborate and systematic plan of action.

SWOT analysis   It is used to identify and prioritize the key aspects of strengths, weaknesses, opportunities, and threats of the organization.

Task   A piece of work that is undertaken to contribute towards the achievement of objectives.

EXERCISES

Concept Review Questions

1. What is meant by plan and planning? Describe briefly the steps in planning.
2. 'Planning is a continuous process' and 'planning facilitates control'. Comment.
3. Distinguish between:
   (i) Policies and objectives
   (ii) Rules and procedures
   (iii) Policies and strategies
4. 'Planning is beneficial to all'. What are the benefits of planning?

Critical Thinking Question

Planning is an important function of management? Do you agree or disagree with this statement? Why or why not?

Project Assignments

1. Identify three companies in a particular industry and find out from the information given on their websites and in the annual reports about their strategic objectives. Compare and contrast their strategic objectives. Comment on the success of the company's competitive position vis-à-vis its strategic objectives.
2. Take a company from the IT or steel industry. Use SWOT analysis to prioritize the strengths, weakness, opportunities, and threats of the company. On the basis of SWOT analysis, propose a business strategy.

REFERENCES

Brenneman, D. Sonders (1975), 'Management by Objectives: A Process for Educational Administration' in C.P. Heaton (ed.) *Management by Objectives in Higher Education*, National Laboratory for Higher Education, Durham, NC.

Chris, Frank (1997), *Using MBO to Create, Develop, Improve and Sustain Learning Assistance Programs*, Proceedings of the 17th and 18th Annual Institute for Learning Assistance Professionals: 1996 and 1997, University of Arizona, pp. 43–51.

Drucker, Peter F. (1955), *The Practice of Management*, Heinemann, London, http://www.pvc.maricopa.edu/~lsche/proceedings/967_proc/967proc_christ.htm, accessed on 15 June 2007.

Harvey, L.J. (1974), *Management by Objectives in Higher Education: A Guide to Implementation*, McManis Associates, Inc., Washington, D.C.

McConkey, D, (1983), *How to Manage by Results*, 4th edition, Amacom Book Division, New York.

Mali, P. (1986), MBO Updated: *A Handbook of Practices and Techniques for Managing by Objectives*, John Wiley & Sons, New York.

5

Management Control Systems

INTRODUCTION

After taking steps to plan and organize, to achieve the desired goals, an organization needs to put in place a control mechanism to ensure success with a greater degree of certainty. Therefore, apart from planning, organizing, and leading, the fourth key function of management is controlling, which is most crucial. This function ensures that due mechanism has been put in place to monitor the progress vis-à-vis predetermined milestones and take necessary corrective measures for deviations, if any.

In the words of E.F.L. Brech, 'Control is the process of checking actual performance against the agreed standards or plans with a view to ensuring adequate progress and satisfactory performances.' According to Henry Fayol, 'Control consists in verifying whether everything occurs in conformity with the plans adopted, the instructions issued and principles established. It has for object to point out weaknesses and errors in order to rectify them and prevent recurrence.'

Controlling encompasses different aspects such as confirming whether things are happening as planned vis-à-vis instructions issued and framework that has been put in place. An organization needs to put checks and balances to ensure that there is effective and efficient utilization of resources deployed for the achievement of planned goals. The checks will give timely alert signals about the deviations from expected performance and will identify the root cause for variation in performance so as to allow the decision-makers to take timely corrective actions.

Learning Objectives

After studying this chapter, you will be able to:
- Understand the importance of control as a management function
- Understand how control is an essential function for achieving goals
- Learn about important features and characteristics of controlling
- Understand about steps involved in controlling
- Learn about importance of budgeting as a tool of control
- Learn about balanced scorecard as a strategy management control tool

This function gives rise to an insight to the managers about the variations that occur while implementing plans. This insight and experience over a period of time helps develop a greater expertise in managers to visualize various aspects during the planning stage, which can ensure a greater degree of certainty in achieving the goals. This function provides a feedback whether the actual outcomes are in line with the predetermined goals or not. It enables the team involved in implementation and even the concerned decision-makers to make the required changes and adjustments.

All organizations, irrespective of size or nature of activity, pay close attention to the controlling function, as it is this aspect of management that becomes extremely important during the implementation phase. In the fast changing business environment continuous learning, relearning, and changing is now part and parcel of the management process.

WHY IS CONTROL ESSENTIAL?

The best plan, organizational structure, and leader who inspires and motivates the team members may not ensure that activities happen as desired and people in the organization necessarily work towards achievement of the goals. Therefore, control becomes an imperative tool that ensures that organizational goals will be achieved and if not, the reasons for the same (Fig. 5.1). The organization can realize the value of control function mainly in three specific areas—planning, empowering employees, and protecting the workforce (Robbins and Coulter, 2008). Although setting goals by meticulous planning provides purpose to employees and managers, it does not ensure that employees will take the required actions to work towards those goals.

For example, Nita had to travel to Chandigarh from Delhi for an interview, which was supposed to be at 10 am. She planned to travel by taxi early morning and called one to report at her home at 4 am. She wanted to start from home at 4.30 am. The total journey time was expected to be 4 hours as she had started early in the morning, thus giving her a margin of 1.30 hours to take care of any eventuality that may arise on the way or after reaching Chandigarh. Nita had consulted Google map to find out the exact route the taxi driver should take. She also ensured from the taxi owner as well as her friends about the suitability of the proposed route. The taxi driver was however not familiar with the route and she had to guide him. Nita started from her home in South Delhi at 4.20 am and took the Ring Road that connects Karnal bypass via Lajpat Nagar, ISBT. The taxi followed the correct route up to ISBT and thereafter, while Nita dozed off, took a diversion and turned towards Ghaziabad and kept on moving at a high speed for

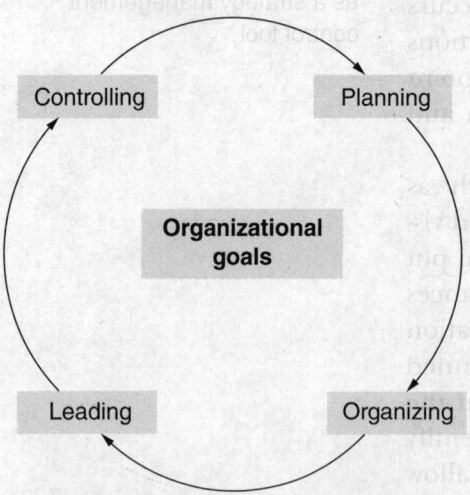

FIGURE 5.1 Management functions to achieve organizational goals

another 40 minutes or so. By the time Nita woke up and realized that the taxi had taken a wrong turn, it had gone forward by about 60 kms. Nita got extremely upset with the driver and asked him to turn back immediately. However, going back to Ring Road, where she had missed the track, would take her 1.30 hours. Therefore, a small mistake of not having a foolproof control mechanism led to an extra travel time, thus wasting the 1.30 hours of cushion time she had kept. Nita was not effective as she went in a wrong direction. Further, resources such as time and petrol were wasted. Although Nita had planned it well, she could not meet her goal of reaching her destination in time for her interview.

ORGANIZATIONAL PERFORMANCE

The ultimate aim of an organization, whether commercial or social, is to be effective, that is, to achieve organizational goals in a cost-effective manner. This implies that an organization wants to achieve organizational performance, which is the sum total of the results achieved by the organization by undertaking various activities. It is complex but very vital for the existence of an organization and provides competitive advantage from its competitors. There needs to be well-defined criteria to measure organizational performance, whether quantitative or qualitative. It basically needs to identify data on well-defined parameters that ought to be gathered, whether organizational goal is achieved or not. While measuring organizational performance, one should be clear regarding organizational productivity, which gives the total output of goods and services from inputs, both physical and human. Every organization wants to get maximum possible output of a certain quality with minimum possible input. Output in the case of a manufacturing company will be the revenue generated through sales of the goods produced, while inputs would be the cost of physical and human resources that go into transforming these inputs into outputs that have a value proposition for the customer. As per systems resource model, organizational effectiveness is the capability and capacity of the organization to deploy resources such that it gives rise to maximum possible outcome in terms of desired goods and services. It is this aspect of organizational effectiveness and organizational performance that requires a well-defined control mechanism in place to ensure that things happen as desired and if they do not, a timely corrective action is taken.

Effective management should ensure that people in the organization are doing what is expected of them and their efforts are leading towards the achievement of organizational goals. Therefore without control, the managers would never know whether plans are helping in achieving those goals. The control function is equally important in empowering people in the organization to undertake and be responsible for the tasks assigned to them. Many organizational managers are unwilling to empower their employees as they do not have the confidence in the employees' ability to perform. However, by having set control mechanisms, it becomes easy to make employees accountable by empowering them. Lastly, control

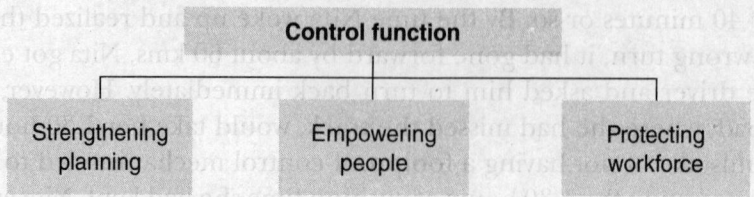

FIGURE 5.2 Control function adds value

systems also help in protecting the employees and the assets of the organization, as control mechanism clearly specifies responsibility and accountability in the organization (see Fig. 5.2).

FEATURES AND CHARACTERISTICS OF CONTROLLING

Controlling is one of the key managerial functions and without incorporation of this aspect, other three functions of management will not be able to give the required results. It is undertaken by managers at all levels, irrespective of their role and functions. It requires an insight to the future, so that deviations that occurred in the past do not recur in future. Some of the key characteristics of controlling function are shown in Fig. 5.3.

Continuous Controlling involves continuous feedback mechanism in the organization on the basis of analysis of objectives, policies, procedures, performance variations, and reasons for the same. As long as an organization is alive, controlling needs to be an inbuilt function.

All levels and all pervasive Controlling has to be at different levels in the organization along with all the activities that are undertaken by different functionaries to achieve overall goals of the organization.

Future perspective Controlling is just an onward looking activity. Analysis of past should give a foresight to the managers to take corrective action and curative measures to overcome the mistakes made in the past.

Corrective and remedial measures The purpose of a control mechanism is to have timely corrective and curative measures, which ought to be based on the factual and objective feedback mechanism. An effective control system would ensure that actions are initiated and implemented timely, so that there is minimum wastage of physical or human resources.

People driven Control is necessarily a people driven process and thus employees need to be vigilant, alert, and self-disciplined to exercise control.

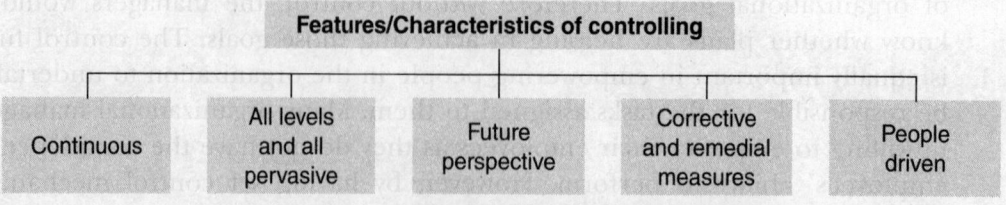

FIGURE 5.3 Features and characteristics of controlling

STEPS INVOLVED IN CONTROLLING

Like the four management functions, there are four steps involved in building an effective control system in any activity or department of an organization. These steps are taken to set the required standards of performance, measure actual performance against set standards, compare the performance with set standards to identify deviations if any, and to initiate corrective measures to ensure that predetermined standards are achieved in future (see Fig. 5.4).

Set Standards of Performance

The core of control lies in setting up of standards against which the actual performance is to be measured; preferably in quantitative terms but could even be qualitative. The standards need to be simple, specific, practical, and achievable with allocated resources—time, money, and effort. It is important to communicate to the concerned people about the importance of achieving the set standards in their work performance. These need to be stated in clear and unambiguous terms, so that people in the organization understand that their performance will be measured. Therefore, to the extent possible, standards should be measurable.

System and Processes to Measure Performance

After setting standards, an organization needs to set the system and process to measure the actual performance. It is important to have accurate facts and figures to measure the deviations from set standards instead of having presumption and deductive reasoning of predetermined standards for achievements. Evaluation becomes relatively simple when standards are set in quantitative terms, which are measurable, as against standards, which are of a qualitative nature.

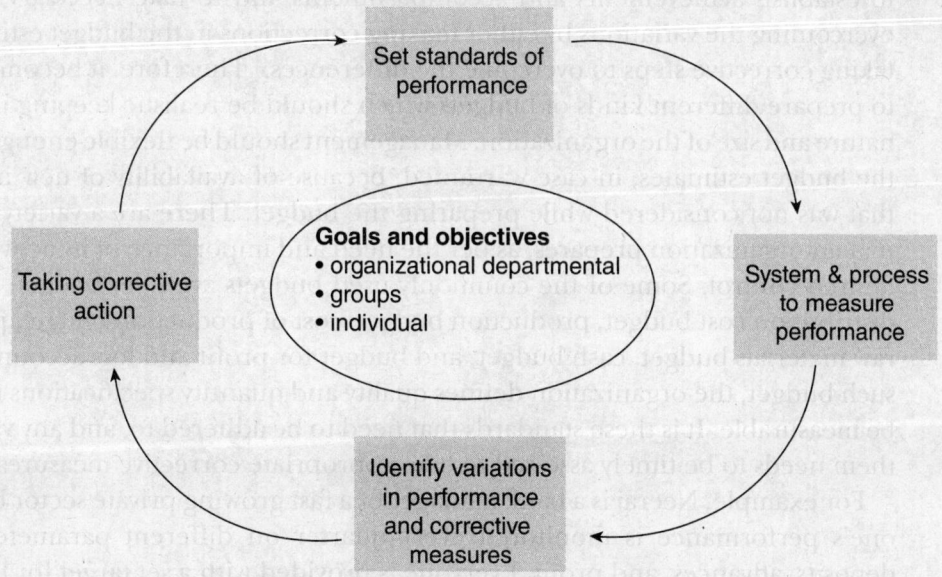

FIGURE 5.4   Steps involved in controlling

Identifying Variations in Performance and Corrective Measures

It is important to get timely reports in well-defined formats that can highlight budgets as compared to the actuals and also reflect the deviations. These reports should be communicated to the concerned people in writing, verbally, or through enterprise resource planning (ERP) systems. Communication of these deviations, which are pertinent and adversely affect in achieving the organizational goals, is important. This step ought to help in identifying important corrective measures that can assist the organization in achieving its well set standards. A team of personnel could help in identifying the critical factors that have led to variations which, if corrected, would go a long way towards achievement of standards. It is important that the variations are corrected by taking the most effective and efficient measures.

Taking Corrective Action

Managers need to take corrective measures by duly implementing them and monitoring whether standards are being achieved or not. In case there are huge variations in the actual achieved status as compared to the set standards, management may need to reset the goals and standards, reassign roles and duties, and reallocate required resources. It may even call for developing new skills, by inducting new people or through training and development of the existing set of people. If the standards are inaccurate, they should be changed.

TECHNIQUES TO CONTROL

One of the prominent techniques used to control is budget, which specifies the expected standards to be achieved. George R. Terry (1974) states, 'Budgetary control is a process of comparing the actual outcomes with the pre-set budget data to establish achievements and accomplishments and to take necessary actions for overcoming the variations by either making corrections in the budget estimates or by taking corrective steps to overcome the differences.' Therefore, it becomes essential to prepare different kinds of budgets which should be realistic keeping in mind the nature and size of the organization. Management should be flexible enough to modify the budget estimates, in case warranted, because of availability of new information that was not considered while preparing the budget. There are a variety of budgets that an organization prepares, as per the need and importance of its activities and its desired control. Some of the commonly used budgets are sales budget, selling and distribution cost budget, production budget, cost of production budget, purchase of raw materials budget, cash budget, and budget for profit and loss account. For each such budget, the organization defines quality and quantity specifications that should be measurable. It is these standards that need to be adhered to, and any variations in them needs to be timely assessed to take appropriate corrective measures.

For example, Neeraj is a bank manager of a fast growing private sector bank where one's performance is monitored every quarter on different parameters such as deposits, advances, and profit. Everyone is provided with a set target for the quarter. Neeraj is expecting a promotion at the end of the year and it depends completely on

TABLE 5.1   Quarterly budgetary targets and actual performance   ₹ in Cr

Items	Ist qtr's budget	Ist qtr's Actual	Variation	% Variation	Remarks
Deposits	15	16	+1	6.67	Favourable
Advances	9	4	−5	−55.56	Adverse
Interest Income	1.75	1.25	−0.50	−28.57	Adverse
Interest Expenditure	1.05	1.10	+0.05	4.76	Adverse
Overall Profit	0.22	0.17	−0.05	−22.73	Adverse

his performance. It is crucial that he achieves his quarterly as well as yearly targets. His Regional Manager monitors his performance after every quarter. He has his team members overlooking various assigned jobs, some of which on a regular basis are interdependent, too, on different departments, about every 10–15 days. He needs to monitor their performance regularly or else he might suddenly get a shock to observe major variations that may be uncontrollable because of lack of sufficient time. Suppose the quarterly targets given to Neeraj was as given in Table 5.1.

Such extreme adverse variations indicate (i) absence of a control mechanism, (ii) no timely corrective actions taken, or (iii) the targets were unrealistic. Neeraj should establish his case with his Regional Manager and ensure that in the next quarter his branch does not suffer any adverse variations in the outcomes.

The purpose of preparing budgets is to ensure that the future is planned in advance. As future activities will be interdependent on different teams and departments, therefore an inbuilt mechanism needs to be ensured to coordinate activities of different departments such that the overall outcome is not adversely affected. In any budgetary exercise, the key cost centre that matters most is efficient utilization of resources, whether it is physical or human. Therefore the budget should be made in such a way that it helps in overcoming any wastage of time and resources. The whole budgetary exercise can fulfill its purpose only if responsibility of different people and departments is clearly assigned. The whole exercise would become futile if people are not held responsible for non-performance.

BALANCED SCORECARD AS A STRATEGIC MANAGEMENT CONTROL TOOL

From early writings by renowned scholars of management, such as Herbert Simon, Peter Drucker, and R.N. Anthony, one can trace the roots of management planning and control systems encompassing both financial and non-financial measurement. Despite the plea from these renowned scholars, the basic management system for most companies till the 1990s relied heavily on budgets and financial control systems to maintain focus on short-term performance.

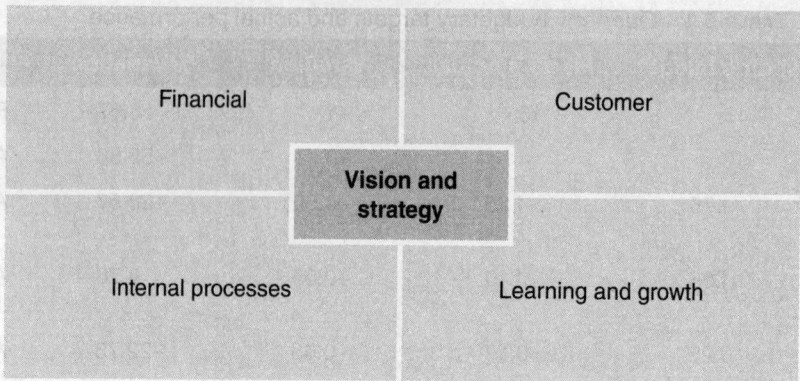

FIGURE 5.5   Balanced scorecard framework

The balanced scorecard was originally introduced by Kaplan and Norton (1992) as a multi-dimensional and multi-stakeholder approach to measure performance. This performance measurement system includes financial measures and non-financial drivers for future financial outcomes. The non-financial drivers are related to customer, internal processes, learning, and growth. It is a framework (refer to Fig. 5.5) that considers both outcome and processes, and internal and external perspectives of different stakeholders' interests. More recently Kaplan and Norton (1996, 2001) have introduced the concept of 'strategy map' that advocates utilization of the balanced scorecard as a strategic control system and that it should be integrated into an organization's strategic management process.

Implementation of balanced scorecard has enabled companies to track their financial results while simultaneously monitoring progress in building the capabilities and acquiring the intangible assets they would need for future growth, that is, as a supra-control system. The scorecard is not actually a replacement for financial measures, it complements it.

SUMMARY

Controlling is a function that ensures that proper mechanisms are used to monitor the progress vis-à-vis predetermined milestones and take necessary corrective measures for deviations, if any. All organizations, irrespective of their size or nature of activity, pay close attention to the controlling function, as it is this aspect of management that becomes important during implementation phase. Organizations realize the value of control function mainly in three specific areas—planning, empowering employees, and protecting the workforce. Without control, managers would never know whether their plans are in place and contributing to achievement of goals. Controlling is a continuous process at all levels, is people driven, and all pervasive in the organization having future perspective to take timely, corrective, and remedial measures. The four steps involved in building an effective control system in any activity or department of an organization is to set expected standards of performance, measure performance against the set standards, compare with standards to identify deviations, if any, and to initiate corrective measures to ensure that predetermined standards are achieved in future.

KEYWORDS

Budgetary control A process to compare actual performance against pre-set budgets to ascertain achievements and to take necessary corrective actions to overcome variations.

Controlling A mechanism used to monitor the progress vis-à-vis predetermined milestones and take necessary corrective measures for deviations, if any.

Organizational effectiveness The capability and capacity of the organisation to deploy resources in such a way that it gives rise to maximum possible outcomes in terms of desired goods and services.

Organizational performance Sum total of the end results that are achieved by undertaking various activities in the organization.

Organizational productivity It gives overall output of goods and services produced by given inputs, both physical and human.

EXERCISES

Concept Review Questions

1. What is meant by control being one of the management functions and why is it said to be a critical function?
2. What are the three specific areas in which value of control function can be realized by organizations?
3. Define organizational performance.
4. Define organizational effectiveness as per systems resource model.
5. What are the four steps involved in controlling? What is the relevance of each step?

Critical Thinking Questions

1. In what way does control function empower people in the organization? Explain by giving an example.
2. Planning function cannot deliver results if there are no control functions in an organization. Explain.
3. What does 'control function has to be a continuous' imply?
4. Why is it said that mostly people play a critical role in effectiveness of control system?
5. Is it possible to have control mechanism that is fully mechanical and does not involve human intervention?
6. What are the weaknesses of balanced scorecard as a management control system?

REFERENCES

Brech, E.F.L. (1972), *Principles and Practice of Management*, Pitman, London.

Fayol, Henry (1949), *General and Industrial Management*, Pitman Publishing, New York, pp. 107–109.

George R. Terry (1974), *Principles of Management,* Sixth Edn, Irwin.

Kaplan, R.S. and D.P. Norton (1992), 'The Balanced Scorecard: Measures that Drive Performance', *Harvard Business Review,* vol. 70, no. 1, Jan/Feb, pp. 71–79.

Kaplan, R.S. and D.P. Norton (1996), *The Balanced Scorecard: Translating Strategy into Action,* Harvard Business School Press, Boston, MA.

Kaplan, R. S. and D.P. Norton (2001), *The Strategy-focused Organization: How Balanced Scorecard Companies Thrive in the New Business Environment,* Harvard Business School Press, Boston, MA.

Robbins, Stephen P. and Mary K. Coulter (2008), *Management*, 9th ed., Pearson, p. 526.

6

Organizational Structure

Learning Objectives

After studying this chapter, you will be able to:

- Understand what is meant by organizational structure
- Comprehend different dimensions of organizational structure
- Understand the dimension of job specialization vs differentiation
- Understand what is meant by formalization dimension
- Understand the dimensions of centralization vs decentralization
- Comprehend different bases for departmentalization
- Understand the effect of size, environment, and technology on organizational structure
- Understand Mintzberg's typology of organization configurations

INTRODUCTION

An organization chart formally represents the division of activities within an organization. It indicates the reporting structure (who reports to whom) and describes vertical channels of communication that link the CEO with the operating level. It also maps different departments, which exist because of functional differentiation horizontally. An enterprise must grow both vertically and horizontally. The question that we will be trying to answer in this chapter will be, primarily, what determines the number of levels in an organization vertically and the number of departments horizontally.

We observe that every human activity gives rise to two fundamental and opposing requirements—(1) the division of labour into various tasks; and (2) the coordination of these tasks to carry out the activity. How is this accomplished in an organization? Further, how is internal consistency in an organization as well as situational consistency (consisting of its environment, size, technology, etc.) achieved? What supports the various functions in an organization—planning, organizing, staffing, leading, and controlling. In short, what are the dimensions along which the structure of an organization is patterned? Organizational structure is thus a framework on which an organization is patterned for coordinating and carrying out organizational tasks. Let us try to understand the concept of organizational structure by describing its dimensions—job specialization, behaviour formalization, and centralization (Fig. 6.1).

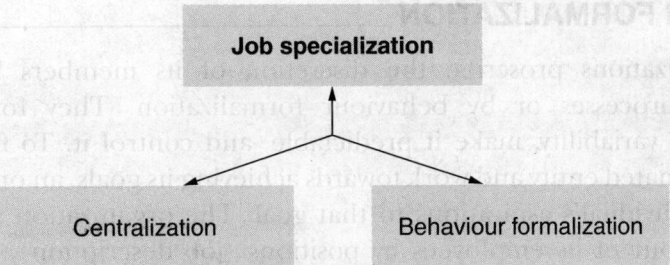

FIGURE 6.1   Organizational structure

JOB SPECIALIZATION

Adam Smith in his famous book *The Wealth of Nations* (1937) gives reasons for productivity increase on account of job specialization. Primarily, the improved dexterity of the workers by specializing in one task, the time saved in switching tasks, development of new methods and machines, and the processes automated on account of specialization led to enormous increases in productivity. He documented the increase in productivity by observing a pin-making process. From 20 pins per worker per day, the productivity rose to 4,800 pins per worker per day. This happened due to the division of labour, the predominant form of job specialization in the horizontal dimension. There are two ways of specializing the jobs—breadth or scope, and depth. Breadth or scope refers to the number of tasks that can be contained in each job and how broad or narrow each of these tasks is (jack-of-all-trades vs master of a few, but highly-specialized tasks). Depth or job specialization in vertical dimension separates the performance of work from its administration. It refers to the level of control the workers have over their work (whether they merely do the work without any thought or whether they control every aspect of the work in addition to doing it). The jobs are specialized in the vertical dimension in the belief that a different perspective is required to determine which and how work needs to be done.

A highly specialized job indicates that the workers' perspective is narrowing, making it difficult for them to relate their work to that of others. The work is often under the supervision of a manager or an analyst responsible for standardization. Job specialization creates problems of communication and coordination that are overcome with intrinsic motivation, threats of punishments, or rewards. In horizontal job enlargement, the worker engages in a wide variety of the tasks associated with producing products and services. In vertical job enlargement (enrichment), not only does the worker carry out more tasks but also gains more control over them. The question that may be raised at this point is 'when to go for job enlargement?' It will pay to go for it when the gains from better-motivated workers in a particular job offset the losses from less than optimal technical specialization.

BEHAVIOUR FORMALIZATION

Organizations proscribe the discretion of its members by standardization of work processes or by behaviour formalization. They formalize behaviour to reduce variability, make it predictable, and control it. To function as a perfectly coordinated entity and work towards achieving its goals, an organization has to align the individual's aspirations to that goal. The organization seeks to formalize the behaviour of its employees by positions (job description), by work-flow (process descriptions), and by specifying rules (regulations, policy manuals, code and conduct rules, etc.). Irrespective of the means used, behaviour formalization is resorted to so that the effect on the person doing the work is the same, that is, his/her behaviour is regulated. Organizations that rely primarily on the formalization of behaviour to achieve coordination are referred to as *bureaucracies*. We can define a structure as bureaucratic to the extent that its behaviour is predetermined or predictable, in effect standardized. Its contrast is organic structure. Highly formalized structures, nevertheless, have some drawbacks. An employee's inherent propensity to resist formalization and impersonalization results in:

- rejection of innovative ideas;
- mistreatment of clients; and
- increase in absenteeism, high turnover, strikes, etc.

CENTRALIZATION AND DECENTRALIZATION

In a centralized organizational structure, decision-making is controlled by one authority.

However, within a decentralized structure, employees at various levels within the organization have the right to make decisions. What prompts an organization to adopt a centralized or decentralized structure? Centralization is the tightest means of coordinating decision-making in the organization. Why then should an organization decentralize? Simply because not all matters of decision-making can be dealt by one centre of an organization. Decentralization can take care of the following:

- handling information overload;
- allowing the organization to respond quickly to local conditions;
- acting as a stimulus for motivation especially for creative people; and
- training middle line managers for higher jobs.

However, centralization and decentralization should not be treated as absolutes but rather as two ends of a continuum. The dispersal of formal power down the chain of line authority is known as *vertical decentralization*. By formal power, we mean the power to make decisions and authorize them and not to informal power, which refers to power arising from expertise and execution. Before adopting the structure of vertical decentralization certain issues need to be clarified. What decision-making powers should be delegated down the chain of authority? How far down the chain should they be delegated? How should their use be coordinated? For example, in service industries, the empowerment of frontline personnel becomes imperative if we have to ensure the quality of service delivery. The extent to which non-managers (staff and support personnel) control decision processes is termed as *horizontal decentralization*. It occurs when there is a shift of power from line managers to staff managers, analysts, etc. (e.g., new product development team, ISO 9001 implementation task force, etc.) There can be two other kinds of decentralization. In *selective decentralization*, the power over different kinds of decisions rests in different places in the organization (e.g., finance decisions by the management, production decision by first line supervisors, etc.). *Parallel decentralization* refers to the dispersal of power for many kinds of decisions in the same place (e.g., finance, marketing, production decisions, etc. would be made by division managers in the middle line).

The power of employees is maximized by their control over various steps in the decision-making process. The process is most centralized when they collect their own information, analyse it themselves, make choices, seek no authorization for it, and finally execute it themselves.

A decision-making process is most decentralized when the decision-maker controls only the making of choice (the least he/she can do and still be called a decision-maker). In the organizational hierarchy, he/she loses some power to the information gatherers and advisors to his/her side, to the authorizers above, and to the executers below.

DEPARTMENTALIZATION

Departmentalization refers to the grouping of activities at every level in the organization and not just at the 'departmental' level alone. It is the first step towards organizing an enterprise. While unskilled manpower may be grouped and departmentalized according to their *number*, skilled manpower within large and complex organizations may be grouped according to the *function* they perform, e.g., production, marketing, finance, and research and development (Fig. 6.2). Apart from grouping manpower on the basis of number and function, organizational activities can be also grouped on the basis of *product or product line* (Fig. 6.3). A company can thus be organized around divisions (or product lines) where the divisional executive takes all the decisions about production, marketing, finance, etc., for a given product.

Another basis for departmentalization can be *territory* (Fig. 6.4), when geographical location becomes the basis for organizing activities. International divisions or national/regional subsidiaries of many organizations are geo-demographically and economically relevant groupings. We can also group an organization's activities according to its *customers*. For example, most mobile service providers have different divisions—those that cater to consumer markets and those that provide solutions to enterprise markets. Sometimes it is logical to group activities based on the *process* (or on the type of equipment) used for production. For example, the production

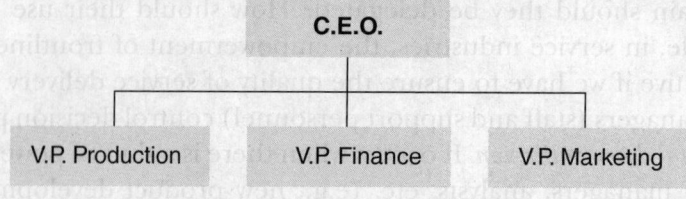

FIGURE 6.2   Functional structure

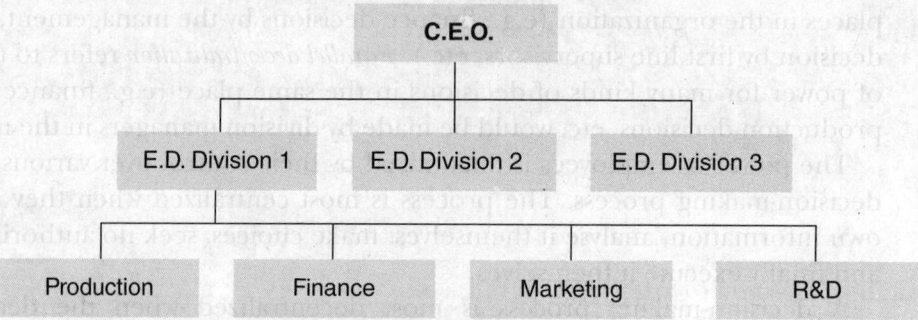

FIGURE 6.3   Divisional structure

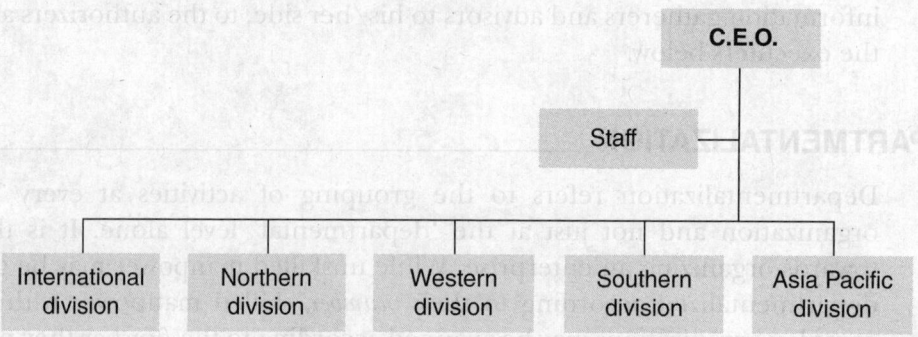

FIGURE 6.4   Territory-based structure

may be organized around machining shop, press shop, electroplating shop, heat treatment shop, assembling shop, etc. with similar type of machines or processes grouped together.

Organizations may be departmentalized at various levels according to different criteria; starting from the primary, that is, the level below chief executive, to the intermediate level, that is, the level/s between primary and ultimate departmentalization level, to the lowest level of the organization.

However, it is also possible to departmentalize, according to two or more different criteria, at the same level within the organization. For example, the matrix structure (Fig. 6.5) combines functional and divisional structures simultaneously. Within this structure, an employee has to report to two bosses, the functional as well as the divisional. The recent add-ons to departmentalization have been the concepts of

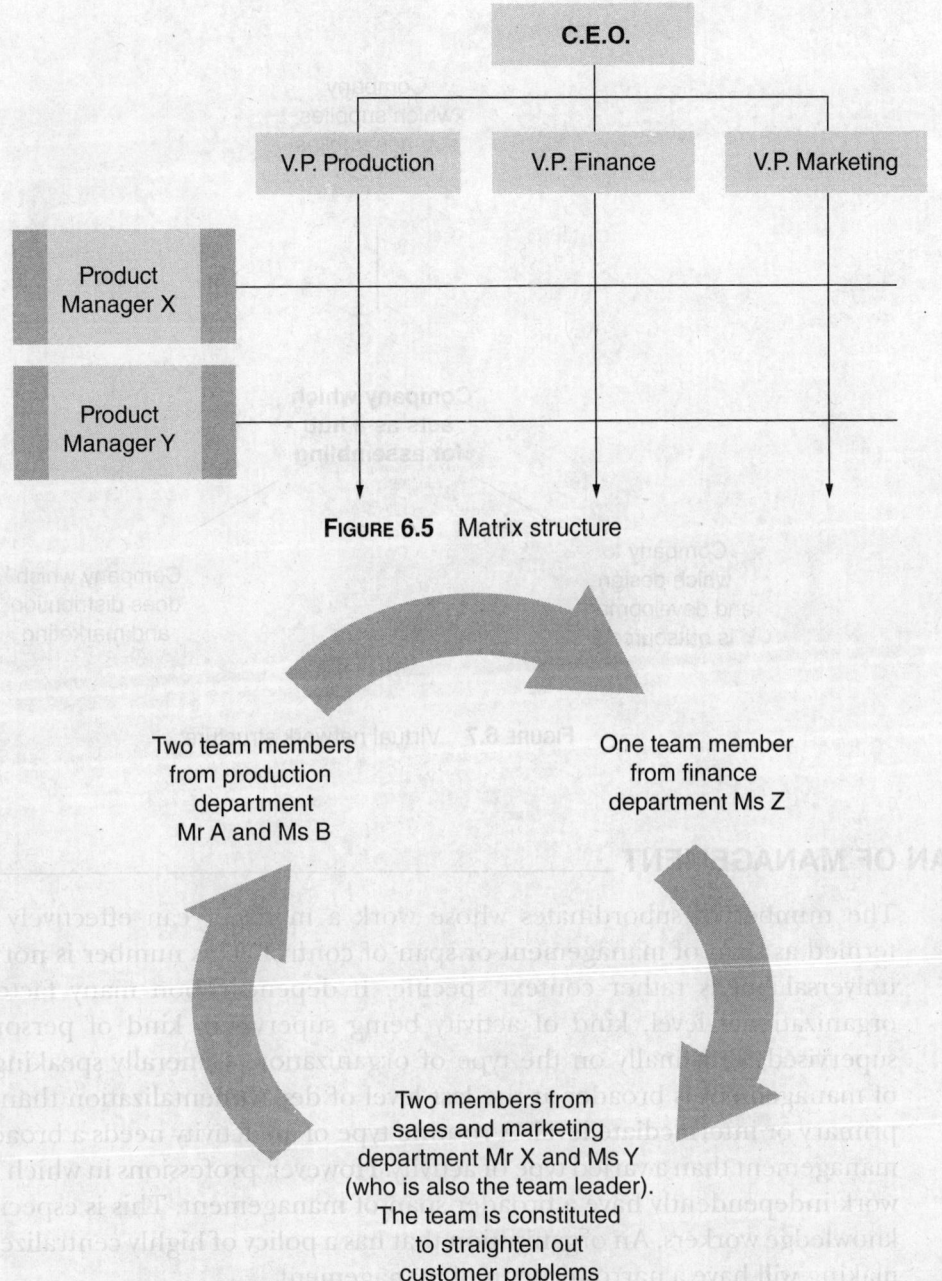

FIGURE 6.5   Matrix structure

FIGURE 6.6   Cross-functional team add-on structure

cross-functional teams (Fig. 6.6) wherein the members are drawn from different functional areas and focus on solving problems of mutual interest and virtual network structure (Fig. 6.7) which is an outcome of focusing on one's core competency and outsourcing most of the secondary activities. As a result, the company's structure is like a spider's web, which can retract and expand as per the changing requirements.

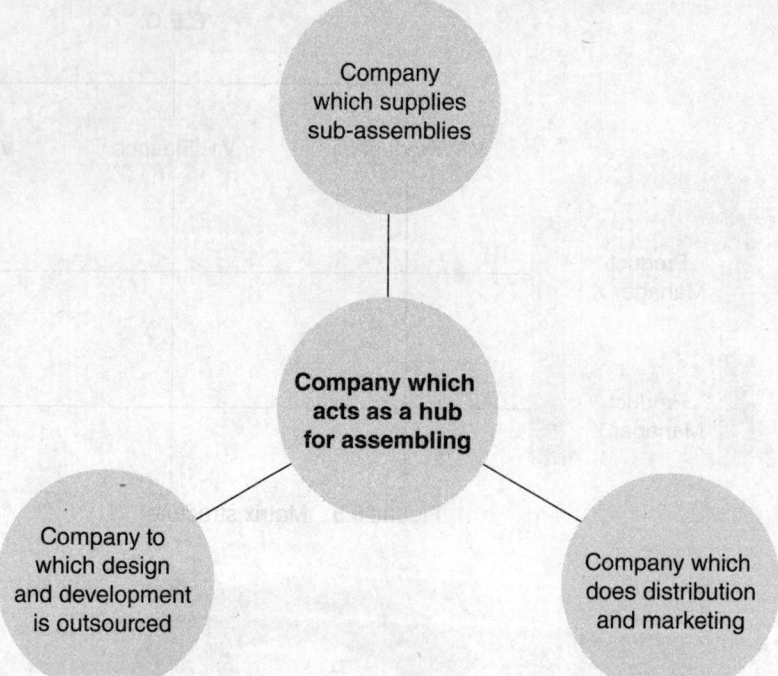

FIGURE 6.7   Virtual network structure

SPAN OF MANAGEMENT

The number of subordinates whose work a manager can effectively manage is termed as span of management or span of control. This number is not something universal but is rather context specific. It depends upon many factors such as organizational level, kind of activity being supervised, kind of personnel being supervised, and finally on the type of organization. Generally speaking, the span of management is broader at the last level of departmentalization than it is at the primary or intermediate level. A routine type of an activity needs a broader span of management than a varied type of activity. However, professions in which individuals work independently have a broader span of management. This is especially true of knowledge workers. An organization that has a policy of highly centralized decision-making will have a narrower span of management.

Other factors being the same, the average span of management determines whether an organization has a tall structure or has a relatively flat structure. A flat structure (Fig. 6.8) has fewer hierarchical levels and a broader span of management, whereas a tall structure (Fig. 6.9) has more hierarchical levels but a narrower span of control. Agile, customer-oriented, and knowledge-work dominated organizations tend to have flatter structures that are both efficient and effective.

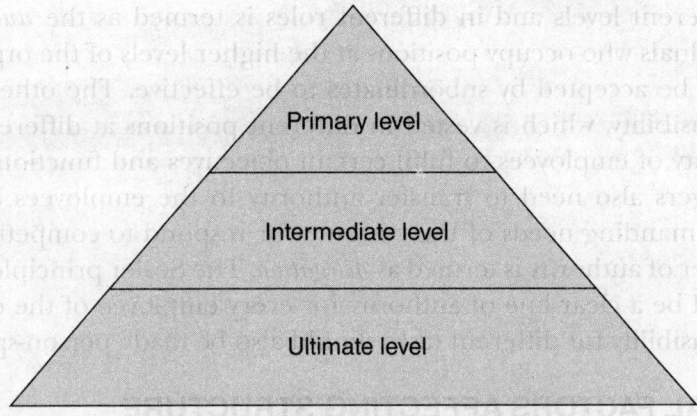

FIGURE 6.8   Flat organization structure

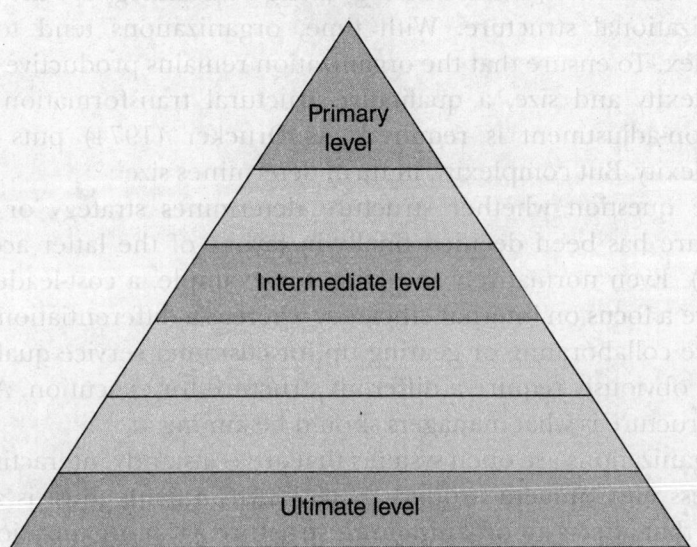

FIGURE 6.9   Taller organization structure

Chain of Command and Line and Staff Relationships

The line activities are concerned directly with attaining the company's output objectives (products or services), whereas the staff activities exist in order to help make line activities more effective and provide support.

In a typical manufacturing company, production, sales, and finance are considered line functions while design, personnel, and purchasing are considered staff functions. The staff function authority may be used as advisory staff (e.g., by design department), service staff (e.g., by transportation and logistics department), control staff (e.g., by inspection department), and functional staff (e.g., by the safety department) responsibility.

Chain of command refers to the unbroken flow of authority originating from the CEO and reaching down to the worker. The legitimate power to make decisions at different levels and in different roles is termed as the *authority*. It is vested in individuals who occupy positions at the higher levels of the organization. Authority has to be accepted by subordinates to be effective. The other side of authority is responsibility, which is vested in different positions at different levels. It refers to the duty of employees to fulfil certain objectives and functions entrusted to them. Managers also need to transfer authority to the employees below them to meet the demanding needs of the customer or respond to competitive onslaughts. This transfer of authority is termed as *delegation*. The Scaler principle demands that there should be a clear line of authority for every employee of the organization and the responsibility for different tasks should also be made person-specific.

SITUATIONAL FACTORS AFFECTING STRUCTURE

Size, environment, and technology along with strategy are the factors that influence organizational structure. With time, organizations tend to grow and become complex. To ensure that the organization remains productive despite its increasing complexity and size, a qualitative-structural transformation and not merely an addition-adjustment is required. As Drucker (1974) puts it, 'Size determines complexity. But complexity, in turn, determines size'.

The question whether structure determines strategy or strategy determines structure has been decided finally in favour of the latter according to Chandler (1962). Even normatively speaking, for example, a cost-leadership strategy would require a focus on internal efficiency whereas a differentiation-focus strategy would require collaborating or gearing up for customer service quality and each strategy would obviously require a different structure for execution. A fit between strategy and structure is what managers should be aiming at.

Organizations are open systems that are constantly interacting with the changing business environment around them. Environment, thus, is another contingency factor that affects an organization's structure as an organization tries to adapt itself to it. The task environment, that is, those elements in the general environment that are of immediate relevance to the organization can be both complex—comprising of many and often interrelated elements as well as dynamic. These elements of complexity and dynamism, which change at a great speed within the environment, make the environment uncertain (Fig. 6.10).

Managers have to work towards creating organizational structures that can deal with this uncertainty. Decentralized structures that have the capacity to process more information as well as respond to the competitor's moves are the solution. In case of a relatively static and simple corporate environment, a mechanical structure may suffice. However, in case of a complex and dynamic environment, a more organic structure, that empowers employees is needed. Many corporations have moved from a functional and divisional structure to more responsive structures in their quest to adapt themselves to the fast-changing environment.

The other factor that influences organizational structure is technology. Perrow (1970) defines technology as a means of transforming raw materials into desirable

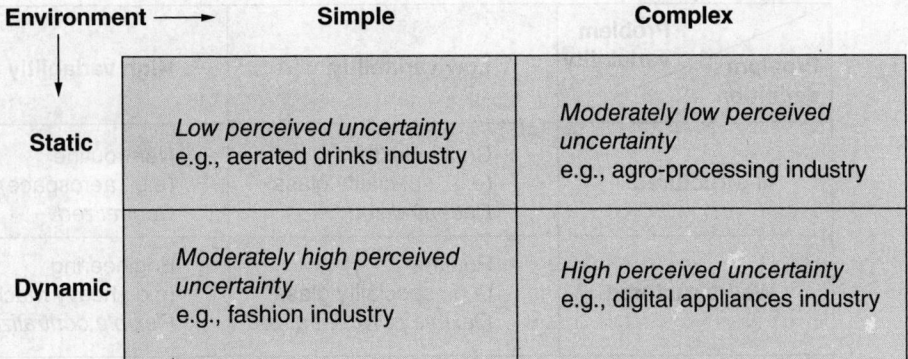

FIGURE 6.10   Effect of complexity and dynamism in the environment

goods and services. Woodword (1965) who conducted one of the first studies of technology and structure found a relationship between organizational structure and organizational effectiveness after grouping the firms according to the type of production system namely:

1. *Batch production* (a mode in which a firm made a few kinds of products for special orders)
2. *Mass production* (e.g., an automobile manufacturing plant operated in this mode)
3. *Process production* (e.g., a cement or chemicals plant operated in this mode)

In Woodward's survey of 100 firms, these three production systems—batch, mass, and process demonstrated an increasing degree of complexity with the spans of management at CEO levels being 2–9, 4–13, and 5–19, respectively. More importantly, firms with average spans for their type of production system were successful, whereas firms deviating from the average span in their production system were not. This was an excellent study that indicated how structure of a successful organization has to take into account technology that an organization employs. However, structural differences may arise within functional departments on account of their using different technologies. Perrow (1970) describes how research, marketing, and production employ different technologies on account of non-routine, less routine, and fully routine nature of tasks and how this leads to their structural differences. Perrow specifies technology type-effective organizational structure fit as a 2 × 2 matrix (Fig. 6.11).

Lawrence and Lorsch (1967) advocated that organization, differentiation, and subsequent integration were means of dealing with complexity and variability.

ORGANIZATIONAL TYPOLOGY

Henry Mintzberg (1979), the organizational theorist from McGill University, Canada has elegantly typified certain organizational configurations based on the *key part* of the organization and the predominating *coordinating mechanism* employed by that type in Fig. 6.12. The key parts of an organization are illustrated in this section.

Problem definition \ Problem variability	Low variabiltiy	High variabiltiy
Ill-structured	Craft industries (e.g., speciality glass) *Decentralized*	Non-routine (e.g., aerospace) *Centralized*
Well-structured	Routine (e.g., speciality glass) *Flexible polycentralized*	Engineering (e.g., heavy machinery) *Flexible centralized*

Adapted from: Perrow (1970)

FIGURE 6.11   Types of technology

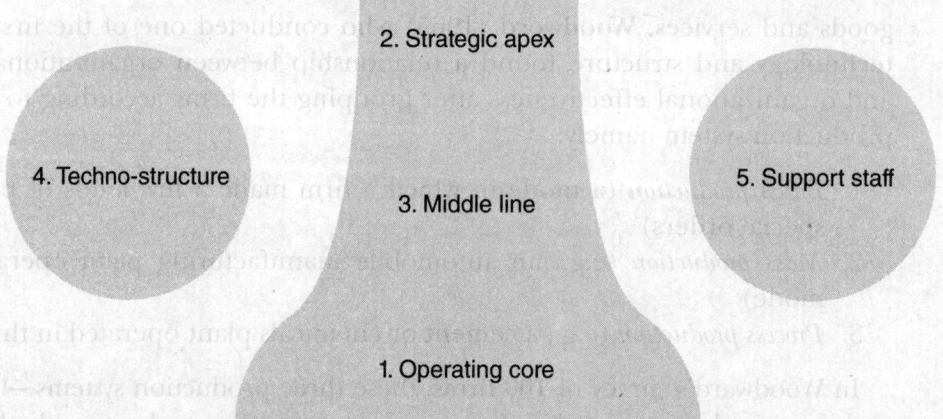

FIGURE 6.12   Five basic parts of any organization

Operating core   The operating core consists of operators who perform the main work directly related to the production of goods and services. For example, lecturers in a university or assembly line workers in an automobile plant would constitute the operating core of an organization.

Strategic apex   It refers to the top level management that has the ultimate responsibility of guiding the organization towards its mission and goals. For example, a company's board of directors, its CEO, and VPs would constitute the strategic apex, primarily responsible to the company's various stakeholders.

Middle line   The top management of a company is joined to its operating core by a chain of middle line managers, who are given formal authority. They play an important role in transferring information between the top-level management and the operating core. For example, general managers, deputy-general managers, divisional managers, factory heads, managers, etc. of a multi-division, multi-unit company would constitute its range of middle-line managers.

Techno-structure   Different departments within an organization control particular forms of standardization in the organization. For example, the inspection department controls the quality of inputs, process, and the final output. The personnel department controls the quality of manpower according to their knowledge, expertise, skills, and attitude norms, while the design department specifies and standardizes product dimensions, processes, etc.

Support staff   This refers to all other departments/units that exist to provide support to the organization outside its main work area. For example, transportation department, canteen, security services unit, etc. Most of the times it makes a greater sense to outsource these specialized services.

Further as per Mintzberg (1979) there exist five types of mechanisms employed by the organizations to coordinate their various activities. These coordinating mechanisms are:

1. *Direct supervision*   When one person supervises the work of others, as in the case of an entrepreneur in a small start-up who supervises his/her workers directly to achieve the objectives thus, acting as the main and only link to achieve coordination.
2. *Mutual adjustment*   This method of coordination can be achieved only when a degree of informal communication happens between different functional experts in a project team.
3. *Work process standardization*   The work process standardization itself can promote coordination between different units as is exemplified, for instance, in the process of an assembly line.
4. *Outputs standardization*   This happens when, for example, finished product or service specifications and standards act as means of coordinating work as the concerned departments have to coordinate till the output meets the specifications.
5. *Skills or knowledge standardization*   Often the qualifications, training, and experience of the personnel may act as a major source of coordination in an organization. For example, in an operation theatre of a hospital, the anesthetist, the surgeon, and the staff nurses coordinate to complete the operation successfully.

As an organization grows big and complex, the preferred means of coordination are from type $2 \rightarrow 1 \rightarrow 3 \rightarrow 4, 5$.

Taking into account the key role that the various parts of an organization play and the predominant or the main coordinating mechanism that they employ, Mintzberg further classifies organizations into the following configurations—simple structure, machine bureaucracy, professional bureaucracy, divisionalized form, and adhocracy.

Simple structure   A medium-sized retail store, a corporation run by an aggressive entrepreneur, a government run by an autocratic politician, etc. are all examples of a simple structure. The key part in this type of structure is the strategic apex that tries to centralize and control. The main coordinating mechanism is direct supervision. The strategic apex, in order to centralize and coordinate by direct supervision, structures the organization as a simple structure.

Machine bureaucracy   A security agency, national post office, a steel company, a custodial prison, national railways, etc. are all examples of a machine bureaucracy. The chief component in this organization is the techno-structure and the main coordinating mechanism is the standardization of work processes. The techno-structure strives to coordinate by the standardization of work processes and to structure the organization as a machine bureaucracy. The primary desire of the key part is to increase its influence.

Professional bureaucracy   A general hospital, a university, public accounting firms, and social work agencies are all examples of organizations that follow the structure of a professional bureaucracy. The key part in this type of structure is its operating core and the main coordinating mechanism is the standardization of skills. The operators within this structure tend to professionalize, coordinate by standardization of skills, and structure the organization as a professional bureaucracy. The main desire of the key part is to maximize their autonomy.

Divisionalized form   The divisionalized structure is followed by a vast majority of private firms. The main part of such organizations is the middle line and the main coordinating mechanism is standardization of outputs. The middle management tries to group together the organization, with coordination restricted to the standardization of outputs, to structure the organization as a divisionalized form. The main desire of the key part is to garner autonomy so as to manage their units.

Adhocracy   A space agency, an avant-garde film company, a factory manufacturing complex prototypes, consultancy organizations, etc. are all examples of adhocracy structures. The chief component in this structure is the support staff and the main coordinating mechanism, mutual adjustment. The support staff tries to coordinate by mutual adjustment so as to structure the organization as an adhocracy. The main desire of the key part is for collaboration and innovation in decision-making.

Hindustan Zinc Limited

Before its disinvestment in April 2002, Hindustan Zinc Limited (HZL) was a public sector company owned by Government of India (GOI). The company was doing fairly well for almost four decades and was recognized as a 'mini ratna'. The procedures and systems were in line with general guidelines issued by GOI and internal control was exercised by periodical reviews by the company's management. After the disinvestment, management control was ceded to Sterlite group, which soon took stock of company's resources, potential, and capabilities for formulation of strategies in terms of increasing the output, metal recoveries, and plant availability and for reducing costs, power consumption, material consumption, etc. These changes in strategy would lead to a progressive change in organization structure which would be reflected in the change in the dimensions of the organization structure. Following are pre- and post-disinvestment dimensions as perceived by employees within the company itself.

(contd)

Exhibit *(Contd)*

Pre-disinvestment	Post-disinvestment
I. Work Specialization	
1. High on specialization	1. High on job enlargement
2. High on horizontal job enrichment	2. High on vertical job enrichment
II. Departmentation	
1. More departments	1. Many departments removed or clubbed with other departments
2. Many departments had huge manpower at the unit level	2. Strategic business unit (SBU) concept introduced at unit level
III. Chain of Command	
1. Hierarchical organization	1. Flatter organization with extensive use of technology
2. Only top management empowered	2. Operations employees also empowered
3. Everything should get approval from top management	3. Expertise-based decision-making
IV. Span of Control	
1. Narrower span of control	1. Wider span of control
V. Centralization vs Decentralization	
1. Bureaucratic organization structure	1. Decentralized structure
2. Decision-making at the highest level	2. SBU heads have all the powers
3. Purchase department centralized	3. Decentralized purchasing for some items
4. Lesser coordination between functions	4. Formation of cross-functional teams
VI. Formalization	
1. Mechanistic organization	1. Organic organization
2. Promotions based on seniority	2. Performance-based promotions
3. Routine nature of working	3. More agile, incorporation of world-class practices, and focus on value-addition chain.

Conclusion

Post-disinvestment, the organization structure is perceived as more 'organic' with decision-making becoming more decentralized. This led to a sense of ownership and participative culture, performance-linked incentive, for executives, and performance-linked bonus for workmen, team work, a culture of honesty, promoted growth strategy, and continuous improvement in work practices.

Source: An unpublished informal study conducted by the author on a small sample (*n* = 35) about employees' perception regarding various organization dimensions before and after disinvestment of HZL. The study was conducted during a training programme in 2005.

SUMMARY

An organization chart formally represents the division of activities within an organization. An organization structure is the skeleton that supports various functions in an organization, namely planning, organizing, staffing, leading, and controlling. The dimensions along which the structure of an organization is patterned are job specialization, behaviour formalization, and centralization. Departmentalization refers to grouping activities in an organization. Departmentalization may be done according to number, function, product line, division, territory, customers, or process. Functional and divisional structuring are the most popular. It is also possible to combine different bases simultaneously in the same part of the organization for structuring purposes, for example, matrix structure combines functional and divisional structures simultaneously. Other innovations are cross-functional team (add-on) structure and virtual network structure. Size, environment, and technology along with strategy are the factors that influence organizational structure. Mintzberg categorizes organizations as simple structure, machine bureaucracy, professional bureaucracy, divisionalized form, and adhocracy.

KEYWORDS

Behaviour formalization The way organizations seek to formalize the behaviour of its employees by the positions (job description), by the work-flow (process descriptions), and by specifying rules (regulations, policy manuals, code and conduct rules, etc.).

Centralized vs decentralized structure When all the power for decision-making rests in the hands of one person, it is known as a centralized structure. When power is dispersed among many people, it is known as a decentralized structure.

Departmentalization It deals with grouping of activities at any level in the organization.

Job enlargement A job design in which the worker engages in a wide variety of the tasks associated with producing products and services.

Job enrichment A job design in which not only does the worker carry out more tasks, but also gains more control over them.

Job specialization It is primarily achieved through division of labour that specializes in one or a few tasks.

Organizational structure A framework or skeleton on which an organization is patterned for coordinating and carrying out organizational tasks.

Span of control The number of subordinates whose work a manager can effectively manage is termed as span of management or span of control.

EXERCISES

Concept Review Questions

1. How are job enrichment and job enlargement related to job specialization?
2. Does structure follow strategy or strategy follow structure? Give reasons.
3. How does formalization take place in the organizations?
4. Why is it important to empower employees in today's competitive market place?
5. What are the new evolving forms of organizing work and how are they related to the changing business environment?

Critical Thinking Questions

1. Is departmentalization on the basis of product lines or divisions an improvement on one based on functions? Give your arguments for and against in light of the matrix structure.

2. Which configuration of organizational structure is more suitable for a hospital and for a university?

Project Assignment

Prepare an organizational chart for your business school and show how it fits into Mintzberg's orga-nizational typology. Also, take any company and contrast its organizational structure with that of your business school.

REFERENCES

Chandler, Alfred D. (1962), *Strategy and Structure*, M.I.T. Press, London.

Drucker, Peter F. (1974), *Management: Tasks, Responsibilities, Practices*, William Heinemann Ltd, London.

Lawerence, Paul R. and Jay W. Lorsch (1967), *Organization and Environment: Managing Differentiation and Integration,* Division of Research, Harvard University Graduation School of Business Administration, Boston.

Mintzberg, Henry (1979), *The Structure of Organizations*, Prentice Hall, Englewood Cliffs, New Jersey.

Perrow, Charles (1970), *Organization Analysis: A Sociological View,* Wadsworth, Belmont, California.

Smith, Adam (1937), *The Wealth of Nations*, Modern Library, New York.

Woodward, Joan (1965), *Industrial Organization: Theory and Practice,* Oxford University Press, London.

7

Organizational Effectiveness

Learning Objectives

After studying this chapter, you will be able to:
- Comprehend organizational effectiveness
- Understand organizational culture and its implications to organizational effectiveness
- Learn about factors that build and nurture favourable organizational culture
- Examine different organization life cycle stages
- Measure organizational effectiveness
- Examine the characteristics of effective organizations

INTRODUCTION

Some organizations develop at an accelerated pace while others exit the market or continue to have a declining performance, leading to their ultimate collapse. Similarly, some organizations respond to change quickly, while others find it very difficult to respond to the changing business environment. What is the difference between successful organizations and unsuccessful ones? What are the life cycle stages through which an organization goes through? The answer lies in understanding the meaning of organizational effectiveness.

Every organization working in a highly competitive environment aspires to excel by improving its effectiveness. However, performance in an organization does not just happen. It is the dedicated and skilful team of human resources that makes it happen. To perform means to achieve predetermined worthwhile organizational goals and objectives. Productivity refers to the accomplishment of objectives through the utilization of resources such as capital, workforce, machinery, and infrastructure. It refers to the relationship between inputs and outputs or the efficiency with which the organizational objectives are achieved by combining and utilizing organizational resources.

For organizational effectiveness, a clear purpose and direction is a must. Organization structure, processes and systems, culture, and people must all be aligned to this purpose and direction to achieve the organization's goals. Some issues that normally come across in this context are listed in this section.

- A high performance organization is enormously valuable, yet few achieve it and many do not even try.
- Organizations are complicated and multidimensional, yet few have identified the culture they need to develop and actively work towards it.
- Even high performance organizations must evolve, yet few rigorously assess organizational health over time.

ORGANIZATIONAL EFFECTIVENESS

Organizational effectiveness is defined as the ability of an organization to maximize its performance within a competitive external environment. It is achieved when organizational resources are optimally utilized by creating suitable structures, processes and systems, culture, and people fully aligned to the organization's business purpose and direction. An organization is a consciously coordinated entity with an identifiable boundary that functions on a relatively continuous basis to achieve a common goal or set of goals. An organizational structure defines how roles are defined, tasks are allocated, relationships are reported, and the formal coordination and interaction pattern that the organization would follow.

Organizations need to be committed to the philosophy of continuous improvement of the processes and systems that they use to transform inputs into outputs. This involves continually assessing and reassessing not only the outcomes of business processes but also the processes and systems to see what improvements can be made to streamline and improve methods, so as to keep making positive contributions to the overall effectiveness. Ahisholm (1998) highlights four key challenges facing organizations in the present context—rapid advancement of technology, globalization, operational and process complexity, and shift in values and beliefs. The secrets of organizational effectiveness, in case of Infosys Technologies Ltd are presented in this section.

Organizational Effectiveness and Culture

Culture is a set of norms, values, and assumptions that are available to the staff, and it is thus inseparable from action and process. It is also defined as a learned set of rules, written and unwritten, that instructs individuals about working effectively with each other and with their environment. It not only defines ways to act, but also ways to react and, therefore, is an essential component of individual capacity to live as a human being in an organizational context. In other words, 'It's the way we do things around here'. Trice and Beyer (1993) have defined culture as the 'unique pattern of shared assumptions, values, and norms that shape the socialization, symbols, language, narratives, and practices of a group of people'.

Schein Edgar defines organizational culture as 'the residue of success' within an organization. According to him, culture is the most crucial and difficult organizational attribute to change as it is long lasting compared to all other physical attributes of the organization. He states that there are three levels of organizational

Infosys Technologies Ltd

Infosys Technologies Ltd (NASDAQ: INFY) provides consulting and IT services to clients globally—as partners to conceptualize and realize technology-driven business transformation initiatives. The company employs more than 187,000 employees worldwide and uses a low-risk global delivery model (GDM) to accelerate schedules with a high degree of time and cost predictability. N.R. Narayana Murthy was the Chairman of the Board and Chief Mentor under whose dynamic leadership the organization reached great heights. Vishal Sikka joined the company as the CEO and MD in 2014. Infosys has been ranked No.1 among the best managed companies in Asia-Pacific in the annual Euromoney Best Managed Companies in Asia survey, 2013.

The company's corporate office is in Bengaluru. Its US headquarters is in Fremont, CA and it has many branches across the world. From an initial capital of US$ 250, the company has grown to become a US$ 9.02 billion company with a market capitalization of approximately US$ 43.8 billion.

Infosys had achieved some major milestones since its inception in 1981, such as becoming a public limited company in 1992, obtaining the ISO 9001/TickIT Certification in 1993, and getting listed on the NASDAQ in 1999. In 2011, it crossed US$ 6 billion revenue mark and had an employee strength of over 125,000. Its annual revenue which crossed the US$100 million mark in 1999 had reached US$9.02 billion in 2014. Today, Infosys has emerged as one of the most successful and effective Indian organizations with a global presence. Its success is mainly attributed to an organizational culture that could only be nurtured by Mr Narayana Murthy and other founders over the years.

Source: http://www.infosys.com/newsroom/features/Pages/best-managed-companies-asia.aspx, accessed on 28 October 2015 and various newspaper reports.

attributes that contribute to its culture namely those attributes that can be seen, felt, and heard by the uninitiated observer. These include facilities, offices, furnishings, visible awards, recognition, dress codes, and the way each person visibly interacts with each other and outsiders. At the second level are the organization's slogans, stories, mission statement, operational creeds, and values that are expressed often and repeatedly. These cultural elements of an organization can be understood by interviewing the employees of the organization about their attitudes. At the third and deepest level are the organization's underlying and tacit assumptions, which are usually invisible and not cognitively identified in everyday interactions among organizational members.

Regular employees of the organization are usually unaware of these assumptions. Only those members of the organization who have been serving the organization for a long time and understand the organizational culture at its deepest can understand these assumptions. They have got acclimatized to these attributes over time, thus reinforcing the invisibility of their existence. Therefore, according to Schein, organizational culture gets formed from shared history, values, and adaptation.

Further, organizational change is not possible without making changes that affect its culture.

Schein states that organizational culture develops in response to two major challenges that every organization confronts—external adaptation and survival, and internal integration. External adaptation and survival refer to the way an organization copes with and responds to its ever-changing environment. Internal integration refers to the establishment and maintenance of effective and harmonious relationships in work situation among members of the organization.

Thus, organizational culture may be defined as the overall attitude of the people within an organization. It contributes a great deal to the achievement of its objectives and in improving its effectiveness. In a recent survey of business leaders, it was found that 70 per cent agreed with the statement 'culture is the true source of competitive advantage'. 91 per cent agreed that 'culture erodes if not actively nurtured'. Many features of organizational performance get blocked due to the inherent diversity of organizational membership. On one hand, it can bring in healthy and necessary differences, while on the other, it may also create conflicts and lack of synergy.

Changing external environment on one hand and shifting expectations of managers as they move along different career stages, on the other, require a change in approach towards managing and leading.

The basics of building and nurturing a favourable organizational culture requires focused attention on teamwork, leadership development, conflict management, inculcating best practices, and values.

Thus, harmonizing, aligning, and integrating people, processes and systems, culture, and organizational structure to the business objective and direction lead to achievement of organizational effectiveness. The way Hewlett-Packard (HP) has aligned and integrated various aspects of organization for organizational effectiveness is given here.

ORGANIZATION LIFE CYCLE STAGES

Every organization goes through various life cycle stages. However, what matters the most is the management of these stages in a manner that it remains on the path of growth. This mainly depends on the leader and his capability to create a culture for innovation in the organization. In growing, highly competitive businesses, the life cycle's predictable patterns help organizations and their managers to develop a greater insight as to what problems need to be corrected first. These problems may be both operational and cultural. The management's ability to handle problems effectively and to create new market opportunities differentiates successful from unsuccessful businesses. Organizational life-cycle stages can be categorized as— entrepreneurial, collectivity, formalization and control, elaboration of structure, and decline stages. Each stage presents different challenges, issues, and problems that need to be appropriately diagnosed to devise right strategies to respond to the same. There are five organization life cycle stages, as shown in Fig. 7.1.

Hewlett-Packard

Known for its overall culture of collaboration, which encourages knowledge sharing and risk-taking on all levels, HP supports even those employees who try out things that do not work. At HP, one of the rules of the garage says 'Share tools, ideas, and trust your colleagues.' The company has Expert Yellow Pages, a knowledge management system that enables employees to register their areas of expertise and competence. Through this system, HP employees can find a person within the organization with knowledge, skills, education, interests, affiliations, and projects that are of interest to them. This tool facilitates the sharing of best practices, answering of questions, and obtaining feedback on ideas.

HP's Vice President, HR, C Mahalingam says the knowledge market needs its own currency to transact knowledge business. 'Organizations will have to define, design, and deliver such a tool as well.' Living up to the 'invent' slogan on its logo, HP has contributed breakthrough innovations in areas such as light-emitting diodes, inkjet printing, RISC technology, 64-bit architectures, nanotechnology, and utility computing.

Over the past several decades, the company has leveraged the creativity of HP Labs, as well as continuing company-wide research and development investments, to bring transformational advances to the technology services arena as well. As a result, HP fields the computer industry's largest technical services organization, with innovative processes and methodologies to help ensure consistent delivery capabilities in every corner of the globe. Some of the core principles around which the company operates to effectively deliver its services are as under:

- eSupport innovation: automated monitoring and proactive problem-solving
- Technology management innovation: end-to-end visibility for enhancing the business value of IT
- 'Better together': integrating remote and onsite service innovations
- Service management innovation: making measurable gains with ITSM

Innovation has become the hallmark of success of HP.

Source: *Business Line*, The Hindu Group, 25 February 2002, www.blonnet.com/life/ Hewlett-Packard website Excellence & Innovation: Technology & Process, h20219.www2.hp.com/services/cache/290966-0-0-225-121.html, accessed on 19 August 2007.

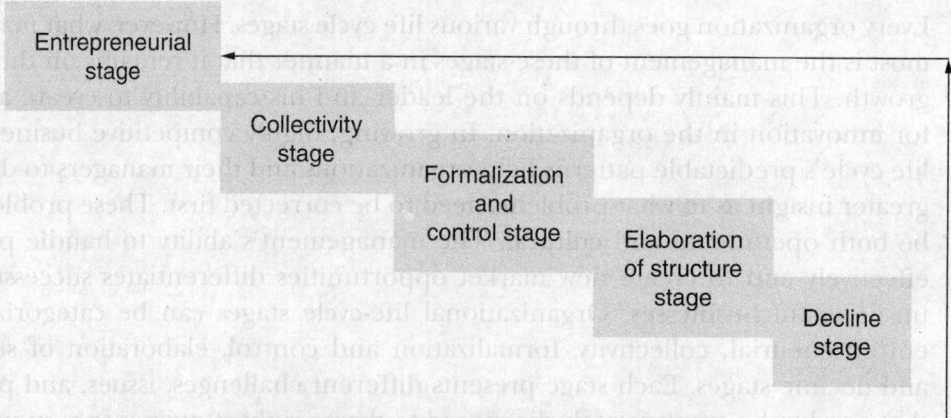

FIGURE 7.1 Organization life cycle stages

Entrepreneurial stage   The organization is in its nascent stage. Although its goals are ambiguous, they have a high level of creativity.

Collectivity stage   Innovations continue in this stage and the organization's mission is clarified. Communication is informal and its employees are highly committed to the organization's objectives and goals.

Formalization and control stage   In this stage the organizational structure stabilizes and formal rules and procedures are put in place. However, innovation is given a back seat while greater emphasis is placed on efficiency and stability.

Elaboration of structure stage   Products and services are diversified at this level. The structure becomes more complex with multiple departments giving rise to multiple reporting relationships. This is the stage in which decision-making gets decentralized.

Decline stage   This is the stage when management looks for ways to maintain market position and look for new opportunities. In this phase organizational effectiveness really matters in terms of coming out with new ideas to exploit existing or emerging opportunities.

ORGANIZATIONAL EFFECTIVENESS CRITERIA

'We rigorously measure everything else in our company. Why don't we measure the effectiveness of our organization?' This is the attitude of most managers.

An organization may achieve its goals, but the ultimate test of its success lies in measurement of the results, which contribute to the achieving of those goals. Those responsible and accountable for directing the organization must first determine where an organization stands and what it wants to achieve in a particular period. This must then be translated into sub-goals (or objectives and results), a component of the goals the organization must achieve. Individual and group performance have to be viewed and evaluated vis-à-vis a predetermined criteria. Certain objectives and goals may be qualitative, while others may be quantitative. Qualitative objectives need to be converted into quantitative objectives as much as possible. To achieve the desired results, individuals and groups at different tiers have to plan and execute a sequence of actions and activities (Fig. 7.2).

Some of the commonly used criteria for evaluating organizational effectiveness such as productivity, efficiency, profit, quality, accidents, growth, absenteeism, turnover, dividend payment, share price, and earning per share, are quantitative in nature and can be measured by using well-defined variables. However, there are a number of criteria that have a considerable impact on achievement of quantitative criteria but cannot be easily measured as they are qualitative in nature. Some of the vital qualitative criteria are—job-satisfaction, motivation, morale, control, conflict-cohesion, flexibility-adaptation, goal consensus, internalization of organizational goals, role and norm congruence, managerial and interpersonal skills, information management and communication, readiness, utilization of environment, value of human resources, participation and shared influence, training and

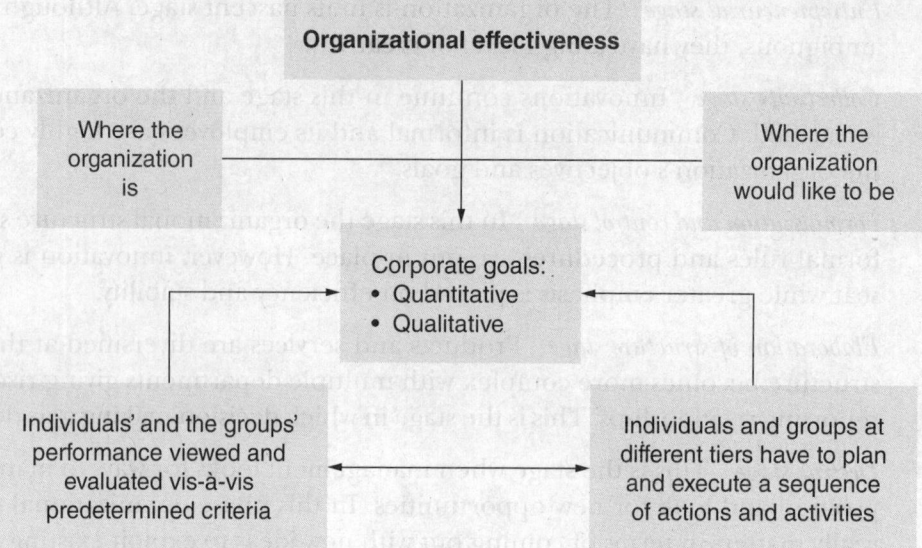

FIGURE 7.2   Model for organizational effectiveness measurement criteria

development, and emphasis on achievement. The criteria used to measure organizational effectiveness by Tata Consultancy Services Limited is illustrated in this section.

High-performance organizations

Research shows that high-performance organizations can be distinguished from the rest by applying a yardstick on certain parameters (Table 7.1).

TABLE 7.1   Parameters of high-performance organizations

Parameters	Yardsticks
• Values and goals	• Clear vision
• Leadership behaviour	• Cohesive leadership
• Decision-making	• Crisp decision
• Management processes	• Value-adding processes
• Talent	• Deep talent
• Measure and incentives	• Meritocracy
• Customer focus	• Consistent high quality
• Frontline support	• Fit
• Performance culture	• High performance
• Capacity to change	• Continuous evaluation

Some of the leading high-performance organizations are Infosys, Bharti Tele Ventures, Reliance Industries Limited (RIL), Dabur India, Oil and Natural Gas Corporation (ONGC), Bharat Heavy Electrical Ltd (BHEL), and Larsen and Toubro

Tata Consultancy Services Limited (TCS)

Tata Consultancy Services Limited (TCS) is the world's leading information technology consulting, services, and business process outsourcing organization that envisioned and pioneered the adoption of the flexible global business practices that today enable companies to operate more efficiently and produce more value. TCS started its operations in 1968, when the IT services industry did not have any presence. Today, the company has over 3,24,000 of the world's best-trained IT consultants in 46 countries and offers a comprehensive range of services across diverse industries. TCS has product range offerings in diverse areas such as banking, insurance, financial services, manufacturing, life sciences, healthcare, energy and utilities, transportation, telecom and more.

The market capitalization of the company crossed US$80 billion during 2014–15, making TCS the most valuable company in India at that time. During the fiscal year ending March 31, 2015, TCS had revenues of $15.5 billion; up 15% Y-o-Y in reported terms and 17% in constant currency; and net income at $3.5B; up 12.8% Y-o-Y.

All this extraordinary financial performance could be achieved because of having a pool of talented human resources that the company inducts, trains, develops, and retains. The emphasis that the company has been laying on human resources has enabled it to become one of the world's leading IT companies. The company's business model is people driven and, therefore, strategically the company is endowed with one of the most enviable pool of talent from across the globe. TCS brings together the most complete team with a rare mix of domain, technology, and project management experts to deal and deliver on every project it undertakes. TCS provides its people with careers across business and technology areas; opportunities to be at the forefront of e-revolution; global exposure with clients, many of them Fortune 500 standouts; world-class training; the opportunity to learn continuously; and an open door energetic environment with world-class infrastructure.

TCS gives the utmost importance to the training and education of its people as a continuous value-adding process. This approach hones, improves, and enhances their skills, making the organization stronger. Its training and development centre introduces young graduates, from some of the best educational institutions in the world, to the TCS way of doing things. Business and technology experts from some of the best organizations in the world bring invaluable insights into their areas of expertise. Industry veterans who laid the foundation of the offshore services business form the backbone of their leadership team. TCS invests a part of its annual revenues in training, a shining example of which can be seen at its state-of-the-art training centres in the country.

(L&T) Limited. Leaders with a clear vision, well-designed management processes, policies to attract and retain talent, customer focus, innovation, and above all, adaptability and capacity to change are some of things that these organizations have in common. Thus, these organizations have been able to earn consistent profits and move on the growth path.

Characteristics of effective organizations

Effective organizations have been found to possess certain characteristics that distinguish them from the rest. The common ones are:

- providing sustained leadership;
- driving effective decisions;

- focusing people on performance;
- aligning the front line; and
- driving a high-performance culture.

Thus, performing, growing, and developing organizations create inbuilt mechanisms to continuously improve their effectiveness by developing a culture that is conducive to creating and responding to the environmental changes. These organizations have transparent systems and processes and an organizational structure wherein communication between different tiers and within groups is encouraged. People are receptive to feedback as measured in quantitative and qualitative terms. It would be imperative for any organization to focus on being effective for its long-term sustainable growth and development.

SUMMARY

A clear purpose and direction is a must for organizational effectiveness. Organizational structure, processes and systems, culture, and employees must all be aligned to this objective for the organization's success. Organizational effectiveness is defined as the ability of an organization to maximize its performance amidst competitive external environment.

The basics of building and nurturing a favourable organizational culture require focused attention on teamwork, leadership development, conflict management, inculcating best practices, and values.

Every organization undergoes various life cycle stages, which can be classified as—entrepreneurial, collectivity, formalization and control, and elaboration of structure stages. However, the management, at all these stages must remain focused on the organization's path of growth. This mainly depends on the leader and his capability to create a culture for innovation within the organization. Some of the commonly used criteria for evaluation of organizational effectiveness are productivity, efficiency, profit, quality, accidents, growth, absenteeism, turnover, dividend payment, share price, earning per share, etc. These yardsticks are quantitative in nature and can be measured by using well-defined variables. However, there are other yardsticks that have a considerable impact on achievement of goals but cannot be easily measured, as they are qualitative in nature.

Sustained leadership, effective decisions, focusing people on performance, aligning the front line, and driving a high-performance culture are some common features of effective organizations. It is these characteristics that distinguish them from non-effective ones.

KEYWORDS

Culture A set of norms, values, and assumptions that are available to the employees. It is thus inseparable from action and process.

High-performance organizations These are organizations that perform exceedingly well in terms of achievement of their goals.

Organizational effectiveness It is the ability of an organization to maximize its performance amidst competitive external environment.

Organizational life cycle stages The various stages an organization goes through in its process of growth.

Productivity It refers to the accomplishment of objectives through the utilization of resources such as capital, workforce, machinery, and infrastructure.

EXERCISES

Concept Review Questions

1. Define organizational effectiveness.
2. How relevant is organizational structure to organizational effectiveness?
3. What is meant by organizational culture? What are the factors that build a favourable organizational structure?
4. Differentiate between entrepreneurial, formalization, and control stage in the organizational life cycle stages.
5. What are the important quantitative and qualitative criteria used to measure organizational effectiveness?
6. What are the important yardsticks on the basis of which high-performance organizations can be distinguished from that of low performance organizations?
7. What are the five distinct characteristics possessed by effective organizations?

Critical Thinking Questions

1. How can meritocracy, which contributes to the organization's performance, be promoted?

2. Identify five distinct companies, each falling under a particular category of organization life cycle stages. Give due justification for categorizing them in each of these categories.

Project Assignments

1. One of the characteristics of effective organization is to 'drive a high-performance culture'. Taking the example of two companies, compare the cultural characteristics that set them apart and have led to one being more effective than the other.
2. Take the example of a company in the service sector and evaluate its effectiveness against the commonly used criteria for evaluation vis-à-vis its competitors.
3. Consider a sample of 15 manufacturing companies and classify them into various organizational life cycle stages. Give justification for your classification. Suggest the possible strategies that would lead to the growth of each of these companies for a given life cycle stage.

REFERENCES

Ahisholm, R.F. (1998), *Developing Network Organizations: Learning from Practice and Theory*, Addison-Wesley, Reading, Massachusetts.

diversity.gsfc.nasa.gov/dcprivate/diversityresources/conflict1.html, accessed on 20 August 2007.

Schein, E.H. (2004), *Organizational Culture and Leadership*, 3rd edition, Jossey-Bass, Wiley, New York.

Trice, H.M. and J.M. Beyer (1993), *The Culture of Work Organizations*, Prentice Hall, Englewood Cliffs, New Jersey, pp. 1–32.

Part II
Economic and Financial Analysis

8

Business—Economic Fundamentals

INTRODUCTION

What is economics and how does it affect business decisions? Does a sound business require a good understanding of economics? These are just some of the questions that arise in the minds of business decision-makers. It is said that management and economics share a one-to-one relationship. Good businesses often have a good grip on economics. They invariably use economic tools and techniques to effectively manage their businesses. Thus, it is essential to equip ourselves with the fundamentals of economics.

ECONOMICS

Economics (derived from the Greek words οίκω (*okos*), 'house', and νέμω (*nemo*), 'rules' referring to household management) is the social science that studies the allocation of scarce resources. This involves analysing production, distribution, trade, and consumption of goods and services. Economics studies choice, decision-making, and optimum allocation of limited resources to fulfil unlimited human needs and wants. Economics is that branch of social science that deals with the production, distribution, and consumption of goods and services and their management. It is the social science that studies production and consumption systems through measurable variables. It involves analysing the production, distribution, trade, and consumption of goods and services with a view to suggest optimum allocation of resources.

Learning Objectives

After studying this chapter, you will be able to:
- Understand the meaning of economics
- Learn the purpose of studying economics
- Examine the types of economic theories
- Understand demand and supply concepts and their relevance to the understanding economic behaviour
- Appreciate how market mechanism operates
- Learn the concepts of elasticity, factors affecting elasticity, and their implications to economic decision-making

Economics is the study of the economy. Classical economics is the result of the pioneering efforts of leading economists who laid the foundation of economic theories. It is said to be the first modern school of economic thought. The major contributors to economic thought in this era were Adam Smith (1723–1790), David Recardo (1772–1823), Thomas Malthus (1766–1834), and John Stuart Mill (1806–1873). Some scholars include the contributions of Karl Marx (1818–1883) and William Petty (1623–1687) as part of classical economics. The classical economics school was active up to mid-nineteenth century and thereafter, neoclassical economists in Britain contributed to the development of economics around 1870. Classical economics concentrates on how the forces of supply and demand facilitate allocation of scarce products, services, and resources. Thus, management and economics are interwoven. There cannot be effective management without understanding the economics of production, distribution, and consumption.

Purpose of Studying Economics

Economics needs to be studied as it provides a logical way of diagnosis, analysis, and solution to a variety of problems that arise within an organization. Economics covers a wide gamut of topics ranging from making sound business decisions, to consumer choices, to tackling some of society's most challenging issues. It would not be possible to understand business decisions, politics, social reforms, technological developments, or international relations without understanding their economic base. An education in economics enables individuals to appreciate, understand, and assist in resolving problems that arise in today's business and society.

Economists believe that individuals and business organizations act with their own self-interest in mind. Market trends are understood and predicted by keeping an eye on the optimization of objectives of different economic agents. For the consumer it is the maximization of satisfaction, for the producer it is the maximization of production, and the businessperson aims at the maximization of profits within existing constraints. Economic theories help in predicting future market trends; analysing the relative merits of different market structures possible (e.g., small vs big business, capitalism vs socialism, monopoly vs competition); and advising consumers, business entities, governments, and international bodies about the likely impact of their economic policies (e.g., taxes, unemployment insurance, free trade) on individuals, industries, and economies. All these reasons make economics a necessary field of study for those involved with business. A classification of economic theories is given in Fig. 8.1.

Positive and normative economics

The word 'positive' is used in context of theories that only attempt to describe how things are, as opposed to how they should be. Economics is said to be positive when it attempts to explain the consequences of different choices given a set of assumptions or a set of observations. Thus, positive economics deals with causal relationships and attempts to find out the causes that lead to a given effect or vice versa. As against this, normative economics is prescriptive in nature and has more to

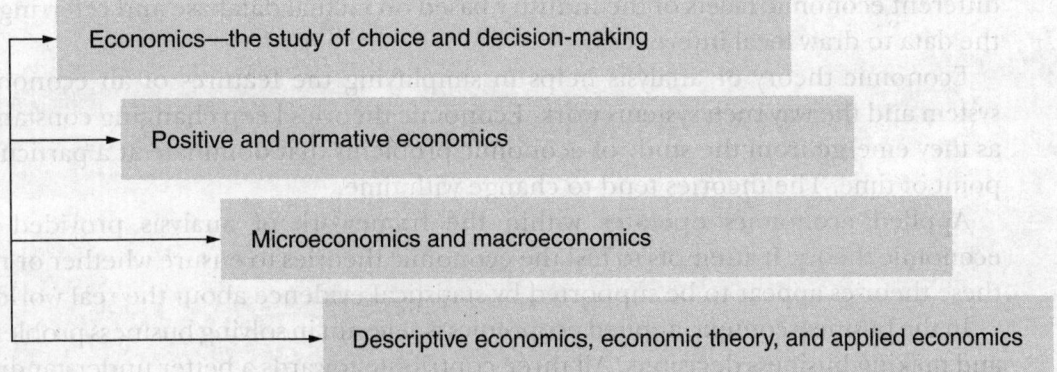

FIGURE 8.1 Classification of different economic theories

do with values. It prescribes the action that should be taken when the organization is facing a certain situation. Normative economics is more in the domain of public policy. However, though we may have a normative perspective before us, when an economic problem arises, it is essential to deal with the reality. At that time, only positive economics can provide us with the answers.

Microeconomics and macroeconomics

The whole gamut of economic theories is divided into two main branches—*microeconomics* and *macroeconomics*. Microeconomics deals with individual behaviour of a householder, consumer, businessperson, producer, etc. It studies the economic behaviour of individual consumers, firms, and industries and the distribution of production and income among them. It considers individuals both as suppliers of labour and capital. It analyses firms—both as suppliers of products and as consumers of labour and capital. It observes the markets that establish relative prices of goods and services and/or allocates resources amongst alternative uses. Thus, understanding of microeconomics provides a basic framework within which sound and effective business decisions are taken.

Macroeconomics considers the economy as a whole and deals with aggregate variables such as aggregate demand and supply for money, capital, and commodities. Aggregate supply is the total supply of goods and services by a national economy during a specific time period. Aggregate demand is the total demand for goods and services in the economy during a specific time period. It is also referred to as effective demand. Aggregate supply and demand can be measured in nominal or real terms. The measurement in nominal terms means at current prices, while measurement in real terms refers to constant price in relation to the base year.

Descriptive economics, economic theory, and applied economics

Descriptive economics refers to the collection of all the relevant facts related to an event and aligning them coherently with emerging implications. For example, the textile industry in India or in a particular state would require an understanding of different economic facets of the industry based on factual database and referring to the data to draw local inferences.

Economic theory or analysis helps in simplifying the features of an economic system and the way such systems work. Economic theories keep changing constantly as they emerge from the study of economic problems that dominate at a particular point of time. The theories tend to change with time.

Applied economics operates within the framework of analysis provided by economic theory. It attempts to test the economic theories to ensure whether or not these theories appear to be supported by statistical evidence about the real world.

In the business context, applied economics is relevant in solving business problems and making business decisions. All three contribute towards a better understanding of the business environment.

DEMAND AND SUPPLY

Demand–supply analysis can be best understood assuming that a model of perfect competition is operating in the markets as this model simplifies reality. The characteristics of perfect competition are homogeneity of the product, large number of buyers and sellers, that is, both the buyer and seller of the product are small to influence the price of the product significantly being bought or sold in the market. There are no artificial restraints, that is, prices move purely on the basis of demand–supply forces. Neither the government nor other institutions intervene in the fixing of prices, mobility of goods, services, and resources in the economy. Although, in reality, it is difficult to come across perfect competition markets, the model provides a good insight into the understanding of reality. Markets such as those for agricultural produce, stock exchange, and foreign exchange, operate more or less under perfect competitive market conditions.

Demand

Demand for a product is defined as the various quantities of the product per unit of a time; daily, weekly, or monthly that consumers are willing and able to purchase at alternative prices, keeping all other things affecting demand as constant. The *law of demand* states that the relationship between a good's price and its quantity demanded is negative, that is, when the price of a good falls from ₹100 per unit to ₹50 per unit, the quantity demanded rises from 50 units to 80 units per unit of time. This is referred to as a 'change in quantity demanded' and in this case as an 'increase in quantity demanded'. Thus, change in the price of a product or service causes movements along a given demand curve. Demand can be expressed in mathematical terms as:

$$X_D = f(P_x, N, T, Y, P_n, R, E) \tag{8.1}$$

Where:

X = Quantity of goods or services

P_x = Price of X: The law of demand suggests that price of a good is inversely related to the quantity demanded

N = Number of consumers under consideration: As the number of people consuming the product increases, the demand for it also goes up and vice versa.

T = Taste and preferences of consumers: Consumer preferences have a major impact on the level of demand. They may be influenced by a wide range of factors, mostly psychological and are, therefore, difficult to quantify.

Y = Consumers' income and distribution: This is the most important determinant of demand. As incomes rise, the quantity demanded should also increase. Again, there are exceptions to this. In poorer countries, there is evidence that some staple goods, such as rice, become less popular as incomes rise even if their prices fall.

P_n = Price of related goods: Some goods are substitutes for one another. If the price of one falls, the demand for the other also falls as it becomes less attractive to the consumer. Holidays in Srinagar and Shimla are good examples of substitute goods. A fall in the prices of holidaying in Shimla would reduce the demand for holidaying in Srinagar. Some goods are complementary; the demand for them moves in tandem. If the price of one of them falls, the quantity demanded of the other will rise. Examples of complementary goods are portable CD players and batteries.

R = Range of products available to consumers: As the number of goods available increases, the demand for each comes down and vice versa.

E = Expectations of consumers: When consumers expect the prices to fall, the demand for the product would fall and if they expect the prices to rise, the demand would also increase.

Demand refers to a demand schedule that lists the different quantities of the commodity that consumers are willing and able to take at alternative prices, keeping all other factors affecting the demand as constant, that is, *ceteris paribus*. For example, the fall in the price of steel will result in an increase in its demand and vice versa (law of demand).

Note that quantity demanded is a number (e.g., 600 tonnes of steel), but demand is the relationship between two variables. The demand relationship can be expressed in the form of a table or demand schedule. The demand schedule for steel is presented in Table 8.1.

The market demand schedule summarizes the behaviour of individual buyers. It shows that buyers respond to a lower price by buying more and vice versa. Price and demand are inversely related. The demand schedule shows the relationship between price and quantity demanded, *ceteris paribus*. The demand relationship,

TABLE 8.1 Demand schedule for steel

Price ₹/tonnes	18,000	16,000	14,000	12,000	10,000	8000	6000	4000	2000
Q_D in *M* tonnes	2000	3000	4000	5000	6000	7000	8000	9000	10,000

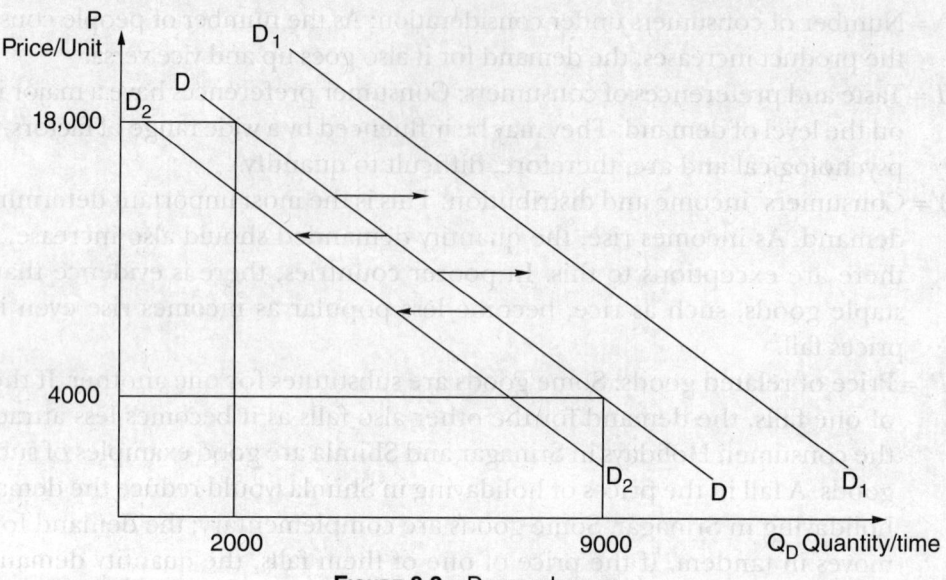

FIGURE 8.2   Demand curve

based on the demand schedule given earlier is graphically expressed in the Fig. 8.2. The graphical representation of demand is referred to as a demand curve.

Change in demand

A change in the demand or a shift of the entire demand curve is caused by a change in any of the other factors other than the price of the product under consideration affecting the demand. Thus, a shift of the entire demand curve would be caused by a change in one of the *ceteris paribus* demand variables. This is referred to as an increase or decrease in demand.

Increase and decrease in demand   When demand increases, the quantity demanded by consumers increases at every price.

For example, when demand increases, the quantity demanded at a price of ₹100 per unit rises from 50 units per unit of time to 70 units per unit of time. Demand would increase if the consumers' tastes shift in its favour or if more people start purchasing the product.

When demand decreases, the quantity demanded by consumers falls at every price. For example, when demand decreases, the quantity demanded at a price of ₹100 per unit falls from 50 units per unit of time to 30 units per unit of time.

$D_1 D_1$ is an upward shift of the demand curve, that is, at each and every price there is an increase in quantity demanded. Similarly, $D_2 D_2$ is a downward shift in the demand curve, that is, at each and every price there is a decrease in the quantity demanded.

The term 'demand' refers to the entire demand curve/schedule. When any of the factors are kept constant while defining demand change, it results in the change in demand resulting in the shift in the demand curve upward or downward depending upon the change in the factor under consideration.

Supply

The concept of supply is defined as various quantities of a product that the seller places in the market per unit of time at alternative prices, keeping all other factors affecting supply as constant. It is basically a relationship between quantities that suppliers are willing to sell at alternate prices. Supply can be expressed in mathematical terms as:

$$X_s = f(P_x, P_n, T, E, P_i) \qquad (8.2)$$

Where:

X = Quantity of goods or service

P_x = Price of X: The law of supply suggests that the price of a product is directly related to the quantity supplied.

N = Number of sellers under consideration: As the number of sellers increase, there is an increase in capacities leading to a shift in the supply curve downward resulting in increased quantity supplied at the same price.

T = Technology to produce the product: As and when better technology to produce the product comes up, there would be increased quantity supplied at the same price.

E = Future expectations of the sellers: When sellers expect that future prices would increase, the supply curve as a whole would get shifted upward, implying that quantity supplied at the same price would fall.

P_i = Price of inputs

Thus, the shift in supply takes place when any one of the factors, other than the price of the product changes. The shift in supply can be upward or downward depending upon the type of change that has taken place in the other factor. The supply schedule for steel is as given in Table 8.2.

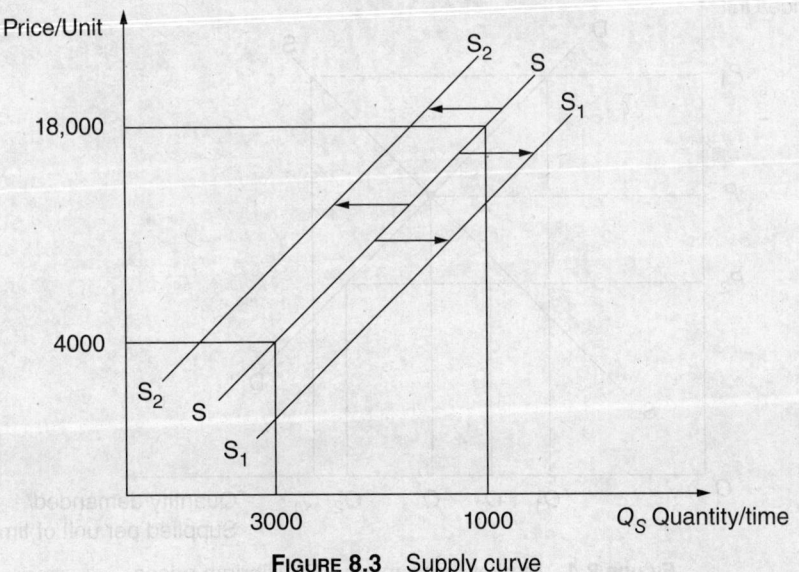

FIGURE 8.3 Supply curve

TABLE 8.2 Supply schedule for steel

Price ₹/tonnes	18,000	16,000	14,000	12,000	10,000	8000	6000	4000	2000
Q_s in M tonnes	10,000	9000	8000	7000	6000	5000	4000	3000	2000

Supply curve The supply curve (Fig. 8.3) plots different points of the supply schedule on a graph. S_1S_1 is an upward shift of the supply curve indicating an increase in the quantity supplied by sellers at each price. This happens due to an improvement in technology or an increase in producers of the product. S_2S_2 is a downward shift of the supply curve, implying fall in the quantity supplied at each price due to an increase in the cost of inputs and/or some sellers leaving the market.

MARKET PRICE

Market price is determined by the forces of demand and supply. In the above analysis, consumer demand was assumed to be independent of the suppliers' activities and vice versa. Equilibrium price P is displayed in Fig. 8.4. OP represents the equilibrium price. OQ is the quantity demanded/supplied at equilibrium price.

Conventional microeconomic analysis states that the price of a product or service and its output is determined at the intersection of supply and demand curves. This is called the equilibrium price. Any price above the equilibrium will result in a situation where the quantity supplied exceeds the quantity demanded. Due to their inability to clear the market, producers may reduce prices. Any price below the equilibrium will see the quantity demanded exceed the quantity supplied, bidding the price upwards.

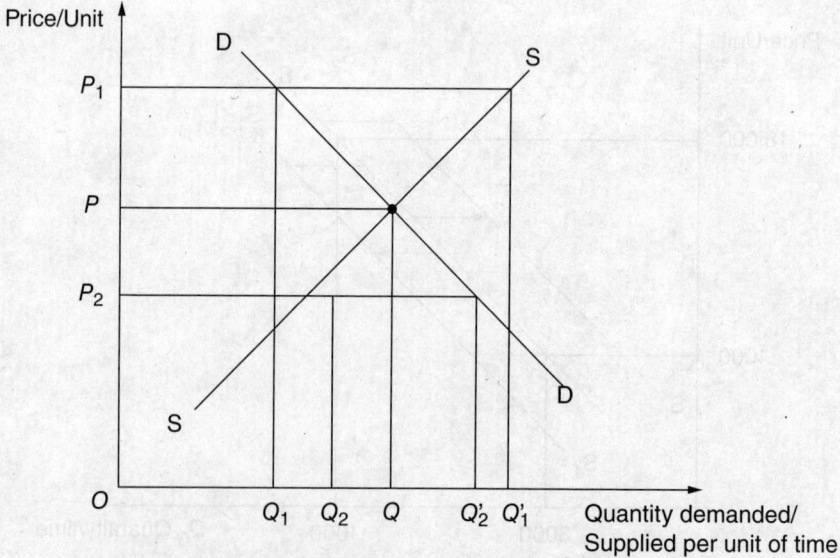

FIGURE 8.4 Market mechanism—Equilibrium prices

Prices should always tend to settle at equilibrium, unless artificial constraints are imposed by government or by collusion amongst producers (cartels). At price level P_1 consumers are willing to buy Q_1 quantity per unit of time. However, sellers are prepared to place Q'_1 quantity per unit of time in the market. Thus, an excess supply of $Q_1 Q'_1$ per unit of time takes place. This gives an incentive to the sellers to reduce the price by undercutting each other to dispose of their quantities supplied. Thus, the sellers would scale down prices; quantities supplied will decrease and quantities consumed will increase pushing the price towards equilibrium. Similarly, in case sellers establish a price P_2, consumers want Q'_2 quantity per unit of time. However, sellers are prepared to place only Q_2 quantity per unit of time in the market, resulting in an excess demand amounting to $Q_2 Q'_2$ per unit of time. This results in shortages in the market and, therefore, consumers will have an incentive to bid against each other to get the product. They will continue to raise prices till the shortage exists and ultimately price P would be reached where there would not be any shortage in the market. The change in demand and supply for milk and its implication on equilibrium prices is given here.

Quantity Demanded $Q_D = 10 - 2P$ where q is in number of units of the product and P is ₹/unit for the product

$$\text{Quantity Supplied } Q_S = 5 + 2P$$

where Q is in number of units of the product and P is ₹/unit for the product. Equilibrium Price will be at point where $Q_D = Q_S$. Thus to calculate equilibrium price, we will have to equate demand and supply equations.

$$Q_D = Q_S \text{ implies } 10 - 2P = 5 + 2P$$

$5 = 4P$ therefore $P = 5/4 = $ ₹1.25/unit and equilibrium quantity will be
$$Q_D = Q_S = 7.5 \text{ Units}$$

Quantity Demanded $Q_D = 10 - 2P^2 - 2P$
Quantity Supplied $Q_S = 5 + 2P^2 + 2P$
where Q is in number of units of the product and P is ₹/unit for the product. Equilibrium price will be at point where $Q_D = Q_S$.

For calculating equilibrium price $10 - 2P^2 - 2P = 5 + 2P^2 + 2P$

$4P^2 + 4P - 5 = 0$

$$P = \frac{-b \pm \sqrt{b^2 - 4ac}}{2a} = \frac{-4 \pm \sqrt{4^2 - 4 \times 4 \times (9-5)}}{2 \times 4} = \frac{-4 \pm 9.798}{8}$$

$P = $ ₹0.72475/ unit or minus ₹1.7247/ unit

As price for any normal good cannot be negative, hence price for the product will be ₹0.72475/unit and equilibrium quantity will be 7.5 units.

Surging demand causes milk prices to touch a peak

Milk prices are rising leaps and bound throughout the world and are not likely to reverse in the near future particularly because of its increasing demand in China and Latin America. Milk production has failed to keep pace with 3 per cent increase in annual milk consumption. Reduction in subsidies has led to elimination of surpluses in Europe and slowed production growth in USA. The situation has been aggravated because of a drought in Australia that is said to be the worst one of this century. 'Over the next several months, we're going to see some pretty strong prices on all milk', said Larry Salathe, an economist and dairy expert at the US Department of Agriculture in Washington. Production needed to bring prices down 'takes at least several months, usually a year to two years, to come'. The prices of skimmed-milk powder has risen 60 per cent during the six months period to touch a record level of $1.58 per pound on the Chicago Mercantile Exchange in May 2007, which is seven times higher than the last five year average.

The biggest candy maker in the US and the largest milk processor, Dean Foods Co., said that higher dairy cost will adversely hit the industry by squeezing profit growth. Domino's Pizza has said that their cost would increase dramatically as they spend 30 per cent of the total cost on cheese. Increasing cost of milk will adversely affect food programmes for children in Indonesia, Mexico, the Philippines, and Algeria. The government will have to scale down these programmes.

Mr Merritt Cluff, an economist with United Nations Food and Agriculture Organization (FAO) in Rome has stated that with the rising prices of milk and milk products, the programmes to feed the poor will face difficulties. Poor people will have to cut down their milk consumption and buy alternatives such as wheat. However, considering that prices of wheat and maize have also risen; poor people will have a tough time surviving.

Source: Based on *Business Standard*, 16 May 2007.

Implications of Taxes and Subsidies

Suppose the government decides to impose a tax amounting to ₹t per unit on a product. The first issue that arises is whether this would affect demand, supply, or both? The answer to this can be found in the shift of either the demand or supply curve, however, with a different interpretation of the equilibrium point. If we model taxes as shifting the supply curve, then the tax is considered as a cost of doing business. In this case, the new equilibrium point measures the total price paid, including the tax. If we model taxes as shifting the demand curve, then the new equilibrium point measures the price excluding the tax. To find the total price paid we have to add the tax back. Usually, we model taxes and subsidies as affecting the supply curve. Then the new equilibrium point measures the total price paid in both the tax and pretax cases. The tax shifts the supply curve up (left) by ₹t indicating that we need an extra ₹t after the tax to supply the same quantity as before the tax. This is a decrease in supply as a result of the tax. Mathematically, the price depicted on the original supply curve is the price producers must receive to induce them to supply the indicated quantity. The new supply curve shows the relationship between the price consumers pay and the quantity producers are willing to supply.

The price consumers pay is not equal to the price producers receive with a tax. In fact, $PP = PC - Tax$. Thus, the vertical distance between the two curves shows the tax per unit at each output level ($PC - PP = Tax$). The demand curve shows the relationship between the price consumers pay and the quantity they are willing to purchase. Therefore, the new equilibrium is the relevant equilibrium and the corresponding price is the price consumers pay. The price producers receive is the consumers' price minus the tax. To find the equation for the new supply curve, the curve needs to be rewritten in terms of Q versus PC, not PP as in the original supply curve. To do this, the relationship $PP = PC - Tax$ described above is used. Now substitute $PC - Tax$ for P in the original supply curve and simplify.

Suppose we try to pass the entire tax on to consumers, the price would be raised by the tax rate say ₹2 per unit resulting in an increase in the price from say ₹5 per unit, that is, the equilibrium price to ₹7 per unit (₹5 + ₹2 tax per unit). At this increased price, suppliers want to supply 5 units per unit of time, but the consumers only want to purchase 3 units per unit of time. This will result in excess supply leading to the accumulation of inventories. Thus, sellers will have to reduce prices to get rid of their excess inventory build-up. As prices fall, the quantity supplied decreases and the quantity demanded increases. This would continue until the new equilibrium price say at ₹6 per unit is reached at which equilibrium quantity of 4 units per unit of time is supplied in the market. Thus, sellers bear half the tax and receive ₹4 instead of ₹5 per unit after the tax and consumers bear half the tax as they pay ₹6 per unit after the tax instead of ₹5 per unit. Will the tax always be shared equally? This depends on the slope of the supply and demand curves.

A subsidy is the exact opposite of a tax. The government pays incentive per unit of the product produced to producers to encourage production of the product. This shifts the supply curve down by the amount of the per unit subsidy. Again, producers and consumers will share the subsidy, with the relative shares determined by the slope of the supply and demand curves. If producers try to capture the entire subsidy, they would increase output, but consumers would not increase the quantity demanded. Their unintended inventories would accumulate. They would lower prices and pass some of the subsidy on to consumers.

PRICE ELASTICITY OF DEMAND

Price elasticity of demand measures the responsiveness of the quantity demanded as the price of the product or service undergoes changes, given the demand curve for the product or service. If the quantity demanded is not too responsive to the change in price, it would result in an increase in the total expenditure on the product for increase in price of the product and vice versa. Similarly, if a product or service is highly responsive to change in price, it would result in a decrease in the total expenditure on the product for increase in its price and vice versa. Thus, depending upon the elasticity of demand for the product, a seller can take an informed decision regarding the increase in price, keeping his/her objectives in mind.

Measuring price elasticity

Alfred Marshall (1891), the well-known British economist, defined price elasticity of demand as the percentage of change in quantity taken divided by percentage change in price, when the price change is small.

$$\text{Price elasticity of demand } e = \frac{\text{Percentage change in quantity demanded}}{\text{Percentage change in the price of the product}} \quad (8.3)$$

So, by taking proportionate changes in the numerator and denominator, the elasticity is computed as a unit less, irrespective of whether goods are measured in pounds, kilos, feet, or numbers.

Numerically, the price elasticity of demand 'η_p' represents the following ratio:

$$\eta_p = (\%\Delta Q)/(\%\Delta P)$$
$$= (\Delta Q/Q)/(\Delta P/P)$$
$$= (\Delta Q/\Delta P)/(P/Q) \quad (8.4)$$

If $(\%\Delta Q)>\%(\Delta P)$ then $|\eta_p|>1.0$ and demand is price elastic.
In the opposite situation $|\eta_p|<1.0$ and demand is price inelastic.
This relationship between price changes and expenditure can be summarized as shown in Table 8.3.

Point and arc elasticity

The elasticity of demand at a given point on the demand curve is referred to as point elasticity of demand. Arc elasticity of demand is computed between two points on the demand curve; for example, two points on the demand curve are described as under:

	Price (₹/metre)	Quantity (M metres)
At Point *L*	40	40,000
At Point *K*	30	60,000

TABLE 8.3 Elasticity of demand and price changes

Elasticity	Demand is price elastic: $|\eta_p|>1.0$	Demand is price inelastic: $|\eta_p|<1.0$	Demand is price unitary elastic $|\eta_p|=1.0$
Price Reduction	Expenditure increases	Expenditure decreases	Expenditure unchanged and maximum
Price Increase	Expenditure decreases	Expenditure increases	Expenditure unchanged and at maximum

$$\text{Elasticity of demand } \eta_p = \frac{20,000/40,000}{-10/40} = -2$$

if we move from point L to K

$$\text{Elasticity of demand } \eta_p = \frac{-20,000/60,000}{10/30} = -1$$

if we move from point K to L

$$\text{Elasticity of demand } \eta_p = \frac{20,000/50,000}{-10/35} = -1.4$$

if we consider arc elasticity between point K to L

Factors that influence price elasticity of demand

The factors that influence price elasticity of demand are availability of close substitutes with the market, the degree of necessity or luxury, proportion of income spent on a product, habit forming products, the time period under consideration, and permanent or temporary price change. The more (and closer) substitutes are available in the market, the more elastic will the demand be in response to a change in the price.

Necessities tend to have a relatively more inelastic demand curve, whereas luxury goods and services tend to be more elastic. For example, the demand for air conditioners is more elastic than that for fans. The demand for holiday air travel is more elastic than the demand for business air travel.

The greater the proportion of expenditure budget spent on the product, greater will be its elasticity. Goods such as cigarettes and drugs tend to be inelastic in demand. If the consumer knows that price change is temporary for a day or week then responsiveness would be different than if the price change is going to be permanent. Demand tends to be more elastic in the long run rather than in the short run.

Concept of elasticity: Application

Clubs

Most metropolitan cities in India have good clubs that offer a variety of services starting from sports, gym, swimming, indoor games, etc. Regular visitors consider it an important feature of their lifestyle. Club managements tend to take their members for granted, as an increase in the annual fee has never led to members quitting their membership. Data suggests that more than 90 per cent of the members pay their annual membership fee through debit cards and get the reimbursement through their employers. Most of them never come to know about an enhancement in their membership fee. For a majority having committed to pay ₹5,000 to ₹10,000 p.a., a marginal rise of ₹500 to ₹700 does not lead to cancellation of membership. This indicates that elasticity of demand for particularly premium clubs membership is inelastic.

Mobile handsets

The prices of mobile sets with similar or better features have fallen by more than 50 to 75 per cent during last three years. With decrease in prices, the number of mobile users has been increasing at a fast rate. Turnover has increased by more than double when prices of mobile handsets have fallen by 50 per cent in a one year period between 2004–05 and 2005–06, indicating highly elastic demand.

Cross elasticity of demand

The quantity demanded of a particular product varies with the change in the price of other products. Cross elasticity of demand measures the responsiveness of the quantity demanded of one product to changes in the price of another. The formula for measuring cross elasticity of demand for product X is:

$$\text{Cross elasticity of demand} = \frac{\text{\% change in quantity demanded of product } X}{\text{\% change in price of another product } Y}$$

Two goods, which are substitutes, will have a positive cross elasticity. An increase in the price of one product will lead to an increase in the quantity demanded of a substitute. An example of substitute products having a positive cross elasticity of demand is the case of Coca-Cola and Pepsi.

Two goods that are complementary to each other will have a negative cross elasticity demand. An increase in the price of one product will lead to a fall in demand of a complement. For example, an increase in the price of computer monitors will lead to a decrease in the demand of its complement—the CPU. The cross elasticity of two goods which are completely independent of each other would be 0; for example, flowers and sugar.

Similarly, one can understand the concepts of elasticity of supply, that is, a proportionate change in the quantity supplied to proportionate change in the price of the product. Thus, it gives the responsiveness of quantity supplied to the change in price by the sellers. On the other hand, income elasticity of demand measures the relationship between change in quantity demanded, that is, percentage change in quantity demanded in response to change in the income, that is, percentage change in the income. The degree to which the demand for a product changes with respect to the change in income depends on whether the product is a necessity or a luxury. The demand for necessities will increase with income, but at a slower rate. This is because consumers, instead of buying more of only the necessity, will want to use their increased income to buy more of a luxury. During a period of increasing income, demand for luxury products tends to increase at a higher rate than the demand for necessities.

Thus, the fundamental tool of demand, supply, and elasticity can be used to understand a variety of real life issues such as effect of price controls, restriction to produce particular quantities, minimum wage payments and their implications to supply, price support to encourage production, subsidies to encourage production, whether to increase or decrease the price keeping in view consumers and sellers responsiveness, etc. The theory of business economics having great implications to business decisions can be best understood by having a better understanding of concepts of demand and supply. Similarly, certain macro policy decisions would have a bearing on business decisions and they need to be understood from a macro perspective. Above all, dimensions of positive and normative economics have to be duly weighed while examining real life business situations. It is important to highlight that tools of economics provide a better understanding about real life business situations but cannot be applied in a simplistic way as understood; keeping all other factors affecting the problem situation under consideration as constant.

Telecom industry—Cross elasticity of demand

The supply side in the telecom industry has been favourably affected because of technological developments. The industry has seen an unprecedented growth rate world over, particularly in developing countries such as India. With the mobile phone becoming affordable by the common man, phone usage has been growing at a phenomenal rate. The demand in India and China together account for around 2.3 billion users. This growth has significant implications. Its greatest impact has been on basic telecommunication services, information, and communication technologies. The cross elasticity of demand is a positive sign with high and absolute number indicating that the goods are substitutes to each other. This has adversely affected landline or fixed services. The same has been getting replaced by wireless technology (mobile phones) mainly because of their better efficiency, low prices, and improved customer service. The challenge is whether a regulator needs to regulate both fixed lines and mobile markets or should they leave it to market forces to operate and lead the prices to an equilibrium in both mobile and fixed line markets.

SUMMARY

Good business decisions require a good grip over economics. Economics is the study of choice and decision-making in a world with limited resources to fulfil unlimited wants. There cannot be effective management without understanding the economics of production, distribution, and consumption.

In the business context, the relevance of applied economics to solving business problems and taking business decisions is the greatest. The concept of demand and supply can be best understood under conditions of perfect competition. Market prices are determined depending upon the forces of demand and supply. The intersection of demand and supply curves gives rise to an equilibrium price. Market forces lead to an equilibrium price where buyers demand and suppliers needs match each other. Price elasticity of demand measures the responsiveness of the quantity demanded as price of the product or service changes, given the demand curve for the product. The concept of elasticity enables a business entity to take an informed decision regarding increase of prices, keeping in view its objectives.

Thus, the theory of business economics having great implications to business decisions can be best understood by having a better understanding of concepts of demand and supply. Similarly, certain macro policy decisions would have a bearing on business decisions and they need to be understood from the macro perspective.

KEYWORDS

Cross elasticity of demand It measures the responsiveness of the quantity demanded of one product to changes in the price of another.

Demand It is defined as the various quantities of a product per unit of a time that consumers are willing and able to purchase at alternative prices, keeping all other things affecting demand as constant.

Economics It is the study of choice and decision-making in a world with limited resources to fulfil unlimited wants.

Economics in business decisions It has been found that good businesses have a good grip over economics and they invariably use economic tools and techniques to effectively manage their businesses.

Elasticity of demand It measures the responsiveness of the quantity demanded as the price of the product or service undergoes changes, given the demand curve for the product or service.

Elasticity of supply It measures the responsiveness of quantity supplied to the change in price by the sellers.

Equilibrium It is a point where demand and supply curve intersects to arrive at the price of a product or service and the output level that would ultimately take place in the market.

Factors affecting demand Change in any of the other factors other than the price of the product leads to change in demand.

Factors affecting supply Upward or downward shift in supply takes place when any of the factors other than price of the product changes.

Market mechanism Market is the place where consumers and sellers interact together and the forces of demand and supply operate to arrive at the equilibrium price under market mechanism.

Supply It is defined as various quantities of a product that the seller will place in the market per unit of time at alternative prices, keeping all other factors affecting supply as constant.

EXERCISES

Concept Review Questions

1. Define economics and its relevance to business decisions.
2. Citing an example, differentiate between normative and positive economics.
3. Differentiate between descriptive economics, economic theory, and applied economics.
4. Define law of demand.
5. Differentiate between quantity demanded and demand.
6. What are the factors that affect supply?
7. What is meant by equilibrium price?
8. Differentiate between taxes and subsidies.
9. In what way does the availability of subsidies affect business?
10. Define elasticity of demand.
11. What is the significance of increase in cross elasticity of demand having a positive sign?
12. What are the factors that influence elasticity of demand?

Critical Thinking Question

For certain commodities demand increases with increase in prices. Explain with the help of economic concepts. Take the example of the rise in the price of mangoes in the initial season that touches a low only to shoot up and touch another peak during the last phase of the season.

Project Assignments

1. According to Paul Samuelson, the economy was characterized as 'stagflation', that is, rising prices and falling outputs in 1973 and 1974. Analyse the situation with the help of demand and supply curves, taking the steel industry as an example. What explanation would you give to such a pressure on the economy?

2. Analyse the reasons for a fall in the prices of mobile handsets over the years coupled with availability of better and sophisticated mobile handsets.

REFERENCES

Fisher, Irving Norton (1961), *A Bibliography of the Writings of Irving Fisher,* Yale University Library, New Haven, US.

Hollander, Samuel (1979), *The Economics of David Ricardo,* University of Toronto Press.

Malthus, T.R. (1978), *An Essay on the Principle of Population with a Summary View* (1830), and Introduction by Prof. Anthony Flow, Penguin Classics.

Marshall, Alfred (1891), *Principles of Economics,* Macmillan and Co., New York.

Marshall, Alfred (1920), *Principles of Economics,* MacMillan and Co. Ltd, London.

McLellan, David (1973), *Karl Marx: His Life and Thought,* Paladin, London.

Mill, John Stuart (2002), *A System of Logic,* University Press of the Pacific, Honolulu.

Mill, John Stuart (1848), *The Principles of Political Economy: with Some of Their Applications to Social Philosophy,* 7th edition, London.

Schumpeter, Joseph A. on William Petty (1954), *A History of Economic Analysis,* Allen & Unwin, London.

Smith, Adam (1776), *An Inquiry into the Nature and Causes of the Wealth of Nations,* The Modern Library (1937), Random House.

Spiegel, Henry William (1991), *The Growth of Economic Thought, on Francis Edgeworth* (1845–1926), Durham & London, Duke University Press.

Vilfredo, Pareto (1857), 'The New Theories of Economics', *Journal of Political Economy,* vol. 5, September, pp. 485–502.

9

Principles of Production

Learning Objectives

After studying this chapter, you will be able to:

- Understand principles of production
- Learn about production function
- Understand the concepts of production function
- Understand optimal resource allocation in production

INTRODUCTION

Understanding the issues pertaining to cost of production of goods and services, supply curves, resource pricing, resource allocation, and distribution requires an understanding of the principles of production. Every business entity that decides to produce a product or a service has to decide the amount that has to be produced so that it may minimize the cost of production, given the prices of input and the expenditure outlay. Producers have to choose the optimum mix in which the resources required for production of a product need to be combined. They also have to choose suitable technology for producing a particular level of output. To understand all these issues, one needs to understand the principles of production, i.e., laws governing production systems in an organization.

PRODUCTION FUNCTION

The production function is the physical relationship between a firm's inputs of resources and the output of goods and services per unit of time, leaving prices aside. Thus, the production function gives maximum output that can be achieved by combining inputs into various combinations, for a given technology and prices of inputs. In mathematical terms, production function is described as under:

$$Q = f(x, y, z) \tag{9.1}$$

Where Q represents a firm's output and x, y, z represent the inputs required to produce the given product. It displays the relationship between the maximum outputs that can be produced with various combinations of inputs. The production process does not necessarily involve physical conversion of raw materials into tangible goods. In this process, an input as well as the output may be intangible. Thus, in economic terms, the production process may take a variety of forms.

The input-input, input-output, and output-output relationships that emerge as a result of a production function mainly depend upon the technology, i.e., techniques of production. Changing the technology of production will change the relationship between input and output quantities. It is also possible that two different technologies can produce the same quantity of output. A profit-maximizing firm chooses the technology that minimizes its cost for a given level of output.

Inputs

An input comprises goods or services that go into the process of production. It is the inputs that a firm buys and adds value to, through production or other processes, to obtain an output. An output is any commodity that the firm produces or processes for sale. It refers to any good or service that is a result of a production process. The inputs are classified into four broad categories namely, land, labour, capital, and entrepreneur.

Fixed and variable inputs

All inputs can be classified into two broad categories—fixed inputs and variable inputs. A fixed input is one whose quantity remains fixed irrespective of the level of production in the short run such as plant, building, and machinery. Their quantities cannot be readily changed as their supply is inelastic in the short run. A variable input is defined as one whose quantity varies with the level of production and, therefore, the quantities of variable input can be changed as the supply of inputs, such as labour and raw materials, is elastic in the short run.

Short run and long run

Short run refers to a period of time (time horizon) in which the supply of certain inputs is fixed or inelastic. The producer cannot readily vary the level of fixed input. However, a variation in them according to the existing market conditions would be beneficial for the producer. The long run refers to a planning horizon in which all inputs can be readily varied for a desirable change in the output. Thus, in the long run the supply of all inputs is elastic. Therefore, an input that is said to be fixed for one period of time may be a variable in another period of time.

Law of variable proportion vs law of fixed proportion

The law of variable proportion is defined as the possibility under which varied levels of outputs can be achieved by combining various amounts of variable inputs together with a fixed input in the short run. The law of fixed proportion relates to the production system in which resources can be combined in only one unique way to get an output. For increasing or reducing the level of output, all inputs have to be proportionately expanded or contracted to maintain this unique ratio among the inputs.

Returns to scale

Constant returns to scale production functions are those in which changes in the quantity of all inputs used in the same proportion result in changes in the quantity of output by the same proportion. This also assumes that the resources used are divisible and can be combined in smaller or larger proportions. If all inputs are raised by a proportion k and output increases by a proportion greater than k, then it is referred to as increasing returns to scale production function. Similarly, if all inputs are raised by a proportion k and output increases by less than k proportion, then it is referred to as decreasing returns to scale production function. Mathematically, we can say that if the production function is given by $Q = f(x, y)$ then it is said to be a homogenous function of degree k if $\lambda^k Q = f(\lambda x, \lambda y)$

In case, $k = 1$, it is a constant returns to scale production function

$k > 1$, it is an increasing returns to scale production function

$k < 1$, it is a decreasing returns to scale production function

Let us consider an example of a company producing potato snacks that are consumed with low calorie soft drinks. Presently, the company uses 1,000 tonnes of potatoes, 1 tonne of salt and other spices, 1,000 people, and Rs 2 crore worth of capital equipment to produce half a million bags of potato chips in different sizes constituting a total of 800 tonnes of chips. If the company decides to expand its operations by adding 10 per cent of additional input— 100 tonnes of potatoes, 0.10 tonne of additional salt, 100 additional people, and Rs 0.20 crore worth of additional capital, constituting equi-proportionate increase in these inputs, how would this decision affect the output? It might increase the output of chips by 80 tonnes, more than 80 tonnes, or less than 80 tonnes. An increase in the output greater than 80 tonnes reveals economies of scale resulting from efficient resource utilization due to the addition of higher levels of input into its production process, proper meshing of capacities in different processes, and division of labour resulting in specialization. However, an increase in less than 80 tonnes of output reveals inefficiency in resource utilization. It indicates inefficient management of the venture and the difficulties associated with organization, coordination, and communication that outweighed the advantages of specialization associated with large scale production. An increase in the output by 80 tonnes implies that the changes in the scale of the firm's output had no effect on the efficiency of resource utilization.

Alfred Marshall (1920) was the first to explain the concept of returns to scale in detail. He focused on the concept of economies of scale—the advantages that accrue to firms by increasing the size of operations and diseconomies of scale—the disadvantages that accrue to the firm by increasing the size of operations. Marshall presented a rationale behind returns to scale either on technical grounds or due to changes in prices—applicable to situations of imperfect competition or both.

It is obvious that when a firm increases its operations from smaller to a bigger scale, it has an advantage in terms of increasing returns to scale because of better deployment and use of resources, particularly by way of division of labour and specialization of skills. The same job repeatedly performed by a labour force would yield increasing efficiency of operations and labour productivity. On the other hand, in case a firm is already producing at a large scale, it will face decreasing returns to scale particularly due to the management issues and challenges faced by the entrepreneur, as it becomes increasingly difficult for the entrepreneur to manage the enterprise effectively. The shift from increasing returns to scale to decreasing returns to scale as output increases is defined as *ultra-passum* law of production by Frisch (1965). As such, a justification behind returns to scale is not simple and straightforward. The major reason that appeals to most for increasing returns to scale is the 'division of labour' argument. Adam Smith (1776) highlighted that with the addition of more labour and machines, specialization of certain sub-tasks in the production process can be done. With the task being performed more efficiently, with greater precision it results in more output per unit of time. Specialization is the advantage that a large scale production has over a small scale production.

CONCEPTS OF PRODUCTION FUNCTION

Production function, as stated earlier, is a function that gives the maximum quantity of output that can be produced with various combinations of inputs. Suppose there is a production system that uses only two inputs namely, labour (L) and capital (K), the production function can be represented in a format such as Fig. 9.1. Thus, production function shows that four units of labour and three units of capital can produce 83 units of output per unit of time. It is, of course, always possible to waste resources and produce lesser than 83 units of output with the same amount of labour and capital. However, the table indicates that no more than 83 units can be produced with the technology available. The production function, thus, contains the limitations that technology places on the firm.

The transmission of the above data into a graph gives rise to isoquants, i.e., all combination of inputs that can produce a certain quantity of output per unit of time. The movement to the right gives rise to higher level of production. The graphical representation of isoquants is illustrated in Fig. 9.2.

Marginal rate of technical substitution

On a given isoquant map, the marginal rate of technical substitution (MRTS) of B (labour) for A (capital) is given by the ratio of the marginal product of B to the marginal product of A. This measures the reduction in one input per unit increase in the other such that the level of output remains constant. Marginal rate of technical substitution of input B for input A at a

A production function		
Labour (*L*)		
5	75	85	93
4	65	75	83
3	53	63	70
2	40	50	58
1	25	32	48
	1	2	3
Capital (*K*)		

FIGURE 9.1   Isoquants

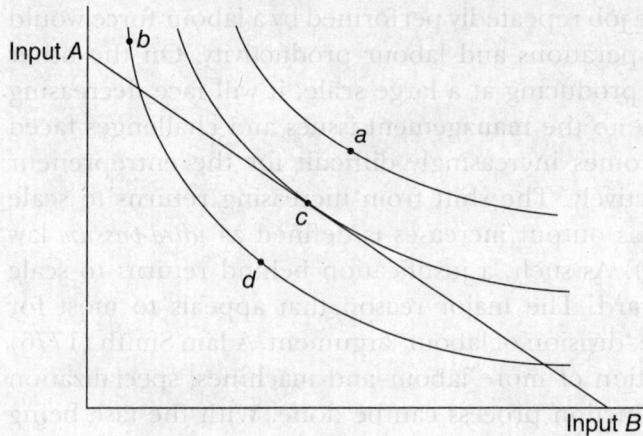

FIGURE 9.2   Isoquants—graphical representation

point on the isoquant is equal to the negative of the slope of the isoquant at that point.

The marginal rate of technical substitution for a fixed proportion production function, i.e., a production in which it is essential to combine the inputs in a fixed proportion to get an output, as is widely applicable in case of chemical industry would be either 0 or ∞. Isoquants under fixed proportion production function are L shaped. The isoquants of a production function for which the inputs are perfect substitutes are straight lines, so the MRTS is constant, equal to the slope of the lines.

Law of diminishing returns

According to the law of diminishing returns, increase in the levels of one input while keeping other inputs fixed would eventually result in smaller and smaller increases in additional output. To see the law in the table above, one must follow a column or row. If the capital is held constant at two, the marginal output of labour (that economists usually call marginal product of labour) can be shown as given in Table 9.1. The first unit of labour increases production by 32 units; however, with the addition of more unit of labour, the increase in production gradually falls.

As additional workers are added to the production system with the amount of equipment remaining fixed, the latter will have to be shared by more workers making the production environment less favourable for the additional workers, diminishing

TABLE 9.1   Marginal product of labour

Labour	Marginal Output
1	32
2	18
3	13
4	12
5	10

the additional output of production, with each successive unit of labour. Thus, the productivity of workers not only depends on their skills and abilities, but also on their work environment.

Total product, average product, and marginal product under short run

In the short run, the production function gives the maximum amount of the total product (output) that can be obtained by combining different amounts of variable inputs with fixed amount of fixed inputs. Marginal product (*MP*) of a variable input is defined as the change in the total product for a unit change in the variable input in the production system. This is known as marginal productivity of an input in the production system. Average product (*AP*), with respect to the variable input, is defined as the output per unit of a variable input used, keeping a particular level

Law of diminishing returns

Malthus (1826) argued that land is a fixed input, but it is the growth of population that makes labour a variable input. He propounded a general law of economics—the law of diminishing returns. According to it, when a fixed input is combined in production with a variable input, using a given technology, increases in the quantity of the variable input will ultimately result in reducing the productivity of the variable input. Malthus had argued that decreasing productivity of labour would result in reducing the incomes. Was Malthus right? The answer is both yes and no.

There is sufficient evidence, both observational and statistical, that the law of diminishing returns is valid. Agricultural economists have carried out various experiments on selected plots of land of identical size and fertility, using different quantities of fertilizers on the different plots of land, i.e., land was the fixed input and fertilizer the variable input. They found that as the quantity of the fertilizer increased, its productivity decreased, validating the law of diminishing returns.

However, in the 200 years since Malthus wrote, the population has increased multifold. However, labour, productivity, and incomes have not declined. In fact, they have increased. Not only that, technology has also improved over the years. Malthus believed that if technology improves, it might postpone the inevitable poverty that is a consequence of rising population. Some economists believe that the Malthusian prediction will eventually come true.

Source: http://william-king.www.drexel.edu/top/Prin/txt/MPCh/firm6.html, accessed on 15 October 2007.

of fixed input. Thus, the average product is an output-input ratio for each level of output obtained for a corresponding level of input. For example, let us consider a production system with one unit of capital employing different amount of labour input per day to produce job pieces per day as given below. The average product of labour (AP_L) and the marginal product of labour (MP_L) are displayed in Table 9.2.

From Table 9.2, it may be inferred that MP_L first increases, reaches the maximum, and thereafter starts falling. It becomes zero and thereafter becomes negative. When the MP_L increases, the AP_L also increases. MP_L cuts AP_L from the top at the maximum of average productivity of labour and thereafter AP_L continuously falls and remains positive, although it tends towards zero. MP_L exceeds MP_L when AP_L shows a declining trend.

As capital units are varied to a fixed input of labour, we observe that marginal product of capital (MP_K) rises, reaches a peak, and then starts declining. While declining, it cuts the average product (AP_K) at its peak and thereafter reaches zero and turns out to be negative. The average product of capital (AP_K) first rises, reach its peak, and thereafter starts declining and moves towards zero, but remains positive. It is observed that increasing AP with respect to the variable input corresponds to a negative MP with respect to a fixed input. From Tables 9.2 and 9.3, it may be inferred that negative marginal product with respect to variable input labour corresponds to an increasing average product with respect to capital, keeping labour input as fixed. On the other hand, negative marginal product with respect to capital, keeping labour input as fixed corresponds to an increasing average product with respect

TABLE 9.2 Output of number of pieces for a single unit of capital employing different levels of labour per day

Capital	Number of labourers	Capital labour ratio	Total product (TP_L) number of job pieces	Average product of labour (AP_L)	Marginal product of labour (MP_L)	Production stages
1	1	1	5	5.00	5	Stage I
1	2	1:2	14	7.00	9	Stage I
1	3	1:3	27	9.00	13	Stage I
1	4	1:4	36	9.00	9	Stage II
1	5	1:5	41	8.20	5	Stage II
1	6	1:6	45	7.50	4	Stage II
1	7	1:7	47	6.71	2	Stage II
1	8	1:8	47	5.87	0	Stage III
1	9	1:9	45	5.00	-2	Stage III
1	10	1:10	41	4.10	-4	Stage III

TABLE 9.3 Output of number of pieces for single unit of labour employing different levels of capital per day

Capital	Number of labourers	Capital labour ratio	Total product (TP_L) number of job pieces	Average product of labour (AP_L)	Marginal product of labour (MP_L)	Production stages
1/10	1	1/10	4.1	41	41	Stage I
1/9	1	1/9	5.0	45	81	Stage I
1/8	1	1/8	5.87	47	62.64	Stage I
1/7	1	1/7	6.71	47	47.19	Stage II
1/6	1	1/6	7.50	45	33.18	Stage II
1/5	1	1/5	8.20	41	21.00	Stage II
1/4	1	1/4	9.00	36	16.00	Stage II
1/3	1	1/3	9.00	27	0	Stage III
1/2	1	1/2	7.00	14	-12	Stage III
1	1	1	5.00	5	-4	Stage III

to labour input, keeping capital input fixed. Thus, a producer would never like to operate in these stages as one of the input contributes negative marginal product, implying that producer would never like to deploy such an input in these stages even if it is available free of cost.

Tables 9.2 and 9.3 clearly show that stage I with respect to labour turns out to be stage III for capital, stage III with respect to labour turns out to be stage I with respect to capital and stage II for labour is also stage II for capital. In stage I for labour, we find that a shortage of labour units exists and any additional unit of labour results in increasing the *AP* with respect to labour. However, increasing *AP* with respect to labour is accompanied with negative *MP* of capital in this stage. Thus, the producer should increase the use of units of labour to the extent that *AP* of labour does no longer increase and *MP* of capital is no longer negative. This would allow production to enter into stage II. In stage III for labour, *MP* of labour is negative that is accompanied by a decrease in the *AP* of capital when the capital labour ratio decreases. This implies an excessive use of labour relative to the capital. Thus, it will be better for the producer to increase the capital labour ratio either by increasing the capital outlay or by reducing the labour employed.

The increase in capital labour ratio should continue till the producer achieves a point where the *MP*, with respect to labour is no more negative. The increase in capital labour ratio will also increase the *AP* with respect to capital. This helps in eliminating stage I and stage III with respect to labour that corresponds with stage III and stage I of capital. A producer should select an input combination falling in stage II of production only. Thus, a rational producer would always carry his/her production in a range of combination of inputs that would be between maximum *AP* with respect to variable input and zero *MP* with respect to variable input. This alone would lead to the most economical use of both the resources.

OPTIMAL RESOURCE ALLOCATION IN PRODUCTION

An important issue that every producer faces is the combination of inputs that should be selected for operation, to produce the output as efficiently as possible. To achieve the said objective, a producer would either like to minimize the cost of production for a given level of output or maximize the production for a given cost outlay. The cost outlay, as a constraint, gives rise to an isocost line faced by the producer. Let us assume that the cost outlay for the firm is E rupees per unit of time that it spends on two inputs x and y used in the production system having the market prices as p_x and p_y respectively. Mathematically, the isocost line can be represented as:

$$xp_x + yp_y = E \tag{9.2}$$

Where x and y are number of units of x and y respectively and p_x and p_y are their respective prices.

Equation 9.2 can also be expressed as:

$$y = E/p_y - xp_x/p_y \tag{9.2a}$$

Where E/p_y is the intercept on the y axis and p_x/p_y is the slope of the line. In case we increase the cost outlay, keeping price of inputs as same, there would be a parallel upward shift in the isocost line. In case input prices x undergo a change, the slope of the isocost line will change shifting inward or outward on the x axis, keeping the y axis point as same. The maximum output that can be obtained by a given cost outlay is the one which gives rise to the highest isoquant touched by the isocost line. Mathematically, the producer aims to maximize $Q = f(x, y)$ for a given cost constraint as $E = xp_x + yp_y$ where x and y are units of inputs and p_x and p_y are the prices of inputs respectively.

We form a Lagrangian multiplier equation for maximization as give under:

$$Z = f(x, y) - \lambda (xp_x + yp_y) \tag{9.3}$$

To maximize, we need to take partial derivative with respect to variables and put them equal to 0.

$$dz/dx = f_x - \lambda p_x = 0 \tag{9.3a}$$
$$dz/dy = f_y - \lambda p_y = 0 \tag{9.3b}$$
$$dz/d\lambda = E - xp_x - yp_y = 0 \tag{9.3c}$$

Dividing equation (9.3a) by (9.3b) we get:

$$f_x/f_y = p_x/p_y \text{ or } f_x/p_x = f_y/p_y \text{ or } MP_x/p_x = MP_y/p_y$$

This means to optimize the production, the producer should operate at a point of input combination at which $MRTS_{xy}$ is equal to the input price ratio or MP per rupee worth of an input must be same for each input used in the production system.

The second order condition for maximization of output is that $d^2y/dx^2 > 0$.

In case there are n inputs in the production system, say x_1, X_2, ... x_n with prices p_1, p_2, ... p_n respectively, the optimum resource allocation will emerge at a point at which input combination is such that the MP per rupee worth is same in case of all the inputs that is equivalent to some constant λ.

Thus, the above discussion enables us to have a better understanding about the issues that a producer, i.e., owner of a business faces regarding procurement of resources, combining resources in optimum combination, minimization of cost of production for a given level of output, or maximization of output for a given cost outlay, selection of technology, etc., in a real-life situation.

SUMMARY

The production function is the physical relationship between a firm's input of resources and output of goods and services per unit of time, leaving prices aside. The input-input, input-output, and output-output relationships that emerge as a result of a production function mainly depend upon the technology, i.e., techniques of production. Isoquants are combinations of inputs that can produce a particular quantity of output per unit of time.

To understand the optimum combination of inputs, one needs to understand concepts of marginal product, average product, and total product as inputs are mixed in different proportions. What is important is that MP with respect to any input should not become negative implying intensive use of that input. Given the cost of inputs and the total cost outlay that an entrepreneur is prepared to incur, every entrepreneur aspires to maximize the output at a given cost outlay.

The optimum resource allocation in production is achieved by arriving at a point which gives rise to highest isoquant that can be achieved for a given cost outlay. To optimize the production, a producer should operate at a point of input combination at which MRTS between two inputs x for y is equal to the input price ratio or MP per rupee worth of an input must be same for each input used in the production system.

KEYWORDS

Average product It is defined as the output per unit of a variable input used, keeping a particular level of fixed input.

Fixed and variable inputs A fixed input is one whose quantity remains fixed irrespective of the level of production in the short run, while variable input is defined as that whose quantity varies with the level of production, such as labour and raw materials, in the short run.

Law of diminishing returns It states that as we keep on adding more of one input while holding other inputs fixed, it would eventually result in smaller and smaller increases in the additional output.

Law of variable and fixed proportion Law of variable proportion refers to the possibility under which a varied level of outputs can be achieved by combining various amounts of variable inputs together with a fixed input in the short run, while law of fixed proportion refers to the production system in which resources can be combined in only one way to get an output.

Marginal product Change in the total product for a unit change in the variable input in the production system.

Marginal rate of technical substitution (MRTS) It is the amount by which the quantity of one input can be reduced when one extra unit of another input is used so as to keep the output level constant.

Optimal resource allocation in production It refers to a combination of inputs that should be selected for operation, so as to produce the output as efficiently as possible.

Production function It is the physical relationship between a firm's input of resources and output of goods and services per unit of time, leaving prices aside.

Returns to scale It refers to a technical property of production function that examines changes in the output as a result of proportional change in all inputs.

Short and long run Short run refers to a period of time (time horizon) in which the supply of certain inputs is fixed or inelastic, while long run refers to a planning horizon in which all inputs can be readily varied for desirable change in the output.

Total product The maximum amount of the total product (output) that can be obtained for different amounts of variable inputs used together with fixed amount of fixed inputs.

EXERCISES

Concept Review Questions

1. Define production function and associated concepts involved in defining the same.
2. What is meant by law of variable proportion and law of fixed proportion? Define with the help of a concrete example.

Critical Thinking Questions

1. Why is it not advisable to produce in the first or third stage of production? Explain by giving economic implications in favour of your argument.
2. Show that if the marginal product of an input lies below its average product curve, then average

product curve must fall. Explain with the help of a diagram.

3. What concepts are highlighted through the following examples?
   (i) A steel plant under consideration is too large to be run efficiently.
   (ii) 'I think we are big enough to use computerized accounting systems in our firm.'
   (iii) By purchasing this machine you can cut your labour force by 40 per cent.

4. Draw an isoquant, considering two input production situations wherein minimum cost position always involves equal amounts of both inputs, regardless of prices or quantity produced.

5. Describe the minimum cost position equilibrium point for a firm whose isoquants are straight lines, downward sloping, and parallel lines. Analyse and interpret the implications of the same.

6. Draw isoquants for two different firms using only two inputs, one firm is facing increasing returns to scale, while the other is facing decreasing returns to scale.

7. Given the cost of inputs and production function and the total cost outlay, what conditions pertaining to MRTS would give rise to optimum production for a given level of cost outlay? What is the implication of a second order condition for the maximization of output?

PROJECT ASSIGNMENT

Economists sometimes come across a situation of 'free disposal of inputs' implying, thereby, that the firm does not want to use them. What would be the implication of this assumption as regards shape of isoquants, TP and MP is concerned?

REFERENCES

Frisch, R. (1965), *Theory of Production*, Dordrecht: D. Reidel Rand McNally and Company, Chicago.

Hollander, Samuel 1997, *The Economics of Thomas Robert*, University of Toronto Press, Canada.

Malthus, T.R. (1826), *An Essay on the Principle of Population*, 6th edition, John Murray, London.

Marshall, Alfred (1920), *Principles of Economics, at the Library of Economics and Liberty*, 8th edition, Macmillan, London.

Smith, Adam (1776), *An Inquiry into the Nature and Causes of the Wealth of Nations*, Edwin Cannan (ed), Random House, Modern Library edn, New York.

10

Markets

INTRODUCTION

In a market place where consumers and sellers interact to achieve their respective objectives, it is the operation of market mechanism that results in expected or unexpected outcomes for consumers, firms, and producers. A business entity has to be aware of the existing and emerging market forces to achieve its goals. Therefore, market structures and their characteristics become crucial for business entities for their sustained growth and success. One should study the different types of markets and forces, the intensity of rivalry among existing firms, the threat of entry, the threat of substitutes, the power of buyers, the power of suppliers, etc., to get an idea of market models in a dynamic framework. This enables managers to make informed business decisions. It is in this context that we shall try to understand market structures and mechanisms within which firms operate.

MARKET

A market refers to a suitable arrangement in which the buyers and sellers could closely interact (physically or otherwise) to arrive at exchange decisions. The demand and supply forces meet in the market to allocate resources. On one hand, firms compete for the scarce resources in order to produce and on the other, consumers compete in the market for their demands.

Market structure refers to the relationship between buyers and sellers, the forms of competition among the firms in the same industry, and the special features of a

Learning Objectives

After studying this chapter, you will be able to:
- Understand markets and their relevance to business decisions
- Learn about different market structures and their implications to business decisions
- Examine the difference between normal and economic profits
- Analyse the mechanism of pricing and output decisions in different markets

market in affecting the demand and supply forces. Markets are classified, broadly, depending upon the importance of an individual firm in relation to the entire market and whether products placed in the market are homogenous or not. Using these two broad criteria, markets are classified into four broad categories—pure competition, pure monopoly, oligopoly, and monopolistic competition (Fig. 10.1). In reality, markets may not fit into any one of these categories; they may be a mixture of two or more types of markets or it may have characteristics close to one of these categories. However, an understanding of the broad classifications of markets provides a framework for analysing the demand curve faced by a firm or a business entity.

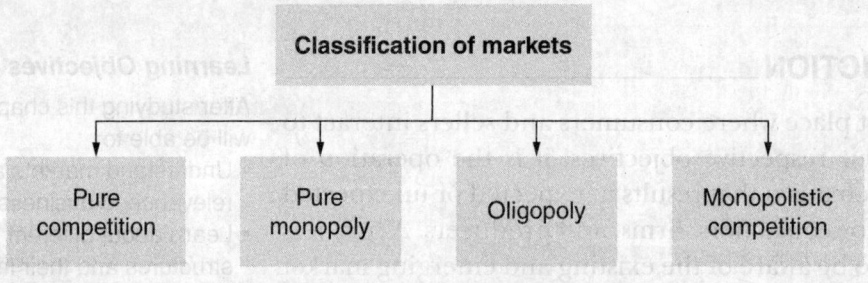

FIGURE 10.1 Classification of markets

PURE COMPETITION

In this market model there are a large number of firms having a homogenous or standardized product. Firms can enter or exit easily and have perfect knowledge about the markets. In brief, the important characteristics of such a market are:

- very large numbers of buyers and sellers;
- standardized product similar in all respects being produced by each firm;
- 'price takers'—firms accept the price as given;
- free entry and exit for sellers; and
- perfect knowledge about the market.

Thus, if one or few firms quit the market, supply does not decrease enough to cause a change in the market price as no seller is big enough to influence it. The market price is determined by the forces of demand and supply operating in the market. Buyers and sellers have to accept the market price as given and are called price-takers. They have complete information about the price, quality, and quantity sold in the market. As a result, there is no role for advertisement in such a market condition. Agricultural markets for wheat, sugar, rice; grocery stores of similar size; restaurants, etc. are examples of markets operating in pure competition.

Demand curve

The demand curve faced by sellers is horizontal at the prevailing equilibrium price. It is said to be perfectly elastic, that is, at the given price, sellers can sell all that they have to offer. However, at any price above the market equilibrium price, firms

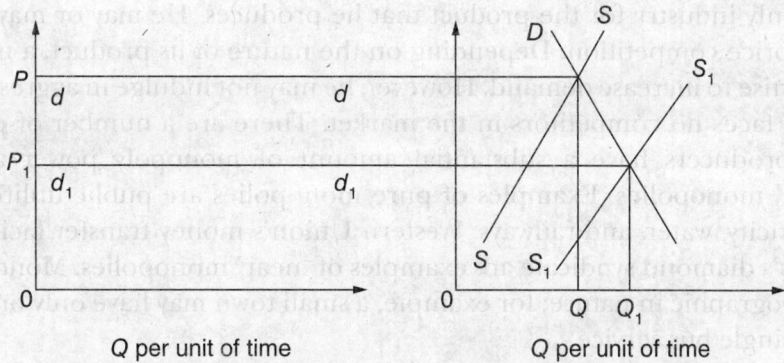

FIGURE 10.2 Pure competition—Firm and market demand curves

would not be in a position to sell any quantity. They can sell all they want to sell at the going market price.

In case of a firm operating under pure competition, it has to adjust itself to the market prices as given. If market supply increases resulting in a decrease in the price to P_1, the demand curve faced by the firm would shift downward to d_1d_1 (Fig. 10.2). The firm has to just adjust itself to the given reduced price and adjust its output accordingly.

Normal profit

A perfectly competitive industry would be in equilibrium when each and every individual firm in the industry is in equilibrium, that is, each firm maximizes its profit by equating marginal revenue with marginal cost and the industry, as a whole, is in equilibrium. It means that no firm enters or leaves the market. This happens when every entrepreneur in the industry earns normal profit—gains that are sufficient to sustain the seller in the industry. Thus, if in the industry, profits of all entrepreneurs rise above 'normal', then new firms will be encouraged to enter the industry leading to an extra supply and reduction in the prices. This will lead to a new equilibrium price at which, again, every entrepreneur will just earn normal profits. Similarly, in case profits for everyone fall below 'normal', some firms will quit the market, decreasing supply, leading to an increase in prices. This will set a new equilibrium price at which all entrepreneurs will just earn normal profits.

PURE MONOPOLY

Pure monopoly operates in a market when a single firm is the sole producer of a product for which there are no close substitutes. There are no similar products in the market whose prices or sales can influence the monopolist's price or sales substantially and vice versa. Thus, cross elasticity of demand for the monopolist's product is either zero or negligible. Neither does he expect a reaction from other firms nor do the actions of other firms in the market affect them. A monopolist is the only industry for the product that he produces. He may or may not engage in non-price competition. Depending on the nature of its product, a monopolist may advertise to increase demand. However, he may not indulge in aggressive marketing, as he faces no competitors in the market. There are a number of products where the producers have a substantial amount of monopoly power and are called 'near' monopolies. Examples of pure monopolies are public utilities such as gas, electricity, water, and railways. Western Union's money transfer facility and the De Beers's diamond syndicate are examples of 'near' monopolies. Monopolies can also be geographic in nature; for example, a small town may have only one bank branch or a single bus service.

Barriers to entry

Economies of scale have one major barrier—in case a production requires a massive investment and a large firm with a large market share already exists, new firms cannot afford to start industries with economies of scale. Public utilities have natural monopolies as they have economies of scale; where one firm is the most efficient in satisfying existing demand. The government usually gives one firm the right to operate a public utility industry in exchange for government regulation of its power. Further, there can be legal barriers for entry in the form of patents and licenses.

Demand curve

The market demand curve would be a demand curve for the monopolist (Fig. 10.3). Since he is the only seller of the product in the market, he can sell exactly the quantity that buyers would buy at a given price.

Being alone in the market, a monopolist is able to exert some amount of influence on the price, output, and demand for the product. A monopolist can increase sales by lowering the price and restrict them by increasing the price, according to market demand. It can change its demand curve by using promotional tactics such as selective price-cutting and advertising. A monopolist can effectively operate on price discrimination strategies, that is, charging different prices from different buyers for the same product, provided it can segregate the market by dividing the buyers into separate categories according to their ability or willingness to pay for the product (usually based on differing elasticities of demand).

The basic condition for effectively operating on price discrimination strategy is that buyers must be unable to resell the original product or service to derive price advantage. Examples of effective price discrimination are airline companies charging high fares from executive

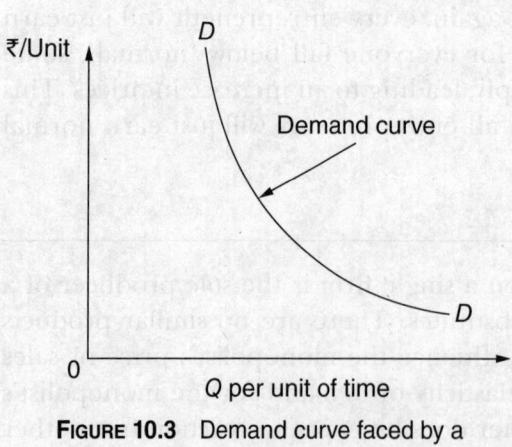

FIGURE 10.3   Demand curve faced by a monopolist

travellers (inelastic demand) than vacation travellers (elastic demand); power companies that frequently segment their markets according to their end uses, such as lighting and heating, commercial users, and agriculture purposes (lack of substitutes for lighting makes this demand inelastic).

OLIGOPOLY

In an oligopoly market situation, there are few sellers and the decision of one affects the other because of the sellers' small size. Thus, changes in the output and price of one firm affect the price and the quantities that another firm would be able to sell in the market. Individual sellers in an oligopoly market are interdependent and not independent. Each of the players in the market has to be very receptive to its competitor's actions. Their goods may be homogeneous or heterogeneous. There are some barriers for entry into this industry arising on account of patents, high set-up cost, or specialized technology. As a result, knowledge and information about each other's operations is imperfect. Sellers in an oligopoly market usually turn to advertising to improve their sales. Some examples of oligopolies are banks, automotive manufacturers, gas companies, insurance companies, telecommunications companies, etc.

Oligopoly markets are normally classified into two broad categories—pure oligopoly and differentiated oligopoly. In a pure oligopoly market, firms produce homogeneous products while in a differentiated oligopoly market, firms produce and sell differentiated products. Although these products are close substitutes to each other and have a high cross elasticity of demand, each firm's product has its own unique characteristics to distinguish it from the other in terms of quality, design, packaging, size, etc. A market structure characterized by two producers is a specialized form of oligopoly, referred to as duopoly.

Demand curve

The interdependence of sellers in an oligopoly market makes it difficult to estimate the demand for each firm. The demand for a firm's products cannot be determined if the firm is unable to predict the reactions of its competitors to changes in its price and output decisions. However, if the firm can predict the reaction of its competitors with some accuracy, the demand curve for the firm can be estimated and would be correspondingly more determinate.

An oligopolistic firm is in a position to influence its demand curve to some extent and, consequentially, its price and output. An oligopolist can shift its demand curve upwards with the help of advertising and other promotional efforts to induce consumers to disassociate from its rivals and switch to its brand. However, the firm's rivals would also be ready with their moves to counter it. Ultimately, firms that succeed in their strategies of advertising campaign or other promotional measures would succeed in increasing the demand for their brands. Whether the firm faces a determinate or an indeterminate demand curve, it knows when it faces a downward sloping demand curve. It can increase its sales by reduction in the price of the product, unless the objective is achieved through upward shift in the demand curve. Generally, the elasticity of demand faced by an oligopolist would be elastic because of the availability of good substitutes. However, elasticity of demand depends on the rival's reactions to the price and output changes of the single seller.

MONOPOLISTIC COMPETITION

Monopolistic competition is a market situation wherein there are many sellers of a particular product that are differentiated in some way or the other. Like those in a pure competitive market, each seller is too small to influence the decision of the other. The relationship between different sellers is impersonal. The products get differentiated by brand name, quality, trademarks, post-sale service, packaging, etc. The cross elasticities of demand are high as though differentiated, and the products are good substitutes of each other. Enterprises that fall under monopolistic competition include beauty clinics, hosiery items, service trades, textile products, etc. For example, there are many beauty clinics in the country and a majority of them are small. The entry is free and people know enough about their hairdressing options, that is, 'sufficient knowledge' is available to the buyers. However, the products of different beauty clinics are differentiated in some way or other and, therefore, are not perfect substitutes. The difference between monopolistic competition and perfect competition is that in monopolistic competition, production does not take place at the lowest possible cost. Due to this, firms are left with excess production capacity. Chamberlin (1946) and Robinson (1933) developed this market concept.

Demand curve

The demand curve faced by the firm has typical basis because of differentiation of products. The demand faced by a firm in a pure competition, wherein products are homogenous, is perfectly elastic. The differentiation makes the consumers attached to the brand and, therefore, the demand curve becomes somewhat elastic from perfectly elastic. It implies that consumers would continue to purchase a product from a particular firm even if there is some degree of variation in the price, but beyond a point they would switchover to another product which is a close substitute. Thus, a firm operating in the monopolistic competition attempts to have a relatively less elastic demand by differentiating its products and creating a niche for its products in the market.

In monopolistic competition, firms may enjoy economic gains, that is, profits over and above normal profits. However, because of free entry (as in pure competition), economic profits will be zero in the long run. As long as there are positive economic profits, there will be new entrants into the industry leading to a squeeze in the economic profits. Therefore, positive economic profits will not be stable in a monopolistically competitive industry. However, some economists believe that a monopolistically competitive industry may have high prices because non-price competition raises costs.

The individual firms in monopolistic competitive markets may be in a position to influence the demand and price of its product to some degree through advertising. However, their influence is limited because of availability of good substitutes in the market. Although a firm in a monopolistic competitive market faces a situation similar to that of a firm in a perfectly competitive market, it operates to some extent like a monopoly, as it has some control over its prices and output. However, if a firm raises the prices of its products beyond a certain tolerable limit, it loses all its customers. At the same time, it does not have to bring its prices too low to secure all the customers it can handle. So, outside a given price range, the firm operates under the forces of pure competition.

Sugar industry in India

In India, the white sugar industry is of utmost economic importance. It is the second largest industry after the cotton textile industry. About 35 million farmers and their families, constituting seven per cent of the rural population are dependent on sugarcane production. The sugar industry employs more than 3,50,000 workers and provides substantial indirect employment through various ancillary activities. There were a total of 571 sugar factories in India as on 31 March 2005 compared to 138 in 1950–51. These 571 sugar mills produce a total of more than 19.2 million tonnes (MT). Sugar production increased from 15.5 MT in 1998–99 to 20.1 MT in 2002–03. Sugar production is cyclic as the production of sugar cane, on which the production of sugar is dependent, is cyclic in nature.

The Indian sugar industry is among the most diversified industry in the world, with an installed capacity to produce 1,000 MW co-generated power against a potential of 7,500 MW. More and more new plants with co-generation facility are being installed. The Government of India, today, recognizes this potential and has committed itself to promote renewable sources of energy. However, down the line, a finer policy tuning substantially deviated from the declared policy, which had sapped further progress as co-generation of power suffered from problems with regard to tariff fixation, third party sale, and timely payments.

The Indian sugar industry is highly fragmented with organized and unorganized players. The producers of *gur* and *khandsari*, the less refined forms of sugar are the unorganized players of the industry. The sugar industry in India is still controlled by the government, which is slowly, yet steadily getting liberalized.

As the Indian sugar industry is fragmented, even leading players do not control more than four per cent market share. However, the situation is undergoing change and players of late are striving to increase their market share either by acquiring smaller mills or by going for green field capacity additions. Another notable trend is the shift from *gur* and *khandsari* to refined sugar in the rural areas. This change in the consumption habits has resulted in further increase in the per capita consumption of sugar in India (currently around 15.6 kg). Besides, the Indian urban market is slowly moving towards branded sugar. The potential for branded sugar market segment seems to be very high. Some of the leading players in the market are Balrampur Chini Mills Ltd, Bajaj Hindustan Ltd, Andhra Sugars Ltd, Thiru Arooran Sugars Ltd, and Dhampur Sugar Ltd.

Source: Based on www.indiansugar.com, accessed on 16 June 2007.

SUMMARY

A market is any suitable arrangement in which the buyers and sellers could closely interact (physically or otherwise) to arrive at exchange decisions. Markets are classified broadly depending upon the importance of an individual firm in relation to the entire market and whether products placed in the market are homogenous or not.

Pure competition is a market model in which there are a large number of firms having homogenous or standardized product. They can enter or exit easily and have perfect knowledge about the markets. Pure monopoly exists when a single firm is the sole producer of a product for which there are no close substitutes. In an oligopoly market situation, there are a few sellers and the decision of one affects the other because of their small size. In a pure oligopoly market, firms produce homogeneous products, whereas in a differentiated oligopoly market, firms produce and sell differentiated products. Monopolistic competition is a market situation in which there are many sellers of a particular product that are differentiated in some way or the other. In this market, firms may enjoy economic profits, that is, over and above normal profits. However, in case of free entry (as in pure competition), economic profits will be zero in the long run.

A clear understanding of the market in which a firm operates helps in taking objective decisions to optimize the firm's objectives such as maximization of profit, maximization of output at least cost, and minimization of cost of production for a given level of output. The strategies of pricing and output that need to be adopted vary with market conditions.

KEYWORDS

Differentiated oligopoly　An oligopoly market situation wherein firms produce and sell differentiated products.

Economic profit　Profits over and above normal profit, that is, revenue less the opportunity cost of inputs.

Market　Any suitable arrangement in which the buyers and sellers can closely interact to arrive at exchange decisions.

Market price　A price where demand and supply curve intersect with each other indicating a match between what consumers and sellers are willing to do.

Market structure　It refers to the relationship between buyers and sellers and the special features of a market that affect the demand and supply forces.

Monopolistic competition　A market situation having many sellers of a particular product that are differentiated in some way or the other.

Normal profit　Profits that are sufficient to sustain and induce a seller in the industry.

Oligopoly　A market situation having few sellers and having interdependency as the decision of one affects the other because of their small size.

Price discrimination　The act of charging different prices to different buyers for the same product.

Pure competition　A market model in which there are a large number of firms having a homogenous product. These firms can enter or exit easily and have perfect knowledge about the markets.

Pure monopoly　It exists when a single firm is the sole producer of a product for which there are no close substitutes.

Pure oligopoly　In an oligopoly market situation firms produce homogeneous products.

EXERCISES

Concept Review Questions

1. Define market and market structure.
2. What are the broad categories in which markets are classified?
3. The demand curve faced by each firm in perfect competition is perfectly elastic. Explain the significance of this perfectly elastic demand curve?

4. In perfectly competitive market conditions, each firm cannot earn more than the normal profit. What is the incentive to produce in such a market, where, in the long run, there is no scope to earn more than the normal profit?

5. What are the major barriers to entry in a pure monopoly market condition?

6. What are the conditions that enable a monopolist to increase his profit by price discrimination?

7. Define oligopoly market situation. What are the different categories of oligopoly markets?

Critical Thinking Questions

1. What are the characteristics of pure competition? Pure competition is an ideal state and does not exist in reality. Comment critically.

2. What type of elasticity of demand would an oligopolist face? Justify your answer.

3. Giving concrete examples, differentiate between monopolistic competition and differentiated oligopoly.

4. The objective of any business entity is to maximize profits. Profit maximization requires the firm to produce an output level at which the difference between total revenue and total cost is maximum. However, it is also said that profits are maximized at a level of output at which marginal cost equals marginal revenue. How do you reconcile these two situations? Explain.

Project Assignments

1. What determines the size of an advertising budget for a monopolist? Do you think a monopolist would extensively spend money on advertising? Give reasons. Give examples highlighting the details of their advertising budget to justify your answer.

2. Would you favour bifurcation of Maruti Udyog Ltd into a number of companies, each producing a specific line of car? Give reasons. Explain using concrete concepts from the oligopoly market structure.

REFERENCES

Chamberlin, E.H. (1946), *Theory of Monopolistic Competition*, Cambridge, Massachusetts.

Fellner, William (1960), *Modern Economic Analysis*, McGraw-Hill, New York.

Hicks, Sir John (1965), *Capital and Growth*, Clarendon, Oxford.

Robinson, E.A.G. (1948), *Monopoly*, Cambridge UK, London.

Robinson, John (1933), *Economics of Imperfect Competition*, Macmillan, London.

11

National Income Accounting

Learning Objectives

After studying this chapter, you will be able to:

- Understand the relevance of macroeconomics to business
- Examine production of output and payments to factors of production
- Understand gross domestic product (GDP) and its relevance to business entities
- Elaborate the techniques used to measure GDP
- Learn about problems associated with measurement of national product
- Examine the relationship between GNP, NNP, NI, and DPI

INTRODUCTION

National and global economies go through ups and downs. These fluctuations are reflected in the unemployment rates, rising or declining aggregate demand for products and services of industries, increasing or decreasing prices of particular commodities, expansion of certain industries as against close down of certain others, etc. All these changes affect the performance of those business entities that are isolated from the global business environment. Businesses that are integrated with global markets, either due to import–export or the policies of the economies, affect involved countries because of greater trade transactions. Therefore, in today's fast changing environment, the economic happenings directly affect businesses and their future operations. Therefore, a business has to keep scanning the aggregate economic environment at the national and global levels. In order to be successful, it needs to work out strategies for responding and adapting to its business environment.

MACROECONOMICS

Macroeconomics deals with the behaviour of economy as a whole such as booms and recessions, aggregate output of goods and services, growth in employment and output, inflation and deflation, balance of payment, balance of trade, exchange rates, etc. It focuses on economic policies that affect consumption and investment and all other related economic indicators in turn. Macroeconomics essentially deals with interactions among goods and services, labour, and capital markets of the economy, and similar interactions amongst national economies that interact with each other.

Effective accounting helps in turning the data into information. National income accounting provides the structure for macroeconomic models that help us in understanding the implications of economic policies and their outcomes on different sectors of the economy—agriculture, industry, and service. National income accounting is the sum total of the value of all goods and services produced in the economy.

PRODUCTION OF OUTPUT AND PAYMENTS TO FACTORS OF PRODUCTION

The production systems in the economy transform inputs—land, labour, capital, and entrepreneurship—into output of goods and services. These inputs are called *factors of production*. Payments made to use these inputs in the form of rent, wages, interest, and profit are known as *factor payments*. Thus, output can be measured by knowing the production function relating to the economy's production. The aggregate production function for the economy is represented as $Y = f$ (land, labour, capital, entrepreneurship).

In this chapter we shall discuss the concepts related to aggregate output and income. *National product* represents the country's total output of goods and services. Goods such as wheat, cars, clothing, and milk are tangible while services such as insurance, transportation of goods, computer programming, etc. are intangible. A common value can be derived for all the goods and services produced in an economy by knowing their market value, that is, whatever is paid for the same. Therefore, expressed in the simplest form, national product is defined as the money value at the given market prices of all goods and services produced in one year.

National income accounts is the data collected and published by the government describing the various components of national income and output in the economy. The Department of Commerce is responsible for producing and maintaining the national income and product accounts that keep track of *gross domestic product* (GDP), which may be defined as the total market value of all final goods and services produced within a given period, by factors of production located within a country. *Final goods and services* refer to goods and services produced for final use. *Intermediate goods* are goods produced by one firm to be used as raw materials by another. The difference between the values of goods as they leave the stage of production and their cost when they entered that stage is known as value added.

For calculating the GDP, we can either sum up the value added at each stage of production, or we can consider final value of sales. We do not use the value of total sales in an economy to measure how much output has been produced. *Gross national product* (GNP) is the market value of all final goods and services produced within a given period, say one year, by factors of production owned by a country's citizens, irrespective of the location at which the output is produced.

Measurement of GDP

There are two approaches to calculating the GDP namely *expenditure approach* and *income approach.* The computation of GDP is based on the total output of goods and services that make up the national product produced for consumption (C). This refers to household spending on durable and non-durable consumer goods and on services in a given period of time. The other vital output relates to investment (I). The gross private domestic investment (I) relates to the spending by firms and households in the economy on new capital—plants, equipment, inventory, building, residential structures, etc., which are produced to facilitate the further production of goods and services, that is, contributing to increased future output some of which is meant for Government (G) consumption and gross investment by the government. Lastly, foreign trade, that is, imports (I) (goods produced abroad and sold in our country) and exports (X) (goods and services produced in the country and sold abroad) contribute to the national product. The net of exports may be calculated as exports (X) – imports (I). Thus, the aggregate demand or output for domestic goods and services is made up of four components—consumption spending by households (C), investment spending by business and households (I), government consumption of goods and services and gross investment (G), and foreign demand for our net exports. This gives us the fundamental national income accounting equation as

$$Y = C + I + G + (E - I) \tag{11.1}$$

The GDP (Y) can also be defined as final sales to the households and government plus change in inventory.

Gross Investment

Gross investment is defined as the total value of all newly produced capital goods such as plants, machinery, equipment, housing, building, and inventory in a given time period. It is important to understand that investment spending is very volatile and causes fluctuations in the GDP. It is the primary link through which interest rates and in turn monetary policy, affect the economy. The tax structure emerging from the fiscal policy also affects investment in the country. Above all, investments determine the long-term plan of growth that the economy will adopt. It is the demand for capital formation that gets affected by aggregate demand for goods and services, prevailing interest rates, taxation system and structure, and other monetary and fiscal considerations. It is important to clarify here that in common terminology we describe buying of existing financial stocks, bonds, and house as an investment. However, in macroeconomics, investment refers to spending that adds to the existing physical stock of capital.

Net Investment

Capital is subject to wear and tear with usage and time. It may also become completely obsolete on account of various factors such as changes in input prices and emergence of new technology. The rate of depreciation depends upon the type of capital and its useful life. The net investment is the difference between gross investment and depreciation.

NATIONAL PRODUCT: PROBLEMS OF MEASUREMENT_____

While measuring the national product with the expenditure approach certain issues need to be taken into account. The most crucial problem is that of double counting. For example, if we add in the computation of national product all the wood pulp; paper, books, newspapers, and stationery produced, we would be counting the wood value thrice; at the first stage with wood pulp, second stage with paper and third stage with books, newspaper, and stationery. This is because the value of books, newspaper, and stationery includes the value of wood. Thus, in order to compute the national product properly one has to avoid adding the value of all intermediate goods, that is, one should count only the final products. Similarly, all second-hand goods already sold once should not be accounted in the national product accounts, as it has already been accounted for either this year or in the earlier years. Even a new gift or exchange, say a father presenting a house to his son, should not be included in national product as it has been already included when it was purchased first by the father. Similarly, in investment, sale and transfer of plant and machinery should not to be included. Also, some investments create new capital while others are channelized towards replacement of old capital. Gross investment takes care of both these categories. However, when only additions to capital are included without counting investment towards replacement, it is called net investment.

There are also certain limitations as far as GDP data is concerned. These exist because some outputs are not traded in the market and are not rightly reflected in the GDP. These include services of a housewife, vegetables and fruits produced in a kitchen garden, etc. Similarly, certain limitations in GDP data arise as government services are not directly priced by the market and, therefore, it is not necessary that a rupee spent by the government is worth its value. Similarly, certain expenses that are added to GDP represent use of resources to contain or overcome social evils such as crime or risk to national economy. The scope of GDP is limited as nothing is subtracted from it towards environmental pollution and degradation. Above all, it does not take into account the improvement in the quality of products such as computers, whose quality and efficiency are improving while the prices are falling, resulting in lesser contribution in GDP for each additional unit produced. Economists have been trying to overcome these limitations and arrive at an adjusted GNP.

Contribution of industry to GNP

The Indian economy has experienced a robust growth with strong macroeconomic fundamentals in 2006–07. However, inflation continued to be a matter of great concern to the planners. The inflation rate in 2006–07 has generally seen an upward trend with *(Contd)*

Exhibit (*Contd*)

intermittent fall in the rate for temporary periods. However, the average inflation rate for the 52 weeks, ending on 3 February 2007, remained high at five per cent. A similar spurt in the inflation rate was observed earlier in the years in 1997–98, 2000–01, 2003–04, and 2004–05.

The economy could achieve a high growth rate of 9.0 per cent and 9.2 per cent in 2005–06 and 2006–07, respectively. It was better than the expected rates. The industry continued to have a lower contribution to GDP growth when compared to the services sector. It was partly because of its lower share in the GDP.

The growth of the industrial sector has improved in recent years as evident from a low of 2.7 per cent in 2001–02, revived to 5.7 per cent and 7.0 per cent in 2002–03 and 2003–04, respectively. After rising to over 8.0 per cent in the next two years, it touched 10.6 per cent in 2006–07 (between April and November). The growth of industry, in proportion to the corresponding growth in services that was 78.9 per cent on an average between 1991–92 and 1999–2000 has improved dramatically to touch 88.7 per cent in the last seven years. It is important to note that since 1951–52, the industry has never consistently grown over a rate of

TABLE 11.1   Annual growth rate of industrial production in major sectors of industry
(based on the index of industrial production)

(*per cent*)

Period Overall	Mining and Quarrying	Manufacturing	Electricity	Total
Weights	10.47	79.36	10.17	100.00
1995–96	9.7	14.1	8.1	13.0
1996–97	−1.9	7.3	4.0	6.1
1997–98	6.9	6.7	6.6	6.7
1998–99	−0.8	4.4	6.5	4.1
1999–00	1.0	7.1	7.3	6.7
2000–01	2.8	5.3	4.0	5.0
2001–02	1.2	2.9	3.1	2.7
2002–03	5.8	6.0	3.2	5.7
2003–04	5.2	7.4	5.1	7.0
2004–05	4.4	9.2	5.2	8.4
2005–06	1.0	9.1	5.2	8.2
2006–07	3.8	11.5	7.3	10.6

Base: 1993–94 = 100
#(April–November)

Source: Based on *Central Statistical Organization* data.

(*Contd*)

Exhibit   *(Contd)*

7 per cent per year, consecutively, for more than three years before 2004–05.

The growth of the services sector has continued to be broad-based. The four sub-sectors of services; trade, hotel, transport, and communication services have been growing at double-digit rates for the fourth successive year. This may be attributed to the progress in information technology (IT) and IT-enabled services, rail-road traffic, and fast additions to existing stock of telephone connections, particularly mobiles. Growth of financial services (banking, insurance, real estate, and business services), after falling to 5.6 per cent in 2003–04 bounced back to 8.7 per cent in 2004–05 and 10.9 per cent in 2005–06. The momentum has been maintained with a growth of 11.1 per cent in 2006–07.

Source: Based on *Economic Survey 2006–07*, Government of India.

Agriculture, forestry and fishing, and mining and quarrying constituted 35.2 per cent of total GDP at factor cost in 1989–90. This persistently declined to reach a level of 27.3 per cent in 1999–00 and further to 21.7 per cent in 2005–06 (quick estimates). The contribution of manufacturing, construction, electricity, gas, and water supply remained around 24 per cent between 1989–00 and 2005–06 (quick estimates). The proportion of contribution from trade, hotels, transport, and communication increased from 18.9 per cent in 1989–00 to 21.7 per cent in 1999–00 and further to 26.1 per cent in 2005–06 (quick estimates). Similarly, the share of financing, insurance, real estate and business services in the total gross domestic product at factor cost increased from 9.5 per cent in 1989–00 to 13.8 per cent in 2005–06. Thus, the contribution of services has been consistently increasing mainly at the cost of primary sector; agriculture, forestry and fishing, and mining and quarrying. The contribution of secondary sector; manufacturing, construction, electricity, gas, and water supply has more or less remained same between 1989–00 and 2005–06.

Another approach to calculate the national product is the income approach. This refers to the measurement of total income earned for production of goods and services in a given time period, say a year. We may recall that it is the factors of production—land, labour, capital, and entrepreneurship that are used for the production of goods and services. All these factors of production earn an income when deployed for the purpose of production. As seen earlier, the income earned by these factors of production is known as rent, wages, interest, or profit. By this approach, we add all these forms of income together to get a national income for the year. This national income is going to be the same as the national product arrived at through the output approach. *National income* is the total income earned by the factors of production owned by a country's citizens. However, while computing the same value by output approach and income approach, cash flows that do not arise from actual production such as transfer payments are not included. Transfer payments refer to the payments that do not represent current production of goods and services. For example, the government pays, in the current year, the pension of employees who do not contribute anything for current production, social security outlays, relief payments, etc. These are payments made for goods and services already rendered and, therefore, counted in the GDP in earlier years. They are towards expenses that are not contributing directly towards the current year's production. Similarly, private transfers also have to be kept out of national accounts.

The relationship between GNP, NNP, NI, and DPI can be shown as under:

	Gross National Product (GNP)
Less:	Depreciation (capital consumption allowance with capital consumption adjustment) equals Net National Product (NNP)
Less:	Indirect business tax and non-tax liability Business transfer payments Statistical discrepancy
Add:	Subsidies less current surplus of Government enterprises equals National Income (NI)
Less:	Corporate Taxes Undistributed Corporate Profit Social Security Taxes
Add:	Government Transfer Payments equals Personal Income (PI)
Less:	Personal Taxes equals Disposable Personal Income (DPI)

Per capita GDP or GNP is a country's GDP or GNP divided by its population. It measures the well being of an average person better than the total GDP or GNP and is also used for inter-country comparison by converting into single currency.

Aggregate demand gets reflected through GDP, its growth and implications to inflation and unemployment over the years gives rise to business cycles, that is, formation of certain pattern of expansion and contraction in economic activity around the path of growth trend. At the peak of a business cycle, economic activity gets a boost compared to normal trend and at a cyclical trough the economic activity is at a low ebb. The growth of output or GDP vis-à-vis the business cycle trend becomes an important input for businesses to plan effectively for their future growth. In short, it is the GDP and its growth, composition from various sectors of the economy, that is, primary (agriculture), secondary (industry), and tertiary (services) that has a direct bearing on inflation and unemployment rates. These economic indicators give rise to a cyclical behaviour; an important aspect to be analysed and understood by business entities for their growth.

Inflation

Inflation, with its roots in supply-side factors, was accompanied by buoyant growth of money and credit in 2005–06 and 2006–07 in the Indian economy. While GDP rose from 7.5 per cent to 9.0 per cent between 2004–05 and 2005–06, the corresponding acceleration in growth of broad money (M3) was from 12.3 per cent to 17.0 per cent. Year-on-year, M3 grew by 21.1 per cent, as of 19 January, 2007. The industrial resurgence and upswing in investment was reflected in, and sustained by, growth of gross bank credit (as per data covering 90 per cent of credit by scheduled commercial banks), industry (medium and large) at 31.6 per cent, and for housing loans at 38.0 per cent in 2005–06. A year-on-year growth of gross bank credit at 32.0 per cent in September 2006, albeit marginally down from 37.1 per cent in 2005–06, was also observed. Reconciling the twin needs of facilitating credit for growth, on the one hand and containing liquidity to tame inflation on the other, remained a challenge. The RBI put a restraint on the rapid growth of personal loans, capital market exposures, residential housing beyond ₹20 lakh, and commercial real estate loans by more than doubling the provisioning requirements for standard advances under these categories from 0.40 per cent to 1.0 per cent in April 2006. Simultaneously, it increased the risk on exposures to commercial real estate from 125 per cent to 150 per cent.

With year-on-year inflation stuck above five per cent from early August 2006, the RBI announced more measures to stem inflationary expectations and contain the credit off-take at the desired growth rate of 20.0 per cent on 31 October, 2006, unlike the previous four times, when both the repo and the reverse repo rates were raised by the same 25 basis points, keeping their spread constant at 100 basis points, this time only the repo rate was raised by 25 basis points. This policy was repeated on 31 January, 2007, when the repo rate reached 7.50 per cent with a spread of 150 basis points over the reverse repo rate. Since deposits are growing at a lower rate than credit, a higher repo rate was an indication to the banks that they would have to pay a higher price of accommodation in case of credit over extension.

Source: Based on *Economic Survey 2006–07*, Government of India.

SUMMARY

National and global economies keep going through ups and downs. These fluctuations are reflected in the unemployment rates, rising, or declining aggregate demand for products and services of typical industries, increasing or decreasing prices of particular commodities, expansion of certain industries as against closure of others, etc. All these changes keep affecting performance of business entities.

Gross domestic product (GDP) is the total market value of all final goods and services produced within a given period by factors of production located within a country. The final *goods and services* refer to goods and services produced for final use. National income accounting can be understood by measuring the sum total of the value of all goods and services produced in the economy.

There are two approaches to arrive at the GDP namely expenditure approach and income approach. While measuring GDP, one should avoid double counting. Investment is defined as the total value of all newly produced capital goods such as plants, machinery, equipment, housing, building, and inventory in a given time period that helps in further production of goods and services.

It is important to understand that investment spending is very volatile and, therefore, contributes a great deal to fluctuation in the GDP. It is the primary link through which interest rates and in turn monetary policy, affect the economy. Per capita GDP or GNP is calculated by dividing a country's GDP or GNP by its population. It measures the well being of the average person better than the total GDP or GNP. Economic indicators giving rise to a particular cyclical behaviour become an important factor to be analysed and understood by the business entities for their sustained growth.

KEYWORDS

Consumption It relates to household spending on consumer goods—durable as well as non-durable and on services in a given time period.
Exports Goods produced in the country and sold abroad.
Government expenditure Consumption of goods and services and gross investment by the government.
Government transfer payments Payments towards expenses that are not contributing directly to the current year production. They are made for either goods or services that have already been rendered and, therefore, counted in the GDP in earlier years.
Gross domestic product (GDP) It is the total market value of all final goods and services produced within a given period by factors of production located within a country.
Imports Goods produced abroad and sold in our country.
Investment Spending by firms and households in the economy on new capital—plants, equipment, inventory, building, residential structures, etc.
Macroeconomics It deals with the behaviour of economy as a whole.

EXERCISES

Concept Review Questions

1. How does economic activity at national or global level affect a business entity?
2. Define macroeconomics. What are the variables with which macroeconomics deals with?
3. Define gross domestic product (GDP). What are the two approaches by which GDP is measured? What precautions need to be used while measuring GDP?
4. Define investment. Differentiate between gross investment and net investment. In what way does investment contribute to growth in GDP?
5. Define the relationship between gross national product (GNP), net national product (NNP), national income, and disposable income.
6. In what way does inflation affect the working of a business entity?

Critical Thinking Question

Economic growth directly affects business prospects. Comment critically.

Project Assignments

1. The service sector in the Indian economy is growing at an accelerated rate. Collect data on the share of primary, secondary, and service sectors in the total GDP for the last five years. Interpret it and estimate which sector is going to have bright prospects in the coming years and why?
2. Indian economy has been gaining a lot by export earnings through the software industry. What are the strengths of the Indian IT industry? Collect details of foreign exchange earnings by the export of IT products during the last 10 years. Analyse the same to comment on the future prospects of IT industry in India.

REFERENCES

Aakley, Gardner (1978), *Macroeconomics: Theory and Policy*, Macmillan, New York.
Boulding, Kenneth (1966), *Economic Analysis*, 4th edn, Harper & Row, New York.

Chalmers, James Anderson (1971), *Economic Principles: Theory and Policy*, Macmillan, New York.
Samuelson, Paul Anthony (2001), *Economics, Tata McGraw-Hill Pub. Co. Ltd*, New York.

12

Goals and Functions of Finance

INTRODUCTION

A finance manager is vital to the success of an organization. An effective financial manager is a team player who plays an integrative and constructive role, vis-à-vis all other departments—marketing, operations, human resources, management information systems, accounts, stores, research and development, etc. Some of the fundamental questions that a finance manager has to deal with are—What should firms do about new investment, mergers, and dividends? Why are share prices important? How much should firms borrow? Why is cash flow and risk analysis so important? How to minimize the cost of borrowing? How to optimize shareholders' wealth? To satisfactorily answer these questions requires a better understanding about the role, functions, and goals of finance.

GOAL OF THE COMPANY

The fundamental purpose for the existence of a business entity is to create value for the shareholders (Fig. 12.1). Although there are many stakeholders in a business entity, key stakeholders are the owners of the company. The owners want the maximization of the share value as represented by the market value of the stock in order to get due returns on the stake that they have in the company. The market value of a company's stock depends upon its investment, financing, and dividend decisions. Every company would like to invest in opportunities that ensure better returns, keeping in view the probable financing options that can minimize the cost of funds, so that the

Learning Objectives

After studying this chapter, you will be able to:
- Understand the goals of a business entity
- Learn about the meaning and implications of profit maximization
- Examine the role and function of finance and financial managers
- Understand value creation for shareholders
- Understand economic value added (EVA)
- Know about corporate social responsibility and business

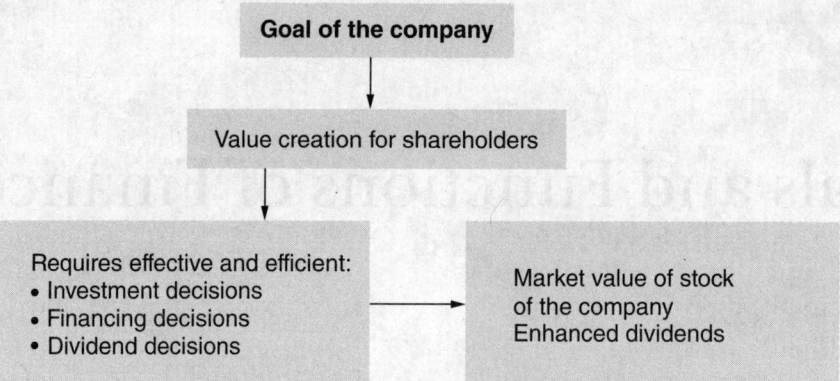

FIGURE 12.1   Goal of the company

company's management can take worthwhile dividend decisions. Thus, a company's main objective is the maximization of the shareholders' wealth by availing profitable business opportunities.

For example, Bharat Forge's return on net worth, which was 8.83 per cent in 2001, increased to 47.2 per cent within the next four years. Shareholders of the company have been amply rewarded, with market capitalization increasing by 24 times between April 2002 and April 2006. The earning per share (EPS) of the company increased from 5.5 in 2001–02, to 32.28 in 2003–04, and further to 39.64 in 2004–05. The company could create remarkable value for its shareholders by judiciously raising and deploying funds.

Profit Maximization

Generally, maximization of profits is considered to be the fundamental objective of a company. This implies that the financial manager should take only those decisions that will contribute towards profit maximization. The profits are measured in terms of EPS, representing profit earned by the company per unit of share during a particular time period. However, both profit maximization as well as maximization of EPS are not reasonable measures of a company's success as these fail to consider the following:

- timings of returns (the rupee earned today is certainly far more valuable than rupee earned after a week);
- availability of cash flows to stakeholders (stockholders' inflows not only depend upon dividends arising from accounting profits, but also on a large share of inflows dependent upon the market price of the stock); and
- uncertainty and risk (profits or EPS does not take care of future risk associated with investment and the expected future flows).

Although the maximization of profits and EPS are important, it is necessary to maximize the shareholders' wealth by the maximization of market price per share. The measurement of the stockholders' wealth by the share price of the stock is dependent upon the timing of returns, magnitude of returns, and other associated risks. Thus, financial mangers should focus on factors that influence the share price of the company.

ECONOMIC VALUE ADDED

Economic value added (EVA) is a popular concept used to find out whether an existing or a proposed investment opportunity would positively contribute to the shareholders' wealth. It is a yardstick that measures the company's financial performance based on the residual wealth calculated by deducting cost of capital from its operating profit after making adjustments for taxes on a cash basis. It is also known as economic profit as it charges opportunity cost of capital, that is, whatever returns the best alternative use of the said capital would have yielded. The formula for calculating EVA is as follows:

$$\text{EVA} = \text{Net operating profit after taxes (NOPAT)} - (\text{Capital} \times \text{Cost of capital}) \tag{12.1}$$

Investment opportunities having positive EVAs increase shareholders' wealth, while those with negative EVAs reduce it. As compared to accounting profits and EPS, EVA is an economic concept and, therefore, requires that businesses must cover both operating costs and capital costs. This concept can be used for setting organizational goals, evaluation of performance of the company, capital budgeting, company valuation, etc.

SOCIAL RESPONSIBILITY

Apart from shareholders, a company has many stakeholders such as employees, customers, suppliers, creditors, government, and the public. A good company not only has the maximization of the shareholders' wealth as its corporate goal, but also adheres to its social responsibility of protecting consumer interests, payment of fair wages, adoption of good hiring practices, hygienic working conditions for employees, awareness of environmental issues, etc. A good business is certain that its existence is for the society in general, and customers in particular, and it cannot achieve its objectives without being sensitive to the needs and requirements of all stakeholders. Responsible governing is part of a good corporate culture and is part and parcel of its ultimate goal of maximizing the shareholders' wealth. A good business believes that corporate existence depends upon social responsibility.

National Thermal Power Corporation—CSR

National Thermal Power Corporation (NTPC) has been a committed and socially responsible corporate citizen since its inception and has formulated a specific set of guidelines for the welfare of project affected persons (PAPs) and community development in and around its

(Contd)

Exhibit   (*Contd*)

power generating plants as early as 1980s. It is one of the first in the corporate sector to formulate a comprehensive resettlement and rehabilitation policy for addressing the issue of PAPs.

The concept of corporate social responsibility (CSR) is deeply imbedded in NTPC's culture. NTPC's mission in the area of CSR is to 'Be a socially responsible corporate entity with a thrust on environment protection, ash utilization, community development, and energy conservation'.

NTPC's approach towards CSR is further articulated in the corporate objectives on sustainable power development. These include:

- Contributing towards sustainable power development by discharging corporate social responsibilities.
- Leading the sector in the areas of resettlement, rehabilitation, and environment protection including effective ash utilization, peripheral development, and energy conservation practices.
- Reflecting its commitment towards community development through formulation of CSR-CD Policy, July 2004, thus establishing NTPC foundation as a trust and initiating a scheme for economic self reliance of physically challenged persons (PCP).

As a member of Global Compact, a UN initiative launched by the former UN Secretary General Mr Kofi Annan, NTPC is committed to its ten principles in the areas of human rights, labour, environment, and anti-corruption.

Environment

Environment protection continues to be the key area of NTPC's activities along with its growth in the power sector. In November 1995, NTPC became the first public utility to bring out a comprehensive document entitled *NTPC Environment Policy and Environment Management System*. Among the guiding principles adopted in the document are the company's proactive approach to environment, optimum utilization of equipment, adoption of latest technologies, and continuous improvement of the environment. The policy also envisages efficient utilization of resources, thereby minimizing waste, maximizing ash utilization, and maintaining a green belt around the plant for maintaining the ecological balance.

Scheme of economic self-reliance for physically challenged persons

NTPC has come out with a scheme for providing vocational skills and sustainable employment opportunities for PCPs, particularly for visually challenged and hearing impaired persons. It supports proposals for schemes that will create sustainable livelihoods for PCPs to be economically self-reliant. NTPC proposes to enable empowered and capable PCPs to become economically self-reliant by supporting specific targeted schemes, which will focus on creating employment opportunities for PCPs. In case of a group or cooperative, the scheme may focus on sustainable self-employment and income generating schemes.

Source: Based on information from www.ntpc.co.in, accessed on 18 June 2007.

ROLE OF FINANCE AND FINANCIAL MANAGERS

Till the 1950s, the main role of financial managers continued to be fundraising and management of the company's cost across various activities. It was in the 1950s that the concept of *present value* led to a change in the role and responsibilities of financial managers. They were required, *inter alia*, to be concerned with capital investment projects as also implications of time value of money on financial decisions. However, in the 1990s, the corporate world changed dramatically in terms of intense competition, technological changes, volatility in inflation and interest rates, worldwide economic uncertainty, fluctuating exchange rates, tax law changes, ethical concerns over certain financial dealings, etc. These changes transformed the role of financial managers and brought them into limelight as key team players.

The finance function makes financial decisions related to acquisitions, financing, and effective management of acquired assets to achieve overall goals pertaining to stockholders and stakeholders. Vital decisions pertain to investment decisions, financing decisions, and dividend/share repurchase decisions. It is the optimum combination of these three decisions that enables the company's management to achieve its objectives within its given constraints. Of the three, the investment decision is the most important one, as it is this decision that determines further decisions related to financing and creating a surplus that can be distributed to the shareholders by way of dividends or share repurchase. Investment decisions deal with the total amount of assets required to execute a plan of action for responding quickly to the available business opportunities, efficient management of current and fixed assets, management of balance sheet of the company, capital structuring, ensuring adequate liquidity, composition of assets, and the type of business risk involved—its assessment and management, in order to maximize the profits and shareholders' worth. Investment decisions also deal with acquisitions and mergers to expand the business as also undertaking new business opportunities in related or diversified areas of operation.

Financial decision is the second vital area, which financial managers have to deal with. This mainly involves optimization of financing mix or capital structure of the company for a given level of investment in the light of the existing balance sheet position. The financing decisions mainly revolve around issues such as determining capital structure of the company; optimum mix of debt, equity, and hybrid securities such as partially convertible or fully convertible debentures; valuation of the company; and whether the value of the company can be further enhanced by changing the capital structure; how to maximize price per share; how best to acquire stocks, bonds, commercial paper, certificate of deposit, and long-term loans; etc. Efficient financing decisions help a company to generate profit by just changing the mix of money raised from time to time, retirement of high-cost debt by substituting it with low-cost debt, changing the short-term and long-term mix of funds deployed in the business, etc.

A company generates good surplus to commensurate with its activity and asset base, if proper and timely investment decisions are backed by good financing decisions. Whenever surplus is available, the company has to mainly decide as to what proportion of the surplus should be used for repurchasing shares/dividends and what proportion should be redeployed within the business for expanding operations or investments in the allied or other areas. Today, a good corporate entity

Tata Motors

Tata Motors, formerly Tata Engineering and Locomotive Co (TELCO), underwent a massive financial crisis in late 1990s. Nobody could have predicted the slide of this leading giant at that time. It was one of the elite blue-chips companies and shareholders were proud to own shares of the company. However, the company's growth stagnated in late 1990s and company's commercial vehicle's sales saw a downslide. The company incurred a loss of ₹500 crore in 2000–01. Investors were surprised as the company's stock price crashed in the market. Finally, it was due to the untiring creative measures taken by Mr Praveen Kadle, Executive Director-Finance & Corporate Affairs, who joined Tata Motors in January 1997, that the company revived. Mr Ravi Kant, MD, Tata Motors stated 'Praveen has demonstrated a leadership role in making the finance department more integrated in the business and in taking several steps proactively in exploring new areas like M&As and the NYSE listing'.

The company earned profits amounting to ₹1,237 crore and around 30 per cent return on capital employed for the year ending March 2005. Its net profit further increased to ₹1,529 crore on net sales of ₹20,602 crore for the year ending March 2006. The company's EPS increased from negative to the tune of 1.98 in 2001–02 to a positive of 9.38 in 2002–03, 34.37 in 2004–05, and further to 40.57 in 2005–06. The company's stock price had risen by around 14 times from a low of ₹60 in 2001 to around ₹850 in 2005. All this was achieved from the lessons the company learnt during the tough times that led to the initiation of tough measures such as cost cutting, optimum mix of finance to minimizing the cost of financial resources, and a decision to go overseas to hedge against the cyclical nature of the commercial vehicles business.

Mr Praveen Kadle initiated a number of strategic financial moves, including having a hand in certain key decisions such as the acquisition of Daewoo's commercial vehicle segment for ₹459 crore, merging Tata Finance with the company, acquisition of the German firm CEDIS Mechanical Engineering, and acquiring stake in the Spanish company Hispano.

Source: Based on *Business Today*, 9 April 2006 and Tata Motors's website www.tatamotors.com, accessed on 15 July 2007.

focuses on building good investor relations, so that the company has their support when it needs it. Dividend and share repurchase decisions are vital tools to building investor goodwill and, therefore, should be considered in the backdrop of various interests of investors including taxation implications, to take care of stockholders' interest to the maximum possible extent. Dividend and share repurchase decisions are market signals to the investing public and other stakeholders regarding the future prospects, profitability, and risk profile of investing in the company.

Thus, the main goal and objective of a business entity is to maximize shareholders' wealth. This can be achieved by simultaneously taking care of interests of various stakeholders of the company such as customers, employees, government, suppliers, creditors, and the community at large. This approach towards financial management has introduced a new dimension for effective operations of the company—social corporate responsibility. More and more corporate entities are focusing their efforts in this direction. Further, profit maximization and EPS maximization are the guiding forces for taking various financial decisions, but these are only partial objectives. The real goal of the organization is maximizing the shareholders' wealth. Thus, the financing decisions relate to three interrelated areas—investment decisions, financing decisions, and dividend/share repurchase decisions. An optimum combination of these three financial decisions helps organizations to have sustainable long-term growth.

SUMMARY

The role of a finance manager is vital to the success of an organization. All financial activities of an organization revolve around him/her. The fundamental goal of the company is to create value for its shareholders. A company attempts to maximize the market value of its stock that depends upon investment, financing, and dividend decisions.

As compared to accounting profits and earnings per share (EPS), economic value added (EVA) is an economic concept and, therefore, requires the business to cover both operating costs and capital costs. A good business gives due importance to corporate social responsibility (CSR) and adheres to good corporate governance practices.

Finance functions refer to making financial decisions regarding acquisitions, financing, and effective management of acquired assets to achieve overall goals pertaining to stockholders and other stakeholders. An optimum combination of these three financial decisions helps organizations to have sustainable long-term growth.

KEYWORDS

Dividend/share repurchase decisions Surplus that can be distributed to shareholders.
Economic value added (EVA) It is a yardstick to measure a company's financial performance based on its residual wealth calculated by deducting cost of capital from its operating profit after making adjustments for taxes, on a cash basis.
Financing decisions Optimization of financing mix or capital structure of the company for a given level of investment in the light of the existing balance sheet position.
Investment decisions It involves dealing with the total amount of assets required to execute a

plan of action so as to respond on time to the available business opportunities.
Profit maximization Generally maximization of profits, that is, difference between total revenue and total cost is treated as the fundamental objective behind the existence of a company.
Shareholders' wealth It is represented by the market value of the stock.
Social responsibility Corporate responsibility towards all stakeholders.
Value creation for shareholders The fundamental purpose for existence of a company is to maximize shareholders' wealth by making use of profitable business opportunities.

EXERCISES

Concept Review Questions
1. What is meant by value creation for shareholders?
2. Differentiate between maximization of profits and maximization of shareholders' wealth.
3. Why is economic value added (EVA) referred to as economic profit?
4. In what way is the EVA concept superior to accounting profit and earnings per share (EPS)?

5. Define corporate social responsibility (CSR).

6. Define investment decisions, financing decisions, and dividend/share repurchase decisions.

Critical Thinking Question

What consequences are faced by a company that has been consistently rewarding its shareholders by way of payment of dividends and appreciation of stock market price yet not committed to social responsibility? Comment critically.

Project Assignments

1. 'Taking care of interest of shareholders and community at large are not compatible with each other.' Analyse this statement with the help of concrete examples of corporate entities. Cite concrete data to support your argument.

2. Take an example of a corporate entity that has grown multifold during the last 2–3 years. Analyse the reasons behind its growth in the light of the role and functions of finance and financial managers.

13

Financial Statements

INTRODUCTION

Financial statements provide the sum total of an organization's commercial activity that needs to be understood by its various stakeholders. By summing up the existing and future health of an organization, a financial statement is used by the different stakeholders to get their perspective about the business. It is important to understand what these statements reveal and what they hide to get a clearer picture about the workings of a business entity and the potential for its future growth. No wonder, they are sometimes referred to as the horoscope of the company. It is said that with experience, business managers and corporate leaders learn to read between the lines of a financial statement. A good financial management system tells us how a particular business is doing, and the reasons for its performance. Therefore, it is essential to understand financial statements.

FINANCIAL STATEMENTS

It is a written record of the financial status of an individual, association, or business organization. A financial statement includes a balance sheet, income statement (also known as operating statement or profit and loss statement), and a statement of cash flows (Fig. 13.1).

It is also defined as a set of reports that summarize a firm's accounting data and indicate its financial condition. The four basic financial statements are the balance sheet, profit and loss account or income statement, statement of retained earnings, and statement of changes in financial position.

Accounting statements provide specific information about a company's financial position. They include profit

Learning Objectives

After studying this chapter, you will be able to:
- Understand financial statements and their utility
- Examine the need and purpose of financial statements
- Analyse different types of financial statements
- Understand balance sheet, profit and loss account, cash flow, and fund flow statements
- Examine the difference between cash flow and fund flow and their implications on business decisions
- Know about the relevance and implication of 'note forming part of accounts' and the 'auditor's report to the shareholders'

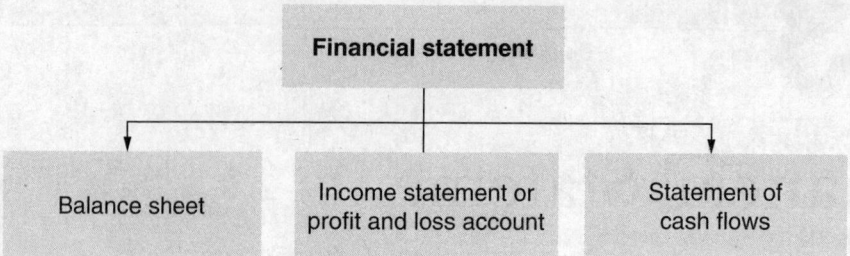

FIGURE 13.1   Different types of financial statements

and loss statement, also known as the income statement, the balance sheet, and the statement of cash flows. Financial statements are prepared by the company's chartered accounting firm or by the company's accountants themselves.

Need for Financial Statements

There are many stakeholders in a business organization such as employees, managers, owners, shareholders, creditors, financial institutions and banks, venture capitalists, customers, government, and public. All of them have a different objective and interest that they would like to fulfil through the business entity. Therefore, each stakeholder would like to have information about the company, which addresses his/her concerns. Some common questions posed by various stakeholders are:

• What is the financial position of the company at present? How does it compare with its past financial position and competitors?
• How has the business performed for the given time period in absolute and relative terms?
• Where do the funds come from into the system and where do they go?

An accountant prepares a financial statement comprising balance sheets, profit and loss accounts or income statements, and fund and cash flow statements to address the aforementioned queries. They help in understanding the financial position of the company and provide the basic data for financial planning and forecasting. It is these statements and information that form the basis of scientific and logical financial decisions. Users of financial statement information do not necessarily need to know about the intricacies of finance or accounting to understand and make use of the information in these statements; however, at the same time they need to be conversant with some of the fundamental characteristics of the same. They can then use this information according to their perspective and interests. In this chapter we shall attempt to understand balance sheet, profit and loss account, cash flow, shareholders equity, and some other related concepts.

BALANCE SHEET

A balance sheet provides information about the financial condition of a company at a given point of time. It provides details about a company's assets, liabilities, and shareholders' equity.

Assets   The resources of a company that have a value and are expected to provide additional benefits in the form of higher cash inflows are known as assets. They can either be sold or used by adding additional value by making products or services that can be sold. Assets include physical property such as plants, trucks, equipment, and inventory. It also includes intangible assets that cannot be touched but nevertheless exist and have value, such as trademarks and patents. Cash in itself is an asset; so are investments a company makes. Assets can be classified into four categories:

Fixed assets: Land, building, plant, machinery, etc. constitute fixed assets. These assets are expected to produce benefits over a period of time.

Investments: Financial securities and bonds owned by the firm are referred to as investments.

Current assets, loans and advances: This includes inventories, debtors, cash and bank balance, loans and advances, and other current assets. A salient feature of these assets is that these can be converted into cash within an operating cycle of the company or in the short run, that is, within a period of one year.

Miscellaneous expenditure and losses: Consists of preliminary expenses incurred during construction, development expenditure, and the debit balance of profit and loss account.

Liabilities   The amount of money that a company owes to others. These include all types of obligations that a company has to others such as money borrowed from a bank to launch a new product, rent for the hired building, money owed to suppliers for materials (creditors), salary that a company owes to its employees, environmental cleanup costs, or taxes owed to the government. Liabilities also include a company's obligations to provide goods or services to customers in the future. They may be classified into the following categories:

Share capital: It includes equity and preference capital, that is, the stake of the owners in the company.

Reserves and surplus: It includes retained earnings out of the profit earned by the business as well as shared premium money and capital subsidy, if any in the system.

Secured loans: Loans taken from banks and institutions or other sources having charge on the assets of the company.

Unsecured loans: Loans taken by the company without extending any charge on the assets of the company.

Current liabilities and provisions: Obligations such as payments to be made to creditors, interest accrued and not due, bills payable, and provision for taxes, dividend, etc., that are expected to materialize within a year.

Shareholders' equity   It is also referred to as capital or net worth of the company. It is the amount that owners invest in the company's stock plus or minus the company's earnings or losses since inception. Sometimes companies distribute earnings, instead of retaining them. These distributed earnings are known as dividends paid.

A balance sheet shows a snapshot of a company's assets, liabilities, and shareholders' equity at any given point of time and is usually provided to all concerned at the end of the reporting period. It does not show the flows into and out of the accounts during the period.

Thus, the balance sheet shows that at any given point of time the total assets of the company equal the total liabilities of the company, that is, outside liabilities and shareholders' equity. It is expressed as:

$$\text{Assets} = \text{Liabilities} + \text{Shareholders' equity} \qquad (13.1)$$

From the above equation, it is clear that if two of the three components are known, the third can be found. For example, if assets of the company are ₹200 crore and its owner's equity is ₹25 crore, then outside liabilities for the company would be ₹175 crore. According to the Companies Act (1956), the structure of a balance sheet could be either in the format of an account form or a report form. It may be displayed as under:

Account Form

Liabilities	Assets
Share Capital	Fixed Assets
Reserves and surplus	Investments
Secured loans	Current assets, loans and advances
Unsecured loans	Current assets
Current liabilities and provisions	Loans and advances
Current liabilities provisions	Miscellaneous expenses and losses

Report Form

Sources of Funds
1. Shareholders' funds
   (a) Share capital
   (b) Reserves and surpluses
2. Loan funds
   (a) Secured loans
   (b) Unsecured loans

Application of Funds
1. Fixed assets
2. Investments
3. Current assets, loans and advances
   Less: Current liabilities and provisions   Net current assets
4. Miscellaneous expenses and losses

PROFIT AND LOSS ACCOUNT

A profit and loss account, also known as the income statement, is a report that shows how much revenue a company earned over a specific time period (usually for a year or some portion of a year) from the sales of its goods and services and the costs and expenses associated with earning that revenue. It provides broad details of income and expenses of the company in a particular time period. In turn, it gives the net earnings or losses incurred in undertaking the business activity in a given time period, say a month, a quarter, half a year, or a year. Certain vital terms to understand profit and loss account are as under:

Net sales: Gross sales – Sales rejected by customer – Excise.

Cost of goods sold: It computes all the cost associated with the goods sold during the accounting period.

Gross profit: Net sales – Cost of goods sold.

Operating expenses: Expenses incurred in running the business during the accounting period. It consists of administrative expenses, selling and distribution expenses, depreciation, etc. Depreciation takes into account the wear and tear on fixed assets, such as machinery, tools, and furniture, which are used over the long term. Companies spread the cost of these assets over the periods they are used.

Operating profit: It represents the profit earned/loss incurred on account of normal business activities of the company and does not consider non-operating gains.

Non-operating gains/losses: Gains and losses on account of transactions that are not related to normal business of the company such as interest and dividend income, profit/loss on account of sale of fixed assets, investments, etc.

Profit before interest or taxes: Profit before interest and taxes (PBIT) measures profit without considering interest and taxes and is arrived at by adding non-operating profit or subtracting non-operating loss from the operating profit.

Interest: Interest relates to the cost of borrowed funds (secured or unsecured) from banks, financial institutions, fixed deposits, promoters, commercial papers, etc.

Profit before tax: PBIT – Interest expenses.

Provision for taxes: Current tax on taxable income as computed under the Income Tax Act.

Profit after tax/Net profit: Profit before tax – Income tax provision.

Prior period adjustments: From net profit certain adjustments such as adding the profit brought forward, adding reserves written back, and subtracting extra burden on account of earlier years taxes/expenses, etc., are done. These are known as prior period adjustments.

Amount available for appropriation: Profit after tax plus prior period adjustments. The provision for payments of dividends is made from this and the balance amount in the profit and loss account is carried forward to the balance sheet.

Income statements also report earnings per share (EPS). This calculation allows companies to calculate the money shareholders would receive if it decides to distribute all the net earnings for the period. It is computed by dividing the net profit by the number of equity shares. It may be mentioned here that companies normally do not distribute all their earnings. A part of the earnings is kept for reinvestment in the business to avail opportunities.

It is the profit and loss account for a given period that indicates the commercial viability of the operations of the business. Every company tries to maximize shareholders' wealth by earning as much profit as it can from fixed and current assets.

Financial highlights of Colgate and Ashok Leyland

Colgate

The financial position of Colgate for the past five years is presented below. It may be observed that its sales have increased from ₹1,160.9 crore in 2001–02 to ₹1217.5 crore in 2005–06 resulting in an average annual growth in sales of 1.20 per cent. However, in the corresponding period, net profit has gone up from ₹69.8 crore to 137.6 crore, resulting in an average annual growth rate of 18.5 per cent. Net profit margins have gone up from 6.0 per cent in 2001–02 to 11.3 per cent in 2005–06. After absorbing ₹24 crore on account of impairment of assets, accelerated depreciation and diminu-

tion in the value of the company's investment in its wholly-owned subsidiary in Nepal, the profit after tax has registered an impressive growth of 21 per cent at ₹137.6 crore as against ₹113.3 crore during 2004–05.

The company firmly believes that the commitment of its employees to living Colgate's values of caring, global teamwork, and continuous improvement is the key reason behind the success of the company. It has been developing and launching innovative new products to strengthen its market leadership position. Its recently established Oral Care Category Innovation Centre works closely with the technology

TABLE 13.1   Financial performance of Colgate (2001–02 to 2005–06)

₹ *in crore*

Items	2001–02	2002–03	2003–04	2004–05	2005–06
Operating results					
Sales	1160.9	1056.9	1042.1	1072.5	1217.5
Other income	30.9	35.8	29.9	34.2	25.6
Net profit	69.8	88.7	108.0	113.3	137.6
Cash profit	91.9	108.1	132.3	135.7	169.0
Financial position					
Fixed assets (Net)	172.3	158.0	94.0	147.2	169.1
Current assets	56.8	29.5	36.8	(62.8)	(49.6)
Others	27.7	89.6	115.7	169.4	156.0
Total assets	256.9	277.2	246.5	253.8	275.4
Share capital	136.0	136.0	136.0	136.0	136.0
Reserves and surplus	111.6	139.0	108.3	113.8	135.1
Shareholders' funds	247.6	275.0	244.3	249.8	271.1
Loan funds	9.3	2.1	2.2	4.0	4.4
Total capital employed	256.9	277.2	246.5	253.8	275.4
Equity share data					
Earnings per share (₹)	5.13	6.52	7.94	8.33	10.12
Dividend per share (₹)	4.25	4.25	6.00	7.00	7.50

Note: Figures in brackets indicate negative.

Exhibit   (*Contd*)

TABLE 13.2   Financial performance of Ashok Leyland

₹ *in crore*

Items	2005–06	2006–07	Increase/(Decrease) %
Gross sales	6053.1	8304.7	37.2
Less Excise duty	805.4	1136.5	41.1
Gross operating margin	540.1	702.7	30.1
Financial expenses	16.5	5.3	(67.6)
Gross profit (PBDT)	556.6	768.2	38.0
Depreciation	126.0	150.6	19.5
Profit before tax	453.3	604.5	33.6
Net profit	327.3	441.2	34.7
Earnings per share (₹)	2.74	3.38	23.4
Dividend per share (₹)	1.2	1.5	25.0

centres in India and USA to shape ideas into products that respond to changing customer needs. The Centre focuses on understanding consumer needs, habits, and product usage and it is this aspect that enables the company to come up with a stream of new product ideas and concepts. The company has been consistently raising the value to its investors, as is evident from continuous increase in the earning per share as also dividend per share between 2001–02 and 2005–06.

Ashok Leyland

The financial performance of Ashok Leyland for the two years ending March 2006 is displayed below:

Company's market share for medium and heavy commercial vehicles has increased from 0.8 per cent in 2005–06 to 28 per cent in 2006–07. Its gross sales increased from 6053.1 crore in 2005–06 to ₹8304.7 crore in 2006–07, that is, a growth rate of 37.2 per cent. The increase

in sales has resulted in 34.7 per cent growth in profits that increased from ₹327.3 crore in 2005–06 to ₹441.2 crore. In 2006–07, the earnings per share have gone up from ₹2.74 in 2005–06 to ₹3.38. Due to its improved performance, the company announced a dividend of ₹1.5 per share in 2006–07 as against ₹1.2 per share in 2005–06. The main reasons for improved performance during 2006–07 was the general buoyancy in the market coupled with initiatives taken by the company to focus on value added products and services, capacity expansion, and improved productivity and efficiency.

Although steel prices fell during the last two years, there were significant cost increases on account of adherence to emission and noise norms. The company achieved better productivity norms in all the plants, through its concerted efforts. The emphasis on Research and Development (R and D) is continuing and the total R and D expenditure, including capital expenditure, accounted for ₹104.9 crore, that is, an

(*Contd*)

Exhibit *(Contd)*

increase of 14 per cent over 2004–05. Ashok Leyland has succeeded in product development because of its emphasis on R and D that gave rise to innovative technologies. The company had initiated a research into alternative fuels even before legislative debates on this issue had even begun in the country. It has enabled the company to come out with CNG technology ahead of the rest, thus promising a breath of fresh air for polluted cities.

Source: Based on www.ashokleyland.com/, accessed on 26 June 2007; www.colgate.com, accessed on 26 June 2007.

FUND FLOW AND CASH FLOW STATEMENTS

Cash flow statements show a company's inflows and outflows of cash. This is important because a company needs to have enough reserves of cash for its expenses and to purchase assets. The profit and loss statement shows whether the company had made any profits from its operations at the end of a given time period. However, profits might not get translated into cash receipts, which matters the most for operations of the company, that is, some of the profits might be locked-up with debtors who have bought the product but have failed to pay the money for the same. The cash flow statement shows changes over time rather than absolute rupee amounts at a given point of time. It uses and reorders the information from a company's balance sheet and income statement. The cash flow statement shows the net increase or decrease in cash during a given period of time. To get a better picture about the inflow and outflow of cash, cash flow statements are divided into three main parts. Each reviews the cash flow from one of the three types of activities—(1) operating activities; (2) investing activities; and (3) financing activities.

As against cash flow, the fund flow statement takes into account the inflow and outflow of all funds—cash or non-cash. There are certain non-cash inflows or outflows affecting the company's ability to fulfil its commitments. For example, depreciation provided in the books of accounts is not paid to anybody and remains in the system. Similarly, on certain investments, the company may have an interest due but not received as a fund inflow. It will not get reflected into cash inflow until the company receives it. The relationship between net cash flow and profit after tax, thus gives the picture about net cash flow. It may be calculated as:

$$\text{Net cash flow} = \text{Profit after tax}$$
$$- \text{Non-cash revenue} + \text{Non-cash expenses} \qquad (13.2)$$

In practice, net cash flow is defined as profit after tax plus depreciation plus amortization.

NOTES TO ACCOUNTS

Other than the financial figures given in the various financial statements, much is recorded by the statutory auditors of the company in the 'note forming part of accounts' and in the 'auditors' report to the shareholders'. These observations reveal much about accounting policies and the situations when the company may have deviated from standard practices. It also provides the details of contingent liabilities, that is, liabilities that may or may not fall on the company and, therefore, on the date of annual accounts. They may not have been settled on time, and thus, not included in the financial statement. Thus, notes to accounts is packed with important information, whose implications should be clearly analysed for the future operations and financial decisions of the company. However, stakeholders have some points of concern with regard to notes to accounts. They are:

- prospects about realization of bad debts;
- status on certain international contracts and their implications, etc;
- payment of income tax and statutory dues;
- pension plans and other retirement programmes;
- stock options;
- significant accounting policies and practices; and
- details on contingent liabilities.

HUMAN RESOURCE ACCOUNTING

Business organizations use tangible assets—fixed and current, intangible assets, and investment assets to create value for the shareholders (Fig. 13.2). Fixed assets refer to land, buildings, equipment, machinery, vehicles, furniture, etc., which are tangible and have a normal life of more than 12 months. Current assets are stocks, debtors, cash, and other current assets that are realizable within 12 months. It is important to understand that some businesses, particularly those in the service

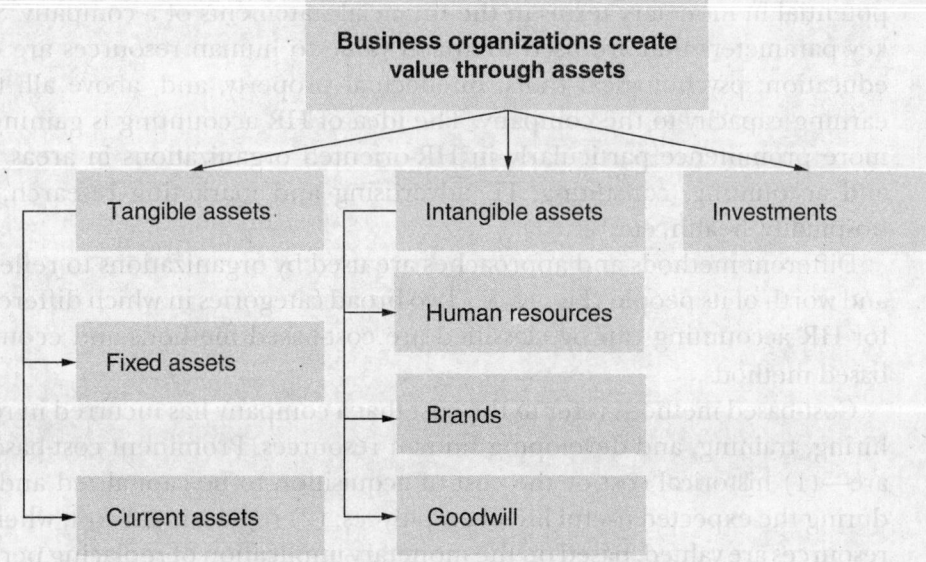

FIGURE 13.2 Types of assets

industry, have low fixed assets and are not capital intensive. However, manufacturing businesses such as steel, automobiles, telecom equipment, etc. are capital intensive and, therefore, require more fixed assets. Most tangible assets exist in the physical form and are easy to evaluate, so their worth can be incorporated in the balance sheet. However, intangible assets such as goodwill, brands, and human resources (HR) are difficult to be valued and, hence, incorporated in the balance sheet. Once their value is ascertained, these assets too depreciate like tangible assets over their useful economic life. It is these assets that play a critical role in the growth of certain businesses and, therefore, their value needs to be ascertained, so as to duly incorporate their worth and give these assets a due accounting treatment.

Importance and relevance of human resource accounting has been appreciated by a number of authors over the past four decades. Rensis Likert undertook research in the area of HR accounting in the 60s (Bowers 1973). He emphasized on the qualitative aspect of HR planning that contributes to long-term gains and benefits.

In the resource theory (Conner 1991) highlighted that the competitive position of an organization largely depended upon its HR. According to Archel (1995), it is HR that provides the rationale for some firms being more productive and profitable as compared to others. According to American Accounting Association (1970), HR accounting is the human resource identification and measuring process and so is its communication to the interested parties. Like any other resource, HR has two sides—asset value and procurement cost. However, in case of HR, as per generally acceptable accounting principles, only the procurement/maintenance cost is accounted for in the balance sheet and not the asset value.

With the knowledge economy playing a greater role in business, human capital plays a critical role within the enterprise and a need to evaluate it in the balance sheet has been felt. Human resource accounting attempts to measure and incorporate its potential in monetary terms in the financial statements of a company. Some of the key parameters that are used to attach value to human resources are experience, education, psychological traits, intellectual property, and, above all, their future earning capacity to the company. The idea of HR accounting is gaining more and more prominence particularly in HR-oriented organizations in areas such as law and accounting, consulting, IT, advertising and marketing research, education, hospitality, health, etc.

Different methods and approaches are used by organizations to reflect the value and worth of its people (Fig. 13.3). Two broad categories in which different methods for HR accounting can be classified are cost-based methods and economic value-based methods.

Cost-based methods refer to the cost that a company has incurred in recruitment, hiring, training, and developing human resources. Prominent cost-based methods are—(1) historical cost or the cost of acquisition to be capitalized and written off during the expected useful life of employees; (2) replacement cost, wherein human resources are valued, based on the monetary implication of replacing personnel; and

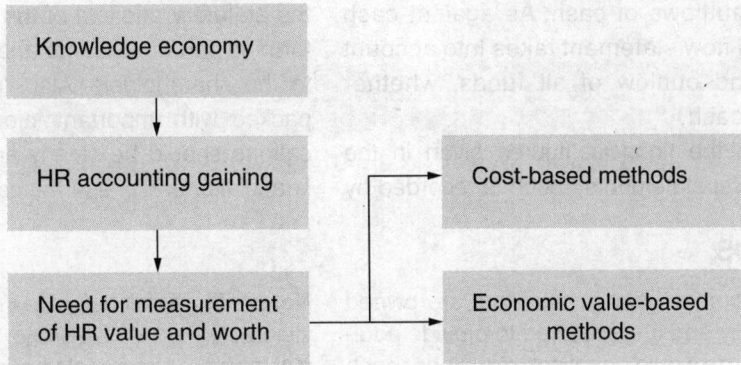

FIGURE 13.3   Human resource accounting

(3) competitive bidding, capitalizing on the earning potential of human resources by using opportunity cost concept.

Economic value-based methods emphasize on the capitalization of a company's earnings. The prominent economic value-based methods are—(1) Jaggi and Lau method, a group-based approach that contributes to productivity and performance in the organization. It is used for estimating the value and worth of human resources; and (2) economic value method that considers net present value of incremental cash flows on account of human resources.

In India, the Companies Act (1956), does not require explicit disclosure of human assets in the financial statements of the companies. However, realizing the benefits derived from these assets, some companies have started disclosing all relevant information in their books of accounts.

Thus, it is the financial statements and the details therein along with the notes to accounts that gives a clear picture about the financial working position of the company. It answers questions such as how far has it been able to utilize the funds optimally? To what extent has it been able to meet the corporate objectives? The information given in the financial statements has different meanings to different stakeholders. The companies that are able to respond to the objectives of various stakeholders to meet their concerns and objectives survive and grow in the long run.

SUMMARY

Financial statements are the most common way in which different stakeholders get their perspective about business. The four basic financial statements are—the balance sheet, income statement or profit and loss account, fund flow, and cash flow.

Financial statements help in understanding the financial position of the company and pro-

vide the basic data for financial planning and forecasting. It provides details about a company's assets, liabilities, and shareholders' equity as on a particular date. Profit and loss account for a given period indicates the commercial viability of the operations of the business. Cash flow statements show a company's inflows and outflows of cash. As against cash flow, the fund flow statement takes into account the inflow and outflow of all funds, whether cash or non-cash.

Other than the financial figures given in the various financial statements, much is recorded by the statutory auditors of the company in the 'note forming part of accounts' and in the auditor's report to the shareholders. Also, 'note to accounts' are packed with important information whose implications should be clearly analysed for the future financial operations of the company.

KEYWORDS

Assets   Resources having value that are owned by the company and are expected to provide additional benefits, as would be reflected in higher cash inflows.

Cost of goods   All the cost associated with the goods sold during the accounting period.

Depreciation   It refers to the wear and tear on fixed assets.

Equity   The amount owners invested in the company's stock plus or minus the company's earnings or losses since inception.

Financial statements   A written record of the financial status of an individual, association, or a business organization.

Gross profit   Net sales minus the cost of goods sold.

Investments   Financial securities and bonds owned by the firm.

Liabilities   The amount of money that a company owes to others.

Net cash flows   Profit after tax minus non-cash revenue plus non-cash expenses.

Net profit   Profit before tax minus income tax provision.

Net sales   Gross sales minus sales rejected by the customer minus the excise duty.

Non-operating gains/losses   These are incurred on account of transactions that are not related to normal business of the company.

Notes to accounts   Observations recorded by the statutory auditors of the company in the 'note forming part of accounts' and in the 'auditor's report to the shareholders'.

Operating profit   Gross profit minus operating expenses.

Reserves and surplus   It includes retained earnings out of the profit earned by the business as also share premium money and capital subsidy, if any in the system.

Secured loans   It refers to loans having charge on the assets of the company.

Unsecured loans   It refers to loans obtained by the company without extending any charge on the assets of the company.

EXERCISES

Concept Review Questions

1. What are financial statements and their relevance to business organizations?
2. Why do we need financial statements?
3. Why are total assets always equal to total liabilities?
4. Differentiate between fixed assets, current assets, and investments.
5. 'Depreciation is a non-cash entry.' What is its implication on cash flow of the company?
6. Define gross profit. What is the difference between gross profit and operating profit?

Critical Thinking Questions

1. It is the profit and loss account for a given period that indicates the commercial viability of the operations of the business. Do you agree with this statement? Give reasons.
2. In case a company is earning profit but is having no cash to continue with its operations, what are the financial implications of such a situation? Should the company continue with the business? Why or why not?
3. What are the areas of concern to different stakeholders as far as 'notes to the accounts'

are concerned? Explain by considering a particular category of stakeholder and area of concern that would attract his/her maximum attention.

Project Assignments

1. Take the latest annual report of two companies and comment on their performance vis-à-vis previous year and compare the performance in terms of profit, reserves, shareholders' equity, turnover, fixed assets, and current assets position. Go through 'notes to accounts' of the companies selected and comment on important issues highlighted by the auditors from a shareholder's perspective.

2. From the cash flow statement of the two companies that you selected for the question above, compare and highlight salient aspects of operating activities, investing activities, and financing activities.

REFERENCES

American Accounting Association, *A Statement of Basic Accounting Theory*, Evanston II, AAA Revised Edition (1970), p. 35.

Archel, P. (1995), *Actives intangibles: analysis de lacunas partidas polemicas*, Revista Tecnica del instituto de censoves jurados de cuentas de espara, vol. 7.

Bowers, David G. (1973), 'A Review of Rensis Likert's Improving the Accuracy of P/L Reports and Estimating the Change in Dollar Value of the Human Organization', *Michigan Business Review*, vol. 25, March.

Carme, B.C., S.M. Gutierrez, S.L. Antonio, V.C. Joseph, and G.M. Carlos (1999), 'Human Resource Accounting', *International Advances in Economic Research*, vol. 5, no. 3, pp. 386–94.

Conner K. (1991), 'A Historical Comparison of Resource Based Theory and Five Schools of Thought Within Industrial Organisation Economics', *Journal of Management*, vol. 17, no. 1, pp. 121–154.

14

Financial Ratio Analysis

Learning Objectives

After studying this chapter, you will be able to:

- Understand the application of ratio analysis to analyse financial statements
- Learn about financial ratios and their utility
- Learn about different types of ratios
- Use ratio analysis
- Examine different types of ratios and their implications on analysis of financial position of the company
- Evaluate the relative strengths and weaknesses of the company by using ratio analysis so that the various stakeholders of a company may make their financial decisions

INTRODUCTION

Financial statements are meaningless if one does not have the ability and skills to use them. The balance sheet and the profit and loss account are essential, but are only the starting points of successful financial management. It is the application of ratio analysis to financial statements that provides the much needed insight into the success, failure, and progress of a company. There are various tools for obtaining information from the financial statements and for taking corrective steps, in case things have not happened as planned, for future planning and, above all, day-to-day financial decisions. Ratio analysis is commonly used to derive relevant information for financial decision-making. A good interpretation of ratios goes a long way in having effective control over the finances of a company.

FINANCIAL RATIOS

Financial ratio analysis is the calculation and comparison of ratios based on the information about the company's performance in its financial statements. The level and historical trends of various ratios can be used to make inferences about a company's financial position, effectiveness of its operations, and viability as an investment. Thus, financial ratios provide the relationship between two or more than two variables, picked up from financial statements, to get more than one perspective about the workings of a company. If we know the variable cost of production and sales, we can work out a contribution and get a ratio indicating a contribution margin to sales. However, suppose we know that the contribution margin for the company is 25 per cent, this information is meaningless in isolation. But, if we know that the competitors have a contribution margin of 10 per cent, then we may conclude that the company's operations up to the stage of variable cost of production are more profitable than of its competitors. Further, if we know that over the last three years the contribution margin is steadily increasing, it implies that the company's management has been implementing effective business policies.

The utility of ratios varies from stakeholder to stakeholder. Each stakeholder views the ratio according to the issues that concern him/her.

Ratio Comparison

As stated earlier, ratios in isolation are of no use. The value of ratios lies in meaningful and relevant comparisons leading to interpretations that facilitate the analysis and diagnosis of a given situation. Ratio comparisons can be made in two ways—cross-sectional and time series (Fig. 14.1). *Cross-sectional analysis* compares the financial ratios of different comparable firms at a given point of time. The comparison can be with the best, worst, or average in the industry depending upon the company's objective that it has kept before it, depending upon its position and in relation to its competitors.

As against cross-sectional analysis, under *time series,* ratios are compared for a given company over a period of time. This helps in evaluating the progress or deterioration that a company has made in its specific areas of operations over time. However, the analysis of time series ratios, without taking into account the fundamental changes in a company's situation or prospects would be futile as regards prediction of future trends. While considering the future prospects of a company, while studying its time series ratios, one has to also consider whether it has undergone a merger, had a substantive change in its technology or market position, change in management, or has been sick in its operations. Above all, one can combine cross-sectional analysis with time series analysis to get the time trend behaviour of the ratio in relation to other companies or industry analysis. Thus, it is essential to go through statements to the notes to accounts, which provides a variety of information, before arriving at a final conclusion about the business entity based on ratio analysis.

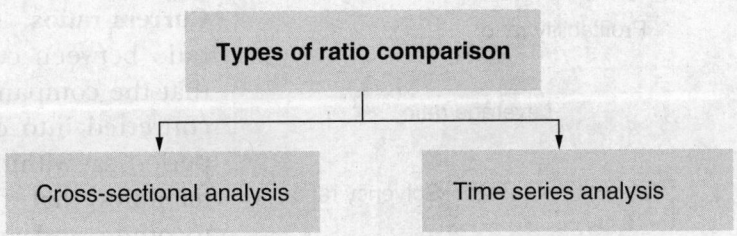

FIGURE 14.1   Types of ratio analysis

Using ratio analysis   Some points to be kept in mind while using ratios are:

- over dependence on a single ratio is not desirable as far as conclusive interpretation of the performance of a company is concerned;
- effect of seasonality needs to be segregated while making comparisons. Further, ratios to be compared should relate to the same time period for all companies;
- to get the true financial analysis, ratios should be computed based on audited accounts data; and
- the definition used for arriving at the value of variables in the ratio should be identical in all respects for all the companies being compared. The implication of inflating on the business performance as also on the computed ratios should be duly taken care of while interpreting the ratios.

CATEGORIES OF RATIOS

Ratios can be broadly categorized into liquidity ratio, operational ratio, profitability ratio, leverage ratio, and solvency ratio (Fig. 14.2).

Liquidity ratio gives short-term financial position or solvency of the company. Operational ratio deals with efficiency of resource and asset utilization in the operations of the company. Profitability ratio indicates the margins realized by the company, that is, various returns on sales and capital employed. Leverage ratio relates to the debt component used in the company's capital structure. Solvency ratio indicates the company's ability to generate cash flow for meeting its overall financial obligations.

Balance Sheet Ratio Analysis

Balance sheet ratio analysis measures liquidity and solvency (a firm's ability to pay its obligations) and leverage, that is, the degree to which a business depends upon its creditors' funding.

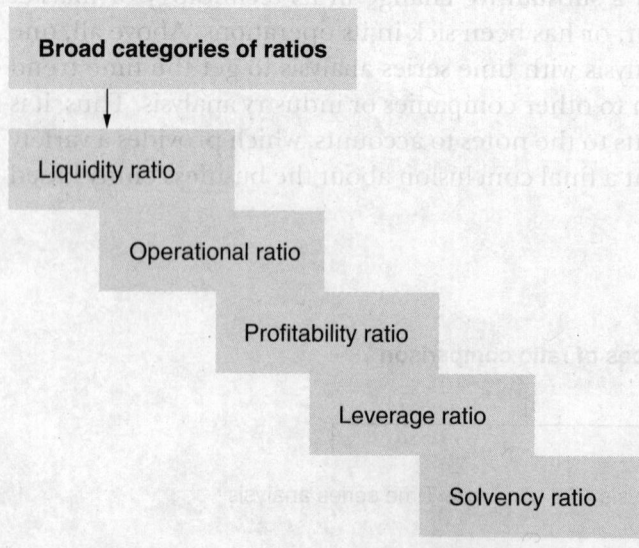

FIGURE 14.2   Different categories of ratios

Liquidity ratios

Liquidity ratios provide information about the company's ability to meet its short-term commitments with its total cash reserves. Important liquidity ratios are the current ratio, quick ratio, and working capital position.

Current ratios   Current ratio is the ratio between current assets; those that the company owns and can be converted into cash within a short period, say within a year, and current liabilities that the company owes to others and are payable within a short time, say within a year.

$$\text{Current ratio} = \text{Total current assets}/\text{Total current liabilities} \qquad (14.1)$$

Current ratio evaluates whether the business has enough current assets to meet its payment obligations and its current debts with an adequately safe margin in case of the non-realization of certain current assets, such as the depletion of the value of inventory or bad debts. A generally acceptable current ratio is 2:1. However, the reasonableness of the adequate current ratio depends on the nature and type of the business and characteristics of its current assets and liabilities. The current ratio of less than 1:1 indicates the difficulties in running the business and is a clear sign that the company is sick. Current ratio can be improved by paying certain current debts, particularly by long-term borrowings infusing equity, channelizing profits into business, or converting non-current assets into current assets.

Quick ratios   The quick ratio is also called the acid-test ratio and is one of the best measures of the liquidity position of the company. It gives the company the ability to meet its short-term obligations with its most liquid assets, that is, in the form of cash, or assets that can be easily converted into cash. It is computed as shown here:

$$\text{Quick ratio} = \text{Cash} + \text{Government securities}$$
$$+ \text{Receivables}/\text{Total current liabilities}$$
$$= (\text{Current assets} - \text{Inventory})/\text{Current liabilities} \quad (14.2)$$

Quick ratio differs from current ratio, as it excludes inventories and only considers mostly those liquid assets that can be easily converted into cash. It attempts to find out whether the business can meet all its current obligations in a situation in which the company realizes no sales revenue. In normal circumstances an acid test ratio of 1:1 is considered satisfactory.

Working capital   It may be defined as the difference between total current assets and total current liabilities. It provides the working capital position of the company and is not a ratio. It is computed as shown here:

$$\text{Working capital} = \text{Total current assets} - \text{Total current liabilities} \qquad (14.3)$$

It is an important indicator that helps banks to determine their decision to give loans to companies. Loans from banks are normally linked to minimum working capital, as it provides a cushion to the bankers about the company's financial strength from the point of view of liquidity position. In general, the higher the liquidity ratios, the better it is. However, very high liquidity ratios far beyond the industry norms are not good and reflect upon the working capital management of the company.

Operational ratios

Operational ratios focus on the management's efficiency in running the business. It is reflected in the speed with which working capital cycle is managed and efficiency with which the total assets of the company are being used.

Inventory turnover ratio   This ratio reveals how well the inventory is being managed as measured through the activity or liquidity of a company's inventory. The greater the speed of the inventory turnover into finished goods, the better it would be to realize greater profits. It measures the speed at which the inventory gets converted into sales by finding out the number of times a company sells its inventory during a year. Inventory turnover ratio is computed as under:

$$\text{Inventory turnover ratio} = \text{Net sales/Average inventory at cost}$$

or $\qquad = \text{Cost of goods sold/Inventory} \qquad (14.4)$

Inventory turnover is normally reported as the inventory period, that is, in terms of number of days' worth of inventory carried by the company. Inventory period is calculated as:

$$\text{Inventory period} = 365/\text{Inventory turnover}$$

365 is the assumed numbers of days in a year.

Average collection period   Average collection period or the average age of account receivables helps in evaluating a company's policies towards its debtors. The comparison of the same with the best in the industry indicates that the company has good collection policies. It is computed as:

$$\text{Average collection period} = \text{Accounts receivables/Average sales per day}$$
$$= \text{Accounts receivables/(Annual sales/365)} \qquad (14.5)$$

This ratio indicates the efficiency with which the accounts receivables are being collected. If they are not being collected in accordance with their terms, the management should rethink its collection policy. If receivables are excessively slow in being converted to cash, liquidity could be severely impaired. The interpretation of this ratio largely depends upon the stipulated collection terms to the debtors.

Average payment period   The average payment period or average age of accounts payable is computed as under:

$$\text{Average payment period} = \text{Accounts payable/ Average purchases per day}$$
$$= \text{Accounts payable/(Annual purchases/365)} \qquad (14.6)$$

Annual purchases are estimated as the given percentage of the cost of the goods sold. This can be understood better in terms of company's strength to get more favourable terms of payment from its creditors.

Total asset turnover   It indicates the efficiency with which a company's assets are being used. This ratio is computed as under:

$$\text{Total asset turnover} = \text{Sales/Total assets} \qquad (14.7)$$

The higher the ratio, the greater the efficiency of asset utilization and better it is for the company.

Profitability ratios

The sum total of a company's performance is measured in terms of its various profitability ratios. These ratios give the margins to sales, on assets, and on owner's investment. Comparison of the margin ratios with the average of the industry or the best performers indicates the performance of the company and the scope the management has to improve efficiency of resource generation, allocation, and value addition to the same. Some of the important profit related ratios are gross margin ratio, net profit margin ratio, return on total assets, leverage ratio, solvency ratio, debt–equity ratio, interest cover ratio, and debt service coverage ratio.

Gross margin ratio   Gross margin ratio is the percentage of amount remaining after the company has paid for the cost of goods sold. The higher the margin the better it is. The gross margin achieved by the company in relation to similar businesses helps in understanding the relative strengths and weaknesses of the company. It is computed as:

$$\text{Gross margin ratio} = \text{Gross profit}/\text{Net sales}$$
$$\text{Gross profit} = \text{Net sales} - \text{Cost of goods sold} \qquad (14.8)$$

Net profit margin ratio   This ratio is the percentage of amount left after subtracting all cost and expenses, including cost of goods sold, administrative expenses, interest, depreciation, taxes, and adding preferred stock dividends. The higher the net profit margin, the better it is. This reveals the overall efficiency of the management in terms of resource procurement, allocation, and value addition to them. The net profit margin ratio is computed as under:

$$\text{Net profit margin ratio} = \text{Net profit (earnings available for}$$
$$\text{common stockholders)}/\text{Net sales} \qquad (14.9)$$

Return on total assets/net worth/equity   A return on total assets, also known as return on investment (ROI) measures the overall effectiveness of the management in generating profits (Fig. 14.3). This measures how efficiently profits are being generated from the assets deployed in the business as compared to the ratios of similar businesses. A low ratio in comparison with industry averages indicates an inefficient use of business assets. The net profit in the formula refers to earnings available for common stockholders. The return on assets ratio is computed as:

$$\text{Return on total assets} = \text{Net profit}/\text{Total assets} \qquad (14.10)$$
$$\text{Return on net worth} = \text{Net profit}/\text{Net worth}$$
$$\text{Return on equity} = \text{Net profit}/\text{Common stock equity} \qquad (14.11)$$

The return on net worth is one of the most important ratios, indicating the percentage of return on funds invested, that is, net worth of the company in the business. This ratio indicates whether all the efforts put into the business have been fruitful or not. If this ratio were less than return on risk-free investment, it would be worthwhile to close the business as continuing it is of no use.

Leverage ratio

Leverage ratio, calculated by total liabilities divided by the net worth of the company, indicates the extent to which the business is dependent on debt financing in relation to owner's equity. A higher ratio would indicate that the owner's stake within the

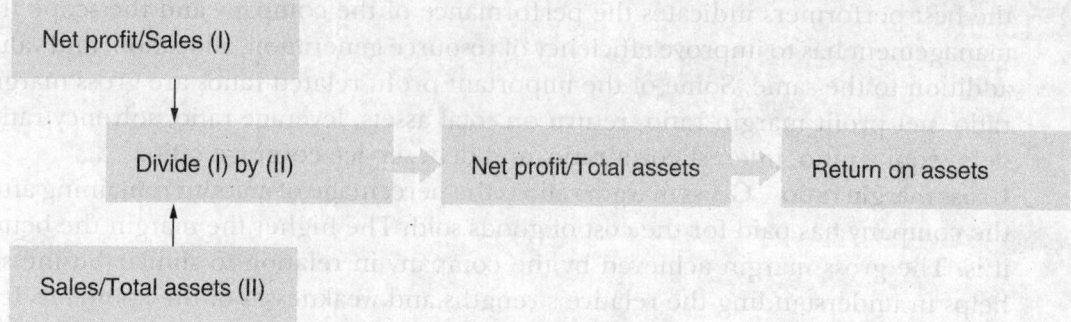

FIGURE 14.3   Return on assets through interrelated ratios

company is relatively low. Banks and financial institutions would perceive a greater risk and they would lay out stricter and costlier terms of financing.

Solvency ratios

The solvency ratios indicate the company's ability to generate cash flow for meeting its overall financial obligations. These ratios help in verifying whether a company has a reasonably normal capital structure or not, and whether it is and would be in a position to service its debt from internal generations or not.

Debt–equity ratio   This ratio indicates the proportion of debt with respect to the equity, that is, owners' stake in the business. In case a company has retained earnings, as shown under free reserves, the owner's stake is considered by taking the net worth of the company. This ratio is computed as:

$$\text{Debt} - \text{Equity ratio} = \text{Debt/Common stock equity} \qquad (14.12)$$

While working with net worth, we will have to consider it as the denominator. In the above ratio as regards debt, one can take overall debt to arrive at the overall debt–equity ratio or secured debt to find debt–equity ratio pertaining to only secured debt component, implying thereby that unsecured debts to the company would not be considered.

Interest cover ratio   This ratio measures a company's capacity to meet its interest commitments. The higher the value of the ratio, the better it is.

$$\text{Interest coverage ratio} = \text{Earnings before interest and taxes/Interest} \qquad (14.13)$$

Earnings before interest and taxes are nothing but the operating income. Normally an interest cover of 2:1 is said to be acceptable. However, the higher this ratio, the greater is the company's ability to further absorb interest-bearing debts for its expansion or otherwise.

Debt service coverage ratio   A company's capability to service its debt obligations is found through the computation of debt service coverage ratio (DSCR). The greater the ratio, the better it is, as it reflects that the company is having adequate capacity to meet its debt obligations. In case the ratio is 2:1, it indicates that the company has double the amount available for servicing its debt. Also called fixed payment coverage ratio, it is computed as:

$$\text{Fixed payment coverage ratio} = (\text{Earnings before interest and taxes}$$
$$+ \text{Lease payments})/\text{Interest} + \text{Lease payments}$$
$$+ (\text{Principal payments} + \text{Preferred stock dividends})$$
$$\times \{1/(1-T)\} \qquad (14.14)$$

Here, T refers to the corporate tax rate. A lower DSCR, indicates a greater risk of default to the lenders and preferred stockholders and vice versa. The various ratios—liquidity, operational, profitability, and solvency—enable business owners and all stakeholders to identify trends in a business and compare its progress with the performance of similar businesses in the same industry. This in turn helps in the identification of relative strengths and weaknesses of the company that enable various stakeholders to make financial decisions.

Financial ratios help in the review and analysis of financial statements of the company. They enable the management to take corrective steps or realize its objectives and goals. It is important to interpret financial ratios with a degree of caution, as certain information given in the financial statements is incomplete without really understanding the implications of notes to accounts and their effect on the financial ratio at a given time or in the future. Therefore, coupled with financial ratio analysis, practising financial analysts with their experience often develop their own measures for particular industries and even individual companies to evaluate financial performance.

SUMMARY

Financial ratio analysis is the calculation and comparison of ratios based on the available information about a company's financial statements. The two types of ratio comparison that can be made are cross-sectional and time series.

Liquidity ratios give short-term financial position or solvency of the company. Operational ratios deal with the efficiency of resource and asset utilization in the operations of the company. Profitability ratios indicate the margins realized by the company, that

is, various returns on sales and capital employed. Leverage ratios relate to the debt component used in the company's capital structure. Solvency ratios indicate the company's ability to generate cash flow for meeting its overall financial obligations.

Financial ratios help in the periodical analysis and review of financial statements of the company, with a view to making decisions as also taking corrective steps for enabling the management of the company to achieve its objectives and goals.

KEYWORDS

Current ratio The ratio between current assets and current liabilities.
Debt service coverage ratio (DSCR) It indicates the capacity of the company to service its debt obligations.
Debt–equity ratio It indicates the proportion of debt with respect to the equity.

Financial ratio analysis The calculation and comparison of ratios based on the available information about the company's financial statements.
Gross margin It provides the percentage of amount remaining after the company has paid for cost of goods sold.

Inventory turnover It measures the number of times a company sells its inventory during a year.

Leverage ratio The extent to which the business is dependent on debt financing in relation to owner's equity.

Liquidity ratios Provide information about company's ability to meet its short-term financial obligations.

Net margin It is the percentage of net profit to net sales.

Operational ratios Deal with the efficiency of resource and asset utilization in the operations of the company.

Profitability ratios Provide the margins in relation to sales, on assets, and on owner's investment, etc.

Quick ratio It gives a company's ability to meet its short-term obligations with its most liquid assets.

Solvency ratio Indicates the company's ability to generate cash flow for meeting its overall financial obligations.

Total asset turnover It is a ratio between sales to total assets that indicates the efficiency with which company's assets are being used.

EXERCISES

Concept Review Questions

1. What are financial ratios and their utilities?
2. Differentiate between time series ratios and cross-sectional ratios with relevant examples.
3. What are the factors that need to be considered while using ratio analysis? Explain the relevance of these factors by giving concrete examples.
4. What is the difference between current ratio and quick ratio? Which is more relevant for assessing the liquidity position of the company and why?
5. Define fixed payment coverage ratio. What is the use of computing it? In case it is less than one, what will be its implication on the financial position of the company?

Critical Thinking Questions

1. Can liquidity ratios, profitability ratios, operational ratios, leverage ratios, and solvency ratios be used independent of each other or do they need to be viewed in an integrated manner? Justify your answer by giving examples.
2. Differentiate between return on total assets, return on net worth, and return on equity. What would be the implication for the business of ABC Ltd, in case its return on total assets is thrice the industry average, while return on net worth is half of the industry average?
3. Interest payments on loans are tax deductible, while dividend on equity is not. Which should be more costly to service and why? Differentiate between fixed assets, current assets, and investments.

Project Assignments

1. A company's current ratio is 3:1. It uses part of its cash for payment of current liabilities including creditors. What would be its implication on current ratio, asset turnover ratio, quick ratio, and debt–equity ratio?
2. For TTC Ltd, the following ratios have been worked out based on the available data from the annual reports of the company, for 2003–2007:

Year ended 31 March, 2007

	2003	2004	2006	2007
Gross margin (%)	76	82	84	75
Operating margin (%)	26	32	32	27
Net profit margin (%)	12	14	13	11
Return on total assets (%)	5	7	8	4
Return on equity (%)	30	35	36	29

Interpret the implications of the above ratios on the financial performance of the company and on its shareholders.

15

Security Analysis and Portfolio Management

INTRODUCTION

Financial system in an economy facilitates the movement of funds from savers who have excess money and are looking at driving returns on it to users of fund who deploy money to multiply it for productive purposes. All the three economic agents, be it consumers (individuals), producers (business), and government, undertake both the roles of users as well as savers of money. However, they may be different entities in the same economy. This flow of funds between demanders of funds and suppliers of funds is carried out by financial institutions and financial markets. Financial institutions constitute entities such as commercial banks, insurance companies, mutual funds, provident funds, and non-banking financial companies.

Financial markets constitute of money market and capital market. Financial system in an economy performs various functions to efficiently channelize flow of funds between users and savers of money. The key functions performed by financial system include payment mechanism, pooling of funds, and channelization of funds for economic activities, price discovery, and dealing with incentive problems.

FINANCIAL AND REAL ASSETS

The two main types of assets are financial and real assets (Fig. 15.1). A financial asset is intangible and is backed up by the monetary value of a physical item or flow of

Learning Objectives

After studying this chapter, you will be able to:
- Understand the role of financial institutions and markets
- Comprehend the difference between money markets and capital markets
- Understand the meaning and purpose of investment and investors' objectives
- Follow concepts related to portfolio and purpose of portfolio management
- Differentiate between various types of market transactions
- Understand and apply concepts related to measurement of risk and return
- Differentiate between systematic and unsystematic risk, and understand how to manage it
- Understand the utility of capital asset pricing model in investment decisions

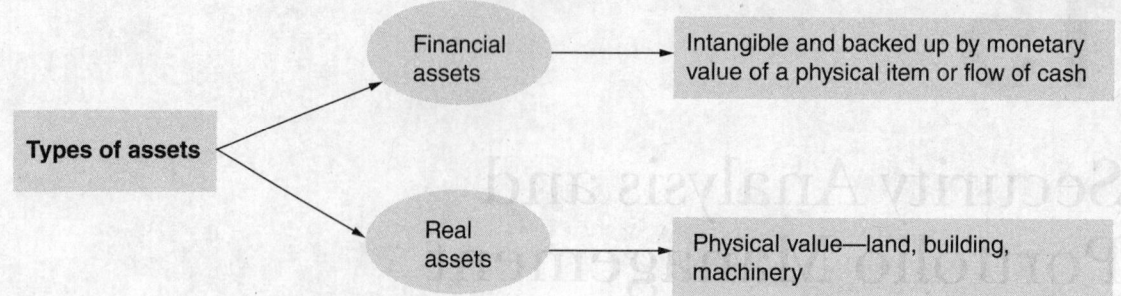

FIGURE 15.1 Types of assets

cash. These assets acquire monetary value from a contractual agreement of what it represents. As against this, real assets such as land, building, machinery, etc., have physical value. However, financial assets are paper securities that have no intrinsic value in themselves until and unless they are converted into cash. Some of the examples of financial assets are certificates of deposits, bonds, stocks, debentures, and bank deposits. Examples of financial assets include cash, equity instruments of business entities, and a contractual right to receive cash or another financial asset from another business entity.

Bonds and stocks are common financial assets. Bonds are offered by corporate, government, or other bodies such as municipal corporations to investors for investing the funds on projects. These are financial papers having legal sanctity showing amount borrowed, period of borrowing, repayment commitments, coupon rate (interest rate), etc. It also indicates whether coupon rate is payable quarterly, half yearly, or is compounded and payable at the time of redemption (repayment). The terms of redemption are also explicitly stated at the time of issue of such bonds. Redemption could be after a certain fixed periods in certain number of installments spread over a period of time or in one go at the time of maturity of these bonds.

Equity is a financial instrument that does not have any contractual obligation to pay cash. It provides an ownership right to the subscriber or buyer of the instrument in a corporate entity. Owner of equity gets paid dividend if the board of the company decides to pay when the corporate entity earns profits, and is entitled to capital appreciation or depreciation based on the demand and supply of these instruments in capital markets.

INVESTMENT

There are individuals who either have more money than their spending and who in turn save the money, or there are individuals who borrow money to fulfill their spending needs. When individuals' current level of income exceeds current consumption, he saves the excess money. These savings may lie idle or may get channelized in such a way that larger amount of money will be available for consumption in future. The saved money which is later deployed for increasing the consumption in future is called investment. The pure rate of interest in market is defined as rate of exchange between future consumption in rupee terms and current consumption in rupee terms. The pure time value of money is defined as the willingness of people to pay for borrowed funds and their willingness to receive surplus on savings and is called interest rate. An investor would further like to ensure that any implication on account of rise in prices called inflation is taken care of to compensate him for today's foregone consumption. He would also like to ensure that risk or uncertainty that correspond to future payment as a result of investment is taken care of by risk premium in the interest rate or the return he is looking at.

Thus, investment is defined as current deployment of funds for a specific time period so as to fetch future payments and takes into consideration the time duration for which funds are deployed, expected rate of inflation, and the risk associated with future payments. Further this definition of investment would include investment by corporate entities in plant and machinery, equipment, land, building, and investments by individuals in stocks, debentures, preference shares, bonds, real estate, or commodities.

Thus, investment relates to different activities undertaken by individuals, businessmen, or government with a common theme of deploying the money or funds to increase investors' wealth in a given time period. These funds could come from money owned, borrowed, or saved. Interest rates and security prices are used by households in their consumption-saving-investment decisions and by firms in their investment and financing decisions.

CLASSIFICATION OF FINANCIAL MARKETS

Following are the five criteria for classification of financial markets (Fig. 15.2).

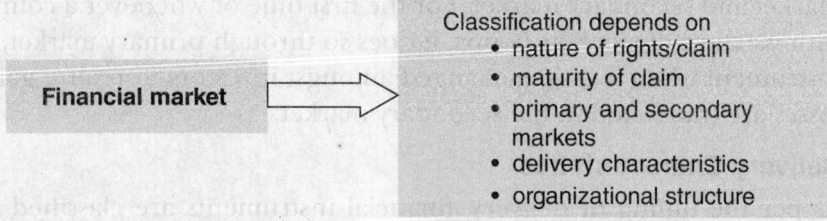

FIGURE 15.2 Criteria for classification of financial markets

Nature of Rights/Claim

As per the nature of rights on the financial instruments markets the market can be classified as debt or equity. Debt market includes fixed income earning securities with a given tenure of maturity. The fixed income can be specified as interest rate or coupon rate in case of bonds, while equity instrument does not have any fixed payment claim by way of interest or coupon rate as also maturity. Equity stake by an investor provides him an ownership right in the corporate entity and is rewarded by way of dividend, in case announced by board of the company subject to earning profit and capital appreciation.

Stocks are equity claims on the net profits earned by the corporate and assets of a corporation. Equity has a residual claim, that is, after taking care of all other outside liabilities. The liability towards equity in private limited or public limited companies is limited to the extent of equity stake in the company. That means in the eventuality of losing money because of business getting wound up, the maximum loss that can occur to an investor is the amount that he has invested as equity in the company. Outside liabilities include creditors' payments, tax payable, debt payable, etc. Equity holders receive dividends or capital appreciation. In case a corporate decides to retain surplus generated, it reinvests in the venture to expand business operations, so as to earn more profit in future to enhance the shareholders' value. Losses to equity holders are limited to the extent of original investment made by shareholders.

Maturity of Claim

As per maturity of claim financial markets can be divided into money markets and capital markets.

Money markets securities are short-term debt securities, that is, having less than one year of maturity and being highly marketable. Examples of money market instruments include treasury bills of Government of India, commercial papers, certificate of deposits, saving deposits, repurchase agreements, time deposits of less than a year maturity, etc. Capital market instruments are riskier in nature and with long-term duration. Examples of capital market instruments include bonds, equity shares of corporates, long-term fixed deposits, LIC policies, long-term bonds, derivatives, etc.

Primary and Secondary Markets

With regard to implications of claim, financial markets are divided into primary market and secondary market. For the first time or whenever a company comes out with issuance of stock or bonds, it does so through primary market, while the same instrument when it gets exchanged amongst investors to realize gains or minimize losses are transacted in the secondary market.

Delivery Characteristics

As per the timing of delivery, financial instruments are classified as cash or spot payment at the time of transaction, forward, or future payment on some future date, as agreed to between the parties involved.

Organizational Structure

Based on organizational structure, financial markets are classified into exchange-traded markets and over-the-counter (OTC) markets. Transactions in case of exchange-traded markets are channelized through a central source, that is, an organization acts as an intermediary to connect buyers and sellers. Therefore, it enables a better enforcement of transactions and protects the interests of buyers and sellers well with regard to payments and delivery of scripts. The examples of exchange-traded markets include National Stock Exchange of India (NSE), Bombay

Stock Exchange (BSE), New York Stock Exchange (NYSE), London Stock Exchange, etc. OTC markets are decentralized and have multiple intermediaries who facilitate interaction between buyers and sellers. Therefore, the transaction cost in such markets is low. However, these markets are a bit unregulated. Some examples of OTC markets are forex markets and markets for certain debt instruments. With fast growth in electronic trading, OTC markets are also growing fast.

OVER-THE-COUNTER EXCHANGE OF INDIA (OTCEI)

This market was incorporated in India in 1990 as a Section 25 company under the Companies Act 1956. Many financial institutions have jointly promoted OTCEI, such as, UTI, ICICI, IDBI, SBI Capital Markets Ltd., IFCI, GIC, and Canbank Financial Services Ltd. This has been recognized as a stock exchange under Section 4 of the Securities Contracts Regulation Act, 1956. OTCEI was established to not only provide a platform to investors to raise funds in a cost effective manner, but also to ensure transparent and efficient mode of trading. Such markets do not have any centralized trading facility as transactions are privately negotiated between the parties. It involves a greater degree of counter party risk because of non-regulation. It is a 'floor-less exchange' where all transactions are computerized, be it trading, billing, payments, etc. OTC designated dealers undertake their operations through computer terminals which are linked to a central computer. All quotes and transactions reached through negotiated deals are recorded and processed. The scripts transacted on exchange-traded markets are not traded on OTCEI in Indian markets.

OTCEI permits trading of only those stocks which are from listed companies. Listing can be obtained by the companies having equity capital in the range of ₹30 lakhs to 25 crores. Closely held companies, venture capital companies, and companies which are not listed on any other recognized stock exchange can be listed on OTCEI, subject to their offer of equity to the public fulfils certain specified criteria and the company is not carrying on the business of investment, leasing, finance, hire-purchase, or amusement parks.

INVESTOR'S OBJECTIVES

Every investor, whether investing in financial instruments or real assets, looks for rewards by way of returns on the amount invested. These returns need to be higher than the safe or risk-free return on deposits. He also looks for returns to be measurable with due cost associated for decision-making, be it by him or some other professional. As expected returns would accrue in the future, there would be uncertainty in the probability distribution of returns called associated risk. Following are the three aspects an investor would like to ensure that expected returns should take care.

(i) Time value to forego consumption as measured by pure *rate of interest* which is defined as the exchange rate between future consumption and present consumption. Market forces would determine this rate.

(ii) Adjustment for inflation to be taken care of in future returns, that is, in case future payment diminishes in value on account of inflation, then the investor will look for an interest rate that will take care of pure time value of money including *expected inflation* expense.

(iii) As future payments on investments involve risk, that is, uncertainty, thus investor will demand an interest rate that also takes care of providing *a risk premium* to cover the investment risk.

Keeping above aspects in view, an investor undertakes an exercise of estimating return and risk for individual securities which is called security analysis, and is to maximize the returns for given risk or to minimize the risk for given returns.

PORTFOLIO CONCEPTS

Every investor combines securities having characteristics of risk and return to optimize his returns for a given risk. Combining different securities with risk and return characteristics is called building a *portfolio*. Portfolio results in combined returns and associated risk which may or may not possess characteristics of their individual parts. *Portfolio analysis* attempts to diagnose risk and return for individual securities and works out the implications of interactive effects of combining securities in terms of associated risk and return. *Portfolio selection* enables an analyst to pick up one best portfolio that would suit the risk return preferences of investors. *Portfolio management* is the dynamic function of evaluating and revising the portfolio consisting of combination of securities so as to achieve the stated investor objectives.

INVESTMENT PROCESS

Investment process involves security analysis that attempts to work out intrinsic value (IV) of security-based projections or expected prices of the stocks and dividends that would be realized on a given stock. In case intrinsic value of a stock is greater than current market price it is advisable to purchase the stock, while if intrinsic value of a stock is less than current price it is advisable to sell the stock.

- If IV > Current Market Price → Purchase
- If IV < Current Market Price → Sale

What matters is the computation of intrinsic value of a stock which basically requires making reasonable and realistic assumptions about the future to arrive at its present value.

TYPES OF MARKET TRANSACTIONS

Investor must know the way orders are placed in the market for transaction of secondary securities. Usually investor is required to instruct his broker about the order. The key concern of the investor is to get the best deal for the transaction he would like to have, that is, the best price to buy or sell stocks. Basically there are two broad categories of transactions namely—buy orders and sell orders. *Buy orders* are placed by the investor when he anticipates rise in the price of a stock. While *sell orders* are further divided into two categories—selling long or selling short. *Sell long order* relates to when the investor who owns the stock anticipates a decline in its price and hence decides to sell it. Such a sell order is called sell long order, particularly as the security is owned by the seller which he decides to sell. An investor exercises a *sell short order* which is peculiar, as in this case the investor borrows stocks and enters into sell short order deal, anticipating price decline. In case the actual price of the stock declines, investor buys the required number of shares of the company at a lower price and returns the borrowed stocks. Investor thus gains by the difference between sale price and purchase price of share. However, incase share price does not decline, he would still need to return the borrowed shares by incurring the loss to the extent of rise in price and other expenses, if any.

PRICE LIMIT ORDERS

While buying or selling of securities, an investor can execute his orders at a price that he would like to or at the prevailing market price. Accordingly, orders are termed as *market orders* and *limit orders*. Market orders are executed instantaneously at the prevailing current price in the exchange. Mostly investors prefer this because of its inherent advantage of execution. Investor is sure of buying or selling stocks he would like to at the prevailing price. The main disadvantage of placing market orders is that investor would not be sure of the price at which order will be executed, unless he receives a confirmation from his broker about execution of the order. Limit orders take care of the major disadvantage of market orders as the investor specifies the price at which he would like his order—buy or sell—to get executed. In case of buy order, the investor specifies the maximum price he would pay for the share and in case of sell order he specifies the minimum price he will accept for the order. Thus the execution of an order is uncertain till such time it materializes at the specified limit orders.

RISK AND RETURN MEASUREMENT

Every investor would like to know the return and risk associated with the investment. Therefore, as an investor he needs to know and understand how to measure the rate of return and associated risk in the investment correctly. One can estimate historical rates of return and risk by accessing concrete data about the past and the same can be used to arrive at expected rates of return and risk by using statistical techniques. For instance if you have bought a stock at ₹50 and after a year sell it at ₹70 and in the interim period you get a dividend of ₹5; you have to consider all these to calculate the return. You may be required to know the point of time when you received the dividend. We are basically interested in change in the wealth as a result of foregone consumption that resulted from this investment decision. Considering the same example, if you do not get any dividend and have sold the share at ₹70 after a year of buying it at ₹50; the period for which you held this investment is called holding period and the return for that period is called holding period return. Following is the formula to calculate holding period return (HPR).

$$\text{HPR} = \text{Ending Value of Investment/Beginning Value of Investment}$$
$$= ₹70/₹50 = 1.40$$

This value can be either 0 or a positive number but can never be a negative. A HPR value greater than 1 indicates an increase in the wealth while a HPR value of less than 1 would indicate decline in wealth. For computing holding period yield (HPY) that is computed in percentage terms we need to subtract 1 and multiply the figure by 100. In this instance, HPY will be $1.40 - 1 = 0.40 \times 100 = 40\%$.

To find annual HPY, one can compute it for a year and subtract 1 from it. For instance, a share bought at ₹500 gets sold at ₹1000 after three years then HPR is 100%, that is, $(2 - 1) \times 100$ for three years. Following are the steps to convert it into annual HPY.

$$\text{HPR} = 1000/500 = 2.0$$
$$\text{Annual HPY} = [(2)^{1/3} - 1] \times 100 = [1.2599 - 1] \times 100 = 0.2599 \times 100 = 25.99\%$$

Following is how we can compute Annual HPY if the same investment is held for about 30 months instead of 3 years.

$$\text{Annual HPY} = [(2)^{1/2.5} - 1] \times 100 = [1.3195 - 1] \times 100 = .3195 \times 100 = 31.95\%$$

Same logic can be extended to find annual holding period return for the number of days for which the investment is held. For instance, if a share is bought at ₹200 and is sold after 100 days at ₹180, the HPR will be 0.90 and HPY will be minus 10%, that is, $[(0.90 - 1) \times 100 = -0.10 \times 100]$. Following is the way we compute annual holding period return for a period of 100 days.

$$\text{Numbers of years} = 100/365 \text{ days} = 0.27397.$$
$$\text{Annual HPY} = [(180/200)^{1/.27397} - 1] \times 100 = [(180/200)^{3.65} - 1] \times 100$$
$$= [0.6807 - 1] \times 100 = -0.3192 \times 100 = -31.925\%$$

It is important to understand that certain inherent assumptions are made to convert HPY into annual holding period, that is, constant annual yield for each year. Mean returns can be calculated for a single investment by arithmetic mean (AM) or geometric mean (GM). The sum of annual HPY is divided by the number of years to arrive at AM mean, that is, AM = Σ HPY/n where Σ HPY is the sum of annual holding period yields and n is the number of years. To calculate GM geometric mean, it would be nth root of the HPRs for number of years, that is, GM = $(\pi \text{ HPR})^{1/n} - 1$, where π is the product of annual holding period returns.

Therefore, GM = $(\text{HPR}_1) \times (\text{HPR}_2) \ldots \ldots \ldots (\text{HPR}_n)$.

Let us consider an example to understand AM and GM concepts with the help of an example.

Year	Beginning Value	Ending Value	HPR	HPY
1	200	250	1.25	0.25
2	250	180	0.72	–0.28
3	180	200	1.11	0.11

$$AM = [\{(0.25) + (-0.28) + (0.11)\}/3] \times 100 = 0.0266 \times 100 = 2.66\%$$
$$GM = [(1.25 \times 0.72 \times 1.11)^{1/3} - 1] \times 100 = [1 - 1] \times 100 = 0\%$$

GM indicates the compound annual rate of return depends upon end value of investment viz-à-viz beginning value of investment. Normally AM returns would be higher than GM while measuring long-term returns from an investment, except when returns are same in different years. In the example given, if 3rd year ending value of the investment is say 280, then AM and GM will be as following.

$$AM = [\{(0.25) + (-0.28) + (0.555)\}/3] \times 100 = [0.175] \times 100 = 17.5\%$$
$$GM = [(1.25 \times 0.72 \times 1.55)^{1/3} - 1] \times 100 = [1.1173 - 1] \times 100$$
$$= 0.1173 \times 100 = 11.73\%$$

When an investment gives the same rate of return every year, the GM and AM will be the same.

When there is risk associated with a stock that can be measured by knowing the probability of different returns that are likely to be derived, one can calculate expected returns on the stock in following manner.

$$n\Sigma P_i \times R_i \text{ where } P_i \text{ is probability of occurrence of } R_i \text{ return } i = 1$$

An investment portfolio is a collection of financial assets. Assuming that the investor is rational, implying averseness to risk, he would always prefer to invest in a portfolio as against a single asset. This would help him in diversifying a portion of risk as against putting all his money in one asset. The diversified portfolio will always help him to better manage the risk.

Expected returns [E(R)] for the portfolio having number of securities is calculated as weighted average of expected profits of each asset in the portfolio.

$$E(R) = w_1R_1 + w_2R_q + \dots + w_nR_n$$

For example, if an individual investor having two stocks in the portfolio A and B is expecting return of 20% from stock A and 5% from stock B, and he has allocated 75% of his money on stock A and 25% on stock B. His expected return from the portfolio can be computed as under:

$$E(R) = (0.75 \times 0.20 + 0.25 \times 0.05) \times 100 = 0.1625 \times 100 = 16.25\%$$

E(R) is not a guaranteed return, however it can be used to estimate future value of portfolio and helps in understanding deviation—positive or negative—from actual return in future. This analysis helps an investor to make a better decision.

Variance (σ^2) of return measures average squared deviation of returns from the mean return. It measures variability from an average return, thus showing volatility which is a measure of risk. Variance in return of a portfolio is computed by finding the probability-weighted average of squared deviations from the expected returns.

Assume that an analyst writes a report on a company and, based on the research, assigns the following probabilities to next year's sales:

Year	Forecasted Return		Expected Portfolio Return (Assuming that investor invests 75% of his total investment on stock A and remaining 25% on stock B
	Asset A	Asset B	
2010	12	18	$[0.75 \times 12 + 0.25 \times 18] \times 100 = 13.5\%$
2011	14	16	$[0.75 \times 14 + 0.25 \times 16] \times 100 = 14.5\%$
2012	16	14	$[0.75 \times 16 + 0.25 \times 14] \times 100 = 15.5\%$
2013	18	12	$[0.75 \times 18 + 0.25 \times 12] \times 100 = 16.5\%$

Therefore, expected value of portfolio return is $(13.5 + 14.5 + 15.5 + 16.5)/4 = 15\%$

Following will be the variance of expected portfolio return.

$$[(13.5 - 15)^2 + (14.5 - 15)^2 + (15.5 - 15)^2 + (16.5 - 15)^2]/N - 1,$$

where N is the number of observations

Standard deviation of the portfolio is given by:

$$\{[(13.5 - 15)^2 + (14.5 - 15)^2 + (15.5 - 15)^2 + (16.5 - 15)^2]/N - 1\}^{1/2},$$

which is the root of the above equation.

$$= (5/3)^{1/2} = 1.2909 - 1 = 0.2909$$

Therefore, associated risk is 29.09%

In comparison, if we consider portfolio of two assets giving the following returns:

Year	Forecasted Return		Expected portfolio return (assuming that investor invests 50% of his total investment on stock A and remaining 50% on stock B
	Asset A	Asset B	
2010	12	18	$(0.5 \times 12 + 0.5 \times 18) \times 100 = 15.0\%$
2011	14	16	$(0.5 \times 14 + 0.5 \times 16) \times 100 = 15.0\%$
2012	16	14	$(0.5 \times 16 + 0.5 \times 14) \times 100 = 15.0\%$
2013	18	12	$(0.5 \times 18 + 0.5 \times 12) \times 100 = 15.0\%$

In that case the standard deviation would work out to be zero, implying there is no risk in this portfolio. It is so because Asset A and Asset B have perfectly negative correlation and investor holds exactly half of his portfolio in each asset. Standard deviation of a portfolio will therefore be zero.

By using correlation between asset A and asset B portfolio variance can also be computed using the following equation:

$$\text{Portfolio Variance} = w_A^2 * \sigma^2(A_A) + w_B^2 * \sigma^2(A_B) + 2 * (w_A) * (w_B) * \text{Cov}(A_A, A_B)$$

where w_A and w_B are portfolio weights, $\sigma^2(A_A)$ and $\sigma^2(A_B)$ are variances and $\text{Cov}(A_A, A_B)$ is the covariance. Covariance helps in finding to what extent returns on two risky assets move together. A negative covariance between two assets would indicate that returns move inversely to each other. However, to identify the strength of relationship between two assets which are directly or inversely related, one needs to use correlation between the assets.

Therefore, in the above equation covariance can be given as $r_{AB}\sigma_A\sigma_B$, where r_{AB} is correlation between asset A and asset B, while σ_A and σ_B are the standard deviation of returns on asset A and asset B respectively. In the instance given above as r_{AB} is -1,

Portfolio variance $= 0.5^2 \times 20 + 0.5^2 \times 20 + 2 \times 0.5 \times 0.5 \times (-1) \times 4.472 \times 4.472$
Standard Deviance $= (0.5^2 \times 20 + 0.5^2 \times 20 + 2 \times 0.5 \times 0.5 \times (-1) \times 4.472 \times 4.472)^{1/2} = 0$

Therefore, standard deviation in investment decision is used to measure volatility of investment which gives historical volatility of an investment. High volatility implies greater risk and low volatility indicates lower risk. It may be noted that correlation coefficient r_{AB} that affects covariance can vary between $+1$ and -1. A value of $+1$ reflects that the assets have positive perfect correlation, implying that returns move together in a completely linear manner in same direction while -1 indicates that returns move in completely linear manner but in opposite direction. A correlation of 0 would indicate that assets are absolutely independent of each other and their returns do not have any effect on each other. Following is summary of the relationship between correlation coefficient returns and risk for a two asset portfolio.

Correlation coefficient	Return	Risk
+1 between two assets	Returns would be between two assets held in isolation	Risk would be between two assets held in isolation
zero between two assets	Returns would be between two assets held in isolation	Risk would lie between risk of most risky asset and less than risk of least risky asset but greater than zero
−1 between two assets	Returns would be between two assets held in isolation	Risk would be between most risky asset and zero

Coefficient of variation (CV) is a measure of relative variability that indicates risk per unit of return and is a better indicator of associated risk on an investment per unit of expected return. It helps in comparing different securities as also different portfolios to know which asset or portfolio is a better proposition amongst the given choices. The following is the formula to calculate CV.

$$CV = \frac{\text{Standard deviation of returns}}{\text{Expected rate of returns}}$$

$$= \frac{\sigma_i}{E(R)}$$

For example, given the following details about two assets:

	Asset A	Asset B
Standard Deviation	0.25%	0.20%
Expected Returns	12.5%	9%
CV	0.20	0.022

Therefore, although asset B has lower standard deviation indicating low risk compared to asset A, but looking at CV asset A should be preferred, as it has lower risk per unit of return.

There are two broad categories of risk to which investor need to respond to manage it. These are called diversifiable, such as unsystematic risk, and non-diversifiable, such as systematic risk. Investor can manage unsystematic risk by adding stocks in his portfolio to derive a benefit of reducing the risk for a given return or maximizing the return for a given risk. However, the benefit of managing unsystematic risk accrues up to a point and thereafter, even if investor keeps adding securities he may not derive much benefit out of it, as shown in Fig. 15.3. Systematic risk cannot be managed by adding securities in the portfolio. This risk affects all securities with different intensity, depending on the industry/sector or the company.

Systematic risk comprises of business risk, financial risk, liquidity risk, foreign exchange risk, and country risk. Business risk arises as a result of nature of business

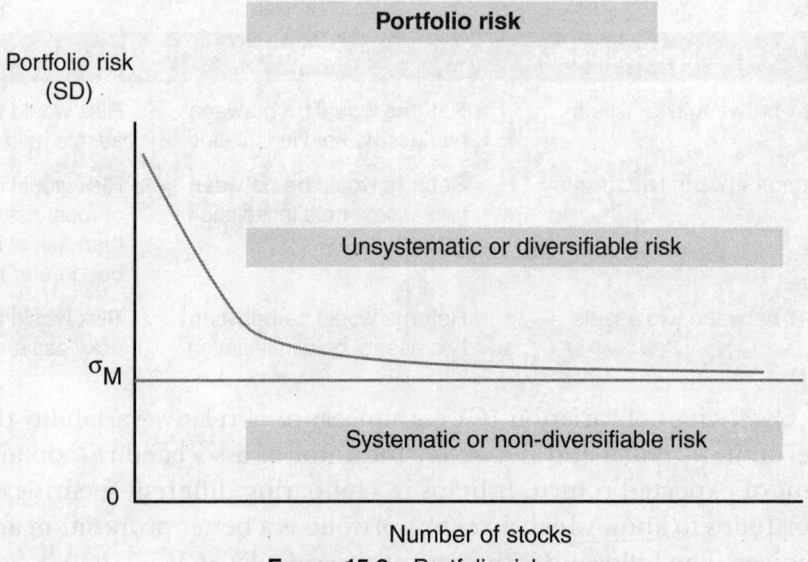

FIGURE 15.3   Portfolio risk

and sector in which it is being operated which results into uncertainty of income flows, volatility in sales, and operating leverage that a business can derive. For example, seasonal businesses, dependent upon weather vagaries, would have uncertainty linked to weather conditions while a business backed up by technology that has patent and good market potential will have good operating margins as also sales. Financial risk arises as a result of debt financing that burden the company with fixed payment liabilities on account of interest and principal repayment, irrespective of earnings. Therefore, debt financing creates uncertainty of stockholders' income and causes an increase in risk premium for the stockholder. Liquidity risk relates to the degree of certainty to get the stock converted into cash in the secondary market and the certainty about the price that can be received for the stock. The uncertainty that arises when an investor buys stocks that are denominated in a currency other than that of the investor, he will be subject to exchange rate risk, that is, to get his returns converted into home currency. The unexpected changes in the political and economic front cause uncertainty in returns from the stock which are associated with country risk. Therefore, in case an investor invests money in a country having political and economic instability, he should look for including country risk premium while determining required rate of return. Therefore, managing systematic risk that affects all stocks cannot be managed by diversification or adding more stocks in the portfolio. These risk factors, as explained earlier, arise because of macro-economic conditions, interest rates, inflation, exchange rates, business cycles, etc. This aspect of risk was studied by Sharpe, Treynor, and Lintner in 1960s to develop an asset pricing model that helps in measurement of systematic risk of a particular asset. To measure this risk they observed that certain factors, such as increase in interest rates affect all stock prices to go down but some stock prices fall more than others and therefore they simply regressed the returns for the 'market portfolio'. Say BSE or NSE returns for all listed stocks against the returns of an individual asset, that is, $Stock_A = \alpha + \beta$. Market returns wherein the slope of the regression line—*beta*— measures an asset's systematic (non diversifiable) risk and α is an intercept that indicates stock A's returns, if market returns are zero. Therefore, beta is a risk coefficient which measures the sensitivity of the particular stock's return to changes in market conditions.

In other words, after estimating beta, which measures a specific asset or portfolio's systematic risk, estimates of the other variables in the model may be obtained to calculate an asset's or portfolio's required return.

$Stock_A$ expected or required return = R_F (risk free rate of return)
+ [β_i (beta for the asset) × k_m (expected return on market portfolio)
− R_F (risk free rate of return)]

Normally cyclical companies like auto companies have high betas while relatively stable companies such as electricity or water, have low betas. β could be positive, negative, or a number zero. If it is 2.5 for a stock, it would indicate that stock is two and a half times responsive to market returns, that is, if market returns increases by

5%, stock returns would increase by 12.5%. If β is 1, it would mean that returns on the stock increases by the same proportion as market, that is, 5% increase in market returns will result in 5% increase in stock return. If β is zero, it would indicate that stock returns are unaffected by market returns. Therefore, capital asset pricing model (CAPM) helps in understanding the expected or required rates of return on risky assets. The model also helps in comparing the estimated rate of return to the required rate of return implied by CAPM so as to know whether stock is over/under valued that can help in taking decision to buy or sell a stock. CAPM model is extensively utilized to make investment decisions from the point of view of managing systematic risk. Some of the drawbacks of CAPM model include that it basically relies on historical data which in reality may mean that the betas may or may not actually reflect the future variability of returns. The model also assumes that markets are efficient, that is, all information is available instantly to all investors and gets absorbed in the market quickly which may be unrealistic. However, studies reveal that there exists expectational relationship described by the CAPM in active markets such as the NYSE. Keeping in view some of the limitations of CAPM model, it should be utilized with certain degree of caution.

SUMMARY

Financial system in an economy performs various functions to efficiently channelize flow of funds between users and savers of money. Bonds and stocks are common financial assets. Bonds are offered by corporates, government, or other bodies such as municipal corporations to investors for investing the funds on projects. Equity is a financial instrument that does not have any contractual obligation to pay cash. It provides an ownership right to the subscriber or buyer of the instrument in a corporate entity. Financial markets are classified based on five key criteria namely—nature of claim, maturity of claim, seasoning of claim, timing of delivery, and organizational structure. Every investor whether investing in financial instruments or real assets looks for rewards by way of returns on the amount invested commensurate with risk taken. Portfolio is combining different securities having risk and return characteristics. Investment process involves security analysis that attempts to work out intrinsic value (IV) of a security based on projections or expected prices of the stocks and dividends that would be realized on given stock. The two broad categories of risk that an investor needs to manage are called diversifiable, such as unsystematic risk, and non-diversifiable, such as systematic risk. Systematic risk comprises of business risk, financial risk, liquidity risk, foreign exchange risk, and country risk which affects all stocks. This aspect of risk was studied by Sharpe, Treynor, and Lintner in 1960s to develop an asset pricing model called capital asset pricing model that helps in measurement of systematic risk of a particular asset. It is measured through a risk coefficient called *beta* which measures the sensitivity of the particular stock's return to changes in market conditions.

KEYWORDS

Beta It is a risk coefficient which measures the sensitivity of the particular stock's return to changes in market conditions.

Coefficient of variation (CV) It is a measure of relative variability that indicates risk per unit of return.

Equity It provides ownership right in a corporate entity and is a financial instrument that does not have any contractual obligation to pay cash.

Financial asset It is intangible and is backed up by the monetary value of a physical item or flow of cash.

Holding period return (HPR) It is the ending value of investment/beginning value of investment.

Investment It is defined as current deployment of funds for a specific time period so as to fetch future payments that need to take care of time duration for which funds are deployed, expected rate of inflation, and risk associated with future payments.

Limit orders When an investor specifies the price at which he would like his order, buying or selling, to get executed.

Market orders They are executed instantaneously at the prevailing current price in the exchange.

Money markets securities They are short-term debt securities, that is, less than one year of maturity and are highly marketable.

Over-the-Trade Counter Exchange of India (OTCEI) It is a market that does not have any centralized trading facility as transactions are privately negotiated between the parties. It is a 'floor-less exchange' where all transactions are computerized, be it trading, billing, payments, etc.

Portfolio It is combining different securities having risks and returns as a characteristic.

Systematic risk It affects all stocks and is not diversifiable. It comprises of business risk, financial risk, liquidity risk, foreign exchange risk, and country risk.

EXERCISES

Concept Review Questions

1. Define equity as a financial instrument and differentiate between debt and equity.
2. What are the key functions played by the financial system in an economy?
3. What is meant by time value of money?
4. Differentiate between bonds and stocks as financial assets. What are the main constituents of systematic risk? Explain.
5. What are the five criteria based on which financial markets can be classified? Explain.
6. Differentiate between exchange-traded markets and over-the-counter market.
7. From the perspective of investors what are the three aspects that an investor attempts to take care while investing in securities?
8. Define portfolio. Differentiate between portfolio analysis, portfolio selection, and portfolio management.
9. What is meant by intrinsic value of a security? Explain.
10. Differentiate between sell long order and sell short order.
11. Differentiate between market orders and limit orders.

12. Differentiate between holding period return and holding period yield.
13. What is the significance of variance and standard deviation of portfolio return? Explain.
14. Why is it said that coefficient of variation (CV) is a better measure of risk? Explain.
15. Differentiate between systematic and unsystematic risk.
16. Explain the significance of Beta in capital asset pricing model.

Critical Thinking Questions

1. Differentiate between investment in physical assets and financial assets. What matters the most for growth of the economy? Explain.
2. 'It is said that OTCEI markets are more efficient and less costly to operate.' Collect a data on operations of BSE and OTCEI market in India and analyse to justify or contradict the above statement and its relevance.
3. Collect the data on Indian money market operations viz-à-viz capital market operations. Analyse the two to understand importance and implications of these markets in Indian economy. What do you think needs to be further strength-

ened to develop financial markets in India? Explain.

4. 'Wealthy individuals having no time to take care of their savings provides a great opportunity to financial intermediaries to develop their business.' What type of specific opportunities may lie to be efficiently tapped? Explain.

5. 'It is said that bundle of assets combined into a portfolio can better help in managing risk.' Explain

by considering a set of five stocks from BSE and working out necessary measures to prove that risk can be managed well by combining which set of stocks and why?

6. Consider five stocks from BSE from the IT sector and estimate their Beta. Analyse and interpret the values of Beta from investor(s) perspective.

REFERENCES

Fisher, D.E., and R.J. Jordan (1995), *Security Analysis and Portfolio Management*, 6th edition, Prentice-Hall/Pearson Edu, New Delhi.

Francis, J.C. (1991), *Investments: Analysis and Management*, 5th edition, McGraw Hill, Singapore.

Fuller, Rusell J. and James L. Farell, *Modern Investment and Security Analysis*, McGraw Hill, International Ed, New York.

Harrington, D.R. (1987), 'Modern Portfolio Theory', *The Capital Asset Pricing Model and Arbitrage Pricing Theory: A User's Guide*, 2nd edition, Prentice Hall, Englewood Cliffs, NJ.

Jones, Charles. P (2004), *Investments—Analysis and Management*, John Wiley and Sons (Asia) Pte. Ltd.

Lintner, John (1965b), 'Security Prices, Risk and Maximal Gains from Diversification', *Journal of Finance*, vol. 20, December, pp. 587–615.

Ranganatham, M. and R. Madhumathi (2006), *Investment Analysis and Portfolio Management*, Pearson Education, New Delhi.

Reilly, Frank K. and Keith C. Brown (2007), *Investment Analysis and Portfolio Management*, 8th edition, Thomson Learning, Australia.

Sharpe, W.F. (1964), 'Capital Asset Prices: A Theory of Market Equilibrium under Conditions of Risk', *The Journal of Finance*, vol. 19, no. 3, pp. 425–442.

Treynor, J.L. (1965), 'How to Rate Management of Investment Funds', *Harvard Business Review*, vol. 43, pp. 63–75.

Part III
Excelling through People

16

Overview of Human Resource Management

INTRODUCTION

Organizations have been becoming complex over the past few years due to the fast-changing business environment and growing uncertainty. Human resource management (HRM) is essential to the management of an organization to effectively respond to the demands of this complex environment. The difference in the performance of two organizations having the same physical resources can only be traced to the difference that they have in their human resource base and the management practices followed to manage human resources.

What is HRM? What does it constitute? What helps in creating a distinct edge over competitors by investing in HRM? We shall be focusing our attention on organizations that have been successful due to HRM.

HUMAN RESOURCE MANAGEMENT

There are various definitions of HRM. Some of them are given here.
- It deals with the staffing functions of the organization such as human resources planning, recruitment, training, career planning, compensation package, and performance appraisal.
- It deals with all aspects of human resources that enable effective use of the same to improve organizational effectiveness.

Learning Objectives

After studying this chapter, you will be able to:
- Understand the concept of human resource management (HRM)
- Examine HRM in the current complex business environment
- Understand the objectives of HRM functions
- Analyse the steps in HR planning process
- Learn about the various facets with which HRM deals with

- It supports activities such as training, recruitment, orientation, motivation of employees, and compensation-related issues.
- It refers to the practices and policies related to management of people (Dessler 2002).
- It consists of various activities required to enhance the effectiveness of an organization's people to achieve organizational goals and objectives (Lewis, et al. 2001).

Thus, the HRM function deals with various activities ranging from staffing needs of an organization such as deployment of required staff through contractors, recruitment, and training of staff to create an efficient working environment. Human resource management also includes devising practices that encourage the staff to work efficiently, and to develop and ensure that personnel and management practices of the organization adhere to various regulations. It directs an organization's approach to employee benefits and compensation, employee records, and personnel policies. Human resource management enables the most effective and efficient contribution from human resources so as to achieve organizational and individual goals (Fig. 16.1). It can also be described as effective managing, that is, planning, organizing, directing, and controlling the functions related to employing,

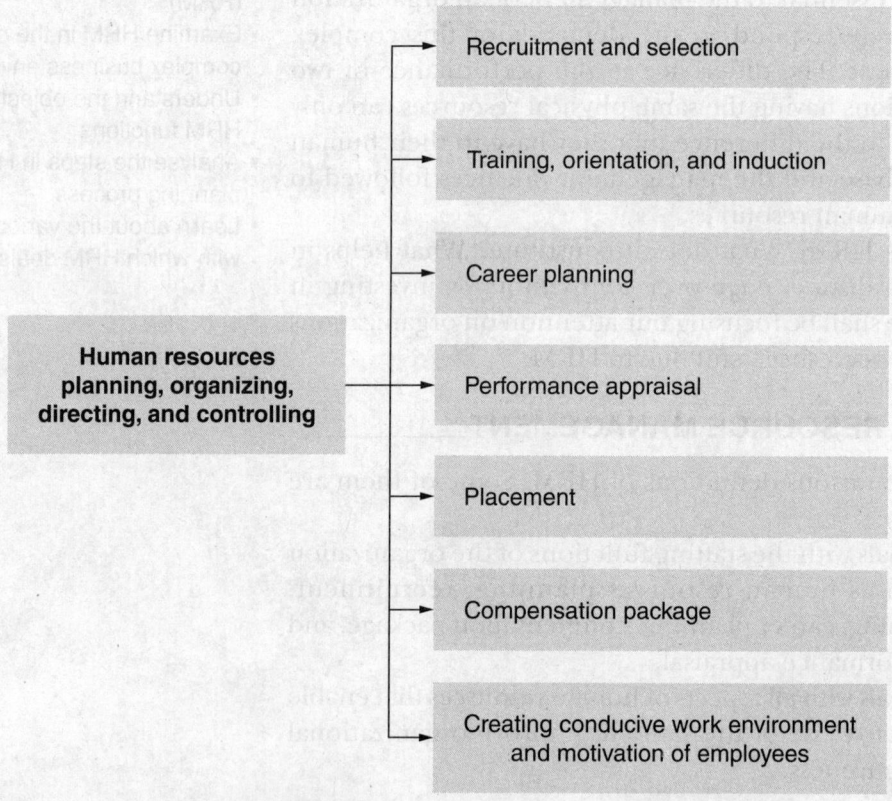

FIGURE 16.1   Functions of HRM

developing, and duly compensating human resources. This lead to healthy relationships at work and employees feel motivated to deliver their best to the organization.

Objectives of HRM

The objectives of the HRM function are as under:
- facilitating achievement of organizational goals;
- effective and efficient deployment of human skills, abilities, and knowledge;
- providing inspired, motivated, and trained employees;
- communicating HRM practices and policies to employees;
- providing scope for creativity and innovation to employees;
- enhancing job satisfaction to employees;
- improving the quality of professional life in the organization;
- creating healthy work relations in the organization;
- operating on ethical policies;
- complying with statutory requirements;
- to work towards corporate social responsibility (CSR); and
- managing change.

Some of the organizations that have successfully implemented HR policies to
effectively respond to the HR-related challenges and in turn contributed to the
achievement of HRM objectives are National Thermal Power Corporation (NTPC),
Bharat Heavy Electrical Limited (BHEL), Oil and Natural Gas Corporation (ONGC),
Tata Consultancy Services (TCS), Infosys, Wipro, Ranbaxy Ltd, Canara Bank, etc.

Importance of HRM

In the fast changing complex environment, human resource managers need to function within the context of fast changes. These changes take place because of information
explosion and technological advances and developments occurring almost every day
(Holman 1996). The role of HRM within an organization is becoming more crucial in
the present scenario. Other managerial inputs such as machines, materials, methods,
and markets are far more predictable than the response of human resources.
Therefore, given all other resources, what matters the most is human resources and
HRM in achievement of organizational goals. Today no organization can:
- risk employing the wrong person for the job;
- have a high employee turnover, particularly when substantial investment gets
  made on a new employee by imparting him/her with the requisite in-house
  training;
- have demotivated employees;
- have employees who waste their time on the job;
- get quoted as an organization not adhering to statutory provisions;
- make employees feel that they are not being paid commensurate with their
  contribution to the organization; and
- lag behind in imparting training to its employees that would adversely affect
  their effectiveness and overall performance.

All the above factors make the role of HRM crucial to the achievement of organizational goals in the current business environment. Organizations, today, have to focus on creating a distinctive competitive advantage within an organization by focusing on HRM. The employees of an organization create value through cost reduction, quality improvement, and creating unique products and services for their customers. Their competencies, capabilities, and knowledge are rare and probably difficult to be reproduced or imitated. It can be honed only through organized teamwork to ensure multiplicative returns.

Tata Consultancy Services Limited (TCS)

Tata Consultancy Services Limited (TCS) is the world's leading information technology consulting, services, and business process outsourcing organization that envisioned and pioneered the adoption of the flexible global business practices that today enable companies to operate more efficiently and produce more value. TCS started its operations in 1968, when the IT services industry did not have any presence. Today, the company operates in 34 countries across six continents and offers a comprehensive range of services across diverse industries. TCS has a product range offerings in diverse areas such as banking, accounting, insurance, financial services, security, manufacturing, life sciences and healthcare tools, government, energy and utilities, and transportation.

Its total revenue earnings increased from ₹7703 crore in 2003–04 to ₹13245 crore in 2005–06, that is, 31 per cent average annual growth rate in revenue. Its net profit increased from ₹1697 crore in 2003–04 to ₹2883 crore in 2005–06, that is, 30 per cent annual average growth rate. The company has been earning a gross margin of around 45 per cent and a net margin of around 21 per cent during the last three years. All this extraordinary financial performance could be achieved because of having a pool of talented human resources that the company inducts, trains, develops, and retains.

The emphasis that the company has been laying on human resources has enabled it to become one of the world's leading IT companies. Six of the Fortune Top 10 companies are among its valued customers. The company's business model is people driven and, therefore, strategically the company is endowed with one of the most enviable pool of talent from across the globe. TCS brings together the most complete team with a rare mix of domain, technology, and project management experts to deal and deliver on every project it undertakes. TCS provides its people with careers across business and technology areas; opportunities to be at the forefront of e-revolution; global exposure with projects in over 50 countries and 800 clients, many of them Fortune 500 standouts; world-class training; the opportunity to learn continuously; and an open door energetic environment with world-class infrastructure.

TCS gives the utmost importance to the training and education of its people as a continuous value-adding process. This approach hones, improves, and enhances their skills, making the organization stronger. Its training and development centre introduces young graduates, from some of the best educational institutions in the world, to the TCS way of doing things. Business and technology experts from some of the best organizations in the world bring invaluable

(Contd)

Exhibit *(Contd)*

insights into their areas of expertise. Industry veterans who laid the foundation of the offshore services business form the backbone of their leadership team. TCS invests about 4 per cent of its annual revenues in training, a shining example of which can be seen at the state-of-the-art training centre in Thiruvananthapuram in the state of Kerala.

Source: Based on the information from www.tcs.com, accessed on 18 July 2007.

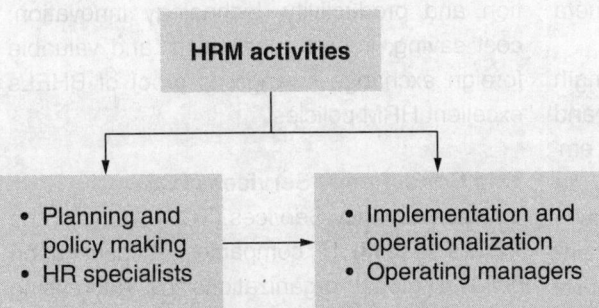

FIGURE 16.2 HRM activities

Who Performs HRM Activities?

In majority of medium to large organizations, HRM functions are performed by both professional HR managers as well as operating managers, supervisors, departmental heads, group heads, etc. (Fig. 16.2). Although devising HRM policies is the exclusive task of HR specialists, operating managers operationalize the same policies. The involvement of operating managers becomes imperative, as they have to effectively manage all resources at their disposal. However, smaller organizations may not be able to afford professional HR specialists and, therefore, operating mangers have to deal with various HRM functions such as scheduling work, recruitment and selection, compensation, rewards, and training.

Of all the resources in an organization, the only one that can be unpredictable is HR. With HR gaining more importance in the present information and knowledge age, companies need to devise effective HRM policies and practices to gain a distinctive advantage over their competitors. HRM planning, programming, review, and evaluation ensure that the right number and kind of people are made available at the right time to effectively implement the company's business plan. The main challenge that lies before HRM is to manage change by eliminating systems and practices that come in the way of effective implementation, and have ethical leaders at different tiers of the organization, outsourcing functions, services, and production processes.

HRM in Indian organizations

Bharat Heavy Electrical Limited (BHEL)
Bharat Heavy Electrical Limited (BHEL) is the largest engineering and manufacturing company in India in the energy-related/infrastructure sector. It was set up more than 40 years ago, ushering in the indigenous heavy electrical equipment industry in India; a dream that has been translated into reality. The company has a consistent

(Contd)

Exhibit   (*Contd*)

track record of performance as is reflected in its profits, earned continuously since 1971–72 and paying dividends since 1976–77.

BHEL's vision is to become a world-class engineering enterprise, committed to enhancing its stakeholders' value. The company is striving to give shape to its aspirations and fulfil the expectations of the country to become a global player.

The single and the most important strength of BHEL is its highly skilled, dedicated, and committed workforce of more than 42,600 employees. Every employee is provided with an equal opportunity for development and growth in his career. Continuous training and retraining, career planning, a positive work culture, and participative style of management have engendered development of a committed and motivated workforce setting new benchmarks and records in terms of productivity, quality, and responsiveness.

The company has a Human Resource Development Institute (HRDI) that develops skills in the areas of management training, research, consultancy, organizational development, and manpower planning. Over the years, the institute has acquired proficiency in imparting training to professionals in the field of strategic management, contract management, marketing management, project management, human resource management, activity-based costing, performance management, emotional intelligence, values laboratory, human-process laboratory, leadership development, team building, trainer development, and other functional and behavioural areas of management.

The company gives a lot of importance to training employees. The institute has acquired core competency in consultancy services, specifically in the field of contract management,

performance management, HRM, and organization development. It is a ground for experimenting with innovations in HRM and has set a number of benchmarks. The fact that the maximum number of Prime Minister's Shram Awards in 2004 were conferred to BHEL employees for their outstanding contribution towards production and productivity, technology innovation, cost saving, import substitution, and valuable foreign exchange savings, is proof of BHEL's excellent HRM policies.

Tata Consultancy Services (TCS)

Tata Consultancy Services (TCS) is one of the world's leading IT companies. It focuses on building global organizations by addressing their business challenges effectively. It continues to invest in new technologies, processes, and people, which can add the much needed value to its customers. It keeps coming out with novel concepts and ideas through TCS Innovation Labs and academic alliances, drawing upon the expertise of key partners. It keeps clients operating at the very edge of technological possibility.

Whether TCS is envisioning a business advantage, engineering an IT solution, or executing an outsourcing strategy, it helps its customers experience certainty in their every day business. The company reported 2006–07 global revenues of US$4.3 billion.

Working for and being with TCS is all about possibilities, growth, learning, teamwork, and leading change. At TCS, there is much more than just technology and software development. It encourages and inspires its people to think different, challenge the conventional, and innovate. There are people from diverse cultural and educational backgrounds who bring in a wealth of knowledge and experience that gives

(*Contd*)

Exhibit *(Contd)*

an opportunity to its employees to keep learning and expanding their horizons.

Ranbaxy Pharmaceuticals Inc.

Ranbaxy believes that human capital forms a critical part of an organization's portfolio of privileged assets. Ranbaxy Pharmaceuticals Inc. (RPI) is a multicultural company offering diversity within a fast-paced entrepreneurial environment. Whether it is the manufacturing or administration, it offers employees ample opportunities to grow, take control, and be decision-makers.

Being a small company, its employees can develop multiple areas of expertise to positively influence the company; along with the advantages of having global operations with many successful years of experience. Its lean and thin organizational structure enables each individual to exercise responsibility within the given framework of authority. The values, which guide the human resource function at RPI provide opportunities to all employees to realize their full potential and, in this process, build the Ranbaxy of tomorrow.

SAP Labs India

SAP Labs India, today, employs over 3,000 people. It is a place for ambitious, dedicated professionals who can deliver high-end software products and services for operations in Bangalore, Gurgaon, and Chandigarh. Its vision is to be a role model for software organizations worldwide and the talent pool at Labs India helps it achieve this. The unique corporate culture of SAP Labs India is based on open communication, flat hierarchies, strong emphasis on teamwork, and a high level of employee responsibility. This culture allows employees to adopt the challenges facing SAP as their own and inextricably tie in individual achievements to the success of the company.

SAP Labs India offers exceptional career opportunities for high achievers in a variety of areas. It is dedicated to providing employees with a fulfilling and career-enhancing work environment. Their core values are customer focus, quality, product excellence, integrity, commitment, and passion. On the road to realizing SAP's vision for 2010 is to become the leader in the business processes platform industry and, thus, contribute to large-scale economic growth by helping companies accelerate their business innovation. Agility, high performance, simplicity, co-innovation, and talent development are the company's values.

Working with the company provides the following to the employees:

- Opportunities to take on challenging assignments and work on the best of technologies
- Avenues to develop skills in niche areas. Strong emphasis is given on enhancing technical skills and business knowledge, facilitating a keen insight into business processes while pioneering e-business solutions
- Uninhibited growth through a unique learning system that focuses on individual interests and competencies

Employees can choose a career path in technical, managerial, production, or quality streams based on their interest and competency in relation to job requirements.

SAP Labs India is a truly global organization, providing growth opportunities and transfer across various subsidiaries of SAP and covering more than 50 countries.

Source: Based on the data from www.bhel.com/bhel/, accessed on 25 July 2007; www.tcs.com, accessed on 18 July 2007; www.ranbaxy.com, accessed on 25 July 2007; and www.sap.com/india/company/saplabs/index.epx, accessed on 31 July 2007.

HR PLANNING PROCESS

'Give me the right number of people, with the right knowledge and skills at the right time, and I will give you the results', is easier said than done. To accomplish this goal requires a strategic human resource planning that has three interrelated steps—planning, programming, implementing, review, and evaluation (Bateman and Snell 2004). Human resource managers have to synchronize their activities with the business plan of the organization to ensure that the right type and number of people are made available to different departments of an organization, in line with their contribution to the organizational goals. Keeping a plan in mind, the organization is expected to take steps for synchronizing human resources activities, such as recruitment, selection, placement, training, recognition and reward system, performance appraisal, and labour relations, with the organizational business plan. Lastly, HRM has to review and evaluate its actions to ensure that the steps taken are producing the expected results as per business plan and the corrective measures that need to be taken, in case they are not. The evaluation of human resource activities focuses on productivity, quality, quantity, innovation, and employee satisfaction levels.

DIFFERENT FACETS OF HRM

Human resource management is a key input to all other functions of the organization for the achievement of organizational effectiveness. A proper synchronization of HRM activities with all other activities of the organization gives the organization a competitive edge. Some of the key facets with which HR managers have to deal with are as given in Exhibit 16.1.

Exhibit 16.1   Key facets of HRM

- Recruitment and retention of employees
- Planning for staff requirement
- Defining jobs, roles, and responsibilities
- Recruitment process
  - applications and resumes
  - examinations, group discussions, and interviews
  - reference checks
  - personality tests
  - integrity tests
  - ensure reliability and validity of various tests used

- Induction of new employees
- Outsourcing certain stages of production, functions, and services
- Creating and providing an environment conducive to growth
- Determining employees benefits and compensation package
- Training and development
- Career planning for different groups of employees
- Arranging training in-house or outside
- Leadership development

(Contd)

Exhibit 16.1 *(Contd)*

- Self-development
- Team training
- Diversity training
- Training need assessment
- Training evaluation
- Regulatory compliance to be ensured
- Personnel database management
- Framing and devising personnel policies
- Statutory compliances
- Employee rules and regulations and other related issues
- Ethical practices to be followed
- To ensure non-discriminatory treatment to employees
- Arranging conducive and safe working environment by:

- developing employees' assistance programmes
- handling drug abuse situations in the workplace
- ensuring safe working facilities
- promoting welfare schemes for employees
- retaining high-performance employees
- performance measurement and management
- group performance management
- enhancing personal productivity
- rewarding employees and groups for their special achievements
- timely promotions and career advancement prospects

SUMMARY

Human resource management is essential for any contemporary organization to manage and effectively respond to the demands of a complex and fast changing work environment. It deals with the staffing functions of the organization such as human resources planning, recruitment, training, career planning, compensation package, and performance appraisal.

The strategic impact of human resources is crucial because employees are the people in the organization who create value through cost reduction, quality improvement, and providing something distinct and unique to its customers. Some employees' competencies, capabilities, and knowledge are rare and difficult to be reproduced or imitated; it can be honed only through organized teamwork to ensure multiple returns.

Human resource managers have to synchronize their activities with the business plan of the organization to ensure that the right type and number of people are made available to different departments in line with their contribution to the organizational goals. Evaluation of human resource activities focuses on productivity, quality, quantity, innovation, and employee satisfaction levels.

Although devising HRM policies is the exclusive domain of HR specialists, operating managers operationalize the same policies. The main challenge that lies before HRM is managing change.

KEYWORDS

HR planning process It attempts to synchronize its activities with the business plan of the organization to ensure that the right type and number of people are made available to different departments in line with their contribution to the organizational goals.

Human resource management (HRM) It deals with all aspects of human resources that enable effective use of the same to improve organizational effectiveness.

Outsourcing The process by which an organization gets certain non-core functions/operations performed by an external entity that has specialized in management of those functions/operations.

Recruitment It is the process of identifying the qualified and skilled people for a particular task or function within the organization.

Retention Strategies by which an organization retains its productive employees.

Training and development It deals with design, development, and delivery of specific inputs related to knowledge, skills, and attitudes among employees to improve organizational performance.

EXERCISES

Concept Review Questions

1. What is HRM?
2. What are the vital functions of HRM?
3. What are different objectives of HRM functions?
4. What are the key facets that need to be taken care of to ensure regulatory compliances?
5. What are the main steps involved in HR planning process?
6. What are the important aspects that need to be taken care of for the recruitment and retention of employees?

Critical Thinking Questions

1. What is the relevance of corporate social responsibility (CSR) to HRM? In what way CSR contributes to organizational growth?
2. Why is the role of HRM becoming more crucial in the knowledge and information age?
3. One of the objectives of HRM functions is 'providing scope for creativity and innovation to employees'. In what way does this function contribute to organizational effectiveness?
4. What are the risks that an organization cannot afford to take in today's fast-changing environment in the domain of human resources?

5. 'Retaining high performance employees is very important for the growth of an organization.' What steps, from the HR policy point of view does an organization need to take to retain its high-performing employees?
6. 'Effective operationalization of HR functions requires an integrated involvement of both professional HR managers as well as operating managers.' Comment.
7. Retention and recruitment are two vital challenges before the HRM team. Which one out of the two is more critical and crucial? Cite real life situations to justify your answer.

Project Assignment

'To develop competitive capability, organizations keep innovating ways to obtain, retain, and engage their most critical resources, that is, human resources.' Identify two fast-growing manufacturing companies and find from their websites, as also other Internet sites, about the innovative ways deployed by them to develop competitive capability through HRM.

REFERENCES

Bateman, Thomas and Scott A. Snell (2004), *Management New Competitive Landscape*, 6th edition, McGraw-Hill Irwin, International Edition, New York, p. 301.

Dessler, Gary (2002), *Human Resource Management*, Pearson Education, New York, p. 2.

Holman, L. (1996), 'Globalization in the Information Age', *Lessons in Leadership Newsletter*, October, p. 3.

Lewis, Pamela, Stephen H. Goodman, and Patricia M. Fandt (2001), *Management Challenges in 21st Century*, 3rd edition, South-Western College Publishing, Thomson Learning, Ohio, p. 320.

17

Job Design

INTRODUCTION

In the previous chapter we saw the importance of HRM amidst the fast-changing profile of the economy. We also noted that the role of human resources has always been important but it has never been more important and more necessary than it is now, in the information and knowledge economy. In the current fast-changing environment, jobs and demands made on the jobs are ever increasing and changing. Work profiles are undergoing continuous changes due to technological, social, economic, legal, cultural, and demographic factors. These changes have posed a major challenge before human resource professionals, who have to continuously keep analysing job profiles and placing the employees with the requisite capabilities and competencies so as to get the best out of them. This has necessitated the need for a continuous understanding of the nature of jobs and, in turn, job designs that specify various requirements that enable a right matching of people with the requirements of the job. The importance of job analysis, job description, and job specification cannot be underestimated, if the organization wants to excel in their domain of operations (Dessler 2002). *Job analysis* examines tasks and sequence of tasks that are to be performed for the completion of a well-defined job. It studies individual elements and duties required to accomplish it.

Job description refers to a list of general tasks, functions, and responsibilities of a designation within an organization. It is an overall view of what needs to be done for the performance of a job at any level. It defines responsibilities and relationships within the organization and the expected

Learning Objectives

After studying this chapter, you will be able to:
- Learn about the concept of job design
- Understand its significance for HRM professionals
- Know about job design related factors that affect work performance
- Learn about changes that the job design perspective has undergone over the years
- Understand the issues that job design addresses
- Examine different approaches to job design
- Analyse implications of viewing an organization from the socio-technical systems model point of view

outcomes of a job. *Job specification* helps in profiling the kind of professional required for a certain job or function. For example, a human resource specialist in The Boston Consulting Group (BCG) Consultants collects information on various aspects, such as work activities, human behaviour, machine tools, performance standards, job context, and human requirements, through job analysis (McCormick 1976).

JOB DESIGN

Job design refers to the way in which sets of interrelated tasks—leading to a desired and expected outcome—are organized (Fig. 17.1). Parker and Wall (1998) have highlighted that while designing jobs, the needs and goals of the employees and the organization need to be considered and aligned. It requires a stepwise diagnosis of a job to deal with the following issues with a view to getting a total picture about what would be needed to effectively perform a given task:

- task to be performed (content);
- how they are to be performed (method and mechanism);
- how many actions are to be performed within the task (steps involved);
- in what order the actions have to be done (sequencing); and
- the knowledge skills and attitudes required to perform the task efficiently and effectively (optimum performance).

Thus, job design is defined as the process of defining the content of a job in terms of its duties and responsibilities; the methods, techniques and systems, and procedures for carrying out the job; and the relationships that should exist between the job holder and his superiors, subordinates, and colleagues. An important objective of job design is to meet organizational requirements of productivity, quality of production, and to satisfy individual job-related needs by integrating them with organizational requirements.

Job design takes into account all factors that affect work performance. It precisely defines the job content and the activities required to be undertaken so that an employee develops confidence to effectively perform the job, once he has been equipped to carry out the same. Job design also deals with the administrative issues such as:

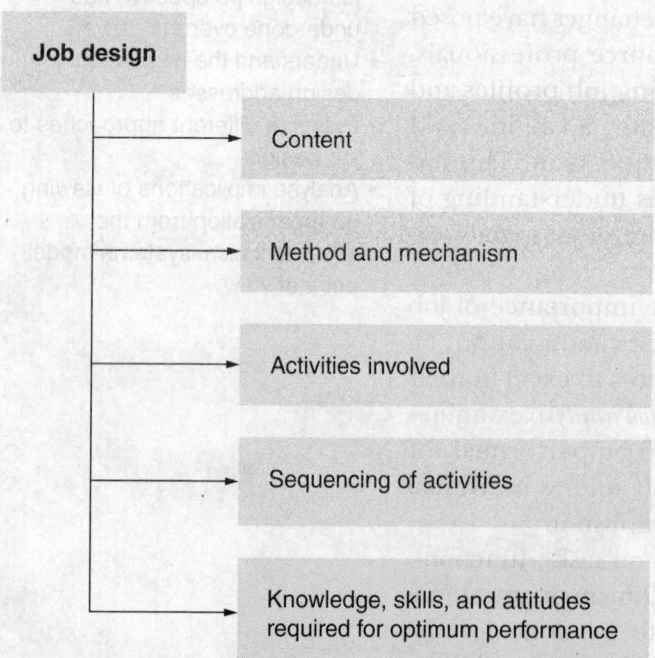

FIGURE 17.1 Job design

(Figure labels: Job design → Content; Method and mechanism; Activities involved; Sequencing of activities; Knowledge, skills, and attitudes required for optimum performance)

- job rotation;
- job enlargement;
- job enrichment;
- job engineering;
- task/machine pacing;

- work breaks;
- working hours;
- working environment; and
- working relationships.

A well-designed job encourages a variety of 'good' body postures, has reasonable strength requirements, and requires adequate mental activity. It helps in inculcating feelings of achievement, motivation, and self-esteem.

Importance of Job Design

As stated earlier, job design and work organization deal with the specifications of the content, methods, and relationships of jobs in an integrated manner to satisfy technological and organizational requirements as well as the personal needs of employees. During the 1970s, the challenge before HRM professionals dealing with job designs was to find out how organizations achieve results in the wake of loss of productive effort resulting from industrial actions and absenteeism, increased demand for employee participation, and imposition of various employee legislations. During the 1980s a major change occurred in the working environment in the form of introduction of new technologies and a shift in the cost of production in favour of machines as against workforce. In this period of recession, the need for retrenchment of employees also arose. All these factors changed the perspective of job design. It was only in the 1990s that a real challenge in terms of optimum job design and work organization arose to respond to the fast-changing environmental conditions. This resulted in giving a greater importance and adopting a new approach towards job design.

Job Design: Issues

Job design principles help in tackling and managing the following issues:
- work overload;
- work underload;
- repetitiveness leading to drudgery and adverse effect on productivity;
- work and people isolation;
- multiple shifts;
- managing pending filling-up of vacancies;
- excessive working hours; and
- lack of understanding of the whole job process.

Job design and workplace design are interrelated concepts as both contribute to keeping the physical requirements of a job reasonable. Job design focuses on the need for administrative changes that can help in improving working conditions. Workplace design focuses on the physical setting of the workplace, such as workstation, tools, and body posture, which contribute to an individual's work performance.

IBM Corporation

American companies and their employees have almost never faced an environment as dynamic and challenging as the one they face today. Fast changing technological advances, dynamic marketplace, highly demanding customers, mounting global competitive pressure, and increasing expectations from investors have become a reality. A competitive business model in the twenty-first century requires the optimum outsourcing of products, services, and people. Organizational success would greatly depend upon their ability to innovate. The difference between winners and losers will depend a lot on the quality of a company's workforce—equipped with adequate and appropriate skills on a continuous basis.

Bureau of Labor Statistics' (USA) projections show that over the 2002–12 period, computer related jobs, especially network specialists, computer systems engineers, and database specialists, are among the occupations expected to show the fastest growth. Further, the Department of Labor, USA (2004) predicts that the rate of growth of jobs in computer and mathematical science occupations will grow twice as fast as other private employment.

IBM is the world's largest professional services company and its success depends on the skills of its employees. Matching skills to a fast changing environment is the greatest challenge. Some of the IT skills are fast becoming obsolete as is evident from their shifting from being in high demand, or 'hot', to be standardized, or 'cold' at a much quicker pace. The driving force behind these emerging trends are the rapid emergence of new technologies, the low-cost availability of commodity skills (e.g., HTML and C++ coding) in emerging countries, and the growing shift in demand for more specialized IT skills that require higher levels of thinking, industry knowledge, and business process expertise. In just two years, eight new skill categories entered the top 12 in- demand jobs, according to a survey based on job vacancy advertisements. On the contrary, eight skill categories, previously popular, exited the list (according to Tech Skills Demand Index, Techies.com). All this has posed a great challenge for HR professionals, who have to be on their toes to develop and devise job designs to suit emerging knowledge and skills needs.

While the standardized or 'cold' skills are fast shifting to emerging markets, that is, India and China, in the US there's an increasing demand for sophisticated skills that would require unification of industry knowledge, high-level IT expertise, and business process expertise coupled with the convergence of technologies. According to META Group, the skills most requested by executives in 2004 are split 38 per cent for business (business acumen, project management, and leadership skills) and 62 per cent for IT (e-commerce and Internet, Java, networking). IBM's own assessments of market data conclude that the demand is rising for new IT jobs in areas such as business analysis, security analysis, vendor management, service management, and system integration.

In response to these market needs, IBM has created new job designs to target candidates with a broader mix of business and IT backgrounds. Security consultant and logistics consultant are just two examples of new job profiles. The qualified degrees for these jobs are bachelors or masters degrees in accounting, business administration, computer science, electrical, industrial engineering, mathematics, mechanical engineering, management, marketing, management of information systems, etc.

Source: Based on www.dol.gov/ebsa/pdf/Barnes070505.pdf, accessed on 15 September 2007.
Reprint Courtesy of International Business Machines Corporation, © International Business Machines Corporation.

Common Approaches to Job Design

Achieving a good job design requires devising administrative practices that determine what the employee does, for how long, where, when, and how he does it; as also giving the employee choice, wherever feasible and workable. While working out a job design, the focus may be on examining the various tasks of an individual's job or the design of a group of tasks, depending upon the nature and characteristic of the job involved.

There are different approaches to job design (Fig. 17.2). Each places different emphasis on performance and satisfaction, depending upon the desired outcomes. While some approaches to job design focus primarily on improving performance, others emphasize on employee satisfaction. Some of the approaches of job design are described in this section.

Job enlargement

Job enlargement for a particular task attempts to enhance the scope of the job to include a variety of tasks that need to be performed by the individual. It adds interest and enjoyment to working, without necessarily handing over extra responsibility to the employees. The expanded job is not as specialized or as routine as a job designed according to scientific management principles. It basically attempts to increase job satisfaction by allowing an employee to perform a greater variety of activities and tasks, requiring more advanced skill sets. It is more applicable to satisfy higher level needs of employees by including higher variety in their jobs (Wright and Cordery 1999).

Job rotation

Job rotation moves employees from one task to another to add variety and reduce boredom by allowing them to perform a variety of tasks. It also helps in broadening the understanding of employees about all aspects of the business (William, et al. 1992). It not only distributes the group tasks among a number of employees, but also trains the employees on different tasks, so that job output does not suffer in absence of an employee who may have an exclusive command over a particular job. It also helps in curbing any vested interest that employees may develop by permanently working on a particular seat,

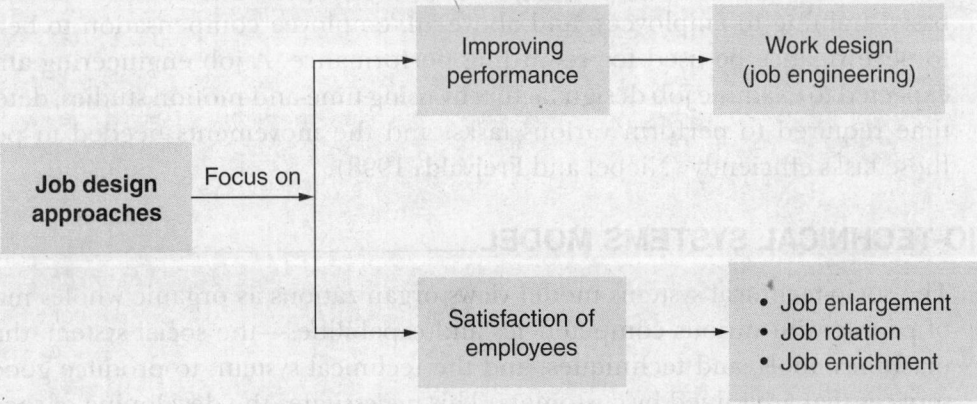

FIGURE 17.2 Approaches to job design

particularly in sensitive positions. However, in case all the tasks involved are similar and of routine nature, the strategy of job rotation may not be helpful in improving employee effectiveness and job satisfaction. As stated by Kenneth and Latham (1981), there are several methods to improve the success of job rotation programmes. What is important is to tailor the needs, interests, and capabilities of the individual trainee rather than to have a standardized sequence of job rotation for all trainees.

Job enrichment

Job enrichment, as per Orsburn and Moran (2000), empowers employees to assume greater responsibility and accountability for planning, organizing, performing, controlling, and evaluating their own work. It enables and allows employees to assume more responsibility, accountability, and independence while learning new tasks. Job enrichment attempts to design jobs in such a way that it helps employees in satisfying their needs for growth, recognition, and responsibility. Job enrichment differs from job enlargement, as it adds new dimensions to the job by expanding it vertically; employees are given more responsibility. The employees need satisfaction to get greater prominence while designing jobs, according to Herzberg (1959), who propounded the two-factor theory of work motivation. His basic idea is that employees will be inspired, encouraged, and motivated in undertaking jobs that enhance their feelings of self-worth.

Work design

Work design (job engineering) allows employees to understand and appreciate the linkage between work methods, layout, and handling procedures as also the interaction between people and machines. Job design was central issue in Taylor's (1856–1915) model of scientific management. His perspective on the importance of job design is an excellent example of rational approach to scientific management practices and shows how certain perspectives focus more on productivity than on satisfaction. Taylor's recommendations emphasize the need for scientific job analysis; arranging work in such a way that workers turn out to be efficient, recruitment be linked one to one with job descriptions and job specifications, continuous need-based training to employees, and above all, employee compensation to be linked to performance be used for rewarding performance. A job engineering analyst is expected to examine job design factors by using time-and-motion studies, determine time required to perform various tasks, and the movements needed to perform those tasks efficiently (Niebel and Freivalds 1998).

SOCIO-TECHNICAL SYSTEMS MODEL

The socio-technical systems model views organizations as organic wholes made up of people with various competencies and capabilities—the social system, that uses machines, tools, and techniques, and the technical system, to produce goods and services that are valued by customers. This necessitates the developing of social and technical systems in such a way that they become interdependent in a unified whole to fulfil the demands made on them by customers, suppliers, and other stakeholders in the external environment.

From the nineties, job designs are becoming more and more critical in improving the effectiveness of organizations by getting the best out of their human resources. This involves job analysis to understand the demands of the jobs, the competencies and capabilities required, so as to develop a profile of people needed and putting them in place to successfully perform their roles. The techniques for job design and analysis include visionary interviews to explore links between organizational objectives, values and culture, and the attitudes expected from people within the organization.

SUMMARY

Work profiles are undergoing constant changes due to technological, social, economic, legal, cultural, and demographic factors. These changes have posed a major challenge before human resource professionals who now need to continuously keep analysing job profiles and placing human resource with requisite capabilities and competencies to get the best out of them.

Job design refers to the way in which sets of interrelated tasks leading to a desired and expected outcome are organized. The relevance of job design is changing with time; with changes occurring in the working environment particularly with

the introduction of new technologies. Job design and workplace design are interrelated concepts as both contribute to keep the physical requirements of a job reasonable.

The different approaches to job design are—job enlargement, job enrichment, and job rotation. Each places different emphasis on performance and satisfaction depending upon the desired outcomes. Job design mainly revolves around job analysis to understand the demands of the jobs, the competencies and capabilities required, so as to develop a profile of people needed to successfully perform their roles.

KEYWORDS

Job analysis Examines tasks and sequence of tasks, which are necessary for the completion of a well-defined job.
Job description Relates to listing of general tasks, functions, and responsibilities of a position.
Job design The way in which sets of interrelated tasks, leading to a desired or expected outcome, are organized.

Job enlargement It attempts to bring in changes in the jobs so as to include a variety of tasks to be performed by the individual involved.
Job enrichment It enables and allows employees to assume more responsibility, accountability, and independence while learning new tasks.
Job rotation It involves moving employees from one task to another to add variety and reduce boredom.

EXERCISES

Concept Review Questions
1. Define job design.
2. What are the issues that need to be diagnosed, step-by-step, to have a total picture of the administrative issues with which the job design has to deal with? Explain the significance of each administrative issue.

3. How has the role of HRM professional dealing with job design changed over the years? What challenges has this change posed to HRM professionals?
4. What are the important issues that job design addresses?

5. Explain the common approaches used for effective job design.
6. How does a socio-technical system model view organizations?

Critical Thinking Questions

1. Job analysis and job description are interrelated functions and one without the other is of no use. Comment critically with an example.
2. Consider a position of an accounts manager in the service industry such as a hotel. What needs to be taken care of at the time of designing his job to provide him with job enrichment? Explain.

Project Assignments

1. Take an example of a company in the business process outsourcing (BPO) domain having a high attrition rate of more that 50 per cent. The management has identified two major reasons for high attrition—monotony and drudgery at work. Assuming that you are the head of the HR department, the top management in a meeting with you has asked you to come out with a solution to the problem. Keeping job design in mind, what concrete strategies and suggestions will you propose to the management?
2. In the banking industry, to avoid the possibility of frauds by employees, jobs are rotated, especially in the case of sensitive positions. What are the main advantages and disadvantages of job rotation in the banking industry?

REFERENCES

Dessler, Gary (2002), *Human Resource Management*, 8th edition, Pearson Education Asia, p. 84.

Hecker, Daniel E. (2004), 'Occupational Employment Projections to 2012', *Monthly Labor Review*, USA, vol. 127, no. 2, February.

Herzberg, Frederick, B. Mausner, and B.B. Snyderman (1959), *The Motivation to Work*, John Wiley & Sons, New York.

McCormick, Ernest (1976), 'Job and Task Analysis', in Marvin D. Dunnette (ed), *Handbook of Industrial and Organizational Psychology*, Rand McNally, Chicago, pp. 651–96.

McCormick, Ernest (1976), *Human Factors in Engineering and Design*, 4th edition, McGraw-Hill Book Company, New York.

Niebel, B.W. and A. Freivalds (1998), *Methods, Standards, and Work Design*, 10th edition, McGraw-Hill, New York.

Orsburn, J.D. and L. Moran (2000), *The New-Self Directed Work Teams: Mastering the Challenge*, McGraw-Hill, New York.

Parker, S. and T. Wall (1998), *Job and Work Design: Organizing Work to Promote Well-Being and Effectiveness*, Sage, Thousand Oaks, California.

Rothwell, William, H.C. Kazanas, and Daria Haines (1992), 'Issues and Practices in Management Job Rotation Programs as Perceived by HRD Professionals', *Performance Improvement Quarterly*, vol. 5, no. 1, pp. 49–69.

Taylor, F.W. (1947), *Scientific Management*, Harper & Row, New York, pp. 66–71.

Wexley, Kenneth and Gary Latham (1981), *Developing and Training Resources in Organizations*, Scott Foresman, Glenview, p. 118.

Wrigh, B.M. and J.L. Cordery (1999), 'Production Uncertainty as a Contextual Moderator of Employee Reactions to Job Design', *Journal of Applied Psychology*, vol. 84, pp. 456–63.

18

Recruitment and Selection

INTRODUCTION

Management is the sum total of the achievement of organizational goals and targets by the workforce. Therefore, employees are the most crucial and critical input for any organization to achieve predetermined goals. The success or failure of an organization largely depends upon the quality and quantity of right people, at the right time and right place. Induction of qualified, experienced, and motivated professionals in the organization is an important function of human resource management (HRM). The consequences of an unprofessional approach to recruitment can be disastrous for the organization, as human resources can turn out to be an asset or a liability, depending upon their suitability or otherwise to the organization. Thus, the process of selection and recruitment is important for the success of any organization. In this chapter, we shall try to understand the need and importance of recruitment, after having identified human resource needs and requirements and the process of recruitment. This enables the organization to induct suitable human assets/capital leading to a multiplier effect on the organizational turnover and, in turn, on shareholders' wealth.

RECRUITMENT

Recruitment is a specialized task. Effective recruitment is becoming more and more important and challenging in the present business environment. Effective recruitment contributes a great deal in the achievement of organizational goals. One of the major challenges in recruitment

Learning Objectives

After studying this chapter, you will be able to:
- Examine recruitment and selection as an HRM function
- Understand the significance of recruitment and functional aspects for developing an effective recruitment process
- Examine the different steps required for effective recruitment
- Understand the importance of proper induction of employees and professional approach to induct new employees

lies in recruiting the right person who would have a long-term relationship with the organization. As such, tight labour markets have brought a new paradigm. It is believed that generation X employees, especially those born between 1963–77 are less likely to have a long-term employment relationship with the organization compared to their predecessors. Turnover rates have suddenly shot up and as per a study published in *BNA Bulletin to Management* (1998), it has touched as high as 14.5 per cent in case of employees in the high-tech sector. Once HRM planning identifies the need for further induction of employees, the task of staffing the organization begins. The staffing task involves recruitment, selection, and outplacement. The selection process helps in identifying a pool of suitable candidates who might meet the expected human resource requirements of a company. Recruitment decisions should be made in the context of an overall staffing plan, which takes into account long-term operational needs, known retirements, and resignations vis-à-vis the growth plans of the company. Recruitment can be internal through promotions and transfers from within the organization or external through the infusion of new talent and skills from outside the organization (Fig. 18.1). Both approaches have their own advantages and disadvantages (Terpstra 1996).

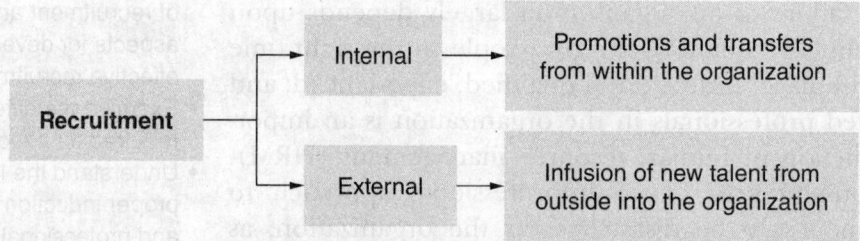

FIGURE 18.1 Approaches to recruitment

Having identified the organization's needs, the tasks of recruitment, selection, and placement are undertaken to ensure the availability of the right number of employees at the right place and at the right time (Fig. 18.2).

The functional aspects for developing an effective recruitment process are as under:

- Identification and analysis of requirements; at organizational and job levels
- Inviting applications, processing applications, and taking steps for selection; internal and external markets
- Standardization of selection process within the broad framework of policies to reduce risk while filling vacancies
- Deploying reliable, valid, and cost-effective methods of selection
- Taking care of legal constraints and contracts of employment
- Recruitment system should maintain and deliver quality service
- Recruitment process should be strategic and proactive

Internal Recruitment

Internal recruitment refers to the promotion or relocation of existing employees to fill up specific personnel requirements. It also refers to upgrading the skills of

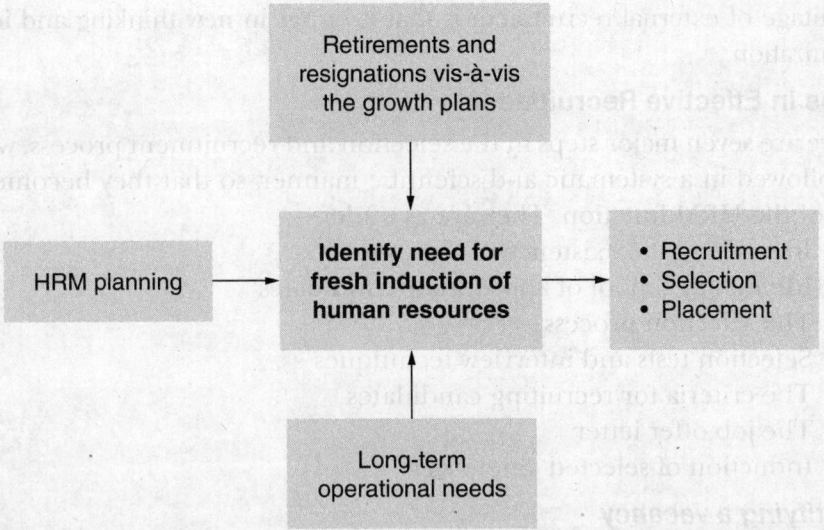

FIGURE 18.2   HRM planning—inputs and tasks

people and then redeploying them as per changed requirements. A major advantage of internal recruitment is that employers know the employees and vice versa. The challenges related to adaptation that arise when external candidates are inducted get minimized. Further, providing opportunities to employees within the organization encourages employees across the board to stick to the organization, work hard, and give their best. On the other hand, according to Bateman and Snell (2004), the major drawback of internal staffing, particularly when existing employees lack the requisite knowledge and skills required for the job, is limiting the pool of candidates for the selection process. This leads to poor selection decisions.

External Recruitment

External recruitment refers to hiring of new employees from outside the organization. It infuses new talent, skill, and thinking into the organization that, in turn, leads to innovations. External recruitment can be done through advertisements, employee referrals, professional recruiting organizations, and campus placement selection process. Advertisements are the most popular way of recruiting people, as they are relatively less expensive and help in generating a large number of responses. In case requirements are limited and the staff dealing with the recruitment process is small in numbers, organizations assign the job of preliminary selection or, even, final recruitment to outside professional recruiting organizations. As per Morehart (2001), employee referral is another frequently used source of applicants. Some companies actively encourage employees to refer their friends by offering cash rewards. According to Talbott (1996), the advantage of campus recruiting is that there is a large pool of people from which the company can draw out applicants with up-to-date training and innovative ideas. There are certain organizations that have started advertising for the vacancies available in their company on their websites or on specially-designed websites or job sites. The major advantage of external recruitment is that it brings in new thinking and ideas into the organization.

Steps in Effective Recruitment

There are seven major steps in the selection and recruitment process, which have to be followed in a systematic and scientific manner, so that they become an integral part of the HRM function. They are as under:

1. Identifying the existence of a vacancy
2. Identifying a pool of appropriate candidates
3. The selection process
4. Selection tests and interview techniques
5. The criteria for recruiting candidates
6. The job offer letter
7. Induction of selected employees

Identifying a vacancy

The first step towards an effective recruitment process is to verify whether the organization needs a person to perform a certain task or a function. It is necessary to analyse the tasks, objectives, and benefits involved with the job. Is the work really necessary to accomplish overall goals? Can it be avoided, relocated, mechanized, or subcontracted? What would be the consequence, if the job were not undertaken? Questions such as these need to be answered. It is important to rationalize the requirement of personnel, keeping in view the tasks required to be performed for achieving the objectives from a particular activity/department. It is pertinent to note that there are managers with inflated egos, who aspire to build an empire. Therefore, it is imperative to analyse the financial implications of additional personnel compared to the additional or incremental benefits that would accrue to the organization. Having ensured the requirement for additional hands, one has to precisely define the duties, responsibilities, hierarchy, and grade in which the prospective candidate will be placed. A job description is a key document in the selection and recruitment process, and must be the first to be finalized before embarking on the process of looking for an employee. It should clearly spell out the following:

- the job title;
- the location of the job, that is, department/group/division;
- grade of the post;
- whom an employee for a given job would be responsible to;
- who all would be reporting to the person occupying a particular position;
- main purpose of the job;
- duties and responsibilities involved; and
- any special working conditions.

Job description should have an inbuilt flexibility to include any other duties that the post holder will carry out, which are within the scope, spirit, and purpose of the job. It should help in formulating personnel specification information about the prospective candidate such as (1) physique, health, and appearance including height, build, hearing, eyesight, health, looks, grooming, voice, or for that matter any disabilities; (2) accomplishments, which include educational qualifications, training, learning, and experience; (3) conceptual and reasoning ability, that is, knowledge base, perception, intellectual capacities, special aptitudes (speech/writing); (4) interests, intellectual, cultural, practical, physically active; (5) disposition, that is, acceptability, relationships, leadership/initiative, motivation and drive, reliability, stability/adjustment, proactively influencing; (6) circumstances such as age, plans, domestic responsibilities, mobility, domicile.

This information needs to be further classified into essential, desirable, and disqualifier categories depending upon the profile required for a particular job description. The purpose of such a detailed diagnosis is to clarify the qualifications, skills and abilities, experience, and aptitudes expected from the prospective candidate. Thus, a job description should spell out the skills, experience, abilities, and expertise that are required to effectively perform the job.

Identifying a pool of appropriate candidates

The sources to identify the appropriate pool of candidates depend, to a large extent, upon the benefits that are likely to accrue to the organization after a candidate is hired. Therefore, the choice of source that has to be tapped for recruitment would depend upon the need, vis-à-vis, the cost and efficiency of various sources. Some of the prominent sources to identify a pool of candidates from are (Fig. 18.3):

- people already known, including ex-employees and past applicants;
- direct advertising;

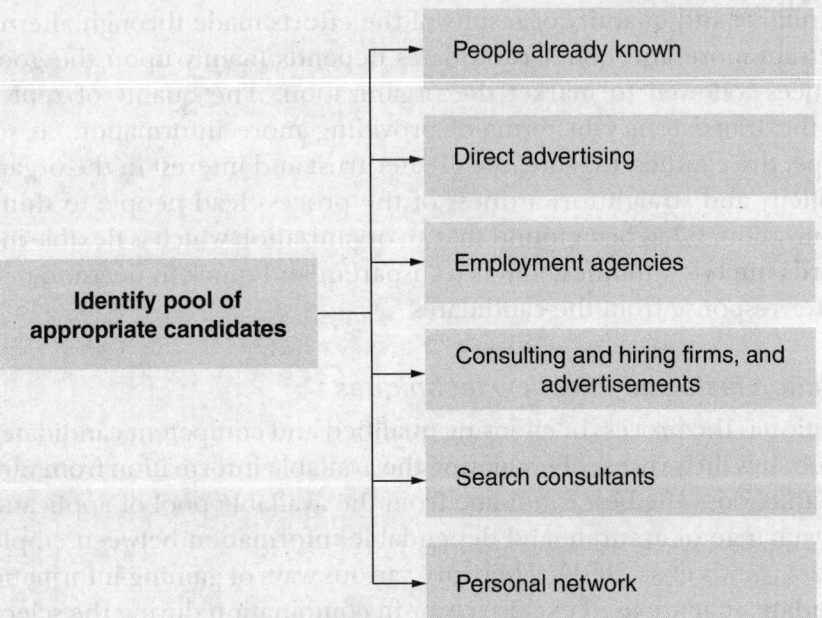

FIGURE 18.3   Methods of identifying candidates

- employment agencies;
- consulting and hiring firms, along with advertisements;
- search consultants; and
- personal network for head hunting.

To identify an appropriate pool of people for the job through advertising requires two vital issues to be addressed—media to be used and construction of an advertisement (Hunger 1985 and Bob 1987). An advertisement specifying the job description and candidate profile should include details such as a title of vacancy, salary details with breakup, brief details of the job, key details of personal specification, duration of appointment, how to obtain further information related to the vacancy, closing date for applicants, and if possible, date of interview.

Hiring an employee through recruiting agencies and consultants may be a relatively expensive channel of recruitment. However, because of their special professional competence they are able to satisfy an employer's needs. As a customer, the organization has to decide whom to assign the task. The quality of service by the consultants depends much upon the input that the organization provides them. Clear and explicit disclosure by the client goes a long way in getting the best out of professional consulting firms providing recruitment services. Thus, the task would basically involve identification of the right source from amongst alternative sources through agencies such as recruitment consultants, head hunters, media, advertising, and online recruitment to attract the maximum possible relevant applicants for recruitment.

Selection process

The quality and quantity of results of the efforts made through alternative sources to attract more and better candidates depends mainly upon the good marketing practices followed to market the organization. The quality of reply instructions and the transparency in terms of providing more information, as sought by the prospective candidates, generate greater trust and interest in the organization. The simplicity and straightforwardness of the process lead people to think well of the organization. It has been found that an organization which is flexible in its approach towards interview timings, and is transparent and quick in decision-making attracts greater response from the candidates.

Selection tests and interview techniques

Selection is the process of choosing qualified and competent candidates suitable for the job. It is the process of evaluating the available information from various sources, so as to choose the best candidate from the available pool of applicants. It involves the exchange of accurate and dependable information between employer and job seekers (Lewis et al. 2001). There are various ways of gaining information about the candidate, that are used exclusively or in combination during the selection process, depending upon the nature and level of the job. These methods should be reliable,

Colgate's selection process

Colgate has a systematic, well defined, and objective process of selection and recruitment. The company has clearly defined the process of shortlisting; what aspects should be looked into and evaluated in the preliminary assessment and final interview. Actual steps involved in the recruitment for the filling up the vacancies in the company are as under:

Application shortlist: In this step, the company shortlists the CVs received from various sources based on the suitability of the requirement as identified by the company.

Preliminary assessment: The shortlisted candidates go through a preliminary round of interviews, which lays a great emphasis on finding out functional competencies of the prospective employees. For a better insight into their functional skills, the candidates may be evaluated according to their analysis and presentation of a business case. However, this step is followed for only certain specific positions.

Final interview: In this step the candidates who successfully clear the first round of interview go through the second round of interview with one or more of the functional heads of the company.

Medical evaluation: Selected candidates are asked to undergo a medical test before they join duty.

Source: Based on the data from www.colgate.co.in, accessed on 28 July 2007.

valid, cost-effective, and acceptable. Some of the commonly used methods are—application form, bio-data; structured/unstructured interviews such as one-to-one panel, references screening; ability tests: paper based, practical, social, aptitude, intelligence; and personality tests in groups or in assessment centres. Depending upon the nature and type of job and the level at which the vacancy exists in the organization, a decision is made about the methods to be used for conducting selection tests.

The purpose of the interview is to assess the candidate's credentials as well as his potential, with objective reasons for rejection. An interviewer should necessarily have due qualities, competence, and knowledge to perform this task. Therefore, the criteria for evaluation of candidates should be clearly laid down in advance and the selection committee constituting experts should necessarily examine the suitability of each candidate by using techniques that can scientifically help in assessing the knowledge, skills, competence, and above all, the attitudinal aspects of a candidate vis-à-vis the job requirements.

Criteria for recruiting a candidate

After having gone through the tests, interviews reviewing the track records, and having obtained references without damaging the candidate's current employment and position, one should be able to arrive at a yardstick to identify the most suitable, second best suitable candidate, and so on (Fig. 18.4). Professionally-managed organizations, having scientific approach to arrive at the decision, are able to take quick and prompt decisions. It has been found that good organizations are able to

The interview

Preparing for an interview

Appearing for an interview is an art and requires special preparation. It is not enough to have adequate knowledge in the area that the prospective employer is looking for. Some aspects an interviewee has to focus on are discussed in this section.

Making a good impression

One should prepare before facing an interview, irrespective of who you are going to meet. Be serious about it; even if it starts informally there are chances of it becoming formal. It is important to remember that your success depends upon influencing and leaving a memorable mark in the mind of person(s) on the other side of the table. When expressing yourself and responding to the questions, always be polite, speak slowly and clearly, and make sure they have all your details right. Be courteous and always maintain eye contact while talking.

Getting the basics right

Ensure that you have collected accurate details about the date, time, and, location of your interview. Although this sounds obvious, but candidates still manage to reach late for interviews with varied excuses. This reflects a lack of organization and attention to detail that would have a bearing on your candidature. It is better to inform over the telephone, ahead of time, if there are any exceptional circumstances that may delay your arrival on time on that day. Dress in the same style as the representatives of the organization, and pay full attention to different facets of your appearance and personal hygiene; right down to your shoes. Try to fit in with the employer's image and if in doubt, dress conservatively. Maintain pleasing manners throughout the interview, especially in the beginning and in the end.

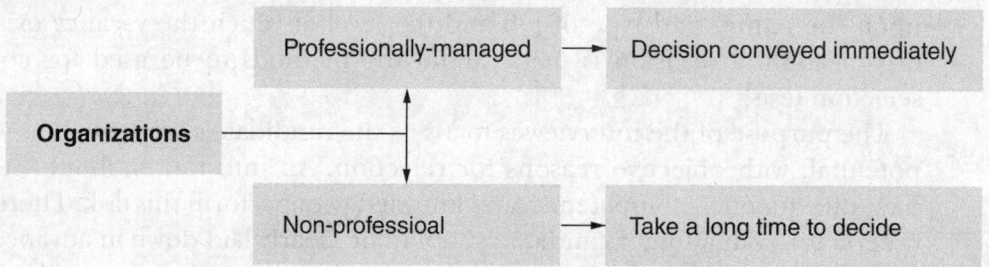

FIGURE 18.4   Professional and non-professional approaches to selection

communicate the decision on the spot or immediately after the interview, giving a rationale and reason for selection or otherwise to the candidate. It is important that there is no point in selecting a candidate whom the organization cannot afford or motivate.

Job offer letter

Once a candidate has been selected, a job offer letter has to be given to the selected candidate(s), comprising the terms and conditions of the job. This is a crucial step in the recruitment of a candidate However, after the selected candidate accepts the stipulated terms and conditions, the offer letter becomes a contract between the two parties. The candidate, before accepting an offer letter, should feel free to seek any information or clarification that may help him in making a decision to join or otherwise.

Induction of new employees

Induction refers to the smooth entry of new employees into their jobs and organizational culture. It is, yet another crucial part of the selection and recruitment process. It has been found that lack of emphasis on the part of the organization to induct prospective employees, costs heavily, in terms of time and money. Inadequate and inappropriate induction has been found to be the reasons for de-motivation, increased turnover, employee–employer disputes, and above all, damages to the reputation of the organization. Professionally-managed organizations have a detailed checklist to scientifically and systematically induct people into the organization, so that new employees are able to get right information from the right sources. In the absence of proper induction, people may make assumptions or ask the wrong person that may lead to getting incomplete or incorrect information resulting in their getting dissatisfied and, in turn, quickly quitting the organization.

One of the biggest challenges facing HR managers today is recruiting and retaining employees with the right skills. Selection and recruitment is very crucial for the success of the organization. Appointments should be made on the basis of merit, through a fair, transparent, well defined, and open selection process. Basic principles underlying the recruitment process are those of fairness, credibility, equal employment opportunity, merit, and the optimization of career prospects.

EMPLOYEE RETENTION—A GREAT CHALLENGE

Retention of talented and hard-working employees is crucial for the long-term sustainable growth of the organization. Employee turnover is a costly affair for the organization as it leads to loss of investment on training, recruitment, and above all, knowledge. Retaining employees has become a great challenge, particularly, in the business process outsourcing (BPO) and information technology enabled services (ITES) industries. Attrition rates are as high as 35 per cent in non-voice BPOs and 45 per cent in voice call centres. More than two-thirds, who quit, look for better career openings within the same industry. Some of the vital reasons identified for the high attrition rate are the lure of higher salary, monotonous job, and unnatural working hours.

Organizational culture and the relationship with bosses emanating from the quality of supervision is also a critical factor in reducing attrition rate. Exit interviews sometimes reveal that employees feel that they lack an identity in the organization. Good organizations provide opportunities for employees to share their knowledge via training sessions, presentations, mentoring others, and team assignments. Above all, the BPO sector should endeavour to have a work–leisure balance by taking concrete policy decisions and initiatives to reinforce the retention strategies.

SUMMARY

Human resources can turn out to be an asset or a liability to the organization. It is in this perspective that the process of selection and recruitment becomes important. The staffing task involves selection, recruitment, and outplacement. Recruitment process enables the identification of a pool of suitable candidates who might meet the expected requirements of people for different activities. The process should be strategic and proactive.

A major advantage of internal recruitment is that employers know the employees and employees know their organization. External recruitment infuses new talent, skills, and thinking into the organization that further leads to innovation. External recruitment can be done through advertisements, employee referral, professional recruiting organizations, and campus placement selection process. In case requirements are limited and staff dealing with recruitment process is small in numbers, organizations assign the job of preliminary or even final recruitment to external professional recruiting organizations. The sources to identify the appropriate pool of candidates depends largely upon the benefits that are likely to accrue to the organization after the recruitment of a candidate.

A job description is the key document in the recruitment process, and must be finalized prior to taking any other steps in the process. It has been found that good organizations are able to communicate the selection decision on the spot or immediately after the interview.

Induction is a crucial part of the recruitment process. Professionally managed organizations have a detailed checklist to scientifically and systematically induct people in the organization, so that new employees are able to get right information from the right sources. Recruitment is a very sensitive and crucial aspect for the success of an organization, thus, they should have very well-defined recruitment policies.

KEYWORDS

Contract of employment   Terms and conditions to be mutually agreed by employee and employer result in contract of employment.

External recruitment   It infuses new talent, skill, and thinking into the organization.

Human assets/liabilities   Human resources can turn out to be an asset or a liability, depending upon their suitability or otherwise to the organization.

Induction   The smooth entry of new employees into their jobs and organizational culture.

Internal recruitment   The promotion of existing employees or relocation of employees to fill up specific personnel requirements.

Interview techniques   Methods and processes used for assessing prospective employees.

Recruitment   A process to identify a pool of suitable candidate(s) who meet the expected requirements of the job profile.

Selection   The step of choosing qualified and competent candidates suitable for the job from an available pool of candidates.

EXERCISES

Concept Review Questions

1. Why in the present era, recruitment and selection are considered as critical HRM functions?
2. What are the functional aspects for developing an effective recruitment process?
3. Differentiate between internal recruitment and external recruitment. Give advantages and disadvantages of both.
4. What are different steps required for effective recruitment?
5. 'Induction of a new employee in the organization is very crucial.' How do professionally-managed organizations induct new employees?

Critical Thinking Questions

1. 'For attracting talent in the organization, selection decision needs to be quick and prompt.' Why?
2. It is always desirable to recruit from within the organization rather than from outside. Comment critically.
3. Between middle- and senior-level positions, for a company that is continuing with its existing business profile, it is said that recruiting people from outside would be desirable in case of senior positions rather than middle-level positions. Comment critically.

Project Assignment

Select five advertisements that have appeared during the last 3–4 months for the position of senior-level personnel in the manufacturing or banking sector. Analyse the content and presentation of these. Which one of them is the best? Give reasons.

REFERENCES

Bateman, Thomas and Scott A. Snell (2004), *Management New Competitive Landscape*, 6th edition, McGraw-Hill Irwin, International Edition, p. 304.

Bob, Martin (1987), 'Recruitment Ad Ventures', *Personnel Journal*, vol. 66, August, pp. 46–63.

Dessler, Gary and Jean Philips (2008), *Managing Now,* Houghton Miffin Company, Boston, quoted in 'High Stakes in Recruiting in High-Tech' , BNA Bulletin to Management (1998), 12 February, p. 48.

Hunger, Barbara (1985), 'How to Choose a Recruitment Advertising Agency', *Personnel Journal*, vol. 64, no. 2, December, pp. 60–62.

Lewis, Pamela, Stephen H. Goodman, and Patricia M. Fandt (2001), *Management Challenges in 21st Century*, 3rd edition, South-Western College Publishing, Thomson Learning, USA, p. 330.

Morehart, Kerri Koss (2001), 'How to Create an Employee Referral Program that Really Works', *HR Focus*, January, vol. 78, no. 1, pp. 3–5.

Talbott, Shannon Peters (1996), 'Boost Your Campus Image to Attract Top Grads', *Personnel Journal*, March, pp. 6–8.

Terpstra, David E. (1996), 'The Search for Effective Methods', *HR Focus*, May, pp. 16–17.

19

Training and Development

Learning Objectives

After studying this chapter, you will be able to:
- Appreciate the relevance of training in a fast-changing business environment
- Understand the difference between training, training and development, and learning and development
- Learn the scope of training
- Examine the steps involved in designing a good training programme
- Appreciate the significance of systems approach to training
- Examine the sources of data for training that need assessment
- Examine various methods of training and their relevance to training objectives
- Appreciate the relevance of training evaluation, techniques, and approaches used to evaluate training

INTRODUCTION

Advances in technology, knowledge, and information pose a great challenge before organizations. Any organization that does not take into consideration these changes faces a real threat. Coping with these challenges requires a continuous investment on training and development for upgrading knowledge and skills of its workforce. People working in some of the fastest growing organizations spend as much as one to two months in a year in training. The need for greater investment on human resources through training has become imperative due to the fast obsolescence of human capital in the present era of knowledge and information society. Therefore, continuous training and development has become an important input to get the best out of human resources. It is in this backdrop that we shall focus on the various issues related to training.

TRAINING

The Manpower Services Commission (UK), which was set up by the 1973 Employment and Training Act that was replaced in 1988, defined training as 'A planned process to modify attitude, knowledge, or skill behaviour through learning experience to achieve effective performance in an activity or range of activities. Its purpose, in the work situation, is to develop the abilities of the individual and to satisfy the current and future needs of the organization.'

Training may be distinguished from development. Training usually refers to teaching lower-level employees how to perform their present jobs, while development involves teaching managers and professional employees broader skills needed for their present and future jobs (Bateman and Snell 2002).

David Kolb (1984) has focused on experiential learning, that is, experience as the source of learning and development. He emphasized on how learners can transform learning into an experience, and later, use it to perform their assigned duties. Each learner has his/her preferred method of learning, which gets developed like any other facet of his/her personality. Therefore, for understanding the value and relevance of learning inventory, a learner must have basic understanding of experiential learning mode and his/her preferred style. Kolb had identified four learning styles that are associated with different ways of problem solving. The *divergers style* views a problem situation from multiple perspectives and depends a lot on brainstorming and generation of ideas. People having a diverger style are imaginative, creative, open, and receptive to new ideas. They are good in recognizing problems and identifying opportunities. *Assimilators* depend on the processing of information based on the inductive reasoning process that enables them to develop a theoretical model that can be applied in similar situations. Assimilators have the ability to build theoretical models for the specifically defined problem based on well-defined hypothesis, established criteria for evaluation, and comparing alternatives by using inductive reasoning. *Convergers* go by hypothetical deductive logic and reasoning to come out with their rationale and logic for the decision. They have a practical approach, are good in making decisions, and do exceedingly well when faced with only one answer. *Accommodators* respond by adapting to given circumstances. They are effective in carrying out plans/instructions, use trial and error style, and set objectives and deadlines to achieve the same.

A different pedagogy applies to each learning style. As highlighted by Kolb, the suitable pedagogy for an activist is problem solving, small group discussion, and peer feedback. The trainer has to be a model professional who allows the learner to pick his/her own criteria for evaluating the alternatives and available information and material. For the reflector, the pedagogy that works best is lecture-based and the trainer needs to be a taskmaster and guide. A theorist learns the most by studying case studies, reading, and thinking. A pragmatist gains a lot from peer feedback, skill-based activities, and a trainer needs to act as a coach, as a pragmatist is a self-directed learner. According to Kolb there are four processes in the learning cycle that result in learning to take place and gives rise to four different types of personalities (Fig. 19.1).

The four styles (displayed above) emerge as an outcome of a learning process that undergoes four stages—(1) reflection and observation that has a focus on review and watching minutely; (2) abstraction and generalization that is considered to be a stage involving thinking; (3) hypotheses testing involving planning and doing phase; and (4) ultimately the stage that results in concretization and an experience linked to a phase of doing, sensing, and feeling. The ultimate purpose of learning is to ensure that the different stages of learning get ingrained in the

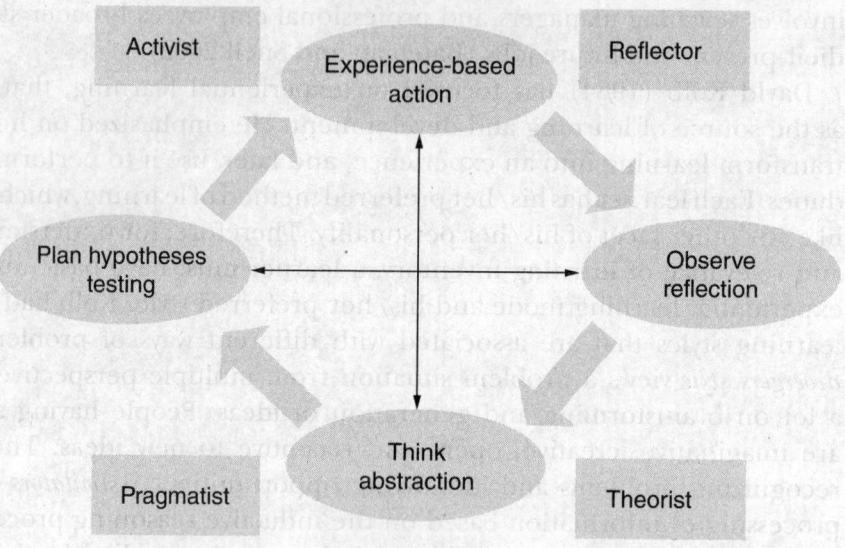

FIGURE 19.1   Kolb's experiential learning model

learner's personality. This ensures effectiveness, as a learner starts doing what he/ she is expected to do, so as to achieve a given level of performance.

The field of training and development (T&D) deals with the design and delivery of workplace learning by imparting required changes in the knowledge, skills, and attitudes to improve job performance. Therefore, in some organizations, the term *learning and development* is used instead of T&D in order to emphasize the importance of continuous learning for the individual and the organization.

Training and development provides an opportunity that enables an employee to acquire more than just knowledge. It offers the added advantage of networking and learning by sharing others' experiences. A trainee gains by learning the way in which his/her peers have tackled certain problems effectively while facing similar constraints, even when the training notes do not give a participant(s) the key to some of the solutions that he/she faces in the workplace.

Thus, training and career development are an integral part of the HRM programme that should be properly aligned with corporate strategy. Figure 19.2 displays the link between training, learning, individual, and organizational development.

Need for Training

Until a decade ago, organizations considered training to be a formality rather than an activity that was a must for the growth of the organization. In fact, line managers used to depute people for training out of sheer compulsion and for the sake of deputing. At times employees could easily be denied training because of their non-performance.

In the current scenario of advanced technology and information boom, human resources, knowledge, and skills are fast becoming obsolete. However, organizations

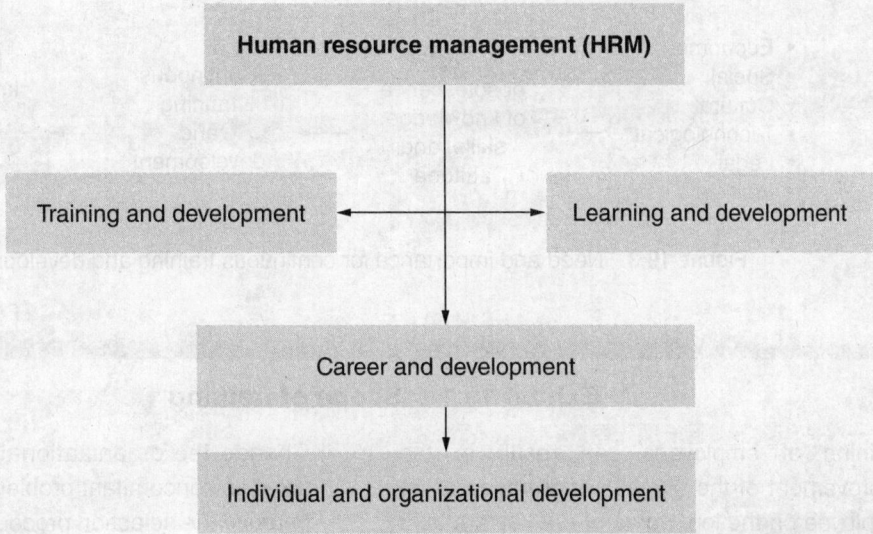

FIGURE 19.2 HRM—Linkages

are waking up to the need and importance of training not only because of a competitive global environment but also because of the success of economies such as Japan, Sweden, USA, wherein corporate entities have been making substantial investments in human resources training. In companies, such as Hewlett-Packard (HP), Xerox, IBM, and Marks & Spencer, human resource development (HRD) is seen as a major key to the success of the organization and is heavily emphasized at all levels (Beardwell and Holden 1996). Companies that spend the most on training typically average about 3.2 per cent of the payroll on training and provide employees with an average of 3.4 days of training per year (Kimmerling 1993). Alan Greenspan, the former Chairman of Federal Reserve Board, has rightly stated at the National Skills Summit, US Department of Labour that:

'The heyday when a high school or college education would serve a graduate for a lifetime is gone; basic credentials, by themselves, are not enough to ensure success in the workplace. Today's recipients of diplomas expect to have many jobs and to use a wide range of skills over their working lives. Their parents and grandparents looked to a more stable future—even if in reality it often turned out otherwise. Workers must be equipped not simply with technical know-how but also with the ability to create, analyse, and transform information and to interact effectively with others. Moreover, learning will increasingly be a lifelong activity.'

Thus, learning has to be a lifelong activity, considering the fast changes in economic, social, cultural, technological, legal, and political environment (Fig. 19.3). The need for T&D would continue becoming more and more crucial for the existence and long-term success of the organizations. The scope of training has been illustrated in Exhibit 19.1.

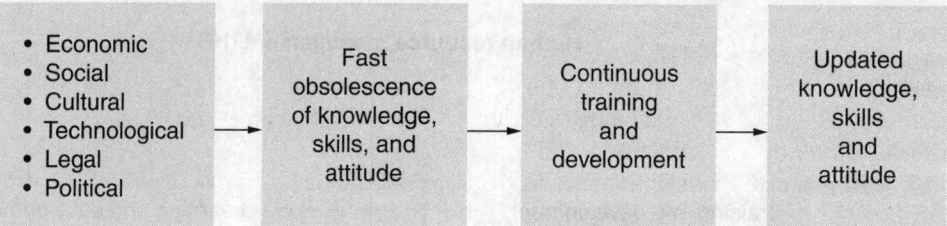

FIGURE 19.3 Need and importance for continuous training and development

Exhibit 19.1 Scope of training

Training of employees can result in the improvement of the overall performance of an employee on the job. Some of the key areas in which training can bring in positive change in the work environment are as under:

- Improve the method and system of working
- Increase the work output of the trained employee
- Increase employee versatility
- Improve communication and cooperation among employees and with clients
- Lower absenteeism
- Motivate employees to give their best to the organization
- Equip employees to deal with and handle new technology
- Help in overcoming resistance to change
- Increase employee satisfaction and lower grievances
- Reduce overtime
- Help superiors to delegate their responsibilities
- Let the trainee learn new skills at a very fast rate

It is equally important to know that training is not a panacea for all ills. Training cannot do the following:

- Change the organizational structure or solve its concomitant problems
- Improve the selection process or a substitute for it
- Solve problems, which are caused by organizational shortcomings such as shortage of manpower, lack of delegation, conducive work environment, and shortage of tools and technology

The steps to design a good training programme are as under:

1. Organizational analysis: Start with broad training needs of the organization
2. Based upon needs assessment: Assesses corporate and individual goals
3. Moves to specific tasks: Objectives should be phrased in terms of specific behavioural, knowledge, and attitudinal criteria
4. Employee analysis: Which employees need training?
5. Training evaluation: Pre and post change
6. Change in behaviour and performance on the job

Figure 19.4 illustrates the concept further.

(Contd)

Exhibit 19.1   (*Contd*)

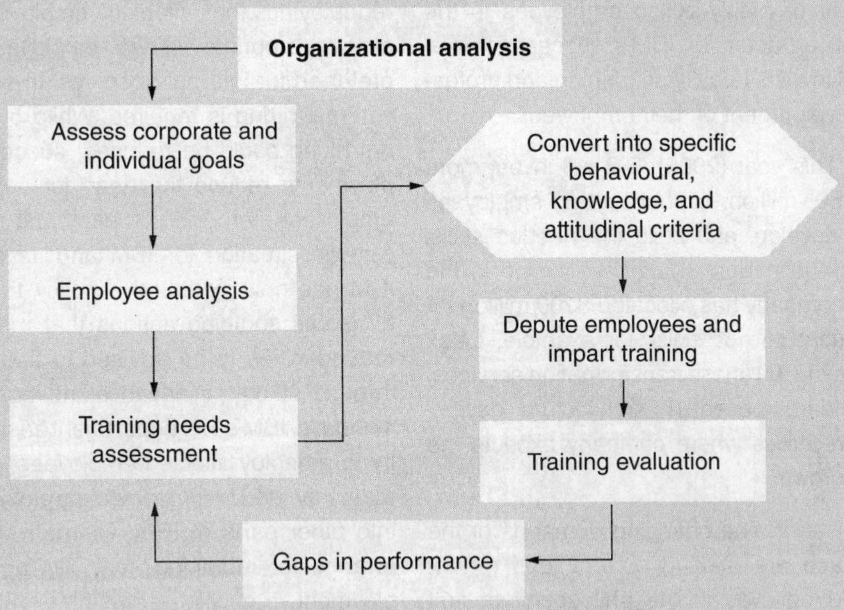

Organizational analysis

Assess corporate and individual goals

Convert into specific behavioural, knowledge, and attitudinal criteria

Employee analysis

Depute employees and impart training

Training needs assessment

Training evaluation

Gaps in performance

FIGURE 19.4   Steps in designing a good training programme

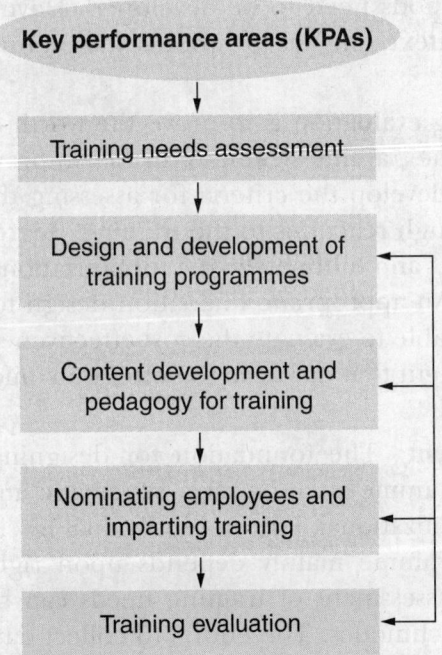

Key performance areas (KPAs)

Training needs assessment

Design and development of training programmes

Content development and pedagogy for training

Nominating employees and imparting training

Training evaluation

FIGURE 19.5   Complete cycle in development of effective training programmes

Systems Approach to Training

To realize the optimum benefits from investment made on training, the systems approach to training is imperative. The systems approach emphasizes on three major steps, which have been described in this section.

Assessment emanating from key performance areas It requires systematic identification of training needs by finding out what the organization needs at the organizational, work, and individual levels. At all the three levels, one has to precisely define the KPAs that are used to evaluate the performance. Key performance areas are the guiding force behind instructional objectives.

Development of training programmes Before conducting a training programme, one needs to keep the target participants in mind. A training programme needs to be devised with a focus on the profile of participants and learning principles (Fig. 19.5). After deciding upon the learning

IBM's investment in employee skills

Availability of highly-skilled employees is the most critical factor for IBM's success. Therefore, IBM invests heavily on training and professional development of their employees.

Training: This year (2005) IBM will invest more than $750 million to help their employees acquire, develop, and build the needed skills. Of this, $400 million would be invested in the US. The company has allocated $200 million for development of 'hot' skills; for example, Linux programming, business transformation services, and standards-based IT architecture design. These are areas where company expects the greatest growth.

Redeployment: The changing demands of the marketplace are making current jobs redundant. IBM believes in the philosophy of first redeploying the affected employees. Wherever appropriate, these employees will be preferred for internal openings. In some cases external hiring is required. While overall external hiring could be reduced, successful redeployments reduce the need for separation of employees from the company and results in a win-win situation for IBM and its employees. IBM has now instituted a policy that requires all global sourcing actions that may result in redundancies to be advised to the HR with a target of 90 days in advance and more desirably 180 days. IBM's HR department has the authority to redeploy affected employees, and others that may not be impacted by global sourcing, into other parts of IBM. Alternatively, HR can arrange for retraining, that will facilitate redeployment.

Source: Based on IBM Corporation, www.dol.gov/ebsa/pdf/Barnes070505.pdf, accessed on 15 October 2007.

environment, the training material and methods need to be developed. Having developed the training content in a given context, one has to conduct the training programme to achieve training objectives.

Training evaluation   The purpose of training evaluation is to prove the worth of training as also to bring an improvement in the training system to further improve its effectiveness. Training evaluation should develop the criteria for assessing the outcome of training as may be reflected through reactions to the training, degree of learning acquired, change in behaviour, and ultimately the organizational performance as contributed by the trainee. An appropriate evaluation design for training should be developed that should be able to evaluate the cost-effectiveness of training as also the performance improvement that may lead to better outcomes as desired from training.

Sources of data for training needs assessment   The foundation for designing, developing, and conducting a training programme is laid after a systematic and scientific assessment of training needs at organizational, job, and individual levels. The whole effectiveness of a training programme mainly depends upon right assessment of training needs. The data for assessment of training needs can be collected from various sources by different techniques. The efforts to collect data needs to be coordinated and integrated. Some of the prominent sources of data for training needs analysis are presented in Exhibit 19.2.

Exhibit 19.2   Data sources for training needs

Organizational analysis

- Organizational goals and objectives through strategic plans, business plans, departmental/divisional plans
- Personnel inventories giving detailed profiles of people
- Skills inventories
- Efficiency indices
- Changes in machinery, equipment, and technology
- Changes in systems and procedures
- Changes in policies
- Mandate from top management and executives for training
- Exit interviews

Job analysis

- Job description

- Job specification
- Performance standards
- Steps involved in performing the job
- Diagnosing jobs in consultation with departmental/divisional employees
- Operating problems involved in effectively performing the job

Person analysis

- Performance appraisal data
- Interviews with job performers and their supervisors
- Questionnaires
- Attitude surveys
- Assessment centres

Sources of data for training needs assessment is given in Fig. 19.6

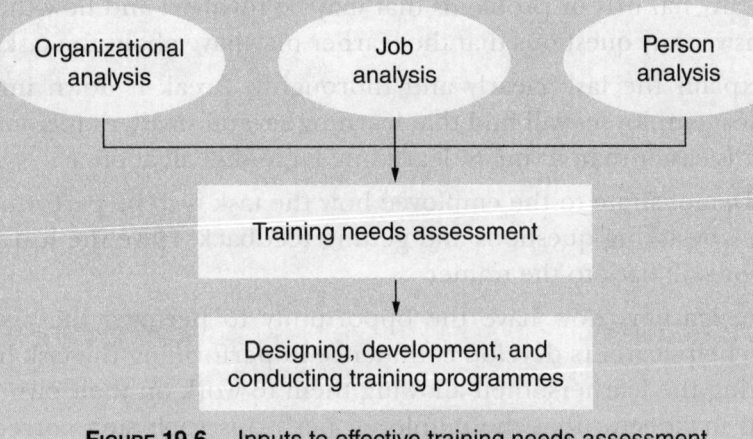

FIGURE 19.6   Inputs to effective training needs assessment

Before starting on a training programme, the needs of the organization should be assessed clearly by getting a three-dimensional matrix highlighting training inputs that would be required in terms of knowledge, skills, and attitudes at organizational, job, and human resource levels to achieve particular organizational objectives. This analysis needs to be proactive so that the details of this assessment are available over a period of time on an ongoing basis. Instructional objectives should emerge from the needs assessment and should clearly spell out the abilities, knowledge, and attitudinal changes that the trainee would be able to acquire at the end of the training programme.

Pre-training environment and conditions   A trainee should be open and receptive to learning. This means he/she should be motivated and should have the ability to learn. Trainees should cooperate with the trainer to create an environment conducive to learning. This can be best done by informing in advance the trainee about the benefits that would accrue from training. Some organizations even prefer to have some incentives linked to training, so that trainees get motivated to learn, retain, and practice what they have gained from the training. Further, its advantages can only be realized if the organization's management is committed to the training and attaches a great value to it. This is reflected in the organizational policies towards training and the kind of budget that gets allocated to training.

STEPS IN TRAINING

The teaching/learning process can be broken down into five steps—prepare, tell, show, do, and review. A closer look at each of these steps helps an employer or trainer to understand the process of learning. This five-step process is drawn from publications on training by Dr Bernie Ervin of The Ohio State University.

Prepare   The first step in this process is to prepare the learner. The trainer should put the learner at ease and explain why it is important to learn a particular skill. Explain any hazards or problems that may be involved and how they may be dealt with. Answer any questions that the learner may have about the task.

Tell   Explain the task clearly and thoroughly. Break it down into key parts or steps. Most employees will find that learning several smaller tasks and putting those together is easier than trying to learn one large skill all at once.

Show   Demonstrate to the employee how the task is to be performed. Involve the employee by asking questions and getting feedback. Have the learner explain the process or skill back to the trainer.

Do   The learners now have the opportunity to perform the task. The trainer needs to help learners develop confidence in performing the task by first carefully monitoring the learners, then allowing them to work on their own. The employer needs to make sure that the employee performs each step correctly and avoids developing any bad habits.

Review   Provide honest feedback to the learner in terms of encouragement, constructive criticism, and additional comments to enable him/her to further improve and excel in performing the task. This is a great opportunity to praise or correct the employee.

TRAINING METHODS

Learning normally takes place through informational methods of training or through experiential training methods (Fig. 19.7). The effectiveness of each varies

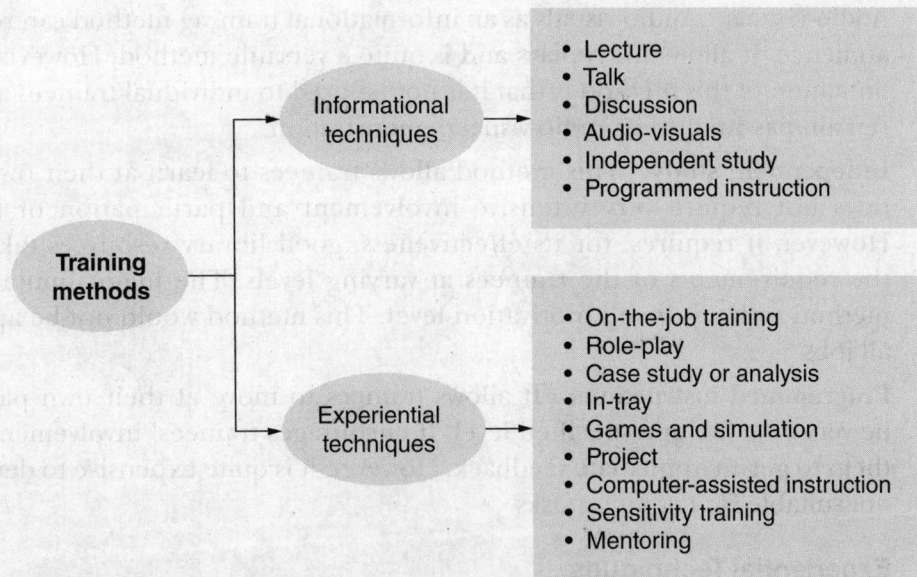

FIGURE 19.7   Various training methods

from the context and type of training. Informational methods are normally used to teach factual material, skills, or attitudes. Generally, they do not require the trainee to actually experience or practice the material taught during the training session (Simon and Werner 1996). Some of the commonly used techniques for training are described in this section.

Informational Techniques

Various informational techniques such as lecture, talk, discussion, etc. are used as training methods.

Lecture   A talk given to the trainees about the essential components of the task involved, without much participation in the form of questions or discussions on the part of the trainees. It is suitable for a large audience. The timing and information that has to be shared has to be worked out beforehand. It is as good as programmed instruction and is low-cost. The major limitation of the lecture method is that the learner is passive and it is not tailored to suit an individual trainee. As a result, the transfer of knowledge may be poor.

Talk   It allows the participation of trainees. It could be through questions asked by either of the party and discussions during the session. It is suitable when the number of participants is small, say less than 25. The main advantage of this method is greater interaction and the involvement of trainees that facilitates learning.

Discussion   Knowledge, ideas, and opinions on a particular topic are freely exchanged among the trainees and instructors. This method is suitable where the application of information is a matter of opinion, when attitudes need to be induced or changed, and obtaining feedback from the instructor about the way in which trainees may apply the knowledge they learnt.

Audio-visuals   Audio-visuals as an informational training method can reach a large audience. It allows for replays and is quite a versatile method. However, the major limitation of this method is that it is not tailored to individual trainees and learners remain passive during audio-visual demonstration.

Independent study   This method allows trainees to learn at their own pace and does not require very intensive involvement and participation of the trainer. However, it requires, for its effectiveness, good library resources taking care of the requirements of the trainees at varying levels. The major limitation of this method is the trainee's motivation level. This method would not be applicable to all jobs.

Programmed instructions   It allows trainees to move at their own pace and can be very effective at a specified level. It encourages trainees' involvement and helps them to get an immediate feedback. However, it is quite expensive to develop and is not suitable for cognitive tasks.

Experiential Techniques

On-the-job training, role-play, case study, etc. are used as experiential techniques of training.

On-the-job training   A session during which a job or part of a job is learned through explaining and demonstrating the ideal way of performing it and, thereafter, asking a trainee to do the job under supervision. This can be done through talk, demonstration, and practice. The method ensures that the required skills and knowledge are transferred to the trainee and involves limited trainer cost. The effectiveness of this method largely depends on the trainer's skills and willingness.

Role-play   Trainees are asked to enact, in the training situation, the role they will be called upon to play in their work. It is mainly used for the practice of dealing with face-to-face situations. This method ensures active learning under simulated situations that are close to reality. However, this method may not be suitable, if trainees do not take the role enactment seriously.

Case study or analysis   A history of some event or set of circumstances, with relevant details, is examined by the trainees. Case studies may focus on diagnosing the causes behind the problem or a solution to it. It helps in developing decision-making and problem-solving skills. The method ensures active learning. However, the case studies need to be continuously updated and trainer should be careful not to dominate the discussions.

In-tray   Trainees are given a series of files, papers, and letters similar to those they will be required to deal with at the place of work, to take action on each piece of work. The results are marked or compared with one another. This method is suitable for giving a trainee desk worker a clear understanding of the real-life problems and their probable solutions.

Games and simulations   Trainees are provided with information about a company's financial position, products, market, etc. They are given different management roles to perform. These groups/individuals run the company. Decisions are made and actions are taken. The probable results of these decisions in terms of profitability are then calculated. This method is suitable for giving trainee managers a practice in dealing with management problems. It provides feedback to the trainee and presents him/her situations involving realistic challenges. However, this method is highly competitive, time consuming, and may stifle creativity.

Project   This gives an opportunity to the trainee to display his/her initiative and creative ideas. The trainer lays down the particular task but the lines to be followed to achieve the objectives are left to the trainee to decide. This method can be used where initiative and creativity need stimulating or testing.

Computer-assisted instruction   This method allows trainees to move at their own pace. The training gets standardized over a period of time. Feedback is provided to the trainee. This method is relatively costly and provides very limited opportunity and flexibility for trainee interaction.

Group dynamics   Trainees are put into a situation in which the behaviour of each individual is subject to examination and comment by the other trainees. Feedback is made available to the trainee. This method is effective in developing interpersonal skills.

Sensitivity training   In this method a small group of trainees, say 8–14, work together to develop interpersonal skills. Sensitivity training can help a lot in improving self-concept, reducing prejudice, and changing interpersonal behaviour. However, this method may at times become threatening to the trainee.

Mentoring   The trainee is attached to a mentor, that is, an experienced member of the organization who serves as a friend, adviser, and confidant to a trainee to acquire knowledge and skills under one-to-one guidance. The relationship with the mentor in an organization or outside the organization may be formally planned or informally developed.

TRAINING IN THE INFORMATION AGE

There are various ways of training employees in today's complex environment. A training session can be organized in a classroom of the organization's training centre, on-the-job training, in corporate universities, community colleges, apprenticeship training, etc. The focus of training can be on imparting knowledge in specific areas to fill up the gaps, developing management development programmes to inculcate skills, or having a focus on attitudinal change. Today, organizations are emphasizing on training programmes such as basic computer skills, technical skills/knowledge, management skills/development, communication skills, supervisory skills, new methods and procedures, customer service, executive development, personal growth, secretarial skills, industrial relations, personnel management practices, etc.

NIIT

NIIT is a leading skills and talent development corporation that is building a manpower pool for global industry requirements. The company, which was set up in 1981 to help the nascent IT industry overcome its human resource challenges, today ranks among the world's leading training companies owing to its vast, yet comprehensive array of talent development programs. With a footprint across 40 nations, NIIT offers training and development solutions to individuals, enterprises, and institutions.

Let us now look at an example of a BPO service provider in the Philippines catering to various banking entities around the globe. The company has credit card and mortgage processes, and caters mostly to Australian customers.

In order to maintain consistent quality across the floor, the Filipino agents not only needed training on product/process, but also needed to be able to communicate effectively with customers. There was a need to neutralize their accent and train them on various customer interaction parameters, which would help them converse professionally with customers from Australia as well as other parts of the world.

Evolv, NIIT's soft skills arm, offers soft skills training, content development, and assessment services to clients. It studied the Filipino speech patterns by monitoring live and recorded calls of a sample of agents on the floor. The training program covered voice and accent, customer service, culture and listening comprehension. Filipino agents were helped to acquire a neutral accent by eliminating their speech idiosyncrasies and creating awareness of Australian idioms and speech nuances. Agents were also trained on Australian culture to help them relate better with the average Australian customer. The agents were trained, and then monitored when they hit the floor. Shop floor customer interactions were recorded and used during short burst refresher capsules to help agents relate with real-time environment and come up the curve faster.

Performance was measured during training as well as the monitoring phase. The same assessment metric was used so that progress could be tracked and areas of concern/improvement for each agent were immediately given attention. Evolv monitoring scores were mapped with the Customer Satisfaction Scores for the agents. Focused training inputs were given to the agents who were off the benchmark.

Source: http://www.niit.com/, accessed on 5 February 2016.

TRAINING EVALUATION

As Sloman (1996) says, 'If training in the organization is to become more effective, action will be required from trainers, academics, business schools, consultants, and government.' However, the trainer, trainee, and management play a crucial role in the success of a training session. Udai Pareek (2005) has rightly focused on managers as training partners for improving training effectiveness. In his paper, he has emphasized upon the need for line management to become partners in training. He has dwelt upon five key points of continuum for partnering by the work system management—hostility to training, critical attitude about training, supportive orientation to training, participating in the training function, and sharing training responsibilities.

After having spent huge funds on training, the credibility of the training system would depend upon the concrete benefits that the organization derives as a result of training. Therefore, it becomes important to determine the value of training to the organization. It is in this perspective that training departments have started placing greater emphasis on documenting their efforts and the valuable services provided. Certain organizations have started computing returns on investment on training and cost–benefit analysis to find out the worth of training. The task of measuring the benefits of training is quite difficult as number of benefits that accrue to the organization are intangible in nature and occur over a long-term period. Still, efforts are being made to find out the worth of training and training programmes to the organization vis-à-vis the investment made. The evaluation of training programmes helps in taking corrective steps in terms of change in methodology of training, content of training, type of training, duration of training, etc. Some of the commonly used techniques and approaches to evaluate the training are as follows:

- participants' opinions and reactions;
- extent and degree of learning by the participants;
- change in the behaviour of participants;
- to what extent have the proposed training goals and objectives been achieved;
- return on investment and cost–benefit analysis; and
- benchmarking, which is comparing the data with data from companies that excel in those areas.

In a fast-changing environment, it is essential that organizations train their employees to maintain an edge over other business entities in the industry. Training ensures motivated employees who are capable of responding to the emerging challenges on a continuous basis. It is in this backdrop that training and development, a planned continuous effort on the part of the organization to improve employee competency level and organizational performance, is becoming crucial to the growth of the organization. Effectiveness of training largely depends upon the commitment of the top management and the support it is provided with, a systematic approach to determine training needs backed up by solid programme design, and its implementation. One important condition that helps increase the chances of success of a training program is the cooperation from the trainee's superior. If the latter does not allow the trainee to use his/her newly acquired skills on the job, then he/she will soon forget the skills. Above all, a credible training system gives due importance to training evaluation. It is the outcome of training evaluation that would help the organization to keep improving its effectiveness and elicit further commitment from the top management to conduct training programmes in future.

SUMMARY

Advancements in technology and the information boom have made training of human resource very important for any organization, as human resource, capital, and knowledge tends to get obsolete fast. Training and development not only provides knowledge to the employee but also offers an added advantage of networking and learning from others' experiences.

Training can improve the overall performance of an employee on the job. To realize the optimum benefits from investment made on training, the systems approach to training is important. It requires the systematic identification of training needs by conducting needs analysis at organizational, work, and individual levels. The teaching/learning process can be broken down into five steps—prepare, tell, show, do, and review.

The purpose of training evaluation is not only to prove its worth but also to improve the training system. Learning normally takes place through informational methods of training or through experiential training methods. One needs to identify the form(s) of training to be adopted to achieve training objectives in a given context.

Training evaluation should develop the criteria for assessing the outcome of training as may be reflected through reactions to the training, degree of learning acquired, change in behaviour, and ultimately the contribution of the trainee in improving organizational performance. The training evaluation helps in taking corrective steps in terms of change in methodology of training, content of training, type of training, and duration of training.

KEYWORDS

Key performance areas (KPA) These are the measures that specify the optimum performance level expected of a particular job role.

Learning and development It emphasizes the importance of continuous learning for the individual and the organization.

Person analysis It is a component of job analysis that is used to identify who needs training.

Post-training Information, knowledge, skills, and attitude obtained after the training process.

Pre-training Information, knowledge, skills, and attitude possessed prior to the training.

Training and development (T&D) Training is a planned process to modify attitude, knowledge,

or skill behaviour through learning experience to achieve effective performance while development involves teaching managers and professional employees broader skills needed for their present and future jobs.

Training design, training programme, training evaluation These deal with the measurement of impact of training.

Training methods Methods used for imparting training to ensure desired learning.

Training needs A gap between what is required to perform a job competently as against what they actually know.

EXERCISES

Concept Review Questions

1. Define the concept of training. How does it differ from training and development?
2. What is the scope of training? Explain giving justification.
3. What are the steps involved in designing a good training programme?
4. What is meant by systems approach to training? What is the rationale behind it?
5. Training needs assessment is the first step in designing, developing, and conducting an effective training programme. What are the different sources of data for training needs assessment?
6. What are the different methods of training? Explain the relevance of each method and

its suitability for the achievement of training objectives.

7. To establish credibility of investment on training requires training evaluation to establish the benefits vis-à-vis the cost of training. What are the different techniques and approaches used for evaluation of training?

Critical Thinking Questions

1. Why is training and career development an integrated part of HRM? Explain.
2. 'The importance of training has been particularly influenced by the global competitive environment.' What is the rationale behind this statement? Explain.

Project Assignments

1. You have been assigned a task to justify, or otherwise, the investment on training abroad in the area of leadership of the top-level management. The cost has been growing at the rate of 20 per cent per year for the past three years. How will you go about identifying costs and benefits of training on leadership, particularly in an institution abroad?
2. Collect data from various sites on the investment on training and the amount time spent by employees in training systems in different companies belonging to different industries. Analyse this data to highlight the significance of training investment in different types of industries.

REFERENCES

Alan Greenspan, Chairman of Federal Reserve Board, National Skills Summit, US Department of Labor, www.dol.gov/_sec/skills_summit/p1s3.htm, accessed on 20 October 2007.

Bateman, Thomas S. and Scott A. Snell (2002), *Management Competing in the New Era*, McGraw-Hill Irwin, Boston, p. 321.

Beardwell, Ian and Len Holden (1996), *Human Resource Management: A Contemporary Perspective*, Macmillan India Ltd, New Delhi, pp. 337–338.

Fielding, M. (1994), 'Valuing Difference in Teachers and Learners: Building on Kolb's Learning Styles to Develop a Language of Teaching and Learning', *The Curriculum Journal*, vol. 5, no. 3, pp. 393–417.

Gibbs, G. (1988), *Learning by Doing: A Guide to Teaching and Learning Methods*, Further Education Unit, London.

Kimmerling, G. (1993), 'Gathering Best Practices', *Training and Development Journal*, September, pp. 28–36.

Kolb, D. (1984), *Experiential Learning: Experience as the Source of Learning and Development*, Prentice-Hall, Eaglewood Cliffs, New Jersey.

Pareek, Udai (2005), 'Managers as Training Partners', *Indian Journal of Training & Development*, vol. XXXV, no. 3, July–Sept, pp. 26–32.

Simon, S.J., and J.M. Werner (1996), 'Computer Training through Behaviour Modeling, Self Paced, and Instructional Approaches: A Field Experiment', *Journal of Applied Psychology*, vol. 81, no. 6, pp. 648–659.

Sloman, Martyn (1996), *A Handbook of Training Strategy*, Jaico, Mumbai.

Part IV
Managerial Competencies

20

Motivation

INTRODUCTION

What inspires people to do what they do? Why are some people more enthusiastic than others? Why do some people succeed and others do not, given the same environment and challenges? The answer to some of these questions lies in 'motivation'. How can one motivate the self and others? What are the factors that motivate? Which motivating factor would be the most suitable and under what circumstances and among what kind of personalities?

Motivation is a drive, an energizing force that directs and sustains a person's effort to achieve a given objective and goal. The first and foremost step that stimulates a person is the conscious setting of goals. The pursuit of the ultimate goal that has to be realized, stimulates, energizes, and directs a person's thoughts and behaviour. Thus, goal setting is extremely important for motivation and success. When a group has to perform and achieve results, cooperation becomes a basic prerequisite. It is essential to set goals for the team.

Motivation is need based and, therefore, can be defined as 'what one does not have that one wants, one works to achieve that which one needs'. Hence, if we know what people want and need, then we know what they will work for, and like working for, and so excel to achieve.

Motivation towards improved and better performance depends on the satisfaction of employees' needs for responsibility, achievement, recognition, and growth. Needs are basically felt, and their intensity differs and varies from person to person and from time to time, and so does the extent to which they can motivate. Behaviour is acquired

Learning Objectives

After studying this chapter, you will be able to:
- Understand the meaning of motivation
- Appreciate the theories of motivation
- Examine motivating and demotivating factors
- Learn how to motivate the self and employees

and learned. The desired behaviour could be encouraged and reinforced for even better performance through rewarding an individual or group of individuals for having achieved existing objectives and goals. One does get motivated by others or by factors that are available externally.

However, the motivation that comes from within an individual really makes the difference. Thus, a highly motivated person works very hard to achieve performance goals as they are set before him. Such a person develops a proper understanding of the job and turns out to be highly productive.

There are various theories that have been propounded to understand what motivates whom. Some of the prominent ones are explained in this section.

HIERARCHY OF NEEDS

One of the most well-known theories of motivation is Maslow's (1954) hierarchy of needs. Maslow highlighted on primary needs as motivators as per hierarchy of needs (Fig. 20.1).

The primary needs of an individual are as follows:

Physiological The need to survive; for example, for food, drink, health.

Safety Physical and emotional security, such as clothing, shelter, protection against unemployment, and old age pension.

Social needs/love and belonging The desire for affection and the need to belong within the family and in society.

Esteem Accomplishment and achievement that is recognized and appreciated by someone who matters brings a sense of self-respect and bolsters self-esteem. The achiever feels good about the self.

Self-actualization To utilize one's potential to the maximum, working with and for one's fellow beings.

Usually, the fulfillment of primary needs leads to higher order needs and, thereby, the primary needs related motivators become redundant for some people.

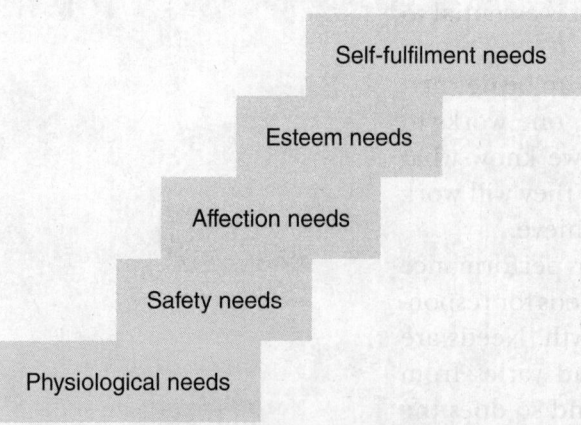

FIGURE 20.1 Maslow's hierarchy of needs

Self-fulfilment needs

Esteem needs

Affection needs

Safety needs

Physiological needs

THEORY X AND THEORY Y

Douglas McGregor (1960) proposed two distinct views of human beings—theory X that was labeled negative, and theory Y, that was labeled positive. Under theory X, managers assume that the employee does not like work, and given a chance would avoid it. Employees need to be coerced and controlled, or punished to achieve goals; they will avoid responsibilities and basically seek formal direction. The majority of workers like security and place it above all other factors. As against these negative assumptions about human behaviour under theory X, managers make positive assumptions under theory Y. They believe that employees view work as something natural such as play, rest, or relaxation; people are basically self-directed and self-controlled; an average person accepts and seeks responsibility; and above all, the ability to innovate is widely distributed throughout the population and is not necessarily among those who hold managerial positions. The major contribution by McGregor was in line with the framework given by Maslow in the hierarchy of needs. Theory X assumed dominance of lower level needs in individuals, while theory Y assumes the dominance of a higher order of needs in individuals. McGregor himself believed that theory Y is more valid and dependable than theory X. The major application of this theory lies in managers making assumptions about the employees and turning to motivators that would work under each of the assumption.

RELATED THEORIES

Some factors motivate while other do not. The need for job satisfaction acts as a motivator. Herzberg (1966) identified hygiene and comfort related environmental factors as leading to improvement in productivity. According to him, it is not the work but the way work is being performed that motivates people.

In his book *Professional People and Manual Workers*, Myers (1964), stated that people are motivated by the challenge in a job, which brings a feeling of achievement, responsibility, growth, advancement, fulfillment, enjoyment of work itself, and earned recognition. Workers become dissatisfied when opportunities for meaningful achievement are lacking or eliminated. Herzberg had also considered that feelings of job satisfaction were more important than money for persuading people to contribute more and increase productivity (Fig. 20.2). Myers, however, defined job satisfaction in more detail. Once the basic factors for job satisfaction were met by the worker, attempts were made to take the satisfaction to another level by job enlargement and job enrichment. *Job enlargement* consists of making

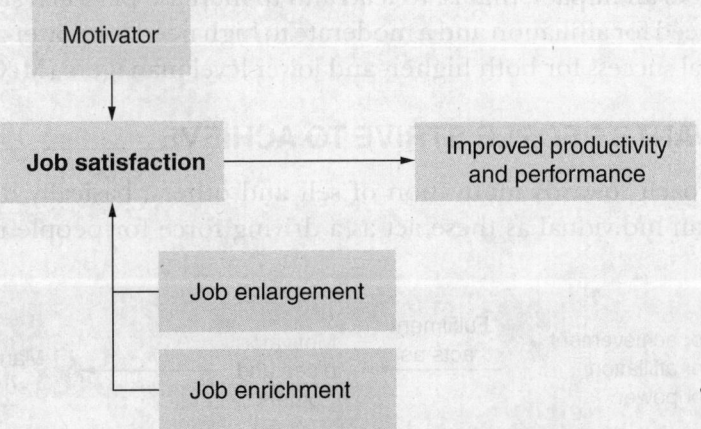

FIGURE 20.2 Job satisfaction—key to motivation

jobs more challenging and interesting by increasing the variety of the tasks to be carried out. *Job enrichment* refers to providing greater growth opportunities to the employee. Hence, motivation towards better performance depends on the satisfaction of needs for responsibility, achievement, recognition, and growth. The intensity of these needs varies from person to person and from time to time, and so does the extent to which they are motivated. The term 'recognition' in the definition includes money rewards. Note that both job satisfaction and money are motivating factors. One works to achieve what one needs and does not have. This could be either one of the two factors or both.

In reaction to Maslow's hierarchy of needs, Alderfer propounded the theory of existence, relatedness, and growth (ERG). Alderfer's ERG theory was first published in 1969 in an article titled 'An Empirical Test of a New Theory of Human Need' in *Psychological Review*. The ERG theory approaches the question of 'what motivates a person to act?' or 'why do we ever do anything?' The theory assumes that all human activity is motivated by needs. Existence (E) needs are material and physiological desires. Relatedness (R) needs are relationships with other people that are fulfilled by sharing thoughts and feelings with others. Growth (G) needs motivate people to change themselves or their environment.

These needs are realized by the complete utilization of existing capacities and developing new capacities. David McClelland (1961) proposed that each of us have three fundamental needs that exist in different proportions. These affect both how we are motivated and how we attempt to motivate others. The most important needs for a manager, according to McClelland, are the needs for achievement, affiliation, and power (Fig. 20.3).

Need for achievement A manager seeks achievement, this is realized by the attainment of goals and advancement, a strong need for feedback, sense of accomplishment, and progress.

Need for affiliation Need for friendship, interaction, and to be liked.

Need for power Managers are motivated by authority and seek to exercise influence and to make an impact, that is, to lead and to increase personal status and prestige.

A low need for affiliation and a moderate to high need for power are associated with managerial success for both higher- and lower-level managers (McClelland 1982).

NEEDS AND WANTS PEOPLE STRIVE TO ACHIEVE

The approach towards motivation of self and others, basically depends upon the needs of an individual as these act as a driving force for people to behave and act

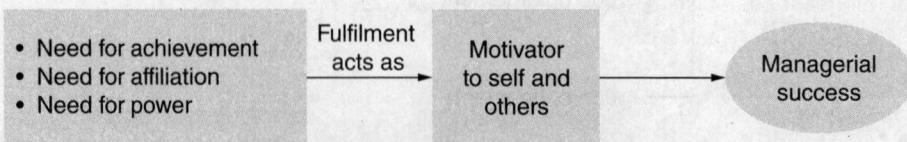

FIGURE 20.3   Fundamental needs as per McClelland

the way they do. The motivators may differ from person to person and time to time, depending upon the intrinsic profile of needs of the person. A broad spectrum of needs, as identified based on various theories of motivation in order of hierarchy, are presented in Exhibit 20.1.

One should also be careful not to use certain methods and attitudes that demotivate people (Fig. 20.4). Some of the demotivating factors are—negative criticism, humiliation in public, rewarding non-performance, lack of clarity about objectives and goals, negative attitude, discriminatory treatment, frequent transfers, changes in the assigned roles, responsibility not backed up by adequate authority, etc.

Similarly, the factors that motivate an individual are—recognition by way of praise, promotion, respect; making work interesting; attentive listening; assigning challenging tasks; support at critical junctures; encouraging people to do what they are expected to do; etc. The organization should create an environment wherein people, in general, aspire to cultivate motivation. Achievement-oriented groups of employees propel an organization to continuously grow, develop, and

---

Exhibit 20.1   Spectrum of needs

- Food and shelter, clothing, and warmth
- Affection and esteem
- Friendly and trustworthy cooperation and companionship
- Security from external threats
- Independence from domination by others
- Security from internal threats (losing job, criminal activities, or political persecution)
- Housing, education, and good health
- Help when in need
- Constructive work
- Constructive leisure activities
- Challenging work
- Maintaining, and the chance for improving one's position relative to colleagues
- Recognition of success by others
- Fair share of the national income and wealth
- Fair share of the international income and wealth

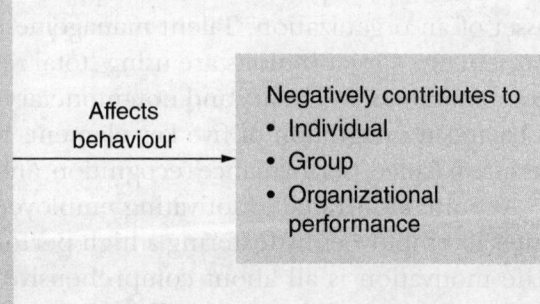

FIGURE 20.4   Factors that demotivate

Motivation

The trek towards the famous Sikh pilgrim centre Hemkund Sahib, a Sikh shrine begins at Govind Ghat. However, pilgrims trudge on foot to reach this sacred shrine, situated on the bank of the Hemkund lake (4,320 mt). Hemkund Sahib, is believed to be the spot where Guru Gobind Singh, the tenth and the last guru of the Sikhs, attained self-realization in his last birth.

It is trek of 14 km from Govind Ghat by foot or pony/horse to Ghangaria. The trek between Govind Ghat and Ghangaria takes about 6–8 hours on foot for a normal healthy individual and 8–15 hours for others. From Ghangaria, the 8 km trek upto Hemkund Lake (also known as Lokpal) is very steep.

Despite the distance and the obstacles, pilgrims of various faiths, apart from Sikhs, aged from 4 to 100 years can be seen walking to the shrine. Even physically handicapped individuals; some on crutches, can be seen making their way towards it. On enquiring about the distance left, the response is always that one is very close to the shrine. On the way, people keep helping each other selflessly; there is physical help to move, and glucose and other energy boosters are constantly distributed. At the end of this long tread, a majority of pilgrims find it surprising and miraculous to have reached the shrine and touched the holy place. What motivates these people to achieve something that seems next to impossible? Is it faith, will to achieve, the desire to enjoy nature's beauty, social support, friends, commitment to one's pledge, sense of belonging, or the sense of recognition? The answer is unknown. However, this example only proves motivation comes from within an individual and a motivated individual can motivate others.

aspire for excellence. Some of the important characteristics found in achievement-oriented people are—creativity, calculated risk taking, learning from failures, hard work, taking personal responsibility, openness to feedback, self-confidence, positive attitude, time consciousness, innovativeness, enjoying challenging assignments, initiative for continuous improvement, quick grasping power, and high tolerance for ambiguity.

HUMAN RESOURCES

It requires a completely different approach to motivate human resource, the key asset of an organization. Talent management is becoming more challenging in the present era. Organizations are using 'total reward' as a strategic tool for HRM. It is a combination of monetary and non-monetary gains provided to employees. It involves a balanced integration of five key elements namely—compensation, benefits, work–leisure balance, performance recognition, and development and career opportunities.

At Pantaloon Retail, motivating employees involves their families. Sapient motivates its employees by fostering a high performance culture, while at Max New York Life motivation is all about comprehensive and progressive people policies. Rajit Mehta, Executive Director of HR, training and internal communication at Max New York Life highlighting on non-monetary gains says, 'In today's competitive environment, playing just a monetary game to attract and retain talent is a losing proposition.

What matters the most is building an emotional bond with employees by extending a comprehensive value proposition'. Anil Sachdev, Chairman and Managing Director of Grow Talent, states that the intangible benefits, particularly, by way of reward and recognition amidst large gathering of employees have become a part and parcel of strategies to retain employees. Binod Wadhwa, Director of People Strategy at Sapient Technologies, highlights on value proposition, 'A critical component of our people success strategy is to make employees feel that they are recognized'. According to Sanjay Jog, HR head, Pantaloons, 'Employee engagement is more important than employee retention'. He attributes Pantaloon's low level of attrition at 23.6 per cent to the group's rewards programme.

What matters the most is an analysis of the needs of an individual and the group that employees strive to meet. It is this analysis that gives rise to a set of motivators that would click for a particular person or group of persons for performing and contributing their best for the achievement of set objectives and goals.

Experience has shown that people will do a lot for money, more for a good leader, and do most for a belief (Khera 2000). The challenge before managers is to change their own belief system and set an example whereby others develop a positive thinking and belief system conducive to channelization of their energies for achievement of worthwhile individual and group goals. The ultimate motivation is in self-motivation that comes from within, that is, when people act and perform on their own initiatives. What is needed for the same is developing a belief that we are responsible for our actions and behaviour. It is empowerment coupled with a sense of responsibility that leads to quality, efficiency, effectiveness, cost reduction, relationship building, cooperation, involvement, commitment, and, above all, achievement of worthwhile goals. At the organizational level, it is empowerment, fairness in dealings and processes, and designing programmes that creates a work environment that enhances employees' well-being through fair compensation, healthy environment, scope for personal growth, and freedom that leads to employees contributing more to enhance work output and productivity.

Motivation and performance level

Two companies X and Y producing 40 count cotton yarn with similar levels of investment, size, and labour force have been competing with each other. All their costs, such as raw materials, power, wages, administrative, sales, interest, and depreciation expenses, have been the same. Company X has been earning around 1.2 times of the net profit level when compared to the net profit earned by company Y.

The management of company Y appointed a task force to find out the reasons for the same. On detailed analysis carried over by the task force, it was found that the motivation level of employees of company X was relatively far higher than that of company Y. It was mainly on account of certain facilities provided in company X such as environment on the shop floor in terms of space for movement, lighting

(Contd)

Exhibit (Contd)

arrangement, canteen facility, pick-up and drop facility from home to company and back, and a free membership of a local club.

It was also found that employees of company X had free access to the top management and every month employees' achievements used to be recognized by giving them token prizes; handed over to them by the top management in person in a function organized by the company. The effect of these motivators resulted in a higher performance of employees in company X as estimated by their productivity being 1.4 times that of employees of company Y.

SUMMARY

Motivation is a drive, a force that directs and sustains a person's effort to perform for a given objective and goal. Motivation towards better performance depends on the satisfaction of needs for responsibility, achievement, recognition, and growth. Fulfilment of primary needs, that is, physiological, safety, affection, esteem, and self-actualization lead the employees further to needs of a higher order and thereby primary needs related motivators become redundant for some.

The most important needs for managers, according to McClelland, are the needs for achievement, affiliation, and power. What matters the most is the diagnosis and analysis of individual (self and others) and group needs that people strive and struggle to satisfy. It is this diagnosis and analysis that gives rise to a set of motivators that would click for a particular person or a group of persons for performing and contributing to their fullest extent for the achievement of a set objectives and goals.

KEYWORDS

De-motivating factors Factors that do not motivate a person to perform a task that he is expected to do.

Hierarchy of needs Maslow had defined a hierarchy of five levels of primary needs—physiological, safety, affection, esteem, and self-actualization needs.

Job satisfaction Factors contributing to job satisfaction act as motivators.

Motivation It is a drive, a force that directs and sustains a person's effort to perform for a given objective and goal.

Motivators Factors that encourage, inspire, and lead individuals to do what they are expected to do.

Need for achievement It seeks attainment of goals and advancement.

Need for affiliation Need for friendships, interaction, and to be liked.

Need for power Desire to exercise influence.

EXERCISES

Concept Review Questions

1. Define motivation and its relevance to self and managers.
2. Define Maslow's hierarchy of needs and its contribution to the theory of motivation.
3. What has been Herzberg's contribution to the theory of motivation?

Critical Thinking Questions

1. In what way does McClelland's three fundamental needs differ from Maslow's hierarchy of needs. Do you think that there is any relevance of McClelland's three fundamental needs to the workers of an organization? Give reasons.

2. Do you think any one theory of motivation can work effectively to get the best out of an individual? Comment critically.

Project Assignment
Prepare a case identifying a particular incident related to an adamant employee who has posed a great challenge to the manager. After diagnosing the situation, what methods would you use to motivate the employee?

REFERENCES

Alderfer, C. (1972), *Existence, Relatedness, and Growth: Human Needs in Organisational Settings*, Free Press, Glencoe.

Herzberg, F. (1966), *Work and the Nature of Man*, World Publishing Co., Cleveland.

Khera, Shiv (2000), *You Can Win*, Macmillan India Ltd, p. 99.

Maslow, A. (1954), *Motivation and Personality*, Harper & Row, New York.

McClelland, David (1961), *The Achieving Society*, D. Van Nostrand, Princeton, New Jersey.

McGregor, D. (1960), *The Human Side of Enterprise*, McGraw-Hill, New York.

Scott, Myers M. (1964), 'Professional People and Manual Workers', http://www.solhaam.org/articles/motvtnsu.html, accessed on 10 August 2014.

21

Team Effectiveness

Learning Objectives

After studying this chapter, you will be able to:
- Examine the importance of team building in organizational effectiveness
- Use inputs that design successful teams
- Evaluate rules of team development
- Understand the principles of team building
- Understand team effectiveness

INTRODUCTION

A team may be defined as a group of interdependent individuals who work together to accomplish a common goal or purpose. The critical prerequisites for building an effective team are interaction, mutual influence, interdependence, and a well-defined common goal. However, forming a team cannot ensure success. For a team to succeed, it is essential that members work consciously to maintain, build, and develop effectiveness. What matters the most is the composition of a team and the roles that its members play, given the inputs and skills that they possess. The first step in developing team building skills is to identify each team player's style. Without knowing what style each one follows, it is very difficult to form an effective team that will complement an individual's strengths and weaknesses. All members of the team have to synchronize themselves with each other to build an effective team. One can always accomplish more as a group than as an individual. Teams can contribute a great deal to modern organizational life. Positively working teams encourage flexibility, involvement, and efficiency. An introduction to teamwork is known to have entirely transformed companies. Almost all fast growing and sustainable business organizations use a team-based approach to produce goods and services, manage projects, and run the company effectively (Cohen and Bailey 1997).

SUCCESSFUL TEAMS

An organization has to form effective teams to achieve its goals. Important inputs to design effective teams are as under:

- size of the team;
- team goals;
- composition of members: skills, talents, and knowledge;
- roles: task-oriented, relationship-oriented, and self-oriented;
- characteristics: personalities, skills, and abilities; and
- diversity: heterogeneous or homogeneous.

All the aforementioned inputs are crucial for the success of a team. However, for a team to succeed it is essential that it is clear about its team goals, only then can the team have a sense of direction and purpose and can all team members be motivated to contribute their best for the accomplishment of a goal. Common understanding and sharing of goals among team members compels them to work harder and longer on the task required for high performance (O'Leary-Kelly et al. 1994).

Roles

A critical factor in designing and developing a team is related to individuals who comprise the team. Team composition depends largely upon the mixture of individual inputs and the skills that are available in the team (Lewis et al. 2001).

For a team to be effective each team member should be clear about their role within it. A role may be defined as a set of behaviours and attitudes that characterize an individual in a given situation. This behaviour is governed by a combination of individual, team, and organizational expectations. The development of roles on the part of individuals gets governed by the process of internalization on the part of employees about the expectations of these three sources. It is important to understand that people have multiple roles to play within the same group (Johnson & Johnson 1994). While working in a group, associated individuals have to perform and fulfil several roles. Member roles mainly fall into three broad categories—task-oriented, relationship-oriented, and self-oriented. Each category has its own set of associated behaviours (Quick 1992). For these three categories of roles, the associated behaviour characteristics are as under:

Task-oriented roles: The team member plays the role of an initiator, informer, clarifier, summarizer, energizer, reality tester, and consensus taker.

Relationship-oriented roles: The team member takes on the responsibilities of a harmonizer, gatekeeper, encourager, compromiser, observer, and commentator.

Self-oriented roles: The team member plays the negative role of an avoider, help seeker, aggressor, blocker, and dominator.

Effective teams are the ones that are able to integrate the relationship and task-oriented roles well. A good team has the following characteristics:

- it has clear sense of itself as a group;
- it interacts positively with outsiders;
- it cultivates positive assumptions and beliefs;
- it communicates clearly;
- the team and its members must establish a clear approach to the team's work; and
- the members must have a sense of mutual accountability.

TEAM DEVELOPMENT

Team development refers to different stages of team building, ultimately, leading to a situation wherein a team member, leader, and facilitator is prepared to work effectively, and contribute his best for the achievement of team goals.

- start modestly;
- be very clear about your goals and objectives;
- remember that the unknown is usually more threatening than the known;
- remember that development is basically self-regulated;
- be prepared to grab other opportunities that may arise as a result of your actions;
- ensure everyone's agreement;
- if required, be prepared to accept outside help;
- consult widely and genuinely; and
- encourage open and frank discussions.

Types of Teams

There are six basic types of teams as shown in Fig. 21.1—functional teams, problem-solving teams, cross-functional teams, virtual teams, self-managed teams, and advisory teams.

A *functional team* comprises of a group of people engaged in performing a particular function in the organization. Such teams mainly exist in an organization within functional departments such as marketing, production, finance, human resources, quality, and research and development. *Problem-solving* teams are meant for solving work-related problems pertaining to all aspects of group working. These teams are often empowered to take action within well-defined limits (Rose & Buckley 1999). *Cross-functional teams* comprise diverse membership with varied professional background and focus on undertaking a conceptual work that is occasionally temporary in nature. Such teams are especially required to handle situations that require adaptability, speed, and a directed focus to respond to fast-changing customer needs (Michalski & King 1998). *Virtual team* members are physically located at different places and are linked by technology. They work together to achieve team goals. These teams are the most effective to deal with situations wherein team members need to work across distances, time zones, and, increasingly, across organizational boundaries (Hellriegel et al. 2001). Virtual teams use computers and Internet-based technology to interact with distant members of the team, while working towards a common goal (Cohen 2003). *Self-managed teams* focus on doing well-defined day-to-day work as a coherent group. In a self-managed team, members may develop themselves to perform different jobs required to be undertaken for the completion of the task. These teams undertake

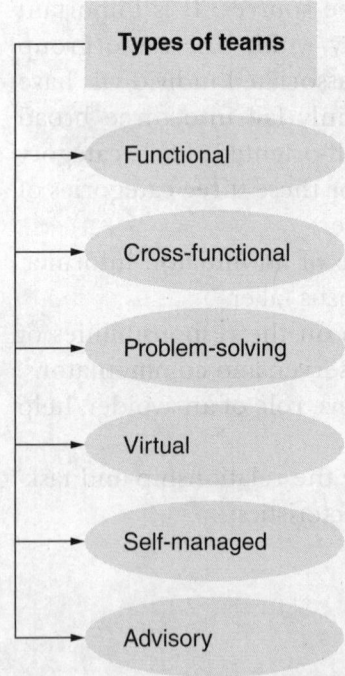

Types of teams

- Functional
- Cross-functional
- Problem-solving
- Virtual
- Self-managed
- Advisory

FIGURE 21.1   Different types of teams

a variety of managerial tasks involving work scheduling, rotation of tasks and assignments among members, ordering materials, deciding on team leadership, setting team goals, budgeting, hiring replacements when required, etc. (Purser & Cabana 1999). *Advisory teams* are formed to provide suggestions for improvement. They are usually set up for overseeing team operations and extend guidance and support related to team projects or goals. They usually comprise part-time members.

Principles of Team Building

Team building is a well-planned process that results in improved communication and working relationships amongst the team members to contribute towards the achievement of a well-defined goal. The basic principles of team building are as under:

1. Each team member performs both a function and a team role.
2. A team needs an optimal balance between functional and team roles, depending on its task.

Different teams

Mr Topiwala has a group comprising 12–15 members of his organization working in the production department. He operates on the principle of getting jobs done in the fastest and most efficient way possible without producing a single defective piece. Mr Topiwala usually allows his group members to have a moderate degree of authority over their work and allows the group to decide the goal towards which it would like to work within the framework of monthly targets given by the production general manager. As a part of the organization's management team, Mr Topiwala has little involvement in directing the group. He has been observing that his team has been effectively delivering results and responds to emergency situations and challenges with a lot of involvement and commitment. His own experience has been that creating an environment to build self-managed work teams goes a long way in organizational success.

Mr Abhishek Rathi, an engineer from IIT Delhi, has been serving in a software development company for the past 5 years. He has been elevated to the position of project leader last year. A team of 12 young engineers, some fresh campus recruits, and others, having two-three years of experience have been working with him. The company gets software assignments from its clients spread across different continents. Assignments need to be delivered on time and with the coordinated effort of team members. Abhishek discusses the project in detail with his team and then leaves it to them to decide about the work schedules. He meets the team twice a week on Monday and Friday between three and four p.m. to review the progress.

All team members, after the initial rounds of discussions and planning, go back and start working from their homes. Sometimes, during the course of their work they may come back to office and work till late in the evening. The whole group, usually works on a specific assignment under the leadership of one of the members (leadership keeps rotating) who interacts with them through the Internet. A team leader interacts with the client to clarify doubts, if any, and also to keep them abreast with the progress of the work. The arrangement has been working well and all the overall objectives and goals of the organization are being met with. This kind of virtual team operation has been quite common in a number of software development companies.

Exhibit 21.1   Nine steps for building good teams

A good team has some basic features. They are as under:

- Clearly defines the problem
- Looks for commonalities
- Respects all contributions
- Recognizes multiple interests
- Respects all individuals
- Looks towards solutions
- Moves from WIIFM (what's in it for me) to WIIFU (what's in it for us)
- Focuses on benefits
- Allows time to evaluate and make decisions

3. Team effectiveness depends on how the team members balance themselves within the team.
4. Some team members fit into certain team roles better than others, depending on their personalities and mental abilities.
5. A team can only deploy its technical resources to the best advantage when it has a suitable range and balance of team roles.

Exhibit 21.1 illustrates the steps towards building good teams.

Team building skills

Team building skills are important for a leader or manager to be effective. In today's environment, teams take on different forms such as inter-departmental, inter-divisional, physical or virtual, members constituting equal level of hierarchy, or different levels of hierarchy. Effective leaders have to consciously inculcate various skills among their team members that would contribute to good team building. Some of the important skills required for building a team are as follows:

- building interpersonal relationship;
- interaction process analysis;
- roles;
- clarifying purpose;
- goal;
- measures;
- communication;
- participation;
- decision-making;
- problem-solving;
- team spirit factor;
- feedback rules; and
- team effectiveness review.

TEAM EFFECTIVENESS

Team effectiveness refers to the efficient achievement of well-defined set of objectives. Successful organizations continuously keep working towards improving their teams' effectiveness by becoming responsive to the fast-changing internal and external environment. It requires a diversity of skills and talents that need to be complemented amongst team members. Some of them are:

- providing the team with a vision;
- establishing clear and well-defined goals;
- defining roles and their complementarities;
- attempting to build consensus;

Dell Inc.

Dell Inc. is a trusted and diversified information technology supplier and partner employing 65,200 employees worldwide working towards selling a comprehensive portfolio of products and services to customers worldwide. Dell is recognized by *Fortune* magazine as America's most admired company and is ranked number three globally. It designs, builds, and delivers innovative, tailored systems that provide customers with exceptional value. The company's revenues for the last four quarters were $54.2 billion.

The core principles of Dell articulate the company's commitment to people development. 'We believe our continued success lies in teamwork and the opportunity each team member has to learn, develop, and grow.' This includes a pledge to provide learning opportunities to maximize team and individual performance as well as utilizing job assignments and experiences to build global leadership capability. The company's philosophy is to manage its talent as a key asset and invest in its people's capability to build a competitive advantage.

Dell recognizes that most learning and development happens on-the-job, while the remainder includes interacting with others through networking, coaching, mentoring, and formal learning programs. The company believes in the philosophy of learning through others and building a strong culture based on team building. It encourages coaching and mentoring that would help its employees to improve their performance. The informal networking within the organization increases effectiveness as team members and establishes productive relationships with co-workers and key individuals across the company.

Source: Based on the data from www1.ap.dell.com/hybrid/careers/content/0de1e3f6-bdab-49bb-8202; www.dell.com/content/topics/global.aspx/corp/soulofdell/, accessed on 24 August 2007.

- deciding to perform key tasks via a democratic process;
- encouraging voluntary sharing of work experience, professional expertise, and essential information;
- inculcating in team members the need to show respect for and courtesy towards each other;
- promoting free discussion cross-fertilization at planning stage;
- using brainstorming techniques to trigger creativity;
- providing organizational support; and
- having a performance-linked objective reward system.

Thus, an ideal team member is the one who has the appropriate technical skills, knowledge, good listening and communication skills, ability to build trusting relations among team members and with the management, and a willingness to be committed to team goals. Such a member would contribute the most to team effectiveness. The team building approach in an organization goes a long way in ensuring ultimate organizational success, irrespective of external constraints and challenges. Team building, in short, entails rigorous planning and commitment involving team members and their development, training team members in a variety of skills, monitoring, and rewarding them for its success, so as to enthuse them for the next venture.

The core of today's organization is to recognize the value of teams, to specify why teams are a vital factor for organizations, why they fail in a given situation, and how conflict can contribute positively to a team. It is also necessary to understand and identify non-cooperative team members and suitably deal with them. A manager needs to clearly work out the steps to move from 'I' to 'We' to the 'problem' as a point of focal attention. In today's complex work situations and fast-changing environment, the success of an organization largely depends upon building a team-based culture.

Barriers to Team Effectiveness

Teams often face issues that can decrease their effectiveness, especially its ability to make decisions (Hargreaves et al., cited in Fullan 1993). These problems can relate to—(1) the time trade-offs in decision-making (the time taken by the team to make decisions can take time away from working directly on the relevant issue); (2) problems of 'groupthink' and pressure to conform; (3) the potential for increased conflict over decision-making without adequate training and preparation; it is unlikely that such team(s) will work effectively to develop and realize a shared vision; and (4) without team leadership (as opposed to traditional top-down leadership), the teams will be unproductive. Another potential barrier is individual resistance to working in a team.

Issues in team effectiveness

ABC Ltd, a construction company having a good team, has been doing well over the year. The managing director comes across an advertisement seeking tenders for the construction of a tourist resort in Himachal Pradesh. He discusses the matter with his senior team members. Together, they decide that they would quote for the tender of rupees ₹5 crore. A meeting was called the same afternoon to discuss various aspects of the tender with departmental heads. The discussion was fruitful and a meeting was adjourned to the next day, so that the people involved can do their homework to arrive at more accurate figures as also the competence that it would require on the part of the company to effectively execute the project. The next day, everybody came prepared with details related to their role with regard to the project. After some brainstorming, a decision was arrived regarding the quote to be submitted, delivery, quality, and the team members required in case the company gets the project and the kind of margins that the project would have.

The marketing department was asked to prepare the tender papers and submit the same within two days. The tender papers were prepared in line with the decisions taken by the corporate team and sent across the same day. After ten days ABC Ltd comes to know that the tender has gone in favour of its rival XYZ Ltd, the company's rival at a higher quote than the one decided by the ABC Ltd. The company was perplexed and decided to enquire into the reasons of its failure. Soon, it was found that the tender papers of ABC Ltd had not reached in time as

(Contd)

Exhibit *(Contd)*

the mailing clerk did not dispatch the papers on the same day. Since 'the courier fellow did not turn up that day' an employee had been sent to the local post office to send the papers by Speed Post. But the window was closed by the time he reached and the next day happened to be Sunday. The papers were ultimately sent on Monday by Speed Post which were delivered a day after the last date for submission of tenders. This focuses on a single weak link in the chain of operations to be undertaken by the team for achievement of its goal that jeopardized the whole effectiveness of the team. Further, what appears to be a simple task may turn out to be highly valuable for achievement of results by the team.

SUMMARY

An effective team is essential for the success of a modern organization. Teams that work positively encourage flexibility, involvement, and efficiency. An introduction to team working has been known to transform companies entirely. While developing a team, one should be conscious of different roles that people play, such as relationship oriented, task-oriented, and self-oriented roles, and their relevance and implications to the development of a team. The four basic types of teams are functional, problem-solving, cross-functional, and self-managed. Cooperation is the key element behind building a good team. It is important to understand the steps involved in building cooperation amongst team members. Teams often face issues that can decrease the effectiveness of the team and, especially, its ability to make decisions.

Today organizations strive to recognize the value of teams, why they are a vital to organizations, why teams may fail in a given situation, and how conflict can be a positive team element.

KEYWORDS

Cooperation and team building skills These are skills required in a leader or manager to build a good team. Some of the prominent skills required are cooperation, communication, decision-making, participation, feedback rules, etc.

Cross-functional team It comprises a diverse membership with varied professional backgrounds and focuses on undertaking a conceptual work that is occasionally temporary in nature.

Effective teams These teams are formed to achieve a specific, well-defined purpose and goal.

Functional team It is a group of people engaged in performing a particular function in the organization.

Good team It refers to a team that looks for commonalities, respects all contributions, recognizes multiple interests, respects individuals, looks for solutions, moves from WIIFM (what's in it for me) to WIIFU (what's in it for us), focuses on benefits, allows time to evaluate and make decisions, and follows steps for team building.

Problem-solving team It is meant for solving work-related problems pertaining to all aspects of group working.

Self-managed team It focuses on performing well-defined day-to-day work as a coherent group.

Team A team is a group of interdependent individuals who work together to accomplish a common goal or purpose.

Team building It is a well-planned process that results in improved communication and working relationships amongst team members to contribute towards achievement of well-defined goals.

Team development It refers to different stages of team building, ultimately leading to a situation wherein a team member, leader, and facilitator are prepared to work effectively and contribute their best for the achievement of team goals.

Team effectiveness It relates to achievement of well set and well-defined objectives and goals.

EXERCISES

Concept Review Questions

1. Define positive working teams.
2. What are the different types of roles that individuals play while working in a team? Which particular areas of roles hinder formation of an effective team and which facilitate the formation of an effective team?
3 'In a good team, members must have a sense of mutual accountability.' How does mutual accountability contribute to the formation of a good team?
4. How can cooperation be built amongst team members?

Critical Thinking Questions

1. What are the barriers to effective team functioning? How does individual resistance come in the way of team functioning? Explain giving concrete examples.
2. How does a performance-linked objective reward system contribute to team effectiveness? Explain.

Project Assignments

1. There are a large number of organizations having excellent employees. However, they lack in team effectiveness. What do you think are the major obstacles to teams functioning in Indian organizations?
2. Identify a company and find out the emphasis it gives on team-based culture to promote its effectiveness. Identify the strategies and policies pertaining to team building that it has implemented in achieving organizational goals.

REFERENCES

Cohen, S. and D. Bailey (1997), 'What Makes Teams Work: Group Effectiveness Research from the Shop Floor to Executive Suite', *Journal of Management*, vol. 23, pp. 239–90.

Cohen, S.G. (2003), (ed.), *Virtual Teams That Work*, Josssey-Bass, San Francisco.

Fullan, M. (1993), *Change Forces: Probing the Depths of Educational Reform*, Falmer, Bristol.

Hellriegel, Don, John W. Slocum, Jr., and Richard W. Woodman (2001), *Organizational Behavior*, 9th edition, South-Western Thomson Learning, Singapore, pp. 229–31.

Johnson, D.W. and P.F. Johnson (1994), *Joining Together: Group Theory and Group Skills*, Allyn & Bacon, Boston, pp. 18–21.

Lewis, Pamela, Stephen H. Goodman, and Patricia M. Fandt (2001), *Management Challenges in 21st Century*, 3rd edition, South-Western College Publishing, Thomson Learning, p. 449.

Michalski, W.J. and D.G. King (1998), (eds), *409 Tools for Cross-Functional Teams: Building Synergy for Breakthrough Creativity*, Productivity Press, Portland.

O'Leary-Kelly, A.M., J.J. Martocchio, and D.D. Frink (1994), 'A Review of the Influence of Group Goals on Group Performance', *Academy of Management Review*, vol. 37, pp. 1285–301.

Purser, R. and S. Cabana (1999), *The Self-Managing Organization: How Leading Companies Are Transforming the Work of Teams for Real Impact*, Free Press, New York.

Quick, T.L. (1992), *Successful Team Building*, AMACOM, New York.

Rose, E. and S. Buckley (1999), *50 Ways to Teach Your Learner: Activities and Interventions for Building High-Performance Teams*, Jossey-Bass, San Francisco.

22

Communication

INTRODUCTION

Effective communication is important, not only for the success of an organization but also the individuals within it. Individuals who are able to communicate their ideas and thoughts influence others within the organization and leave their mark. Similarly, organizations that effectively communicate their purpose as well as the information about products and services tend to be more successful. Information technology has diversified the various ways in which organizations function. Hence, communication is vital in clarifying the diverse and complex methods in which the organization works to achieve its objectives. Communication is further becoming relevant in the information society wherein services have started dominating with regard to wealth creation and accumulation. In this chapter, we shall analyse communication and its relevance to organizations and their dealings.

EFFECTIVE COMMUNICATION

Communication refers to a series of interrelated activities such as reading, listening, managing, interpreting information, serving clients, writing, speech making, and the use of symbolic gestures (Conger 1991). Development and integration of technology with professional life has made traditional communication activities much more complicated.

Learning Objectives

After studying this chapter, you will be able to:

- Understand the importance of communication in improving personal and organizational effectiveness
- Learn how communication enhances personal effectiveness
- Understand the communication process
- Examine the barriers to effective communication
- Examine the basic rules for ensuring effective communication
- Learn about improving organizational effectiveness through communication

Communication and Personal Effectiveness

Organizational communication is the central binding force that permits coordination among people and, thus, allows for organized behaviour, according to Myers and Myers (1982). As per Rogers (1976), the behaviour of individuals in organizations is best understood from a communication point of view. Communication is not only an essential aspect of organizational changes, but effective communication is the foundation of modern organizations (Grenier & Metes 1992; D'Aprix 1996; Witherspoon 1997; Von Krogh et al. 2000).

Effective communication refers to the meaningful transfer of ideas and thoughts from one party (sender) to another (receiver) through the medium of exchange via a monologue or a dialogue. Communication helps us in projecting a positive image; it builds synergies that lead us to achieve goals, it helps others to estimate an idea's true potential; and above all, it helps us in displaying our knowledge and facilitates feelings, so that we are prepared to absorb new and fresh ideas. It is also very important to appreciate and understand that a major part of communication between individuals, groups, and organizations is non-verbal, implying thereby, that when we attribute meaning to what someone else is saying, the verbal part of the message actually means less than the non-verbal part that includes body language and tone. These aspects should be given special importance in ensuring effective communication.

It is in this backdrop that we need to appreciate the power of communication for each one of us in our different roles and particularly the managers who spend a major part of their valuable time communicating through meetings, face-to face discussions, memos, letters, emails, reports, etc. Further, technological developments and transformation have drastically changed the role of workers, managers, and executives in an organization.

Communication Process

The communication process has four important aspects—the message, decoding of the message, encoding by the receiver, and the message receiver (Fig. 22.1). A message is a tangible form of coded symbols that are intended to give a particular meaning to the information or data (Lewis, et al. 2001). The sender gives a meaning to the message and the situation under consideration. As highlighted in the best practices from corporate leaders, at times messages are conveyed in a way that they get misinterpreted. Miscommunication, misinterpretation, or errors in communication can take place while decoding or encoding the message. Therefore, it is not enough for the sender to have an impressive command over the language or the content. He has to be careful that the message is received in its true sense at the other end. The receiver has to act as expected by the sender after having received the message. It is important to realize that the medium of communication matters the most. The communicator has to choose from written, oral, non-verbal, and electronic methods of communication.

Communication is said to be complete when it serves the intended purpose. Therefore, it should have a balance between emotion and intelligence, speaking

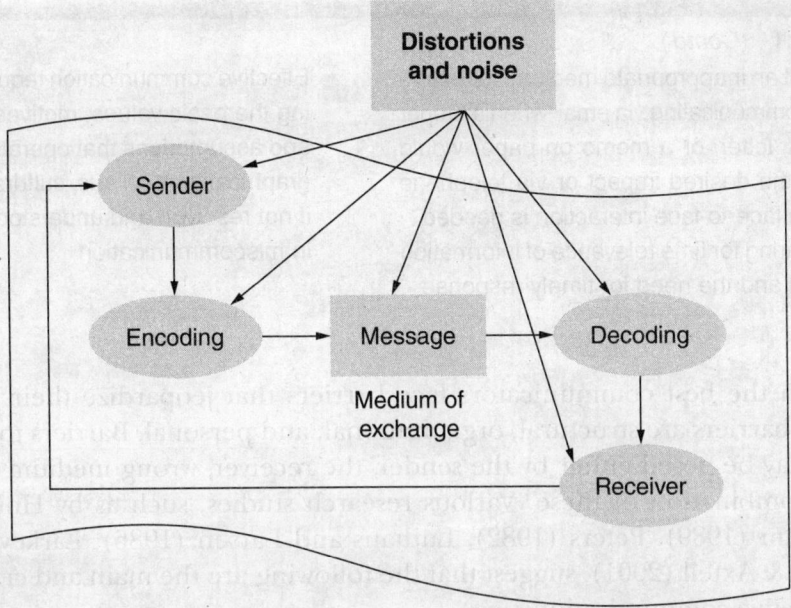

Figure 22.1   Important stages in the communication process

and listening, and above all, should ensure that the audience grasps its content and purpose. Effective communication is creative and caters to its audience's needs.

To ensure value addition to the target audience, a communicator must plan, prepare, and finalize the message beforehand and should be clear about the target audience. Effective communication also involves good body language, understanding, voice modulation, and a good grip over the language. In short, communicators have to articulate and must be able to communicate their ideas and thoughts clearly. In order to communicate effectively, it is necessary to eliminate the barriers to communication. Exhibit 22.1 illustrates the concept further.

Exhibit 22.1   Barriers to effective communication

Some of the important barriers to effective communication that need to be carefully attended to are as under:

- A bad choice of words, unclear sentences, or phrases
- Defensiveness, distorted perceptions, guilt transference, or distortions from the past
- Body language, tone, and other non-verbal forms of communication
- Receiver distortion comes in the way due to

selective hearing, ignoring non-verbal cues
- Assumptions that others see situations as you do and have similar knowledge level and feelings
- Perceptual differences
- Communication is affected by the professional relationship between two individuals. Information may be misunderstood due to lack of understanding

(Contd)

Exhibit 22.1 *(Contd)*

- Use of an inappropriate medium, for example, communicating via email when a proper report, letter, or a memo on paper would have the desired impact or via telephone where face-to-face interaction is needed
- Not caring for time relevance of information arrival and the need for timely response

- Effective communication requires deciphering the basic values, motives, aspirations, and assumptions that operate across geographical areas. Thus, cultural differences, if not resolved and understood, may result in miscommunication

Even the best communicators face barriers that jeopardize their effectiveness. These barriers are structural, organizational, and personal. Barriers to communication may be posed either by the sender, the receiver, wrong medium of exchange, or a combination of these. Various research studies, such as by Holman (1993), Farnham (1989), Peters (1982), Luthans and Larsen (1986), Larkey (1996), and Parker & Axtell (2001), suggest that the following are the main and critical barriers to effective communication:

- different status of the sender and the receiver;
- use of jargons that mean differently to different individuals;
- incomplete, incorrect, or selective information transmission;
- wrong timing of conveying information;
- presence of conflict between sender and the recipient;
- cross cultural diversity;
- lack of trust and credibility;
- gender differences; and
- information explosion and overload.

Fast growing and progressive organizations put in special efforts to improve communication by overcoming various communication barriers that come in their way. These companies distinguish themselves in many ways, including developing a management team that makes effective communication a top priority in the organization. Exhibit 22.2 illustrates the rules of effective communication.

Exhibit 22.2   Rules of effective communication

There are three basic rules to effective communication:

- Tell them what you are going to tell them
- Tell them
- Tell them what you told them

Some of the main rules for ensuring effective communication are as under:

- Choose right words to convey your thoughts
- Speak from your knowledge and experience

(Contd)

Exhibit 22.2 *(Contd)*

- Do not make sure shot statements, unless confident
- Always intermittently confirm the meaning of the words from the receiver
- Do not begin sentences with 'everyone knows ...'
- Avoid jargons and complex sentences
- Do not try to impress others with your vocabulary, you may miscommunicate
- Be an attentive listener
- Be calm and poised
- Make a positive first impression
- Synchronize body language with verbal communication
- Modulate your content appropriately
- Use motivating statements and positive strokes wherever required
- Always give a concise summary
- Create an environment open to the flow of communication
- Keep the receiver in mind
- Do not communicate under emotionally disturbed conditions
- Be conscious and aware of the differences in language, culture, accent, etc.
- Choose effective and appropriate non-verbal cues
- Always pick up the most suitable medium for the exchange of communication
- Collect and analyse the feedback
- Above all, add humour in a natural and spontaneous way in your dealings with people.

ORGANIZATIONAL COMMUNICATION

Tom Peters (1997), the best-selling business author, emphasizes the role that communication plays in defining successful companies that are rated highly by employees. Organizational effectiveness is the ability of the organization to achieve its goals and objectives. Communication plays a very vital role in organizational effectiveness. Organizational communication refers to the way organizations respond, adjust, and adapt themselves to changing external and internal environment. The key focus has to be on interaction among different stakeholders and, within the organization, among co-workers. In all these interactions different perceptions need to be appropriately dealt with to create common understanding in each transaction that is guided by organizational objectives. Communication is interwoven in all aspects of the organization that includes channels to all stakeholders and the external environment in the following forms:

- organizational structure;
- official channels;
- unofficial channels;
- communication devices/technology; and
- communication cultures (organizational level).

To improve organizational effectiveness through effective communication, organizations need to devise systems and structures wherein downward, upward, horizontal, and informal communication take place amongst people—interpersonal, intra-personal, inter-group, inter-department, inter-organizational, and the organization and the environment—with complete understanding and commitment.

Downward communication   The flow of information from higher to lower levels in the organization's hierarchy is referred to as downward communication. The efficacy of downward communication may get affected due to information overload, lack of openness, and filtering of information over different layers. Normally, it is found that the filtering effect leads to transmission of just 20 per cent of information from the board level to the workers' level (Fig. 22.2). It has been found that greater the transparency in sharing information from top to bottom, the higher would be its effectiveness. Some of the best performing organizations have been found to operate on the principles of open-book management that revolves around sharing of financial and operating information with employees, turning the management of a business into a game that employees can win, empowering people in the organization, having accountability of employees, and sharing and celebrating success.

It is important to note that downward communication often tends to suffer from serious inaccuracies due to the amount of information loss that occurs from the time a message is sent until it is received and understood (Kirmeyer & Lin 1987). Research studies show that organizations, such as Intel and Hewlett-Packard (HP), that encourage effective downward communication have greater stability of work force (James 1996).

Upward communication   The flow of information from lower to higher levels in the organization's hierarchy is referred to as upward communication. However,

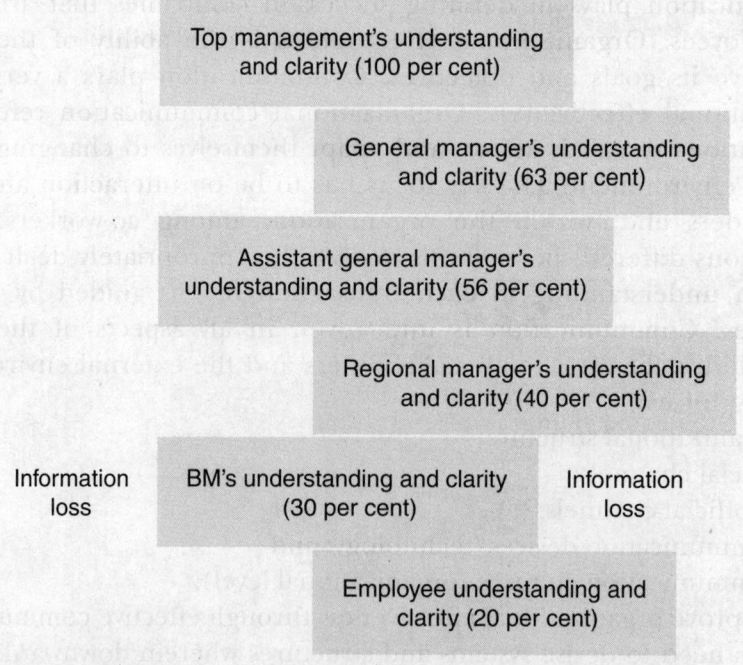

Top management's understanding and clarity (100 per cent)

General manager's understanding and clarity (63 per cent)

Assistant general manager's understanding and clarity (56 per cent)

Regional manager's understanding and clarity (40 per cent)

Information loss   BM's understanding and clarity (30 per cent)   Information loss

Employee understanding and clarity (20 per cent)

FIGURE 22.2   Information loss in downward communication

subordinates usually suppress bad news from their higher-ups because of mistrust and fear, which can hinder upward communication. For upward communication to be effective, an organizational culture wherein higher-ups facilitate upward communication and motivate people down the line to provide relevant and reliable information pertaining to business needs to be cultivated.

A study has revealed that less than 15 per cent of the managers' total communication was directed toward their superior (Luthans & Larsen 1986). When managers communicate upward, their conversations tend to be shorter than discussions with peers, and they often highlight their accomplishments and downplay their mistakes if the mistakes will be looked upon unfavourably (Glauser 1984).

Horizontal communication   The flow of information amongst people on the same hierarchical level is known as horizontal communication. It plays a very important role in contributing to organizational effectiveness by particularly sharing information, coordination, and problem solving in and among teams, groups, and departments.

Formal and informal communication   Formal communication is official and can move upward, downward, or horizontally for performing a specific task. However, informal communication is unofficial. Grapevine is the social network of informal communication that translates management's formal messages into the employees' language. However, grapevine can also generate irrelevant or erroneous information and messages within the organization. Managers, for their effectiveness, need to respect the grapevine, since it is prevalent in all organizations as a reliable form of communication (Lewis et al. 2001). In fact, one well-known study found that approximately 80 per cent of the information transmitted through the grapevine was correct (Walton 1961).

Diagonal communication   It refers to communication between managers and workers located in different functional departments/divisions. The concept of diagonal communication has become prominent, especially, to capture communication challenges that are associated with new organizational forms, such as matrix and project-based organizations. Also, with the emergence of the network organization (internal and external), communication flows can no longer be restricted to vertical and horizontal. As such, it is diagonal communication that has brought out a new dimension in organizational communication.

Effective communicator

Mr Gabriel, CEO of a multinational manufacturing company and a charismatic leader, accomplishes his goals and usually communicates to his staff face-to-face. As a principle, he meets all his staff members at least once a month in a formal or informal meeting and discusses company specific issues with them. He makes rounds of his company, obtaining feedback not only on official matters but also about his employees' families' well-being. He also sends a bouquet to each of his employees on their birthdays. All this makes him a good corporate communicator.

Borderless organizations   Those organizations in which the flow of information takes place without any barriers are known as organizations without borders. These are the organizations wherein information flows to where it is needed the most (Fig. 22.3).

The fundamental prerequisite to effective communication lies in building trustworthy relationships. These cannot be built by policies or directives from the top. Subordinates can have a trustworthy relationship with their superiors and peers not only through responsible behaviour but also by communicating regularly with them, expressing genuine concern for others in formal and informal relationships, being receptive to feedback, and accepting mistakes.

Personal, group, and organizational success revolves around organizational communication. However, the importance of communication has increased multifold in the information and knowledge society. Effective communication and technologies provide competencies and capabilities to individuals and organizations to continuously keep improving their effectiveness. Both researchers and the business community agree that effective communication skills are essential for success in today's knowledge-based society.

It is important to be sensitive to the process of communication, so that its purpose is achieved under different contexts. Individuals and organizations should be sensitive to barriers to effective communication, so that the same gets identified under different situations and is duly tackled to ensure that the purpose behind communication is achieved under different situations. Effective communication, basically, involves interaction and collaboration, ability to read and manage emotions, motives,

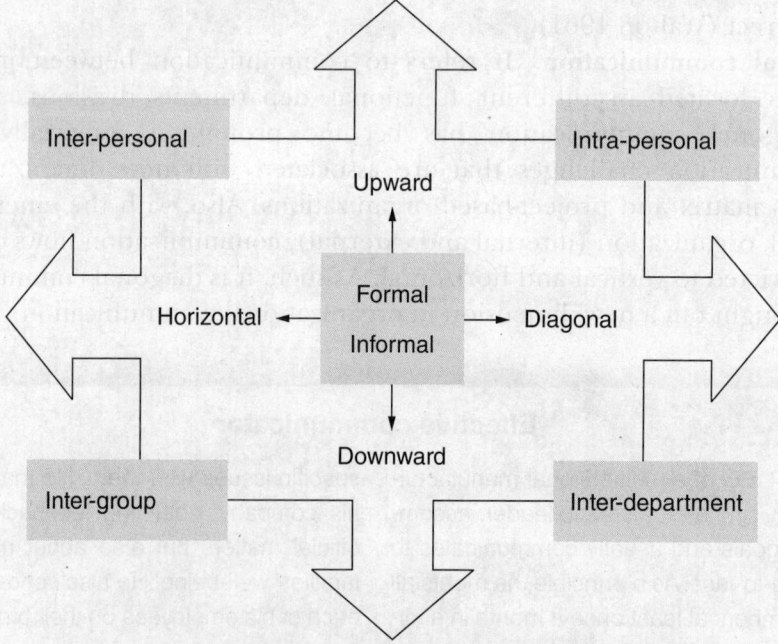

FIGURE 22.3   Flow of information in borderless organizations

attitudes, and behaviours of self and others: knowledge about the subject matter being handled; coupled with ability to apply the same, effectively, under different situations; and above all, the expertise to generate meaning to the people involved through exchanges using appropriate modern tools, transmissions, and processes.

SUMMARY

Personal and professional effectiveness depends, to a great extent, upon our ability to influence others to act as we desire through effective communication. Effective communication is a process involving meaningful transactions and transfer of ideas and thoughts from one party (sender) to another (receiver) through a medium of exchange via a monologue or a dialogue.

To ensure value addition to the target audience through communication, the communicator must plan, prepare, and finalize the contents of the message beforehand and should be aware of the target audience. To ensure effective communication, one should be very clear about the various barriers that come in its way and take appropriate measures to overcome the same. These barriers are posed either by the sender, receiver, wrong medium of exchange, or a combination of these.

Organizational communication relates to the way organizations respond, adjust, and adapt them to changing external and internal environments. To improve organizational effectiveness through effective communication, organizations need to devise systems and structures wherein downward, upward, horizontal, and informal communication takes place among people.

The importance of communication has increased multifold in the information and knowledge society. Effective communication and technologies provide competencies and capabilities to individuals and organizations to keep improving their effectiveness.

KEYWORDS

Borderless organizations It refers to organizations wherein the flow of information takes place without any barriers.

Communication process It has four important aspects namely, the message to be sent, decoding of the message, encoding by the receiver, and message receiver.

Diagonal communication The communication between managers and workers located in different functional departments/divisions.

Downward communication It is the flow of information from higher to lower levels in the organization's hierarchy.

Effective communication It is the meaningful transfer of ideas and thoughts from one party (sender) to another (receiver) through a medium of exchange via a monologue or a dialogue.

Formal and informal communication Formal communication is official and can move upward, downward, or horizontally for performing a specific task. However, informal communication is unofficial.

Horizontal communication The flow of information amongst people on the same hierarchical level.

Organizational effectiveness It is the ability of the organization to achieve its goals and objectives through effective and efficient communication.

Upward communication The flow of information from lower to higher levels in the organizational hierarchy.

EXERCISES

Concept Review Questions

1. Define effective communication. Explain giving an example of a situation from your own experience.

2. How does effective communication enhance personal effectiveness?

3. Explain the communication process. What are the factors that can cause a break in communication? Explain citing an example.

4. What are important barriers to effective communication? How do perceptual differences cause a barrier to effective communication? Explain giving an example.

5. What are the important rules for ensuring effective communication?

6. Explain the meaning and purpose of organizational communication? In what way does personal communication differ from organizational communication?

7. Differentiate, in context of organizational communication, between upward and downward communication with the help of an example.

Critical Thinking Questions

1. What is meant by borderless organization? Is it good to have an organization which is characterized as borderless for organizational effectiveness? Give reasons.

2. One of the rules for ensuring effective communication states that one should not begin sentences with 'everyone knows…'. Explain how does this adversely affect the purpose of communication.

Project Assignments

1. How does communicating a call for a meeting face-to-face differ from that of issuing an office note? What is the advantage and disadvantage of each? Identify a situation and state which method would be more effective under what circumstances and why?

2. Recollect a situation in which people do not speak the same language. How does this impede communication? How would you make an effective communication when the person with whom you have to communicate does not understand your language?

REFERENCES

Catalyst Guide (1998),The Best Practices from the Corporate Leaders, Advancing Women in Business—The Catalyst Guide, Jossey-Bass, Francisco.

Conger, J.A. (1991), 'Inspiring Others: The Language of Leadership', *Academy of Management Executive*, vol. 5, no. 1, pp. 310–45.

Farnham, A. (1989), 'Trust Gap', *Fortune*, 4 December, pp. 56–78.

Glauser, M.J. (1984), 'Upward Information Flows in Organizations: Review and Conceptual Analysis', *Human Relations*, vol. 37, pp. 113–43.

Grenier, R. and G. Metes (1995), *Going virtual. Upper Saddle River*, Prentice Hall, New Jersey.

James, J. (1996), *Thinking in the Future Tense*, Touchstone, New York.

Kirmeyer, S.L. and T. Lin (1987), 'Social Support: Its Relationship to Observed Communication with Peers and Superiors', *Academy of Management Journal*, vol. 30, pp. 138–51.

Lewis, Pamela, Stephen H. Goodman, and Patricia M. Fandt (2001), *Management Challenges in 21st Century*, 3rd edition, South-Western College Publishing, Thomson Learning, pp. 386, 402.

Luthans, F. and J.K. Larsen (1986), 'How Managers Really Communicate', *Human Relations*, vol. 39, pp. 161–78.

Myers, M.T. and G.E. Myers (1982), *Managing by Communication—An Organizational Approach*, McGraw-Hill Book Company, New York.

Parker, S.K. and C.M. Axtell (2001), 'Seeing Another View Point: Antecedents and Outcomes of Employee Perspective Taking', *Academy of Management Journal*, vol. 44, pp. 1085–1101.

Peters, J.T. and H.R. Waterman Jr (1982), *In Search of Excellence*, Harper and Row, New York.

Peters, Tom (1997), 'The Search for Excellence Continues', *Forbes*, 2 December, pp. 238–40.

Rogers, Everett M. (1976), *Communication and Development: Critical Perspectives*, Sage Publications.

Von Krogh, G., K. Ichijo, et al. (2000), *Enabling Knowledge Creation*, Oxford University Press, New York.

Walton, E. (1961), 'How Efficient is the Grapevine?', *Personnel*, vol. 28, pp. 45–8.

23

Conflict Management

INTRODUCTION

Conflict is part of human existence in groups, teams, and organizations. The complexity of interdependencies within organizations leads to the creation of opportunities, resulting in conflict among groups and teams. Some conflicting situations are constructive for the organization, whereas others can be destructive. However, the management of conflict is most important. Conflict, on one hand, can destroy people, while on the other can lead to collective upliftment. The fundamental cause behind any conflict is the difference in the feelings and behaviour of two or more entities, namely individuals, social groups, teams, companies, nations, etc. If not handled appropriately, conflict can lead to a clash between the individuals and the parties involved. It can affect performance and impede the achievement of goals. Kramer (1999) has highlighted that management of conflict requires an ability to diagnose, dissect, and understand it correctly.

CONFLICT

Conflict refers to a process in which one party (person or group) perceives that its interests are being opposed or negatively affected by another party (Brown and Clarkson (1998) and Walls Jr. (1995)). This basically implies a mismatch in the concerns of people involved in a particular event. Conflict is a state of disagreement resulting from individuals or groups that differ in attitudes, beliefs, values, objectives, and goals. It occurs due to the difference in the feelings and behaviour of two sets of individuals (Fig. 23.1).

Learning Objectives

After studying this chapter, you will be able to:
- Understand conflict and its causes
- Identify types of conflict and their sources
- Identify the root cause of conflict
- Learn how to manage conflict in organizations
- Understand the linkage between creativity and managing conflict

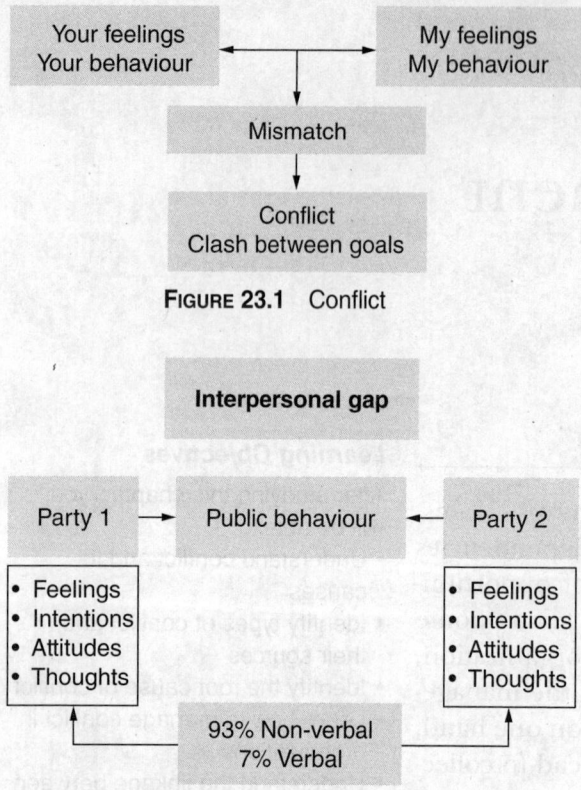

FIGURE 23.1 Conflict

FIGURE 23.2 Manifestation of conflict through human behaviour

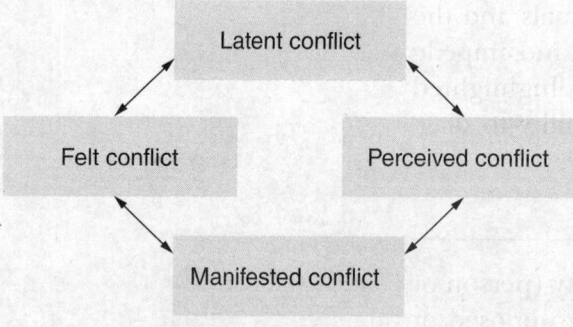

FIGURE 23.3 Stages of conflict manifestation

Differences in heredity, environment, and personal choices of individuals are also a leading cause of conflict. One of the fundamental reasons of conflict is that most of us are normally concerned with winning rather than achieving. The desire to win at any cost leads to an increase in the intensity of conflict among the parties involved in the situation.

Conflict mainly gets manifested through human behaviour as shown in Fig. 23.2. When conflict manifests itself non-verbally mainly through actions and reactions to the situations, it is referred to as latent. *Latent conflict* can further result in felt and perceived conflict that ultimately manifests itself in an interpersonal gap, as shown in Fig. 23.3. Latent conflict is the first sign of a visible conflict and may lead to an active conflict. In this stage, the involved parties feel the conflict building up, although it is still in an invisible state.

Perceived conflict normally results from partial availability of information that is likely to jeopardize the interest of one of the parties involved in the situation. It is the confluence of many factors that ultimately results in manifestation of conflict as evident from behaviour and actions among involved parties. The phase wherein the conflict manifests itself verbally or materially is the stage of *manifested conflict. Felt conflict* is the stage wherein one or the other involved parties undergo a stage of felt emotions including fear, mistrust, and anger. Thus, a feeling of anxiety and aggression becomes visible in one or the other involved parties.

Varieties of Conflict

Contradictions in organizational perspective usually gets reflected at the interdepartmental level, within the department and intergroup level, management versus union level, interorganization level, particularly among competitors, and above all, within intraconflict, which is conflict within oneself as regards views, attitudes, feelings, and actions about a particular situation. On the other hand, there are conflicts that arise between two communities, nations, continents, etc. Any conflict within the organization or between organizations arises mainly due to lack of common understanding about goals and for cognitive, affective, and procedural reasons (Hellriegel et al. 2001). *Goal conflict* arises because of a mismatch between the expected and the actual outcomes of an event/action. This also includes inconsistencies arising between individuals and groups because of their variation in value systems leading to different behaviours. Confusion within an individual resulting from his ideas and thoughts on a particular issue gives rise to *cognitive conflict*. On the other hand, inconsistency in feelings and emotions within an individual or between individuals results in *affective conflict*. When individuals and groups have differing opinions about the process to be used for responding to an issue, it results in *procedural conflict*. These concern matters such as who would be involved, how and where the issue should be discussed, variation in interpretation of the outcomes, etc.

Sources of Conflict

Conflict can arise due to variety of reasons. Some of the prominent sources of conflict are as follows:
- diverse goals or objectives;
- different values and beliefs;
- status: incongruence, salary differences, and education level;
- decision-making: considerations, pressures;
- role pressure or clarification;
- differences in perception of the situation;
- group associations, status, or identity;
- race, ethnicity, or gender differences;
- personality clashes;
- competition for limited resources or competition to achieve similar goals;
- inadequate or poor communication;
- resource inadequacy: disagreements about 'who does what';
- leadership problems, including inconsistent leadership, lack of knowledge for avoiding conflict;
- disagreement on the process of doing things;
- personal-, self-, or group-vested interests;
- power and influence;
- getting into win–lose situation;
- role ambiguity and lack of role clarity; and
- communication: limited, lack of, under, or distorted.

All organizations work towards a predetermined goal in mind, which they have to achieve within a given time frame with the help of limited resources. The effective and efficient achievement of goals requires people to have a shared vision and common understanding of what they are striving to achieve. This also requires clear objectives for each group/department and people therein. Above all, there needs to be a mechanism, system, and a culture in an organization to identify, recognize, and resolve conflicts at different levels and among different groups at the same level. Conflict in the planning stage can be utilized constructively to come out with more creative and better solutions to the problem. However, conflict needs to be minimized in the implementation stage, so that productive energies do not go waste.

Root cause of conflict

To understand and identify the root cause of conflict between groups and parties, one needs to identify the factors that lead to conflict. It adversely affects the ultimate goal achievement, if the right cause of conflict is not tackled appropriately at the right time.

Needs Needs are those essentials—material or non-material, tangible or intangible—required for the well-being of individuals and/or groups associated and involved in the task. If we ignore or fail to give due weightage to others', our own, or the group's needs, it would lead to conflict. While diagnosing the cause of conflict within a group, one should identify the essential, fulfilled, and unfulfilled, needs of the people involved.

Perceptions There might be a lot of differences between what we perceive and the reality. These perceptual variations can result in variations in the way people view causes and consequences of problems. These variations may arise due to differences in self-perceptions and others' perceptions. Therefore, it is important that perceptual variations to be resolved based on facts, to develop a common understanding.

Sociocultural backgrounds People's sociocultural background is reflected in their grooming, attitudes, and values in life. A person's reaction to situations depends largely upon their sociocultural background. Therefore, in any conflicting situation, it becomes necessary to identify individual values that are rooted in their sociocultural backgrounds and consider them while working out solutions to the problem situation.

Power The way power is defined in an organization and the manner in which people use the same may lead to conflicts. Conflicts also arise when people try to make others change their actions or to gain an unfair advantage. Power also determines how conflict is managed.

Values Values or the set of beliefs, principles, norms, or attitudes of the individuals involved in a particular situation are a very important factor in conflict. One of the major reasons for conflicts is incompatibility between the values of individuals or misunderstanding of each other's values. It becomes necessary to identify the values of individuals involved in the situation and bring them together for the achievement of the common purpose.

Feelings and emotions The difference in feelings and emotions over a particular issue gives rise to conflict. Feelings and emotions influence the way we react in a given situation and, therefore, identification of the same and giving them due weightage is very essential to handle a conflict situation.

Consequences of Conflict

Conflict need not always be destructive or damaging. If it is dealt with effectively, it works as a potential source for creativity, innovation, and finding different ways for solving the problem. By handling conflict appropriately, not only does the organization set itself on the path of sustained growth but also builds a healthy spirit of creativity and innovation that further helps in the development of multiple and productive options for the management to solve problems. It is important to diagnose the underlying causes of conflict to come out with effective implementable solutions through a democratic process by arriving at a consensus that meets the needs of involved individuals and their organizations. This approach to resolving conflicts results in mutual benefits and, in turn, builds trusting relationships among involved individuals/groups. The goal should be for all to 'win' in some way or the other, by meeting their needs.

MANAGING CONFLICT

Conflict can be effectively managed in three steps:
1. Define conflict and get concerned about it when it is at latent or felt stage
2. Identify the root causes behind conflict by diagnosis and analysis
3. Work out an implementable and acceptable management strategy through negotiations

Defining conflict   The first step in managing conflict is to identify its causes. This requires a thorough analysis of its nature by asking open-ended or close-ended questions relevant to the issue. The answers to the specific questions may come from experience, partners, or the local media. This stage may necessitate interviewing some of the groups concerned with the conflict as stakeholders. It is important at this stage to identify the groups involved by posing questions such as:
- Who are the groups involved?
- Whom do they represent?
- How strong are they in their organization?
- What is their strength and power base?
- Are the groups capable of working together?
- What are the historical relationships among the groups?

Identifying causes   The basis of a conflict can be diagnosed by posing questions such as:
- What has led to conflict?
- What are the main and secondary issues related to conflict?
- Is it possible to reframe the issues positively?
- Are the issues negotiable?
- Are there any common interests among involved parties in the conflict?

- What information is available and what other information would be required to understand the problem situation?
- Are there any values or interests of the involved group, which are challenged?

Strategy formulation Once you have a general understanding of the conflict, the groups involved will need to analyse and select the most appropriate strategy. In some cases, it may be necessary to have a third party or a neutral facilitator to help the groups arrive at a consensus. After having defined and understood the conflict, one has to work out strategies that can help in resolving it. While working out the strategies to manage conflict, the following aspects need to be looked into:

- Would consensus help in taking care of all interests?
- Are there any outside influences and external constraints that must be accommodated or taken care of?
- Have the groups worked together in the past?
- What is the time frame for arriving at a decision?
- How would the involved groups be informed in case of further developments?
- Will an external negotiator be needed?

Managerial actions to manage conflict Some of the commonly used tactics by managers to manage and handle conflict are as under:

- review job descriptions and seek employees' inputs about them;
- build relationships with all subordinates; get involved with their accomplishments, challenges, and issues;
- receive regular written reports from various departments covering current issues, needs and expectations from management, and future plans;
- conduct trainings on how to have effective interpersonal communication, management of conflict, etc.;
- standardize the procedures for routine tasks with employees' involvement;
- hold regular meetings to communicate new initiatives and status of current programmes; and
- use a suggestion scheme to involve people in problem solving.

Managing conflict

In XYZ company, the management and workers are in conflict with each other over the issue of removal of an employee whose integrity is under question. This conflict has resulted in substantial loss of money to the company. The two recognized workers' unions in the company have both joined hands against the management over this issue and are demanding for reinstatement of the worker. Initially, workers have gone on a 'go slow move' for a month, but now they have threatened the management with a ten-day notice to go on an indefinite strike, if the worker is not reinstated immediately. This has become a difficult situation for the management. What are the stages through which the whole process should be taken to resolve the matter? What are the key skills that the management needs to possess to successfully tackle the situation?

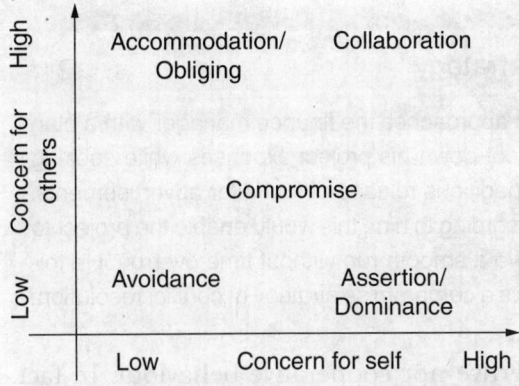

FIGURE 23.4 Conflict management strategies

Conflict management strategies

Individuals manage and handle conflict in different styles (Thomas 1992). The styles have been categorized, based on two prominent factors that an individual considers, while dealing with any conflicting situation—concern for self and concern for others. Based on these two dimensions, five different styles that emerge are highlighted in Fig. 23.4. These are collaboration, compromise, avoidance, assertive/dominating, and accommodation.

Collaboration When the group has a high level of concern for its own interests and matches it with a high concern for the interests of its other partners, it tries to resolve conflict through collaboration. This method involves strong cooperative and assertive behaviours. It has a 'win–win' approach towards resolving interpersonal conflict. Individuals and groups using this method view conflict as natural, helpful, and a source of arriving at creative solutions to the problem. The greatest advantage of this method is that it develops mutual trust among the individuals and groups involved. Conflict is recognized transparently and evaluated by all concerned. Sharing, examining, and assessing the reasons for the conflict should lead to development of an alternative that effectively resolves it and is fully acceptable to everyone involved (Blanchard and O'Connor (1997)). This strategy is generally adopted when concern for others is important to resolve the issue. It is also generally the best strategy to manage conflict and more so when the society's interests are at stake. This approach helps build trust between the groups and commitment on the part of involved individuals in the groups. A major drawback of this strategy is that it is time, effort, and energy consuming. In addition, some partners may take advantage of others' trust and openness. Generally regarded as the best approach for managing conflict, the purpose behind this strategy is to arrive at a consensus.

Compromise When there is a high level of concern for a group's own interests along with a moderate concern for the interests of other partners, conflict resolution is approached through compromise. This method involves an intermediate level of cooperation and assertiveness. The approach involves give and take so that a series of concessions for each party is worked out. This style, as against a collaborative style, does not maximize mutual satisfaction. It enables involved parties to achieve partial satisfaction. The outcome is 'win some/lose some'. This strategy is generally used to achieve temporary solutions, to avoid destructive power struggles, particularly in time-pressure situations. One of the drawbacks of this strategy is that partners may lose sight of important values and long-term objectives. This approach can also distract the partners from the merits of an issue and create a cynical climate. This method is usually followed by positive feelings from others (Rahim 1992).

Compromise strategy

Mr Landmark, the manager of the marketing department for ABC Ltd, is engaged in a conflict situation with the manager of the finance department of the firm. Mr Landmark has to complete a project within a specific time frame and needs to submit his decision to the CEO within two days.

He approaches the finance manager with a plan to cut down his project expenses while seeking expeditious release of funds for advertisements. According to him, this would enable the project to have a smooth run without time overrun. He follows a compromise strategy of conflict resolution.

Avoidance   This style involves neither assertive nor cooperative behaviour. In fact, the employees try to remain away from conflict by not caring for disagreements. As ignoring important issues often frustrates others, the consistent use of the avoidance style usually results in unfavourable evaluations by others (Sorenson et al. 1995). In case, unresolved conflicts have a direct bearing on organizational goals, the avoidance style would negatively affect the achievement of organizational goals. This style may be effective when an issue has a minor bearing on organizational goals and is not worth worrying about. It may be a desirable strategy when the decision-maker does not have adequate information to effectively deal with the problem situation. Employees adopt the avoidance method when they have less concern for the group's interests, coupled with a disregard for the interests of others. The outcome is 'lose–lose'. This strategy is generally used when the issue is trivial or other issues are more pressing. It is also used when the confrontation is potentially damaging or more information is needed. Its drawbacks are that important decisions may be made by default.

Assertion/dominance   This strategy results from a high concern for your group's own interests while having less concern for other groups. It refers to assertive and uncooperative behaviour. The concern for achievement of self-goals dominates this style, which includes aspects of coercive power and dominance (Weider-Hatfield and Hatfield Superiors 1996, Dana 2000). This method presumes that only one person/party has to win and the other must lose; an attitude that creates an atmosphere of fear and subordinates work more out of compulsion than with willing involvement and commitment. The outcome is 'win–lose'. This strategy includes bargaining and is generally used when basic rights are at stake or to set a precedent so that a similar situation does not recur. However, it can escalate the conflict and the losing party may try to retaliate and become negative a contributor in the whole process. This style may be effective when urgent actions are required to be taken for organizational survival or during situations that need an immediate response.

Accommodation/obliging   It is an approach that results from less concern for an individual's own group's interests combined with a high concern for the interests of other partners. This is also referred to as cooperative and unassertive behaviour. A cooperative approach towards others may seem purely unselfish, but when used to elicit support from others due to incompetence and non-assertive behaviour, then individuals are perceived as weak and submissive. This style is also known as

Dominating approach

Mr Godbole, owner of a company, has a very aggressive personality with little regard for the feelings of others. He loses his temper very easily and does not usually listen to the views of his executive team. The company has an average profit margin compared to its competitors. He is known to actively engage in open confrontation with executives of his firm and shouts at them to command theirs as well as others' attention during corporate meetings. He has a dictatorial approach in dealing with problem situations. According to him, 'I am the owner of the company so it must be done the way I want it to be done'. He gives orders such as, 'Ensure that this gets done by 3 pm tomorrow'. He feels uncomfortable whenever he stands to lose an argument based on facts and figures. Mr Godbole's follows a forcing or dominating approach to resolve conflicts.

Accommodating approach

Mrs Dogra is polite to everybody in the organization. She demonstrates her concern for employees by paying heed to their personal and official requests. She manages her job by accepting the ideas of employees working with her. She has rarely challenged or turned down an employee's request. One of the reasons for her behaviour, which the management has identified, is her weakness to leave the office before time. In one of the review meetings taken up by the managing director of the company, it was observed that over the months Mrs Dogra's department performance had slipped compared to her predecessor's. Ultimately, the management has decided to move her to the accounts department from her existing position in the sales department. Her style of conflict management can be labelled as accommodating and obliging.

'buying peace in an organization' by showing concern about the feelings of others at the cost of organizational goals. This style is futile when used as a dominant style and its outcome is 'lose–win'. This strategy is generally used when the issue is more important to others than to the self. It should be used as a goodwill gesture. It is also an appropriate style that can be adopted when individuals recognize that they are wrong and want to accept their mistakes. The drawbacks of this style are that an individual's own ideas and concerns do not get the required attention. The individual may also lose credibility and future influence. It is generally ineffective when used as a dominant style in managing conflicts (Martocchio and Judge 1995).

NEGOTIATION PROCESS

Negotiation is a systematic process in which two or more individuals or groups having common and/or conflicting goals, discuss alternate possible solutions involving specific terms for a possible agreement (Brett et al. 1999). Negotiation is possible and feasible only when involved parties have faith and belief that some sort of mutually beneficial agreement is possible. There are three stages to the process of negotiation—pre-negotiation, negotiation, and post-negotiation.

Pre-negotiation   To achieve successful breakthrough of any conflict, it is essential that sufficient groundwork is done before entering the negotiation stage. One out of the two parties needs to take the initiative for negotiation. In case, no one is prepared to take this as a first step, a trusted outsider can be brought in as facilitator. It should be ensured that right conditions have been created and right time has come to initiate the negotiation. Key stakeholders should be identified and present during the negotiation. Above all, it should be ensured that all individuals/groups have the will to collaborate. Reasonable deadlines and adequate resources to support the whole process must be ensured. Spokespersons for each group must be identified and involved. A clear understanding about the negotiable and non-negotiable issues should exist. The stakeholders/groups must agree on basic ground rules for communication, negotiation, and decision-making. The objective of the negotiating process must be well-defined and agreed upon between the groups. All vital issues that are required to be tackled to arrive at a solution need to be identified in advance.

It is important to define the logistics for the meeting, including time and place for negotiation. People involved should be contacted and invited. The agenda should be laid out in advance and minutes of meetings should be meticulously recorded and shared among all involved parties. Facts related to the conflict should be jointly identified, so that groups involved are at a common wavelength.

Negotiation   During the negotiation phase, the interests of the parties involved are discussed openly. Negotiation must aim at the greatest possible satisfaction of interests of all parties involved within the given constraints. A variety of creative solutions that serve the interests of all involved parties need to be identified and considered. Minutes should be prepared during every stage of negotiation to ensure common understanding. This ensures that the agreements are remembered and communicated clearly. Each should be confident that the agreements will be adhered to. Discuss and agree upon methods to ensure that the parties involved understand and honour their commitments.

Post-negotiation   Once the negotiation is over, the group will need to implement the decisions made. To ensure the smooth implementation of decisions taken, the partners must elicit support for the agreement from the involved parties. Each organization needs to follow its own procedures to review and adapt the agreement. Communication and collaboration should continue as the agreement is carried out over a period of time. A plan to monitor progress, document success, resolve problems, renegotiate terms, and celebrate success should be part and parcel of the implementation process.

CREATIVE CONFLICT MANAGEMENT

Resolving conflict, particularly for those issues that have been dragging for a very long time between the groups, requires imagination and creativity. This basically implies that alternative solutions need to be identified by lateral thinking.

One has to accept the fact that conflict is inevitable in any human group and, therefore, positive steps need to be taken to resolve it. The issues involved should be discussed openly with the stakeholders, and each has to be tackled at a time. Someone needs to take on the role of a leader and identify various issues involved in the conflict. Tackling one issue at a time helps in addressing complicated problems systematically and at arriving at long-lasting solutions. If there is another problem from the past that is acting as a major block, then that needs to be tackled first.

One should be careful in choosing the right time to handle conflict. The concerned parties must be ready to discuss and resolve the impending issue. In general, when people feel that they have been dragged into the negotiation process, they are likely to resist, delay, procrastinate, or display lack of seriousness.

While resolving conflicts, an individual should not react to unintentional remarks. One should appreciate that use of words, such as always, never, impossible, etc., are unintentionally used during negotiation at the spur of moment and may not be meant by the speaker. The use of such words by the opposing group need to be overlooked as else it may lead to dissipation of energies without any fruitful outcomes. Never personalize negotiation. There needs to be a focus on the problem rather than on the group(s) or individual(s) involved and ensure the dignity and self-respect of all the involved parties. One should not insist on being right. There is usually more than one workable and right solution to every problem.

Creatively managing conflict

A bank with a professional approach towards business development mobilized an excellent account and could succeed in lending ₹100 crore at 15 per cent p.a. fixed interest on simple basis to a successful company as against the normal practice of charging interest quarterly. The loan was to be repaid after a moratorium of one year in four equal yearly instalments. Both the company and the banker had smooth and harmonious relationship for the first one and a half year.

The company paid its interest as well as the principle amount that had fallen due from time to time. Subsequently, the rate of interest started falling and the prime lending rate (PLR) fell by 2 per cent. This resulted in relatively increased cost to the company, as it was in a position to raise loan from alternate bankers at around 12.5 per cent to 13.0 per cent payable annually. The company's finance director was under pressure from the top management to do something to repay this loan and borrow from alternate sources so as to reduce the overall cost of borrowing for the company and improve upon the bottom line. Banks usually charge a premium for the prepayment of loans to compensate for the loss in future income. In case the bank charges a full premium, the company does not gain anything, even by raising loan from alternate sources.

A company's concern is to repay the loan by seeking a waiver on premium payment, while a banker's job is to get the full premium. However, the banker also knows that if the company is forced into difficulty by paying the complete premium, they will never come back to the bank for future borrowing and they would also be able to dissuade other good companies from coming to the bank by sharing their difficult experience in crisis. Both the banker and the company now have to come out with a creative solution to resolve this conflict, so that both gain by solving the problem in the long run. Thus, resolving a conflict under such a situation requires a creative solution leading to win–win situation for both parties.

SUMMARY

Conflict is part and parcel of human existence in groups, teams, and organizations. It arises chiefly due to a mismatch between the feelings and behaviour of two sets of individual(s). Conflict can arise due to diverse goals, different values, pressure of the role that has to be performed, race differences, personality clashes, poor communication, resource inadequacy, ambiguity of roles, etc.

To understand and identify the root cause behind the conflict between groups and parties involved, one needs to identify factors that lead to a conflict. Conflict need not be always destructive or damaging. If it is handled and managed effectively, it can be a potential source of creativity and innovations. One needs to find different ways of solving the problem.

Conflict can be resolved by adopting strategies such as collaboration, compromise, assertion/dominance, accommodation, and avoidance. The use of a particular strategy of conflict management depends chiefly upon the nature of conflict, its causes, and the parties involved. However, the most effective is the collaborative strategy, as it usually leads to a smooth and harmonious resolution of conflict. Resolution of conflict requires sufficient homework to take care of pre-negotiation, negotiation, and post-negotiation stages. Conflict management, particularly for those issues that have been dragging for very long periods between the groups, requires imaginative and creative ways of resolution. This basically means to identify alternative solutions by lateral thinking.

KEYWORDS

Accommodation It is the strategy to elicit cooperation from others by appeasement or submission at your own expense because of lack of competence and knowledge.

Assertion/dominance This style to resolve conflict emphasizes on concern for achievement of self-goals through assertive and dominating approach and behaviour.

Avoidance To remain away from conflict by not caring for disagreements.

Collaboration It is a give and take approach resulting in a win–win situation and is regarded as the best approach for managing conflict through consensus.

Compromise It involves give and take so as to offer a series of concessions in the process to each other.

Conflict It is a state of disagreement resulting from individuals or groups that differ in attitudes, beliefs, values, objectives, and goals.

Felt conflict The stage wherein one or the other involved party undergoes a stage of felt emotions including fear, mistrust, and anger.

Latent conflict The first stage of visible conflict as is evident from the difference in values between involved parties that is likely to lead to active conflict.

Managing conflict Handling conflict situations by identifying alternative solutions by lateral thinking.

Manifested conflict It is the confluence of many factors that ultimately result in the verbal or material manifestation of conflict as evident from behaviour and actions among involved parties.

Perceived conflict It normally results from partial availability of information that is likely to jeopardize the interest of one of the parties involved in the situation.

EXERCISES

Concept Review Questions

1. Define conflict. What are the sources of conflict?
2. How can one diagnose the root cause of conflicts?
3. What are the important steps involved in managing conflict? Consider a conflicting situation and explain the importance of each step.

4. Differentiate between the collaboration and avoidance method of managing conflict. Which of the five methods is the most effective? Give reasons.
5. What is the role of creativity in conflict management?

Critical Thinking Questions

1. 'Conflict results in destructive and damaging outcomes'. Comment critically.
2. 'Involving team members and communicating with them helps a lot in identifying and resolving conflicts'. Do you agree with this? Give reasons.

Project Assignments

1. Consider a situation of conflict between a buyer and a seller that has arisen because of a major fault in the new washing machine purchased by the buyer that has gone out of order within a warranty period of one year, that is, somewhere on 360th day from the day of purchase. However, because of her remote location, the buyer was not able to send a communication to the dealer within a year from the date of purchase. Subsequently, under this pretext, the dealer is asking for a full payment towards the replaced parts which the buyer is not prepared to pay. Analyse the whole situation and suggest a concrete way to manage conflict.
2. Identify companies that stimulate conflict within the organization. What is the rationale behind this culture? Identify concrete measurable gains that might have accrued to the organization from building such a culture.
3. Assume that you have taken over as a new supervisor of a company. Within the first few weeks of taking over you come to know that one of your subordinates who is politically connected has been spreading malicious rumours about your capability and competence among other members of your department and in the organization. How would you tackle the situation?

REFERENCES

Blanchard, K. and M. O'Connor (1997), *Managing by Values*, Berrett-Kohler, San Francisco.

Brett, J.F., G.B. Northcraft, and R.L. Pinkley (1999), 'Stairways to Heaven: An Interlocking Self-regulation Model of Negotiation', *Academy of Management Review*, vol. 24, no. 3, pp. 435–451.

Brown, L.D. and A.E. Clarkson (1998), 'Conflict', *The Concise Blackwell Encyclopedia of Management*, Blackwell, Oxford, England, pp.105–107.

Dana, D. (2001), *Retaliatory Cycle: Introducing the Elements of Conflict* in E. Block (ed.), *The 2000 Annual*, vol. 2, pp. 45–49, Jossey Bass/Pfeiffer, San Francisco.

Hellriegel, Don, John W. Slocum, Jr., and Richard W. Woodman (2001), *Organizational Behavior*, 9th edition, South-Western Thomson Learning, Singapore, pp. 294–295.

Kramer, R.M. (1999), 'Trust and Distrust in Organizations: Emerging Perspectives, Enduring Questions', *Annual Review of Psychology*, vol. 50, pp. 569–598.

Martocchio, J.J. and T.A. Judge (1995), 'When We don't See Eye to Eye: Discrepancies between Supervisors and Subordinates in Absence of Disciplinary Decisions', *Journal of Management*, vol. 21, pp. 251–278.

Rahim, M.A. (1992), *Managing Conflict in Organizations*, 2nd edition, Praeger Publishers, New York.

Sorenson, P.S., K. Hawkins, and R.L. Sorenson (1995), 'Gender, Psychological Type and Conflict Style Preference', *Management Communication Quarterly*, vol. 9, no. 1, pp. 115–126.

Thomas, K.W. (1992), 'Conflict and Negotiation Process in Organizations' in M.D. Dunnette and L.M. Hough (eds), *Handbook of Industrial and Organizational Psychology*, 2nd edition, vol. 3, Consulting Psychologists Press, Palo Alto, California, pp. 651–717.

Walls, J.A. Jr. 1995, 'Conflict and its Management', *Journal of Management*, vol. 21, pp. 515–558.

Weider-Hatfield, D. and J.D. Hatfield (1996), 'Superiors' Conflict Management Strategies and Subordinate Outcomes', *Management Communication Quarterly*, vol. 10, pp. 189–208.

24

Dynamics of Leadership

Learning Objectives

After studying this chapter, you will be able to:
• Understand leadership
• Examine theories of leadership
• Examine the difference between leaders and non-leaders
• Appreciate different leadership styles

INTRODUCTION

Mahatma Gandhi, Bill Gates, J.R.D Tata, Walt Disney, Azim Premji, Nararayana Murthy, Kiran Majumdar-Shaw, and Dhirubhai Ambani epitomize success, power to influence, and achievement in today's world. The common thread of leadership links these personalities in different walks of life together and differentiates them from non-achievers.

Leadership is defined, primarily, by what we do and not by the role we have been assigned. Good leadership starts 'in here' and comprises values, clarity, and vision. People instinctively follow good leaders. Leadership is all about influencing people to act, behave, and perform as desired by the leader. Leadership is congruent with self-expression that requires clarity, consciousness, and courage to create value.

The quality of an organization is determined by the leader and the leadership. A leader, who lacks intelligence, virtue, and experience, cannot hope for success. Good leaders are those who can survive in adverse conditions while bad leaders can lose even in favourable conditions. Therefore, good leaders constantly strive to improve themselves.

They may use legitimate power, reward power, coercive power, referent power, and/or expert power to influence those around them; motivate and make them behave accordingly. The powers are used depending upon the situation and the personalities of the followers. There are various theories that define leadership such as traits theory, behavioural model of leadership, and the situational approach.

Traits theory   It assumes that certain characteristics, primarily those of personality, when combined with an individual, bring forth a successful leadership. These characteristics are consistent over a variety of situations.

Behavioural model of leadership   It focuses on what leaders do and how they do it. Some share *task-centered* relations with employees that focus on the quality and quantity of work accomplished, while others have a *considerate and supportive* relationship with employees who attempt to help employees achieve their personal goals such as, work satisfaction, promotion, and recognition. In this relationship, leaders work hard at settling disputes, keeping people happy, providing encouragement, and giving positive reinforcement. The behavioural model focuses on specific attitudes of leaders, implying thereby that leadership can be taught. According to this model, programmes that inculcate specific leadership traits can be designed and imparted to individuals who would like to become effective leaders (Robbins and Sanghi 2005).

Situational approach   Paul Hersey and Ken Blanchard (1974) have developed a leadership theory that has gained popularity among management development specialists. It is a contingency theory that focuses on the followers, according to which what matters is selecting the right style of leadership in a given situation, depending upon the level and degree of preparedness on the part of the followers. This theory asserts that adaptability is the key and the successful leader adapts his/her behaviour according to the situation. They disagreed with the trait approach and denied that leaders showed a certain amount of behavioural consistency across situations.

LEADERSHIP TRAITS

History refers to personalities such as Mahatma Gandhi, Margaret Thatcher, Jack Welch, the former Chairman and CEO of General Electric, Henry Ford, founder of Ford Motor Company, and N.R. Narayana Murthy, the former Chairman of Infosys and World Entrepreneur of the Year 2003 (Ernst & Young), as leaders in their own right. Their names are associated with charisma, enthusiasm, vision, inspiration, and courageous leadership. They are examples for the world to follow. What makes a leader? Various research studies have attempted to identify traits in leaders that distinguish them from the rest. A review study in the late 1960s of 20 studies identified 80 leadership traits. However, five of the traits were found to be common to four or more of the studies (Geier 1967). By the 1990s, as a result of several studies, seven vital traits that differentiated leaders from non-leaders were indentified. They are— ambition, energy, the desire to lead, honesty, integrity, self-confidence, intelligence, high self-monitoring, and job-relevant knowledge (Kirkpatrick and Locke 1991).

The traits model of leadership focuses on the empirically tested characteristics of leaders—successful as well as unsuccessful—to predict leadership effectiveness. Some research studies suggest that the traits normally found in most of the successful leaders are intelligence, maturity and breadth, inner motivation, the drive to achieve, and honesty. Another study has observed the following six traits amongst successful leaders:

Integrity   100 per cent commitment to the highest personal and professional standards.

Loyalty   Faithfulness to superiors, peers, and subordinates, and above all, to the organization.

Commitment   100 per cent devotion to duty and purpose.

Larsen & Toubro Ltd

Larsen & Toubro Limited (L&T) is a technology-driven engineering and construction organization. It is one of the largest companies in India's private sector. The company has additional interests and contributions in the manufacturing, services, and IT. Its strong and dedicated customer-focused approach and the continuous quest for top-class quality has enabled it to attain and sustain leadership in its major lines of business across seven decades.

The company has achieved a gross sales and service revenue from operations to the tune of ₹17,901 crore for the financial year ending 31 March 2007, resulting in growth of 20 per cent. The share of revenue from international operations constituted 18 per cent of the gross revenue. Profit after tax (PAT), including exceptional gains, at ₹1,403 crore for the year ended 31 March 2007 increased by 39 per cent over the previous year. The company achieved 7.8 per cent net margins on gross sales.

There are several reasons behind L&T's success. The company has been deploying cutting-edge HR technologies for evolving into a performance-based, value-creating organization of the future. It has been emphasizing on identification of leadership talent from its high-performers who will grow and lead the business under its management leadership programme.

The technology leadership programme identifies leaders from strategically critical technology areas, keeping in view its emerging thrust on knowledge-based businesses.

L&T launched an execution leadership programme to nurture high performers to build functional expertise in domain areas of business services, technical services, sales and marketing, project management, construction, and manufacturing. The supervisory leadership programme identifies high-potential top performers from the supervisory cadre and gives them opportunities for focused development and faster career progression to managerial positions.

To develop these potential leaders, the competency enhancement programme through coaching was launched by the company to help in leadership development. For technology leaders, the strategic management of technology programme was launched to build capabilities for innovation, technology development, and technology management. Training and development is focused on strengthening strategically competitive capabilities through functional and behavioural development programmes. The company continuously keeps inducting talent from outside for improving its talent mix. It has prepared a strategic plan to attract the best talent from the industry as well as from college campuses.

Source: Based on the data from http://www.larsentoubro.com/lntcorporate/common/ui_templates/homepage_news.aspx?res=P_CORP, accessed on 28 August 2007.

Energy   Enthusiasm and drive to take an extra initiative.

Decisiveness   Willingness to act.

Selflessness   Prepared to sacrifice personal objectives and gains for a bigger cause, that is, group and organizational objectives.

Another way of defining the six prominent traits and qualities of leaders are as under:

Live by integrity, lead by example   This helps in building a trust and confidence amongst followers, which is the prerequisite for high-performing organizations:

Develop a winning strategy   Leaders have to be absolutely clear on what the organization does best and build upon it.

Build a great team   Good and great leaders build a team around them with complementary skills and experiences but with the same passion, attitude, and values.

Inspire people around them   Leaders communicate constantly and listen attentively, carefully, and intensively; encourage risk-taking and even failure, as learning experience.

Create a flexible organization   Leaders build an organizational structure that is responsive to the changes. It is the flexibility in the organization that enables them to quickly respond, adapt, and create change.

Implement relevant systems   The leaders are action-oriented and it is this trait in them that focuses on creating systems that are focused on implementation.

LEADERS AND NON-LEADERS

Peters and Austin (1985) have differentiated between leaders and non-leaders on many grounds (Fig. 24.1). A leader is a coach appealing to the best in each person, he/she is always open to suggestions, is a problem-solver, an advice giver, and a

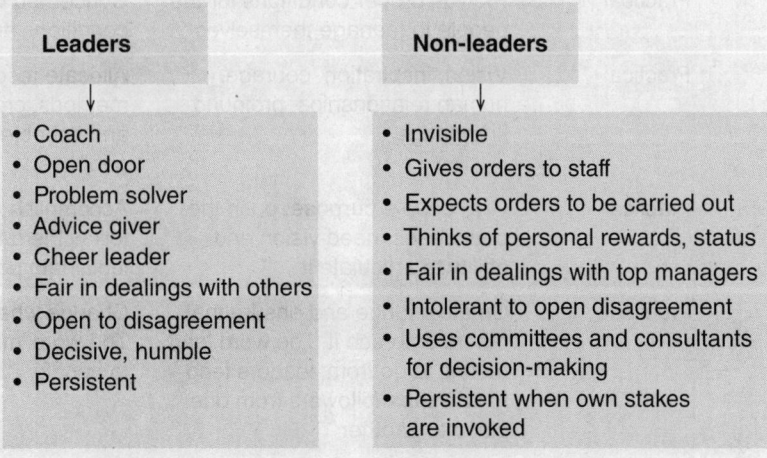

Leaders	Non-leaders
• Coach	• Invisible
• Open door	• Gives orders to staff
• Problem solver	• Expects orders to be carried out
• Advice giver	• Thinks of personal rewards, status
• Cheer leader	• Fair in dealings with top managers
• Fair in dealings with others	• Intolerant to open disagreement
• Open to disagreement	• Uses committees and consultants for decision-making
• Decisive, humble	• Persistent when own stakes are invoked
• Persistent	

FIGURE 24.1   Difference between leaders and non-leaders

cheerleader. A non-leader is invisible and yet gives orders to the staff expecting them to be carried out. A leader thinks of ways to make people productive, focuses on organizational goals, and rewarding performers, as against a non-leader who thinks of personal rewards, status, and how he/she looks to outsiders. A leader is fair while dealings with others, decisive, humble, persistent, tough, yet tolerant to disagreement as against a non-leader who is fair only while dealing with the top management, uses committees and consultants for decision-making, arrogant, persistent only when his/her stake in the situation is high and, above all, is intolerant of open disagreement.

The difference between leaders and managers, as regards their focus on conceptual or practical aspects is given in Table 24.1.

TABLE 24.1   Differences between leaders and managers

Author(s)	Focus	Leaders	Managers
Bennis and Nanus (1985)	Conceptual	Do the right thing, consider people as great assets, are committed, focus on outcomes, what and why some steps should be taken, sharing information networks	Do things right, consider people as liabilities, try to control, make rules, how things should be done, compliance, secrecy, formal authority (hierarchy)
Czarniawska-Joerges and Wolff (1991)	Conceptual	Symbolic performance, expressing the hope of control over destiny	Introducing order by coordinating the flow of things and people towards collective action
Spreitzer and Quinn (1996)	Conceptual	Transformational	Transactional
Zaleznik (1977, 1992)	Practical	Energize the system, their working environment is often chaotic	Ensure the stability of the system
McConkey (1989)	Practical	Provide proper conditions for the people to manage themselves	Concerned with controlling conditions and others
McConnell (1994)	Practical	Vision, inspiration, courage, human relationships, profound knowledge	Allocate resources, design work methods, create procedures, and set objectives and create priorities
Buhler (1995)	Practical	Give people purpose, push the boundaries, need vision and ability to articulate it	Accomplish work through others, follow the rules, and rely on legitimate power
Sanborn (1996)	Practical	Create change and ensure that others embrace it. The word lead means to go from; leaders tend to take their followers from one place to another	Change when they have to. The word 'manage' means to handle

(contd)

TABLE 24.1   (*Contd*)

Author(s)	Focus	Leaders	Managers
Fagiano (1997)	Practical	Help others do the things they know need to be done to achieve a common vision	Get things done through other people
Sharma (1997)	Practical	Innovation	Conformity
Maccoby (2000)	Practical	Leadership is a relationship that involves selecting, motivating, coaching, and building trust	Management is a function that involves planning, budgeting, evaluating, and facilitating

Source: Based on John Kotter (1988), *The Leadership Factor*, and http://www.business.ualberta.ca/rfield/papers/LeadershipDefined.htm, accessed on 23 September 2007.

LEADERSHIP STYLES

Vroom and Jago (1988) developed a model that focuses on the leadership role of managers in decision-making situations. The Vroom–Jago time-driven leadership model (1999) prescribes a leader's choice(s) among five leadership styles based on seven situational factors, recognizing the time requirements and other costs associated with each style.

Five core styles that vary in terms of the levels of empowerment and participation of the subordinates in the decision-making processes are presented in Fig. 24.2.

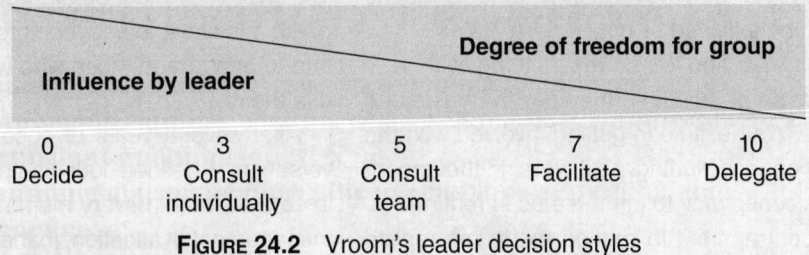

FIGURE 24.2   Vroom's leader decision styles

Decide style   The leader makes the decision and either announces or sells the same to the subordinates. The role of employees is limited to providing information as desired by the leader but has nothing to do with generating or developing solutions.

Consult individual style   The leader consults individuals of the team without bringing them together as a group. The decision may or may not be the outcome of this consultation.

Consult team style   The leader places the problem before the group in a meeting and gets their suggestions. However, the decision may or may not be the outcome of their suggestions.

Facilitate style   The leader presenting the problem to the team acts as a facilitator. The objective is to get the views of the team members and a concurrence to a decision.

The leader is open and receptive to the solutions given by the team and is willing to accept and implement the solution that has the backing of the entire team.

Delegate style   The leader allows the team to make decisions within the given limits. This style implies the highest degree of empowerment to the subordinates.

Thus, leadership is nothing but the power to influence people for performing a task that leads to the achievement of given objectives and goals. James MacGregor Burns (1978) identifies a leadership style as '…inducing followers to act for certain goals that represent the values and the motivations—the wants and needs, the aspirations, and expectations—of both leaders and followers'. Various empirical studies have identified various traits that are found among successful as well as unsuccessful leaders. The leader's effectiveness mainly revolves around—(1) being a pathfinder, creating vision, and clarifying goals; (2) empowerment, inculcating skills among subordinates to become relatively independent and partly interdependent, that is, having self-directed and self-managing teams; and (3) team building, involving people in activities that improve the team's productivity and cooperation.

Why leaders can't lead

Lead, not manage; there is an unimportant difference between the two. Many institutions are well-managed and yet very poorly led. It may be able to handle all routine inputs of each day and yet, may never ask whether a routine should be followed or not.

All of us find ourselves dealing with routine problems because they are the easiest to handle. We hesitate in getting involved with the bigger ones; colluding, as it were, in the unconscious conspiracy to immerse us in routine.

My entrapment in routine made me realize another thing: people were following the army game. They did not want to take the responsibility for or bear the consequence of the decisions that they ideally should be making. The motto was, 'Let's push up the tough ones.' The consequence was that everybody and anybody were dumping his 'wet babies' on my desk, when I had neither the diapers nor the information to take care of them.

Leaders must create clear-cut and measurable goals for their organizations based on opinions from all sections of the community. They must be allowed to proceed towards these goals without being crippled by bureaucratic machinery that saps their strength, energy, and initiative. They must be allowed to take risks, to make mistakes, to use their creativity to the hilt, and to encourage those who work with them to use theirs.

After several years of observation and conversation, I defined four competencies evident to some extent in every member of the group—management of attention, management of meaning, management of trust, and management of self.

Leadership can be felt throughout an organization. It gives pace and energy to the work and empowers the work force. Empowerment is the collective effect of leadership. Ultimately, in great leaders and the organizations surrounding them, there is a fusion of work and play to the point where, as Robert Frost says, 'Love and need are one.' How do we get from here to there? I think we must start by studying change.

Source: Republished with permission of American Society for Training and Development, from 'Why Leaders can't Lead', Bennis, Warren (1989), Training & Development Journal, American Society for Training & Development, vol. 43, no. 4, pp. 35–39; permission conveyed through Copyright Clearance Center, Inc.

SUMMARY

Leadership is about influencing people to act, behave, and perform as desired by the leader. Various theories such as traits theory, behavioural model of leadership, and the situational approach have tried to describe leadership. The traits model of leadership focuses on the empirically tested characteristics of leaders, successful as well as unsuccessful, to predict leadership effectiveness. Good and great leaders build a team around them with complementary skills and experiences with the same passion, attitude, and values. Numer-ous research studies have identified the difference between leaders and managers. There are five distinct leadership styles namely decide, consult individually, consult team, facilitate, and delegate. These vary in terms of the levels of empowerment and participation of the subordinates in the deci-sion-making process. The leader's effectiveness is in being a pathfinder; creating vision and clarify-ing goals; empowerment, and team building; and involving people in activities that improve the team's productivity and cooperation.

KEYWORDS

Behavioural model of leadership   It focuses on what leaders do and how they do it.

Leaders and non-leaders   A leader is a coach, appealing to the best in each person, is open to suggestions, is a problem-solver, and an advice giver, a cheerleader as against a non-leader who gives orders to staff and expects these to be car-ried out.

Leaders vs managers   They have been dis-tinguished based on conceptual and practical aspects such as leaders do the right thing while managers do things right; leaders energize the system while managers ensure the stability of the system.

Leadership   It is about influencing people to act, behave, and perform as desired by the leader.

Leadership style   It focuses on the leadership role of managers in decision-making situations.

Situational approach   It asserts that the suc-cessful leader adapts behaviour according to the situation; adaptability is the key.

Trait theory of leadership   It focuses on the empirically tested characteristics of leaders to pre-dict leadership effectiveness.

EXERCISES

Concept Review Questions

1. Define leadership.
2. What are different theories of leadership? Explain the significance of the statement 'leaders inspire people around them'.
3. Differentiate between leaders and non-leaders by citing examples.

Critical Thinking Questions

1. Differentiate between leaders and managers. Who is more essential to the success of an organization—leader or manager? Comment critically.

2. What are different styles of leadership? Which style of leadership would be applicable under what situations? Explain considering a particular situation in context to a particular organization.

Project Assignments

1. What are your strengths and weaknesses as a leader? Assess yourself to identify the weak-nesses that you would like to overcome to improve your effectiveness as a leader.
2. Who are your role models as leaders? What makes them leaders? What have you learnt from them?

REFERENCES

Bennis, Warren (1989), 'Why Leaders can't Lead', *Training & Development Journal*, American Society for Training & Development, vol. 43, no. 4, pp. 35–39.

Bennis, Warren and B. Nanus (1985), *Leaders: The Strategies for Taking Charge*, Harper & Row, New York.

Buhler, Patricia (1995), 'Leaders vs. Managers', *Supervision*, vol. 56, no.5, pp. 24–26.

Czarniawska-Joerges, Barbara and Rolf Wolff (1991), 'Leaders, Managers, Entrepreneurs on and off the Organization', *Organization Studies*, vol. 12, pp. 529–547.

Fagiano, David (1997), 'Managers vs. Leaders: A Corporate Fable', *Management Review*, vol. 86, no. 10, p. 5.

Geier, J.G. (1967), 'A Trait Approach to the Study of Leadership in Small Groups', *Journal of Communication*, December, pp. 316–323.

Hersey, P. and K.H. Blanchard (1974), 'So You Want to Know Your Leadership Style?', *Training and Development Journal*, February, pp. 1–15.

Kirkpatrick, S.A. and E.A. Locke (1991), 'Leadership: Do Traits Matter?', *Academy of Management Executive*, May, pp. 48–60.

Maccoby, Michael (2000), 'Understanding the Difference between Management and Leadership', *Research Technology Management*, January/February, vol. 43, no. 1, pp. 57–59.

MacGregor, B.J. (1978), *Leadership*, Harper & Row, New York.

McConkey, Dale (1989), 'Are You an Administrator, a Manager, or a Leader?' *Business Horizons*, September–October, vol. 32, no. 5, pp. 15–21.

McConnell, John (1994), 'On Lemmings, Managers and Leaders', *The Journal for Quality and Participation*, vol. 17, no. 2, pp. 26–29.

Peters, Tom and Nancy Austin (1985), *A Passion For Excellence*, Random House, New York.

Robbins, Stephen P. and Seema Sanghi (2005), *Organizational Behavior*, Pearson Education, Singapore, p. 316.

Sanborn, Mark (1996), 'Are You a Leader or a Manager?', *American Agent & Broker*, vol. 68, no. 12, pp. 43–47.

Sharma, Anand (1997), 'Leadership: The Manager vs. the Leader', *IIE Solutions*, vol. 29, no. 9, pp. 34–35.

Spreitzer, Gretchen M., and Robert E. Quinn (1996), 'Empowering Middle Managers to be Transformational Leaders', *The Journal of Applied Behavioral Science*, vol. 32, no. 3, p. 237.

Vroom, V.H. (1999), 'New Developments in Leadership and Decision-making', *OB News*, Briarcliff Manor, Organisational Behavior Division of the Academy of Management, headquartered at Pace University, New York, Spring, pp. 4–5.

Vroom, V.H. and A.G. Jago (1988), *The New Leadership*, Prentice-Hall, Englewood Cliffs, New Jersey.

Zaleznik, Abraham (1992), 'Managers and Leaders: Are They Different?', *Harvard Business Review*, March/April, vol. 70, no. 2, pp. 126–135. First published in May/June 1977, vol. 55, no. 3, pp. 67–76.

25

Decision-making

INTRODUCTION

Managers are often confronted with unmanageable situations. They have to continuously tackle both simple and complex problems. Some problems require immediate action, while others unfold slowly and need consistent action. Managing problems depends upon the decision-making ability of a manager. Is decision-making an art or science? What are the characteristics of managerial decisions? How can one take objective, rational, and right decisions? Thus, the answer to managing problems lies in the ability of a manager to take decisions and face the consequences of his actions. A good executive must be good at decision-making.

Learning Objectives

After studying this chapter, you will be able to:
- Understand decision-making and its relevance to managers
- Examine systematic and structured decision-making
- Learn the steps involved in decision-making
- Evaluate the tools and techniques for decision-making
- Learn about the 'six thinking hats'

DECISION-MAKING

Decision-making is the cognitive process of selecting a course of action from among multiple alternatives. A decision is a choice made between two or more available alternatives. There are two basic types of decisions, namely programmed decisions and non-programmed decisions (Fig. 25.1).

- programmed decisions are routine and repetitive; and
- non-programmed decisions are one shot occurrences and are usually less structured

Decision-making is the cognitive process of selecting a course of action from among multiple alternatives.

Table 25.1 indicates that non-programmed decisions are important, difficult, and therefore, demand creative problem-solving approaches (Bateman & Snell 2002).

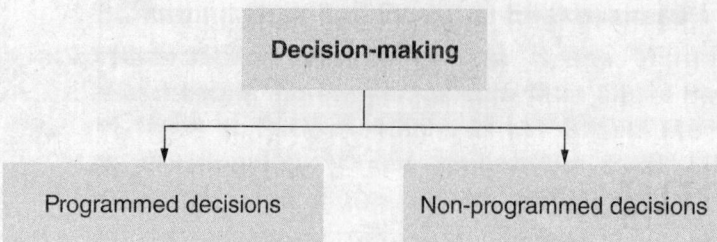

FIGURE 25.1   Types of decisions

The scope of the decision depends upon the level at which it has been taken, its implications on the total management system of the organization, and to what extent it affects people at different tiers of the organization. The broader the scope of the decision, the higher would be the designation of the manager responsible for making that decision.

Uncertainty and Risk

If a decision-maker has the required information and is in a position to predict the consequences of the action about to be taken, then he is said to operate under a condition of certainty. The decision-maker knows the exact consequences of the action that would be taken.

In case decision-makers have inadequate or insufficient information about the consequences of their actions, then they operate under uncertainty. Uncertainty is the situation in which decision-makers have no idea about the outcome of their chosen alternative. When decision-makers can estimate the various outcomes vis-à-vis the decision taken, and yet are not sure of the ultimate outcome, then they are said to be operating under risk.

Systematic and Structured Decision-making

The systematic and structured decision-making requires recognition and analysis of important components of decisions—context, objectives, options, and criteria.

Context: The context describes the clarity and circumstances of the situation surrounding the decision.

Objectives: A clear understanding of desired and expected outcomes should be the guiding force behind the decision-making process. When there is clarity about objectives, decision-making becomes easier, logical, and less stressful.

TABLE 25.1   Programmed and non-programmed decisions

	Programmed decisions	Non-programmed decisions
Type of problem	Frequent, repetitive, routine, much certainty regarding cause-and-effect relationships	Novel, unstructured, much uncertainty regarding cause-and-effect relationships
Procedure	Dependence on policies, rules, and definite procedures	Necessity for creativity, intuition, tolerance for ambiguity, creative problem solving
Examples	Business firm: Periodic reorders of inventory	Business firm: Diversification into new products and markets

Source: Based on Gibson, et al. (1985).

Alternatives: A significant effort must be made to identify various available alternatives, studying how each may be implemented and what would be the cost, time, and quality implications to arrive at the expected outcome of each. Usually people limit their thinking and perceptions to a few choices, and do not explore unusual ideas.

Criteria: To adopt a scientific, logical, and objective approach to decision-making necessarily requires a predetermined criteria to select the best possible alternative and are determined by the context and objectives.

Successful decisions are based on reliable information and verifiable data. The various alternatives, implications, or the outcome of each alternative should be analysed thoroughly before arriving at a final decision. Decisions based on past experience and gut feelings are difficult to defend as they are not backed by data and logic and, therefore, frequently encounter unexpected obstacles and resistance when implemented. Decision-making requires time and effort that should be spent in proportion to the importance of the decision in a given context.

Steps in Decision-making

Professionally managed organizations institutionalize the decision-making process involving the following seven steps:

1. Identify, diagnose, and precisely define the problem
2. Work out alternative solutions
3. Evaluate each alternative solution
4. Choose the best alternative
5. Implement the decision
6. Evaluate the decision
7. Review and learn the lessons for future

The steps involved in systematic and scientific way of making decisions are shown in Fig. 25.2.

The first step in decision-making is to recognize that there is a problem that needs to be tackled. Apart from this, the decision-maker must have the will to do something about the issue and must believe that the resources and abilities needed for resolving it exist (MacCrimmon & Taylor 1976). The problem and its boundaries should be understood well by proper diagnosis. To do so one may have to resolve the following issues:

- What is happening and what was expected to happen?
- Explain the deviations and their causes
- The critical objectives that need to be met in the given context
- Cause of the problem
- The decision
- Should I make this decision?
- What decisions have already been made?

Answers to the above questions would help in defining the precise goals and objectives within the framework of available resources and restrictions/constraints faced.

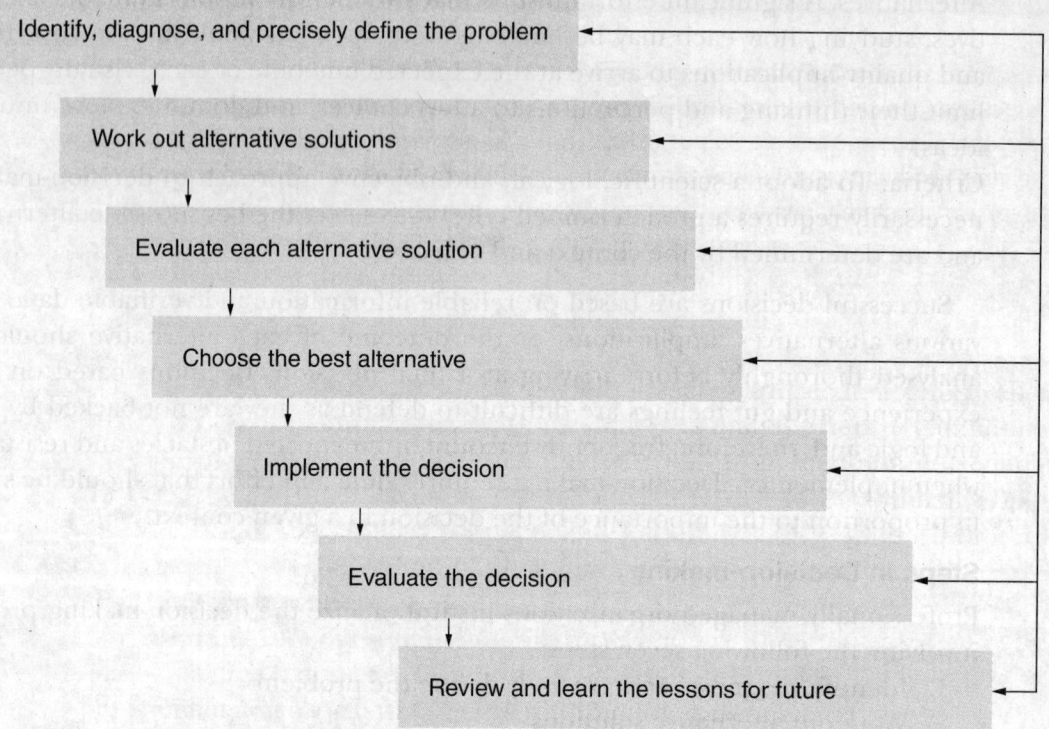

FIGURE 25.2   Steps involved in decision-making

The importance of each objective needs to be evaluated. Once the problem has been defined in a given context, it should be analysed to track down its causes, which will give further insight about working out its alternative solutions. The solution to the problem may be ready-made or custom-made (Alexander 1979).

Ready-made alternatives are based on precedents or on the advice of others who have faced similar problems in the past. Custom-made solutions are designed and developed to tackle the particular problem. This requires a creative input to look beyond for arriving at a solution.

After having worked out various alternatives to solve the problem, one has to evaluate each alternative solution in terms of various parameters such as cost, time, quality, efficiency, and benefits. The main purpose of evaluation of alternatives is to find out the expected consequences of each alternative, if put into action and to what extent the various objectives would be met or not met under each alternative solution. The evolution of various alternatives should also give rise to an insight about the contingency plans that may need to be implemented depending upon the way the future unfolds. Several techniques are available for analysing the options in order to understand their implications. Interpretive structural modeling or concept mapping can be used to analyse the interrelationships of the options.

Based on the evaluation of various alternatives, that is, after having weighed the consequences of various options, the decision-maker has to choose the best possible decision that optimizes achievement of objectives within given constraints, maximizes the benefits, and satisfies the involved individuals to the greatest extent. The process of selection of the best alternative becomes easy and logical, when the criteria for selection are laid down in the initial stage itself. It is the criteria that should help in rating the various alternatives. One should rate each criterion according to its importance. Criteria are basically clear conditions that must be satisfied to arrive at a useful, objective, effective, and good decision. While arriving at the best decision, a decision-maker should ensure its feasibility.

For ensuring that the results, as envisaged, are achieved from the best decision, it should be effectively implemented. For effective implementation what matters the most is that the people involved in implementing the decision understand the problem as well as an alternative choice made to solve the problem and are fully committed to its successful implementation. For effective implementation, managers should plan the implementation process very meticulously and carefully. Implementation analysis can provide a clear view of resource requirements, people and groups affected, and any cautions to exercise when implementing the option.

After having implemented the decision, the next step requires evaluating the decision to obtain an insight into what is happening/has happened as against what was expected. This means that one should consider the efficacy of the solution. Irrespective of positive or negative feedback, evaluating a decision is always useful. A positive feedback reassures that the decision has worked well and should be continued and/or applied elsewhere in similar situations. However, a negative feedback implies that the decision is ineffective requiring additional time, effort, resources, etc. The continuous review of decisions helps in building a feedback mechanism, so that we may learn from them. The review mechanism sheds light on the weak links in the various steps in decision-making. Accordingly, taking corrective actions to strengthen various steps involved leads to improvements in the quality of decisions and institutionalizes the decision-making process.

TOOLS AND TECHNIQUES FOR DECISION-MAKING

Various tools and techniques are being used in decision-making so that the problem situation is scientifically diagnosed and analysed. Some of the commonly used tools and techniques for this specific purpose are highlighted in Fig. 25.3.

Pareto analysis   It is a simple technique that helps in making the most effective changes to achieve the desired results. The underlying principle is the Pareto principle—the idea that by doing 20 per cent of work one can generate 80 per cent of the advantage required for doing the entire job. It is an analytical technique for effecting changes, whereby relatively higher benefits could be derived. It is a useful principle to take decision when many possible courses of action are competing for the decision-maker's attention.

Paired comparison analysis   It is helpful in working out the relative importance of a number of available choices. It is particularly useful where the decision-maker

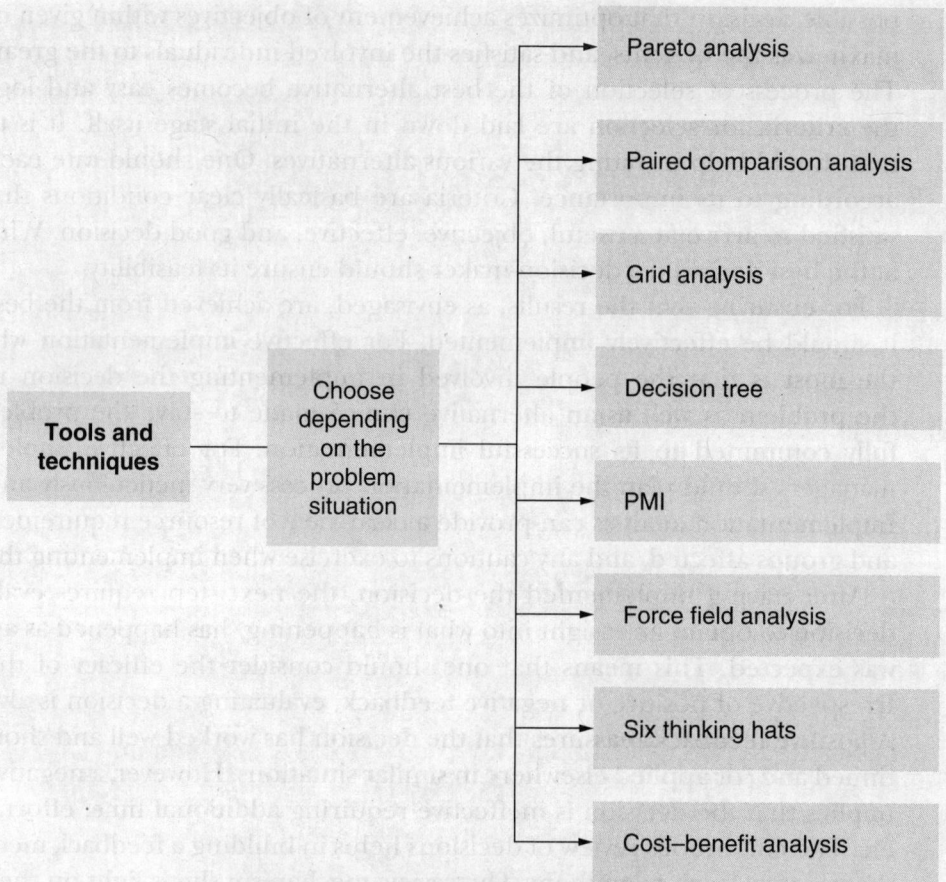

FIGURE 25.3 Tools and techniques for decision-making

does not have any objective data to base the decision on. This tool helps in picking up the most important problem that needs solution, or selects the solution that would give the highest benefits. Paired comparison analysis enables the decision-maker to prioritize the conflicting demands on available resources.

Grid analysis It is an effective tool, which can be used to its advantage when a decision-maker has a number of good alternatives/options and many other factors to take into account. Firstly, one has to list the available options and then the important factors involved for making the decision. Then tabulate them, labeling the rows as 'options' and columns as 'factors'. The relative importance of each factor in a given problem situation is marked by assigning weights according to their increasing or decreasing importance on a scale of say 1–5 or 1–10. In case of any difficulty in assigning weights, one can use paired comparison. As a second step, one has to work one's way across the table, scoring each option for each of the important factors vis-à-vis the decision. Score each option from zero (poor) to three (very good). Note that you do not have to have a different score for each option— if none of them are good for a particular factor in your decision, then all options should score zero. Now multiply each of the scores by the values for your relative importance in terms of weights assigned to factors. This will give the correct overall weightage of the choices available. Finally, add up these weighted scores for your options, the one that scores the highest, wins.

Plus/minus/implications PMI stands for 'plus/minus/implications'. Draw a table with three columns, with the headings plus, minus, and implications headings on the top. In the column below 'plus', write down all possible positive results and outcomes flowing from the action. Below 'minus', write down all possible negative outcomes and effects that would flow from the action. In the 'implications' column write down the implications and possible outcomes of a certain course of action, whether positive or negative. By this process, one can determine whether or not to implement a decision. If it is still not clear, consider each of the points and assign appropriate positive or negative score to it. It is likely that the assigned scores may be quite subjective. After assigning the scores, add up the total scores. A strongly positive score indicates that an action is worth taking, on the other hand a strongly negative score indicates that the proposed action should be avoided.

Six thinking hats De Bono (1985) proposed the concept of Six Thinking Hats—a method that provides a framework of thinking incorporating lateral thinking for decision-making. It is a powerful technique that enables us to view decisions from various perspectives and think out of the box. The six hats connote six vital modes of thinking. As such the purpose of using these hats is to think proactively and come out with solutions about the problem situation. The purpose and reasons to

Where to pursue higher education?

You have appeared for the class 12 Central Board of Secondary Education (CBSE) examination. You are confident of scoring around 88 per cent marks in the examination. You want to enroll for a degree in computer engineering in a reputed institution such as IIT. You have been working hard towards the same. You are attending coaching classes in a reputed coaching centre in Delhi. Your parents have paid ₹2,00,000 as fees for two years. You have appeared in various competitive examinations such as Joint Entrance Examination (JEE) for admission in IIT, BITSAT examination for admission in BITS, and All India Engineering Entrance Examination (AIEEE), widening your choice of colleges and reputed universities you can enroll in. Your rank of 3465 in JEE can get you admitted into one of the less preferred branches of textile engineering or metallurgy in IIT. Your rank of 188 in the BITSAT examination makes you eligible for admission into mechanical engineering and some 50 per cent chances for entry into electrical engineering branch. Your rank of 680 in the AIEEE examination is likely to fetch you an assured seat in electronics engineering in Malviya National Institute of Technology, Jaipur. However, you are assured of getting a seat in the computer sciences programme in Guru Nanak Dev Engineering College, Ludhiana. These are the various choices available to you. Which one you will pick up and why?

use this style are to allow and develop parallel thinking, take advantage of the full thinking spectrum and, above all, to segregate ego from performance. Each hat represents a type of thinking and, therefore, it is important to put on and take off a hat. However, when problem solving is attempted in a group, each member wears the same hat at the same time.

A white hat represents thinking with a focus on facts, figures, and information gaps to dwell upon the problem. A red hat thought process focuses on intuition, feelings, and emotions without much justification for the same. A black hat thinking signifies judgement and caution while making decisions. It is used to find out the reasons for facts, policies, and past experiences differing from suggestions. A yellow hat thinking helps in deriving logical conclusions about workability of solutions and the benefits it would offer. It also helps in finding something of value as an

Decision for retirement planning

Mr Prasad Iyenger has retired at the age of 65, after serving for more than 40 years in a multi-national company. He has two sons and two daughters. All are married and settled in their professions. He had taken a repayable loan from his provident fund for his daughters' marriages amounting to ₹5,00,000 carrying interest at the rate of 8 per cent. An outstanding amount of the loan was ₹2,00,000 that has been deducted from his superannuation benefits that he got on the day of retirement. His job was not pensionable. He got a total sum of ₹38.5 lakh after deduction of all outstanding dues. He bought a house in Delhi at ₹18.5 lakh from his retirement benefits and was left with ₹20 lakh to take care of his and his wife's future requirements.

Mr Iyengar does not want to depend upon his children for his future financial requirements. He has to take a number of decisions about investment of retirement benefits in alternate avenues. The most crucial decision is about uncertainty regarding future life expectancy. He and his wife's normal monthly financial requirements would be around ₹16,666. He has to decide about maintaining his principal amount. In his case, it seems possible to retain his principal amount and invest in alternate avenues to generate returns that can fetch him more than ₹16,666 as income per month. He can think of investing all his money in fixed deposits with bank and post office for a five-year period at an interest rate of 10 per cent per annum payable monthly.

If Mr Iyenger is prepared to take risk, he can invest part of his money in mutual funds to earn higher average returns, so as to increase his standard of living. This may mean his assured income would be less than ₹16,666 per month by depositing balance amount in post office and bank. He may be required to withdraw part of the principal amount, in the eventuality of not getting expected returns from his investment. He also has the third option of withdrawing the accumulation in installments based on his and his wife's life expectancy. This proposition may seem to be attractive, as it guarantees that the entire accumulation will be withdrawn within the projected life expectancy of both of them. However, if his calculation on life expectancy goes wrong and they happen to outlive their expectancy, the principal will be exhausted and Mr Iyenger may need another source of funding. What would you have done in Mr Iyenger's place, what decision will you take, and why? How would you arrive at your decision?

outcome of what has already happened. Green hat denotes creativity, imagination, and alternative ideas that would bring in change and provocations. A blue hat is a process control hat that may give rise to the need for some more green hat thinking to come out with alternative creative solutions.

Cost–benefit analysis Cost–benefit analysis is a relatively simple and useful technique that decides whether or not to accept or reject a proposition leading to making a change. It basically requires computation in financial terms of the net benefits that would accrue from a particular course of action, that is, add the value of all benefits and subtract from that all associated costs to a particular course of action. One needs to pick up an alternative course of action amongst alternative possible set of decisions that gives rise to greatest net benefits. Thus, a decision giving highest net benefits would be the best decision.

The ability to make decisions is vital for the success of a manager, executive, or leader. Decision-making is a scientific process that defines, understands, and solves the problem. What matters the most in the whole process of decision-making is that it is implemented smoothly. Therefore, it is necessary to focus on alternative solutions rather than the right solution. A decision, basically, is a choice between alternatives that would help the most in achieving predetermined goals and objectives. Effective decision-making has to ensure smooth implementation by ensuring that people who matter the most in the implementation are committed. This can be ensured by making them participate responsibly in discussions at different stages of problem solving. It is important to ensure that specific responsibility for taking action is clearly assigned to the people who are capable of carrying it out.

SUMMARY

Managing problems depends upon the manager's ability to make decisions. Decision-making is the cognitive process of selecting a course of action from among multiple alternatives. There are two basic types of decisions—programmed and non-programmed. Systematic and structured decision-making requires recognition and analysis of important components of decisions—context, objectives, options, and criteria. Effective and good decision-making involves seven vital steps—(1) identify, diagnose, and precisely define the problem; (2) work out alternative solutions; (3) evaluate each alternative solution; (4) choose the best alternative; (5) implement the decision; (6) evaluate the decision; and (7) review and learn the lessons for future. For scientific diagnosis and analysis of the problem situation, various tools, and techniques such as Pareto analysis, paired comparison analysis, grid analysis, weighing the pros and cons of a decision, force field analysis, six thinking hats, and cost–benefit analysis are used in decision-making.

KEYWORDS

Cost–benefit analysis It is a useful technique to decide whether to accept or reject a proposition leading to making a change based on net benefits from alternative decisions.

Decision-making It is the cognitive process of selecting a course of action from among multiple alternatives.

Grid analysis   An effective tool which can be used with advantage when a decision-maker has a number of good alternatives and many factors to take into account.

Non-programmed decisions   These are one shot occurrences and are usually less structured.

Paired comparison analysis   A tool that helps in picking up the most important problem that needs solution, or select the solution that would give the highest benefits.

Pareto analysis   A simple technique that helps in making the most effective changes to achieve the desired results.

Programmed decisions   These are routine and repetitive decisions.

Six thinking hats   It is a method that provides a framework of thinking with incorporation of lateral thinking for decision-making.

Steps in decision-making   Concrete steps involved from defining the problem to evaluating the decisions to review for learning future lessons.

Systematic and structured decision-making   It requires recognition and analysis of important components of decisions—context, objectives, options, and criteria.

EXERCISES

Concept Review Questions

1. Define decision-making and its importance to managers. What is the difference between programmed and non-programmed decisions?
2. What are the requirements of systematic and structured decision-making?
3. What are the vital steps involved in decision-making?
4. Why is there a need to evaluate decisions? Does this step come after implementation or before implementation? Explain.
5. What is Pareto analysis? How does it help in decision-making?
6. Explain cost–benefit analysis as a tool and technique used in decision-making.

Critical Thinking Questions

1. Do you think that managers follow decision-making steps in reality? Why or why not? Which particular steps, according to you, can be overlooked and why?
2. What do you think are the advantages and disadvantages of using computers to assist in decision-making?

Project Assignment

How did you decide upon the institution where you would pursue higher studies after class 12? While evaluating in retrospect, after having gone through this chapter, do you think you would have taken some other decision? If so, why?

REFERENCES

Alexander, E.R. (1979), 'The Design of Alternatives in Organisational Contexts: A Pilot Study', *Administrative Science Quarterly*, vol. 24, pp. 382–404.

Bateman, Thomas S. and A. Scott Snell (2002), *Management—Competing in the New Era*, 5th edition, McGraw-Hill Irwin, pp. 71.

De Bono, Edward (1985), *Six Thinking Hats*, Penguin, UK.

De Bono, Edward (1991), 'Why do Quality Efforts Lose Their Fizz? Quality is No Longer Enough', *The Journal for Quality and Participation*, September.

Gibson, J., J. Ivancevich and J. Donnelly Jr. (1985), *Organizations*, 5th edition, Plano, Texas.

MacCrimmon, K. and R. Taylor (1976), 'Decision Making and Problem Solving', in *Handbook of Industrial and Organisational Psychology*, M.D. Dunnette (ed), Rand McNally, Chicago.

26

Emotional Intelligence

Anyone can become angry—that is easy. But to be angry with the right person, to the right degree at the right time, for the right purpose and in the right way is not that easy!

ARISTOTLE IN *NICHOMACHIAN ETHICS*

INTRODUCTION

In recent years, organizations have been demanding a set of key competencies from their managers; emotional competence being one of these. Thorndike (1927) was probably the first researcher to identify the social dimension of emotional intelligence. He defined it as the 'ability to understand and manage men and women, boys and girls to act wisely in human relations'. Howard Gardner (1983) with his conceptualization of multiple intelligence factors once again resurfaced emotional intelligence by incorporating intrapersonal and interpersonal types of intelligence factors in his model of multi-factor intelligence. However, the concept of emotional quotient (EQ) was first coined by Reuven Bar-On in 1988 in his doctoral dissertation (Bar-On 2000). However, the term emotional intelligence was first used by Salovey and Mayor (1990) who defined it as 'the ability to monitor the feelings of the self and others, discriminate among them and use this information to guide one's thinking and action'.

Goleman (1998) defines emotional competence as 'a learned capability based on emotional intelligence that results in outstanding performance at work'. To be adept at an emotional competence, for example, in customer service or conflict management necessitates an

Learning Objectives

After studying this chapter, you will be able to:

- Learn about emotional intelligence
- Understand the relevance of emotional intelligence and emotional competence to work performance
- Examine the relationship between emotional needs and emotional intelligence
- Understand the emotional competence framework
- Analyse the empirical evidence about the relevance of emotional competencies
- Evaluate the effect of emotional intelligence on the company's productivity

understanding of emotional intelligence especially, those of social awareness and relationship management. However, possession of social awareness or skill at managing relationships does not guarantee skills in handling a customer adeptly or resolving a conflict as it simply refers to the potential. In fact, emotional competencies are learned abilities. A study of Harvard graduates in the fields of law, medicine, teaching, and business found that scores of entrance examinations, a surrogate for IQ, had zero or negative correlation with their eventual success in careers. Being intelligent and gaining expertise in one's line of work are not enough to ensure success, according to Goleman (1995). In addition, he says, people in business must be judged on 'how well we handle ourselves and each other'.

Emotional intelligence refers to an individual's ability to manage the self as well as others. It is the individual's capacity for recognizing his own as well as others' feelings, for motivating the self and others, and for managing emotions and relationships. It stands for abilities distinct from, but complementary to, academic intelligence or the purely cognitive capacities measured by IQ. Emotional quotient has more to do with a person's success and happiness in life than IQ and it can be learned. Intelligence quotient is a measure of a person's intelligence as indicated by an intelligence test; the ratio of a person's mental age to their chronological age (multiplied by 100). It is the measure of cognitive abilities, such as the ability to learn or understand; the skilled use of reason; to apply knowledge to manipulate one's environment, or to think abstractly as measured by objective criteria (as tests); mental acuteness; and logical and analytical skills. Emotional quotient is a measure of one's emotional intelligence, or one's ability to use both emotions and cognitive skills in life and work. These competencies include, but are not limited to empathy, intuition, creativity, flexibility, resilience, coping, stress management, leadership, integrity, authenticity, intrapersonal skills, and interpersonal skills.

The model proposed by Mayer and Salovey (1997) embraces four types of abilities. First, there is a complex set of skills that allow an individual to perceive, evaluate, and express emotions. These skills include identifying emotions, expressing one's emotions, and discriminating between those expressed by others. Second, there exists a set of skills for using emotions to facilitate and prioritize thinking and to aid judgement, recognizing that mood swings can lead to a consideration of alternative viewpoints, and understanding that a shift in emotional state and perspective can stimulate varied types of problem solving. Third, there is a set of skills including labelling and differentiating emotions, understanding a complex mixture of feelings, and evolving rules relating to feelings. Finally, there exists a general set of skills that direct emotions towards a social goal. These skills allow individuals to selectively engage in or detach from not only their emotions but also others' emotions.

EMOTIONAL NEEDS

All humans have basic emotional needs. These needs can be expressed as feelings; for example, the need to feel accepted, respected, and important. While all humans share these needs, each differs in the intensity of the need, just as some of us need more water, more food, or more sleep. One person may need more freedom and independence, another may need more security and social connections. One may have a greater curiosity and a greater need for understanding, while another is content to accept whatever he/she has been told.

Managing Emotions

Our emotions are important to our lives. Nature has developed our emotions over millions of years of evolution. As a result, our emotions have the potential to serve us today as a delicate sophisticated internal guidance system. Our emotions are a valuable source of information. They help us to make decisions. Studies show that when a person's emotional connections are disturbed, he cannot make even simple decisions. The reason is that individuals do not know how they will feel about their choices. When we feel uncomfortable with a person's behaviour, our emotions alert us. If we learn to trust our emotions and feel confident about expressing ourselves, we can let the person know that we feel uncomfortable as soon as we are aware of our feelings. This will help us set our boundaries, which are necessary to protect our physical and mental health. Our emotions help us communicate with others. Our facial expressions, for example, can convey a wide range of emotions. If we look sad or hurt, we are signalling to others that we need their help. If we are verbally skilled, we will be able to express more of our emotional needs. If we effectively listen to others' emotional troubles, we would be able to help them feel understood, important, and cared about. The only real way to know that we are happy is when we feel happy. When we feel happy, we feel content and fulfilled. This feeling comes when our needs are met, particularly our emotional needs. We can be materially prosperous, but still be unhappy.

Our emotions and feelings let us know when we are unhappy and when something is missing or is needed. The better we identify with our emotions, the easier it will be to determine what is needed to be happy. Our emotions are perhaps the greatest potential source of uniting all members of the human species. Clearly, our various religious, cultural, and political beliefs have not united us. Far too often, in fact, they have tragically and even fatally divided us. Emotions, on the other hand, are universal. The emotions of empathy, compassion, cooperation, and forgiveness, for instance, all have the potential to unite us.

EMOTIONAL COMPETENCE FRAMEWORK

The first step towards emotional intelligence is being aware of our emotional needs. This determines our potential for learning the practical skills. As per Goleman (1998), the five dimensions or competencies are—self-awareness, motivation, self-regulation, empathy, and adeptness in relationships (Table 26.1).

An emotional competence is, therefore, a learned capability based on emotional intelligence that results in outstanding performance at work.

TABLE 26.1   The five components of emotional intelligence

Dimensions	Definitions
Self-awareness	The ability to recognize one's emotions as well as its effect on those around us.
Self-regulation	The ability to control one's impulsive judgement and reactions.
Motivation	The ability to pursue goals persistently as a higher calling and not for money or status alone.
Empathy	The ability to empathize with emotional state of others and respond accordingly.
Social skill	The ability to network and build rapport with others.

Source: Based on Goleman (1998)

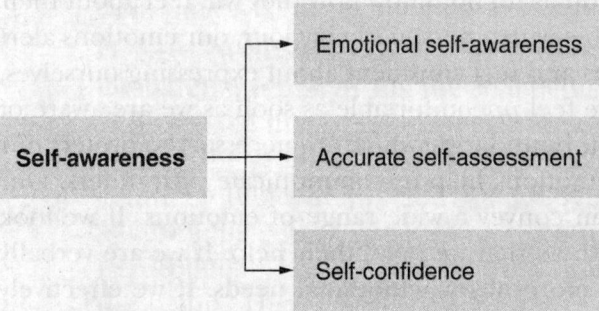

FIGURE 26.1   Components of self-awareness

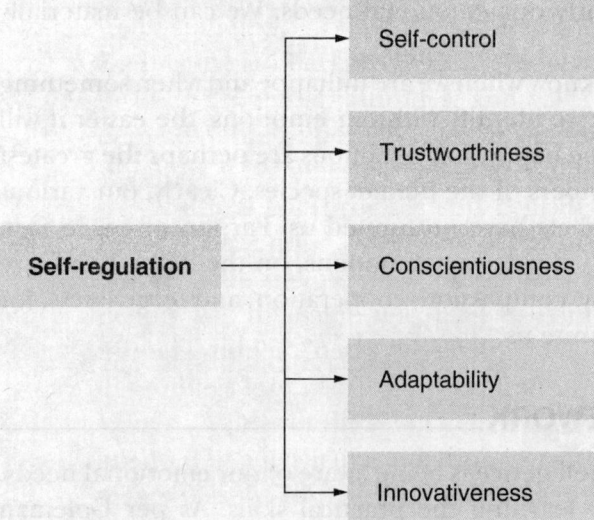

FIGURE 26.2   Components of self-regulation

The five dimensions of emotional competency framework are based on studies conducted in several multinational companies; Sandoz Pharmaceuticals and American Express being two of them. Further, this framework has 25 competencies categorized as five dimensions as given in Figs. 26.1, 26.2, 26.3, 26.4, and 26.5.

Subsequently, using factor analysis, Boyatzis et al. (2000) narrowed down the 25 competencies to twenty and finally to four major categories as given in Table 26.2. This classification labels one axis as awareness and management and the other axis as self and others.

EFFECT OF EMOTIONAL INTELLIGENCE ON A COMPANY'S PRODUCTIVITY

In today's competitive, knowledge-driven organizations, leadership is more important than ever. Leaders—from top executives to line managers—must have more than just the right technical skills and IQ. They must possess the right values, behaviour, and emotions—the right emotional intelligence. Emotionally intelligent leaders help organizations create competitive advantage through emotional competencies.

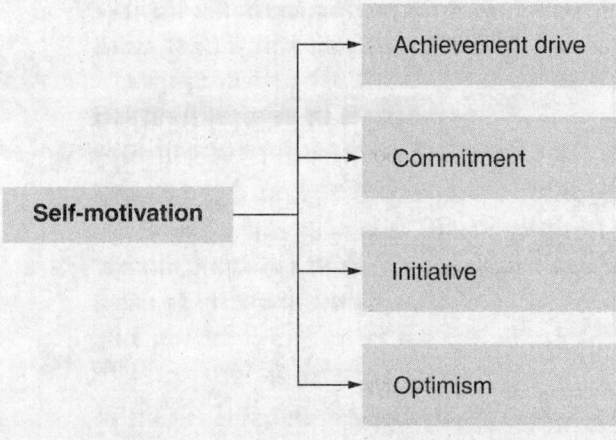

FIGURE 26.3   Components of self-motivation

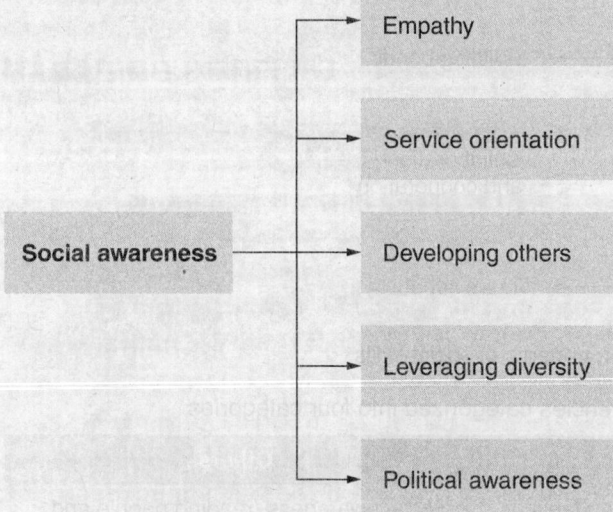

FIGURE 26.4   Components of social awareness

The results are outstanding work and increased productivity (Table 26.3).

Empirical Evidence on Emotional Competencies

There is a close relationship between the success of an organization and the emotional intelligence of its leader. Goleman (2000) analysed data collected from 188 companies to come to a conclusion that emotional intelligence related competencies (e.g., the ability to get along with others, effectiveness in leading change, etc.) are twice as important as competencies related to technical skills (e.g., accounting, business planning, etc.) and cognitive skills (e.g., analytical reasoning). Business executives have to be emotionally competent in a dynamic and complex global environment.

Most effective leaders are alike in a crucial way and that is that all of them invariably have a high level of emotional intelligence. It does not mean that IQ and technical skills are irrelevant. Indeed, they matter but merely as threshold capabilities, that is, as entry-level requirements for executive positions.

A CEO reported that emotional competencies enabled his company to accomplish a growth rate of 30 per cent per annum during the preceding years and that its recruitment and selection processes are exclusively based on the evaluation of emotional intelligence. A study of 300 top-level executives from 15 global companies by Spencer et al. (1997) showed that six emotional competencies differentiated the 'stars' from the 'average'. These competencies included influence, team leadership, organizational awareness, self-confidence, achievement drive, and leadership. Spencer et al. (1997) also found that sales agents selected on the basis of emotional competencies outperformed their counterparts selected by using the company's traditional selection procedures.

McClelland (1999) in his study of a large beverage company found that almost half of the divisional presidents who were selected using traditional measures

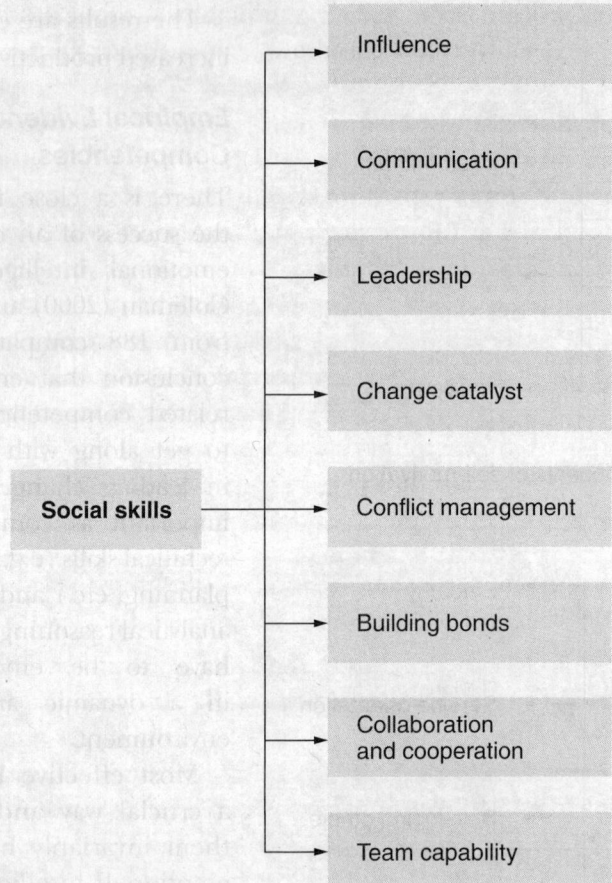

FIGURE 26.5 Components of social skills

TABLE 26.2 Emotional competencies categorized into four categories

	Self	Others
Awareness	Self-awareness (understanding feelings and accurate self-assessment)	Social awareness (reading people and groups accurately)
Management	Self-management (managing internal states, impulses, and resources)	Relationship management (inducing desirable responses in others)

Source: The Emotional and Social Competency Inventory is available worldwide through The Hay Group (http://www.haygroup.com/leadershipandtalentondemand/ourproducts/item_details.aspx?itemid=58&type=7). Copyright © 2000 by Richard E. Boyatzis. Reprinted by permission of Richard E. Boyatzis.

of competencies left the company within two years due to poor performance compared to a miniscule six per cent who left after the company started the selection based on emotional competencies (i.e., on leadership, self-confidence, initiative, etc.). Boyatzis et al. (2000) found that the mastery of a 'critical mass' of emotional competencies was necessary for superior performance and as Boyatzis (1999) proved, the 'self-management' cluster of emotional intelligence produced the highest level of profits for a large financial services company.

TABLE 26.3 Competitive advantage through emotional competencies

1. Increased performance	5. Improved and enhanced innovation
2. Effective leaders	6. Effective use of time and resources
3. More teamwork	7. Restored trust
4. Initiative and infectious enthusiasm result in quality customer service	8. Courage and resilience in times of adverse environment

Several studies have pointed out the positive impact of training on emotional competencies; for example, Cherniss and Adler (2000) describe the varied outcome of a training programme for insurance advisors at American Express.

In India, apart from non-empirical studies by Dasari (2001) and Mathur (2000), there exist only a few empirical studies. Mishra and Dhar (2001) conducted a survey of 210 management students to explore the relationship between thinking orientation and emotional intelligence. Dwivedi (2002) conducted a study of 60 highly successful managers of profit-making Indian organizations and found their score on emotional intelligence components from moderate to high.

SUMMARY

Goleman (1998) defines emotional competence as 'a learned capability based on emotional intelligence that results in outstanding performance at work'. Emotional intelligence merely relates to the potential, but emotional competencies are learned abilities. It refers to the capacity for recognizing our own feelings and those of others, for motivating ourselves, and for managing emotions. Emotional quotient (EQ) is a measure of one's emotional intelligence, or one's ability to use both emotions and cognitive skills in life. Studies show that when a person's emotional connections are disturbed, he cannot make even simple decisions. An emotional competence is a learned capability based on emotional intelligence that results in outstanding performance at work. Today's leaders, from top executives to line managers, must have more than just the right technical skills and IQ. They must possess the right values, behaviour, and emotions—the right emotional intelligence. Emotionally intelligent leaders help organizations create competitive advantage. Research shows that for all kinds of jobs, emotional intelligence is twice as important as IQ and technical skills. The higher the complexity of a job and its authority, the greater the impact of a company's leaders' emotional intelligence on its productivity.

KEYWORDS

Emotional competence It is a learned capability based on emotional intelligence that results in outstanding performance at work.

Emotional intelligence It is the ability to monitor the feelings and emotions of the self and others to discriminate among them and use this information to guide one's thinking.

Empathy The ability to empathize with the emotional state of others and respond accordingly.

Motivation The ability to pursue goals persistently as a higher calling and not for money or status alone.

Self-awareness The ability to recognize one's emotions as well its effect on those around us.

Self-regulation The ability to control one's impulsive judgement and reactions.

Social-skill The ability to network and build rapport with others.

EXERCISES

Concept Review Questions

1. Define emotional intelligence and emotional competence.
2. Define emotional quotient (EQ). How is it different from intelligence quotient?
3. Describe emotional competence framework. What aspect as per emotional competence framework helps in better self-management?

Critical Thinking Questions

1. What are the success factors of emotionally intelligent organizations? Explain citing concrete examples from the corporate world.
2. Most effective leaders are alike in crucial ways. All have, invariably, a high level of emotional intelligence. Does this mean that technical skills and IQ are not important compared with emotional intelligence? Comment critically.
3. Studies show that when a person's emotional connections are disturbed, he/she cannot make even simple decisions. Why?

Project Assignment

Emotional intelligence makes an impact on the company's productivity. Identify two companies from the same industry, one having excellent consistent financial performance and other performing erratically. Collect information on these two companies from various sources, particularly pertaining to emotional intelligence aspects. Is there any relationship between the performance of the company with that of emotional competence of their leaders, managers, and employees? Explain.

REFERENCES

Bar-on, R. (2000), 'Emotional and Social Intelligence: Insights from the Emotional Quotient Inventory', in R. Bar-on and J.D.A. Parker (eds) *Handbook of Emotional Intelligence*, Jossey-Bass, San Francisco.

Boyatzis, R. (1999), 'The Financial Impact of Competencies in Leadership and Management of Consulting Firms', *Department of Organizational Behaviour Working Paper*, Case Western Reserve University, Cleveland.

Boyatzis, R., D. Goleman, and K. Rhee (2000), 'Clustering Competence in Emotional Intelligence: Insight from the Emotional Competence Inventory (ECI)' in R. Bar-On and J.D.A. Parker (eds), *Handbook of Emotional Intelligence*, Jossey-Bass, San Francisco.

Cherniss and M. Adler (2000), *Promoting Emotional Intelligence in Organizations*, American Society for Training and Development (ASTD), Alexandria, Virginia.

Dasari, R. (2001), 'Emotional Intelligence: Why It Matters', *Pratibimba*, August, pp. 42–46.

Dwivedi, R.S. (2002), 'Identifying Emotional Intelligence Related Competencies among Highly Successful Managers for Corporate Success: An Empirical Study', *Paradigm*, vol. 6, no. 1, January–June, pp. 10–28.

Gardner, Howard (1983), *Frames of Mind*, Basic Books, New York.

Goleman, D. (1995), *Emotional Intelligence*, Bantam, New York.

Goleman, D. (1998), 'What makes a leader', *Harvard Business Review*, November–December, pp. 93–102.

Goleman, D. (1998), *Working with Emotional Intelligence*, Bantam, New York.

Goleman, D. (2000), 'Leadership That Gets Results', *Harvard Business Review*, March–April, pp. 78–90.

Mathur, D.M. (2000), 'Emotional Intelligence in Effective Management', *Indian Management*, November, pp. 19–21.

Mayer, J.D. and P. Salovey (1993), 'The Intelligence of Emotional Intelligence', *Intelligence*, vol. 17, pp. 433–443.

Mayer, J.D. and P. Salovey (1997), 'What is Emotional Intelligence?' in P. Slovey and D. Sluyter (eds), *Emotional Development and Emotional Intelligence: Educational Implications*, Basic Books, New York.

McClelland, D.C. (1999), 'Identifying Competencies With Behavioral Interviews', *Psychological Science*, vol. 9, no. 5, pp. 331–339.

Mishra, P. and U. Dhar (2001), 'Emotional Intelligence as a Correlate of Thinking Orientation among Future Managers', *Indian Journal Of Industrial Relations*, January, pp. 323–337.

Salovey, P. and J.D. Mayer (1990), 'Emotional Intelligence', *Imagination, Cognition and Personality*, vol. 9, no. 3, pp. 185–211.

Spencer, L.M. (1997), *Competency Assessment Methods*, in L.J. Bassi and Russ-Eft (eds), *What Works: Assessment, Development, and Measurement,* American Society for Training and Development, Alexandria, VA.

Thorndike, Edward L. (1927), *The Meaning of Intelligence*, Macmillan, New York.

27

Stress Management

Learning Objectives

After studying this chapter, you will be able to:
- Understand stress
- Learn about eustress and distress
- Understand the human stress response and stressors
- Learn about stress and the organization
- Examine levels of stress, and stress and individual behaviour
- Learn about stress management

INTRODUCTION

We keep oscillating between very happy and very sad moments in life. In our daily lives we face stressful situations. On one hand, tension is not good but on the other hand, it is said that there is no life without pressure, as we tend to perform far more effectively under stress. Thus, our performance depends a great deal on the degree, nature, and type of pressure or tension we undergo under different situations. We do not have any control over the events of our day-to-day living. However, we can control our response to the events. The physical, psychological, and intellectual response to the same event differs a great deal from one person to another. What matters is the way we handle, respond, and manage a given situation. Therefore, stress is a must in life but what matters for individual effectiveness is the way stress is managed.

UNDERSTANDING STRESS

Which of these is stress?

- you receive double promotion at work;
- your car has a flat tyre on the highway at midnight amidst a jungle;
- you go to a marriage party that lasts till two a.m.;
- your wife is hospitalized;
- your new house is ready for possession;
- your distant relatives come to stay at your house for a week;
- your son fails in an exam;
- your parents have fixed your marriage without consulting you; or
- all of the above.

The most popular definition of stress is tension that is an outcome of anxiety and fear about a current event or a future one. Thus, the chief cause of stress is 'anxiety' resulting in feeling of discomfort in mind that further leads to body ailments. In management, stress is defined as the human body's response to the demands made on it. Stress can, however, be a desirable condition that motivates a person to do the best for accomplishing set targets. Stress also occurs when the need to act arises, mainly, as a result of fear that the results might not meet the expectations of the self or others. If a person does not react to stress, it does not imply that he/she is out of the state of stress. Stress continues to act within the human body and mind. Each individual handles stress differently. A person can either use stress or suffer from it. He/she can also reduce it for others.

Stress can be defined as the non-specific response of the body to any demand put upon it. It is the body's automatic response to challenge. It is not an event or a circumstance but a response to it. It is not necessarily bad, damaging, or unhealthy. It is always over stimulating or exciting. Anxiety is a vital signal that something is out of balance.

Stress is a situation wherein an individual is faced with an opportunity, constraint, or demand related to what he desires and for which the outcome is likely to be both uncertain and important (Schuler 1980). Thus, stress although being seen and understood in a negative context, has a positive value too (Cavanaugh et al. 2000).

Stress need not necessarily be avoided. In fact, it is an essential aspect of life. It is not only impossible to have a life without a certain minimum amount of stress, but also undesirable to have a life without it. Stress is an open and democratic process, that is, the individual is aware, conscious, and knows when he/she undergoes stress, its cause, and implications on the human system. However, unmanaged stress can take its toll on the human body. Its early effects on the response mechanism and system are tough to detect as they are very subtle. Thus, stress can have a positive or negative impact on the human system depending upon the way one views, handles, responds, and adapts to it. The human body responds to stress according to our thoughts, the biochemical and physiological changes in the body, and the way our mind responds to situations.

Stress may be categorized into two types—eustress and distress (Fig. 27.1). The idea of *eustress* or healthy stress was first proposed by Richard Lazarus (1974). It is a condition wherein the individual feels a positive drive and wants to fulfil his/her needs and achieve his/her goals. The level of motivation is high. The individual is optimistic about achievement and the situation appears not only challenging but also stimulating. Stress disappears when the need is fulfilled and success is achieved.

However, on the contrary, when an individual faces a condition of distress, he/she feels a sense of helplessness about the target to be achieved. This results in frustration and disappointment that leads to health problems such as high blood pressure or a cardiac condition. The individual's efforts go waste as one is not able to channelize one's energies properly. The person meets with failure. At times an individual continues to be in this condition of stress as no further attempts are made even to achieve the goal, as success is already considered as elusive.

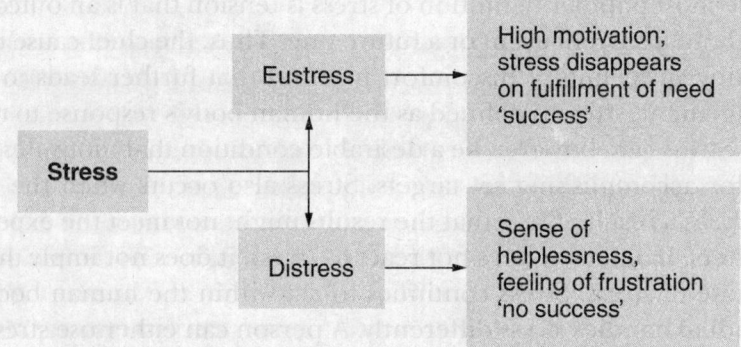

Figure 27.1 Response of the body to the demands put upon it

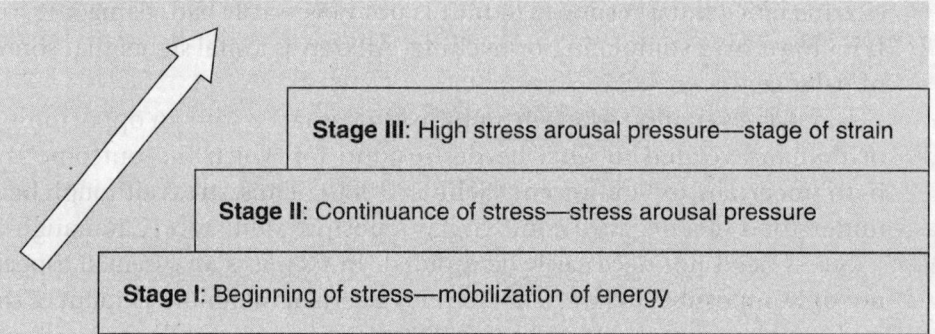

Figure 27.2 Manifestation of stress—Three stages

The human body goes through the following three stages (Fig. 27.2) when it faces an external challenge, crisis, or emergency:

Beginning of stress: In this stage the individual responds to stress through mobilization of energy.

Continuance of stress: The stage of stress arousal pressure.

Stage of strain: The end result of high stress arousal pressure or strain.

HUMAN STRESS RESPONSE

When faced with a challenging situation or event, a small pocket of chemicals in a part of the brain called the hypothalamus instantly triggers off a complex chain of chemicals and nerve reactions and transformations. These changes are brought about by two systems acting together—the hormonal system (particularly the pituitary–adrenal link) and the branch of the nervous system called sympathetic. The main parts of the body that are affected are heart and blood circulation, lungs, stomach, and the internal organs. These changes trigger a significant increase in energy, speed, and strength often far in excess of what is necessary to meet the everyday challenges of life.

Stressors

Stressors refer to those events and situations that trigger stress. Some of common stressors in life are death of a close relative, termination of services of an employee, transfer of residence, transfer, separation due to divorce or change of job, getting married, inadequate finances, serious illness, likelihood of unpleasant secrets becoming revealed, etc. Even situations such as falling in love, welcoming and entertaining important visitors, acting as a chief guest in a public gathering, or delivering a speech for the first time can cause considerable amount of stress. Some common stressors at the workplace include:

- non-fulfillment of needs that could be needs for power, for fulfillment, for use of knowledge, for achievement, etc.;
- not being invited as part of a group you want to belong to;
- not being cared for, recognized, respected, or valued for one's competence;
- having a feeling that one is not fully equipped to perform the assigned task, particularly when compared to peers;
- neglected, not cared for, or denied what is due to you;
- monotony or boredom resulting from an assigned job role;
- not having enough freedom to take initiative at work;
- being over or closely supervised;
- inequity in rewards and work assignments;
- lack of growth opportunity;
- work overload, deadlines, or boredom at work;
- inadequate resources to effectively and efficiently perform the assigned work, thus increasing chances of failure;
- conflict between personal and organizational values at work. Being forced to do what one does not like to do;
- excessive and conflicting demands at work;
- responsibilities not well defined. Ambiguity and confusion about what is expected;
- unpredictable behaviour on the part of the boss supervisor;
- unknown and completely unfamiliar work situations; or
- being made scapegoat for group failures.

On close analysis, we would find that all these situations, in some way or other, cause perceptions of possible failure, non-recognition, and consequent loss of self-esteem in work-related situations. Thus, potential sources of stress mainly emanate from environmental, organizational, and individual factors (Robbins and Sanghi 2005). Environmental factors include economic, political, technological, and terrorism related uncertainties. Organizational factors include lack of knowledge about the task in hand, time pressure to complete the task, work overload, demanding and indiscriminate behaviour on the part of the boss, unpleasant colleagues, etc. These factors can be categorized around task, roles, and interpersonal demands; and organizational structure, organizational leadership, and organization's life stage

(Frew and Bruning 1987). Individual factors include employee's personal life emanating from family issues, economic problems, and personal characteristics. Various studies have shown the presence of these stress symptoms at individual level causing stress (Nelson and Sutton 1990).

Stress and the organization

Ambiguity of role in the workplace can adversely affect the employees' performance. Seeking employee participation in the decision-making process can help in reducing role related stress. Therefore, managers need to consider increasing employee participation and involvement in decision making (Jackson 1983). A large number of professionally managed organizations have developed wellness programmes by setting up employee welfare programme departments. These programmes basically focus their efforts on employees' total physical and mental condition (Leonard 2001). However, what matters the most is the individual's preparedness to manage and handle stress effectively to improve effectiveness.

Levels of stress

Stress gets reflected at four different levels (Fig. 27.3). At the first level, it is characterized by palpitation, increased blood pressure, dilation of pupils, sweaty palms, and reduced activity in the stomach.

At the second level, stress symptoms manifest themselves as irritability, stuttering and stammering, lack of concentration, restlessness, lack of appetite, and a heightened tendency to smoke or drink. At the third level, it is visible in the form of headaches, stomach ache, diarrhoea, sweating, insomnia, depression, etc. Finally, at the fourth level it gets characterized by ulcers, strokes, alcoholism, drug addiction, psychosis, etc.

Stress and individual behaviour

Psychologists have divided people into two broad categories—type A and type B, depending upon their behaviour patterns. The typical traits of these two personality types are shown in Table 27.1.

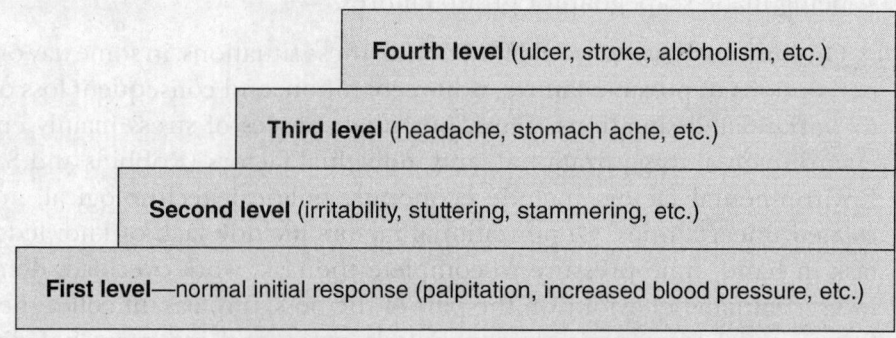

FIGURE 27.3 Four levels of stress symptoms

TABLE 27.1   Type A and type B personalities' responses to stress

Type A individual	Type B individual
• Chronic struggle with the environment	• Balanced interplay with the environment
• Hard driving (over achiever)	• Rational approach to achievement
• Time urgency (hyper responsive)	• Relaxed
• Hostility	• Positive interpersonal relations
• Workaholics	• Balance between work and other events

Type A people are considered to be having 'hurry sickness'. Their tendency to hurry is reflected in their behaviour in terms of eating fast, talking fast, moving fast, etc. They are caught in the never ending struggle to achieve more in less time. They are normally preoccupied with themselves and are not happy with life. Friedman and Rosenman (1974) identified type A personality when they observed recurrent personality behaviour patterns having tendency of hurry sickness in their patients who were identified to be suffering from premature heart disease. Besides being concerned with time deadlines and commitments, most type A persons are competitive and aggressive in their social and business relationships. Type B personalities are easy-going and relaxed, less perturbed by time pressures, and are less likely to overreact to situations in an aggressive manner. Type A behaviour can be checked by following these guidelines:

- Restrain from being centre of attention by constantly and continuously talking.
- Try to take charge of your time directed life by making yourself aware of it.
- Reflect and assess the cause of your hurry sickness. Is there a need to feel important?
- Understand and be clear that majority of your work and social life do not really require 'universal acclaim'.
- Broaden yourself. Indulge in outdoor activities such as theatre, reading, music, games, etc.
- Try not to make unnecessary appointments and unachievable deadlines.
- Protect your time by learning to say no.
- Do something that relaxes you.
- Try to make yourself aware of your behaviour and its impact on others.
- Do not be an idealist.
- Take time off to develop social relationships.

STRESS MANAGEMENT

There is no challenge without stress. It is a state of mind that drives individuals to take on difficult situations. The tendency to give up in difficult situations would make life too easy, uncomplicated, and boring. As such one will not even succeed in doing what one is easily capable of, because even the normal faculties, capabilities, and energy will not come into play if he/she remained inattentive and unfocused, even at the last minute.

There are two ways of managing stress. The first is that one should not allow stress to develop to the extent that one becomes non-functional. The second, is to develop a mechanism to get back to normal as quickly as one can and not to continue in a state of stress for too long.

Developing a positive attitude towards life by rational and logical thinking and realizing that one's perceptions can often distort reality is essential to handling stress effectively. The situation may not be as bad as it may seem to be and failure is not an irreversible situation. It is not possible or even necessary to succeed all the time. One failed effort does not imply that the individual is no good. Even world champions sometimes lose the first round of the match to an unseeded player. Marconi and Edison succeeded in their inventions after many failed attempts. They did not give up and learnt from their failures. They perceived failures as stepping stones to success.

One must understand that worry and anxiety do not improve a situation; on the contrary, they only disturb one's peace of mind and impair one's health. If one watches different passengers' response to a delayed flight at an airport or the late departure of a train at railway stations, one notes that some of them remain relaxed and even sleep while others make continuous enquiries from officials about extent and causes of delays. Such constant enquiries only irritate officials and do not help in any way whatsoever in expediting solutions. They as such multiply and add, not only to their own stress, but also of others.

Stress management at the individual level

Individual level planning to manage stress focuses on developing individual behaviour that helps in the elimination of sources of stress. It helps in developing a perspective to view things that enables the person to cope with stress in a more effective manner. Some effective approaches to managing stress are provided in Fig. 27.4.

Above all 'can' and 'positive' attitude matter the most in managing stress. It has been rightly said 'They can because they think they can'.

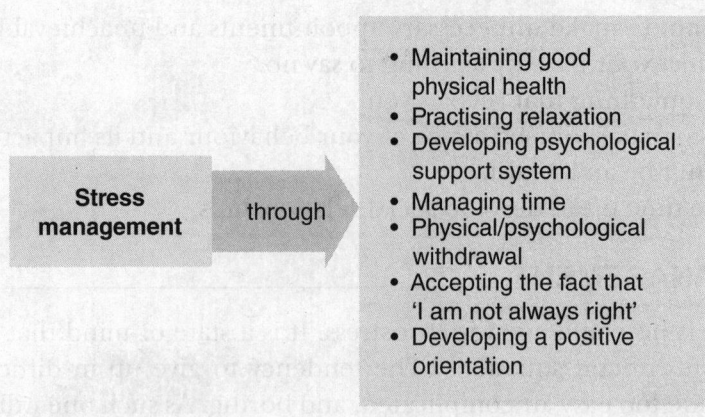

FIGURE 27.4 Individual level planning for stress management

Maintaining good physical health   Regular physical exercises, such as aerobics, walking, jogging, swimming, cycling, etc., help in dealing with excessive stress. Regular sleep, and timely and healthy eating habits also help the individual to tackle stress better. Today, yoga is fast gaining popularity not only as a stress reliever, but also as an exercise that can balance the individual's physical, psychological, and emotional being. These physical exercises help in building heart capacity, lowering the at-rest heart rate, providing mental diversion from work pressure, and offering a means to 'let off steam' (Kiely and Hodgson 1990). While exercising, the body releases a hormone known as endomorphine that makes one feel good about the self.

Practising relaxation   Techniques such as meditation, hypnosis, and bio-feedback reduce tension (Robbins and Sanghi 2005). As per Forbes and Pekala (1993), the objective of practising relaxation techniques is to feel physically relaxed, somewhat detached from the immediate environment and from body sensation. Practising transcendental meditation, yoga, ego-void activity—an activity without the sense of doership such as voluntary work in an NGO or religious place, having faith in a higher power, reading, and practising spirituality can also reduce stress to considerable levels.

Developing a psychological support system   It helps in effectively managing stress. Similarly, expanding social support network and finding an emphatic listener to hear and suggest an objective and broader perspective about the problem situation is beneficial. If the issue is work related, then an organizational solution is required to help the individual. Some of the strategies that the management may consider are scientific and involves improving personnel selection and placement process, training, realistic goal setting, redesigning jobs, increasing employee involvement, improving organizational communication, offering employees vacation allowances, extending sabbaticals, and setting up corporate employee welfare programme departments (Robbins and Sanghi 2005).

Time management   It contributes a great deal in handling stress. The individual should firstly avoid the superhuman urge to do more than what he/she is capable of. They should learn to say 'no' to tasks that are beyond their capacities of time and energy. Scheduling meetings and prioritizing tasks leads to the completion of tasks, both simple and complex, within a given time frame. However, the individual has to be disciplined and needs to stick to the daily, weekly, or monthly agenda so as to achieve the target goals. This not only reduces stress but also ensures that targets are met on time.

Physical and psychological withdrawal   Scheduling of activities has another advantage. The worker is able to keep some time away from the workplace to relax and be with oneself. This time may be spent in relaxation, with family and friends, recreational activities, hobbies, travelling, or simply introspecting. Employees who keep some time aside to physically and psychologically withdraw from work-related responsibilities are able to tackle work with renewed vigour the next day. Annual vacations and weekly offs are ways in which organizations aid the worker in withdrawing from work. Apart from that, many companies organize vacations and picnics exclusively for their staff; not only to reward them for their year round hard work but also to entertain and rejuvenate them.

Accepting your mistakes   Mistakes are a part of human life and work. In fact, as noted earlier, an individual's mistakes are stepping stones to success. An individual can avoid considerable amount of stress by avoiding egoistic behaviour and owning up to errors in actions and decisions, as and when applicable. The world need not be always as the individual expects it to be. In an organization, employees may clash over technology, skills, methods, and knowledge. Excessive worry or adamant behaviour not only causes stress, but is also viewed by others as immature behaviour. An intelligent employee not only accepts mistakes but is also open and receptive to change. This attitude is relevant to the top-level management as it is their openness to change that directs the organization towards new avenues. Hopeless cases are rare. One should never lose faith in the possibility of change.

Developing a positive attitude towards life   Adopting a positive attitude towards life goes a long way in dealing with stress. It helps the individual to deal better

Stress management

Stress management has been recognized as an important part of employee wellness by organizations. Work-related stress is being considered as a lifestyle risk factor and is considered as alarming as physical inactivity and obesity.

One of the most common solutions adopted by organizations to manage employees' stress is by offering flexible working hours and work-from-home options. Other solutions adopted by employers include organizing stress management options such as workshops, yoga, and education and awareness campaigns to help their employees manage stress. The current trend has also seen an increased presence of stress management institutes and corporate yoga centres offering training across the country. Fitness centres are also trying to tap this segment and have started fitness workshops and meditation sessions for corporates who are investing in healthy stress busters.

Many organizations which send their employees for skill sharpening and management training insist on including stress management sessions in the training programme. Government

employees also have an opportunity where alongside all other training, they are also taught to manage and handle stress. Many of the corporate programs are three-month engagements, so members get to take a break or reach a certain goal or level of expertise during that period.

The security forces too realize that stress is a major contributor to demotivation and ill health. The Border Security Force has launched a string of yoga classes and stress management sessions for its people in combat.

However, there is still a long way to go. According to an Asia Pacific edition of the Staying@Work survey (2014), while issues such as stress, lack of exercise, and poor nutrition are driving employee health and productivity issues to the fore, employers still have to work out a successful action plan in order to accomplish this goal. Many organizations still do not have a framework, and as a result may be seeing mixed results in the programs that have been introduced. Many are still facing issues of high cost and misallocation of resources due to lack of monitoring systems.

Source: Staying@Work™ Survey Report 2013/2014, Asia Pacific (2014); PTI (2014); PTI (2015); Roy (2015).

with the problems of daily life. Positive orientation and attitude towards life bring optimism in responding to the situations and help in overcoming worry and anxiety. Having a positive attitude helps us in seeing the bright side of life and expecting the best to happen. It is basically a state of mind worth developing as it prepares and enables us to handle, cope with, and manage stress. An individual should learn to enjoy life and recollect happy memories. One should understand that obsession with difficulties or indulging in self pity does not help.

SUMMARY

Stress is defined as 'the non-specific response of the body to any demand put upon it'. It is, in fact, 'the body's automatic response to challenge'. The human body responds completely to stress, this includes our thoughts, the body's biochemical and physiological processes, and our behaviour. There are two kinds of stress—eustress and distress. Eustress or healthy stress is a condition wherein an individual has the drive and energy to achieve his/her goals. He/she is positive about the outcome. The other state of mind is distress, wherein an individual feels a sense of helplessness and frustration about achieving targets. Stress is not caused by any external factor. It is an individual's reaction to the events of the external world. It is our perception of possible failure at work, non-recognition and consequent loss of self-esteem.

Psychologists have divided people into two broad categories—type A and type B, depending upon their behaviour patterns as reflected through particular characteristics. There are two aspects to stress management. First is that one should not develop stress to the point that one becomes non-functional and the second is to try to get back to normal as quickly as possible and not remain in a state of stress for too long. At the individual level, stress can be managed by maintaining a good physical health, practicing relaxation, developing a psychological support system, time management, physical and psychological withdrawal, and developing a positive orientation towards life.

KEYWORDS

Distress   It is the condition when there is a sense of helplessness in fulfilling the need.

Eustress   It is the condition in which there is drive and effort to fulfil needs.

Human stress response   Under stress, a small pocket of chemicals in a part of the brain called the hypothalamus instantly triggers off a complex chain of chemicals, nerve reactions, and transformations.

Levels of stress   Stress symptoms affect our body at four different levels starting from increased heart beat rate and blood pressure to ulcers, stroke, alcoholism, drug addiction, psychosis, etc. at the fourth level.

Positive orientation   It brings optimism in responding to the situations and helps in overcoming worry and anxiety.

Stress   The non-specific response of the body to any demand put upon it.

Stress management   The way one tackles stress. It has to do with the way we view and handle events in our life.

Time management   It includes techniques, tools, and strategies to make effective and efficient use of time.

Type A individuals   They struggle with the environment and are always in a hurry to act.

Type B individuals   They have a balanced attitude to life and work and are poised and calm.

EXERCISES

Concept Review Questions

1. Define stress.
2. Why is it said that stress should not necessarily be avoided?
3. What are the two kinds of stress and what is their relevance to success?
4. How does human stress response get activated? What are the main changes it produces?
5. What are stressors? What are some of the important stressors in a workplace?
6. Differentiate between type A and type B personalities. How can type A behaviour be checked?
7. What are the vital steps that can be taken to manage stress at the individual level?

Critical Thinking Questions

1. Stress takes its toil in different ways. Therefore, it should be avoided. Comment critically.

2. Without stress in life, human body would become a junk. Do you agree or disagree with this statement? Justify your answer.

Project Assignments

1. Identify major stressors that cause stress to class 12 students.
2. You are always late for class and you feel guilty about it. You have been scolded by your teachers a number of times. Once you could not board a train, as you could not reach the station on time. Even your friends have expressed displeasure about your late arrivals. What specific steps, in the light of the concepts learnt in this chapter, would you like to take to overcome this habit of reaching late?

REFERENCES

Cavanaugh, M.A., W.R. Boswell, M.V. Roehling, and J.W. Boudreau (2000), 'An Empirical Examination of Self-Reported Work—Stress Among U.S. Managers', *Journal of Applied Psychology*, February, pp. 65–74.

Chand, Sharmila, 'The Magic of Dreams' and Chopra, Praveen, 'Bettering the Best', http://www.lifepositive.com/mind/work/corporatemanagement.html, accessed on 15 November 2007.

Forbes, E.J. and R.J. Pekala (1993), 'Psychological Effects of Several Stress Management Techniques', *Psychological Reports*, February, pp. 19–27.

Frew, D.R. and N.S. Bruning (1987), 'Perceived Organizational Characteristics and Personality Measures as Predictors of Stress/Strain in the Work Place', *Journal of Management*, pp. 633–646.

Friedman, M. and R. Rosenman (1974), *Type A Behavior and Your Heart*, Knopf, New York.

https://www.towerswatson.com/en-IN/Insights/IC-Types/Survey-Research-Results/2014/01/Staying-Work-Survey-Report-2013-2014-Asia-Pacific, accessed on 8 March 2016.

'Indian Employers Rank Stress Number One Lifestyle Risk Factor: Survey', http://articles.economictimes.indiatimes.com/2014-04-20/news/49266199_1_stress-management-indian-employers-tai-chi, accessed on 8 March 2016.

Jackson, S.E. (1983), 'Participation in Decision Making as a Strategy for Reducing Job Related strain', *Journal of Applied Psychology*, February, pp. 3–19.

Kiely, J. and G. Hodgson (1990), 'Stress in the Prison Service: The Benefits of Exercise Programs', *Human Relations*, June, pp. 551–572.

Leonard, B. (2001), 'Health Care Costs Increase Interest in Wellness Programs', *HR Magazine*, September, pp. 35–36.

Nelson, D.L. and C. Sutton (1990), 'Chronic Work Stress and Coping: A Longitudinal Study and Suggested New Directions', *Academy of Management Journal*, vol. 33, no. 4, December, pp. 859–869.

Robbins, Stephen P. and Seema Sanghi (2005), *Organizational Behavior*, Pearson Education, Singapore, pp. 544–546, 549–550.

Schuler, R.S. (1980), 'Definition and Conceptualiza-tion of Stress in Organizations', *Organizational Behavior and Human Performance*, April, p. 189.

28
Creativity and Entrepreneurship

INTRODUCTION

Joseph A. Schumpeter (1961) in his much-celebrated work *The Theory of Economic Development* credits an entrepreneur for initiating and carrying out economic activity by combining new means of production. He places entrepreneurs at the centre of economic development and solely identifies them with creation of an enterprise and, hence, totally negating the traditional theory of circular flow of economic life. According to Schumpeter, some basic motivations of an entrepreneur are—the joy of creating, of getting things done, or simply exercising one's energy and ingenuity. The entrepreneur seeks difficulty, changes in order to change, and takes delight in new ventures. The second motive that Schumpeter attributes to them is their will to conquer, the impulse to fight, and prove themselves superior to others. They want to succeed for success' sake, something akin to indulging in a sport. Although pecuniary gain is indeed a very accurate indicator of success, especially relative success and from the perspective of a man who strives for it—it has an additional advantage of being an objective indicator that is largely independent from the opinion of others.

NEED FOR CREATIVITY

An entrepreneur can take an idea and produce an entirely new set of possibilities. Even organizations, who by their very nature are more structured and given to produce an order out of constantly shifting dynamic imperatives, are to survive and grow, they have to earmark certain domains

Learning Objectives

After studying this chapter, you will be able to:
- Learn about entrepreneurship
- Examine the need for creativity and the relationship between creativity and innovation
- Learn about creativity in a knowledge economy
- Examine entrepreneurship and creativity
- Understand the attitudes of a successful entrepreneur

where they have to give a free run to their in-house entrepreneurs (known as intra-preneurs). For example, engineers at Google are encouraged to utilize some of their time to work on company-related issues that interest them. Creativity needs a particular environment to blossom and grow. In today's competitive environment, only companies that know how to manage creativity, how to organize for creative results, and who willingly implement new ideas, can triumph.

Creativity and Innovation

According to John Kao (1996) who taught at Harvard Business School, Stanford University, and MIT Media lab and is the author of *Managing Creativity* and *The Entrepreneur*, business creativity, is the entire process by which ideas are generated, developed, and transformed into value. It encompasses what people commonly understand as innovation and entrepreneurship. It includes both the art of innovating new ideas and the discipline of shaping and developing those ideas to the stage of realized value. It is worthwhile to remember that though the entrepreneurs are innovators as much as they are capitalists, they are innovators not by nature of their function but by coincidence. Innovations need not be inventions at all. As long as they are not practised or used, inventions are economically irrelevant. According to Schumpeter (1961), economic leadership must be distinguished from invention. Kao (1996) thinks that the business world is already launched on a new quest, that of seeking a new advantage—delicate and dangerous, and absolutely vital—the creativity advantage.

IBM—Innovation is the key to success

IBM's key strategy for growth is to lead in the invention, development, and manufacture of the industry's most advanced information technologies, including computer systems, software, storage systems, and microelec-tronics. The company translates technolo-gies into value for its customers through its unique and professional solutions, services, and consulting businesses worldwide. The IBM turnaround is one of the business world's most prominent success stories to have revi-talized the company to achieve still greater heights. It was all an outcome of meticulous and detailed strategic planning and execu-tion as displayed by former IBM CEO Louis Gerstner.

IBM's present CEO, Sam Palmisano, says, 'Either you innovate or you're in commodity hell,' referring to IBM's current organizational strat-egy to become more of a business consultancy. Big Blue cannot sustain itself as a technology supermarket—not on those slender margins and with 3,16,000 employees worldwide. IBM's strategic focus on innovation to respond to fast-changing customer needs is evident from its having received 2,974 US patents from the USPTO in 2005. It continues to be on the top of the list for the thirteenth consecutive year for getting US patents. The company is actively involved in delivering these innovations through its products and services that has been the main reason for its success.

Creativity in a Knowledge Economy

The Nomura Institute, Tokyo, a think-tank in the areas of IT services and consultancy, has identified four economic eras—agricultural, industrial, informational, and creative. Throughout history, business practices have undergone huge changes from the time information has become widespread. When in 1450 Gutenberg published the first book, or when Luca di Pacioli devised the first double-entry bookkeeping system in 1494, or when British Parliament passed the Public Libraries Act in 1850, suddenly everyone had an unprecedented access to information and ideas, regardless of social rank or organizational position. This impacted everything from daily lives, to local businesses, to world affairs.

Today, it is information technology that has dramatically transformed the space for speculative thought as well as fundamentally altered the nature of collaboration. Information technology is evolving into the technology of relationships, facilitating the flow of creative interaction through computer-based communication networks, groupware, knowledge representation, management systems, videoconferencing systems, and convergence of different forms of traditional media. With Moor's Law (that deals with the exponential decrement in cost of computing power) and Metcalfe's Law (that deals with the exponential increase in value of network as number of users on a network increase) in place, it is almost definite that the power of creativity will rise exponentially with diversity and divergence of those users.

In an age that values knowledge; business creativity adds value to knowledge and making it more useful. Kao (1996) writes in his book on business creativity titled *Jamming* that when we add information technology to the mix of creativity and knowledge, we get a particularly potent combination—capabilities to represent, deploy, and track knowledge coupled with technologies to promote collaboration across divergent disciplines and perspectives. In these times of shifting competitive dynamics, technological change, demographic shifts, and capricious consumer tastes, no business is safe unless it reinvents itself continuously.

CREATIVITY AND ENTREPRENEURSHIP

Peter Drucker (1974), the well-known management guru, thinks that an entrepreneur always seeks change, responds to it, and exploits it as an opportunity. The entrepreneur has a mindset that sees the possibilities than the problems created by change. A leading theorist of entrepreneurship at Harvard Business School, Howard H. Stevenson (1991), defines the heart of entrepreneurial management as 'the pursuit of opportunity without regard to resources currently controlled.' Both of these definitions emphasize essentially that creativity is all about imagination, inspiration, ingenuity, and initiative—a mindset of unrestrained pursuit of potentialities.

Professor J. Gregory Dees (2001) in his paper *The Meaning of Social Entrepreneurship* expands the domain of entrepreneurship and calls for a need to engender social entrepreneurship to help us find new avenues towards social improvement

Business—A passion

For IIM graduate Satya Narayanan R., an interest in teaching led him to quit a lucrative and high profile job with Ranbaxy and become an entrepreneur. He initiated Career Launcher in 1995. Today, after 12 years, Career Launcher has turned out to be a well-established business in education and training industry. It has grown on the strength of the franchisee marketing model. The governing principle behind extending franchisee status is the interest in teaching. The company has grown and diversified into various areas both by way of acquisitions and also by expanding on its own. The acquisition mode for the growth has been a strategic move for the firm. Till date, the firm has acquired four firms. It has acquired www.compassboss.com, an online tutoring firm based in Middle East; www.lawentrance.com, a firm that specializes in the preparation for law exams; www.powermath.org, a firm in Texas; and Arun

Roy classes, a firm in IIT entrance preparation space. However, 70 per cent of Career Launcher's revenue continues to come from the coaching for MBA entrance exam. The company has also entered into mainstream education through its subsidiary—Career Launcher Education Infrastructure & Services (CLEIS). Its three Indus World Schools, that have adopted radically different educational methods as compared to the regular Indian schools, are already operational at Noida, Indore, and Hyderabad. It is expected to increase to eight by 2008. Thus, business is becoming more capital intensive with investments in real estate and buildings.

Five years down the line, Career Launcher's revenue mix will be totally different from what it is today. The company is likely to undergo a change in ownership by way of strategic investor and/or public equity. However, it will continue to focus on its passion for teaching.

Source: Based on article from *The Economic Times*, 18 May 2007.

in this century. How do individuals know that they have the potential to be entrepreneurs? To succeed individuals must feel passionate about the work they have chosen. Launching your own business entails long hours of toil. You must be sure that you want to give up a secure social life in order to focus all your energies on the venture. You must have the mental stamina and concentration to meet the demands of your project. Besides, you need to be flexible and open minded, because no matter how carefully you plan, you are bound to run into unforeseen problems that will demand a change of course. Learning from one's mistakes without getting derailed is a quality that will serve potential entrepreneurs good. They should be good at concentrating on the details. In terms of backup resources, as banks and financial institutions seldom lend money to start-up businesses, an entrepreneur might also depend on family members or friends to invest in the company.

Attitudes of a Successful Entrepreneur

A successful entrepreneur needs to take fear out of failure, have a worthy goal, never give up, be ready for work–life imbalance, believe in his/her vision, and be ready to change course, if the need arises. See Fig. 28. 1.

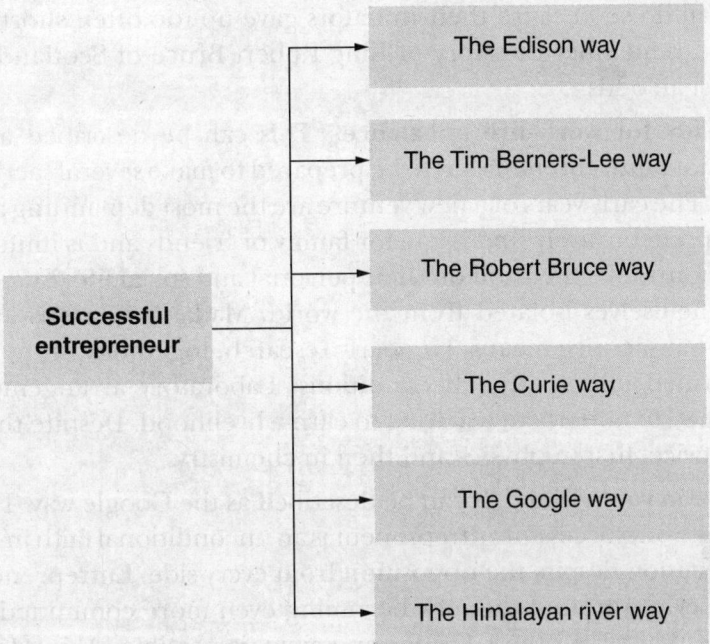

FIGURE 28.1 Attitudes of a successful entrepreneur

Take fear out of failure   It can also be described as the Edison way. An entrepreneur has to take calculated risks shaking off the fear of failure. When starting out, most of the successful entrepreneurs put their entire savings at stake and burned all bridges so that there is no looking back. It is but natural for people to feel fear at the prospect of losing all and entrepreneurs try to take fear out by reducing the risks out of their ventures, by learning from their failures, and by persisting through their failures.

Have a worthy goal   It can also be described as the Tim Berners-Lee way. Entrepreneurship is not just money, power, or influence. If you are afraid of losing money, you may not take the prudent risks that all entrepreneurs must take to succeed. 'If you think money is a real big deal you will be too scared of losing it to get it' as one founder-entrepreneur of a major international broadcasting company put it. The inventor of the Internet and the Director of the world wide web consortium, Tim Berners-Lee has not patented his invention as he believes that the goal of helping the people to connect is a worthy goal and, hence, beyond money consideration. Berners-Lee along with Robert Cailliau invented the world wide web (www) in 1989 while he was working at CERN, the European Particle Physics Laboratory.

Never give up   It can be described as the Robert Bruce way. It is characterized by a dogged determination along with resilience to succeed in the face of what seems like impossible odds is the defining characteristic of entrepreneurs. Most projects that fail do so because their initiators gave up too often short of it. Entrepreneurs should remember the story of King Robert Bruce of Scotland, who won his battle against all odds.

Be ready for work–life imbalance   This can be described as the Curie way. An ambitious entrepreneur has to be prepared to make several sacrifices on the personal front. The early years of a new venture are the most demanding and challenging. The entrepreneur rarely finds time for family or friends and is immersed in work. These long hours take their toll on their personal and social life. Entrepreneurs ultimately find themselves isolated from the world. Madame Curie is a shining example of what that sacrifice means. Her early research, together with her husband, was often performed under difficult conditions. Laboratory arrangements were poor and both had to undertake teaching to earn a livelihood. Despite this she won the noble prize twice, first in physics and then in chemistry.

Believe in your vision   It can be described as the Google way. The ultimate defining attribute of a successful entrepreneur is an unconditional faith in the business idea and its execution despite the opposition from every side. Entrepreneurs tend to respond to the cynics around them by becoming even more committed to their ideas. They believe that what others think impossible, is possible. Akio Morita, the co-founder of Sony Corporation, shares an anecdote, 'Two shoe salesmen find themselves in a rustic part of a country. The first salesman wires back to his head office, "there is no prospect of selling shoes to the natives, as they don't wear shoes." The other salesman wires, "no one wears shoes here. We can dominate the market. Send all possible stock."' True entrepreneurs are eternal optimists and passionate about their vision, just like Larry Page and Sergey Brin, the founders of Google. The Google philosophy can be expressed in five general principles—work on things that matter, affect everyone in the world, solve problems with algorithms if possible, hire bright people and give them lots of freedom, and do not be afraid to try new things. As a general practice, Google also requires that its engineers spend 20 per cent of their time working on personal technology projects unrelated to their primary projects.

Be ready to change your course   The entrepreneurs need to be flexible enough to change their course like a mighty Himalayan river if the situation so demands. Every couple of years or so the gushing mountain rivers change their course on account of flash floods and cover the surrounding land with alluvial soil. The result is a constant replenishment of the fertility of the soil in the sprit of creative destruction. Steadfastness and flexibility at the right time is a defining characteristic of successful entrepreneurs. It can be described as the Himalayan river way.

Entrepreneurs need to be creative in their attempts. Creativity begins with the generation of ideas. It is also very much at work in the selection, development, and implementation of ideas. The highest form of art is perhaps business. It is an extremely creative form and can be more creative than all the things we classically think of as creative. In business, the tools with which an entrepreneur works are dynamic—capital, people, markets, and ideas. Taking these tools and reorganizing

Hiranandani brothers

The Hiranandani brothers started their construction business around 1981 with a meagre capital of ₹5,00,000 and big dreams. The group has slowly and steadily grown by developing competence and has taken up a project in Chennai requiring estimated investment of ₹2,000 crore. This clearly shows that if you dream big and passionately work towards the realization of your dream, you are bound to succeed. They started from scratch. 'We did not even have a family background in business and so we started by learning everything about the business we wanted to do,' says Surendra, the younger brother. Elder brother, Niranjan has been the visionary while the younger one has been the innovator.

On the issue of government regulation, Niranjan says, 'We have too many regulations in this industry. It is essential to deregulate this business. We need liberalization. We had liberalization in IT, in telecom, and in aviation. But there has been no liberalization in the housing sector so that affordable housing is accessible to all in the country.'

What is the secret of their success? 'You need to have a great risk-taking ability. You need to work very hard and apply your common sense. If you have these qualities then I think you can succeed in any business,' says Niranjan. One needs to be focused, inspired, and motivated. 'We started off at Versova (Mumbai) in 1981. In the first four years, we did about 12 buildings. However, we are not able to produce the desired level of quality.' So in 1985 they created their own R&D division and training programme. The initial efforts were put in on concrete (1985–90) and then on architecture, followed by plumbing, waterproofing, plasters, etc. 'We have always been motivated by the urge to constantly improve and innovate. Long before water conservation became mandatory, we introduced systems for 100 per cent sewage recycling and rainwater harvesting in all our projects as early as 1989. The Indian government amended IS Code 456 on 14 August 2000, but we had implemented these specifications well before 1989. We were pioneers in the usage of flyash and we were the first to introduce copper plumbing in the country,' informs Surendra. 'I think it is the attitude towards work, passion for your profession, and the desire to provide value to the customer that really matters.'

Source: Based on articles from *The Economic Times*, 1 May 2007.

them in new and different ways, turns out to be a very creative process. This is actually what an entrepreneur attempts to do.

New Generation Entrepreneur

The new generation of entrepreneurs want to pursue their own dreams rather than be just a cog in the wheel of big traditional businesses. For a growing number of young people, creating a business has become a calling, a vocation, and a mission. Stuart Crainer and Des Dearlove (2000) in their book *Generation Entrepreneur* write about this new breed of young men and women who are not only driven by business ideas but also by technology. This new breed of wealth creators and shapers of businesses are the new generation of e-literate knowledge workers who think differently about life in general. These new entrepreneurs are better educated than their predecessors, dislike hierarchy, and are shamelessly entrepreneurial. Michael Dell of Dell Corporation, Jeff Bezos of Amazon.com, and Marc Andreessen of Netscape are some iconic generation entrepreneurs who have been hugely successful. About half the businesses in America are now started by people who are 35 or under. Many of them are serial entrepreneurs with a string of start-ups already under their belts by their early twenties. In India, a growing proportion of B-school graduates are shunning secure jobs with blue chip companies in favour of becoming entrepreneurs in their own right.

SUMMARY

An entrepreneur can take an idea and produce an entirely new set of possibilities. Creativity needs a particular environment to blossom and grow. Business creativity, writes John Kao, is the entire process by which ideas are generated, developed, and transformed into value. In an age that prizes knowledge, business creativity adds value to knowledge and makes it progressively more useful. It is worthwhile to remember that though the entrepreneurs are inventors as much as they are capitalists, they are inventors not by nature of their function but by coincidence. Innovations need not be inventions at all. As long as they are not practised or used, inventions are economically irrelevant. Today, information technology has dramatically transformed the space for speculative thought as well as fundamentally altered the nature of collaboration, influencing entrepreneurship.

Information technology is evolving into the technology of relationships, facilitating the flow of creative interaction through computer-based communication networks, groupware, knowledge representation, management systems, videoconferencing systems, and convergence of different forms of traditional media. A successful entrepreneur has to take fear out of failure, have worthy goals, never give up, be ready for work–life imbalance, and believe in their vision. Entrepreneurs need to be creative in whatever they attempt. The new generation of entrepreneurs wants to pursue their own dreams rather than be just a cog in the wheel of big traditional businesses.

KEYWORDS

Business creativity It is the entire process by which ideas are generated, developed, and transformed into value.

Entrepreneurship The pursuit of opportunity without regard to resources currently controlled.

Generation entrepreneur The new breed of entrepreneurs who are technology savvy, dislike organizational hierarchy, and want to establish themselves in their own right.

Innovation Products and service, emerging from the combination of new ideas and concepts.

Invention An innovation that has a value and is widely used.

Knowledge economy The new economy in which the knowledge worker has a central role characterized by conversion of information into value-creating products and services.

Social entrepreneurship Entrepreneurial undertaking that is committed to both good business as well as social improvement.

EXERCISES

Concept Review Questions

1. What is the relationship between creativity and entrepreneurship?

2. Why should an entrepreneur be creative?

3. Define innovation and its relevance to the development of an enterprise.

4. What are the salient features of a 'knowledge economy'? What is the relevance of creativity in the knowledge economy?
5. What are the basic prerequisites of a successful entrepreneur?

Critical Thinking Question

A leading theorist of entrepreneurship at Harvard Business School, Howard H. Stevenson, defines the heart of entrepreneurial management as 'the pursuit of opportunity without regard to resources currently controlled'. What is the significance and implication of this to the development of entrepreneurship?

Project Assignments

1. For the long-term sustainable growth of the organization, entrepreneurship is a basic prerequisite. Identify two companies from any industry and analyse their performance in the light of successful innovations introduced by them.
2. Take three leading entrepreneurs and diagnose their personality traits as also success factors that have contributed the most in their growth.

REFERENCES

Bibb, Porter (1997), *Ted Turner: It Ain't as Easy as It Looks: A Biography,* Johnson Books Boulder, Colorado.

Crainer, Stuart and Des Dearlove (2000), *Generation Entrepreneur*, Pearson Education Ltd, Great Britain.

Dees, J. Gregory. (2001), 'The Meaning of 'Social Entrepreneurship', Draft paper, http://www.fuqua.duke.edu/centers/case/documents/dees_SE.pdf, accessed on 30 August 2005.

Drucker, Peter F. (1974), *Management: Tasks, Responsibilities, Practices*, William Heinemann Ltd, London.

Kao, John Jamming (1996), *The Art and Discipline of Business Creativity*, HarperCollins Business, London.

Morita, Akio (1988), *Made in Japan*, Signet.

Schumpeter, Joseph A. (1961), *The Theory of Economic Development*, translated by Opie Redvers, Galaxy Books, USA.

Stevenson, Howard H. and W.A. Sahlman (eds) (1991), *Introduction to the Entrepreneurial Venture,* Harvard Business School Press, Boston, Massachusetts.

29

Organizational Change and Development

Learning Objectives

After studying this chapter, you will be able to:

- Understand the importance and implications of change in the organization
- Know the meaning, key activities, and assumptions of organizational development (OD)
- Understand key characteristics of OD
- Understand the reasons and implications of resistance to change and learn about various ways to manage it
- Understand the relationship between innovation and change management
- Learn about the models for introducing change management in organizations

INTRODUCTION

The fast-changing environment in an organization, whether it is economic, social, technological, political, or cultural, poses a great challenge to the organization to survive and grow. Organizations that can foresee emerging trends and developments can cope better and are able to manage change by opting for appropriate strategies to respond with, whereas organizations that are not prepared in advance lose their competitive edge in the market and face downturn in their performance.

Concerns related to performance arising because of change are common for all organizations irrespective of the industry. Organizational development through change management mainly requires people management strategies to be aligned to business development strategies.

Organizational change takes place as an outcome of strategies created to respond to the ever-changing environment, be it a crisis-ridden situation or otherwise. Effective organizations manage change successfully by developing appropriate strategies and capabilities, and systems and processes to effectively implement those strategies.

As per as study undertaken by McKinsey for 1,536 companies that had over five years undergone organizational change (Isern and Pung 2007), 38 per cent of the company managers claimed that the process helped in improving the work performance, implying the challenges involved in organizational development

(OD). Organizational change is usually induced because of changes in external environment such as cuts in budgets; introduction of new product by competitor; dramatic increase in raw material costs; and changes in government policies such as taxation, incentives, and subsidies. Usually, as a result of change, organizations initiate steps involving technical, organizational, or other strategic steps to move to the next growth level in their life cycle.

Change is inevitable and has to be managed in a well-planned manner. Change management is the responsibility of the corporate leaders and is done by developing appropriate skills and changes in the employees' mindset. Each employee is gifted with certain skills and talents, which the corporate leaders should tap by providing appropriate opportunities to each employee.

If employees lack certain knowledge, skills, or attitude to perform their jobs effectively, it is the responsibility of the management to ensure that such employees get the required training. Therefore, primary responsibility for managing change is of the management of an organization. The management has to create conditions conducive to change by understanding the situation from an objective viewpoint.

ORGANIZATIONAL DEVELOPMENT

Organizational development (OD) is an activity that focuses on behavioural dimensions to develop and enhance an individual's capabilities by organizational interventions to enhance knowledge, expertise, productivity, satisfaction level, improved interpersonal relationships, and other preferred outcomes for personal or team initiatives that benefits the organization, community, nation, and the whole of humanity(see Fig. 29.1). OD looks at 'the total system and the linkage between all

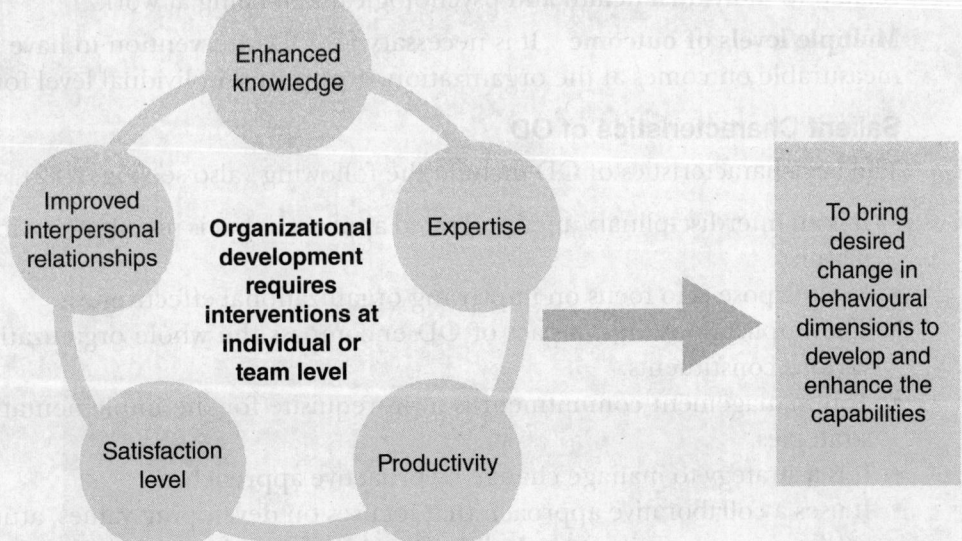

FIGURE 29.1   OD interventions and outcomes

parts of the organization, and at how change in one part will affect the other parts' (Holbeche 2009).

The American Society for Training and Development has defined OD as 'an effort planned, organization-wide, managed from top, to increase organization effectiveness and health through planned intervention using behavioural science knowledge'. Therefore, OD requires an integrated and holistic approach encompassing synchronization with organizational objectives that needs to be an ongoing process with long-term perspectives. It needs to be process and system driven, requiring collaboration among individuals in different parts of the organization.

OD incorporates the following key activities and assumptions.

Planned intervention   This basically attempts to diagnose the need for change, the prospects of a specified plan of action, confirmation, and validation of outcomes after intervention.

Organization-wide programmes   This process involves analysis of various aspects of the organization as a whole, although strategies of an OD intervention will focus upon specific departments, sub-units, or work groups that would matter the most in improving organizational effectiveness.

Knowledge-based action   OD mainly deals with the application of behavioural science knowledge, principles, and research, so as to achieve desired outcomes. This knowledge base spreads over organizational psychology, human resource management, organization sociology, and other relevant topics in organization behaviour.

Pragmatic improvement of organization capabilities   This aspect attempts to enhance intra organizational efficiency and performance, including capabilities related to individual health and psychological well-being at work.

Multiple levels of outcome   It is necessary for OD intervention to have potentially measurable outcomes at the organization, group, and individual level for analysis.

Salient Characteristics of OD

The key characteristics of OD include the following (also see Fig. 29.2).

- It is an interdisciplinary and integrated approach that is mainly behaviour science driven.
- Key purpose is to focus on improving organizational effectiveness.
- The implications and impact of OD encompass the whole organization and its various constituents.
- Top management commitment is a prerequisite for the implementation of OD strategies.
- It is a strategy to manage change by proactive approach.
- It uses a collaborative approach that focuses on developing values, attitudes, and management practices that build a conducive and harmonious environment in the organization.

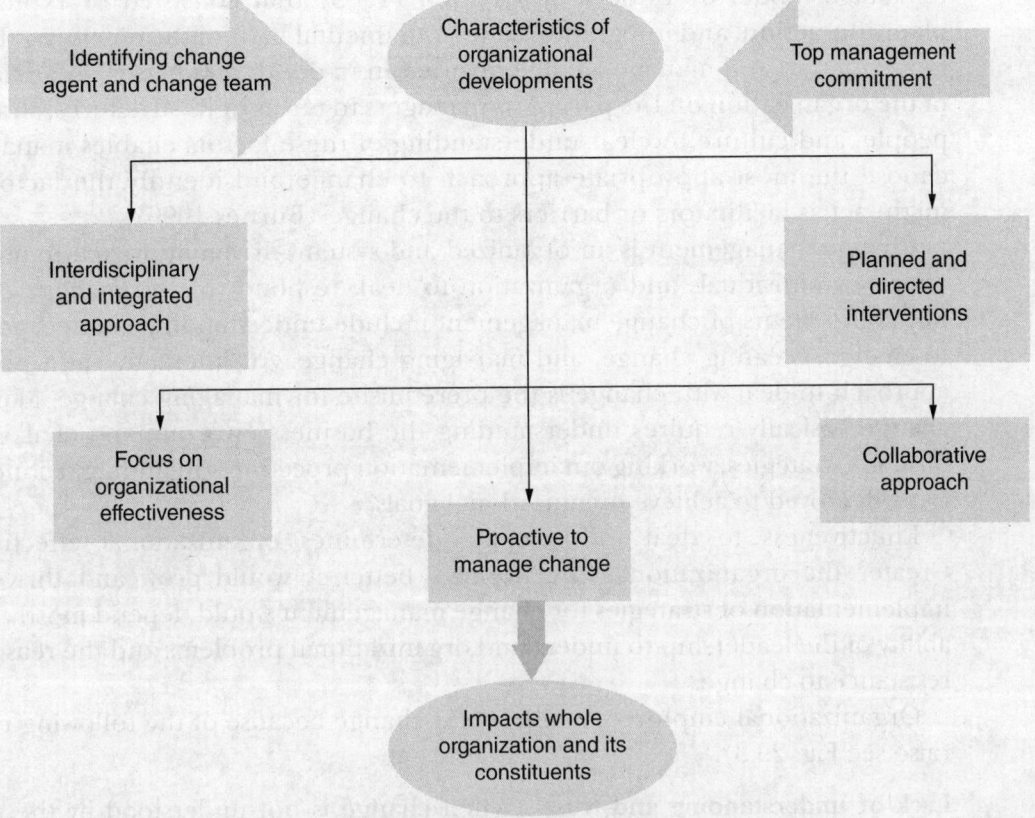

FIGURE 29.2 Characteristics of OD

- The success lies on identifying a change agent and a change team that acts as facilitator and coach.
- It requires planned and directed interventions and improvements in an organization's systems, structures, and strategy.

ORGANIZATIONAL CHANGE

Change is said to be the only constant and is becoming an ever-present characteristic of organizational life (Burnes 2004). Different studies reveal that although majority of the organizations understand and appreciate the need for change but somehow as many as 70 per cent of the change programmes do not achieve their anticipated and desired outcomes (Balogun and Hailey 2004). 'Planned approach' to change management involves a three stage process, namely unfreezing current behaviour, moving on to the new behaviour, and, finally, refreezing the new behaviour. This three-stage model was used for many years as the main framework for understanding the process of organizational change (Todnem 2005). Subsequently, the three stages were developed into a four-stage model by Bullock and Batten (1985) that consisted of exploration, planning, action, and integration. The fundamental basis of the emerging theories to respond to and manage change involves an in-depth and better understanding of the organization on the part of its managers in terms of its structures, strategies, people, and culture. A clear understanding of these factors enables managers to choose the most appropriate approach to change and identify the factors that might act as facilitators or barriers to the change (Burnes 1996).

Change management is an organized and systems-driven approach to align the efforts of individuals and organization to deal, respond to, and manage change. Key components of change management include understanding change, adapting to change, creating change, and managing change. An interactive and proactive approach to deal with change is the prerequisite for managing change. Managing change basically requires understanding the business environment, chalking out business strategies, working out implementation procedures including technologies to be deployed to achieve organizational goals.

Effectiveness to deal with change determines organizational effectiveness. Greater the organizational effectiveness, better it would grow and thrive. The implementation of strategies for change management would depend mostly on the ability of the leadership to understand organizational problems and the reasons for resistance to change.

Organizational employees mainly resist change because of the following reasons (also see Fig. 29.3).

Lack of understanding and trust   When change is not understood by the people who would get affected by it and they also have a reason to believe in vested interests on the part of the group that would like to introduce it, they resist change. Even ambiguity about certain key aspects such as cost implications, technology required, the related skills requirement, and lack of clarity as to the rationale for change causes resistance. This normally happens when the need for change and change per se is not communicated well to the employees. Therefore, building mutual trust even at the cost of delays is at times a worthwhile proposition on the part of the leadership team.

Economic factors   Even though there might be overall qualitative and quantitative benefits that arise as a result of change, there will be people who may get displaced, who may lose income and growth prospects, or fear job insecurity. It is essential to see how such inhibitions and problems felt by the existing employees are dealt with. Any proposal involving lay-offs, voluntary retirement, etc., needs to be handled in a sensitive manner. It is always essential to consult existing people who would get affected and bring them into confidence before initiating steps for introducing changes. It is natural for the people irrespective of their level in the organization to know about what is going on and is likely to happen in advance as they will be getting affected in whatsoever manner. The organizations that keeps their workers informed about things that are happening in the organization, always find less resistance in introducing new practices, systems, or technologies.

Inconvenience and required change in behaviour Usually change requires modified patterns of working relationships between people and introduces new ways and means of control. This would always result in certain inconvenience to people who have over the years learnt only a specific way of doing things. To ensure that such resistance gets minimized, there is a need for training interventions, which could be on the job or a well-designed training system.

Employees' Inhibitions and Fear of New Technology

Normally change requires the need to handle introduction of new technology and deal with new situations posing organizational challenges. Employees including middle- and senior-level managers feel inadequate while using it or at times have fixed notions that it would not work in their set up to respond to the achievement of organizational goals. This would require employee training and clear communication highlighting the need for new technology and possible benefits that would accrue to the organization along with the employees and other stakeholders as a result of adoption of new technology. Before introducing any new technology in an organization, it is essential that a thorough assessment of users from the point

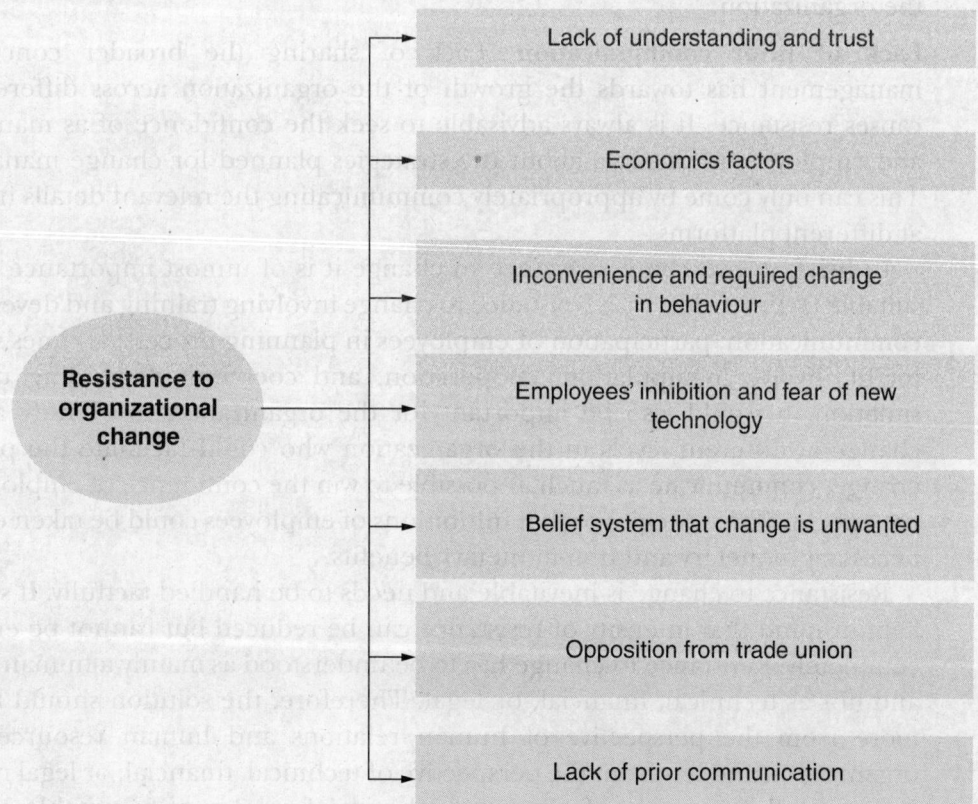

FIGURE 29.3 Resistance to organizational change

of view of their capabilities to identify gaps, if any, should be undertaken. A clear technology transfer strategy needs to be worked out for the organization, which should take care of the implementation mechanism by particularly focusing on effective use of user networks to transfer information.

Belief that change is unwanted People feel they are in a comfortable zone as long as they keep doing things the way they have been doing for years. A general tendency among leaders is to block change and this belief influences other employees in the organization. Normally, as long as the present system and structure is delivering results, employees would have greater tendency to continue with the belief that change is unwanted. Therefore, it becomes necessary to recognize the problem, seek its solution from the employees, have better solutions to deal with it, and handle it by involving employees in the process right from the beginning.

Opposition from trade union Management should necessarily recognize that a trade union's main motive is to protect the interests of workers and in the process, at times, even to bargain better they would resist any change. It is natural for trade unions to show their power in this manner. Therefore, management should necessarily keep them in confidence while initiating any steps to bring a change in the organization.

Lack of prior communication Lack of sharing the broader concern that management has towards the growth of the organization across different levels causes resistance. It is always advisable to seek the confidence of as many groups and employees as possible about the strategies planned for change management. This can only come by appropriately communicating the relevant details frequently at different platforms.

In brief, to overcome resistance to change it is of utmost importance to devise suitable tactics to deal with resistance to change involving training and development, communication, participation of employees in planning process; at times strategies might involve manipulation, cooperation, and coercion, depending upon the situation. It would also be important for the organization to identify agents of change at different levels in the organization who could facilitate the process of change, communicate as much as possible to win the confidence of employees, and use appropriate strategies so that inhibitions of employees could be taken care of by necessary monetary and non-monetary benefits.

Resistance to change is inevitable and needs to be handled tactfully. It should be kept in mind that intensity of resistance can be reduced but cannot be eradicated completely. Resistance to change has to be understood as mainly a human problem and not as technical, financial, or legal. Therefore, the solution should be found more from the perspective of human relations and human resources in the organization and less from the perspective of technical, financial, or legal measures. It is normally a question of winning the hearts of employees by suitable, workable, and economically viable strategies.

Kotter and Schlesinger's Contingency Approach for Overcoming Resistance

The model by Kotter and Schlesinger's (1979) contingency approach for overcoming resistance to change focuses on some basic principles that can be effectively utilized (see Fig. 29.4).

Communication   When it is identified that there is inaccurate or lack of information about introduction of change management strategies, the best way is to communicate and educate employees by providing all relevant information that would be of concern to them. This helps in providing a rationale for change with logic and facts and also helps in overcoming unfounded rumours in the organization. While educating employees, the focus needs to be on the rationale behind the proposal, benefits that would accrue to employees and the organization, and refute and confront misrepresentations through facts and figures.

Participation   Participation and involvement of employee groups who are going to get affected the most helps in buying the idea well and minimizes any resistance to it. This allows people to own the change that would affect them. Participative approach to management wherein it is expected that there is a strong power and lobby to resist change helps in gaining wider commitment.

Facilitation and support   When resistance is more of an outcome of adjustment process on the part of employees, it would be desirable that the superiors extend complete support, as it helps the employees to overcome their anxiety and fear that they might have in their mind. After identifying and exploring areas of resistance, special, and directed training modules for specific groups of employees and individuals for counselling goes a long way in persuading employees and have their commitment to change. The main purpose of counselling is to facilitate attitude and behavioural change among employees.

Negotiation   When people who have the power to resist protest strongly because their interests would get adversely affected, it is desirable for the organization to negotiate with them and extend certain incentives to take care of their concerns. In the extreme situation, when introduction of change is inevitable and such lobbies or powerful groups would not allow it to happen even after offering certain incentives, the organization may think in terms of extending voluntary retirement options to employees, if at all feasible. Negotiation could be formal or informal, depending upon the situation and what would be workable. During negotiation, if the situation

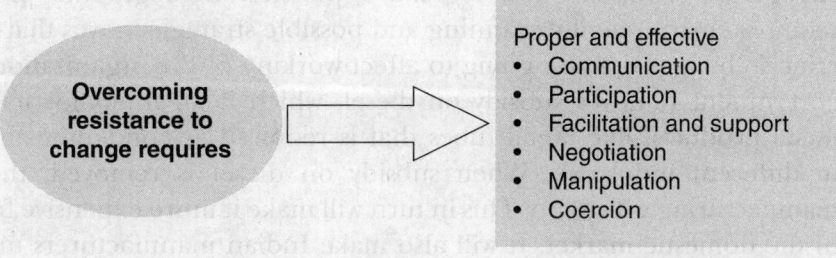

FIGURE 29.4   Contingency approach for overcoming resistance

so demands, one can involve a third-party arbitrator who is neutral, understands problems faced by both sides, and is trusted by both parties.

Manipulation In case other approaches do not work and the resisters have a strong power to resist, a manipulation strategy to co-opt persons, especially resistance leaders, in the change management process for the sake of appearance, rather than looking for a concrete contribution from them, works well. These leaders can be given a figurative role in decision-making without adversely affecting the change initiative and effort. Manipulation at times also can be exercised by offering actual or potential rewards to leaders who come in the way of change.

Coercion In extreme situations, explicit or implicit, coercion techniques can be used when management is convinced about introduction of change and there lies a strong resistance for the same by threatening with loss of jobs, transfers, and lay-offs. The purpose is to threaten existing unacceptable behaviour on the part of the select few who are adversely influencing others in the organization. This approach basically involves use of authority that lies with the management to enforce acceptance of the change by people working in the organization. This is mainly adopted when speed in introduction of change is essential for the survival of the organization. In crisis situations, change agents have considerable power. However, it is important to remember that there are ill effects of using coercion that get reflected through frustration and revenge, which in turn give rise to overall poor performance, dissatisfaction, and turnover (Woodman and Pasmore 1989).

Drivers of Change

As per Burke–Litwin (1992) environmental factors play the most crucial role and act as the most important drivers of change. It is important to recognize that a key aspect of growth of an organization depends more on and originates from environmental factors—be it social, cultural, technological, economic, or legal. Therefore, it becomes important to identify, analyse, and understand the implications of these external factors on the organization in a proactive manner (see Fig. 29.5).

External environment The changes in the external environment are inevitable and keep on occurring. One needs to assess them in advance and prepare the organization to respond to them. External factors that keep affecting organization(s) include competition, change in social milieu, cultural changes taking place, change in economic and legislative policies, demographic profile, etc. This requires environmental scanning and possible strategic moves that can respond to critical changes that are going to affect working of the organization. For example, government removes subsidy on diesel, which is an input for manufacturing of metal products, like metal tubes that is required as condenser and heat transfer in different industries. When subsidy on diesel is removed, the cost of tube manufacturing will go up. This in turn will make it more expensive for the customer in the domestic market. It will also make Indian manufacturers uncompetitive in the global markets for exports. It would require scientific analysis to understand the

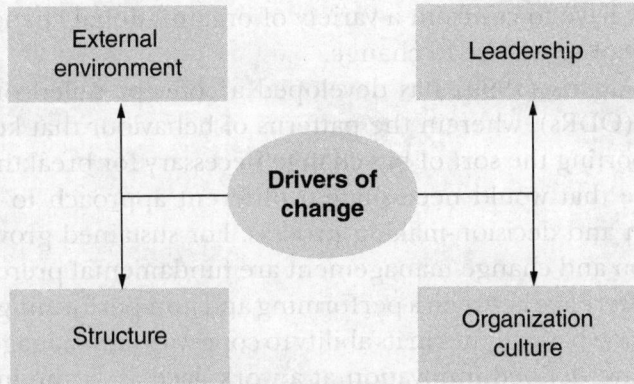

FIGURE 29.5 Drivers of change

impact and implications to decide about strategic actions that need to be taken, in case the price rise is not acceptable to customers.

Leadership Being a driver of change requires understanding the attitude and behaviour of the top management team of the organization. It is essential to understand whether the top management team of the organization is committed to change or is not responsive to change. In case it is not, it would be essential for the organization to first put in place a dynamic team at the top that is responsive to environmental changes.

Organization culture This plays an important role in organizational transformation and change management, and acts as a driver of change. Organization culture is defined as 'the way we do things'. It encompasses the beliefs, behaviours, values, and practices that become part and parcel of an organization. It cannot undergo change overnight, as it is something that evolves over time because of multiple factors. Therefore, it is necessary to work out a desired state from the cultural point of view to respond to the change and work towards creating it in the organization.

Structure Changes in strategy often requires a change in the structure of the organization to ensure effective implementation of strategy. Any change in structure results in change in the human dynamics as reflected in relationships, responsibilities, and ways of working. Whenever changes in structure are introduced, it becomes the responsibility of the management to ensure that employees understand the rationale and its implications to them and their working. Any structural change should not adversely affect the motivational level of employees, as that is the key to effective change.

INNOVATION AND CHANGE MANAGEMENT

It is usually said that innovation is nothing but change management. As innovation implies to offer something new and different in response to the problem that would necessarily require a degree of change in the organization, therefore innovators invariably have to confront a variety of organizational change issues arising mainly as a result of resistance to change.

Chris Argyris (1999) has developed a concept called organizational defensive routines (ODRs), wherein the patterns of behaviour that keep companies backing and supporting the sort of big change necessary for breakthrough innovation, that is, change that would necessitate a different approach to prioritize the resource allocation and decision-making process. For sustained growth of an organization, innovation and change management are fundamental prerequisites.

The difference between a performing and non-performing, growing, and stagnant organization basically lies in its ability to cope with and manage change. West and Farr (1990) have defined innovation at a workplace as '…the intentional introduction and application within a role, group or organization of ideas, processes, products or procedures, new to the relevant unit'. The process is designed and developed in such a manner that it should benefit the individual, group, organization, or wider society significantly. The innovation has been characterized by West and Farr (1990) and King and West (1987) as follows.

- An innovation is a tangible product, process, or procedure within an organization.
- An innovation must be intentional rather than accidental.
- An innovation must not be a routine change.
- An innovation must be aimed at benefitting the organization, some subsection of it, and/or the wider society.
- An innovation must be public in its effects.

There are various techniques that can be used to come out with innovative solutions to the problem at hand at different levels of an organization. One of the most commonly used techniques is brainstorming. This technique was first described by Alex Osborn (1953) and has since been used in many types of organizations around the world to tackle a variety of issues and challenges faced by an organization. It is based on the observation that one of the main hurdles in having creative ideas in an organization is 'evaluation apprehension'—the fear that a new idea will be met with ridicule or hostility by colleagues or superiors. As a result, new ideas may simply never be voiced. The essence of brainstorming mainly lies in making no judgments and encouraging number of ideas that would give rise to quality of solutions best suited to deal with and respond to problems. Four major rules and prerequisites are followed while undertaking brainstorming sessions, namely (i) no criticism of ideas, (ii) freewheeling is welcomed, (iii) number of ideas is encouraged, and (iv) combination and improvement are sought.

It is only after compiling all ideas irrespective of weighing them against any criteria that the next step of evaluating ideas is undertaken to come out with a viable, desirable, and preferred solution to the problem. Osborn recommends a five-person evaluation group, whose members have a direct responsibility to the problem at hand and therefore with an actual stake in the quality of the decision arrived at. A checklist of criteria is frequently used, against which each of the listed ideas can be assessed; for instance, the evaluators might consider the (i) cost, (ii) skills required for implementing, (iii) time taken to implement, and (iv) probable reactions of groups and individuals in the organization.

MODEL FOR ORGANIZATION DEVELOPMENT

Kurt Lewin had developed a model for change management involving three key stages namely—unfreezing, changing, and refreezing. The model embodies and signifies a simple and practical approach to diagnose, understand, and manage the change process. According to Lewin, the process of change management demands creating the situation and awareness in the organization about a change that is inevitable and required, which should lead an organization to move towards a well-defined desired level of behavioural state and which should ultimately help in embodying new behaviour as the norm. The model is widely accepted and used even today as the basis for newly developed models for change management.

A seven-stage model of OD was proposed by Edger Huse in 1980 based on Lewin's original model, which has the following key stages and associated processes to effectively ensure organization development.

Scouting   This is the process that involves unfreezing of the issue by consultation and sharing. Organizational people meet with OD experts to recognize and discuss the need for change in the organization. The change agent and organizational personnel involved in OD interventions together search and identify problems that need urgent consideration.

Entry   This stage helps in working out mutual understanding and accord for business and psychological contracts. Organization clearly highlights the expectations from the change while agreeing to OD interventions.

Diagnosis   In this stage, OD experts or the consultants diagnose and dissect the critical organizational problems based upon their previous experience, knowledge, and training interventions in the organization. This stage aspires to come out with specific improvement goals for the organization and a planned intervention strategy to achieve those goals.

Planning   This stage of change management through OD involves detailing a series of intervention techniques and actions, which can be taken at different points of time. One of the crucial steps taken during the planning phase is identifying and recognizing areas of resistance from employees that are likely to be confronted and the possible moves that can be taken to neutralize their effect.

Action   The change interventions as planned and agreed to are initiated at this stage. This stage also involves implementation of established action steps of the past.

Stabilization and evaluation   This is also called the stage of 'refreezing' the system in the organization. The task is to internalize among employees' codes of action, practices, and systems as an integral part of the organization. A mechanism is also developed to evaluate the impact of OD interventions on the evaluation vis-à-vis expected impact, so as to identify any need for further action to improvise. Main purpose becomes to make new system, processes, and behaviour an integral part of the system.

Termination   In the termination phase, having realized the advantages through OD and internalized the processes, OD consultant or change agent either quits the organization or takes up an entirely new project within the same organization.

Therefore, the seven-stage model propounded by Edger Huse is a useful tool to understand the complexity involved in organizational change. However, in reality, with the rapid pace of organizational change, the 'refreezing' stage may never be concluded. This would imply that organizational systems often go through a continuous process of change interventions and hardly ever regress to a stabilized state.

Normally, OD consultants or the people involved in organization development from within the organization attempt to establish the urgency for the same so that the top leadership gets convinced and extends all commitment to the change initiatives. They clearly define the vision for the organization and communicate it throughout the initiative. A due empowerment is inbuilt in favour of change agents as also for others who become part of the process of change. It normally attempts at short-term wins, so that people's confidence and trust gets reinforced in the whole chain of events. The whole purpose is to institutionalize new approaches, processes, and systems in the organization.

SUMMARY

Organizations that foresee emerging trends and developments are able to cope better and manage change by preparing themselves with appropriate strategies to respond. Organization development (OD) is an activity that focuses on behavioural dimensions to develop and enhance the capabilities in individuals by organizational interventions to enhance knowledge, expertise, productivity, satisfaction level, improved interpersonal relationships, and other preferred outcomes for personal or team initiatives that result in benefitting the organization, community, nation, and the whole of humanity. The OD incorporates a number of key activities and assumptions, including—planned intervention, organization-wide programmes, knowledge-based action, pragmatic improvement of organizational capabilities, and multiple levels of outcome. Suc-cess of OD efforts mainly depend on top management's commitment in identifying change agent and change team that acts as a facilitator and coach. Organizational employees mainly resist change because of lack of understanding and trust, economic factors, inconvenience, inhibitions, trade union, and above all lack of communication. Overcoming resistance to change requires proper and effective communication, participation, facilitation and support, negotiation, manipulation, and coercion. Innovative organizations have better defences as well as proactive measures to manage change. There are different OD models, one such model was proposed by Edger Huse, based on Lewin's original model, involving seven key stages and associated processes: scouting, entry, diagnosis, planning, action, stabilization and evaluation, and termination.

KEYWORDS

Evaluation apprehension   The fear that a new idea will be met with ridicule or hostility by colleagues or superiors.

Innovation   When you offer something new and different in response to the problem.

Knowledge-based action Spread over organizational psychology, human resource management, organization sociology, and other relevant topics in organization behaviour.

Multiple levels of outcome OD intervention must have potentially measurable outcomes at the organization, group, and individual level for analysis.

Organizational development An activity that focuses on behavioural dimensions to develop and enhance the capabilities in individuals by organizational interventions.

Organization-wide programmes Involves analysis of various aspects of the organization as a whole.

Planned approach to change management A three-stage process, namely unfreezing current behaviour, moving on to the new behaviour, and, finally, refreezing the new behaviour.

Planned intervention Attempts to diagnose the need for change, prospects of a specified plan of action, confirmation, and validation of outcomes after intervention.

Pragmatic improvement of organization capabilities It attempts to enhance intra-organizational efficiency and performance, including capabilities related to individual health and psychological well-being at work.

EXERCISES

Concept Review Questions

1. What leads to organizational change?
2. Why is it said that it is the primary responsibility of corporate leadership to manage change? Explain.
3. What is meant by organizational development? What is its relevance in the 21st century? Explain.
4. What are the key activities and assumptions incorporated in OD?
5. Differentiate between OD interventions from the point of view of knowledge-based action and pragmatic improvement of organization capabilities.
6. What are the key reasons that results in employees resisting change? Explain.
7. What are the principles that Kotter and Schlesinger's contingency approach in overcoming resistance to change focuses on? Explain.
8. As per Burke–Litwin, what are the key drivers of change and how an organization needs to take care of those drivers for effective implementation of change strategies? Explain.
9. In what way is innovation and change management related? Explain.
10. What are the key criteria that can be used to assess the innovative ideas that may emanate while solving a given problem through brainstorming technique? Explain.
11. Explain the seven-stage model propounded by Edger Huse for organizational development.

Critical Thinking Questions

1. What are the key characteristics of OD? Which characteristics are more crucial for success of the organization from the point of view of OD and Why? Analyse by giving concrete examples from the corporate world.
2. 'Lack of prior communication normally results in great resistance to change from employees.' Identify a situation of introduction of change which was not properly communicated to employees from the corporate world and the consequences that it had on the organization.
3. 'Belief that change is unwanted' in the organization normally comes in the way of introduction of change. How does such a belief system get formed in the organization? How should the organization attempt to handle such a belief system? Explain.
4. Although coercion approach to manage change is not desirable, however, under certain specific circumstances, it becomes inevitable for the organization to take recourse to it. Identify a situation from the corporate world wherein an organization adopted coercion approach and

explain the rationale for adopting it in the given identified circumstances.

5. Each step involved in a seven-stage model of OD as proposed by Edger Huse is critical. It may not be desirable to skip any step out of the chain of steps involved. Critically examine this statement with the help of examples.

REFERENCES

Argyris, Chris (1999), *On Organizational Learning*, 2nd edition, Malden, MA: Blackwell.

Balogun, J. and V. Hope Hailey (2004), *Exploring Strategic Change*, 2nd edition, London, Prentice Hall.

Bullock, R.J. and D. Batten (1985), 'It's Just a Phase We're Going Through: A Review and Synthesis of OD Phase Analysis', *Group and Organization Studies*, vol. 10, December, pp. 383–412.

Burke, W.W. and G. Litwin (1992), 'A Causal Model of Organisation Performance and Change', *Journal of Management*, vol. 18, no. 3, pp. 523–545.

Burnes, B. (1996), 'No such thing as ... A "One Best Way" to Manage Organizational Change', *Management Decision*, vol. 34, issue 10, pp.11–18.

Burnes, B. (2004), *Managing Change: A Strategic Approach to Organisational Dynamics*, 4th edition, Prentice Hall, Harlow.

Holbeche, L. (2009), 'Organisational Development — What's in a Name?', *Impact*, vol. 26, pp. 6–9.

Burnes, B. (2004), *Managing Change: A Strategic Approach to Organisational Dynamics*, 4th edition, Harlow, Prentice Hall.

Isern, J. and A. Pung (2007), 'Harnessing energy to Drive Organizational Change', *McKinsey Quarterly*, vol. 1, pp. 16–19.

King, N. and M.A. West (1987), 'Experiences of Innovation at Work', *Journal of Managerial Psychology*, vol. 2, no. 3, pp. 6–10.

Kotter, J. andL. Schlesinger (1979), 'Choosing Strategies for Change', *Harvard Business Review*, vol. 57, pp. 106–114.

Todnem, R. (2005), 'Organisational Change Management: A Critical Review', *Journal of Change Management*, 5, 4, pp. 369–380.

West, M. A. and J. L. Farr (1990), *Innovation and Creativity at Work*, Chichester: Wiley, pp. 3–13.

Woodman, R.W. and W.A. Pasmore (1989), '*Research in Organizational Change and Development*', vol. 2, Greenwich, CT: JAI Press.

Part V
Creating and Delivering Customer Value

Part V

Creating and Delivering Customer Value

30

Marketing Research

INTRODUCTION

One of the greatest fears of marketing managers is about losing market share on account of defective products, bad service by sales people, better deals offered by the competitors, or simply due to customers' whims. Shifting consumer loyalty and steeper costs of attracting new customers have led companies to seek greater insights into the consumer's process of decision-making. This has enabled marketeers to develop an effective marketing mix to retain customers.

A marketing manager is increasingly called upon to play a greater role in strategic decision-making where the environment needs to be scanned continuously for changing economic, sociocultural, politico-legal, and technological trends. With increasing failure of new products and the cost of launching a new brand being high, managers are under tremendous pressure to gather and use relevant information about customer preferences in order to reduce the risks associated, than base their decisions on instincts alone.

How do the marketeers spot opportunities and most importantly, how do they spot the problems? How do they design methods to collect information? How do they analyse this information to generate, refine, and evaluate alternative marketing actions? How do they present and communicate their findings effectively so that they can persuade the management to implement their recommended actions? And finally, how does it improve their understanding of the marketing process in general? These are the questions that market research aims at answering.

Learning Objectives

After studying this chapter, you will be able to:
- Understand the concepts of marketing research
- Examine the purpose and importance of marketing research
- Learn about research designs
- Evaluate different sources and methods of collecting information
- Learn the applications of marketing research
- Understand problems associated with marketing research
- Learn to carry out marketing research
- Learn to design a questionnaire
- Examine the aspects of marketing research in India

MARKETING RESEARCH

The process of marketing consists of creating, communicating, and delivering customer value profitably (Kotler 1999). Marketing research seeks to provide information relevant to all aspects of marketing research, thus, aiding the fine-tuning of the marketing mix to ensure maximum customer response. Marketing research and the marketing system are shown in Fig. 30.1.

American Marketing Association (AMA) defines marketing research as the function which links the consumer, customer, and public to the marketeer through information. This information is used to identify and define marketing opportunities and problems; generate, refine, and evaluate marketing actions; monitor marketing performance; and improve understanding of marketing as a process. Marketing research specifies the information required to address these issues; designs the method for collecting information; manages and implements the data collection process; analyses the results; and communicates the findings and their implications.

Essentially, research uncovers the relationship between variables. A relationship that can be sufficiently generalized, can be unearthed by following a scientific method so that the validity and reliability of the results is ensured. The framework for carrying out the research is known as a research design. Suppose a marketing manager seems worried about a constant fall in market share of his/her company's brand in a particular sales territory. The manager wishes to undertake a quick research study to understand the possible reasons that could be orchestrating this downfall. Perhaps a meeting with the distributors could throw some light on the phenomenon or perhaps the customers could provide a better explanation. There could be many possible explanations; vis-à-vis problems related to quality, price, packaging, competitor's prices, quality of servicing, or availability of spare parts, courteousness of salespersons, etc.

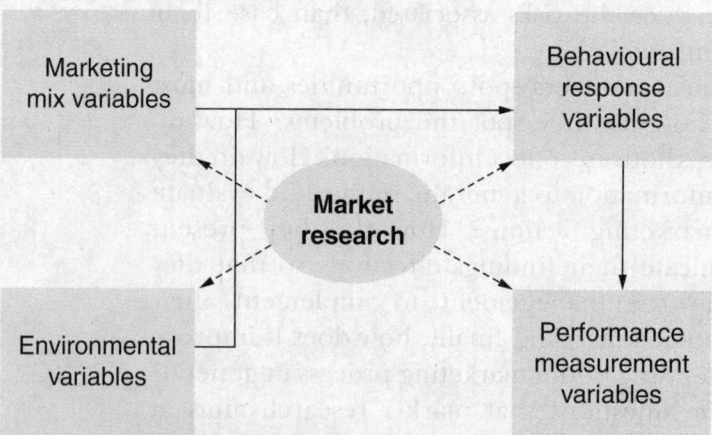

FIGURE 30.1   Marketing research and the marketing system

Research Design

There are mainly three types of research frameworks or designs that are used to carry out marketing research—exploratory, descriptive, and experimental.

Exploratory research design

A research design that explores these possible independent (causes) variables on which the dependent variable (effect such as declining sales figures) depends and ranks them in some order, is referred to as exploratory research design. It may not even qualify the scientific research grade since at the most it is of reporting nature, a far cry from descriptive or predictive or control aspects of scientific research. However, it is most often relatively speedier, low-cost, and quite insightful as far as qualitative aspects of the problem are concerned. At other times it may be an adjunct to the more detailed survey or descriptive research in terms of formulating of the hypotheses. Exploratory research is mostly carried out through the:

Study of secondary sources of data   This consists of study of published data in newspapers, periodicals, journals, websites, government publications, research project reports, trade association publications, etc. as well as study of internal company records.

Survey of individuals (depth, projective, and focus group)   It includes qualitative research for deriving rich insights from the individual (as in case of depth interview) or groups of individuals (indirectly in case of projective and directly in case of focus group).

Analysis of selected cases   This includes selecting extreme cases for study to unearth possible relationships, which are then investigated through conclusive research.

Descriptive research design

A more detailed research, which is often conducted through a survey research form and aims to statistically pin down one or more independent variables to the dependent variable and also tests these relationships for statistical significance is known as descriptive research. A systematic collection of data from populations or samples of population through use of personal interviews, questionnaire, and other data-gathering devices is termed as a survey (Festinger and Katz 1976).

It is often necessary to back up empirical findings from a survey with statistical tests of significance so that the decision-makers can have sufficient confidence in basing their decisions on the researcher's findings. This type of research design is known as descriptive research design. Many times it may be used to segment different target groups that might then be targeted through different marketing mix. The survey could be a one-time study known as a cross-sectional study or it could take the form of taking the responses of the target group over a period of time, which is known as a longitudinal study. A longitudinal study typically uses a panel that is recruited to provide measurements over time. The sample size of a survey is dependent upon the accuracy desired; and the effort level, time, money, etc., at the disposal of the marketeer; and the extent of population variance. The sample may be drawn either through probabilistic or non-probabilistic sampling methods.

Experimental research design

Experimental or causal research design goes beyond aiming at statistical association but seeks to explain the relationship. The special research designs in experimental research isolate the experiment from extraneous variables that might otherwise confound the experiment. The errors that can affect the validity of conclusions are due to:

History   Caused due to non-recurring external events.

Maturation   Caused due to changes in the experimental units.

Testing   Caused by sensitizing respondents by testing and, hence, biasing their responses.

Instrumentation   Caused by changes in the measuring instrument.

Test unit mortality   Caused by dropping out of some experimental units during the study.

Selection bias   Caused by selection of a non-random procedure in the selection.

Experimental research designs can be of the following types—quasi- and true experimental design, ex-post facto design, and x-sectional and longitudinal. Three conditions need to be satisfied for inferring causality:

Antecedence   The causing variable has to occur prior to the effect.

Internal validity   Causal link can be established if and only if we take care of extraneous variables.

Concomitant variation   The independent and dependent variables must move jointly. They may move in reverse directions (inversely correlated) or they may move in the same direction (directly correlated).

This criterion, though, needs to be satisfied for inferring causality but the state of marketing science is far from the exact nature of physical sciences. The most noteworthy fact is the dynamic nature of the world of business. The experimental research design requires more than one experimental and control group (that are to remain unaffected throughout the period of giving the treatment to the experimental group). The treatment could be a change in the product packaging, advertising campaign, or a change in the price. Yet the world of commerce will seldom allow the risk of stopping and experimenting with such a cost. However, there are occasions, for example, before choosing to launch a brand nationally, where fine-tuning the marketing mix in terms of test marketing is often resorted to in order to reduce the probability of product failure.

Problems Associated with Marketing Research

Marketing research problems, like most of the social science problems, are multidimensional in nature and were almost intractable in terms of their analyses till the advent of powerful personal computers. Market researchers frequently use many user-friendly multi-variate statistical analytical software tools such as SPSS, SYATAT, MINITAB, BMPD, SAS, etc. In the hands of an expert they can give a

Seven steps to designing a research project

1. Specifying research objectives
2. Preparing a list of the needed information
3. Designing the data collection project
4. Selecting a sample type
5. Determining sample size
6. Organizing and carrying out the fieldwork
7. Analysing the collected data and reporting the findings

powerful insight into the data collected and, thus, act as useful aids to marketing decision-making and marketing action, but in the hands of a novice the conclusions can often be misleading. One needs to be aware of the assumptions on which these techniques are based as well as learn the fine art of interpretation.

Sources of data can be primary or secondary. Usually, in a survey research, a questionnaire is used as an instrument to collect primary data. Most often a sample of respondents is chosen for the survey. In order to select a sample we must have the sampling frame, that is, the list of respondents. How do we select our sample is of considerable importance for sample statistics to give us as much an accurate idea about the parameters of the population as desired by the managers. Higher accuracy would demand broader sample size, *cetris paribus*. A randomly drawn sample will be able to represent the population better. Sometimes, it not possible to draw the sample by any of the probability sampling methods and then the choice may be exercised based on judgement or simply convenience, but the accuracy of the results of that study will consequently be relatively lower.

It is equally important to communicate the findings of the marketing research clearly and persuasively. A good marketing research report will include—(1) an executive summary describing the management problem and the research problem, the research methodology, and some of the major findings or insights along with the recommendations, very briefly, in a page or two; (2) an introductory chapter explaining the objectives of the research; (3) a chapter on research methodology; (4) an analysis chapter; (5) a findings and recommendations chapter; and (6) references, reports, and sources of secondary information.

These are the components of an ideal report. Many an ideal report has not led to marketing decisions for the simple reason that managers would rather base their decisions on gut feeling and intuition.

APPLICATION OF MARKETING RESEARCH

Marketing research is frequently used for identifying market segments, forecasting demand, product positioning, new product development, advertising research, pricing research, and sales and distribution research.

Some authors differentiate between market research and marketing research, the difference being in the greater emphasis of the latter on the generalization (i.e.,

Exhibit 30.1 Questionnaire design checklist

- Information required
- Type of questionnaire
- Content of questions
- Framing questions
- Scale of measurement used for different questions

- The sequence of questions
- Form and layout of questions
- Method of questionnaire reproduction
- The shortcomings in the questionnaire revealed by pre-testing
- The final draft

external validity) of the results so obtained, that is, the probability that the results are valid across contexts is relatively higher.

First, any business problem, needs to be converted into research problem/s and further into research objectives (Green et al. 1996). The data can then be collected through questioning or through observation. The questioning method is much efficient and can take the form of interviewing or collecting data through a questionnaire. The questionnaire design checklist is given in Exhibit 30.1.

The communication methods of data collection can further be classified (Boyd and Westfall 1990) on the basis of whether the communication is direct (vs indirect) and structured (vs unstructured), as displayed in Table 30.1.

Observational methods can be either through gadgets or delegated to humans. However, in the latter case, the objectivity of the data collection method can be greatly compromised through perceptual dysfunctions. This can be rectified to some extent through ethnographic research, where the researcher becomes the insider. This methodology is being increasingly resorted to where one wants to infer motivations rather than merely record the behaviour that most observational methods achieve.

Data analysis   The methods of data analysis used in marketing research range from descriptive and graphical to inferential statistical tools. The inferential statistical tools include univariate, bivariate, and multi-variate methods of statistical analysis. Multivariate tools are categorized (Kinnear and Taylor 1971) under interdependence methods when the entities–attributes matrix is subjected to analysis for patterns without differentiation between dependent and independent variables, while as in the category of dependence methods this differentiation is relevant. The popular

TABLE 30.1   Classification of communication methods of data collection

	Direct	Indirect
Structured	Formal structured questionnaires	Projective techniques
Unstructured	Unstructured personal interviews	Unstructured freewheeling interview by personal interviewer

interdependence methods are factor analysis, cluster analysis, and multidimensional scaling whereas the popular dependence methods are multiple-regression, conjoint analysis, and discriminant analysis.

ACNielsen ORG-MARG Pvt Ltd

As market research is a cost-effective way of finding out what people think, want, need or do, businesses use market research to help them produce goods and services taking into account their customers' needs, and to fine-tune their marketing strategies to make them effective. Most successful organizations recognize that inadequate research significantly increases the risk of failure in the marketplace. Social and government bodies also use market research to gauge public opinion, as an input to policy generation, or to measure the success of government communication campaigns. However, market research works if the people that are sampled are representative of the total group of interest, if the right questions are asked, and if the answers are interpreted correctly. For this reason, research needs to be conducted by skilled and experienced practitioners who can design, conduct, and deliver information and insight to their customers.

In 1923, Arthur C. Nielsen started the company that would provide information about evolving consumer markets and retail buying trends—first in the United States and then, internationally. Nielsen produced the first retail drug index in 1933 in the US, followed by a food index and a department store index. These, in turn, were followed by other indices that, taken together, came to constitute the ACNielsen retail index. Whilst developing these audits, he coined the phrase 'market share' to describe the measurement in percentage terms of the amount of goods sold by each manufacturer

in each product category, relative to their competitors.

The erstwhile ORG (Operations Research Group) launched retail audit in 1961. It was among the first few to be established in Asia. Since then it has continuously grown in size and sophistication and now covers 65,000 retail outlets in over 400 towns and 1,000 Indian villages. To support this mammoth operation, it has an extensive permanent field infrastructure, which includes 750 full-time field staff spread across 155 locations in India. Later on, ORG merged with Marketing and Research Group (MARG). The coming together of the two strongest players in the Indian market research industry in 1995 gave birth to a new entity called ORG-MARG Research Limited (OMRL). In 1997, OMRL created history by crossing the national boundary and setting up new ventures in Nepal, Bangladesh, and Sri Lanka. It was in 1999 that OMRL became an integral part of VNU—a Dutch company in the information business and operating across the globe. With VNU's global acquisition of ACNielsen in 2001, OMRL, the national leader and ACNielsen, the global leader in the arena of market research, were brought under the same roof and re-christened as ACNielsen ORG-MARG Private Limited.

The breadth and depth of ACNielsen ORG-MARG's infrastructure and services are unmatched. The company investigates the market through many different 'windows'—retail and consumer, quantity and quality, syndicated and customized data, one-off, periodic, and

(Contd)

Exhibit *(Contd)*

continuous studies. Together, ACNielsen ORG-MARG has the largest field network among all the market research agencies in the Indian subcontinent. The market research agency employs more than 250 full-time research professionals with specialization in fields such as market research, business management, economics, statistics, engineering, psychology, and sociology. These professionals are based in 10 full-fledged branch offices at Baroda, Mumbai, Delhi, Kolkata, Chennai, Bangalore, Hyderabad, Pune, Lucknow, and Bhubaneswar. In addition, the company has 48 field offices across the country, and over 750 research investigators operate from these field offices.

The organization maintains a strong and modern computer set-up, critical to the massive data gathering and analysis operations. With VNU as the main shareholder and the alignment with ACNielsen ORG-MARG, already the largest market research company in India, is now poised for significant growth through consolidation of existing businesses as well as the launch of new products including database management and other information services, precision marketing, and innovative data solutions.

ACNielsen ORG-MARG holds a majority stake (60 per cent) in ORG–GfK, a joint venture with GfK for consumer durable retail tracking in India. It also controls the management of its subsidiaries—ACNielsen ORG-MARG Bangladesh, ACNielsen ORG-MARG Sri Lanka, and ACNielsen ORG-MARG Nepal. The field offices organize the primary data collection from the panel dealer/panel doctor. The branch offices primarily look after business development and client servicing. A 50:50 joint venture with IMRB in India called TAM India, provides advertisers and the media industry with television ratings, advertising expenditure analysis, and message evaluation. ACNielsen ORG-MARG is committed to the continuous development of retail measurement service by constantly embracing new technology and listening to the needs of its consumers. With their global expertise and local knowledge, ACNielsen ORG-MARG India, today, is in a unique position to provide clients with the whole story—a comprehensive understanding of what's happening in their markets, its reasons, and what is likely to happen in the future.

ACNielsen ORG-MARG has two main areas of activity—retail measurement service and customized research. This is indicated in the following table:

1. Consumer products/Food products (CP/FP) audit	8. Lubricant audit
2. Pharmaceutical audit	9. Liquor audit
3. Prescription audit (scrip count)	10. Sanitary ware audit
4. Soft drinks audit	11. SIM card
5. Ice cream audit	12. Durable audit
6. Media audit	13. Hot tea shop audit
7. Cigarette audit	14. Contact lens solution audit

The aforementioned services are managed by the respective strategic business units mentioned here:

Retail measurement service SBU: Consumer products/food products (CP/FP) audit, cigarette, lubricant, liquor, SIM card, sanitary ware,

Exhibit (*Contd*)

tea shops, durables, soft drinks, and ice cream audits.

Pharmaceutical services SBU: A joint venture with IMS in India, the organization operates under the ORG-IMS banner and offers clients a pharmaceutical audit, prescription audit (scrip count), and lens audit.

Media services SBU: A 50:50 joint venture with IMRB in India called TAM India; it provides advertisers and the media industry with television ratings, advertising expenditure analysis, and message evaluation.

MARKETING RESEARCH IN INDIA

It is clear from Table 30.2 that a majority (86 per cent) of Indian firms spent very less money (<= ₹10 lakh) on marketing research in 1986. Also, for majority of the firms (for 91 per cent of the firms) the spend on marketing research was less than or equal to 0.4 per cent of their sales. Although the authors are not aware of any published data on marketing research spend in 2006, that is, after two decades, it is assumed that this too would have shown growth after liberalization and globalization of the Indian economy. What must be still of concern is that marketeers spend far too much on advertising than on marketing research.

Marketing research and organizations Only large consumer goods firms seem to utilize services of marketing research firms (refer Table 30.3) while marketing research for smaller firms was conducted either by advertising agencies or consultants. Sales staff and in-house marketing researchers were used by firms across the entire spectrum.

TABLE 30.2 Expenditure on marketing research by Indian firms

Expenditure amount	Percentage of respondents
Less than ₹1 lakh	40.0
₹1 lakh to ₹10 lakh	46.0
More than ₹10 lakh	14.0
	100.0
(Marketing research expenditure as a percentage of sales)	
Up to 0.01	28.0
0.02–0.09	34.0
0.10–0.40	29.0
More than 0.40	9.0
	100.0

Source: Based on *Business India*, November 17–30, 1986.

TABLE 30.3 Organizational arrangements for conducting marketing research in India

Arrangement	Percentage of firms	Nature of the firms preferring the arrangement
Firms' sales staff	69	Firms of all sizes, industrial goods, and services marketers
Marketing research agencies	52	Large firms, consumer goods marketers
In-house marketing researchers	44	Large firms, industrial goods, and services firms
Advertising agencies	35	Smaller firms
Consultants	34	—
Syndicated research services	22	Large firms and consumer goods firms

Source: Based on *Business India*, November 17–30, 1986.

Application of marketing research The use of marketing research in fifteen areas (refer Table 30.4) of marketing strategy and marketing mix decision-making indicate the wide array of application of marketing research in India.

Exhibit 30.2 lists some of the prominent marketing research firms operating in India. This sector has seen a lot of mergers and acquisitions as fallout of consolidation at the global level in recent times.

TABLE 30.4 Application of marketing research in India

S. no.	Area of application	% of companies using marketing research
1.	New product decisions	58
2.	Estimating market share	49
3.	Gathering competitive information	47
4.	Demand estimation	46
5.	Product modification decisions	44
6.	Measuring consumer satisfaction	43
7.	Product positioning decisions	42
8.	Diversification decisions	40
9.	Market segmentation decisions	38
10.	Advertising theme/Message decisions	31
11.	Pricing decisions	30
12.	Customer service decisions	27
13.	Product elimination decisions	21
14.	Evaluating advertising effectiveness	20
15.	Channel modification decisions	9

Source: Based on *Business India*, November 17–30, 1986.

Exhibit 30.2 Major market research firms in India

- ACNielsen ORG-MARG
- Gallup India
- Hansa Research
- IMRB
- Indica Research
- IDC
- Market and Research Team (MART)
- National Council of Applied Economic Research (NCAER)
- NFO MFL
- Pathfinders
- Quantum Market Research
- Research International
- Synovate
- Taylor Nelson Sofres Mode

Source: Based on the data from Market Research Society of India (MRSI).

SUMMARY

Marketing research is the function which links the consumer, customer, and public to the marketeer through information. This information is used to identify and define marketing opportunities and problems; generate, refine, and evaluate marketing actions; monitor marketing performance; and improve understanding of marketing as a process. Marketing research specifies the information required to address these issues; designs the method for collecting information; manages and implements the data collection process; analyses the results; and communicates the findings and their implications.

The framework for carrying out research is known as a research design. A research design that explores possible independent variables, supports dependent variables, and ranks them in some order, is known as exploratory research design. The type of research which seeks to explore the relation between independent and dependent variables and most often takes the form of a survey research is known as descriptive research. Experimental or causal research design goes beyond aiming at statistical association but seeks to explain the relationship. Special research designs in experimental research isolate the experiment from extraneous variables that might confound the experiment. Marketing research is applied frequently for identifying market segments, forecasting demand, product positioning, new product development, advertising research, pricing research, and sales and distribution research.

KEYWORDS

Descriptive research It enables one to describe the extent and direction of relationship among variables.

Experimental research It enables one to make causal inferences about relationship among variables.

Exploratory research It is undertaken to identify major variables of interest and as a precursor to conclusive research either by descriptive or by experimental research.

Qualitative research Collection and analysis of data that does not lend itself easily to quantification (numbers).

Questionnaire A set of questions designed to generate data, which is then analysed to accomplish research objectives.

Research design Basic framework for carrying out research.

Research objectives The goals of any research problem that are sought to be attained by an appropriate research design and provide information for marketing actions.

Sampling method The method of selecting a fraction of the population to infer about population parameters.

Survey research A systematic collection of data from samples of population through use of personal interviews, questionnaire, and other data-gathering devices.

EXERCISES

Concept Review Questions

1. How is a business problem converted to marketing research problem and, finally, to research objectives?
2. What is the major difference between exploratory research design and descriptive research design? Illustrate with examples.
3. How is survey research carried out? Discuss in detail.

Critical Thinking Questions

1. It is said that Akio Morita of Sony Corporation went beyond the findings of formal marketing research when he decided to market the Walkman. What must have prompted him to go for that?
2. Should formal marketing research replace decision-making using gut feeling and experience alone?

Project Assignment

Prepare a detailed market research proposal for carrying out demand forecasting, pricing research, positioning research, and consumer research in terms of features desired for Simputer (a low-price, few-features computer) for the Indian market.

REFERENCES

Boyd, Harper W. Jr., Ralph Westfall, and Stanley F. Stasch (1990), *Marketing Research—Text and Cases*, 7th edn, Richard D. Irwin, Homewood, Illinois.

Festinger, L. and D. Katz (1976), *Research Methods in the Behavioural Sciences*, Indian Reprint, Amerind Publishing Co. Pvt. Ltd, Calcutta.

Green, Paul E., Donald S. Tull, and Gerald Albaum (1996), *Research for Marketing Decision*, 5th edn, Prentice Hall of India, New Delhi.

Kinnear, Thomas C. and James R. Taylor (1971), 'Multivariate Methods in Marketing Research: A Further Attempt at Classification', *Journal of Marketing*, Vol. 35, No. 4, October.

Kotler, Philip (1999), *Marketing Management— The Millennium Edition*, Prentice Hall of India, New Delhi.

31

Marketing Planning

INTRODUCTION

A marketing plan helps a marketeer to establish, direct, and coordinate marketing efforts. Preparing a marketing plan based on clear, measurable, and time-marked marketing objectives forces firms to assess what is going on in the marketplace and how it affects their business. It also provides a benchmark for later measurement. Often, simply embarking on the process of preparing a marketing plan aids the marketeer in developing an effective and successful marketing strategy.

MARKETING PLAN

A marketing plan contains information about the company and its products, marketing objectives, and strategies. It specifies the yardstick by which the success of a firm's marketing activities would be measured. It describes all the marketing activity that is performed during a specified time period (usually a year). Any background information and research that has been used to arrive at a particular marketing strategy is also included. Finally, the costs associated with the planned marketing activities as well as the measures that will be used to determine success is included in the marketing plan. Most often, a marketing plan is a component of a business plan. A business plan basically states how the business will be run, specifies goals, the capital required, and the business strategy. Marketing strategy is part of the business strategy.

Marketing plans should always support and be closely linked to a company's business objectives. In order

Learning Objectives

After studying this chapter, you will be able to:
- Understand a marketing plan
- Elaborate different elements of a marketing plan
- Frame marketing objectives and goals
- Prepare a marketing action plan
- Understand marketing controls

to develop a good marketing plan one should have a thorough understanding of products and services, their benefits and features, the target market and its characteristics, and finally enough knowledge about current and potential competing products or services. Just as a road map guides us on a journey, a good marketing plan guides all the people concerned in reaching their goals and prevents them from going off-course. Regarding the marketing plan components, there are no hard and fast rules and they vary according to the industry, size of the company, and its stage of growth. The structure of the plan is not as important as the process of preparing it—as it makes a firm think about its business goals and what the marketing strategy should be, to achieve those goals. A business can be very good at strategic and tactical marketing and yet fail if it is not also good at administrative marketing. Administrative marketing refers to the capacity to prepare and carry out sound marketing plans. All strategies that can be effectively executed by the marketing organization must be integrated in a marketing plan.

To determine whether a firm has created a plan that is realistic as well as profitable, the issues of costs, break-even, and payback period of the investment are critical. A disguised example from the real world will illustrate this point (Table 31.1).

The two important things that a marketing manager should consider are variable and fixed costs, and the break-even point, that is, the point at which the fixed costs are recovered from the sale of goods but no profit is made. As is evident from the calculations for the XYZ Detergents Limited, the company would break even by selling 108,163 kg of detergent, generating sales revenue of ₹1,297,956.00. However,

TABLE 31.1 Break-even calculation

S. no.	Particulars	Cost	Cost type
1.	Retail sales price	₹12.00/kg	
2.	Selling price to distributors	₹8.40/kg	
3.	Raw material cost	₹2.00/kg	Variable
4.	Processing cost	₹0.88/kg	Variable
5.	Packaging cost	₹1.10/kg	Variable
6.	Shipping cost	₹0.50/kg	Variable
7.	Overheads	₹100,000	Fixed
8.	Production equipment rental	₹24,000	Fixed
9.	Promotional expenses	₹300,000	Fixed
*	Break-even volume =	Fixed costs/unit contribution	= (100,000 + 24,000 + 300,000)/ [8.40 − {2.0 + 0.88 + 1.10 + 0.50}] = 108,163 kg And the break-even Rupee Sales were 108,163 × 12 = ₹1,297,956

it is not enough for the company to achieve a mere break-even point. It needs to generate a target profit. The same equation can be used to calculate target volume to yield a target profit.

$$\text{Target volume} = (\text{Fixed cost} + \text{Profit})/\text{Unit contribution} \qquad (31.1)$$

For example, the target volume for a target profit of say ₹100,000 would be 133,763.47 kg [(₹424,000 + ₹100,000)/₹3.92], that is, approximately 30 per cent more volume than was required to attain break-even point. It is evident that the marketing manager has to revise the original marketing plans to achieve a target profit. Another parameter used by companies to evaluate marketing projects, when they have a choice, is payback period which is calculated as below:

$$\begin{aligned}\text{Payback period} &= \text{Initial investment}/\text{Annual profit}\\ &= ₹424,000/₹100,000 = 4.2 \text{ years}\end{aligned} \qquad (31.2)$$

It is for the company to decide whether a period more than four years is suitable for a risky venture or is it just right, as per the industry norms. Finally, it takes great skill to develop a plan that is internally consistent and mutually supportive.

A marketing plan should be simple and precise. It should incorporate goals, strategy, and the estimated cost of carrying out the plan. Nevertheless, at the minimum a formal plan should contain the following sections (Kotler 1999):

- situation analysis;
- marketing objectives and goals;
- marketing strategy;
- marketing action plan; and
- marketing controls.

Situation Analysis

The situation analysis includes four components—(1) the current situation; (2) SWOT analysis; (3) issue analysis; and (4) assumptions.

The current situation

The planning process begins with an objective assessment of the current situation. This may be done by carrying out an audit of external (uncontrollable) variables and internal (controllable) variables. The external audit is carried out in the areas of business and economic environment, the market, and competition. The industry analysis may be carried out using Porter's (1980) five forces framework.

Business and economic environment The opportunities and threats constitute these issues:

Politico-legal Issues such as nationalization, union legislation, regulatory considerations, fiscal policies, custom and excise duties regime, taxation, etc.

Economic Issues such as savings rate, disposable income, GNP, inflation rate, unemployment rate, volatility, etc.

Sociocultural   Issues such as education, environment, demographics, family, changes in consumer lifestyle, etc.

Technological   Issues such as new technologies, methods and systems, availability of substitutes, production processes, cost savings, new materials, R&D, etc.

The external environment poses both threats as well as opportunities. It is scanned in the domains described earlier, and specifically in those areas that have the potential to affect the company in particular. This subset of general environment then constitutes the task environment that is of immediate concern to the business.

The market   It is analysed in terms of the total market and market characteristics and trends.

Total market   The total market is described in terms of its size, growth, and trends both in value and volume terms. A description of consumers in terms of changing demographics, psychographics, and their varied purchasing behaviour is also undertaken at this point.

Market characteristics and trends   This section is described in terms of the marketing mix (McCarthy 1996) vis-à-vis products, prices, physical distribution channels, communication, and industry practices.

Market planning includes studying—(1) product characteristics, end-use of products, accessories, packaging, etc.; (2) prices include sticking to normal trade practices, setting price levels and range, terms of sale, etc.; (3) physical distribution strategy decides the principal method of physical distribution; (4) a study of channels examines studying principal channels, purchasing patterns, purchasing ability, geographical location, turnover, profits, needs, tastes, attitudes, decision-makers, etc.; (5) communication finalizes the principal methods of promotion vis-à-vis advertising, sales force, direct response, public relations, sales promotion, etc.; and (6) industry practices such as adhering to norms set by trade associations, government bodies, inter-firm comparisons, and benchmarking, etc. is important. All of these elements are reviewed based on their relevance to the firm.

Competition   An analysis of the competition involves the following:

Industry structure   Factors to be considered are make-up of companies in the industry, market standing/reputation, diversification, new entrants, mergers, acquisitions, key strengths and weaknesses, competitive arrangements, production capacities, etc.

Industry profitability   Factors to be considered are barriers to entry; industry profitability and relative performance of individual companies; structure of operating costs; return on investment and its relationship with price, volume, cost of capital, structure of operating costs, etc.

Company   The internal audit of a company's resources vis-à-vis environment, market, and competition is carried out. A review of the following may be carried out:

Sales   Sales (by location, product types, customers), market shares, profit margins, marketing mix variables, marketing organization, sales and marketing control data, etc.

Marketing objectives and marketing strategy   One has to consider whether the marketing objectives are clearly stated and whether they are aligned with corporate objectives. The company should formulate a marketing strategy and ensure that the resources are utilized optimally.

Marketing intelligence system   One has to consider whether the marketing intelligence system is geared to provide accurate, timely, and sufficient information to help marketing managers to make effective decisions.

Organization structure   It has to be considered whether the organizational structure facilitates effective and efficient response by interacting with both internal and external constituents.

Planning and control systems   One has to ensure that the planning is well-conceived and are there effective control systems in place to guide the execution.

Cost-effectiveness analysis   The marketing activities should be within the budget and should not be excessively costly. The scope for reduction should always be maintained.

Profitability analysis   It has to be decided based on issues such as whether the profitability will be monitored by product category, segments served, and can they be ranked in terms of where and in which segment and product category the best profits are made and the largest costs incurred.

Each of these areas should be critically examined to determine factors that are critical to the company's performance. The vast amount of data that is generated in both external and internal marketing audit has to be screened for validity and relevance before it can be organized and complemented with prudent judgement in certain areas, to arrive at viable results from the analysis.

SWOT analysis

SWOT (strengths, weaknesses, opportunities, and threats) analysis is carried out by relating the internal strengths and weaknesses, and external opportunities and threats. It should highlight internal *differential* strengths and weaknesses vis-à-vis competitors and *key* external opportunities and threats. The analysis should be conducted for each important segment, considering its future potential. A summary of good or bad performance should be included, which should be concise, relevant, and well-presented. All information that is not central to the company's marketing problems should be omitted. The whole emphasis should be on creative analysis. It should begin with the opportunities and threats list, elucidating the attractive opportunities present before the firm. There is no such thing as a mature product without opportunities; there are only managers lacking in imagination and creativity. Similarly, the plan should detail significant threats facing the business. A company that does not see trouble ahead is headed for real trouble. To be hit by unforeseen threats is the worst that can happen to a company.

Issues analysis

An issues analysis briefly lists key external issues that present potential challenges or opportunities for a business. Most CEOs would want their managers to present an honest list of the problems and choices facing the business such as a new legislation or impact of a technological advancement.

Assumptions

Managers implicitly hold certain assumptions about the environment, competitors, and market structure for the planning process to proceed. These should be made explicit. Managers' assumptions about the future may vary dramatically, thus making market planning an exercise in futility. So if possible, these assumptions should be few in number, concerning certain key determinants of success for the company.

Framing Marketing Objectives and Goals

The next step in marketing planning is the clarification of marketing objectives and goals. It is a step from the analysis to the decision-making, considering the current phase that the company is in. The broad objectives that are to be achieved in the coming period should be feasible, pragmatic, and also internally compatible. For example, the objectives could be increasing customer satisfaction, improving the brand image, increasing the market share, increasing the margins, etc. Goals must be derived from these broad objectives. The objectives, when recast in terms of a magnitude and a target date of achievement, are termed as goals. They have to be explained in precise terms; for example, 'to increase the market share by 10 percentage points from the current 31 per cent by the end of next fiscal year'.

Marketing Strategy

An objective is what a company wants to achieve while, a strategy is how it plans to achieve its objectives. The strategy can be crafted around six areas. They are the—target market; core positioning; total value proposition; price positioning; promotion strategy; and distribution strategy.

The target market Critical to the success in marketing any product, is aiming an organization's whole marketing effort at a target market. Planning marketing strategy without knowing the target market is like planning a party without knowing anything about the people attending.

Describe the size of target market. Remember, a market is group of people with common wants, not a place or a thing. So it is necessary to be specific and include statistics about the size of the target market. Include information on whether the size of the target market is growing, shrinking, or staying the same. If the size of the target market is changing, give valid reasons.

Markets may be described according to the—(1) demographic characteristics they share such as age, income, sex, race, number of children, marital status, where they live, etc.; (2) psychographics such as their attitudes, interests, opinions, habits and hobbies, etc.; and (3) buying habits, media habits, store preferences, etc.

For business markets the target market description should specify the industries, size of companies, product applications, and locations the company aims to reach with its products. The company's offering should have a core idea or benefit in terms of quality, low prices, safety, durability, prestige, best value-for-money, etc. around which the positioning should be enacted. The firm's strategy in terms of pricing can be more for more, more for same, same for less, less for much less, or more for less.

Core positioning The brand can be differentiated on the basis of its attributes, benefits, applications, quality/price, etc. with respect to competitor's positioning. The specific positioning of the brand needs to be specified.

Total value proposition The marketing plan should also state the firm's value proposition, the single reason that the buyer should buy from the firm and not from its competitors.

Price positioning The firm needs to decide whether it is going to be a product differentiator, a nicher, or a low cost provider.

Promotion strategy The communication strategy should be described for advertising, sales promotion, public relations, sales force, and direct marketing in terms of resources to be allocated and its consonance with the strategic objectives for each of them.

Distribution strategy Next, the distribution strategy as to reach the target segment should be outlined. Finally, the plan should be reviewed to make sure that there is consistency among all these areas.

Marketing Action Plan

The marketing strategies should now be converted into specific action programmes specifying the plan of action, its timing, those responsible for it, and the estimated cost. The action plans will have a supporting budget that will have an estimate of the number of units that are expected to be sold and the net realized price on the revenue side. On the expense side it will show the cost of production, physical distribution, and cost of marketing. Action plans are communicated to all important constituencies so that they know what and when to expect it.

Marketing Controls

A mechanism to review whether or not the actions are proceeding as envisaged is incorporated in terms of monthly or quarterly benchmarks which enables the managers to take corrective action, at the strategic level, if need be.

Exhibit 31.1 Marketing plan of Mangalam Wedding Consultants Limited

Executive Summary

Mangalam Wedding Consultants Limited which will start its operations in Chennai, Tamil Nadu, aims to help clients celebrate their weddings in a special and unique way by taking the load off their shoulders. From choosing the venue, deciding the décor and wedding theme, to selecting the menu, Mangalam Wedding Consultants Limited will ensure that everything happens exactly the way their clients want it. Whether they want the entire wedding to be planned or a specific event managed, they will find Mangalam's services truly affordable and valuable.

(Contd)

Exhibit 31.1 *(Contd)*

Mangalam's highly professional and experienced team ensures 'high value for money', giving the entire event a modern, state-of-the-art feel. Mangalam will seek to combine professionalism with personalized attention.

Situational Analysis

Weddings are the most extravagant events in Indian societies and the money invested in them are increasing at tremendous rates. They are a display of status and are, hence, organized with a lot of pomp and show. Currently, theme weddings are in fashion, that is, dress codes, interior decoration, food, etc., follow a particular theme. With the increasing number of NRI brides and bridegrooms, global standards are expected when it comes to celebrating weddings.

Market Summary

India spends $11 billion (₹49,500 crore) annually on weddings and it is growing at 25 per cent annually. According to the National Council for Applied Economic Research (NCAER), the middle class makes $4,545 (₹2,04,525) to $23,000 (₹10,35,000) a year. NCAER projects that the market for all categories of products (from daily consumables to consumer durables) will double in annual sales by 2010. With the economy expected to maintain steady 6–7 per cent annual growth, India is widely seen as one of the world's largest emerging markets for wedding planners.

SWOT Analysis
Strengths

- Professional team
- Adequate market research skills
- Flexibility of a start-up

Weakness
- Difficulty in developing trust and brand awareness as a start-up company
- Pricing is challenging
- Capital requirements for a rapid built up

Opportunities
- Weddings are grand occasions in the Indian society when people splurge
- Changing trend of seeking convenience and increasing willingness of people to pay for such services
- Can diversify into various other such event management markets

Threats
- A slump in the economy could have a negative effect on the people's spending patterns
- Entry barriers are low
- Laws of the land may change as society may shun conspicuous consumption

Competition

Indigenous vendors: Local vendors, who are already having faithful customers and are well-established in the business, are major competitors.

Wedding sites: Wedding sites such as www. shaadi.com, www.weddingsutra.com, etc. which offer online planning and budgeting services as well as the addresses of different vendors in different locations are serious competitors for Mangalam's business. People find it easier to seek services from online sites rather than approaching wedding consultants. In this case, it is more important for Mangalam to gain their trust and confidence.

Objectives

First-year: Mangalam is aiming at 1.6 per cent market share of the wedding market in Chennai.

Second-year: In the second year it hopes to acquire a market share of 2.4 per cent.

Third-year: By the third year the objective is to achieve a 27.2 per cent increase in profit and acquire a market share of 3.2 per cent.

Marketing Strategy

Target market: Mangalam's marketing strategy is based on positioning itself as a wedding

Exhibit 31.1 *(Contd)*

consultancy service for people who want to hold their weddings in Chennai city. Its primary target is upper-middle and upper class people.

Positioning: It is positioning itself as a time-saving wedding consultancy and service provider, that lets its clients to be 'guests' at their own weddings.

Marketing Action Plan

Product offering: Mangalam offers the following services:

- planning, organizing, and budgeting weddings
- ensuring a smooth wedding

Distribution: Mangalam Consultants Limited will be operating from a centrally located office in Chennai. The company will reach its clients by building a good network among the vendors. It will effectively advertise and promote its business through them. It will initially restrict itself to newspaper ads. Later, it will start putting public hoardings and advertise through websites.

Service strategy: Mangalam offers combined service offerings as packages, consistent with the clients' needs. Services such as video and photography, transportation, invitation stationery, and interior decoration are mandatory components of the package. Selection of clothes, jewels, priests, beauty salons, etc. are left to the choice of clients.

Seasonality strategy: Mangalam plans to promote itself heavily during the peak wedding season by intense publicity and special offers.

Pricing strategy: Services provided by Mangalam are priced slightly higher than what it would cost clients if they were to organize the wedding themselves. The premium is justifiable on account of better quality and speed of service provided.

Promotional strategy: The company should follow these promotional strategies.

- Develop affiliate relationships with other service providers (florists, hair stylists, caterers).
- Word-of-mouth referrals—generating sales leads in the local community through customer referrals.

Advertising strategy: Apart from advertising in the Yellow Pages with two by three ads describing its services, Mangalam will advertise in *The Hindu* (the largest circulating newspaper in South India) in the first year; advertise in newspapers as well as public hoardings in the second year and; continue to advertise in newspapers and public hoardings and start advertising on websites from the third year.

Marketing Research

Using marketing research, Mangalam will identify vendors who will cooperate with the company. Feedback from clients and vendors will help them improve their services. Mangalam will also find out other needs of their clients through client satisfaction studies.

Finances

Mangalam will charge its clients 5 per cent of the wedding budget as its fees. On an average, a wedding is estimated to have a budget of ₹100,000. It will also earn additional revenue in terms of commissions from each vendor.

Mangalam would earn ₹10,000 per wedding by providing mandatory services, such as video and photo facilities, transportation, and other services that are part of the package. Considering the 20, 30, and 40 weddings booked by Mangalam in its first, second, and third year of the operation respectively, the financial statement of Mangalam is forecasted in Table 31.2.

(Contd)

Exhibit 31.1   (Contd)

TABLE 31.2   Financial statement of Mangalam Wedding Consultants Ltd

S.no.	Particulars	Year 1	Year 2	Year 3
1.	Average wedding earning	79,800	79,800	79,800
2.	Less: Variable cost	39,000	33,800	32,955
3.	Contribution margin (CM)	40,800	46,000	46,845
4.	CM for the entire year	8,16,000	13,80,000	18,73,800
5.	Less: Overheads	2,80,000	3,56,000	4,47,200
6.	Net CM	5,36,000	10,24,000	14,26,600
7.	Marketing and other investments	3,50,000	6,25,000	9,00,000
8.	(6) – (7)	186,000	399,000	5,26,600
9.	Less: Depreciation**	10,000	7,500	5,625
10.	PBIT	176,000	391,500	5,20,975

Marketing Controls Implementation

Tight quality control measures and proper feedback will be collected to closely ensure quality of service and customer satisfaction. This will easily spot Mangalam's mistakes and will help it in correcting any problems.

Marketing Organization

Though Mangalam does not have a marketing department operating separately, it will give marketing top importance.

**Depreciation rate 25%

Source: A proposed hypothetical company visualized by student entrepreneurs at BITS Pilani that has been refined for the present purpose.

SUMMARY

The purpose of a marketing plan is to establish, direct, and coordinate a seller's marketing efforts. A marketing plan contains information about the company, its products, marketing objectives, and strategies, as well as the yardstick for measuring the success of its marketing activities. Most often, a marketing plan is a component of a business plan. Administrative marketing involves preparing and carrying out sound marketing plans. A marketing plan should be simple and to the point and contain the situation analysis, marketing objectives and

goals, and marketing strategy. Situation analysis includes four components—a description of the current situation, SWOT analysis, main issues facing the business, and main assumptions about the future. Marketing objectives and goals should be feasible, pragmatic, and internally compatible. The marketing strategy can be crafted around six areas vis-à-vis the target market, core positioning, total value proposition, price positioning, promotion strategy, and distribution strategy.

The marketing action plan specifies the plan of action, its timing, and the responsibility for its estimated cost. The action plans will have a supporting budget that will have an estimate of the number of units that would be sold and the net realized price on the revenue side. On the expense side it will show cost of production, physical distribution, and cost of marketing. Marketing controls are a mechanism to review whether or not the actions proceed as envisaged.

KEYWORDS

Marketing action plan   It specifies the plan of action, its timing, those who will be responsible for implementing it, and the estimated cost.

Marketing control   It is the mechanism to review whether or not the actions are proceeding as envisaged.

Marketing objectives and goals   Goals are objectives quantified which are arrived at after SWOT analysis.

Marketing strategy   It includes segmenting, targeting, and positioning strategy.

Situation analysis   It includes a description of the current situation.

SWOT analysis   It analyses the main issues in terms of strengths, weaknesses, opportunities, and threats facing the business and main assumptions about the future.

EXERCISES

Concept Review Questions

1. How is situation analysis carried out? Explain.
2. SWOT analysis evaluates opportunities and threats in the environment against the backdrop of strengths and weaknesses of the company. Discuss.
3. How is marketing strategy crafted? Elaborate.
4. What are the elements of a marketing action plan? Explain.

Critical Thinking Question

If we take Igor Ansoff's perspective about business strategy, which he delineates through product/ market grid, the marketing strategy and business strategy appear to be one and the same thing. Do you agree with this position? Give reasons.

Project Assignment

Bio-diesel presents an attractive opportunity for an economically growing and developing country like India. Formulate a strategic marketing plan to promote bio-diesel in a big city such as Bengaluru, targeting a substantial share of the automobile fuel market in the first year itself.

REFERENCES

Kotler, Philip (1999), *Marketing Management: The Millennium Edition*, Prentice Hall of India, New Delhi.

McCarthy, Jerome E. (1996), *Basic Marketing—A Managerial Approach*, 12th edn, Irwin, Homewood, Illinois.

Porter, Michael E. (1980), *Competitive Strategy: Techniques for Analyzing Industries and Competitors*, Free Press, New York.

32

Designing Marketing Mix

Learning Objectives

After studying this chapter, you will be able to:
- Understand the purpose of designing marketing mix
- Understand the different elements of a marketing mix
- Explore marketing strategies
- Examine the concept of the product life cycle
- Appreciate the relevance of pricing, distribution, and promotion strategies

INTRODUCTION

Marketing has long suffered from a tarnished image because of dubious selling practices adopted by sellers. Good marketing results in a loyal and satisfied set of customers. An organization cannot survive for long if it does not realize the full value of a customer's lifetime purchase. The range of activities that marketing encompasses is referred to as a 'marketing mix' (Borden 1964). They should be combined well to ensure the maximum impact. Companies should determine the cost-effectiveness of different marketing mix tools and should formulate the most profit-maximizing marketing mix.

MARKETING MIX

Professor Jerome McCarthy (1996) in early 1960s proposed a marketing mix consisting of four Ps—product, price, place, and promotion. The four As from the customer point of view include acceptability (in terms of customer value), affordable price (in terms of cost to the customer), available and accessible (in terms of convenience) products and services, and awareness about the product among the customer (in terms of communication of benefits, etc.). They may be construed also as the four Cs, that is, customer value, cost, convenience, and communication. The four P framework, displayed in Fig. 32.1, is a convenient marketing mix.

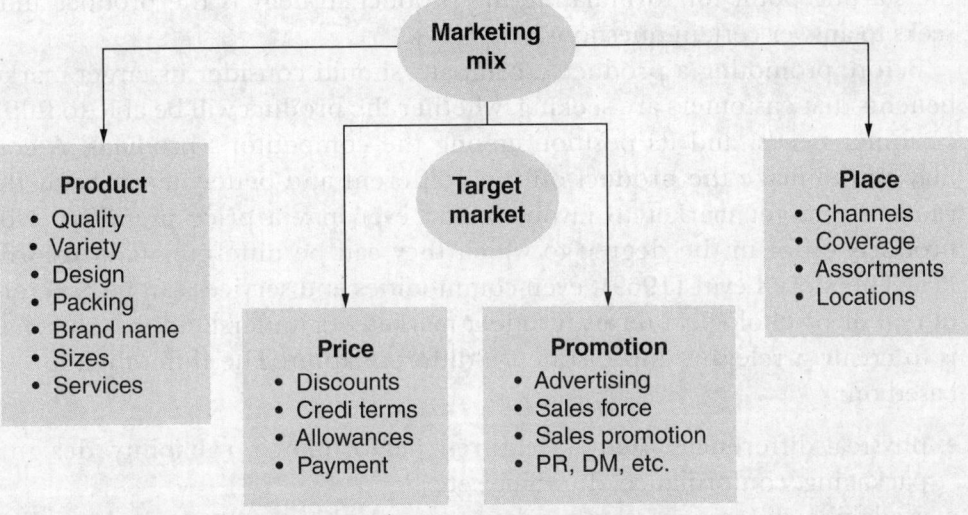

FIGURE 32.1 Marketing mix

Products and Services

The basis of any business is a product or service. However, the customer's perception of a good or a service is complex. The product may be perceived through the layers of tangibles (features, benefits, or packaging) or intangibles (emotional involvement, brand image, or advertisement aesthetics). The product–service hybrid may also be conceptualized as the core product. The tangible product indicates design, colour, styling, packaging, etc. or any other physical dimension that provides benefits to the customers. The intangibles comprise provisions of warranty, service, company image, and psychological benefits conveyed by the product. For existing products

Product strategy

- QC 3 headphones from BOSE provide high sound quality as a core benefit. The product has been augmented further in terms of benefits such as noise reduction and comfortable fit. The tangible part of the product is its form (that of a smaller 'on-ear' alternative rather than an 'around-ear' headphone) as well as its fold-flat design for easy storage.
- HP Color LaserJet multi-function printers provide a core benefit of colour printing, copying, scanning, and faxing in one printer

and, thus, boosting the performance of the business. The tangible benefit of the product is in terms of saving on office space and money. Further augmentation is carried over by including a one-year onsite warranty, a built-in Ethernet, expandable RAM, etc.
- EverYuth Daily SunBlock Lotion from Cadilla provides a core benefit of adequate sun protection with tangible attributes of being sweat-resistant and non-greasy. The product is further augmented with an attribute of having been scientifically tested.

the starting point for formulating the product strategy is the product audit that seeks to answer certain questions.

Before promoting a product, a company should consider its target market, the benefits that customers are seeking, whether the product will be able to fulfil these customer needs, and its position among the competitor's products. A company may aim to make the product offering different and better in some way that will cause the target market to favour it and even pay a price premium. However, products differ in the degree to which they can be differentiated. According to Prof Theodore Levitt (1969), even commodities and services can be differentiated in real or psychological terms. Product marketeers understand that the challenge is to create a relevant and distinctive differentiation. The differentiation may be based on:

- physical differences, that is, features, performance, reliability, design, style, packaging, conformance, durability, etc.;
- availability differences whether they are available from stores or through phone, mail, fax, Internet, etc.; or
- services differences in terms of delivery, installation, training, consulting, maintenance, repair, etc.

The product may be differentiated according to the differences in image; real and perceived. This includes symbols, endorsers, atmosphere, events, and media.

Product differentiation

- Brand Maggi noodles is differentiated from other brands of noodles with a tangible differentiation—it is very convenient to cook in (2 minutes) and is accompanied by different 'taste makers' available for vegetarians and non-vegetarians.
- Ferns 'N' Petals delivers a wide range of flowers (including designer bouquets) all over India with speed and exceptional quality. It is differentiated by its speed of delivery, quality, and convenience.
- Raymond, which has India's largest and exclusive chain of showrooms for men's apparel can be differentiated because of its range of over 5,000 designs and 20,000 patterns in its Expressions Collections. Besides this differentiation on the variety

available the chain has sought to create an image of 'The Complete Man'.
- Oriflame, the Swedish direct selling cosmetics company, differentiates its products on attributes such as its products are not tested on animals but on human volunteers; that it uses ozone friendly aerosols; it packages its products in recyclable material that is safe for environment; that its natural based products are guaranteed to be pure and of high quality, manufactured in a modern equipped factory under strict quality and environmentally controlled conditions. Again the differentiation is achieved through unique channel of distribution (sold only through Oriflame consultants and not in shops) as well on the aforementioned attributes.

Services

- Hotel Taj West End, Bengaluru claims minimal time for check-in, baggage delivery, room service, etc. along with an access to 24-hour business centre with computer facilities so that business professionals, its target segment, find this service attractive and convenient.
- Delhi Public School (DPS), a quality brand in school education has differentiated itself through its process of admission, good infrastructure, and a unique way of developing well-rounded, confident, and articulate students. However, the greatest differentiator of all is the quality and commitment of its teachers and their activity-based teaching style.
- Shoppers' Stop ads have the punch line 'feel the experience while you shop' that seeks to differentiates itself as a centre for relaxed shopping (lingering over accessories, while listening to the music). The store chain is also differentiated on exclusive ambience which it claims is of international standards.

In the services industry, companies try to differentiate their offering on the basis of efficiency of service, varied facilities, speedy service, quality, and cooperation of its employees.

Most of the lifestyle products such as branded jewellery, expensive cars, and premium watches are differentiated on the bases of brand image and personality. The individuals sporting these brands are considered to have qualities that set them apart from the rest. Brands such as Tanishq, Nakshatra, Asmi, and Tag Heuer differentiate themselves through their brand image and the glamour they exude. They promote themselves by appointing movie stars as their brand ambassadors.

While marketing a product, two effective differentiators are its features and design. Although a competitor may be able to copy the design eventually, the original will enjoy at least a short-term lead. The innovator has a choice of lowering the price to protect the market share and accept lower profits, or maintain the price and lose some market share and profits. The company may alternatively find a new basis to differentiate the product and maintain the current price. Out of

GoodKnight

GoodKnight, a product originally from Tran-selectra and since acquired by Godrej, was conceived as a mosquito repellent mat with the Japanese firm Sumitomo supplying the know-how as well as allathrin, the main chemical. The next innovation was a heater and a pack of mats which was followed by a low priced cord-less version. The company then introduced a sophisticated liquid vapourizing plug-in model called GoodKnight Liquidator and followed it with GoodKnight Turbo-timer, a still more sophisticated product which switches off automatically. Its market leadership is maintained largely due to its constant innovation of the product while adding value to the offering by keeping the customer's need in focus.

all the above choices, the last one offers the best hope of maximizing its long-run profitability. The firms cannot just rest at that. They have to constantly search for the next advantage in the hope of finding one utopian 'long-lasting, sustainable advantage' in a hyper-competitive global marketplace. One example is that of GoodKnight.

Marketing strategies

The four basic product strategies are often presented in the form of the Ansoff matrix (Table 32.1).

TABLE 32.1   The Ansoff matrix

Market \ Product	Present	New
Present	Market penetration	Product development
New	Market development	Diversification

Source: Based on Kotler (1999).

The matrix indicates that a firm can follow four main strategies to promote its business.

Market penetration   It can seek to achieve a greater penetration of its existing market by lowering prices, increased usage, and product differentiation.

Market development   It can aim to develop new markets for its existing products by getting new customers, and expanding its national and international markets.

Product development   The firm can develop new products for its existing markets, exploiting the firm's marketing and innovative capabilities.

Diversification   The firm can aim to diversify away from its existing activity by developing new products for new markets.

Peter Drucker (1974) has, similarly, identified three kinds of marketing opportunities—additive, breakthrough, and complementary.

Additive   The additive opportunity exploits almost all the already existing resources and does not change the character of the business. In Ansoff's matrix, it corresponds to a new product in an existing market (product development) or the existing product in a new market (market development).

Breakthrough   This typically changes the fundamental economic characteristics and capacity of the business. It is the high risk extreme of *diversification*, which Ansoff warns against.

Complementary   The complementary opportunity will change the structure of the business. It offers something new, totally larger than its parts. It has also been called a convergent diversification because it utilizes at least some of the skills and knowledge of the organization in contrast to conglomerate diversification that moves into completely new areas. New types of opportunities, in the form of collaborations and alliances have developed between firms to gain a global edge.

Product life cycle

According to the theory of the product life cycle, the marketing mix of a product should reflect all the stages of introduction, growth, maturity, and decline that a product goes through. Even though much attention is focused on new product launches, most products are in their maturity stage, a phase when their promotion needs to be carefully managed, in order to either prolong their life cycle or lead to a graceful retirement. The development of a product mix needs to consider both the width and the depth of product lines and may require line stretching or line rationalization. In doing so, the firm must carefully consider the implications of such product policies on sales, profits, and relationships with customers and suppliers. A product is the most visible component and serves as the focal point for all marketing mix aspects.

Pricing

Setting a price for any product or service is a very important aspect of marketing mix. It singularly produces revenue while all other elements create costs. Firms try to differentiate their products from the competition so that they may command higher prices in the market. However, they have to consider the price elasticity of demand for their product, for the volumes are important for maximization of profits. Companies try to estimate the impact of a higher price on their profits. According to Marn and Rosiello (1992), an estimate of the impact of one per cent price increase on the profits of some multinational companies, for example, will lead to an increase in profit of twenty eight per cent for Philips, seventeen per cent for Nestlé, and six per cent for Coca-Cola respectively. This illustrates the importance of accurately determining this element of the marketing mix.

Companies may practice either value-based pricing strategy or cost-based pricing strategy. In value-based pricing the companies estimate the most that the buyer would pay for the offering. They then charge slightly less than that to leave a consumer

Maruti Udyog Limited

Maruti Udyog Limited sold its 976cc hatchback in early eighties by differentiating the product on the basis of fuel efficiency, affordability, and safety. It promoted itself in metros, mini-metros, and class-I towns. It then pursued a market development strategy by entering class-II and class-III towns. Simultaneously, it added new range of cars in its stable (Gypsy, Omni, Maruti 1000, Zen, Alto, Esteem, Wagon-R, Bolero, etc.) following a product development strategy, to target different market segments. Later on, it pursued a diversification strategy by getting into auto-financing and second-hand cars market businesses.

ITC

Launched by ITC in 1912, Scissors brand of cigarettes at its inception was not just another brand of cigarettes but was promoted as a generic product to wean away potential customers from traditional smoking habits such as *chillum, beedi, hookah*, etc. Promotion and distribution were the initial pillars of the marketing strategy, which along with a low-price left low margins in this initial stage. During the next three decades the brand grew rapidly and ITC started making decent profits as the promotional and distributional expenses as a proportion of sales decreased. Panama brand of cigarettes was launched by National Tobacco Company in the early 1940s and directly positioned against Scissors by pricing it lower than the latter. Panama, because of its contemporary packaging, promotion, and aggressive advertising differentiated itself and grew rapidly at the cost of Scissors. At one stage, market share of Scissors reached a dismal 6.5 per cent in 1961–62 and it was felt that the brand was now beyond redemption. The company then decided to reposition the brand and changed the packaging, improved the blend and quality, and created a distinctive image for the brand aiming at young and active consumers. Scissors once again overtook its main competition. This would be just one of the revival stories of the brand in its product life cycle of almost a century. It would go into its second decline in 1974 and would require a second revival.

with some surplus. The seller, in order to generate profits has to keep costs less than the value price. Many companies add a 'mark-up' to their estimated costs, which is known as cost-based pricing. It assumes that the companies can estimate their costs with some degree of accuracy and then add a factor, which will cover the uncertainties and leave the desired profit.

There is a difference between the list price and the realized price. A buyer may receive a discount, a rebate, a gift, or a free service as a result of customer incentives. Companies may not realize that these practices may result in unprofitability unless they have an accounting system such as activity-based costing in place. Smart marketeers will often bundle their product with additional benefits and then price the total offering at different price differentials for customers to have an opportunity to make a choice. Some companies will create a range of products or a product line at different prices to create a safety net for migrating customers who may be otherwise attracted to competitors' lower priced offerings. Companies will also try to motivate customers to buy the whole range of products by pricing it less than the sum of separate prices.

Pricing new products offers a different set of challenges. In general, two main opposing strategies may be observed—skimming, that is, keeping the price high to skim-off the short-term profit and penetration, that is, keeping the price high to maximize long-term market share. Prices may also be set at levels that are perceived to be psychologically appropriate. For example, ₹299.95 may be perceived as substantially lower than ₹300.00.

In the industrial goods market, prices are often negotiated or offered as per different options. Prices are also used as an indicator of quality or for elevating the status of the product. Organizations may resort to price competition for several reasons but such a price war has its own drawbacks, as it can give the company a bad image and only a temporary advantage, thus leading to losses.

Distribution

Broadly speaking, there are two choices available to companies to make their goods available to the target segment. One, is to sell goods directly and the other, to sell through intermediaries. Before a product reaches the end consumer, it must frequently go through a chain of intermediaries, each one passing the product down to the next organization. This process is known as the distribution chain or channel. Distribution channels include retailers, wholesalers, and agents, or direct distribution through a sales force or mail order. Distribution channels have a number of levels ranging from zero, where the contact between the manufacturer and the end user is direct without any role for any intermediaries to many levels in elaborate distribution systems. In the recent years, rapid changes in technology have influenced distribution channels.

Technology has led to innovations in the field of distribution, thus, increasing the competition between the different channels of distribution, as well as between partners within a distribution channel. A fast-paced lifestyle, with little time for shopping, has led to a trend in home shopping. Stores that charge higher prices, but provide poor service and dull environment will lose the battle to creative retailers who are enhancing the shopping experience by adding fun, entertainment, and games to attract customers. Channel members would need to add value to the distribution process or else be eliminated. Today's customers have an option to order many products through a number of channels such as catalogues, direct mail, home shopping programmes on TV, offers on newspapers and radio, telemarketing calls to the home, and web-based orders.

Promotion

Marketing mix also concerns the communication tools that can deliver the message to the target audience. The tools can be classified under five broad categories as explained in this section.

Direct distribution

When Avon, a cosmetics company, could not persuade retailers to give it shelf space, it resorted to *direct distribution*. It built its own sales force of more than a million 'Avon ladies', who sold Avon products door-to-door. Subsequently, many companies adopted its distribution model adding other features as party selling (Tupperware) and *multilevel marketing* (Amway). Similarly, while most personal computer manufacturers such as Hewlett-Packard, Compaq, and Lenevo sell their PCs through retailers, who give them national distribution coverage at a lower cost, Dell Computers chose to distribute through telephone or through Internet, thus increasing its margins as well as offering greater customization.

Advertising   The seller may promote the product through print and broadcast ads, packaging inserts, brochures, posters, leaflets, directories, billboards, display signs, point-of-purchase displays, audio-visual material, symbols and logos, videotapes, motion pictures, etc. Advertising is the most potent tool for building brand awareness, comprehension, changing attitudes towards a brand, and building brand image. Advertising is most effective when it is narrowly targeted. It involves making decisions on the five Ms—mission, message, media, money, and measurement. The first task is to decide upon the objectives or mission of a particular ad campaign. Is it to inform, persuade, or remind target customers? The content is shaped by the characteristics of the brand's intended target market and the value proposition. The challenge is to creatively present the value proposition by employing a power idea and professional execution. The message decision interacts with the media decision. For example, if the product features are to be communicated to the target audience through comparative advertising then the print media is a better choice due to its imperishability. If the message has the objective of changing or creating brand image of a particular type, then television is a better media choice because of its unlimited possibilities of incorporating sound, movement, contrast, colour, etc. in advertising communication. Various media such as, newspapers, magazines, radio, TV, billboards, direct mail, or telephone are considered depending upon their characteristics, advantages and disadvantages, and harmony with the advertising strategy. The advertising budget is decided on criteria such as competitive parity, affordability, objectives, and task basis. Decisions about a particular media vehicle is then taken on factors such as audience profile, reach, impact, cost per millennium, and editorial quality. Finally, the company may measure some variables such as ad recall, brand comprehension, brand preference, and attitude towards the brand to determine the effectiveness of their advertising expenditures.

Sales promotion   Advertising tries to influence the customer's mind while sales promotion tries to influence customer behaviour. When a customer is motivated to purchase an item for a gift, a prize, or an offer of two for the price of one, it generates sales in the short run. However, these strategies may not work in the long run. They may not augur well, especially for the brand's equity or customer loyalty if the sales promotion offers are withdrawn. In contrast, a good percentage is spent on trade promotion as incentives to the channel partners to push the product. Sales promotion is warranted when the company has a superior brand but low visibility. Then sales promotion will help the customer base to grow. However, most sales promotion brings in switchers and deal-prone customers. Companies have to trade-off advertising budget expenditure (pull strategy) with sales promotion expenditure (push strategy).

Public relations   Philip Kotler (1999) devised an acronym PENCILS for the seven tools of public relations (PR).

Publications   It includes company magazines, annual reports, helpful customer brochures, etc.

Events   The company can gain visibility by sponsoring sports or art or trade shows, etc.

News   A business can promote itself by publishing favourable stories about the company, its people, products, and practices in newspapers and magazines. For example, Reliance India Ltd has obtained positive media coverage about its ventures.

Community involvement activities   It refers to contributing time and money to local community needs, etc.

Identity media   It includes stationery, business cards, corporate dress codes, etc.

Lobbying activity   It involves efforts to influence favourable or dissuade unfavourable legislation and rulings.

Social responsibility activities   It involves building a good reputation for corporate social responsibility, etc.

Investing in PR helps in building and promoting a positive image of the company to the target market and the various stakeholders of the business. Unlike advertising in which the sponsor is identified, a PR effort has high source credibility, as it is not perceived to be self-serving. In certain industries, particularly high-tech, the opinion of influential leaders carry more weight than high blitz advertising.

Sales force   It is a communication tool that is more effective than a series of ads or direct mail. These set of individuals strive to make direct contact with the customers, not only convincing them to buy the product but also assuring them about its quality. The human element in this promotional element makes all the difference when there is little differentiation between products or when the product or service is more complex in nature. As the sales force and buyers become more comfortable with electronic commerce, sales travel costs will go down. The customer saves time, and the selling company saves considerable time and money by turning its sales force into competent telemarketeers.

When one considers that the average sales person is with customers only 30 per cent of the time and spends the remainder learning about the products and selling techniques, filling out reports, attending sales meetings, traveling, and so on, it becomes clear that this resource should be managed carefully. Another approach would be to sell through the distributors. Distributors have their own sales force and normally represent several non-competing suppliers. However, as the company's business grows, it becomes increasingly dissatisfied with the distributor's sales coverage, effort, or cost, and hires its own set of sales personnel. Managing the sales force involves complex issues in recruiting, selecting, hiring, training, motivating, compensating, and evaluating sales people. Companies are increasingly organizing their sales teams by vertical markets because in this way the sales personnel learn more about customer needs within an industry and are in a better position to make useful suggestions. Some companies are setting up key account management systems on the premise that a few customers account for a large share of their sales and profits.

Eureka Forbes

Eureka Forbes is a pioneer in direct-to-customer selling and uses a strong sales force of 5,000. The company with 25 years of experience of bringing state-of-the-art products for Indian consumers has a customer base of over 50 lakh customers across the country. They were the first to innovate and make the Indian homes realize the need for vacuum cleaners. Next in line was Aquaguard for purifying domestic water to make it potable—a pioneering innovation for the Indian market. Anticipating the needs of Indian homes, Eureka Forbes has been in the forefront of innovation bringing vacuum cleaners, water purifiers, and air purifiers to India much ahead of their time. Today, Euroclean, their vacuum cleaner, and Aquaguard water purifier are leaders in their categories. Both the brands have been bestowed with innumerable awards and honours such as the prestigious Superbrand award and the *Mera* Brand award. Consumers have chosen the brand as the most preferred of brands in its category, making Eureka Forbes one of the largest direct sales organizations in Asia. It has also attained national and international recognition. It has been the subject of a case study by the prestigious Harvard Business School. The company has proved the increasing relevance of direct marketing in today's competitive marketplace. Eureka Forbes is an iconic brand trusted by its customers.

Direct marketing   Fragmentation of media and exponential increase in the number of media vehicle options with a specific audience profile has made it possible to deliver ads and editorial material to a specific customer group. Marketing, based on available sources of customer data, can be used to detect various customer groupings or clusters which will respond in a similar way to unique marketing stimuli. In database marketing, a data warehouse comprising a huge customer database is operated upon by data mining tools, which are advanced statistical and mathematical tools, to yield market targets that have a high response rate. The companies collect and scan their database regularly to unearth marketing opportunities and then communicate with the prospective customers through direct marketing.

Companies now realize that an integrated marketing communications approach calls for recognizing all contact points where the customer may encounter the company, its products, and its brands and then strive to deliver a consistent and positive message at all these contact points. All the promotional tools, thus, need to be integrated to communicate a clear value proposition in the most effective manner.

SUMMARY

Professor Jerome McCarthy in early 1960s proposed a marketing mix consisting of four Ps, that is, product, price, place, and promotion. From the customer's point of view, the product should be acceptable (in terms of customer value), the price affordable (in terms of cost to the customer), the products and services should be available and accessible (in terms of convenience), and the customers should be aware of the offering (in terms of communication of benefits, etc.).

A product or service may be perceived through the layers of tangibles (features, benefits, or packaging) or intangibles (emotional involvement, brand image, or advertisement aesthetics). The product may be differentiated according to the differences in image—real and perceived. Before promoting a product, a company should consider the target market, the benefits that customers are seeking, whether the product will be able to fulfil customer needs, and its position among the competitor's products. According to the theory of the product life cycle, the marketing mix of a product should reflect all the stages of introduction, growth, maturity, and decline that a product goes through.

The Ansoff matrix indicates that the firm can follow four main strategies to promote its business. They are market penetration, market development, product development, and diversification. Drucker (1974) has identified three marketing opportunities—additive, breakthrough, and complementary. Companies may practice either value-based pricing or cost-based pricing. Setting the price of a product or service is a very important aspect of marketing mix. There are two kinds of prices—list price and realized price. Two main opposing pricing strategies may be observed—(1) skimming strategy is used to keep the price high to skim-off the short-term profit; and (2) penetration strategy maintains a high price to maximize long-term market share. Prices may also be set at levels that are perceived to be psychologically appropriate.

Companies may sell their products to their customers either directly or through intermediaries. Before a product reaches the end consumer, it must frequently go through a chain of intermediaries, each one passing the product down to the next organization. This process is known as the distribution chain or channel. New technology has radically altered distribution. E-commerce and home shopping (through television) are fast gaining popularity. The five tools that can communicate the benefits and contents of the product to the target audience are advertising, sales promotion, publicity, sales force, and direct marketing. Public relations can build a positive image of the company to the target market and the various stakeholders of the business.

KEYWORDS

Advertising   A means by which marketeers communicate with potential buyers persuading them to buy their brands in preference to the rival's brands.

Ansoff grid   Categorization of business growth strategy options using product–market dimensions.

Cost-based pricing   Pricing method that adds a standard mark-up to a product's cost.

Data-based marketing   A data warehouse comprising a huge customer database is operated upon by data mining tools, which are advanced statistical and mathematical tools, to yield market targets that have a high response rate.

Direct marketing   A form of marketing in which a marketeer dispenses with distribution intermediaries and directly contacts customers.

Distribution strategy   The selection of appropriate distribution channels through which the firm's products will reach its selected markets.

Marketing mix   The range of measures by firms to market their products in terms of product offering, pricing, promotions, and place of distribution.

Product differentiation   The means by which marketers attempt to distinguish their products from those offered by competitors.

Product life cycle   The sales pattern of a product over time characterized by four stages—introduction, growth, maturity, and decline.

Publicity   A general means of promoting the company's image.

Sales force   The sales people employed by a firm to sell its products or services.

Sales promotion   The measures used by firms to increase the sale of their brand by using promotional offers.

Value-based pricing   Pricing method which seeks to set the price on customer's perceived value of the product.

EXERCISES

Concept Review Questions

1. Compare market penetration with market development strategy.
2. How is the product life cycle concept helpful in revitalizing a declining brand?
3. Differentiate the approach used in cost-based pricing with respect to the approach used in value-based pricing.

Critical Thinking Questions

1. Compare advertising with public relations by explaining the strengths and weaknesses of each.

2. What does it take to be a successful direct marketeer? Give examples to support your arguments.

Project Assignment

1. Develop a marketing mix plan for a small eating joint in your college campus. Also, reflect on how it would change as your eatery gains in popularity.

REFERENCES

Borden, N.H. (1964), 'The Concept of the Marketing Mix', *Journal of Advertising Research*, vol. 24, no. 4, pp. 7–12.

Drucker, Peter F. (1974), *Management: Tasks, Responsibilities, Practices*, William Heinemann Ltd, London.

Kotler, Philip (1999), *Marketing Management: The Millennium Edition*, Prentice Hall of India, New Delhi.

Levitt, Theodore (1969), *The Marketing Mode*, McGraw-Hill, New York.

Marn, Michael V. and Robert L. Rosiello, 'Managing Price, Gaining Profit', *Harvard Business Review*, Sept–Oct.

McCarthy, E. Jerome (1996), *Basic Marketing—A Managerial Approach*, 12th edn, Irwin Homewood, Illinois.

33

Customer Relationship Management

INTRODUCTION

Customer refers to partners, agents, third parties, employees, and other stakeholders who fulfil their needs through an organization. Put simply, a customer is any individual who has a relationship with the company from time to time. In earlier times individuals chose to associate themselves with a particular brand or organization because of the personal relationship they formed with its managers (e.g., opening an account in the local bank, because the manager is a distant relative) or because only certain companies produced certain branded products deemed as trustworthy. However, the markets today have changed radically due to changing business trends, technological convergence, commoditization, deregulation, globalization, and growth of the Internet. Competition has increased, and today the existence of multiple brands has made it almost impossible to show competitive differentiation, and even harder to earn profit.

In today's globalized world, a typical organization has thousands of local, regional, national, and global competitors. Consumers now play an active role in creating value not only because of their rising awareness about products and lifestyles, but also because of their increasing levels of disposable income. Organizations have to adopt the motto 'customer is king' to stay ahead in the competition. Today's consumer, unlike before, is willing to take risks and experiment with new products and brands. In today's business scenario a competitive enterprise has to profile its customers, understand their needs, build cordial relationships, and communicate intelligently with them to

Learning Objectives

After studying this chapter, you will be able to:
- Understand the concepts of customer relationship management (CRM)
- Examine how CRM affects businesses
- Understand how CRM is implemented
- Appreciate classification, data warehousing, and data mining
- Learn various steps for personalizing the CRM function

stay ahead of the competition. Customer relationship management (CRM) plays an important role in the success of any enterprise.

Customer relationship management is neither a product nor a service, but a business strategy to learn more about customers' behaviour and requirements in order to create long-term relationships with them. In other words, CRM is a comprehensive approach that provides seamless integration of every aspect of a firm's business that comes in contact with the customer at various stages such as marketing, service delivery, and after-sales-service.

CRM AND THE ORGANIZATION

Studying the profiles of customers, keeping their preferences in mind, and taking care of their needs has its advantages. Sometimes companies can experiment with their own products to improve them, while offering the customer a new product for a lesser price or for free. For example, Microsoft tests beta versions of its Windows software through thousands of its customers, thus, avoiding some of the usual mistakes that software companies make. Prahalad and Ramaswamy (2002) suggest co-creating personalized experiences for the customer. He talks about the increasing realization that the product is subordinate to the consumer experience and advocates that the new frontier for managers is to create the future by harnessing competence in an enhanced network that includes customers. It is prudent to thus adopt a comprehensive view of the customer as part of a continuum, not just a sale, and to manage the life cycle of the relationship, not just a series of transactions.

Customer relationship management is a strategic concept, which focuses on competencies, processes, and technologies required to effectively service customers. It not only helps in retaining existing customers but also in attracting new customers. Many companies have become adept at the art of CRM. They have collected data on preferences, attributes, and behaviour of their customers for further segmenting them and for directing their marketing effort at them to evoke the necessary responses. However, seldom do these companies as per Seybold (2001), bother to look at customer scenario, that is, the broad context in which customers select, buy, and use products and services. According to her, thinking in terms of customer scenarios has always been useful, but the arrival of Internet makes the technique more powerful than ever.

Tesco, a UK-based supermarket chain, rejected one of the basic tenets that online grocers adhered to as an appropriate strategy, that is, consolidating inventory and conducting operations from a central warehouse. Instead, the company launched Tesco-direct, its on-line sales channel based on its insight about a typical grocery shopper's customer scenario, which was supported through a combination of stores and direct Internet sales. The venture became the world's most profitable Internet grocery store because it was based on customer feedback. The consumer insight was that they liked to examine and touch the fresh produce and enjoyed exploring store shelves for new products, etc. Tesco thus set out to tightly integrate its offline and online offerings so that customers could have the best of both worlds. There is no substitute to companies putting themselves in their customers' shoes.

Implementing CRM

Customer relationship management is a comprehensive strategy that integrates people, process, and technology, and works on the process of acquiring, retaining, and partnering with select customers to create superior value for the company and its customers. Organizations usually spend billions of dollars on CRM, which ultimately pays off by:

- restoring the personalized services atmosphere;
- fostering greater long-term loyalty through relationship building;
- maximizing lifetime value of each customer through cross-selling;
- enabling immediate action to retain the most valuable customers;
- identifying high-risk customers and adjusting the service accordingly;
- fulfilling customer needs at the right time with the right offer; and
- increasing the rate of return on marketing initiatives.

A company's success in the field of CRM fully depends on its ability to achieve customer intimacy, which can be built through relevant, uninterrupted, and personalized communication. Its objective is not only to attract new clients/customers or retain valuable ones, but also to boost the profitability of every individual client/customer and, hence, the company as a whole. In other words, the major goal of CRM is to build a single, integrated, organizational image of the customer, enabling the company to maximize the customer's experience.

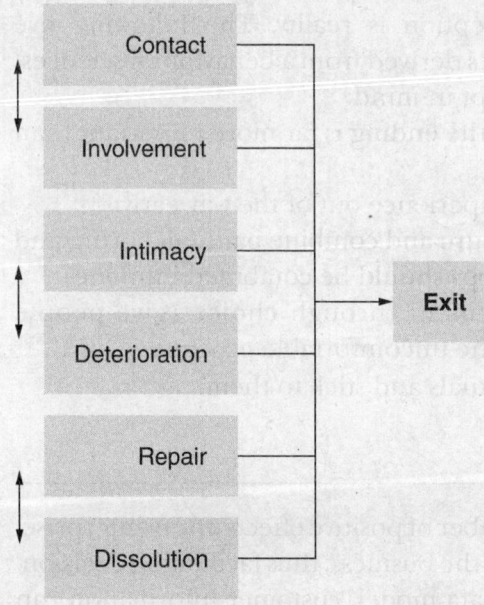

FIGURE 33.1   Stage model of relationship

Customer relationships are not built overnight. They pass through different stages namely contact, involvement, intimacy, deterioration, repair, and dissolution (Fig. 33.1). A relationship can terminate at any of these stages. It is, therefore, essential to understand the stage at which it could sell services efficiently. Cross-selling or up-selling can be attempted at certain stages to get better results. Recent research indicates that some of the behavioural traits, such as adaptation, trust, commitment, communication, cooperation, conflict resolution, interdependence, past satisfaction, and power equation pave the way to build relations and to sustain them over a long period.

Some essential factors that aid the building of a strong bonds between the customer and the organization are—(1) adaptation, the companies need to tailor their resources to meet the specific needs of the individual customer; (2) alignment of a firm's resources with the customer's needs is directly proportional to the quantum of trust injected into the relationship, both by the firm as well as its customer; (3) commitment, a firm has to be committed towards the customer for nurturing a fruitful relationship; and (4) continuity of a relationship, which is the process of communication and interaction extending into cooperation.

The three other dimensions of a customer–organization relationship are continuance, normative components, and effective components. During this phase, disagreements that creep into the business transaction are resolved. In the final analysis, it is the power equation—the ability of one party to evoke a change in other partner that greatly influences the continuity of any relationship.

Berry (2001) did extensive research on dozens of retailers and found that it is not the techniques of emailing customers, hidden cameras to observe customer behaviour, or analysis of scanner data to tailor special offers and manage inventory that can offer lasting solutions in this era of fickle customers and price-cutting customers. He has suggested creating value for customers in five interlocking ways (Fig. 33.2). According to him, today's shoppers want the total customer experience—superior solutions to their needs, respect, an emotional connection, fair prices, and convenience. The seller has to offer all these components together for the venture to be successful.

Today, behavioural science offers new insights into better service management, thus enhancing customer experience in a service encounter. According to Chase and Dasu (2001), in any service encounter, from a simple pizza pickup to a complex, long-term consultancy engagement, perception is reality. The following five operating principles derived from a behavioural sciences' study should be kept in mind:

- finish strong, the ending is far more important than the beginning;
- get the bad experience out of the way early;
- segment pleasure and combine pain (all boring and unpleasant steps should be combined into one);
- build commitment through choice (give people control over the uncomfortable processes); and
- give people rituals and stick to them.

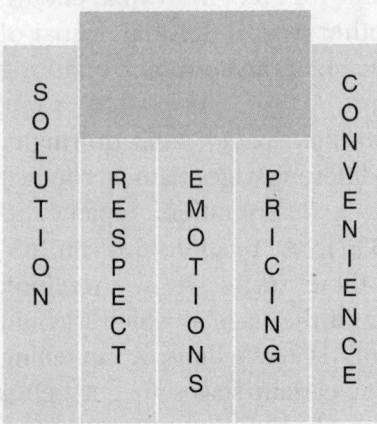

FIGURE 33.2   Five pillars of new retailing

EFFECT OF CRM ON BUSINESS

Customer relationship management has a number of positive effects on an enterprise. It provides management with a clear picture of the business, thus facilitating decision-making. Using a common architecture and data model, customer information can be shared faultlessly between the front-end staff facing the customers to deliver services and the back-office staff who structure the deals. Front-end staff can profile a customer, create, and maintain a customer account with contacts, manage activities, and explore business development possibilities. For example, a call centre can maintain client data/information, produce call notes, reply to customer inquiries, and address and track customer service requests, while the back-office aims to nurture a long-term relationship with the customer. In a nutshell, the implementation of the CRM concept can result in the following advantages:

- speed and accuracy in information analysis;
- foundation for organization-wide data and information;
- understanding customer behaviour;
- facilitating business process re-engineering;
- promoting multiple products;
- creating multiple distribution channels—branch, Internet, call centre, field sales, etc.; and
- creating multiple customer groups—customers, small business, corporation, etc.

Customer Classification

To start with, companies must realize that all customer profiles can differ. Customer profitability varies from person to person and context to context. Not all customers are evenly desirable for the company. Firms must differentiate their customers based on the value criteria or the profit the customer adds to the firm's account. Put simply, a more profitable customer is a 'high value' customer and a less profitable customer is a 'low value' customer.

An organization's CRM system must also capture customers' taste, preference, behaviour, living style, age, education, cultural background, physical and psychological characteristics, sensitivity etc., while differentiating them according to their value criteria. By combining the profitability potential of a given customer and his personality profile, including their expectations, customers can be grouped into four categories:

1. Low value/less profitable customer desiring high-grade service
2. Low value/less profitable customer with potential to become high value in coming days
3. High value/more profitable customer desiring high-grade service
4. High value/more profitable customer requiring low-grade service

Once the firms differentiate their customers vis-à-vis profitability and other traits, it becomes easy for them to customize their services and offerings to maximize the overall value of their customer portfolio.

Retaining a customer

Boosting loyalty can retain a customer. Customer loyalty can be defined as 'making a customer come again and again to the same organization'. Firms must keep their customers serviced and happy so that they keep transacting with them.

CRM and organizations

Royal Bank of Canada was considering to invest in an expensive CRM system but had important issues to discuss with its vendor, Siebel, such as the cost of the system, the time for the system to be functional operationally, the payback period of the investment, and lastly, the long-run return on investment (ROI) that the bank will get from the CRM system.

Today, customers use Internet search engines, comparison engines, expert evaluation engines, and customer evaluation engines to make their decisions. Amazon.com uses customer managed relationships (CMR) instead of CRM to gain intimacy with the customers. Its customers are at the centre of CRM and drive the whole process.

In India, mobile service providers initially paid more attention to customer acquisition than CRM. In the early phases of the market lifecycle operations, mobile operators invested millions of rupees in customer acquisition by giving away mobile phones to increase network subscription. Now the market is beginning to mature and the mobile operators are giving equal attention to CRM systems.

FIGURE 33.3 A customer's journey

A customer's journey from a suspect to an advertiser of word of mouth is illustrated in Fig. 33.3. Customer loyalty can be differentiated into two categories—active loyalty and passive loyalty. Active loyalty refers to repeat purchases and contracts made over a long period of time, while passive loyalty is a term used to describe the retention of customers who have not transacted with the firm for a long time, or those who stick with the firm in the absence of a better alternative. Unfortunately, most of the firms fail to distinguish between active loyalty and passive loyalty. They make the mistake of assuming customer satisfaction is present even in the case of passive loyalty, thus failing to retain their customers.

To boost customer loyalty, firms must have a clear understanding of their customers' unfulfilled needs and must come out with products/services that will satisfy those needs. They have to innovate to meet every need of their loyal customers so that they become their active advertisers. Turning a suspect into an active advertiser will definitely boost referral sales that are known as 'low cost and high margin sales'.

A firm's competitive advantage lies in understanding and meeting the expectations of its customers. Any company that is in the race of implementing CRM technology in its business should follow the steps provided in this section.

Data warehousing

An organization's effort to expand its customer base and retain the existing ones begins by building the data warehouse. An organization's data warehouse is an architectural component that is subject oriented, integrated, non-volatile, and time variant. The data warehouse exists to enhance the firm's ability to make informed decisions.

Data can be of two types—function-oriented and subject-oriented. Subject-oriented data is organized along the lines of the subjects of the firm. Function-oriented data is data that is organized around the functions of the firm. In order to understand the difference between a subject orientation and a functional orientation, one needs to understand the differences between subjects and functions. Each function will have some data that relates to each subject. Mapping the data from each function to each subject area shows that there is a fundamental restructuring and realignment of data that must be done in order to build data warehouse. Data must be read in a functional format and written in a subject-oriented format. Two important steps in data warehousing are—designing the database and data mining.

Designing the database   The first step in this process is to design a comprehensive database. The database acts as a 'memory box' where summary data about the businesses is retained. This includes information about the customers, services/products bought by them, etc.

Data mining   It follows database designing where the firm's strategists analyse the past trends/patterns to forecast the future behaviour/demand from customers for varied services and products and take action accordingly. They analyse the collected data to determine the customer's behaviour according to the product, price, and distribution channel. Firms need not always go for expensive and highly sophisticated data mining systems. The customer information gathered by them in their day-to-day business is often sufficient for effective data mining. Answers to simple questions are enough to form a precise picture of the business.

- What happened to the service offered by the company during a particular period?
- Was the customer's reaction towards that service positive or negative?
- If it is negative, why is it so?
- Are the present economic activities of the customer and the needs thereof fully met with? If not, how to bridge the gap?
- How much of the customers' financial businesses does the firm actually handle?
- How many products does it sell to these customers?
- What is the history of institutional clients' transaction?

A CRM set consists of front-end operations that interact with the customers such as counter staff, call centres, and target marketing initiatives, and gather data about them. This is generally merged from various touch points and directed into the database. A touch point is wherever the customer interacts with the company. The database consolidates not only business transaction data but also data collected from outside sources/agencies. The availability of huge data (both internal and external) helps in creating an environment for better analysis.

The output is interpreted and new information is transferred to a central customer database that would be assessed by all the employees working with different terminals. This enables them to customize responses. Needless to say, data mining provides the intelligence behind the CRM initiative.

PERSONALIZING CRM

Personalization is not only a critical cornerstone of CRM but also one of the most challenging features to accomplish. A company must be able to effectively learn from each customer interaction, record the results of that learning to gain a better understanding of each customer's preferences, and determine how the company can best serve that customer. This understanding will allow the company to communicate the right information to the customer at the right time using the right channel, and will ensure that all of those interactions are complete and consistent. As one would imagine, this repeated analysis and tuning of business processes requires time and money. There is considerable effort involved with capturing each and every customer interaction and then attempting to build customer loyalty through a personalized experience.

Companies that want to enhance customer relationships with personalization are dependent on taking certain actions before moving into the implementation stage. As obvious as some of these actions may seem, many companies still experience problems that keep them from realizing the full benefits of a personalization strategy. Figure 33.4 outlines some pre-implementation actions that impact project success.

The personalization process seeks to answer various questions regarding the data quality, objectives and measures, teams, and personalization model, strategy, scope of the project, and infrastructure design.

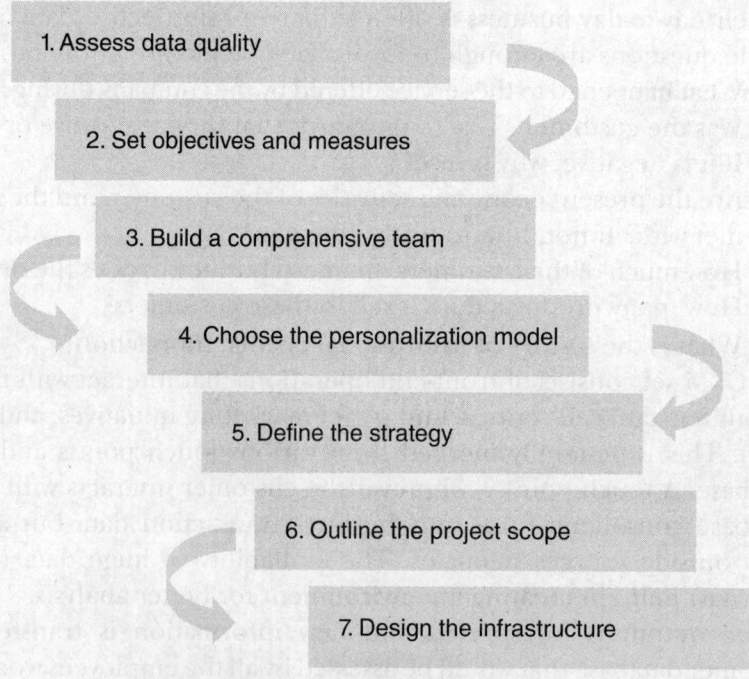

1. Assess data quality

2. Set objectives and measures

3. Build a comprehensive team

4. Choose the personalization model

5. Define the strategy

6. Outline the project scope

7. Design the infrastructure

FIGURE 33.4   The DNA for personalization

1. *Assess data quality*: Is a personalization strategy possible? Without reliable and accessible data, moving forward with personalization will be futile.
2. *Set objectives and measures*: What is the business need or/and the available opportunities? The objectives and measures of success form the foundation for the strategy.
3. *Build a comprehensive team*: Who needs to be involved? The team must include representatives from business, technology, and all groups managing the customers.
4. *Choose the personalization model*: How will offers and content be matched to customer needs? Dynamic personalization based on self-learning analytics is emerging as a favourite over rules-based profiling.
5. *Define the strategy*: How will personalization analysis translate into changed customer behaviour and increased profits? The strategy must be designed to profitably meet customer needs for long-term satisfaction and loyalty.
6. *Outline the project scope*: Where is personalization first implemented and to what level? The goal of a corporate-wide personalization effort may begin on a limited scale for learning, testing, and budget purposes.
7. *Design the infrastructure*: What technology will meet the needs for short-term and long-term personalization strategies? Data flowing into and throughout the organization is essential to establish a single dialogue between the customer and company.

Finally, how do companies succeed in motivating the front-line workers who are often paid low wages, have low hope of being promoted up the hierarchy, and generally care little about the company's performance. The answer as per Katzenbach and Santamaria (1999) is a unique approach to motivation—mission, values, and pride. The authors maintain that minor changes in a company's standard operating procedures can have a powerful effect on front-line motivation and can result in substantial payoffs in a company's performance.

Has relationship marketing delivered on its potential and promise? According to Susan Fournier et al. (1998), a close look suggests that relationships between companies and customers are troubled ones, at best. Companies are caught up in their enthusiasm for information gathering capabilities and the potential opportunities that long-term engagements with customers hold; forgetting the fundamentals of relationship building—trust and intimacy. Loss of control, vulnerability, and stress are the recurrent themes that emerge from consumers' feedback when they talk about products, companies, etc. Customer relationship management can work if it delivers on the principles on which it was founded—technology is not a substitute for gaining consumer's trust and insight, rather it is a great enabler.

SUMMARY

Customer relationship management (CRM) fosters greater long-term loyalty. It maximizes lifetime values of each customer through cross-selling. By aligning the firm's resources with the customer's needs and by injecting trust into the relationship, the firm is able to fulfil the customer's needs at the right time with the right offer. A firm has to necessarily be committed towards the customer for nurturing a fruitful relationship. Customer relationship management is a comprehensive strategy, which through the integration of people, process, and technology, works on the process of acquiring, retaining, and partnering with select customers to create superior value for the company and its customers. In CRM, front-end staff can profile a customer, create and maintain a customer account with contacts, manage activities, and explore business development possibilities, while the back-end staff can work towards maintaining a long-term relationship with the customers.

A company's success in the field of CRM fully depends on its ability to achieve 'customer intimacy'. Understanding and influencing a customer's behaviour through relevant, uninterrupted, and personalized communication can lead to customer intimacy. To start with, companies must realize that all customers are not equal. Customer profitability varies from person to person, context to context and not all customers are evenly desirable for the company. Firms must differentiate their customers based on the value criteria, that is, the potential profit that the customer can bring to the firm's account. A more profitable customer is a high value customer while a less profitable customer is a low value customer. Boosting loyalty can retain a customer. Firms must keep their customers serviced and happy so that they keep transacting with them.

Customer loyalty can be differentiated into two categories—active loyalty and passive loyalty. An organization's effort to expand its customer base and retain the existing ones begins by building the data warehouse. For this purpose, data can be categorized as function-oriented data and subject-oriented data. Subject-oriented data is organized along the lines of the subjects of the firm, while function-oriented data is organized around the functions of the firm. The database acts as a memory box where summary data about the businesses carried out, customers entertained, services/products bought by them etc., are stored. The database consolidates not only business transaction data but also data collected from outside sources/agencies. The two steps involved in data warehousing are—designing the database and data mining. Effective CRM involves personalization. This involves assessing data quality, setting objectives and measures, building a comprehensive team, choosing the personalization model, defining the strategy, outlining the project scope, and designing the infrastructure.

KEYWORDS

Back-office   A company's point of processing of those requests to consumers' satisfaction.

Customer loyalty   It can be defined as making a customer come again and again to the same firm. Firms must retain their customers serviced and happy so that they keep on transacting with them.

Customer relationship management (CRM)   It is the use of competencies, processes, and technologies required to effectively service customers.

Data mining   It follows database designing where firm's strategists analyse the past trends/patterns to forecast the future behaviour/demand from customers for varied services and products and take action accordingly.

Data warehousing technology   An organization's data warehouse is an architectural component that is subject-oriented, integrated, non-volatile, and time variant.

Front-end   A company's interaction point with customers to receive their orders, requests, complaints, etc.

Personalization of relationship with customer   This capability exists when a company is able to communicate the right information to the customer at the right time using the right channel, and will ensure that all of those interactions are complete and consistent.

Touch points   The point of customer interaction with the company in whatever form.

EXERCISES

Concept Review Questions

1. How can CRM help in personalization of relationship with customer?
2. How and in what ways do CRM interventions benefit organizations?
3. What operating principles derived from insights from behavioural sciences should be kept in mind while delivering a service to enhance customer experience?

Critical Thinking Questions

1. An executive from Gartner Group stated that a CRM programme is typically 45 per cent dependent on the right executive leadership, 40 per cent on project management implementation, and 15 per cent on technology. Do you agree with this comment? Give reasons.
2. Does CRM make more sense in data-rich industries such as banking, insurance, and telecommunications and least sense in mass consumer markets selling low-priced goods? Discuss.

Project Assignment

Search for two companies who have successfully incorporated CRM and achieved considerable value addition for their customers and shareholders. Contrast their performance with two other companies who have tried to incorporate CRM but have failed. Try to infer the cause of their failure and elaborate whether these reasons are endemic.

REFERENCES

Berry, Leonard L. (2001), 'The Old Pillars of New Retailing', *Harvard Business Review*, April.

Chase, Richard B. and Sriram Dasu (2001), 'Want to Perfect Your Company's Service? Use Behavioural Science', *Harvard Business Review*, June.

Fournier, Susan, Susan Dobscha, and David Glen Mick (1998), 'Preventing the Premature Death of Relationship Marketing', *Harvard Business Review*, Jan–Feb.

Katzenbach, Jon R. and Jason A. Santamaria (1999), 'Firing up the Front line', *Harvard Business Review*, May–June.

Prahalad, C.K. and Venkatram Ramaswamy (2002), 'Co-opting Customer Connection, *Harvard Business Review*, April.

Seybold, Patricia B. (2001), 'Get Inside the Lives of Your Customers', *Harvard Business Review*, May–June.

34

Advertising Management

Learning Objectives

After studying this chapter, you
will be able to:
• Understand advertising
• Learn about effective advertising
• Examine characteristics of great
  advertising
• Understand the impact of
  advertisements and advertising
  response
• Learn about various types of
  advertisements

INTRODUCTION

No business can progress without taking active steps to
promote itself; this makes advertising essential to business.
Advertising can be used to motivate consumers to buy
goods, change attitudes, encourage retailers to stock the
products, or at certain times to dissuade people from
indulging in certain socially unacceptable behaviours.
Modern advertising industry has its roots in the industrial
revolution. Technological progress improved production
techniques, thus making mass-production possible for
a number of goods and services. Producers had to find
new consumer markets and expand existing ones to
maintain profits and keep a control over prices. They
branded goods and advertised them. Manufacturers
identified the mass media as a vehicle to stimulate the
demand. The promotional efforts of large firms focused
almost exclusively on mass media advertising, increasing
promotional costs, and pricing potential competitors
out of the most concentrated markets. The term
advertising came to be defined as 'paid-for mass media
communication', rather than promotional activity.

According to the American Marketing Association,
advertising is any paid form of non-personal presentation
and promotion of ideas, goods, and services by an
identified sponsor. Advertising is often used to increase
the sale of a product or use of a service. However, this is
not always the most important objective of a firm; it may
conflict with the long-term profit goals. Long-term profits
are a more useful indicator of a firm's objectives than
increasing sales. Achieving a direct sales effect is actually

one of the least effective aspects of advertising. Industry estimates suggest that the immediate response can be as little as 0.01 per cent. Advertisers have generally given up on the claim that advertising has a direct and discernible effect on sales. A stronger reason to advertise is portraying a trustworthy image of the company. Most image advertising is designed not to challenge bad images but to challenge people's perceptions of the company. In social advertising too, the goal is to try and influence people's behaviour and not profit-maximization.

The goal of good advertisement is to ensure that the message that the company intends to convey to the masses, is done in a clear and attractive way. The message should be able to evoke a widespread and positive response in the target market towards the company's goods and/or services.

Consumer behaviour dynamics take place when consumers shift from one company's brands to its rivals' in the same product class and vice versa (Fig. 34.1). Also, consumers may shift from the company's or its competitor's brands to brands which are considered as generic substitutes and not falling in the same product class. On the other hand, the company and its competitors may be getting customers who were earlier buying the brands from the substitute product class. It is in this context of behavioural dynamics that advertising has to perform its job effectively and efficiently.

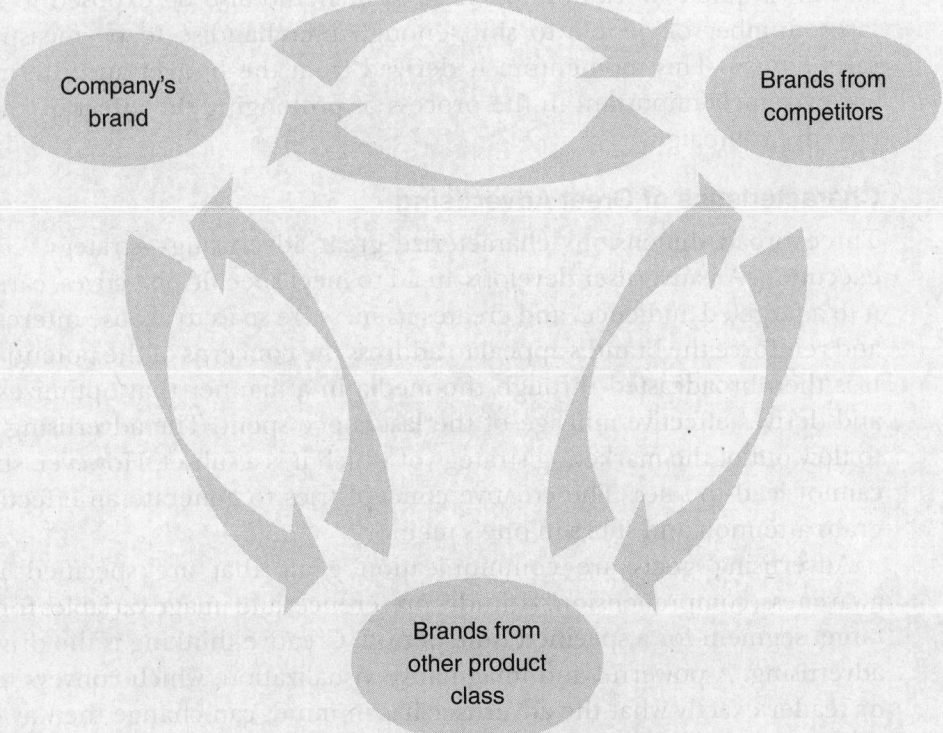

FIGURE 34.1   Consumer behaviour dynamics
Source: Based on Batra, et al. (1996), p. 115.

EFFECTIVE ADVERTISING

Effective advertising is the end product of focused and coordinated work of two parties—the client and the agency. Without the client's contribution, an advertising campaign, no matter how significant or how demonstrable its merits, will have no perceptible effect on sales. As per Jones (1998), the success of new categories of goods and services depends upon four factors—latent demand, discretionary purchasing power among the target group, the presence of strong brands, and heavy advertising and promotional support. However, the last factor alone cannot do the job. In mature markets large-scale evidence shows that increasing the advertising expenditure is not sufficient to influence the market size. Demand in these markets is driven by technological innovations; in others it is driven by changing lifestyles, etc.

All successful brands have some degree of functional superiority over their competitors in at least some respects. Further, the brand's price must be acceptable to the consumers. The third responsibility of the client is to make sure that the brand is available through an efficient distribution network; otherwise, the customer will get very impatient and start looking for it in the stores. Effective advertising by the agency can now play its role by taking care of the—(1) creativity of the campaign; (2) media budget; and (3) media plan.

The advertising stimulus must be effective enough in terms of human psychology and must quietly work in implicit ways. It should also be exposed to a sufficiently large number of people to shift enough merchandise to be measurable in the sales figures. This momentum is derived from the budget and the media. These are extremely important in the process of prolonging the effect of an intrinsically effective campaign.

Characteristics of Great Advertising

Three broad dimensions characterize great advertising—strategy, creativity, and execution. An advertiser develops an ad to meet specific objectives, carefully directs it to a targeted audience, and creates its message so as to arouse interest, persuade, and reinforce the brand's appeal to address the concerns of the potential consumer. It is then broadcasted through the media in a manner that optimizes the budget and derives effective mileage of the last rupee spent. The advertising strategy has to flow out of the marketing strategy of which it is a subset. However, strategy alone cannot lead to sales. The creative concept tries to generate an effective idea that grabs attention and sticks in one's memory.

Advertising goals are communication goals that are specified in terms of awareness, comprehension, attitude, preference, and image variables for a particular target segment for a specified time period. Creative thinking is the driving force of advertising. A powerful and imaginative visualization, which conveys to the viewer or reader exactly what the advertiser has in mind, can change the way the product appeals to the consumer and create a new target audience. The most famous example of creative advertising creating an impression in the minds of consumers is the advertisement for Marlboro Cigarettes, which tried to create a 'macho man' image for the brand. The old positioning and image for Marlboro had been as a woman's cigarette. Both television commercials and print ads depicted the Western Rockies as Marlboro country and tried to associate the potential customer with that aspect of American history considered to be rough, rugged, and manly—the American cowboy. Finally, every great ad is well-executed. That means that the details, the techniques, and the production values, all have been finely tuned. Technology plays a dominant role in execution. While the strategy decides what needs to be conveyed, an ad's creativity and execution decides its overall impact.

Impact of advertising

Advertising has been avidly studied by social scientists in recent times. It has been hypothesized that mere exposure to advertising can create liking with no cognitive activity at all. Such a phenomenon has been demonstrated for nonsense syllables and could provide insights into how repetition affects the impact of advertising.

Research suggests that television advertising, operating under low-involvement and perceptual defenses, creates changes in perceptual structure that can trigger a behavioural act, which, in turn, affects attitude. This low-involvement hierarchy where behaviour change precedes real attitude change is posited in contrast to high-involvement hierarchy where behaviour follows attitude change. In another model referred to as elaboration likelihood model (ELM), two routes to persuasion are suggested—the *central route*, which describes the in-depth processing of information when the audience member is motivated to process the information and has also ability to do so; and the *peripheral route*, which takes peripheral cues such as source credibility, etc. without actively and consciously processing the ad information. Finally, when the audience gets totally involved, it cognitively processes the ad information generated to both support as well as counter arguments regarding the claims of the ad. It then becomes the job of advertisers to increase the proportion of support arguments to the number of counter arguments.

In Fig. 34.2 adapted from Batra et al. (1996), it is shown how intervening variables moderate the way ad exposure creates attitude change through brand awareness, brand comprehension, brand image, and personality and its association with social groups/experts.

Advertising response

There are two types of advertising response functions (depicting sales effect of additional amounts of advertising) that are debated and contested. First, an advertising response function with threshold (S-shaped curve) conveys that extra advertising causes sales to increase at a growing rate, building up to a threshold (inflexion point) where the increasing sales increments change to diminishing ones (Fig. 34.3). The amount of advertising that leads the greatest sales effect is measured at the inflexion point. This is where a marginal dose of advertising produces the greatest return. This theory is based on the belief that a fixed number of exposures

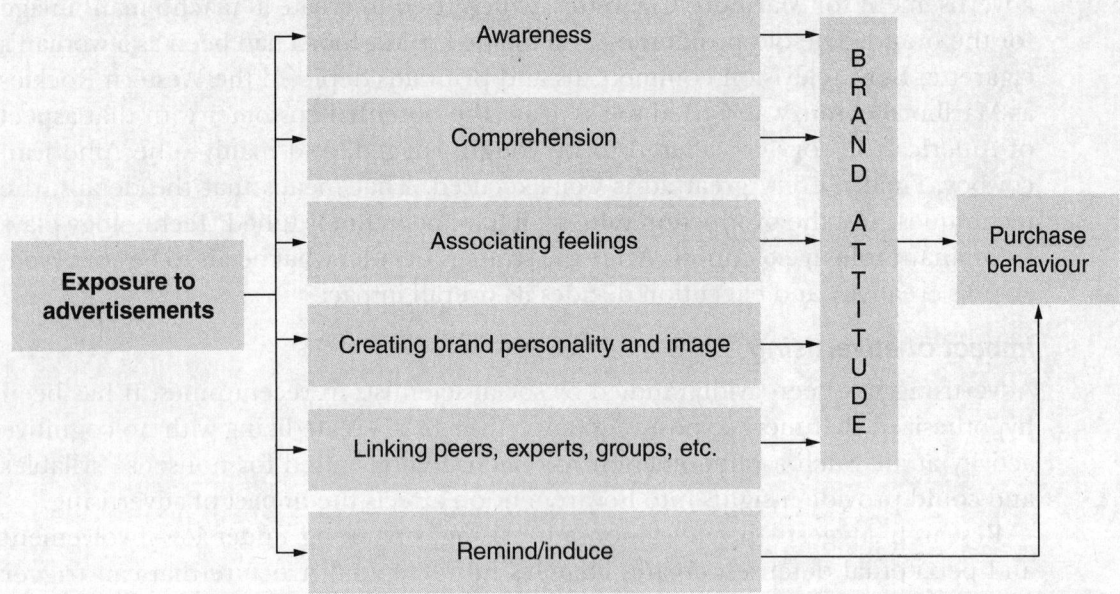

FIGURE 34.2   How advertising works

Source: Based on Batra, et al. (1996), p. 48.

(considered to be three for TV ad exposures) have to be received by the consumer before he/she gets affected.

The alternative diminishing-returns advertising response function posits a different perspective. According to it, all doses of advertising produce results but with diminishing returns. Here, the first dose of advertising is seen to be most effective and the succeeding ones less so, even though they cost the same in terms of the advertising budget. The strategy advocated here is thus to cover large audience exposure than repeat exposures.

Advertising gurus emphasize upon three essential qualities of these ad campaigns– (1) they must be *likeable*; (2) they must be *visual* rather than verbal; (3) they must

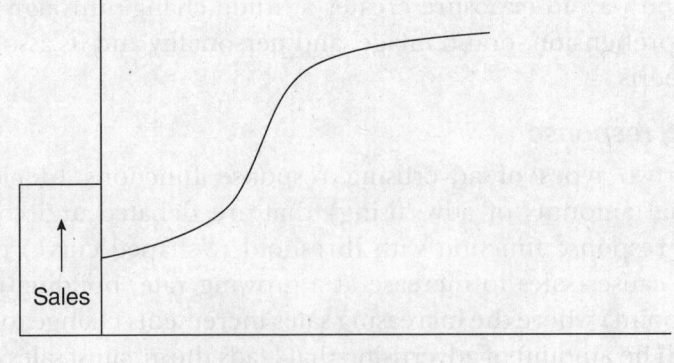

FIGURE 34.3   Advertising response function

have a *balanced appeal* in terms of rationality and emotional appeal. The last one is also connected with how accurately marketeers seek to position their offerings vis-à-vis the competitors in terms of the brand's functional and non-functional features.

Advertising builds a brand's value over time. Other supporting factors, such as a brand's penetration, purchase frequency, price elasticity of its demand, and consumer price relative to the competition, when measured can add further value to the brand. Advertising campaigns, which involve a series of ads conveying the same message in diverse ways help in creating a long lasting impact on the consumer's mind. Sometimes advertisements may use the element of suspense to generate curiosity about the product.

INDIAN MARKET TRENDS

Television advertising (especially in Hindi) has made major headway in the past ten years, especially with the advent of satellite TV. Most major international advertising firms have chosen local Indian partners for their work in this market. Mumbai remains the centre of the advertising business in India.

India has a diverse and growing number of daily newspapers. Since 1991, the increase of business and financial news reports in English language and vernacular

EXEL-AD LAB

A professionally managed company, EXEL-AD LAB offers services in brochure, catalogue, posters, designing, photography, and media related activities. Standing on the grounds of creativity and innovation, EXEL-AD LAB has maintained a lead in the industry. They have developed core competence in the field of designing, publishing, media, photography, and interior design. The background of years of experience coupled with expertise gives it an edge in understanding the customized requirements. They are developing unique and ingenious ways to offer proactive services to their clients. The services that are offered are:

Creative and Designing Services
- Pre-press activities
- Exhibition and stall designing
- Brochure and catalogue designing
- Folders, dockets, posters, and danglers designing
- Craft paper, carry bags, and packaging

- Offset printing
- Hoarding and calendars
- Sales promotion and gift items for corporate institutions
- Multimedia presentation
- Digital large printout services
- Interior designing for commercial and residential locations
- Photography

Media Relations
- Artists, art shows, and art galleries
- Sales promotion services
- Product launch services
- Exhibitions and designing services
- Media monitoring
- Creative services
- Spokesperson and corporate training

Photography
- Offering offset printing solutions
- Catalogue designing and printing service

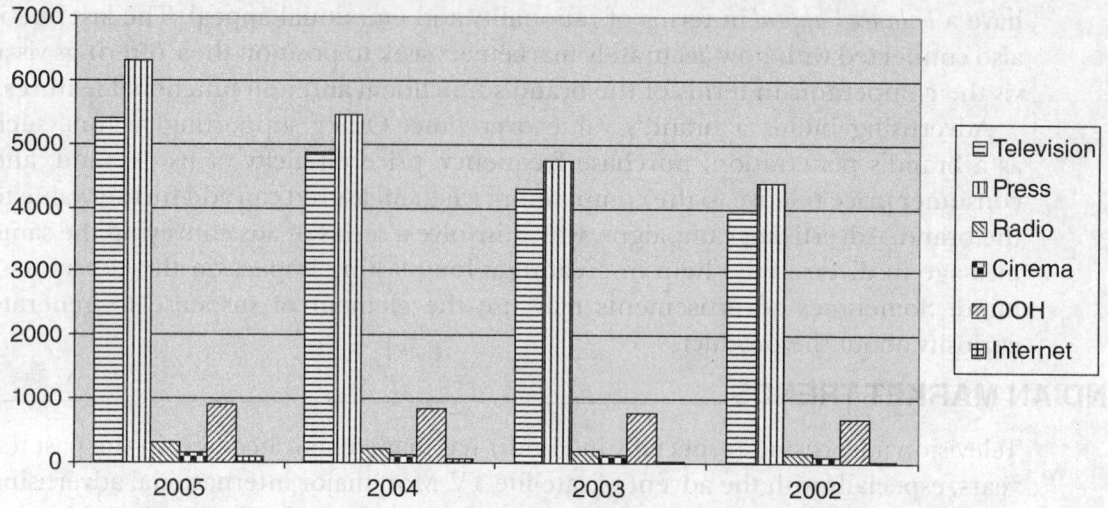

FIGURE 34.4 Advertisement expenditure in (₹ in crore) by media-type (2002–2005)

Source: Based on the data from *The Businessworld Marketing Whitebook 2006*; AdEx India
(A division of TAM Media Research).

dailies has paralleled the economic reform programme and the movements of the stock markets. Most leading publications have their circulation audited by the Audit Bureau of Circulation, headquartered in Mumbai, India. The leading Indian business newspapers include *Business Standard* and *The Economic Times*. Magazines include *India Today, Business India, Business Today*, and *Business World*.

In addition to advertising, other kinds of trade promotion activities are also well developed in India. The most successful direct marketeers in India today are the millions of door-to-door sales representatives who visit neighbourhoods and villages across India. From ice cream vendors to carpet sellers, India's residential neighbourhoods are frequently visited by merchants offering a variety of products.

The Internet revolution has radically impacted brand building. A website can create an integrated brand experience that constantly reinforces brand positioning. Brands more than ever will help people break through the communication clutter. Advertisements can also experiment in terms of design.

Figures 34.4 and 34.5 illustrate the advertisement expenditure by media-type and companies respectively. OOH in Fig. 34.4 refers to out-of-home advertising.

TYPES OF ADVERTISING

Advertising may be classified into the following categories according to its scope and purpose.

Corporate advertising It identifies clients' strengths and highlights them in the right way. By selecting the right media, it makes the clients' corporate identity come shining through. Everything an ad agency does for clients—from strategy to creative conceptualizing to media planning, fulfils the client's fundamental need to be recognized by its target audience as per the company's choice.

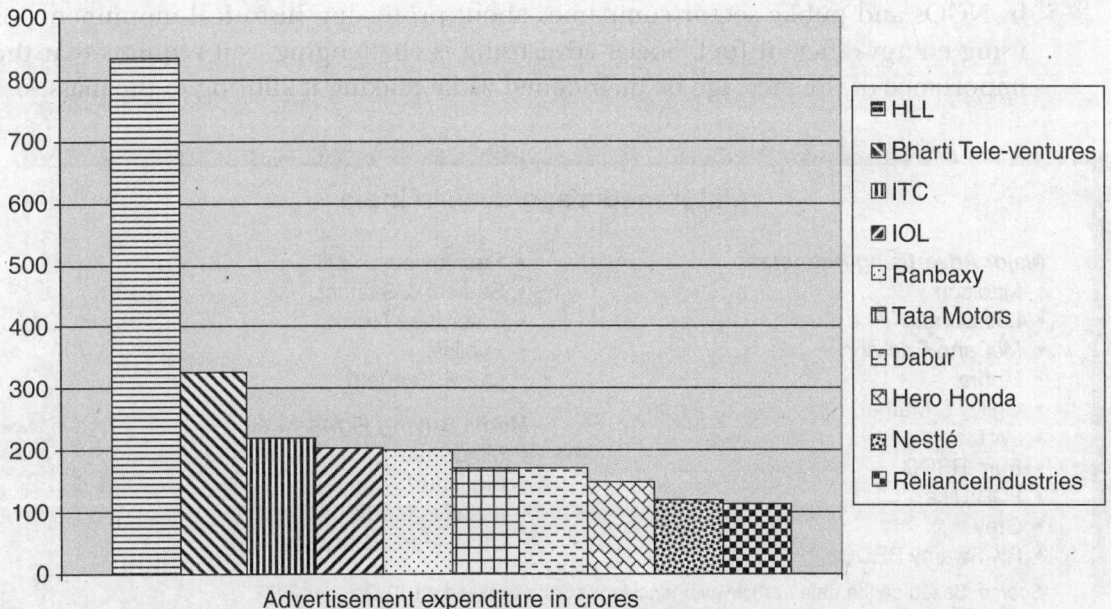

FIGURE 34.5   Ad expenditure by companies during 2005

Source: Based on the data from *The Businessworld Marketing Whitebook 2006*; AdEx India
(A division of TAM Media Research).

Financial advertising   It combines an in-depth understanding of the financial market with superb creative skills to deliver campaigns that influence both institutional and retail investors' decisions.

Brand advertising   Outstanding creativity bring brands to life, creating an everlasting image of the product in the minds of the consumer. Today, brands have more value than the product in itself, to the extent that young consumers are willing to pick up fake goods sporting a popular brand name such as Lacoste, Nike, or Adidas because they are associated with status. Branding has become such an important aspect of advertising that brand management today, as we shall see in the next chapter, is a business activity in itself.

Government advertising   This category includes corporate campaigns, product campaigns, public service campaigns as well as a vast array of design and print jobs for conveying the messages of the government to its people. Messages include information about diseases, family planning, vaccines, government bonds, etc. This involves understanding the complexities and procedures involved in a large number of government and state-owned organizations both at the national and state level.

Recruitment advertising   Recruitment is a key corporate activity. A recruitment advertisement should not only describe what it looks for in a candidate but also what it can offer, make it more appealing, not only to the aspiring candidate but also to the reader in general. Most importantly, it must motivate the right people to respond.

Social advertising   The objective of social advertising is to change public attitude and behaviour and stimulate positive social change. This includes advertisements by NGOs and public sector companies about protecting historical monuments or using energy-efficient fuel. Social advertising is challenging as it requires that the importance of the message be maintained while making it alluring to the masses.

Major media agencies in India

Major Advertising Agencies
- Madison
- Leo Burnett
- McCann-Erickson
- Mudra
- Ogilvy & Mather
- JWT
- Euro RSCG
- FCB Ulka
- Grey
- RK Swamy BBDO

- Rediffusion-DY&R
- Saatchi & Saatchi
- Enterprise-Nexus
- Publicis
- Law & Kenneth

Media Buying Firms
- MindShare
- Mediaturf
- Initiative Media
- Carat Media Services

Source: Based on the data from www.agencyfaqs.com, accessed on 10 October 2007.

SUMMARY

Advertising can be used to motivate consumers, encourage retailers, or dissuade people from indulging in certain socially unacceptable behaviours. It may be defined as any paid form of non-personal presentation and promotion of ideas, goods, and services by an identified sponsor. Effective advertising is the end product of focused and coordinated work of two parties—the client and the agency. Without the client's contribution, an advertising campaign, no matter how significant or meritorious, will have no perceptible effect on sales. As per Jones, the success of new categories of goods and services depends upon latent demand, discretionary purchasing power among the target group, the presence of strong brands, and heavy advertising and promotional support. Three broad dimensions characterize great advertising—strategy, creativity, and execution.

An advertiser develops the ad to meet specific objectives, carefully directs it to a targeted audience, and creates its message to arouse interest, persuade, and reinforce the brand's appeal to address the concerns of the potential consumer.

The advertiser broadcasts it through the media in a manner that optimizes the budget and drives effective mileage of the last rupee spent. The advertising strategy has to flow out of the marketing strategy of which it is a subset. There are two types of advertising response functions (depicting sales effect of additional amounts of advertising) that are debated about and contested. First, an advertising response function with threshold (S-shaped curve) conveys that extra advertising causes sales to increase at a growing rate, building up to a threshold (inflexion point) where the increasing sales increments change to diminishing ones. The amount of advertising that produces the greatest sales effect is measured at the inflexion point. This is where the marginal dose of advertising produces the greatest return.

According to the diminishing-returns advertising response function, all doses of advertising produce results but with diminishing returns. Here, the first dose of advertising is seen to be most effective and the succeeding ones less, although they cost the same in terms of the advertising budget.

Advertising may be categorized as corporate advertising, financial advertising, brand advertising, government advertising, recruitment advertising, and social advertising. In India, growth of the media and the Internet has radically changed the face of advertising.

KEYWORDS

Advertising goals Communication goals that are specified in terms of awareness, comprehension, attitude, preference, and image variables for a particular target segment for a specified time period.

Advertising Non-personal communication which is paid for by identified sponsors through media.

Alternative diminishing-returns The point where all doses of advertising produce results but with diminishing returns.

Consumer behaviour dynamics It takes place when consumers shift from one company's brands to its rivals' in the same product class and vice versa.

CPM Cost of reaching 1000 people in a medium's audience.

Creative department It comprises copywriters and artists who come up with creative ideas about presenting the message.

Full service advertising agency An agency equipped to serve its clients in all areas of communication and promotion.

Inflexion point The point on the advertising response function (S-shaped curve) that conveys that extra advertising has caused the sales to reach a threshold. It is the point where increasing sales increments change to diminishing ones.

Media planning The process of selecting appropriate mix of media type or vehicles that directs advertising messages to the right people in the right place at the right time.

Media vehicles It refers to specific media programmes and publications.

Message The verbal, non-verbal, and technical components used to convey a company's or a product's features.

EXERCISES

Concept Review Questions

1. Are advertising goals different from marketing goals?
2. What are the attributes of great advertising?
3. How does advertising work?

Critical Thinking Questions

1. How can the returns on advertising be evaluated and justified on a short-term and a long-term perspective?
2. How appropriate is the use of children for brand endorsements in TV commercials?

3. Surrogate advertising by liquor and cigarette companies is increasingly termed as unethical by many consumer activist groups. How would you feel about the whole issue if you happen to join the marketing department of one of these companies?

Project Assignment

Prepare a detailed creative brief for a herbal fairness soap targeted at men. Also formulate an advertising strategy, which includes advertising goals, message strategy, media strategy, media plan, and advertising budget:

REFERENCES

'The Marketing Whitebook' (2008), *Businessworld*, ABP Pvt. Ltd, New Delhi.

Batra, Rajeev, John G. Myres, and David A. Aaker (1996), *Advertising Management*, Prentice Hall of India Pvt. Ltd, New Delhi.

Jones, John Philip (1998), *How Advertising Works: The Role of Research*, Sage Publications Inc, Thousand Oaks, California.

www.agencyfaqs.com, accessed on 10 October 2007.

35

Brand Management

Learning Objectives

After studying this chapter, you will be able to:

- Understand the concept of branding
- Appreciate the importance of brand building
- Learn about brand management
- Appreciate the relevance of brand equity

INTRODUCTION

A brand is a term, name, sign, symbol, design, or a combination that identifies a company's product from its competitors. The brand mark is a symbolic or pictorial design or a logo that identifies a product along with its brand name. It is also the legal way by which the owner claims exclusive access for trademark purposes. Brands are also conceptualized as a focal platform for articulating and implementing an organization's strategic intent. Kapferer (1992) defines them as gestalts larger than the sum total of its elements. Brands can also be construed as performing essentially consumer-centric roles such as facilitating decision-making, reducing risks, and providing symbolic value. Brands as personalities evolve in the context of consumer–brand relationships by co-creation of value and meaning. This is created through collaboration and competition between organizations and consumers.

There are various kinds of brands. A premium brand typically costs more than other products. An economy brand is a brand targeted at a highly price elastic market segment. A fighting brand is created specifically to counter a competitive threat. When a company's name is used as a product brand name, it is referred to as corporate branding. When one brand name is used for several related products, it is referred to as family branding. When all a company's products are given different brand names, it is referred to as individual branding. When a company uses the brand equity associated with an existing brand name to introduce a new product or product line, it is referred to as brand leveraging. Private brands can be differentiated from manufacturers' brands (also referred to as national brands). When two or more brands work together to market their products, it is referred to as co-branding. Brand rationalization refers to reducing the number of brands marketed by a company. Companies tend to create more brands and product variations within a brand than economies of scale suggest they should.

BRAND BUILDING

Building fast moving consumer goods (FMCG) brands require a lot of sensitivity as the scope for product differentiation on functional elements is minimal, and recourse to brand image building on feelings and emotions is often the only alternative. Besides this, the quantum of investment on advertising is relatively large on FMCG brands than on consumer durables. A way of looking at building brands has been formulated through a grid by FCB, a reputed advertising agency. It is given in Table 35.1.

TABLE 35.1   FCB grid

	Thinking	Feeling
High Involvement	Informative	Affective
Low Involvement	Habitual	Satisfied

According to the grid, consumers have high and low degrees of involvement in brand purchases and for consumers it is often a mix of rational (thinking) and emotional (feeling) reasons. Research unearths the best route to follow in terms of advertising in a particular product category. In case of consumer durables where the frequency of purchase is low and financial risk high, advertising may have to focus on features, price–value offering, and after-sales service. Advertising is also used to create company brand image and reduce post-purchase dissonance. Creating a service brand is very challenging as the brand is created through the services rendered and the brand image. Creating brands in the services sector involves creating responses from various target groups while retaining the look and feel of the brand. Al Ries and Jack Trout (1981), relate the brand building exercise to the concept of brand positioning. Through brand positioning one can successfully brand products, services, ideas, events, people, and even countries.

BRAND MANAGEMENT

Brand management is the application of marketing techniques to a specific product, product line, or brand to increase the product's perceived value to the customer and, thereby, increase brand franchise and brand equity. Branding refers to a lot more than giving a brand name to a product and publicizing it. Brands are a direct consequence of market segmentation and product differentiation. Companies, in a move to meet the expectations of a specific customer segment, concentrate

Brand rebuilding in the Indian market

Maggi Noodles By the time Nestlé India Limited (NIL) had firmly established the brand Maggi, it was working on extending its brand in an area where it thought of elevating the brand and making a handsome profit. It decided to enter the ketchup market with the brand Maggi. At that time Kissan was the market leader with 65 per cent share. Nestlé further diversified by introducing flavours such as hot and sweet tomato sauce. These additions gave Maggi an edge over Kissan. One of the main reasons why the brand name Maggi has helped in the success of Maggi Ketchup and sauces is the fact that the target customers for both the 2-minute noodle and sauces are the same—mothers and housewives. The efficient distribution system that Nestlé has in India made sure that the new brands be available at all the outlets from where the target population normally buy their requirements. The Maggi brand was a well-known as well as a trusted brand in the eyes of the housewives.

In the early 2000s, NIL started introducing new 'healthy' products in accordance with the Nestlé Group's global strategy to transform itself into a health and wellness company. NIL also adopted the same distribution strategy for the Maggi brand with the launch of the Maggi Vegetable Atta Noodles, a healthy instant noodles product made of whole wheat flour and vegetables (instead of refined flour) in 2005. The Dal Atta Noodles is another variant of Maggi's 'healthy' instant noodles.

Bank of Baroda The bank's new corporate brand identity is much more than a cosmetic change. According to the bank, it is a signal that they recognize and are geared up for a new business paradigm in a globalized world. It also always want to stay in touch with the Indian heritage and the enduring relationships on which the bank is founded. By adopting a symbol as simple and powerful as the Baroda Sun, it hopes to communicate both. Coinciding with the unveiling of the new logo, the bank also announced that it would be launching a number of customer-centric initiatives, including IT products and expansion of electronic delivery channels. However, the most challenging task is creating a lasting, perceptible difference in the consumer's mind about the changed style of functioning.

Bajaj Auto The company, which had earlier marketed itself as a scooter company with the punch line Hamara Bajaj, posing itself as the scooter of middle class Indians, would today like to present itself as a motorcycle company. There was increased thrust on R&D and several new products were launched. Some of its current models include Bajaj Pulsar DTS-i, Bajaj Discover, and Bajaj Kristal DTS-i. The company had also taken initiatives to upgrade its dealer network and service workshops. The change in logo reflected these changes which had taken place within the company. Last year, the company replaced its more than 40-year old logo with an open, abstract form of a stylized B, or 'the flying B' as it has been named, to represent style and technology.

Kinetic The company that manufactures bikes, scooters, and utility vehicles rolled out its new logo and brand identity as the group was posed to undertake several new initiatives. Some of the brands in the Kinetic stable include motorcycles such as Comet 250 and the Kinetic Stryker. Among scooters, Kinetic has brands such as Kinetic Blaze, Nova, and Zing.

Cinthol The sales of Cinthol, a flagship brand of Godrej consumer Products Ltd, increased when it was marketed as a toilet soap with deodorizer for the body. Its target market is the

(Contd)

Exhibit *(Contd)*

Indian middle class. This repositioning was vital for Cinthol since the competition was closing in and the market share was shrinking every year.

Dabur Honey A product of Dabur India, it was originally positioned on 'purity'. This positioning may not have worked as wild honey is seen as pure in India. To aid brand recognition and probably aiming at the urban audience, the positioning changed to nutrition and health.

Mint-O A brand owned by the ITC group, when launched, Mint-O was positioned as 'adult candy'. However, the brand failed to attract consumers. In 1995, Mint-O faced stiff competition from Nestlé Polo which positioned itself as 'the mint with a hole'. To counter it Mint-O positioned itself as 'all mint, no hole'. One advertisement even argued, 'if your head doesn't have a hole, why should your mint'. Positioning the brand head-on with Polo gave it a distinct focus.

Odomos mosquito repellant cream This brand of the Balsara group was one of the first mosquito repellents in the market. It was essentially positioned as an indoor mosquito repellant. For sometime, it was very popular. Later, mosquito mats entered the market and creams became less popular as they were considered to be messy. One way of countering the mosquito repellant mats was positioning the cream for indoor as well as outdoor use; since outdoor locations normally have no power supply to support mosquito repellant mats. This broadened the competitive space, increasing occasion for use.

Parle Bisleri The market leader in bottled mineral water is now confronted by many other brands that sell 'pure' water. It has now made a concerted move from railway platforms, retailers, and floating tourists to a 50-crore target market in the home segment, and is trying to consolidate its position with trendier ad campaigns to give water a new 'young' face. In keeping with that image makeover, its catchphrase from 'pure and safe' has been changed to 'play safe', wherever you are.

Air India The 71-year-old Maharaja of Indian skies is now taking off on a major image building flight. With competition from domestic rivals and international majors growing by the day, Air India has appointed an independent image consultant to help rejuvenate the Air India brand and emerge as a global airline of choice. The exercise involves revamping every customer touch point, from reservation counters to in-flight entertainment and interiors.

Cadbury Dairy Milk Cadbury India has re-launched its flagship brand, Cadbury Dairy Milk (CDM), as part of a global re-launch which has been kicked off in India. The company plans to leverage the equity of the CDM brand across its entire moulded chocolates portfolio, a concept known as 'master-branding' in marketing jargon. Flavours such as Fruit 'N Nut and Crackle are being brought under the CDM fold as part of this initiative. Cadbury Diary Milk constitutes about 30 per cent of Cadbury India's turnover, with a volume share of 26.7 per cent in the urban market and a value share of 30.7 per cent. With profit margins under pressure in a competitive market, the re-launch is expected to help the company extend the benefit of advertising on CDM to positively impact a larger product portfolio. As part of the master-branding strategy, the company plans to launch several variants under the CDM umbrella.

Milkmaid Nestlé's Milkmaid has been a class example of repositioning. Nestlé introduced Milkmaid as a whitener for tea and coffee. Again like Horlicks, when the milk scarcity eased, it changed its positioning to topping for cakes and puddings and use in dessert recipes.

(Contd)

Exhibit (Contd)

Appy A product offered by Parle Agro, Appy got a makeover in 2003 when the white packaging was replaced with a new black pack. The pack also had graphics of champagne glasses, symbolizing party and celebration. After the repackaging, the company claims the drink was particularly successful in student-heavy cities such as Vizag and Pune. Along with an increase in off-take, the company enhanced its reach. Employees were trained to teach retailers the importance of visibility. Finally, in 2004–05, the company felt the time was right to leverage the brand's equity. As a stroke of luck, the pesticide controversy had hit cola drinks, and consumers were looking for alternatives. Appy had the colour and the fizz. Appy Fizz was launched in August 2005. However, this time the company paid special attention to its packaging. Appy Fizz shed the Tetra Pak to be covered in champagne-style PET bottles. The champagne glass graphics were retained. The fizz promise opened new consumption channels. Appy could soon enter discotheques, pubs, and five star bars as the company believes Appy Fizz mixes well with a range of drinks and can be a substitute to alcohol.

Medimix It is a herbal soap offered by Cholayil Pvt Ltd. For years Medimix marketed itself as a herbal soap for skin problems, aiming at the traditional Indian woman. However, today it has changed its profile and addresses itself to the modern Indian woman, promising the same benefit.

Colgate Toothpastes were redefined as 'gels'. The brand that braved this redefinition was Colgate through its brand extension Colgate Gel.

From the above examples it is obvious that rebuilding brands is a regular exercise for products and services.

on providing them, consistently and repeatedly, with the ideal combination of attributes. Companies want to stamp their mark on different sectors and make their imprint on their products.

Successful brand management can help in giving a personality to the brand, such that the consumer subconsciously starts relating to some of the qualities of the brands to the self. In the process of building brand personality, companies may use filmstars, models, or sportspersons as official promoters or ambassadors of their brands. They endorse and support the brand's publicized qualities. In India, some well-known brand ambassadors are Shahrukh Khan for Tag Heuer watches, Aishwarya Rai for L'Oreal, Amitabh Bachchan for Dabur, Sachin Tendulkar for Aviva Life Insurance, etc.

One of the most effective tools to hedge against market risk and distance a company's products or services from competitors is the organization's underlying brand identity. Marketeers seek to set themselves and the brand apart from competitors by focusing the company's resources on the strategic intent of creating a difference. They see a brand as an implied promise that the customers have come to expect from the company and that the customers would continue to make future purchases of the same product. This practice may increase sales by making comparisons with competitors' products more favourable. The value of the brand is determined by the amount of cash flows it generates for the manufacturer. This results from a combination of increased sales and increased price. The reason why so many distributors have created their own brands is because they have discovered this as profitable. At the same time, they should also take into account the opposite situation, that is, the fact that certain brands tend to lose value with time. The challenge for the brand manager is to revitalize the brand using the existing brand equity as leverage. There are several problems associated with setting objectives for a brand or product category. Many brand managers limit themselves to setting financial objectives, while others limit themselves to setting short-term objectives because their compensation packages are designed to reward short-term action.

Thus, the major challenge for a brand manager is to create and sustain brand identity by developing coordinated marketing strategies across diverse markets, media options, and work cultures. Branding may increase sales by making a comparison with competing products more favourable. It may also enable the manufacturer to charge more for the product. The value of the brand is determined by the amount of profit it generates for the manufacturer. This results from a combination of increased sales and increased price. The current approach to branding is multidimensional and comprises functional, emotional, relational, and strategic dimensions. The added brand equity is through higher quality perception created through branding.

Branding reinforces customer loyalty and ensures repeat purchases. Brands by themselves can guard against the excesses of competition. The symbolic value of a brand permits the buyer to restore their faith in the firm due to brand identification. It is here that brand communication plays an important role by furthering its recognition, preference, and loyalty. Brands do not exist in all markets. Research on brand sensitivity has revealed that customers in many product categories do not look for a brand in particular, while exercising their choice of buying.

Brand Equity

The value of a brand as an asset is termed as brand equity. We have to remember that brand is not a physical entity but a collection of consumer cognitions, perceptions, visualizations, and feelings whenever he sees the brand's name or symbol. Super brands evoke a richer and consistent association—associations that, as per Biel (1991), are both 'hard' such as functional attributes and 'soft' such as anthropomorphic attributes such as personality characteristics.

The annual list of the world's most valuable brands, published by Interbrand and *Business Week*, indicates that the market value of companies often consists largely of brand equity. A study by McKinsey & Company, a global consulting firm, in the year 2000 suggested that strong, well-leveraged brands produce higher returns to shareholders than weaker, narrower brands. Taken together, this means that brands seriously impact shareholder value.

Aaker (1991, 1996) describes a framework (Fig. 35.1) that is based on the rationale that brand equity with customers is attained through high awareness and strong association while with the trade it is through proprietary and patented assets.

Brand management at P&G

The discipline of brand management (or product differentiation) was started at Procter & Gamble (P&G) as a result of a famous memo by Neil H. McElroy. Brand management as a business technique was one of the signal innovations in American marketing during the twentieth century. It epitomized the persistent theme of balancing centralized oversight with decentralized decision-making based on who in the company had the best information about the decision at hand.

Neil McElroy changed marketing forever when he wrote the classic McElroy memo at P&G, which led to the creation of the discipline of brand management.

Keller (1993, 2003) argues that it is brand knowledge that is a composite of brand awareness and brand image that leads to greater consumer preference.

Kapferer (1992, 2005) contends that brand image is volatile and peripheral and hence the strategic marketeer needs to go beyond the superficial and investigate the brand at its core level so as to imbue it with a brand identity that is coherent, durable, and realistic. He forwards a six-sided configuration for brand identity namely physique, personality, relationship, reflection, culture, and self image.

Jagdeep Kapoor (2004) of Samsika Marketing Consultants a leading brand management consultant, who has worked on a large number of well-known Indian brands such as Mother Dairy, Fevicol, Safal, Blue Dart, Nirma, Frooti, Cinthol, and Aptech provides twenty seven brand practices to build winning brands. His numerous books are replete with insightful and successful Indian cases of brand building that illustrates that brand building frameworks probably need to be culture specific.

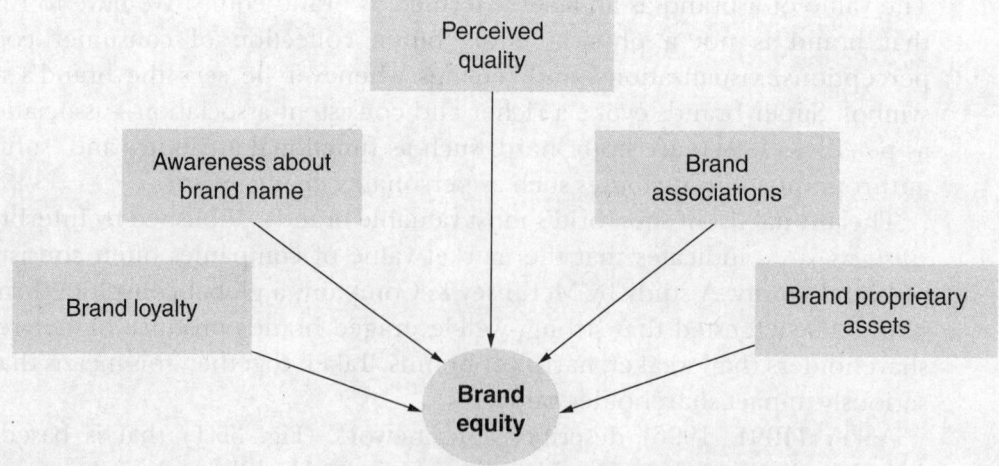

FIGURE 35.1   Brand equity

SUMMARY

Brands evolve in the context of consumer-brand relationships by co-creation of value and meaning. A good brand name should suggest the company or product image. Brand management is the application of marketing techniques to a specific product, product line, or brand. It seeks to increase the product's perceived value to the customer and, thereby, increase brand franchise and brand equity. It is the process for capitalizing and realizing brand value. The major challenge for the brand manager is to create and sustain brand identity by developing coordinated marketing strategies across diverse markets, media options, and work cultures. Branding may increase sales by making a comparison with competing products more favourable.

The current approach to branding is multi-dimensional and comprises of functional, emotional, relational, and strategic dimensions. The added brand equity is through higher quality perception created through branding. Branding reinforces customer loyalty and repeat purchases. Brands do not exist in all markets as most of the staples and cereals are not branded in largely underdeveloped markets. Research on brand sensitivity reveals that the customers in many product categories do not look for a brand while exercising their choice. A premium brand typically costs more than other products. An economy brand is a brand targeted at a high price elasticity market segment. A fighting brand is a brand created specifically to counter a competitive threat. When a company's name is used as a product brand name, it is referred to as corporate branding. When one brand name is used for several related products, it is referred to as family branding. When all a company's products are given different brand names, it is referred to as individual branding. When a company uses the brand equity associated with an existing brand name to introduce a new product or product line, it is referred to as brand leveraging.

Private brands can be differentiated from manufacturers' brands (also referred to as national brands). When two or more brands work together to market their products, it is referred to as co-branding. Brand rationalization refers to reducing the number of brands marketed by a company. Companies tend to create more brands and product variations within a brand than economies of scale suggest they should. Frequently, they will create a specific product or brand for each market that they target.

Repositioning a brand (sometimes called re-branding), wastes the brand equity built up in the past, and also confuses the target market with multiple brand positions. However, old brand images may tend to fade with time. The challenge for the brand manager is to revitalize the brand using the existing brand equity as leverage. There are several problems associated with setting objectives for a brand or product category. Many brand managers limit themselves to setting financial objectives, while others limit themselves to setting short-term objectives because their compensation packages are designed to reward short-term behaviour. It is sometimes difficult to translate corporate level objectives into brand or product level objectives. In a diversified company, the objectives of some brands may conflict with those of other brands. Research will unearth the best route to follow in terms of advertising in a particular product category. Advertising is also used to create company brand image and reduce post-purchase dissonance. Creating a service brand is very challenging as here the brand is created through the services rendered and the brand image. Through brand positioning one can successfully brand products, services, ideas, events, people, and even countries.

KEYWORDS

Brand A distinctive name, term, sign, symbol, or design that is used to identify a firm's product from that of competitors, and which may be given legal protection through use of trademarks and copyright.

Brand ambassador A well-known personality who endorses and supports the brand and its publicized qualities.

Brand equity The goodwill associated with a brand name which adds a tangible value to a company through higher sales and higher profits.

Brand image The perceptions and beliefs held by consumers about a particular brand of product or a service.

Brand leveraging When a company uses the brand equity associated with an existing brand name to introduce a new product or product line, it is referred to as brand leveraging.

Brand management Developing and implementing competitive strategy for brand/brands.

Brand positioning Creation of appropriate associations with a brand so that it occupies the sought after position in the perceptual map of the customer.

Brand rationalization It refers to reducing the number of brands marketed by a company.

Co-branding When two or more brands work together to market their products, it is referred to as co-branding.

Corporate branding When a company's name is used as a product brand name, it is referred to as corporate branding.

Economy brand A brand targeted at a high price elasticity market segment.

Fighting brand A brand created specifically to counter a competitive threat.

EXERCISES

Concept Review Questions

1. What is a brand?
2. How is brand management carried out?
3. What are different problems associated with brand management? Discuss.

Critical Thinking Questions

1. Can brand equity of a brand be measured? How? Discuss.
2. Branding communication has become increasingly abstract and full of imagery with the result that consumers think of it as more confusing and far-fetched than useful. Do you agree with this point of view? Give reasons for your answer.

Project Assignment

Compare and contrast two leading brands of your choice in the same industry segment in terms of their brand management strategies. Next, prepare brand management strategies in terms of positioning these brands for different segments altogether and list down the major challenges and problems that you are likely to face and how you are going to solve them.

REFERENCES

Aaker, David A. (1991), *Managing Brand Equity,* Free Press, New York.

Aaker, David A. (1996), 'Measuring Brand Equity Across Products and Markets', *California Management Review,* vol. 38, Spring, pp. 102–20.

Biel, Alexander L. (1991) 'The Brandscape— Converting Brand Image into Equity', *Admap,* October, available from the www.warc.com database, accessed on 1 July 2015.

Kapferer, Jean-Noel (1992), *Strategic Brand Management,* Kogan-Page, London, England.

Kapferer, Jean-Noel (2005), *The New Strategic Brand Management,* Kogan-Page, London, England.

Kapoor, Jagdeep (2004), *27 Brand Practices,* Macmillan India Ltd, New Delhi.

Keller, Kevin Lane (1993), 'Conceptualising, Measuring, and Managing Customer-based Brand Equity', *Journal of Marketing,* vol. 57, no. 1, p. 7.

Keller, Kevin Lane (2003), *Strategic Brand Management: Building, Measuring, and Managing Brand Equity,* 2nd edition, Prentice Hall, Upper Saddle River, New Jersey.

Ries, Al and Jack Trout (1981), *Positioning: The Battle for Your Mind,* McGraw-Hill, New York.

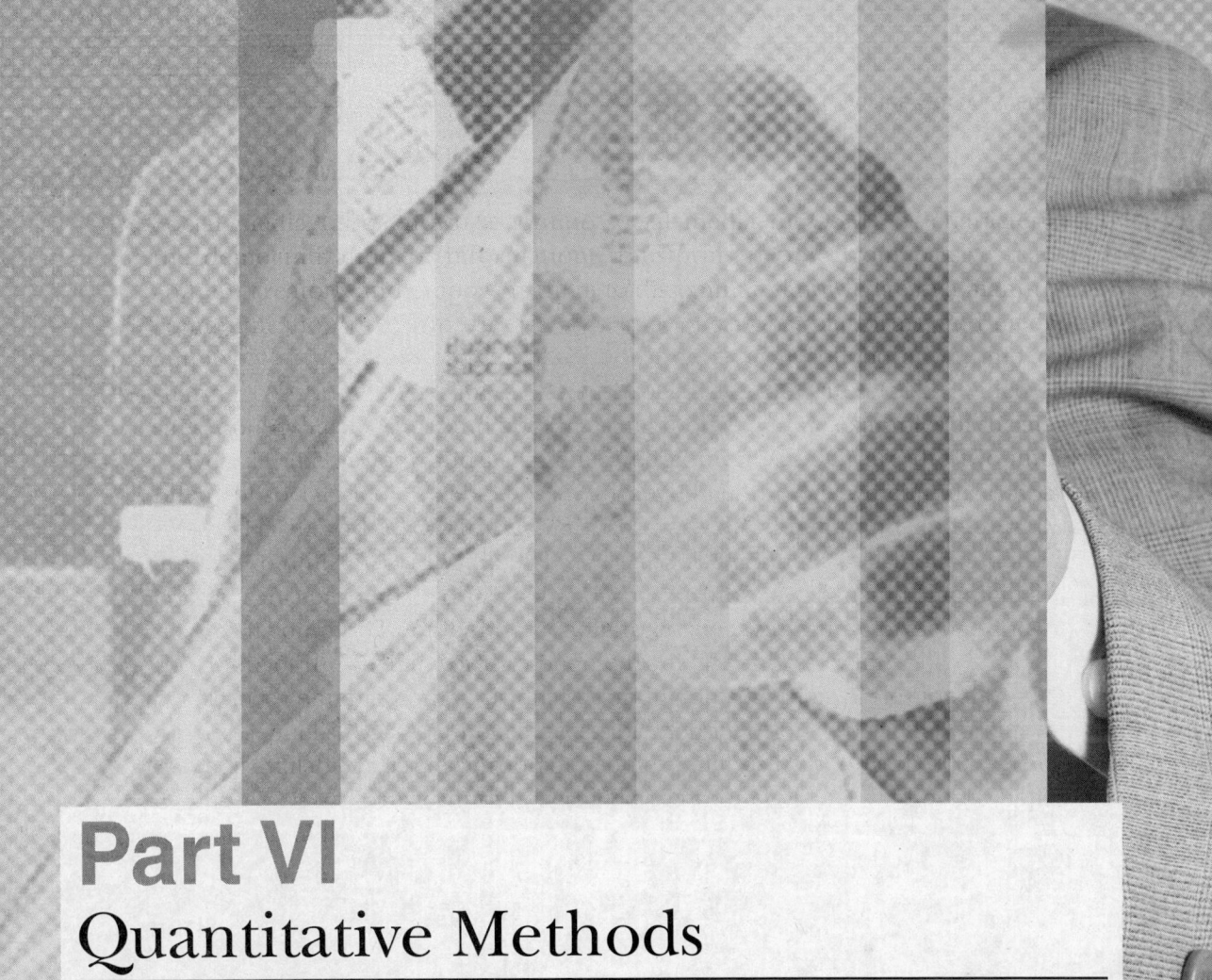

Part VI
Quantitative Methods

36

Statistical Inference

INTRODUCTION

Benjamin Disraeli once said that there are three types of lies—lies, damn lies, and statistics. That hierarchy perhaps reflected the image the usage of statistics evoked in the general public a century back. It also conveyed the feeling, which persists till today, that one can prove anything with the help of statistics. However, we have moved ahead from that deprecatory notion of statistics. Vital statistics may now be used to describe the figure measurements of a model to the variables that characterize the state of economy. In today's competitive, global, and dynamic economic environment, a vast amount of statistical information is available. Managers who can understand this information and base their decisions on it are more likely to be effective and successful.

The use of statistics is common to almost all areas of management. In accounting, for example, an audit firm cannot review and validate every account because that will be too expensive and time-consuming. Instead, the common practice for auditors is to select a subset of accounts referred to as a sample and review the accuracy of that sample to draw conclusions as to whether the accounts shown on the financial statements are acceptable.

Financial advisors use a lot of statistical information about stocks, their price/earning ratios, and dividend yields to draw a conclusion as to whether a stock is under-priced or over-valued compared to stock market averages, to make investment decisions. Marketing managers collect a variety of statistical information about existing and potential consumers on many demographic,

Learning Objectives

After studying this chapter, you will be able to:
- Learn about statistical analysis
- Appreciate data and statistical inference
- Understand probability theory and statistical inference
- Examine type I and type II errors
- Understand chi-square and analysis of variance tests

psychographic and socio-economic factors, and usage patterns to base their marketing strategies. They also purchase syndicated statistical reports, retail audit data, and promotion and sales data to fine-tune their marketing mix plans. In the area of production management the emphasis on quality and quality control is based on statistical theory. An *X*-bar chart helps to correct a production process when necessary and leaves it undisturbed when it is running within limits. Sampling is used for checking the acceptable quality level of a batch of in-process components and assemblies or even the final product. The quality level of the sample is used to infer the quality of the whole batch.

Economists use statistical information and methods to forecast various aspects of the economy. For instance, while forecasting inflation rates, economists use statistical information on such indicators as wholesale price index, the unemployment rate, and manufacturing capacity utilization.

DATA AND STATISTICAL INFERENCE

Data may be defined as the facts and figures that are collected, analysed, and summarized for presentation and interpretation. Data collected in a particular study are together referred to as data set. Elements are the entities on which data is collected. They are sometimes also termed as cases or objects. Data may further be categorized as qualitative (that uses nominal or ordinal scale of measurement) or quantitative (that uses interval or ratio scaled measurement). Most of the statistical information in company reports, magazines, and newspapers is presented in a tabular, graphical, or numerical form, which is easy to understand for the reader. When the characteristics of a particular data set are described without generalizing about other similar data sets, the technique is known as the descriptive statistical technique.

In many situations, data is sought for a large group of elements (voters, consumers, companies, households, products, individuals, and so on) but for considerations of time, cost, effort, etc. data is collected from only a small proportion of the group. The larger group of elements is referred to as a population, while the smaller group is referred to as a sample. A major function of statistics is that data from the sample can be used to make estimates and test hypotheses about the characteristics of the population. This process is referred to as statistical inference and the techniques are known as inferential statistical techniques.

Probability Theory and Statistical Inferences

How can one be sure that the generalization from the sample is valid? When can we infer that the likelihood of it is true? What is the relationship between statistical inference and theory of probability? What is meant by a random variable and by different types of probability distribution? In what way does the central limit theorem permit the use of sample statistics to make inferences about the population parameters? What is the role of hypotheses testing in statistical inference? And finally, what are some of the most common statistical testing procedures that are used? These questions will be addressed in this section.

Random variable   A random variable is a variable that takes on different values as a result of outcomes of a random experiment. One may think of a random variable as a value or magnitude that changes from occurrence to occurrence unpredictably. Some instances of a random variable are—the number of patients seen daily by a doctor in a clinic, the number of cars passing under a flyover at peak hour of traffic, etc.

Probability distribution   A probability distribution is a listing of the probabilities of all the possible outcomes that could result if the experiments were done. It can be viewed as a theoretical frequency distribution.

Normal distribution   It is a distribution of a continuous random variable. Some important features are:

- the curve has a single peak (uni-modal);
- the mean lies at the centre of its normal curve;
- symmetry, that is, mean, mode, and median lie at a single point; and
- two tails of normal distribution extend infinitely and never touch the horizontal axis.

We can determine the probability (area) that a normally distributed random variable will lie within a certain distance from the mean of the distribution.

Estimator   An estimator is a sample statistic used to estimate a population parameter. A good estimator should have the following properties:

- unbiased (more or less equal values);
- efficiency (small standard error);
- consistency (as sample size increases the difference between the estimator and the parameter decreases); and
- sufficiency (uses most of the information in the sample).

Significance of central limit theorem   The significance of the central limit theorem is that it permits us to use sample statistics to make inferences about population parameters without knowing anything about the shape of the distribution of the population other than what we can get from the sample. It assures us that the sampling distribution of the mean approaches normal as the sample size increases.

Hypothesis testing

In hypothesis testing we begin by making a tentative assumption about a population parameter. This tentative assumption is referred to as the null hypothesis and is denoted by H_o. The opposite of null hypothesis is referred to as alternative hypothesis and is denoted by H_a. The hypothesis testing procedure involves using data from a sample to test the two competing statements indicated by H_o and H_a. The purpose of hypothesis testing is not to question the computed value of the sample statistic but to make a judgement about the difference between the sample statistic and a hypothesized population parameter. For example, if a market researcher has a hunch that the average monthly disposable income of households in an affluent neighbourhood is far greater than the national average of say ₹2500, she will put up a null hypothesis conservatively as H_0: $\mu = 2500$ and an alternative hypothesis as H_a: $\mu > 2500$. However, the market researcher cannot accept or reject this hypothesis about the population parameter (i.e., the average monthly disposable income of households in the affluent neighbourhood) simply by intuition but she needs to accept or reject this hunch objectively (by collecting information from a sample of households from the neighbourhood) through hypothesis testing. The crux of the hypothesis testing is whether such a population is likely to produce a sample such as the one that we have got.

The next step, after stating the null and alternate hypothesis, is deciding the criterion for deciding whether or not to reject the null hypothesis. The choice of a minimum standard for an acceptable probability is termed as the significance level.

Type I and type II errors The null and alternative hypotheses are competing statements about the population. Either the null hypothesis or the alternative hypothesis is true, but not both. Since, hypothesis tests are based on sample information, we must allow for the possibility of errors.

- Type I error: Rejecting H_0 when H_0 is true.
- Type II error: Accepting H_0 when H_a is true.

To arrive at an appropriate level of significance, decision-makers have to examine the trade-off involved in type I and type II errors. For example, while checking the quality of outgoing finished parts through sampling and inferring the quality of the whole batch from the sample data, rejecting the whole lot and making a type I error may involve considerable effort in terms of reworking the finished good whereas accepting and making a type II error may involve the risk of passing defective finished goods and losing loyal customers.

One-sample test of hypotheses We use one-sample test of hypotheses testing to decide whether it is reasonable to conclude from the analysis of the sample that the entire population possesses a certain property or not. We state our hypotheses and select a level of significance appropriate for this decision. Next we decide the appropriate distribution either z or t depending upon whether the sample size is greater than 30 or equal to or less than 30 respectively. We then calculate the standard value of the observed sample value using standard error of the sample statistic and compare that with the critical value from the table. If the sample statistic is within the acceptance region then H_0 is not rejected. We can thus, as emphasized in the earlier example, take the managerial decision to pass the finished goods batch.

Two-sample tests of hypotheses We use two-sample tests of hypotheses to decide whether it is reasonable to conclude from the analysis of the sample, that the two populations are related in some particular way. The hypothesis is selected about the difference of the population parameters from these two populations. The rest of the procedure is similar to the aforementioned one, including z- and t-tests.

Chi-square and analysis of variance

Chi-square is used to determine whether two population attributes are independent of each other. It uses a contingency table to determine a test statistic (chi-square) from observed and expected frequencies. Using the degrees of freedom, the critical value is read from the table and compared with the test statistic to arrive at the conclusion as to whether the attributes of the two sets of population are independent of each other. Chi-square test uses nominal data. It can also be used as a test for equality of several proportions, as a test of independence of attributes and as a test for goodness-of-fit.

To determine whether several samples come from populations with equal means, analysis of variance (ANOVA) is used. The test-statistic F is defined as a ratio of between column variance and within-column variance. Taking into account the degrees of freedom, both for the numerator and the denominator in the aforementioned ratio, the critical value is read from the table. If the sample test statistic falls within the region of acceptance, the null hypothesis is not rejected meaning, thereby, that there exists no reason to doubt the homogeneity of different populations to which these samples belonged. Consequently, the manager may treat them as a single group for all decision-making purposes.

Anderson, et al. (2000), Levin and Rubin (1998), and Srivastava, et al. (1987) have explained the use of ANOVA and chi-square tests of statistical significance very well.

User-friendly statistical application software, such as SPSS, MINITAB, BMPD, SYSTAT, SAS, etc., make it very easy for managers to apply many complex and sophisticated statistical tests especially multivariate tests. However, it should be borne in mind that these tests carry with them appropriate assumptions and violating them would be a great risk as the principle of garbage in and garbage out (GIGO) applies. The manager must further substantiate decision-making with instinct and experience.

SUMMARY

Data collected in a particular study are together referred as a data set. The larger group of elements is referred to as the population, and the smaller group as the sample. The major contribution of statistics is that data from the sample can be used to make estimates and test hypotheses about the characteristics of the population. This process is referred to as statistical inference and the techniques are referred to as inferential statistical techniques.

Normal distribution is a distribution of a continuous random variable, while an estimator is a sample statistic used to estimate a population parameter. The central limit theorem assures us that the sampling distribution of the mean approaches normal as the sample size increases. In hypothesis testing, we begin by making a tentative assumption about a population parameter, that is, null hypothesis (H_o). Alternative hypothesis is the opposite of what is stated in the null hypothesis. The alternative hypothesis is denoted by H_a. The hypothesis testing procedure involves using data from a sample to test the two competing statements indicated by H_o and H_a. The purpose of hypothesis testing is not to question the computed value of the sample statistic but to make a judgement about the difference between the sample statistic and a hypothesized population parameter.

The null and alternative hypotheses are competing statements about the population. Since hypothesis tests are based on sample information, the possibility of errors should be taken into account. In one-sample tests of hypotheses the standard value of the observed sample value is calculated using standard error of the sample statistic and compared with the critical value from the table. In two-sample tests of hypotheses, the hypothesis is put about the difference of the population parameters of two populations. Chi-square test uses nominal data while ANOVA uses either an interval-scaled data or ratio-scaled data. If the sample test statistic falls within the acceptance region, the null hypothesis is not rejected implying that, there exists no reason to doubt the homogeneity of different populations to which these samples belonged.

KEYWORDS

Alternate hypothesis The conclusion that is accepted when the data fails to support the null hypothesis.

Central limit theorem A result that assures that the sampling distribution of the mean approaches normality as the sample size increases irrespective of the shape of the population distribution.

Normal distribution A distribution of a continuous variable with a single peaked, bell-shaped curve whose mean lies at the centre of the distribution and the curve is symmetrical around it.

Null hypothesis The tentative assumption value of a population parameter.

Population A collection of all the elements that are studied to draw conclusions.

Sample A collection of some, but not all the elements of the population under study, used to describe the population.

Statistical inference It is drawn from the sample about population parameters.

Type I error Rejecting a null hypothesis (H_o) when it is true.

Type II error Accepting a null hypothesis when it is false.

EXERCISES

Concept Review Questions

1. Why do you think the central limit theorem is central to statistical inference?
2. When are tests such as ANOVA and chi-square appropriate?
3. How is the sample size determined?

Critical Thinking Questions

1. Why is null hypothesis conservatively put?
2. How important is statistical testing to managerial decision-making?

Project Assignment

Create a data set of different attributes/characteristics of your classmates. Plot the values of characteristics as a histogram. The characteristics could be grade point averages, height, pocket money, etc. Draw inferences about the difference in grade point averages between boys and girls by statistical testing. What are the caveats about drawing wrong inferences from this sample?

REFERENCES

Anderson, David R., Dennis J. Sweeny, and Thomas A. Williams (2000), *Statistics for Business and Economics*, 8th edn, Thomson South-Western, 2002.

Levin, Richard I. and David S. Rubin (1998), *Statistics for Management*, 7th edn, Pearson Education.

Srivastava, U.K., G.V. Shenoy, and S.C. Sharma (1987), *Quantitative Techniques for Managerial Decisions*, New Age International Pvt. Ltd, New Delhi.

37

Forecasting

INTRODUCTION

Managing any business systematically requires decision-making on various fronts such as raw material requirement, sales budget, production plan, people requirement, financial planning, investment analysis, distribution planning, etc. Making the right decisions requires planning for the future—short-, medium-, and long-term. The planning process would necessarily have one major ingredient, that is, forecasting about events likely to happen in the future, such as, predicting trends at the stock exchange. Realization of the fact that 'time is money' in business activities, dynamic decision-making methodologies are necessary tools for successful application in a wide range of managerial decisions where time and money are directly related. Forecasts are needed throughout an organization, and they should certainly not be done by an independent and isolated group of forecasters. As time moves on, the impact of the forecasts on actual performance is measured; original forecasts are revised and updated to take care of actual happenings. Indecision and delays are the cause for failure and missed opportunities. In this chapter we deal with anticipating and managing uncertainty, by using effective forecasting and other predictive techniques.

NATURE AND USES OF FORECASTS

Forecasting is a key element of managerial decision-making process. The ultimate effectiveness of any decision depends upon the sequence of actual events that take place vis-à-vis the events that are likely to take place. The quality of decision-making automatically improves with

Learning Objectives

After studying this chapter, you will be able to:
- Understand the concept of forecasting
- Examine the nature and uses of forecasting
- Evaluate forecasting methods and techniques

TABLE 37.1   Performance measures for different levels of management

Level	Performance measures
Strategic	Return on investment, growth, market share, and innovations
Tactical	Cost, quantity, efficiency, productivity, and customer satisfaction
Operational	Budget, target setting, and conformance with standard

the organization's ability to predict uncontrollable aspects of future events prior to making any decision. Effective planning and control of the operations of an organization requires a good forecasting mechanism.

The measurement of business performance is crucial to find out the achievement of an organization. Therefore, the development of effective performance criteria and measures is seen as increasingly important in almost all organizations. However, the challenges of achieving this in public and non-profit organizations becomes relatively difficult because of either the lack of clarity about objectives or the intangible nature of objectives and the benefits that accrue in such organizations. Table 37.1 provides a few examples of performance measures for different levels of management.

An operational view is needed to improve a system's performance (Fig. 37.1). It is here that one attempts to find out the deviation from the actual performance when compared to the projected one at the time of decision-making, based on the forecasts; arrives at the reasons for such a deviation; and further, takes corrective steps for the future. Such a view looks at how a forecasting system really works. Forecasting activity is a continuous process and needs to be done regularly, perhaps on a daily and weekly basis. The results of the forecasts are useful in a variety of business situations such as inventory management, production planning and

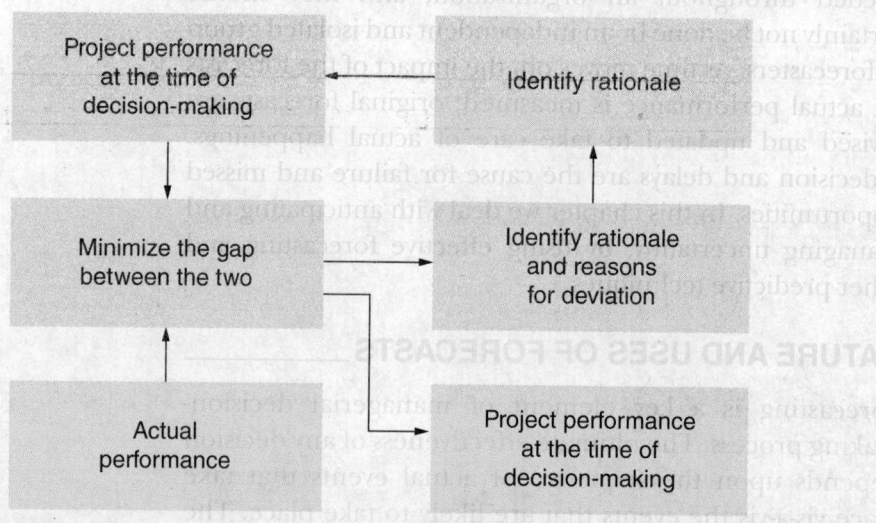

FIGURE 37.1   Improved system's performance through forecasting

control, financial planning, sales budgeting, staff requirements and scheduling, infrastructure planning, raw material procurement, quality management, etc.

A forecasting exercise can be undertaken for three planning horizons—(1) short-term; (2) medium-term; and (3) long-term. Short-term forecast is usually done for a period of less than three months and is used for daily operations and plans of a company. Medium-term forecast covers a period of three months to two years and is used for tactical planning related to cost, efficiency, and productivity issues. Long-term forecast is usually done for a period of more than two years and is used for strategic planning (DeLurgio and Bhame 1991). If the period of forecast is in the past, then the forecast is referred to as ex-post (after-the-fact) forecast. In case, the forecast period is sometime in the future, then the resulting forecast is termed as ex-ante (before-the-fact) forecast.

Forecasting Problem

Forecasting refers to using an estimated model to predict the value or ranges of values of the dependent variable on the basis of the given values of the independent variable(s). Defining the forecasting problem depends on the nature of decision to be made and its implications to the desired characteristics of the forecasting system. The problem situation should clearly enable the forecaster to address the subject of the forecast, the format of the forecast, the time frames involved, and the degree of accuracy required. The level of detail used in forecasting is influenced by many factors such as availability of data, accuracy required, time and cost involved in analysis, and management choices and preferences. The forecasting period is the basic unit of time for which the forecasts are made. The forecasting interval is the time gap after which new forecasts are made. The forecasting interval normally depends upon the frequency at which data processing system provides information about the variables being forecasted. Above all, precise and accurate definition of the forecasting problem largely depends upon the capabilities and the interest of people involved in making forecasts and using the same.

For example, the production, planning, and control department of a scooter manufacturing company that manufactures three varieties of scooters in three different price ranges—high, medium, and low would like to have accurate forecasts of demand, month-wise in the coming year. This will help it to plan for the deployment of facilities available and for putting requisitions to the store department for procurement of various raw materials and parts. In case marketing research and the sales department gives a demand forecast on a far higher side, resulting in a wide variation to actual sales that takes place in first few months, the cost of maintaining inventory would be excessive and this may necessitate the revision of sales and production requirements for the future months.

There are ten steps that are taken sequentially to make a forecast as stated in Fig. 37.2.

1. Determine the use of the forecast
2. Select the items to be forecasted

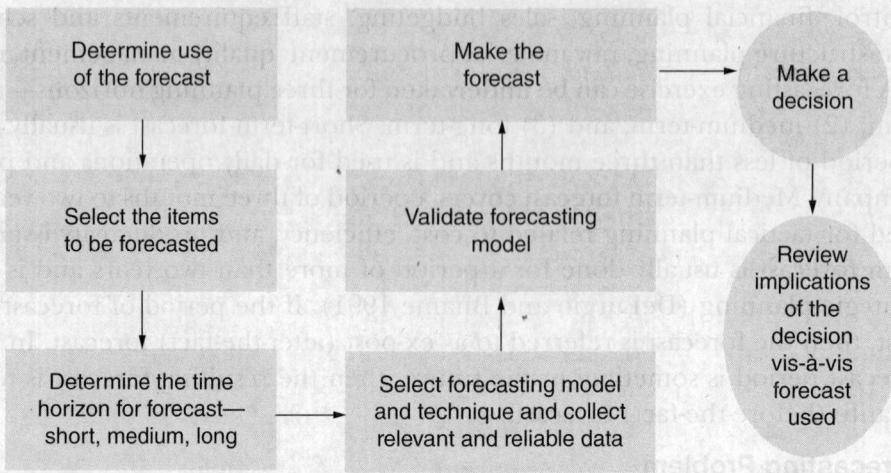

FIGURE 37.2 Steps involved in forecasting

3. Determine the time horizon for the forecast
4. Select forecasting model and technique
5. Collect relevant and reliable data needed
6. Validate the forecasting model
7. Make the forecast
8. Take decision by using the forecast
9. Review the implications of decision vis-à-vis the forecast used
10. Use forecasting methods

FORECASTING METHODS

Forecasting methods can be broadly classified into two categories—qualitative and quantitative, depending upon the degree and extent to which mathematical and statistical methods are used (Fig. 37.3).

Qualitative Methods

Qualitative methods involve subjective estimation based on the opinion of experts such as consolidation of the estimates of sales personnel, by use of Delphi

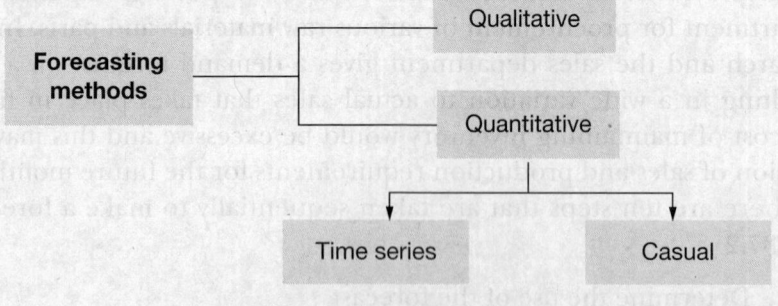

FIGURE 37.3 Forecasting methods

methods to obtain a consensus of opinion from a panel of experts in the field, and customer expectations (Kress 1985). The techniques of judgement are subjective as they rely on intuition, opinions of experts, and the probability of arriving at a forecast (Wilson and Keating 1994). Thus, as against time-series and causal models that depend upon quantitative data, qualitative models attempt to incorporate judgemental or subjective factors into the forecasting model (Render, et al. 2000). The characteristics of qualitative techniques are:

- It is usually based on judgements about causal variables that underlie the demand for particular products or services;
- It is useful for new products and services, as it does not require demand history of the product or service; and
- The approach and degree of complexity to forecast varies from scientifically undertaken surveys to intuitive hunches.

Qualitative techniques for forecasting purpose are used in a wide range of situations and circumstances. However, they may not be of any use under certain situations such as the unavailability of past data to forecast or if the company has come out with a new product for the first time that does not have any substitute in the market. At times qualitative techniques becomes more useful for forecasting purpose, especially when there is insufficient time to collect data, or when circumstances are changing so fast that a forecast based on statistical techniques may not be able to capture the changes that are likely to influence forecasts to a great extent. Above all, it is important to understand that even though quantitative techniques may be effective for forecasting and, therefore, used, the forecasts may be further rationalized by combining qualitative judgements to make final decisions for the given problem.

Quantitative Methods

Quantitative methods use statistical forecasting techniques that explicitly define how the forecast has been arrived at. Qualitative methods used for forecasting purpose varies from intuitive hunches to scientifically conducted surveys. Some of the prominent qualitative methods used for forecasting are educated guess, consensus arrived at by an executive committee, Delphi method, survey undertaken with respect to the sales force and customers, and market research. The logic and rationale is well defined and the techniques and operations used are mathematical. Some of the characteristics of quantitative methods for forecast are as under:

- based on the assumption that the 'forces' that generated demand in the past will generate the future demand, that is, history will tend to repeat itself;
- analysis of the past demand pattern provides a good basis for forecasting future demand; and
- majority of quantitative approaches fall in the category of time-series analysis.

Thus, quantitative techniques for forecasting are useful when the history of the variable being forecasted is available, information is quantifiable, and it is assumed that the past pattern is likely to continue into the future.

Time-series analysis　It is a time-linked sequence of observations of the variable that is used to develop a model for predicting future values. It is important to have a set of observations on the variable that is measured over successive periods of time. The basic objective of time-series method of analysis is to identify a pattern based on past data that can be used to extrapolate into the future. Thus, the forecasts are solely based on past data and/or on past forecasting errors. A time series is a set of numbers where the order or sequence of the numbers is important, for example, historical demand. Analysis of the time series identifies patterns. Once the patterns are identified, they can be used to develop a forecast.

Components of time-series analysis are as under:

- an upward or downward sloping line notes trends;
- cycle is a data pattern that may cover several years before it repeats itself;
- seasonality is a data pattern that repeats itself over the specific time period of one year or less;
- random fluctuation (noise) results from random variation or unexplained causes.

Causal forecasting models attempt to identify the predominant variable that affects the variable of interest. If there appears a cause for the correlation of variables, a statistical model describing the relationship is developed. Knowing the future values of the correlated variable (independent variable), the values for the variable of interest (dependent variable) are forecasted. The major limitation of using causal models is that the independent variable values should be known while making the forecast.

Forecasting Techniques

There are many techniques that can be used for the purpose of forecasting. However, different techniques are applied in different situations depending upon the problem situation, context, degree of sophistication required, available time frame for forecasting, etc. The brief details of these techniques are given in this section.

Multiple regression analysis　It is used when two or more independent variables help in explaining the behaviour of the dependent variable. It is presumed that either a linear or a non-linear relationship exists between independent and the dependent variables. This technique is commonly used for forecasting for a medium-term period. It is also used to identify and assess which independent variables need to be included and which variables to be excluded, depending upon their statistical significance in explaining the behaviour of the dependent variable. Variables, which are strongly linked to explain dependent variables are retained as against those which have a relatively weak relationship with the dependent variable.

Non-linear regression　While calculating multiple regression under non-linear regression, it is assumed that associated variables have a non-linear relationship amongst them such as exponential, binomial, logarithmic, etc. This technique is commonly used when time is the independent variable.

Trend analysis In case of trend analysis involving linear and non-linear regression, time is assumed to be the explanatory variable. This technique is basically used when a particular behaviour and/or pattern is established over time. This technique enables the plotting of aggregated response data on the dependent variable over time. It is especially valuable and useful for conducting a long running survey and helps in measurement of differences in responses over time. The effect on dependent variable with respect to the time factor can be measured on daily, weekly, monthly, quarterly, half yearly, and yearly basis depending upon the problem under consideration. Trend analysis helps in identifying early warning signals of potential problems and issues pertaining to managerial decisions in the area of production planning and control, customer service quality management, etc. This technique also helps in gauging the response rates over time.

Decomposition analysis It is a technique used for identifying several patterns that appear simultaneously in a time-series analysis. This is also used to decompose a series of data into definite multiple patterns.

Moving average analysis A moving average is a smoothing technique to arrive at forecast. This method can be used in two different ways, namely simple moving averages (SMA) or weighted moving averages (WMA). These are used to forecast future values based on past values of a variable. This method is relatively easy to update the forecasts for the future. Thus, simple moving average for a time period is the arithmetic mean of the values in that time period and those close to it (Keller 2005). The moving average is one of the most simple, useful, objective, and analytical tools used for forecasting stock prices. Some patterns and indicators that may emerge from simple or weighted moving average technique can be at times somewhat subjective and, therefore, may result in the analyst questioning whether a pattern is truly emerging or not.

Weighted moving averages This forecasting technique is used when repeated forecasts are required with a need for giving different weights to the values of an independent variable. This method takes care of the trend adjustment by assigning different weights to time periods. As against this, SMAs give equal weightage to all the days in the average that need not be so in reality. For example, if a 15-day moving average is used to forecast stock prices for future, then the obvious question that arises is the logic and rationale for assuming the equal weight to the 15-day old stock price being equally relevant when compared to the weight given to a day's stock prices. It is important to note that by assigning higher weight factors to more recent data under given time frame say days, fortnight, etc. and smaller weight factors for earlier data in time, the trend will be more responsive to recent changes.

Adaptive filtering It is a special type of moving average technique that involves learning from past errors. This technique for forecasting can respond to changes in the relative importance of trend, seasonal, and random factors.

Exponential smoothing It is another form of moving average for time-series forecasting. This technique is simple and an efficient method to forecast evolving seasonal patterns and provides inbuilt flexibility in making adjustments for past errors. It is particularly useful in case of situations where many forecasts need to be prepared. It uses various forms, depending upon the presence of trend or cyclical variations in the behaviour of the dependent variable. In this method of forecasting we select only one weight, that too for the most recent observation. The weights for other data values are computed automatically and tend to decrease as the data points get older. The major advantage of this technique is that it minimizes data storage requirements, as all past data is not required to be saved for arriving at a forecast for the next period. Above all, it is simple in concept and a powerful method because of its weighing process. However, the major disadvantage of this method is that it does not account for the dynamic changes at work that happen on a daily basis, thus making it necessary to constantly update forecasts arrived at by this method to take care of new developments.

Modelling and simulation A model is a representation of reality involving real objects and situations that can be presented in various forms. Mathematical models describe a problem by a system of symbols and mathematical relationships. These are an important part of the objective and quantitative approach to decision-making. These enable testing of impact of changes in various factors considered while developing a mathematical model. A mathematical model depicting a reality normally has controllable inputs, also known as decision variables, and uncontrollable inputs mainly arising from environmental factors. The inputs to the model that are controlled or determined by the decision-maker are referred to as controllable inputs. Uncontrollable inputs can either be definitely known or may be subject to variation and involve uncertainty. Deterministic models are the ones in which all uncontrollable inputs to the model can be known precisely. On the other hand, stochastic or probabilistic models are the ones in which uncontrollable inputs are uncertain and are subject to variation. For example, if a company's liability payments and asset cash inflows are uncertain, a stochastic model is needed to understand the behaviour. The characteristic of stochastic model is that the value of output cannot be found with certainty.

Simulation is a useful technique for evaluating alternative forecasting methods. This can be done retrospectively using past data. Simulation refers to replicating a real world situation by incorporating a mathematical model that does not affect operations. Steps involved in the process of simulation are—defining the problem situation, identifying important variables, developing the simulation model, specifying values of variables to be tested, running the simulation model, examining results/outcomes, and selecting the best course of action. It is a tool that is widely being used by managers because of its flexibility. The availability of software has made development of simulation models relatively easy. It allows the study of the interactive effect of individual components, and above all, helps in analysing complex real world situations that cannot be solved by conventional quantitative techniques. However, it is important to know that simulation models take a long time to be developed and they do not generate optimal solutions such as those generated by other quantitative analysis techniques.

Monte Carlo method of simulation In case a system under consideration involves chance or uncertain elements, the Monte Carlo method of simulation, which relies on experimenting on probabilistic elements through random sampling, is used. The five steps involved in Monte Carlo simulation are:

1. Set a probability distribution for important variables
2. Build cumulative probability distribution for each variable
3. Establish an interval for random numbers for each variable
4. Generate random numbers, and actually simulate series of trials

Certainty models Forecasting models that give only the most likely outcome are known as certainty models. Having arrived at forecasts, one can use advanced spreadsheets to do 'what if' analysis. The implications and effects of changes in the independent variables are used for the purpose of forecasting and their implications on the forecasts of dependent variables have become very easy with spreadsheet/excel applications.

Probabilistic models These models involve uncertainty and use Monte Carlo simulation techniques to deal with the same. This enables to arrive at a range of possible outcomes for each set of events.

Forecasting error All forecasting models involve an implicit or explicit error structure. The objective of forecasting is to minimize this error. The forecast error is defined as the difference between actual or true value and the forecast value or predicted value, as per the prediction model used. One of the measures of accuracy of prediction is arrived at by mean absolute deviation (MAD). It is computed by taking a sum of absolute values of individual forecast errors to be divided by number of errors. Other measures of accuracy of forecast are mean squared error (MSE) and mean absolute percent error (MAPE). Mean squared error is defined as average of squared errors. Mean absolute percent error is the average of the absolute values of the errors expressed as percentage of the actual values. The accuracy of forecasts largely depends on the quality, reliability, and efficiency of data used for the forecasting purpose. The quality of data mainly depends on minimization of errors that may occur at the time of compiling and transmission of data. Therefore, it is important that data should be edited to take care of common and obvious mistakes.

While using any method for forecasting, one must use a performance measure to assess the quality of the method used. Mean absolute deviation and variance are the most useful measures to assess the dependability of the method used. However, it may be mentioned that standard error and not MAD is of more help in making inferences. For arriving at error analysis, variance is preferred indicator, as variances of independent, that is, uncorrelated errors are additive while MAD is not additive.

Thus, realizing that 'time is money' in business activities, the application of dynamic decision methodologies in a wide range of managerial decisions is becoming more and more important. Improving the effectiveness and efficiency of decision-making requires the use of various forecasting methods. The use of an appropriate forecasting method depends upon various factors such as the format of the forecast required, time frame for which the forecast is required, availability of reliable and dependable data, accuracy of the forecast required, cost of development and operation of method used for the forecast, operational ease, and above all, management comprehension, cooperation, and commitment in use and importance of forecasting methods. Greater sophistication needs to be incorporated in the methodology of forecasting to take care of emerging complexities in the business environment. As such, the quality of decision-making greatly depends on the accuracy of forecasts, as they would be a decisive factor for the success of the organization.

SUMMARY

To take right and good decisions requires planning for the future. The planning process would necessarily require forecasting about events likely to happen in the future. The quality of decision-making automatically improves as the competence of the organization improves in predicting uncontrollable aspects of future events prior to making a decision. Forecasting is a continuous process and is useful in a variety of business areas. Forecasting methods can be broadly classified into two categories—qualitative and quantitative, depending upon the degree and extent to which mathematical and statistical methods are used.

Quantitative methods are statistical forecasting techniques that explicitly define how the forecast has been arrived at. A time-series analysis is a time-linked sequence of observations of the variable that is used to develop a model for predicting future values. The major limitation of using causal models is that the independent variable values should be known while making the forecast. If the forecast period is a historical period, then the forecast is referred to as ex-post (after-the-fact) forecast. In case the forecast period is sometime in the future, the resulting forecast is referred to as ex-ante (before-the-fact) forecast.

There are many techniques that can be used for the purpose of forecasting. However, different techniques are applied in different situations depending upon the problem situation, context, degree of sophistication required, available time frame for forecasting, etc. Some of the important techniques used for forecasting are multiple regression analysis, non-linear regression, trend analysis, decomposition analysis, weighted moving averages, adaptive filtering, and exponential smoothing. A model describes a situation through a series of equations and allows testing of impact of changes in various factors. Simulation is a useful technique for evaluating alternate forecasting methods.

KEYWORDS

Certainty models The models whose predictions are the closest to what will happen in future events.

Ex-post and ex-ante forecast If the forecast period is an historical period, then the forecast is referred to as ex-post forecast. In case the forecast period is sometime in the future, the resulting forecast is referred to as ex-ante forecast.

Forecasting It refers to the prediction of uncontrollable aspects of future events prior to making a decision.

Forecasting error It is difference between the model prediction and the 'true' value.

Forecasting interval It is the time gap after which new forecasts are made.

Forecasting methods The methods used for forecasting are qualitative and quantitative, depending upon the degree and extent to which mathematical and statistical methods are used.

Forecasting period It is the basic unit of time for which the forecasts are made.

Forecasting techniques The mathematical or other tools and techniques used for forecasting.

Modelling and simulation Modelling is a representation of reality involving real objects and situations that can be presented in various forms.

Simulation is one of the techniques used to model the system involving a particular problem situation with an input of uncertainty.

Probabilistic models They deal with uncertainty and help in getting a range of possible outcomes for each set of events.

Steps to forecast Determining the use of the forecast to review the implications of decision vis-à-vis the forecast used, the final step being the forecasting model. There are specific steps to be followed for arriving at scientific and objective forecasts.

Time-series analysis It is a time-linked sequence of observations of the variable that is used to develop a model for predicting future values.

EXERCISES

Concept Review Questions

1. What is the necessity and relevance of forecasting techniques to manage business uncertainty? Explain.
2. What are the uses of forecasts in managing business? Explain giving an example.
3. Differentiate between quantitative and qualitative methods of forecasting.
4. Define multiple and non-linear regression analysis used for forecasting purpose.
5. Differentiate between simple and weighted moving average techniques used for forecasting.
6. What is the utility of simulation technique in business forecasting?
7. Define forecasting error. How can forecasting error be measured?

Critical Thinking Questions

1. A reputed mutual fund's regular income scheme has announced the following monthly dividends for the past 12 consecutive months in per cent—0.15, 0.18, 0.125, 0.13, 0.09, 0.08, 0.10, 0.21, 0.11, 0.06, 0.05, and 0.10.
   (i) Find out two and three months' moving averages for the above referred time-series dividends. Which moving average provides a better estimate and why?
   (ii) Find out the moving average expected dividend for the next three months.
   (iii) Will it be advisable for the investor to continue with the said scheme or would you advise her to liquidate the investment? Give reasons.

2. Agriculture scientists have been working on seed development for rice varieties that may lead to increase in productivity by 30 per cent, given all other factors affecting productivity being same. Which forecasting method would be best suited to estimate when such a variety may come in the market? Explain the rationale for your answer.

3. What is the advantage of exponential smoothing forecasting technique? Identify a particular business situation wherein exponential smoothing technique would be best suited for the forecasting purpose.

Project Assignments

1. ABC Ltd has observed that their actual performance has been consistently varying by a wide margin compared to forecasts in terms of sales turnover, net profit, and cost of goods sold. It is losing trust in the group dealing with forecasting because of such wide gap and is thinking of managing without depending upon the forecasts of various business parameters. Based on the concepts learnt in this chapter, what could be the areas contributing to forecasting error beyond bounds? What changes will you suggest to rationalize forecasting efforts?

2. Identify areas of business operations wherein qualitative techniques will be more effective when compared to quantitative techniques. Justify your answer.

REFERENCES

Anderson, David R., Dennis J. Sweeney, and Thomas A. Williams (2006), *Quantitative Methods for Business*, Thomson South Western, Indian Reprint by Kundali, India.

DeLurgio, Stephen A. and Carl O. Bhame (1991), *Forecasting Systems for Operation Management*, Business One Irwin, Homewood, Illinois.

Keller, Gerald (2005), *Statistics for Management and Economics*, 7th edn, Thomson South-Western, First Indian Reprint, (2007), Delhi, p. 701.

Kress, G. (1985), *Practical Techniques of Business Forecasting*, Quorum Books, Westport, Connecticut.

Render, Barry Stair Jr., M. Ralph, and Michael E. Hanna (2000), *Quantitative Analysis for Management*, Pearson Education, Singapore, Indian Reprint, p. 143.

Wilson, Holton J. and Barry Keating (1994), *Business Forecasting*, Richard D. Irwin, McGraw-Hill Education, Europe.

38

Regression Analysis

INTRODUCTION

Regression analysis is a common technique used for forecasting. It is a statistical technique used to analyse and investigate the relationship between two or more variables. Many of the forecasting techniques described in the previous chapter utilize regression methods for parameter estimation. It is a technique used for studying the relationships among variables to predict or estimate the value of one variable from given or assumed values of other variables related to it.

RELATED CONCEPTS

Sir Francis Galton (1877) introduced the term 'regression' as a statistical concept. He denoted the term regression to define the general process of predicting one variable from another. Subsequently, statisticians came out with the term multiple regression to describe the process to predict a variable by using several variables. Regression analysis is a technique to establish relationships between variables by finding the parameters for a function that cause the function to best fit a set of data observations on dependent and independent variables. The best fit line between a dependent and an independent variable gives predicted values of dependent variable to be as close to the observed or actual values as possible. This helps in predicting future values of dependent variable.

The behavioural relationship between variables may be linearly related; implying thereby that the function is a linear (straight line) equation. If the variables are non-linearly related it implies that the function is non-linear. It

Learning Objectives

After studying this chapter, you will be able to:
- Understand the utility of regression analysis in business decisions
- Learn how regression analysis is used for forecasting
- Learn about ordinary least squares (OLS) method to predict value of dependent variable
- Evaluate the various applications of regression analysis

is used to forecast the value of one variable (dependent variable) based on the values of other variables having causal relationship (independent variable) (Keller 2007).

Variables of Interest

To make predictions or estimates, we must identify the effective predictors of the variable of interest (dependent variable). The dependent variable is the item that is estimated/forecasted. Independent variable(s) are items that have causal effect on the dependent variable (Render et al. 2003). It is important to identify the variables that are important indicators in explaining the behaviour of variables of interest and can be measured at the least cost as against those, which carry only a little information, and are redundant. It is important to understand that predicting a change over time or extrapolating from present to future conditions is not the function of regression analysis. Once the relevant variables get identified, model building requires an experimentation that begins with a hypothesis about how several variables might be related to another variable and the form of the relationship. It is important to understand that we often find a causal relationship between variables, that is, the independent variable 'causes' the dependent variable to change (Levin and Rubin 1999). While identifying relevant variables, it is more important to identify the relationships of association rather than the cause and effect relationship. Thus, unless we are able to establish that values of dependent variables are caused by the values of the independent variables, one should not jump to the conclusion that causality is established from the relationships found through regression.

Data is a gathered set of facts representing the values of variables. As it may be unrealistic as also unfeasible in certain situations to collect information on an entire population, a sample, which is a representative subset of the total population is usually selected to collect data on the selected variables related to the problem. Thus, a sample is defined as a small set of individual units, which is drawn from population units for statistical examination. The outcome of the examination is intended to be applied to the population. Therefore, it is necessary that the sample should be representative of the population characteristics (Bartlett et al. 2001; Cochran 1977). Sampling technique is based on two prominent principles of statistics—the law of statistical regularity and the law of inertia of large numbers.

The law of statistical regularity presumes that a random sample selected from the given population represents the characteristics and composition of the population. The law of inertia of large numbers states that keeping other things as same, larger the sample size, greater would be the accuracy in obtaining results.

Random Sampling

The methods used for sampling can be random or non-random (Saha and Mukherjee 2002). Random sampling is a process wherein each member unit of the population has equal chance (probability) of being included in the sample. For example, when one tosses a coin, one has an equal chance of getting head or tail. Similarly, all have an equal chance of picking up a winning ticket from a rotating drum containing all ticket counterfoils. There are four methods that can be used for random sampling—(1) random sampling; (2) stratified sampling; (3) systematic sampling; and (4) multi-stage sampling.

Random sampling   It is the simplest and easiest method of sampling amongst various techniques and is devoid of any personal bias. Picking up an item under random sampling is purely a matter of chance.

Stratified sampling   This method is used when the population under consideration is heterogeneous. Therefore, the population is first divided into several small groups having similar characteristics. Each such group is referred to as a sub-population. Then a small sample is selected from each stratum (sub-group) at random. A combination of all sub-samples forms a stratified sample. Proper stratification ensures homogeneity within the sub-group (*stratum*) and heterogeneity between the sub-groups (*stratum*). Systematic sampling requires arranging a population in some order and thereafter from the first k items, one unit is randomly selected. Thereafter, every kth unit of the serially arranged population coupled with the first unit selected constitutes a systematic sample.

Systematic sampling   The difference between random sample and systematic sample lies in the fact that in random sampling all members are chosen randomly while in case of systematic sampling only the first member is selected randomly and subsequent members are mechanically picked up from the population arranged in an order.

Multi-stage sampling   As the concept suggests, in multi-stage sampling, the process is carried out in multiple stages. This method is especially useful when using sample units from all selected clusters may be very expensive or may not be necessary. A major advantage of this method is its convenience, efficiency, and cost economy in collecting the sample. Under this method a researcher randomly selects units from each cluster as against using all units from the selected cluster. The first step under multiple stage sampling is to form clusters and thereafter to decide the element to use within the cluster. The population is divided into large groups known as first stage units. Thereafter, the first stage units are divided into smaller groups known as second stage units. These units are further divided into third stage units, so on and so forth till the desired sample size is arrived at. For example, in the first stage of studying the consumption pattern of slum dwellers in Mumbai's largest slum area Dharavi, clusters are sub-divided, then sampled. In the second stage, blocks of houses are picked up from within the sub-divisions, and in the third stage individual houses are picked up from within the selected block of houses.

Non-random Sampling Methods

As the term suggests, the choice of individual items in a sample mainly depends upon the judgement of the investigator. Therefore, it is also known as purposive or judgement sampling. The choice of each unit is according to the convenience and personal choice of the individual asking for the sample. Such a sample has limited utility in terms of drawing inferences, as two different purposive samples may give rise to wide variation in the inferences arrived at.

Quota sampling Interviewers are assigned a fixed quota to be covered, based on certain criteria. The interviewer's job is to obtain data from required number of interviewees to fulfil each assigned quota. Within the specified quota, it is the interviewer who selects individuals based on his/her personal judgement.

Convenience sampling A sample is selected from easily available source of information such as telephone directory, stock exchange directory, etc. It is also known as opportunity sampling, as items are selected arbitrarily and in an unstructured manner from the given frame. This method is commonly employed in practical situations because of its ease. It is a useful technique while undertaking opinion surveys and pilot studies.

Sequential sampling Samples are drawn from the population one after the other depending upon the outcome of the earlier sample. Samples are taken sequentially till such time that a final decision to accept or reject the lot is arrived at. This method is commonly used in statistical quality control.

A scatter diagram represents a pair of data in a graphical form. It gives an overall view about the relationship between the variables and in turn helps in understanding the problem better. The diagram enables the analyst to find out whether there exists an apparent relationship between the variables? If so, is it direct or inverse? If the values of variables shown on y axis for each value of the variable on x axis lie within a band described by parallel lines, there exists a linear relationship between the pair of x and y values. Thus, the first step to identify a specific equation that may help in connecting variables is to collect data on the variables under consideration and to plot the same on a diagram. In Fig. 38.1 the data collected on two variables namely X and Y is represented by showing various points in a graphical way. The two different diagrams clearly reveal that X and Y variables are linearly related for one set of data and are non-linearly related for the other set. Regression analysis helps in determining the precise relationship between the two or more variables. Once the relationship is determined, it can be used for forecasting.

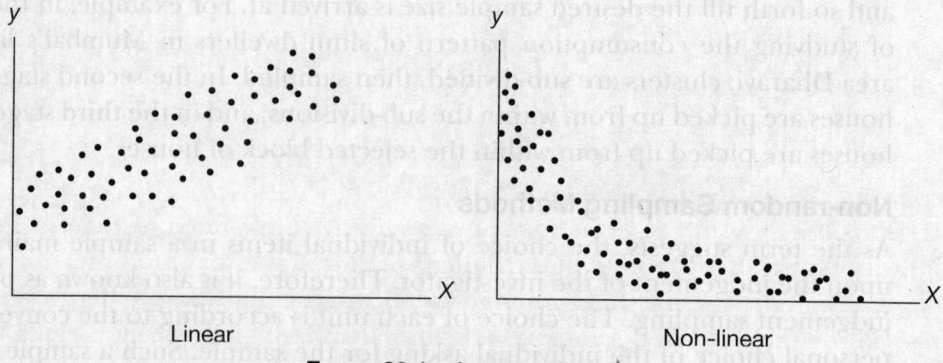

Linear   Non-linear

FIGURE 38.1 A scatter diagram

SIMPLE LINEAR REGRESSION

A regression using only one predictor is referred to as a simple regression; in case of two or more predictors, a multiple regression analysis is employed. A simple regression can be used to determine the relationship between an independent variable, such as time or income and a dependent variable, such as sales or consumption. In case, we assume that the true relationship between these two variables is a straight line and that the observed value of Y (sales or consumption) for any particular value of X (time or income) is a random variable, then we may express the expected value of Y for each value of X in the following form:

$$Y = a + bX \qquad (38.1)$$

Where Y is the dependent variable, X is the independent variable, a is the y-axis intercept, and b is the slope of regression line. The intercept a and slope b are unknown constants. The observed value of Y can be described as:

$$Y = a + bX + e \qquad (38.2)$$

Where, e is defined as a random error term or a disturbance component. This model is referred to as a linear regression model, as it involves only one independent variable that is X. It is also known as repressor variable and Y is known as response variable. We can also define Y as the dependent variable (sales or consumption in the instant case) and X as independent variable (time or income in the instant case). The repressor or the response variable could be time series, and this model is known as time-series regression model. However, the regression analysis can be used for forecasting purposes even on cross sectional data, that is, at a given point of time.

Least Squares Method

Least squares method (Fig. 38.2) is an objective method of producing a straight line drawn through the points so that sum of squared deviations between the points

Forecasting using regression analysis

An expert goldsmith has to decide about a major purchase of gold bullion for the coming year, so that he buys the required amount at the least price possible. However, he needs to forecast the gold prices for the next three years from now. His aim is to earn profit through value addition by making ornaments, and by buying the required gold at its lowest price. He decides to use regression analysis to forecast gold prices. As a first step, he tries to identify all important independent variables such as inflation rate, interest rate, demand for gold jewellery, supply of gold, etc. He has to thereafter build a regression model to explain the price of gold as a function of important independent variables. Having developed the relationship, the past data on variables needs to be collected for using the regression technique to forecast future prices of gold.

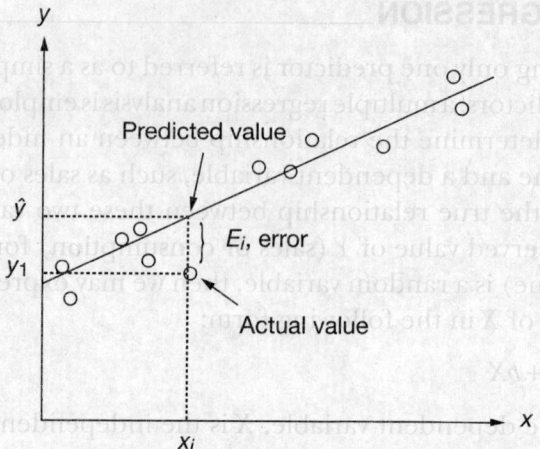

FIGURE 38.2 Least squares method—Predicted
and actual value of dependent variable

and the line is minimized passing from points (Keller 2005). It gives the 'best fit' curve to a sample of data that minimizes the sum of the deviations squared (least square error) between actual values of dependent variable and the estimated values of the dependent variable. Thus, to predict the mean Y value for a given value of X, we need a line which need to pass through the mean value of both X and Y and that should minimize the sum of the distance between each of the points and the predictive line. This approach enables us to identify a line that can be called as a 'best fit' to the sample data.

The least squares method achieves this result by calculating the minimum average squared deviations between the sample Y points and the estimated line. A method used for finding the values of parameters a and b that leads to the solution of simultaneous linear equations (Chatterjee et al. 2000). Simple shortcut methods have been developed to arrive at the values of parameters as an alternative to the solution of simultaneous equations. Matrix algebra techniques can be manually employed to solve simultaneous linear equations to arrive at the values of unknowns. Several well-known computer packages are now available that can be used to simplify the job of the user. These packages can be used to solve both linear and polynomial equations, for example, the BMD packages (Biomedical Computer Programs) from UCLA; SPSS (Statistical Package for the Social Sciences) developed by the University of Chicago; and SAS (Statistical Analysis System). Another package that is also available is IMSL, the International Mathematical and Statistical Libraries, which contain a great variety of standard mathematical and statistical calculations. All these software packages use matrix algebra to solve simultaneous equations. Availability of computational packages have made the job easy and what is now required is greater knowledge and competence on the part of analysts to interpret the results, so as to provide better and objective insight in decision-making (Koop 2005; Hill et al. 2000).

Sample observations and the sample regression line is used to find out the line of 'best fit' based on various data points in the scattered diagram as represented by:

$$\hat{y} = a + bx \qquad\qquad (38.3)$$

requires minimization of $\sum e_i^2$.

To minimize $\sum e_i^2$, calculus is applied to find the following 'normal equations':

$$\sum y = na + b\sum x \qquad\qquad (38.4(1))$$

$$\sum yx = a\sum x + b\sum x^2 \qquad\qquad (38.4(2))$$

Solving equations 38.4(1) and 38.4(2) simultaneously, we get:

$$b = \frac{n\sum xy - \sum x\sum y}{n\sum x^2 - (\sum x)^2}$$

$$a = \frac{\sum y}{n} - b\frac{\sum x}{n} \qquad\qquad (38.5)$$

The formula for calculating the slope b is commonly written as:

$$b = \frac{\sum (x - \bar{x})(y - \bar{y})}{\sum (x - \bar{x})^2} \qquad\qquad (38.6)$$

the numerator and denominator can be expressed as under:

$$
\begin{aligned}
\sum (x - \bar{x})(y - \bar{y}) &= \sum (xy - \bar{x}y - x\bar{y} + \bar{x}\,\bar{y}) \\
&= \sum xy - \bar{x}\sum y - \bar{y}\sum x + \sum \bar{x}\,\bar{y} \\
&= \sum xy - n\bar{x}\,\bar{y} - n\bar{x}\,\bar{y} + n\bar{x}\,\bar{y} \\
&= \sum xy - n\bar{x}\,\bar{y}
\end{aligned}
\qquad (38.7)
$$

and

$$
\begin{aligned}
\sum (x - \bar{x})^2 &= \sum (x^2 - 2x\bar{x} + \bar{x}^2) \\
&= \sum x^2 - 2\bar{x}\sum x + \sum \bar{x}^2 \\
&= \sum x^2 - 2n\bar{x}^2 + n\bar{x}^2 \\
&= \sum x^2 - n\bar{x}^2
\end{aligned}
\qquad (38.8)
$$

When the equation $\hat{y} = a + bx$ is calculated from a sample of observations rather than from a population, it is referred to as a sample regression line.

The constants a and b can also be computed using the following equations:

$$a = \frac{\sum x^2 \sum y - \sum x \sum xy}{n \sum x^2 - (\sum x)^2}$$

$$b = \frac{n \sum xy - \sum x \sum y}{n \sum x^2 - (\sum x)^2}$$

(38.9)

Once the values of a and b are computed, the future value of X can be entered into the regression equation and a corresponding value of Y (the forecast) can be calculated. The value of b, that is, the slope of the line indicates change in y for a unit increase in x. It measures the marginal rate of change in the dependent variable for a unit change in the independent variable. The intercept on the y axis a indicates the value of the dependent variable when the value of x is zero. This may or may not have any actual meaning in reality and would depend upon the nature of problem under consideration.

A sale of the company has steadily grown over the past six years (Table 38.1). We can use time-series regression to forecast the sales for the next three years.

So the simple linear regression works out to be:

$$Y = -1.733 + 2.54X$$

(38.10)

TABLE 38.1 A company's growth chart

Year	₹/Lakh
1	2
2	3
3	5
4	8
5	10
6	15

x	y	x^2	xy
1	2	1	2
2	3	4	6
3	5	9	15
4	8	16	32
5	10	25	50
6	15	36	90
$\sum x = 21$	$\sum y = 43$	$\sum x^2 = 91$	$\sum xy = 195$

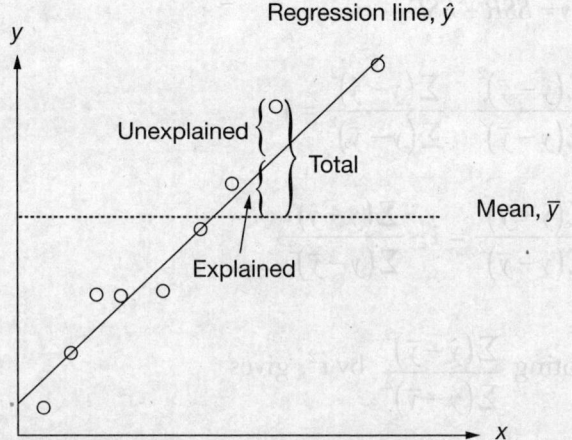

FIGURE 38.3 Relationships between total, explained, and unexplained variations in estimated value of dependent variable

Where Y is the sales and X is the time period in years

The sales for 7th year would be $Y_7 = -1.733 + 2.54 \times 7 = 16.047$
The sales for 8th year would be $Y_8 = -1.733 + 2.54 \times 8 = 18.587$
The sales for 9th year would be $Y_9 = -1.733 + 2.54 \times 9 = 21.127$

Simple linear regression can also be used when the independent variable X represents a variable other than time. In this case, linear regression is representative of a class of forecasting models known as causal forecasting models.

Coefficient of Determination

The obvious question that needs to be answered is how well a least squares regression line fits a given set of paired data? It is important to measure the strength of the linear relationship, particularly when we would like to compare the outcome from several different models. The statistic that enables us to perform the same is known as coefficient of determination (R^2). The coefficient of determination is square of coefficient of correlation (r).

Variation of the y values around their own mean $= \sum(y - \bar{y})^2$

Variation of the y values around the regression line $= \sum(y - \hat{y})^2$

Regression sum of squares $= \sum(\hat{y} - \bar{y})^2$
We have:

$$\sum(y - \bar{y})^2 = \sum(\hat{y} - \bar{y})^2 + \sum(y - \hat{y})^2 \tag{38.11}$$

Thus, the measure of variation in the dependent variable y is explained by the sum of the first term on the right hand side of the equation that denotes the sum of squares for regression and the second term that denotes the sum of squares of errors (Fig. 38.3).

Variation in $y = SSR + SSE$

$$\Rightarrow \frac{\Sigma(\hat{y}-\overline{y})^2}{\Sigma(y-\overline{y})^2} + \frac{\Sigma(y-\hat{y})^2}{\Sigma(y-\overline{y})^2} = 1 \qquad (38.12)$$

$$\Rightarrow \frac{\Sigma(\hat{y}-\overline{y})^2}{\Sigma(y-\overline{y})^2} = 1 - \frac{\Sigma(y-\hat{y})^2}{\Sigma(y-\overline{y})^2}$$

Denoting $\dfrac{\Sigma(\hat{y}-\overline{y})^2}{\Sigma(y-\overline{y})^2}$ by r^2, gives $\qquad (38.13)$

$$R^2 = 1 - \frac{\Sigma(y-\hat{y})^2}{\Sigma(y-\overline{y})^2} = \frac{\text{Explained variation}}{\text{Variation in } y} \qquad (38.14)$$

Thus, R^2 is the coefficient of determination that is the proportion of variation in y explained by a sample regression line and in the instant case by the variation in x.

For example, the value of $R^2 = 0.9523$ in the above example implies that 95.23 per cent of the variation in y is due to their linear relationship with x.

Correlation Coefficient

The correlation coefficient is a statistical concept that measures the way in which well predicted values follow trends in actual values, that is, to what extent predicted values from the forecast model fit into the actual data. The value of correlation coefficient increases as the relationship between the predicted and actual values gets stronger. The value of r will be one in case of a perfect fit. As such, the higher the value of r, the better it is.

$$r = \frac{n\Sigma xy - (\Sigma x)(\Sigma y)}{\sqrt{\left(n\Sigma x^2 - (\Sigma x)^2\right)\left(n\Sigma y^2 - (\Sigma y)^2\right)}} \text{ and } -1 \leq r \leq 1. \qquad (38.15)$$

The formulas for calculating r^2 (sample coefficient of determination) and r (sample coefficient of correlation) can be simplified in a more common version as follows:

$$r^2 = \frac{\left(\Sigma(x-\overline{x})(y-\overline{y})\right)^2}{\Sigma(x-\overline{x})^2 \Sigma(y-\overline{y})^2} = \frac{\left(\Sigma xy - n\overline{x}\,\overline{y}\right)^2}{\left(\Sigma x^2 - n\overline{x}^2\right)\left(\Sigma y^2 - n\overline{y}^2\right)}$$

$$r = \sqrt{r^2} = \frac{\Sigma(x-\overline{x})(y-\overline{y})}{\sqrt{\Sigma(x-\overline{x})^2 \Sigma(y-\overline{y})^2}} = \frac{\Sigma xy - n\overline{x}\,\overline{y}}{\sqrt{\left(\Sigma x^2 - n\overline{x}^2\right)\left(\Sigma y^2 - n\overline{y}^2\right)}} \qquad (38.16)$$

Since the numerator used in calculating r and b (as shown earlier) are the same and both denominators are always positive, r and b will always be of the same sign. Moreover, if $r = 0$, then $b = 0$ and vice versa. The coefficient of correlation, in case of the above example, is 0.9758, implying a strong positive correlationship between x and y. Thus, the coefficient of correlation r explains the relative importance of the relationship between x and y. The sign r shows the direction of the relationship and the absolute value of r shows the strength of the relationship. The sign of r is always the same as the sign of b. r can take on any value between -1 and $+1$. In case r is -1, it indicates a perfectly negative relationship (as x goes up, y goes down by one unit, and vice versa). On the other hand, if r is $+1$, it indicates a perfect positive relationship (as x goes up, y goes up by one unit, and vice versa) and a value of r being 0 indicates that there does not exist any relationship between x and y.

Confidence Intervals

Interval estimates are calculated to find a measure of the confidence in the estimates that a relationship exists between the variables under consideration. These calculations are made using t-distribution tables and help us to derive confidence bands, a pair of non-parallel lines narrowest at the mean values, which express our confidence in varying degrees of the band of values surrounding the regression equation. The strength of the relationship between variables under consideration can be worked out by statistical tests of that hypothesis such as the null hypothesis, which are established using t-distribution, R-squared, and F-distribution tables. These calculations help in obtaining the standard error of the regression coefficient, an estimate of the amount that the regression coefficient b will vary from sample to sample of the same size from the same population.

We have earlier in this chapter seen three different sums of squares namely total sum of squares (SST), regression sum of squares (SSR), and error sum of squares (SSE). Anders Hald (1998) described Sir Ronald Aylmer Fisher (1890–1962), who first introduced these concepts, as a 'genius who single-handedly created the foundations for modern statistical science'. Richard Dawkins described him as 'the greatest of Darwin's successors'. Fisher had made pioneering contributions to statistical analysis. He developed principles of the design of experiments and came out with his original contribution explaining that the total variation in Y can be explained as:

$$SST = SSR + SSE \qquad (38.17)$$

These sums of squares have an associated degree of freedom. SST has $n - 1$ degrees of freedom, that is, n observations minus one degree of freedom, as the sample mean is fixed. SSR has k degrees of freedom, as k independent variables are used. SSE has $n-k-1$ degrees of freedom, as we have used n observations to estimate $k+1$ constants. The concept, known as 'analysis of variance' is a powerful tool of statistical analysis. It is used to test whether difference between means of three or more populations is significant. It is a collection of statistical models and related procedures that enables observed variance to be apportioned into various components arising because of different explanatory variables.

An analysis of variance (ANOVA) table that helps in summarizing the different components of variation can be generated. To compare models of different size (different numbers of independent variables and/or different sample sizes), it is advisable to use the adjusted R-squared, because the usual R-squared tends to grow with the number of independent variables. The standard error of estimate, which is square root of error mean square is a good indicator of the 'quality' of a model used for prediction as it 'adjusts' the error sum of squares for the number of predictors in the model. If the analyst keeps adding irrelevant predictors to a model, the error sum of squares will become less and less stable.

Applications of regression analysis exist in almost every field; in economics, sociology, psychology, and wide-ranging areas of management such as marketing research, sales forecasting, production, finance, and budget forecasting. The dependent variable might be a family's consumption expenditure and the independent variables might be the family's income, the number of children in the family, and other factors that would affect the family's consumption patterns. Thus, the family's consumption expenditure for the future can be estimated (forecasted) using simple linear regression analysis. In business situations one can forecast sales as a function of advertisement expenditure, sales as a function of number of sales people in the territory, profit as a function of cost, output as a function of number of employees, output as a function of number of machines, etc. In sociology, the dependent variable might be a measure of the social status of various occupations and the independent variables characteristics of the occupations (pay, qualifications, etc.). Thus, regression analysis is a vital tool that can be used for objective managerial decision-making, particularly pertaining to aspects involving future forecasts.

SUMMARY

Regression analysis is a technique used for studying the relationships among variables, with an objective to predict, or estimate the value of one variable from a given or assumed values of other variables related to it. A simple regression can be used to determine the relationship between an independent variable, that is, time or income and a dependent variable, that is, sales or consumption. The coefficient of correlation r, explains the relative importance of the relationship between dependent and independent variables. The sign of r shows the direction of the relationship and the absolute value of r shows the strength of the relationship. Interval estimates can be calculated to obtain the measure of the confidence we have in our estimates that a relationship exists. These calculations are made using t-distribution tables.

The strength of that relationship can be assessed by statistical tests of that hypothesis such as the null hypothesis which are established using t-distribution, R-squared, and F-distribution tables.

The standard error of estimate (i.e., square root of error mean square) is a good indicator of the 'quality' of a prediction model since it 'adjusts' the error sum of squares (ESS) for the number of predictors in the model. Regression technique can be used for forecasting purposes in various fields of studies. It is important to establish a relationship between variables and test the reliability and validity of the relationship based on statistical analysis.

KEYWORDS

Coefficient of determination It is the statistic commonly used to find out how well a regression fits, that is, how far the variability in dependent variable is explained with the help of independent variables.

Correlation coefficient It is a statistic that measures the efficiency with which the trends in the predicted values follow trends in past actual values.

Data Gathered facts representing the values of variables.

Error term The difference between the predicted and actual value of the dependent variable.

Least squares method It gives the 'best fit' curve to a sample of data that minimizes the sum of the deviations squared (least square error) between actual values of the dependent variable and the estimated values of the dependent variable.

Regression analysis Statistical technique for modelling to analyse and investigate the relationship between two or more variables.

Scatter diagram Graphical representation of the pairs of data is called a scatter diagram.

Simple linear regression A regression using only one predictor is known as a simple regression.

Variables of interest Also known as dependent variable, its behaviour is proposed to be estimated through regression analysis.

EXERCISES

Concept Review Questions

1. How does regression analysis deal with business situations? Explain.
2. Differentiate between independent variable and dependent variable.
3. What is the relevance of data in regression analysis? How is data collected?
4. What is the purpose of drawing a scatter diagram?
5. Define least squares method used for forecasting in a simple regression analysis. What is the significance of parameters *a* and *b* from the economic point of view?
6. What technique is used to answer 'how well a least squares regression line fits a given set of paired data'? Explain.
7. What is meant by standard error of estimate? What is its utility in regression analysis?

Critical Thinking Questions

1. State and explain whether the relationship between the variables given below is expected to have positive, negative, or no correlation in the following cases.
    (a) Shoe size and intelligence
    (b) Education and income level
    (c) Rent and area in square feet
    (d) Advertising budget and sales
    (e) Profit and variable cost of production
2. What is meant by correlation between two variables? Why should it lie between -1 and $+1$? Prove that correlation coefficient r is independent of units of measurement.
3. A leading college having 625 seats and imparting management education has undergone a following enrolment changes in the last five years at a commercial fee structure:

Year	1	2	3	4	5
Enrollment	600	625	500	490	480

   (a) Work out simple linear equation to estimate the future enrolment trend based on past time-series data.
   (b) Comment critically on the current trend of enrolment in this institute and what is expected trend in the coming three years. Based on your projections, suggest the strategies that the college needs to take to have optimum capacity utilization.

Project Assignments

1. The income and monthly food expenditure data of ten randomly selected families is given here:

(₹ in thousands)

Family	Monthly income	Monthly food expenditure
1	10	4
2	15	6
3	18	8
4	25	7
5	12	5
6	14	6
7	18	9
8	25	9
9	11	5
10	18	8

(a) Assuming a linear relationship between income and monthly food expenditure, determine the regression coefficients related to monthly food expenditure to income. Interpret the significance of these parameters from business related to food industry.

(b) Determine the estimated standard error of monthly food expenditure, based on the family income.

2. You are working in the planning department of a bank. The managing director of the bank is interested in knowing the relationship between bank aggregate deposits (in thousand crore) and gross domestic product (in lakh crore). You have regressed the relationship between the two by using data for the past ten years and have found the following ordinary least square estimates:

Variable	Coefficient	Standard error	't' statistic
Constant	5.85	7.20	0.92
Income	2.88	0.22	22.22
Mean of dependent variable is 57. Error sum of square (ESS) is 2230.	Standard deviation of dependent variable is 12 Standard error of residual is 8.23.	Unadjusted R-squared is 0.93.	Adjusted R-squared is 0.94.

(a) Interpret the regression results to explain to the managing director the significance of your findings as regards deposit planning is concerned.

(b) If the GDP for the next year is going to be ₹450 lakh crore, what will be the deposit level for the bank next year?

(c) What is the implication of value for R^2?

(d) Under certain assumptions the coefficient estimates are unbiased. What assumptions are required in the above model for the estimates to be unbiased?

REFERENCES

Bartlett, J.E., J.W. Kotrlik, and C. Higgins (2001), 'Organizational Research: Determining Appropriate Sample Size for Survey Research', *Information Technology, Learning and Performance Journal*, vol. 19, no. 1, pp. 43–50.

Chatterjee, S., A. Hadi, and B. Price (2000), 'Simple Linear Regression', *Regression Analysis by Example*, 3rd edn, Wiley, New York, pp. 21–50.

Cochran, W.G. (1977), *Sampling Techniques*, Wiley.

Fisher, R.A. (1978), *The Life of a Scientist*, John Wiley, New York.

Galton, F. (1883), *Inquiries into Human Faculty and its Development*, Macmillan, London.

Hald, Anders (1998), *A History of Mathematical Statistics*, Wiley, New York.

Hill Carter, R., William E. Griffiths, and George G. Judge (2000), *Undergraduate Econometrics Using EViews*, 2nd edn, John Wiley, New York.

Keller, Gerald (2005), *Statistics for Management and Economics*, 7th edn, Thomson South–Western, First Indian Reprint, 2007, pp. 122, 578.

Koop, Gary (2005), *Analysis of Economic Data*, 2nd edn, John Wiley and Sons, New York.

Levin, Richard I. and David S. Rubin (1999), *Statistics for Management*, Prentice Hall of India, p.649.

Render, Barry Stair Jr, M. Ralph, Michael E. Hanna, (2003), *Quantitative Analysis for Management*, Pearson Education (Singapore), Indian Reprint, p. 164.

Richard, Dawkins (1995), *River Out of Eden,* HarperCollins, New York.

Saha, S. and S. Mukherjee (2002), *Quantitative Methods*, New Central Book Agency, 5th edn, Kolkata, pp. 98–104.

39

Index Numbers

Learning Objectives

After studying this chapter, you will be able to:

- Understand the meaning and relevance of index numbers
- Know about the prerequisites for computing reliable index numbers
- Learn about various price related index numbers and their applications

INTRODUCTION

We keep coming across news items highlighting that turnover and profits of a company have doubled, the GDP has grown by 1.25 times, etc. The implication behind these numbers needs to be better understood with some degree of caution. According to some salaried people, the standard of life was far better three years back when the salary was just 60 per cent of what is being drawn now. What is the implication of all these? How can we have clearer and better understanding of such information? What is the difference between nominal changes in income and real changes in income? How does inflation affect business and consumer decisions? All these can be better understood with the help of index numbers.

Many business, individual, and economic problems require conversion of data into purely relative numbers, so that the same can have meaningful comparisons. The relative numbers that are relative to a particular base are referred to as index numbers. It is a number that measures the relative change in price, quantity, value, or some other item of concern from interest from one time period to another for a better understanding of such problem situations as highlighted earlier. A simple index number is an index number that is used to measure the relative change in just one variable. It is the ratio of two values of the variable expressed as a percentage. The current period is the period for which one wishes to find the index number. The base period is the period with which the comparison is made. Marris (1958) defines index numbers as 'devices for mitigating deceptions caused by changes in the value of money' and describes the two major kinds of indices—price and volume.

According to Karmel (1957), an index number 'represents the general level of magnitude of the changes between two or more situations of a number of variables taken as a whole.' Bowley (1926) defines an index number as the one 'used to measure the change in some quantity which cannot be observed directly, which we know to have a definite influence on many other quantities which we can so observe, tending to increase all or diminish all, while this influence is concealed by the action of many causes affecting the separate quantities in various ways.'

The chief reasons for computing index numbers are:

- it facilitates a comparison of unlike series;
- it is a convenient way to express the change in the total of a heterogeneous group of items;
- a per cent change is often easier to comprehend than in actual numbers, especially when they are large; and
- it helps in understanding the nominal change and real change in the variables.

To arrive at reliable index numbers, various components used for computation should satisfy certain conditions such as:

- components used to arrive at index numbers should reflect their purpose;
- items included for computation should be true representative of the population;
- data used should be authentic and reliable; and
- relative importance of constituents used keep changing, as also new constituents need to be included. Therefore, the methodology behind the computation of indices should be reviewed in the long run.

PRICE RELATIVE INDEX

The price relative of an item is the ratio of the item in the current period to the price of the same item in the base period. p_n is the price of an item in the current period and p_0 is the price of an item in the base period. The price relative provides a ratio that indicates the change in price of an item from one period to another. Suppose a cup of tea in a particular hotel used to cost ₹5 in 2000 and the same quantity in the same hotel costs ₹12 in 2004. What has been the change in the price of a cup of tea between the year 2000 and 2004? The particular time period 2000 that is chosen to compare against is referred to as the base period. The variable for that period, which in this case is ₹5 per cup of a tea, is then given a value of 100, which corresponds to 100 per cent. The index can then be calculated for the later period of 2004 as a proportionate change as follows:

The index number$/100$ = ₹12/₹5
The index number = $12/5 \times 100 = 240$

Thus, an index number shows that there has been a price increase of 140 per cent since the base period. An index number for a single price change like this is referred to as a price relative.

WHOLESALE AND RETAIL PRICE INDEX

Wholesale and retail price index measures the change in price over time of a range of widely bought goods and services, thus calculating the cost of living. For measurement of inflation wholesale price index is used. Price indices such as wholesale price index (WPI) and consumer price index (CPI) for industrial workers, urban and non-manual employees, and agricultural labourers are computed in India for different purposes. The main difference lies in the basket of commodities considered for computation of each index and the weightage given to different commodities. The WPI is the most widely used price index in India and is an indicator of movement in wholesale prices of 435 commodities. It is available on a weekly basis with a time lag of two weeks. This index is of wide application and utility to business and industry. The base year presently considered for computation of WPI is 1993–94. The consumer price index for industrial workers, CPI (IW) is computed on monthly basis, with a time lag of one month. It measures the changes in the retail prices of a basket of 264 goods and services from 70 centres. The present base year for its computation is 1982. Similarly, the composition of the basket of commodities varies for the computation of CPI for non-manual employees and agricultural labourers. The current base year for CPI (urban non-manual employees) is 1984–85 and for agricultural labourers it is 1986–87.

COMPUTATION OF PRICE INDICES

Suppose a family consumes three vital products—food, milk, and clothing and spends all its income on these items. The prices and the quantities consumed of these three items in the year 2000 and 2004 are mentioned here. We would like to know how index numbers could be used to compare the cost for the base period of 2000 against the cost for a later period (2004). Table 39.1 shows the details of the purchases of these three commodities by the family for those two years.

BSE index—Capital market

For the premier stock exchange that pioneered the stock broking activity in India, 128 years of experience seems to be a proud milestone. Till the decade of eighties, there was no scale to measure the ups and downs in the Indian stock market. The Stock Exchange, Mumbai (BSE), in 1986, came out with a stock index that subsequently became the barometer of the Indian stock market.

Sensex is not only scientifically designed but also based on globally accepted construc-

tion and review methodology. First compiled in 1986, Sensex is a basket of 30 constituent stocks representing a sample of large, liquid, and representative companies. The base year of Sensex is 1978–79 and the base value is 100. The growth of equity markets in India has been phenomenal in the decade gone by. Right from the early nineties, the stock market witnessed heightened activity in terms of various bull and bear runs. The Sensex captured all these events in the most judicial manner. One

(Contd)

Exhibit (*Contd*)

can identify the booms and busts of the Indian stock market through the Sensex.

Sensex is calculated using the 'free-float market capitalization' methodology. As per this methodology, the level of index at any point of time reflects the free-float market value of 30 component stocks relative to a base period. The market capitalization of a company is determined by multiplying the price of its stock by the number of shares issued by the company. This market capitalization is further multiplied by the free-float factor to determine the free-float market capitalization.

The base period of Sensex is 1978–79 and the base value is 100 index points. This is often indicated by the notation 1978–79 = 100. The calculation of Sensex involves dividing the free-float market capitalization of 30 companies in the index by a number called the index divisor. The divisor is the only link to the original base period value of the Sensex. It keeps the index comparable over time and is the adjustment point for all index adjustments arising out of corporate actions, and replacement of scrips.

The Indian capital market witnessed a sharp bullish trend when the BSE Sensex crossed 9,919 mark for the first time in its history on 30 January 2006. It touched highest of 14142.7 in February 2007 and again dipped to 12857.7 in March 2007. India has the third largest investor base in the world and it has one of the world's lowest transaction costs based on screen-based transactions, paperless trading, and a *T* + 2 settlement cycle.

Source: Based on www.bseindia.com, accessed on 31 August 2007.

Index numbers of ordinary share prices

Year	Average BSE Sensitive Index (Base 1978–79 = 100)
1994–95	3975.9
1995–96	3288.7
1996–97	3469.2
1997–98	3812.9
1998–99	3294.8
1999–00	4658.6
2000–01	4269.7
2001–02	3331.9
2002–03	3206.3
2003–04	4492.2
2004–05	5741.0
2005–06	8280.1
2006–07	12277.3

Source: Based on various issues of RBI Bulletins.

Thus, BSE average index has been fluctuating between 1994–95 and 2003–04. However, it has been consistently on a rise for three years ending March 2007. It has increased by 122.77 times between 1978–79 and 2006–07, that is, in 28 years. The increase in the index has been unprecedented during last two years when it grew by 44.2 per cent in 2005–06 and 48.3 per cent in 2006–07.

We can use the above data to compute various index numbers.

Expenditure Index

Changes in the cost of living can be worked out, in the above example, by calculating the expenditure index. For this, the total expenditure incurred by the family in

TABLE 39.1   Family consumption pattern in 2000 and 2004

	2000		2004	
	Unit price p_0	Quantity q_0	Unit price p_n	Quantity q_n
Food	₹10/kg	250 kg	₹12/kg	300 kg
Milk	₹12/litre	300 litre	₹15/litre	280 litre
Clothing	₹25/metre	10 metre	₹26/metre	10 metre

the year 2000 and in the year 2004 is calculated. For making a general rule for computation of index numbers, we make use of the capital Greek *S* known as sigma and written as Σ Mathematicians se to mean 'the sum of everything like ...'

The family expenditure in 2000

$$= \Sigma p_0 q_0 = (10 \times 250) + (12 \times 300) + (25 \times 10) = 6350$$

The family expenditure in 2004

$$= \Sigma p_n q_n = (12 \times 300) + (15 \times 280) + (26 \times 10) = 8060$$

The sign of '₹' has been left out, as the index number is independent of the currency. Now, we work in a similar way, as we did for finding out the relative price for a cup of tea.

$$\text{The expenditure index} = \left(\frac{\text{Family's cost of living in 2004}}{\text{Family's cost of living in 2000}} \right) \times 100$$

$$= \left(\frac{\Sigma p_n q_n}{\Sigma p_0 q_0} \right) \times 100 = \left(\frac{8060}{6350} \right) \times 100 = 126.92 \text{ to } 1$$

It may be mentioned that we have taken account of different quantities for food, milk, and clothing by multiplying the unit prices by the corresponding quantities. This process is referred to as weighting. We could have worked out what is called a simple aggregative index by just taking account of the unit prices as follows: The simple aggregative index is 112.76 to 1 [(12 + 15 + 26)/(10 + 12 + 25)) × 100] but it would not have been very useful as the quantities of different commodities differ so much from each other and the unit prices are themselves for different quantities.

Expenditure in a particular time period is constituted of two elements namely, prices and quantities bought per unit of time; assuming that we are particularly concerned about finding out the implications of price changes over time. In complicated situations, where we need to compare the prices of many items over many different time intervals (such as for the retail price index), we need to work with the different prices, and use quantities to weight them in different ways for different index numbers.

Here is how we would calculate two more index numbers, Laspeyre's price index and Paasche's price index using the above data of family expenditure that provides partial answers to impact of inflation on the welfare of consumers (Leftwitch 1976).

Laspeyre's price index Also known as the base weighted price index, this index concentrates on measuring price changes from a base year. It is known as a base weighted index because we use the quantities purchased in the base year (here 2000) to weight the unit prices in both years. Keeping the quantities constant in this way means any change in the calculated expenditure is solely due to price changes. The Laspeyre's price index is give by $(\Sigma p_n q_0 / \Sigma p_0 q_0) \times 100$.

In this particular case, we have:

$$\Sigma p_n q_0 = (12 \times 250) + (15 \times 300) + (26 \times 10) = 7760$$
$$\Sigma p_0 q_0 = (10 \times 250) + (12 \times 300) + (25 \times 10) = 6350$$

Hence, Laspeyre's price index = $(7760/6350) \times 100 = 122.20$

Here is the general rule for working out the base weighted or Laspeyre's price index using price relatives.

$$\text{Laspeyre's Price Index} = \frac{\Sigma\left[(p_n/p_0 \times 100) \times p_0 q_0\right]}{\Sigma p_0 q_0} \qquad (39.1)$$

Notice that canceling the p_0 above and below the line and taking out the factor of 100 gives us:

$$\left(\frac{\Sigma p_n q_0}{\Sigma p_0 q_0}\right) \times 100$$

as before.

Paasche's price index Also known as the end year weighted price index, it measures the minimum estimate of increase in cost of living from year 0 to year 1, that is, relative change to purchase a year one bundle of goods and services between the years zero and one. This uses the end year quantities as weights. Let us now calculate this for the above example pertaining to the family's cost of living. The Paasche's price index is givn by $(\Sigma p_n q_n / \Sigma p_0 q_n) \times 100$.

In this particular case we have:

$$\Sigma p_n q_n = (12 \times 300) + (15 \times 280) + (26 \times 10) = 8060 \text{ and}$$
$$\Sigma p_0 q_n = (10 \times 300) + (12 \times 280) + (25 \times 10) = 6610$$

Hence, Paasche's price index = $(8060/6610) \times 100 = 121.94$.

Calculation of two different price indices gives us a measure of the fluctuations in prices from a base year. Assuming that the prices remain relatively stable and the quantities of items change, it would then be more useful to calculate an index based on quantities, using prices as weights. The Laspeyre's volume index is given by $(\Sigma p_0 q_n / \Sigma p_0 q_0) \times 100$ using the base period prices as weights. Similarly, Paasche's volume index is given by $(\Sigma p_n q_n / \Sigma p_n q_0) \times 100$ using the end period prices as weights. Thus, the basic issue in the computation of any index number relates to choosing a suitable base period.

We would like to have base period in which prices (or quantities/volumes) were not unnaturally high or low. For example, because of a drought, if prices for food grains have been unusually high in a particular year, it would not be advisable and right to consider that as a base period, as consideration of such a year as the base year would give rise to distorted results. Similarly, it is also not right to consider a base period that is too far in the past. Further, tastes and availability of products and services may change a great deal over time. Therefore, such an index could be seriously misleading. Sometimes a method known as chain-based system is used to overcome and avoid these problems where, in computing successive index numbers, the base used is the previous period. A chain-based index number is particularly suited for period-by-period comparisons. However, fixed-base index number facilitates easier comparison of the movement of prices over time.

We can now appreciate that to get a real change as against nominal change it would be helpful to work out the index numbers. Index numbers are generally used to compute inflation in an economy and based on the rate of change in the prices the salaried employees and pensioners are protected by giving them additional dearness allowance to compensate them for the adverse effect that arises as a result of increase in prices. Normally, employers fully compensate the employees at the lower level and the degree of compensation may be reduced for the high-income employee. The application of index numbers is also very common in countries where inflation rates are high and uncertain, long-term borrowing using nominal debt becomes impossible, as lenders would be completely uncertain about the real value of repayments to be received. Lenders, in such countries prefer to issue bonds that are linked to the rate of inflation to protect their interest.

SUMMARY

The numbers that are relative to a particular base are referred to as index numbers. It is a number that measures the relative change in price, quantity, value, or some other item of concern from interest from one time period to another, for a better understanding of implications of such a change on consumer or producer choices. Index numbers help in understanding nominal change and real change in the variables. The price relative of an item is the ratio of the item in the current period to the price of the same item in the base period. Thus, the basic issue in the computation of any index number relates to choosing a suitable base period. The measurement of various price indexes such as wholesale price index (WPI), consumer price index (CPI) for industrial workers, urban and non-manual employees, and agricultural labourers is computed in India for different purposes. The WPI is the most widely used price index in India and is an indicator of the movement in wholesale prices of 435 commodities.

Expenditure in a particular time period, constitutes of two elements namely, prices and quantities bought per unit of time. The Laspeyre's price index concentrates on measuring price changes from a base year. Paasche's price index measures the minimum estimate of increase in cost of living from year 0 to year 1 to purchase year 1 quantities of bundle of goods, that is, relative change in the level of expenditure required to purchase a year 1 bundle of goods and services between the years 0 and 1.

KEYWORDS

Expenditure index It measures the expenditure incurred by a consumer on a specified basket of goods over a period of time.

Index numbers Used to measure the relative change in price, quantity, value, or some other item of concern from interest from one time period to another from the point of view of better understanding of implications on consumer or producer choices.

Laspeyre's price index Also known as base weighted index, it concentrates on measuring price changes from a base year.

Paasche's price index It measures minimum estimate of increase in cost of living from year 0 to 1 to purchase year 1 quantities of bundle of goods,

that is, relative change in the expenditure required to purchase a year 1 bundle of goods and services between year 0 and year 1.

Price relative index It provides a ratio that indicates the change in price of an item from one period to another.

Reliable index numbers They are computed based on authentic and reliable data and satisfy certain other conditions that matter for reliability of index numbers.

Wholesale and retail price index It measures the change in price over time of a range of widely bought goods and services and in turn gives the cost of living.

EXERCISES

Concept Review Questions

1. What are index numbers and what is the use of computing index numbers?
2. What are the prerequisites for arriving at reliable index numbers?
3. Differentiate between wholesale and consumer price index.
4. Define expenditure index. How can information on expenditure index be used?
5. Differentiate between Laspeyre's price index and Paasche's price index.

Critical Thinking Questions

1. Usually WPI is used to measure inflation. However, it is CPI that actually affects the purchasing power of a consumer. Comment critically.
2. What do you think are the rationale for considering WPI for measurement of inflation?
3. It is said that Laspeyre's price index provides a maximum estimate of increases in the cost

of living over time as against Paasche's price index that provides minimum estimate of such increase. Comment.

Project Assignments

1. Collect details from the latest Economic Survey, Government of India (from the Internet or by referring to books from a library) on index numbers of food grains and non-food grains; and index numbers of area under food grains and non-food grains for the last five years. Analyse these index numbers and their implications to understand the pattern of agriculture growth in production in India during these years.
2. Collect data from Internet on BSE Sensex for the last three months. Interpret this data on index numbers to comment upon the changes that have taken place in the last three months in the capital market and its implications on business.

REFERENCES

Baumal, William J. (1972), *Economic Theory and Operation Analysis*, 3rd edn, Prentice Hall, Englewood Cliffs, New Jersey, pp. 207–221.

Bowley, A.L. (1926), *Elements of Statistics*, 5th edn, P.S. King and Son, London.

Karmel, P.H. (1957), *Applied Statistics for Economists*, Pitman, Melbourne.

Leftwitch, Richard H. (1976), *The Price System and Resource Allocation*, The Dryden Press, Hinsdale, Illinois, pp. 98–101.

Marris, R. (1958), *Economic Arithmetic*, Macmillan, London.

40

Statistical Quality Control

Learning Objectives

After studying this chapter, you will be able to:

- Understand the concepts related to statistical quality control
- Understand different types of quality control charts
- Know about different dimensions of quality
- Understand what is meant by quality circles, PDCA, and the Deming wheel

INTRODUCTION

The quality of a manufactured product or a service, in terms of measurements, taken on its certain variables is always subject to a certain amount of variation due to the element of chance. Statistical quality control, however, deals with variations outside this stable pattern. Tools of statistical quality control separate the tangible causes of quality variation, making it possible to address many production problems, which would result in substantial improvements in product quality and reduction of wastage and rework. Grant and Leavenworth (1972) state that statistical quality control should be viewed as a kit of tools which may influence decisions related to the functions of *specification, production,* or *inspection.* Its effective use requires cooperation among those responsible for these three different functions.

Quality Control Chart

The control chart technique, through its disclosure of process capabilities of a production process, permits better decisions about alternative designs, production methods, and tolerances.

Shewart (1939) devised a graphic method to test continuously, the hypothesis that there is no significant variation in the process and only the chance causes are operating. The control charts (Fig. 40.1) can be classified on the basis of the characteristics being tested (Juran and Gryana 1973):

1. The average $\bar{X}$ of the measurements in the sample $\bar{X}$ (chart)

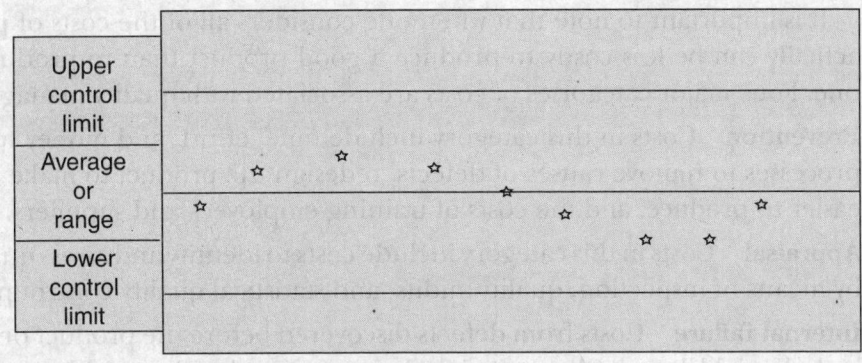

FIGURE 40.1   Shewart control chart

2. The range of the measurements in the sample (R chart)
3. The percent defective in the sample (p chart)
4. The number of defectives in the sample (c chart)

Trial control limits are usually set three standard deviations on either side of the expected value. Then the actual performance is plotted and if all the points fall within the control limits, it is concluded that only chance variation is present and the process is best left unattended.

DIMENSIONS OF QUALITY

Customer-driven definitions of quality must accept that quality has multiple dimensions and that one or more definitions of quality may apply to a product. Conformance to specifications, value, fitness for use, serviceability, support, and psychological impressions are some aspects of quality that consumers are concerned about.

Some quality concerns of consumers are:

Conformance to specifications   Does the product or service meet or exceed advertised levels of performance?

Value   Does the product serve the customers' purposes considering this price?

Fitness for use   Appearance, style, durability, reliability, craftsmanship, etc.

Serviceability   How well does the product perform its intended purpose?

Support   Even when the product performs as expected, if service after the sale is poor, the customers' view of quality diminishes.

Psychological impressions   Atmosphere, image, or aesthetics

The quality of a product is ensured during its production process. Quality control has a long history. While using quality as a competitive weapon, it should be kept in mind that perception is as important as performance. Producers who can match their operating capabilities with consumer preferences have a competitive advantage. Good quality can lead to higher profits in terms of increased volume, increased price, and reduced production cost.

It is important to note that when one considers all of the costs of poor quality, it actually can be less costly to produce a good product than to produce an inferior one. Four major categories of costs are associated with quality management.

Prevention   Costs in this category include time, effort, and money to redesign the processes to remove causes of defects, redesign the product to make it simpler and easier to produce, and the costs of training employees and suppliers.

Appraisal   Costs in this category include costs to identify and assess quality problems by means of inspection, quality audits, and statistical quality control programmes.

Internal failure   Costs from defects discovered before the product or service is sold include yield losses (the material costs associated with scrap losses), and rework effort (time, space, and capacity to store and reroute to correct defects).

External failure   Costs when a defect is discovered after the customer has received the product or service. It could result in loss of market share, warranty service costs, litigation costs, and increased regulation.

Employee involvement is the key element for cultural change and the top management must motivate a cultural change where all employees are expected to contribute. Internal customers are employees in the firm who rely on the output of other employees. An assembly line is a chain of internal customer–supplier relationships, with an external customer purchasing the finished goods.

Quality circles   Teams differ from a more typical 'working group' and should have common commitment towards the final goal with shared leadership roles. The performance should be judged by collective efforts and open-ended discussion is valued in meetings. Team members do real work together rather than delegate. The management's role in successful teams is to assign meaningful projects and create positive environment for meetings. Team members should create clear rules and set some immediate performance-oriented tasks and goals for early successes. They consult people outside the team for ideas and inspiration. Team members should spend lot of time together and initiate incentives other than direct compensation to give the team positive reinforcement. The three types of teams are—problem-solving teams (quality circles), special-purpose teams, and self-managing teams.

The process of continuous improvement is based on the Japanese concept of *kaizen* that follows the philosophy of continually seeking ways to improve operations. It is not unique to quality but applies to process improvement as well. Getting started with continuous improvement requires statistical process control (SPC) training and making SPC a normal aspect of daily operations. It includes building work teams and utilizing problem-solving techniques within the work teams.

Deming wheel   One method of quality control is following the plan-do-check (or study)-act (PDCA) cycle. It is also known as the Deming wheel (Deming 1982) or the continuous improvement spiral. The problem-solving process is based on the Deming wheel (refer Fig. 40.2) which consists of planning an improvement and implementing it and then checking as to whether the goals have been met and if there is a variation. If a variation exists, it involves acting on it and thus moving on

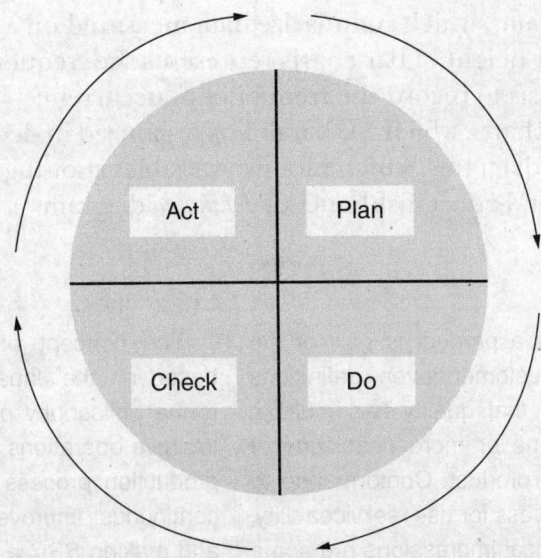

FIGURE 40.2 Deming wheel

to the next level of improvement. It is not unique to quality but applies to process improvement as well. Planning involves selecting a process needing improvement, documenting it, analysing data, setting improvement goals, discussing alternatives, assessing benefits and costs, and developing a plan and improvement measures.

Improving quality through total quality management (TQM) includes purchasing considerations (buyer must emphasize quality, delivery, and price; working with the supplier to obtain defect-free products; specifications must be clear and realistic; allowing time to identify qualified suppliers; improving communication between purchasing, engineering, quality control, and other departments), product and service design (design changes can increase defect rates; stable designs reduce quality problems but may become obsolete in the marketplace), process design (new equipment can overcome quality problems; concurrent engineering ensures that production requirements and process capabilities are synchronized).

SPC method Statistical process control (SPC) method involves measuring the current quality and detecting whether the process has changed, mapping the control charts for variables, monitoring process variability, and removing the causes of variation. While the process is in control, data is collected to estimate the average range of output that occurs. Control limits are based on the mean and variability of the sampling distribution, not the design specifications. The process capability ratio compares the tolerance width (upper specification – lower specification) to the range of actual process outputs.

The tools used in statistical quality control are:

1. Process charts
2. A variety of pictorial formats, such as line graphs and pie charts
3. Flow diagrams

4. Histograms, which summarize data measured on a continuous scale
5. The bar height of bar charts represents the frequency of occurrence
6. Checklists to record the frequency of occurrence
7. Pareto charts, which are bar charts organized in decreasing order of frequency
8. Scatter diagrams, which plot two variables showing whether they are related
9. Cause-and-effect, fishbone, or *Ishikawa* diagram

SUMMARY

Ensuring the quality of a product is part of the production process. Customer-driven definitions of quality must accept that quality has multiple dimensions and that one or more definitions of quality may apply to a product. Conformance to specifications, value, fitness for use, serviceability, support, and psychological impressions are some aspects of quality that consumers are concerned about.

Employees of a firm are internal customers who rely on the output of other employees. Team members do real work together. The management's role in successful teams is to assign meaningful projects and create a positive environment for meetings. The three types of teams are problem-solving teams (quality circles), special-purpose teams, and self-managing teams. It is not unique to quality but applies to process improvement as well. It includes building work teams and utilizing problem-solving techniques within the work teams.

The concept of continuous improvement is based on the Japanese concept of kaizen that is the philosophy of continually seeking ways to improve operations. Quality is ensured during the production process as well. Getting started with continuous improvement requires SPC training and making SPC a normal aspect of daily operations. It includes building work teams and utilizing problem-solving techniques within the work teams. The problem-solving process is based on Deming's plan-do-check-act (PDCA). It involves continuous checking of quality during the production process.

Statistical process control (SPC) method involves measuring of the current quality and detecting whether the process has changed, mapping the control charts for variables, monitoring process variability, and removing assignable causes of variation. Process capability ratio compares the tolerance width (upper specification − lower specification) to the range of actual process outputs.

KEYWORDS

Control charts   A statistical tool used for process control.

Costs of quality Cost towards prevention, appraisal, internal, and external failure.

Deming wheel It includes plan-do-check-act (PDCA). It involves constantly checking for quality in daily routine of the team, project management, vendor development, human resource development, new product development, etc.

Dimensions of quality   Any quality characteristic which contributes to fitness for use.

Process capability   Spread of a process in terms of variability among products manufactured over a period over time.

Quality circles Voluntary teams of workers which meet regularly to devise solutions to quality problems or other work-related problems in their areas of work.

Statistical process control (SPC) method It involves measuring the current quality and detecting whether the process has changed, mapping the control charts for variables, monitoring process variability, and removing the causes of variation.

Statistical quality control Use of statistical techniques for control of product quality.

EXERCISES

Concept Review Questions

1. Customer-driven definitions of quality must accept that quality has multiple dimensions and that one or more definitions of quality may apply. Discuss different dimensions of quality.
2. Describe different types of control charts that are used in statistical quality control.

Critical Thinking Questions

1. Does good quality pay off in terms of higher profits? Give your reasons.
2. Employee involvement is the key element for the cultural change and the top management must motivate to effect a cultural change where everyone is expected to contribute. How important is the above mentioned statement of quality control?

Project Assignment

Education is a difficult field in which quality techniques can be applied. Form a team to first identify the areas in your institution that are critical to improvement of quality and next, recommend a quality plan, both at the strategic and the operational level. Contrast that to the quality appraisal format of National Assessment and Accreditation Council (NAAC) for Indian universities.

REFERENCES

Deming, W.E. (1982), *Out of Crisis*, Cambridge University Press, Cambridge.

Grant, Eugene L. and Richard S. Leavenworth (1972), *Statistical Quality Control*, 4th edn, McGraw-Hill Kogakusha Ltd, Tokyo.

Juran, J.M. and Frank M. Gryana Jr. (1973), *Quality Planning and Analysis*, Tata McGraw-Hill, New Delhi.

Shewart, W.A. (1939) in *Statistical Method from the point of view of quality control*, W.E. Deming (ed.), Graduate School, Department of Agriculture, Washington D.C.

Part VII
Operations and Technology Management

Part VII

Operations and Technology Management

41

Production and Operations Management

INTRODUCTION

The production and operations management function is responsible for planning and coordinating to turn the organization's resource inputs into outputs effectively. The measure of effectiveness and efficiency of that transformation process is termed as productivity. In the generic sense, productivity is defined as the ratio of outputs to inputs. It should be kept in mind that productivity is a relative measure and has meaning only when comparisons are made. Comparisons can be made with respect to productivity of labour, capital, materials, or energy (partial measures of productivity). We can combine some of these (multifactor productivity) or combine the value of all inputs and divide by the value of all outputs (total measure of productivity). This transformation process is illustrated in Fig. 41.1. Chase et al. (2006) categorize transformation process as follows:

- physical (manufacturing);
- location (transportation);
- exchange (retailing);
- storage (warehousing);
- physiological (health care); and
- informational (telecommunication).

This function along with finance and marketing are the primary functions in all product-oriented and service-oriented organizations (Fig. 41.2).

Learning Objectives

After studying this chapter, you will be able to:
- Understand operations management
- Learn about production process and different types of production
- Understand different activities that constitute operations

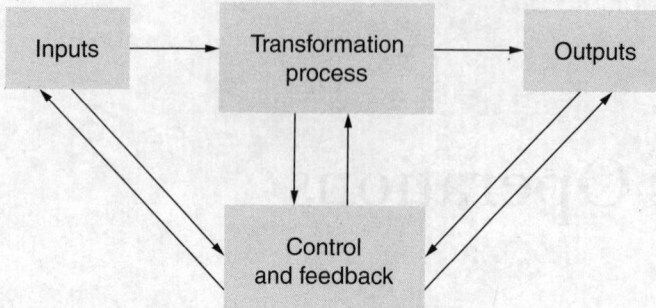

FIGURE 41.1 Transformation process

The emerging view is that every organization is in the services' sector. In manufacturing, such services can be categorized as core services—customers want products that have quality, flexibility in terms of customization, speed in terms of delivery on time, and a competitive price. They also demand value-added services such as information on various aspects of product features and its operation, problem solving in terms of troubleshooting quality problems, sales support in terms of demonstrating the product, and field support in terms of replacement of defective parts. (Fig. 41.3).

In the financial perspective, the options are either revenue growth strategy or productivity strategy. The former encompasses growth through new revenue sources and customer profitability, while the latter concentrates on reduction of cost per unit and better asset utilization. From the customer's perspective, the differentiation can take the route of product leadership, customer intimacy, or

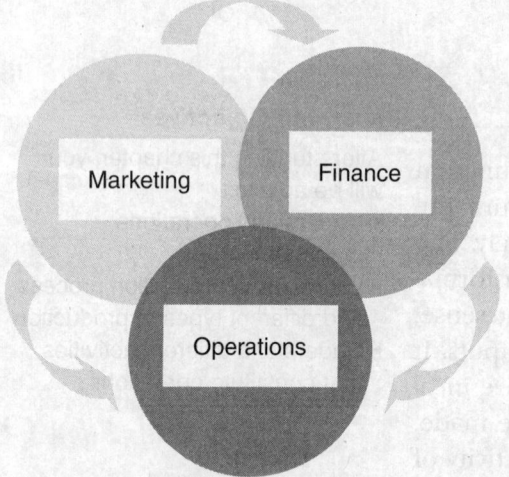

FIGURE 41.2 Primary functions of business

operational excellence. From the perspective of the internal stakeholders, the processes of innovation, customer management, operational processes, and regulatory and environmental processes support the three differentiation strategies mentioned earlier in the customer perspective. The learning and growth perspective define the intangible assets vis-à-vis strategic competencies, strategic technologies, and organizational climate and culture.

Kaplan and Norton (1996) put forth a template for developing corporate strategy that integrates finance,

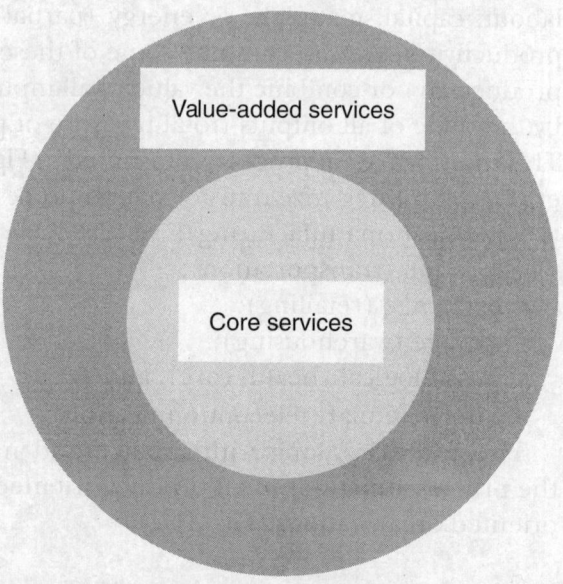

FIGURE 41.3 Operations as core and value-added services

marketing, and operations functions by mapping financial perspective, customer perspective, internal perspective, and learning and growth perspective.

DESIGN AND OPERATING DECISIONS

As operations managers are responsible for creating goods and services, they have to take a number of decisions for many processes that transform inputs into value-added outputs. These decisions can further be classified as design and operating decisions. *Design decisions* relate to product design, process design, and layout of facilities, capacity planning, and selection of locations for putting up facilities. The *operating decisions* relate to project management, inventory management, scheduling, and quality assurance (Fig. 41.4).

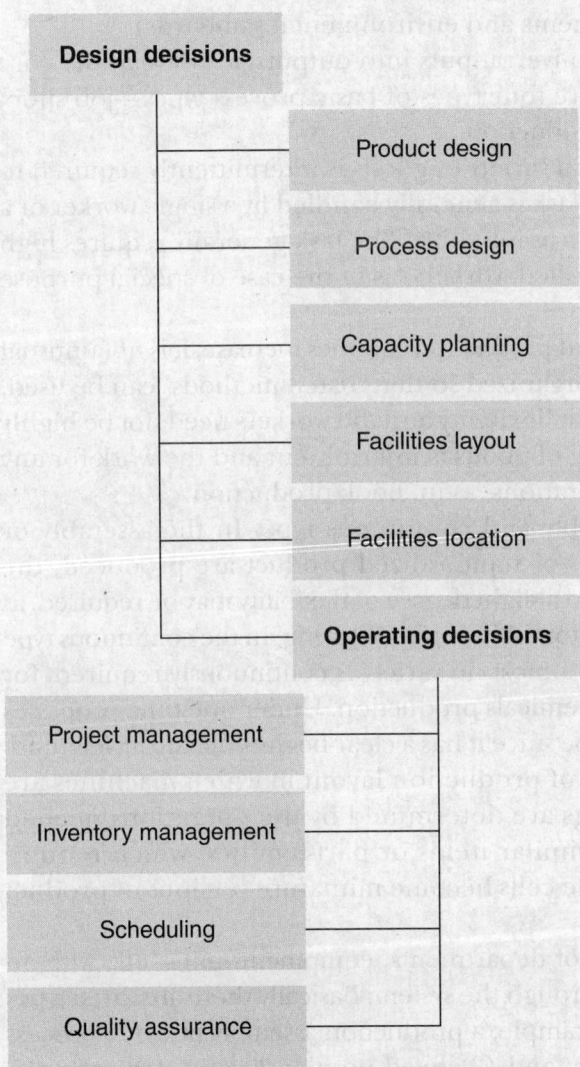

FIGURE 41.4   Design and operating decisions

Design Decisions

The various design decisions pertain to product design, process design, capacity planning, facilities layout, and facilities location.

Product design   Successful product design starts with the identification of customer needs. Quality function deployment (QFD) and market research are some of the ways to get customer inputs. The aim should be to simplify assembly, minimize the number of parts, standardize, and generate a robust design.

Process design   Value engineering is concerned with simplifying products and processes so that an equivalent or better performance can be attained at a lower cost. Japanese companies have been generally able to reduce the time needed to get a new or an improved product to the market. This has helped them achieve a competitive advantage. Computer-aided design (CAD) uses computer graphics for designing the products. Besides CAD, design for manufacturing (DFM) and design for assembly (DFA) are related methodologies that help in simplifying the product and process aspects of manufacturing and assembling.

Capacity planning   The design capacity refers to the maximum amount of output that an operating unit can achieve, whereas effective capacity refers to the maximum possible output the unit actually achieves given various constraints, such as those related to maintenance, quality, scheduling, product mix, and absenteeism. The design capacity is always more than the effective capacity. *Efficiency* is defined as the ratio of actual output to effective capacity. Utilization is defined as the ratio of actual output to design capacity. Stevenson (2002) puts the determinants of effective capacity as:

1. Facilities (size and provision for expansion)
2. Products or services (heterogeneity of output)
3. Processes (quantity and quality of process output)
4. Human considerations (motivation, skill, experience, and absenteeism)
5. Operations (inventory and equipment problems)
6. External forces (legal requirements and environmental standards)

Facilities layout   As the processes convert inputs into outputs, they are at the core of operations management. There are four types of basic process types—job shop, batch type, flow type, and cellular production.

1. *Job shop*: When a low volume of a variety of goods is intermittently required to be produced and the complete task is generally handled by a single worker or a group of workers it is referred to as job shop. The task generally requires high degree of flexibility as well as skilled workers, as in the case of special purpose jigs and fixtures manufacturing.

2. *Batch type*: As businesses grow and production volumes increase, it is not unusual to see the production process organized so that 'batch methods' can be used. Batch methods require moderate flexibility and the workers need not be highly skilled. However, the processing of goods is intermittent and the work for any task is divided into parts or operations, as in, book production.

3. *Flow type*: This includes assembly and continuous type. In the assembly or repetitive type, higher volumes of standardized product are produced, the workers are not highly skilled, and a slight degree of flexibility may be required, as in the case of assembly line for automobile manufacturing. In the continuous type of production a high volume of almost no variety is continuously required, for example, steel production or chemicals production. Under one-time processes we can categorize the project type since it has a clear beginning and a clear end.

4. *Cellular production*: It is a type of production layout in which machines are grouped into a cell. Groupings are determined by the operations needed to perform work for a set of similar items or part-families, which require similar processing. In effect, the cells become miniature versions of product layouts.

Layout refers to the configuration of departments, equipment, units, etc. with an emphasis on the movement of work through the system. Basically there are three types of layouts—(1) product layouts, for example, a production assembly line; (2) process layouts, for example, a machine shop; and (3) fixed position layouts, for example, shipbuilding yard.

Cellular production has the benefits of both batch and flow production in terms of machine utilization and throughput rate. There is the use of flexible manufacturing system (FMS), which is a group of robots, automated control, material handling, and automated processing equipment. Computer integrated manufacturing (CIM) links a broad range of manufacturing activities through an integrating computer system that incorporates design, FMS, and production planning and control.

Facilities location   This decision is made infrequently but has strategic implications for the success of the enterprise. Managers use various techniques such as factor rating method, transportation method of linear programming, and centroid method to finalize the location among a few acceptable locations. Various factors, such as nearness to markets, raw materials, energy sources, labour availability and costs, transportation costs, tax incentives, community, cultural fit, and supply chain considerations are considered while deciding upon the location. Each factor is weighed differently, based upon the industry type, company characteristics, and strategy.

Operating Decisions

Operations function is carried out at the strategic, tactical, and at the operational level. Operations strategy is subordinate to organizational strategy and is related to product design, choice of location, choice of technology, and to the decision regarding setting of new facilities. At the tactical level when the time horizon is moderate, it relates to levels of input and output, facilities layout, and equipment selection. At the operational level when it concerns itself with a short-term horizon, the operations function is concerned with scheduling, inventory management, and purchasing.

For a successful and effective strategy, a company has to have an edge over its competitors, that is, it should have distinctive competencies. In the area of operations as per Stevenson (2002), these distinctive competencies can be on the basis of:

1. Price: As in the case of Nirma detergents
2. Quality: Both in terms of consistency (e.g., Maruti cars) as well as high performance (e.g., Kirloskar pumps)
3. Time: In terms of on-time and speedy delivery (e.g., Delhi Metro Rail Corporation)
4. Flexibility: In terms of variety and volume (e.g., Nirulas restaurants)
5. Service: In terms of superior customer service (e.g., Kingfisher Airlines)
6. Location: In terms of convenience (e.g., PVR multiplexes)

The operating decisions pertain to project management, inventory management, scheduling, and quality assurance.

Project management   Projects are unique set of operations undertaken to achieve a set of objectives in a limited time frame. Projects can be functional or matrix-type when undertaken within an existing organization. They typically have four phases—definition, planning, execution, and termination. As large projects usually involve a large number of activities, a work breakdown structure (WBS) is first undertaken. It defines the hierarchy of project tasks, sub-tasks, and work packages. A work package is a group of activities that can be assigned to a single organizational unit. The Gantt chart is a tool used for planning and scheduling simple projects. However, programme evaluation and review technique (PERT) and critical path method (CPM) are some of the techniques used for planning and coordinating large and complex projects.

Inventory management   Good inventory management is indispensable for conducting smooth operations, for low operating costs, and preventing customer dissatisfaction; in short, it is indispensable for operating a profitable business. Typically, a manufacturing firm may be carrying raw materials, purchased parts, work-in-process, finished goods, replacement parts, tools, consumables, etc. as inventories. Inventories serve a number of functions with respect to smooth production, meeting anticipated demand, preventing stock-outs, hedging against price increases, taking advantage of quantitative discounts, etc. The requirements for effective inventory management are—keeping track of the inventory, forecasting demand, estimating inventory holding costs, and ordering and shortage costs. The ABC classification system recognizes that items held as inventory are not of equal importance. The question of how much to order is determined by using an economic order quantity (EOQ) model.

Scheduling   Timing and coordination of operations is termed as scheduling. Scheduling can affect operations strategy in either way. If scheduling is done well, products or services can be made or delivered on time. Bad scheduling will result in inefficient use of resources and dissatisfied customers. Time-based competition depends on good scheduling. It must be borne in mind that the coordination of materials, equipment use, and employee time is also an important function of operations management. A good design and superior quality cannot compensate for poor scheduling. Simulation models are used to estimate the flow of work through the system to determine bottlenecks and adjust the priorities (Martinich 2003). It is important to avoid sub-optimization, that is, scheduling done well in one part of the organization should not create problems in other parts of the organization.

Supply chain management and total quality management (TQM) are discussed in Chapters 42 and 46, respectively. Some of the important operations management techniques are:

- innovation;
- process design;
- methods study;
- work measurement;
- capacity management;
- inventory management;
- materials requirement planning;
- cost reduction;
- rationalization;
- office automation;
- factory automation;
- just-in-time (JIT) system;

- Tomere, Sugu, and Shouti (TSS);
- poka-yoke;
- visual management; and
- value added network (VAN)

Quality assurance   Without an effective supply chain management, organizations cannot keep up with their customers' ever increasing demands for higher quality products and service. By partnering with suppliers and getting them to think lean, organizations should ensure that the quality standards are met. By using quality function deployment (QFD) technique the organization is able to understand the needs of its customers. Cost, quality, and speed are also dimensions of quality that an effective supply chain management seeks to excel at. Quality assurance means that the quality of the product or service is satisfactory, reliable, and yet economical for the customer.

SUMMARY

The production and operations management function is responsible for planning and coordinating the organization's resources to transform its inputs into outputs efficiently and effectively. The design decisions relate to product design, process design, layout of facilities, capacity planning, and selection of locations for putting up facilities. The operating decisions relate to project management, inventory management, scheduling, and quality assurance. There are several methods of handling the conversion or production processes such as job, batch, flow, and cellular.

Successful product design starts with customer needs. Quality function deployment (QFD) and market research are some of the ways to gather customer inputs. The processes convert inputs into outputs. They are at the core of operations management. The three types of processes are job shop, batch type, and flow type. Capacity planning may be divided into two parts. The design capacity refers to the maximum amount of output that an operat-ing unit can achieve, whereas the effective capacity refers to the maximum possible output the unit actu-ally achieves given various constraints. The three types of layouts are—product, process, and fixed position. The facilities location is made infrequently but has strategic implications for the success of the enterprise. Managers use various techniques, such as factor rating method, transportation method of linear programming, and centroid method to finalize the location among a few acceptable locations.

Projects are a unique set of operations under-taken to achieve a set of objectives in a limited time frame. Projects can be functional or matrix type when undertaken within an existing organization. Good inventory management is indispensable for conducting smooth operations, for low operating costs, and preventing customer dissatisfaction. Timing and coordination of operations is termed as scheduling. It can affect operations strategy in either way. If scheduling is done well, products or services can be made or delivered on time.

KEYWORDS

Design capacity   It refers to the maximum amount of output that an operating unit can achieve.

Design decisions   It relates to product design, pro-cess design, layout of facilities, capacity planning, and selection of locations for setting up the facilities.

Different production processes   These are job shop, batch, flow, and cellular type of production processes.

Effective capacity   It refers to the maximum pos-sible output given various constraints.

Operating decisions   It relates to project management, inventory management, scheduling, and quality assurance.

Operations management   It is responsible for planning and coordination in terms of the organization's resources to transform its inputs into outputs.

Projects   It refers to the unique set of operations undertaken to achieve a set of objectives in a limited time frame.

EXERCISES

Concept Review Questions

1. Compare the job method of production to the batch method of production.
2. How is the facility location decision taken?
3. What is the purpose of scheduling?
4. What are the tools used in planning and scheduling of a project?
5. How is productivity measured?

Critical Thinking Questions

1. Are efficiency and capacity utilization the same concepts? Give an elaborate example to justify your answer.

2. By 2020, radio frequency identification (RFID) will become ubiquitous. In your opinion, how is it going to change inventory management?

Project Assignment

Take three industries from three sectors of economy; primary, secondary and tertiary (e.g., mining, machine tools, and consumer electronics) and compare their production processes in terms of job, flow, batch, and cellular type. Can these be different for two different companies operating within the same industry? Research this question considering a few industries in the economy.

REFERENCES

Chase, Richard B., F. Robert Jacobs, Nicholas J. Aquilano, and Nitin K. Agarwal (2006), *Operations Management for Competitive Advantage*, Tata McGraw-Hill, 11th edition, New Delhi.

Kaplan, Robert S. and David P. Norton (1996), *The Balanced Scorecard*, Harvard Business School Press, Boston, Massachusetts.

Martinich, Joseph S. (2003), *Production and Operations Management—An Applied and Modern Approach*, John Wiley & Sons (Asia) Pte Ltd, New Delhi.

Stevenson, William J. (2002), *Operations Management*, Tata McGraw-Hill, 7th edition, New Delhi.

42

Supply Chain Management

INTRODUCTION

A supply chain is a business process that links manufacturers, retailers, customers, and suppliers in the form of a chain to develop and deliver products as a single virtual organization of pooled skills and resources. Within each organization the supply chain includes all functions involved in receiving and filling a customer request. These functions include new product development, marketing, operations, distribution, finance, and customer service.

Supply chain management (SCM) is the process of synchronizing the flow of physical goods and associated information from the production line of low level component suppliers to the end consumer. This results in the provision of early notice of demand fluctuations and synchronization of business processes among all cooperating organizations in this supply chain. Effective SCM results in the significant reduction of both cost and time in the procurement process, as well as reduction in inventory levels, thus enabling significant gains in the organizational productivity. Some of the formal definitions of a supply chain are:

- It is a network of autonomous or semi-autonomous business entities collectively responsible for procurement, manufacturing, and distribution activities associated with one or more families of related products.
- A supply chain is a network of facilities that procures raw materials, transforms them into intermediate goods and then final products, and delivers the products to customers through a distribution system.

Learning Objectives

After studying this chapter, you will be able to:
- Understand the concept of supply chain
- Learn how to manage a supply chain
- Elaborate the goals of supply chain management (SCM)
- Examine the differences between SCM and logistics management
- Understand the strategic nature of SCM issues

- A supply chain is a network of facilities and distribution options that performs the functions of procurement of materials, transformation of these materials into intermediate and finished products, and the distribution of these finished products to customers.

The management of supply chains is, however, a complex task. The rapid adoption of lean manufacturing techniques such as Just-In-Time (JIT) and flexible manufacturing systems (FMS) has made the timeliness of the materials delivery extremely critical. Today, each company in the chain must be internally 'lean' and must operate in a 'seamless' environment in which all the information relevant to the efficient operation of the total system is available. In this supply chain, the vendor or the supplier assumes a prime position, as organizations are dependent on them. The average manufacturing firm spends over 50 per cent of its revenues on purchased inputs. However, this percentage is rising because companies continue to increase the volume of outsourced work across industries. Consequently, suppliers will have a greater impact on the cost, quality, technology, and delivery of a company's products and services, and, thus, on its profitability. The direct effect of supplier performance on the buyer's bottom line highlights the importance of optimizing the supply chain performance.

The global trends that were predicted to impact careers of logistics professionals as per Lambert et al. (1998) were—the growth of information technology, supply chain management, and globalization. All of these have proved to be correct. As per Braithwaite and Wilding (2004), the experience of applying SCM is that improved visibility and synchronization leads to some or all of these—improved customer service, reduced inventories, lower operating costs, and improved use of fixed assets. In future, companies will increasingly compete on the basis of their total supply chains (Bowersox et al. 2002).

Importance of SCM

As competition increases worldwide, an increasing number of firms are frantically combining domestic and international sourcing as a means of achieving a sustainable competitive advantage. Global competitiveness has led to supply chain functions becoming more geographically dispersed and increased the complexity of supply chain linkages. These changes have brought about a need for greater understanding of these linkages.

Managing the supply chain is an effective method to reduce the operational costs and increase customer satisfaction. Today SCM is rapidly becoming a useful method for reducing inventory costs and increasing customer responsiveness in changing market conditions.

In India, companies are linked to their suppliers and retailers through various sources. Application software is being used to do what was done manually earlier. Supply chain systems analyse information from different points on the supply chain. If one supplier fails to deliver, the SCM software helps managers to find another. For example, consider a customer walking into a Wal-Mart store to purchase detergent.

The supply chain begins with the customer and her need for detergent. The next stage of this supply chain is the Wal-Mart retail store that the customer visits. Wal-Mart stocks its shelves using the inventory that may have been supplied from a finished goods warehouse that it manages or from a distributor using trucks supplied by a third party. The distribution in turn is stocked by the manufacturer such as, P&G. The P&G manufacturing plant receives raw material from a variety of suppliers who may themselves have been supplied by a lower-tier of suppliers. For example, packaging material may come from Tenneco packaging while Tenneco, in turn, receives raw materials to manufacture the packaging from some other supplier. A supply chain, thus, is a business process that links suppliers, manufacturers, wholesalers, retailers, and customers.

Figure 42.1 shows a typical supply chain arrangement in which the supplier, manufacturer, wholesaler, and retailer interact. Supply chain management takes a holistic view of the entire system and emphasizes coordination of all activities. It should be noted that SCM is not the same as vertical integration. Vertical integration normally involves ownership of the complete chain, both upstream and downstream, while in SCM the entities are independent. A supply chain is a dynamic entity and involves a constant flow of information, products, and funds between different stages.

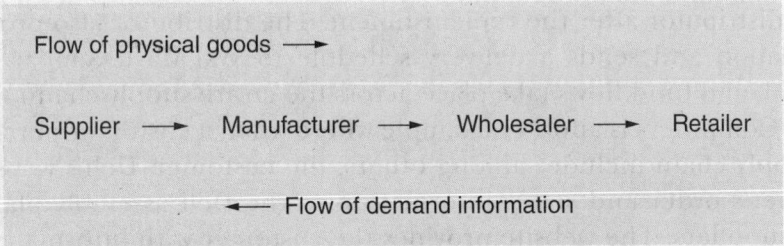

Flow of physical goods ⟶

Supplier ⟶ Manufacturer ⟶ Wholesaler ⟶ Retailer

⟵ Flow of demand information

FIGURE 42.1 Goods and information flow in a supply chain

The primary purpose for the existence of any supply chain is to satisfy customer needs, while it generates profits for itself. Supply chain activities begin with a customer order and end when a satisfied customer has paid for his or her purchase. Thus, most of the supply chains are networks. In fact, it may be more accurate to use the term supply networks. A typical supply chain may have various stages such as customers, retailers, wholesalers or distributors, manufacturers, and component–raw material suppliers.

It is not necessary for each stage to be present in every supply chain. The appropriate design of the supply chain will depend on both the customer's needs and the roles of the different stages involved.

A supply chain is a dynamic entity and involves a constant flow of information, products, and funds between different stages. Figure 42.2 illustrates how Wal-Mart provides the product, pricing, and availability of information to the customer.

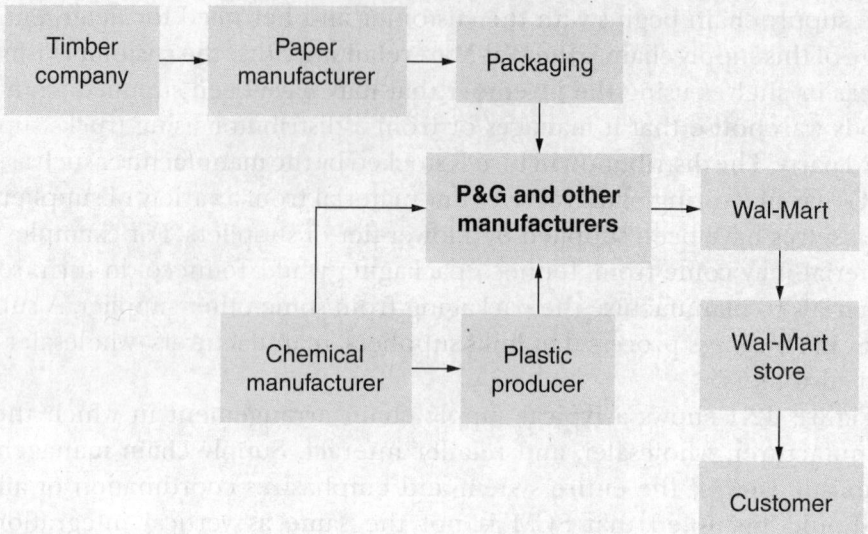

FIGURE 42.2   Stages of a supply chain

The customer transfers funds to Wal-Mart, which in turn conveys point-of-sales data as well as replenishment orders to the warehouse of distributor, who transfers the replenishment order via a truck back to the store. Wal-Mart transfers the funds to the distributor after the replenishment. The distributor also provides pricing information and sends a delivery schedule to Wal-Mart. Similar information, material, and fund flows take place across the entire supply chain.

Dell Computers is another example where when a customer purchases online, the supply chain includes among others, the customer. Dell's website takes the customer's order and sends information to the Dell assembly plant and all of Dell's suppliers. The website provides the customer with information regarding pricing, product variety, and availability. Having a product choice, the customer enters order information and pays for the product. The customer may later return to the website to check the status of the order. Stages further up the supply chain use customer information to fill the order. This process involves an additional flow of information, product, and funds between various stages of the supply chain.

Decision Phases

Supply chain management decisions are often said to belong to one of the following three levels—strategic, tactical, or operational. Figure 42.3 shows the three levels of decisions as a pyramid shaped hierarchy. The decisions on a higher level in the pyramid will set the conditions under which the lower level decisions are made.

Strategic or design level   At the strategic or design level, long-term decisions related to the supply chain's configuration are made. Some of them include resource allocation and the performance of processes at each stage. Strategic decisions made by the

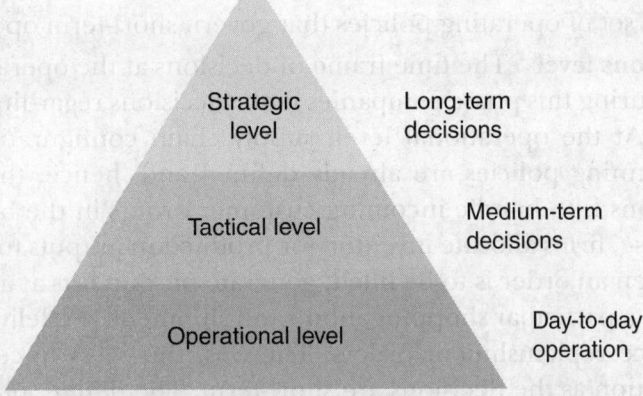

FIGURE 42.3 Decision phases in a supply chain

companies include those pertaining to location, capacities of production, inventory, warehousing facilities, products to be manufactured, modes of transportation, and the type of information system to be utilized. A firm must ensure that the supply chain configuration supports its strategic objectives during this phase. Location decisions are concerned with the size, number, and geographic location of the supply chain entities, such as plants, inventories, or distribution centres. The production decisions are meant to determine the product mix to be manufactured, procurement locations, supplies, etc. Inventory decisions are concerned with the way of managing inventories throughout the supply chain.

Decisions made on the strategic level are interrelated; for example, decisions about the mode of transport are influenced by decisions on geographical placement of plants and warehouses, and inventory policies are influenced by the choice of suppliers and production locations. Modeling and simulation is frequently used for analysing these interrelations, and the impact of making strategic level changes in the supply chain. For example, Dell's decisions regarding the location and capacity of its manufacturing facilities, warehouses, and supply sources are all design or strategic decisions. While taking these decisions, the company must take into account uncertainty in the market conditions over the next few years.

Tactical/planning level For decisions made during this phase, the time frame considered is a quarter to a year. Therefore, the supply chain's configuration as determined in the strategic phase establishes constraints within which planning must be done. Companies start the planning phase by forecasting demand in different markets for the coming year. Planning includes decisions regarding the markets that will be supplied with the goods, the locations from where they would be supplied, the subcontracting or manufacturing, the inventory policies to be followed, and the timing and size of marketing promotions. For example, Dell's planning decisions involves idenfication of specific production facilities and target production quantities at different locations. Planning establishes parameters within which a supply chain must include uncertainty in demand, exchange rates, and competition over this time horizon in their decisions. As a result of the planning phase, companies define a set of operating policies that govern short-term operations.

Operations level The time frame of decisions at the operational level is a week or a day. During this phase companies make decisions regarding individual customer's orders. At the operational level, supply chain configuration is considered fixed and planning policies are already defined and, hence, the goal of supply chain operations is to handle incoming customer orders in the best possible manner. In this phase, firms allocate inventory or production outputs to individual orders, set a date when an order is to be filled, generate pick-up lists at a warehouse, allocate an order to a particular shopping mode and shipment, set delivery schedules of trucks, and place replenishment orders. There is, thus, less uncertainty in the demand information as the decisions are short-term. The design, planning, and operations decisions of a supply chain have a strong impact on profitability and success of a business enterprise.

Process View of a Supply Chain

There are two different ways to view the processes performed in a supply chain—the cycle view and the push–pull view. The processes in a supply chain are divided into a series of cycles in the cycle view. Each cycle is performed at the interface between two successive stages of a supply chain. The processes in a supply chain are divided into two categories in the push–pull view depending on whether they are executed in response to a customer order or in anticipation of customer orders. *Pull* processes are initiated by a customer order whereas *push* processes are initiated and performed in anticipation of customers orders.

Cycle view of supply chain process

The supply chain processes can be broken down into the following four cycles—(1) customer order cycle; (2) replenishment cycle; (3) manufacturing cycle; and (4) procurement cycle. Each cycle occurs at the interface between two successive stages of the supply chain.

Customer order cycle The customer order cycle occurs at the customer–retailer interface and includes all those processes directly involved in receiving and filling the customer's order. Typically, the customer initiates this cycle at a retailer site and the cycle primarily involves meeting the customer's demand. The retailer's interaction with the customer starts when the customer arrives or a contact is initiated and ends when the customer receives the order. The processes involved in the customer order cycle include:

Customer arrival It refers to the customer's arrival at the location where he can make choices and arrive at a decision regarding a purchase.

Customer order It refers to the customer informing the retailer about the products he wants to purchase and the retailer allocating the products to customers.

Customer order fulfilment During this process, the customer's order is met with and the product is delivered.

Customer order receiving   During this process, the customer receives the order and takes ownership.

Replenishment cycle   The replenishment cycle occurs at the retailer–distributor interface and includes all processes involved in replenishing retailer inventory. It is initiated when a retailer places an order to replenish inventories to meet future demand. The replenishment cycle is similar to the customer order cycle except that the retailer is now the customer. The objective of the replenishment cycle is to replenish inventories at the retailer at minimum cost while providing high product availability. The processes involved in the replenishment cycle include:

Retail order trigger   As the retailer tries to meet the customer's demand, the inventory is depleted and must be replenished to meet future demand.

Retail order entry   This process is similar to customer order entry at the retailer. The only difference is that the retailer is now the customer placing the order that is conveyed to the distributor.

Retail order fulfilment   Once the replenishment order arrives at a retailer, the retailer must receive it physically and update all inventory records.

Retail order receiving   This process refers to the movement of the product and related information from the distributor to the retailer and the flow of funds from the retailer to the distributor.

Manufacturing cycle   The manufacturing cycle typically occurs during the distributor–manufacturer (or retailer–manufacturer) interface and includes all processes involved in replenishing distributor (or retailer) inventory. The manufacturing cycle is triggered by customer orders (Dell), replenishment orders from a retailer or distributor (Wal-Mart ordering from P&G), or by the forecast of customer demand and current product availability in the manufacturer's finished-goods warehouse. The processes involved in the manufacturing cycle include the following:

Order arrival   During this process, a finished-goods warehouse or distributor sets a replenishment order trigger based on the forecast of future demand and current product inventories.

Production scheduling   This process is similar to the order entry process in the replenishment cycle where the inventory is allocated to an order. During the production scheduling process, orders (or forecasted orders) are allocated to a production plan. Given the desired production quantities for each product, the manufacturer must decide on the precise production sequence.

Manufacturing and shipping   This process is equivalent to the order fulfilment process described in the replenishment cycle. During the manufacturing phase of the process, the manufacturer produces to the production schedule. During the shipping phase of this process, the product is shipped to the customer, retailer, distributor, or finished-goods warehouse.

Receiving at the distributor, retailer, or customer end   In this process, the product is received at the distributor, finished-goods warehouse, retailer, or customer and inventory records are updated. Other processes related to storage and fund transfers also take place.

Procurement cycle   The procurement cycle occurs at the manufacturer–supplier interface and includes all processes necessary to ensure that materials are available for manufacturing to occur according to schedule. During the procurement cycle, the manufacturer orders the components from the suppliers who replenish the component inventories. The relationship is quite similar to that between a distributor and manufacturer with one significant difference. The retailer–distributor orders are triggered by uncertain customer demand, but component orders can be determined precisely once the manufacturer has decided the production schedule. The orders for components depend upon the production schedule. Thus, it is important for suppliers to be linked to the manufacturer's production schedule. Of course, if a supplier's lead times are long, the supplier has to produce to forecast because the manufacturer's production schedule may not be fixed that far in advance. In practice, there may be several tiers of suppliers, each producing a component for the next tier. A similar cycle would then flow back from one stage to the next.

SUPPLY CHAIN MACRO PROCESSES IN A FIRM

All supply chain processes in a firm can be classified into three macro processes—customer relationship management (CRM), internal supply chain management (ISCM), and supply relationship management (SRM).

1. Customer relationship management (CRM): All processes that focus on the interface between the firm and its customers.
2. Internal supply chain management (ISCM): All processes that are internal to the firm.
3. Supply relationship management (SRM): All processes that focus on the interface between the firm and its suppliers.

These three macro processes manage the flow of information, product, and funds required to generate, receive, and fulfil a customer's request. The CRM macro process aims to generate customer demand and facilitate the placement and tracking of orders. It includes processes such as marketing, sales, order management, and call centre management.

The ISCM process aims to fulfil the demands generated by the CRM process. These processes include the planning of internal production and storage capacity, preparation of demand and supply plans, and internal fulfilment of actual orders.

The SRM macro process aims to arrange for and manage supply sources for various goods and services. Processes include the evaluation and selection of suppliers, negotiation of supply terms, and communication regarding new products and orders with the suppliers.

Supply Chain Coordination and Bullwhip Effect

Supply chain coordination functions effectively as long as all stages of the chain take actions that together increase total supply chain profits. Each participant (phase) of the chain should balance its actions to other participants' and the supply chain in general and make decisions that are beneficial to the whole chain. If the coordination is weak or does not exist at all, a conflict of objectives tends to appear among the participants, who try to maximize personal profits. If the relevant information for some reason can be unreachable to the participants in the chain or the information can get deformed in non-linear activities of some parts of chain, it can lead to irregular comprehension. All these lead to the so-called bullwhip effect resulting from information disorder or increasing fluctuations in orders as they move up within a supply chain from retailers to wholesalers to manufacturers to suppliers. Different chain phases have different calculations of demand quantity, thus, the longer the chain between the retailer and wholesaler, the bigger the demand variation. This distorts demand information within the supply chain, with different stages having very different estimates of what the demand looks like. The result is the loss of supply chain coordination.

P&G has observed the presence of the bullwhip effect in the supply chain for diapers. The company found that raw material orders from P&G to its suppliers fluctuated significantly over time. Further down the chain, when sales at retail stores were studied, it was found that the fluctuations were small. It is reasonable to assume that the consumers of diapers at the last stage of supply chain used them at a steady rate. Although consumption of the end product was stable, order for raw materials were highly variable, increasing costs and making it difficult for supply to match demand.

It is also seen that apparel and grocery industry have shown a similar phenomenon; the fluctuation in orders increases as we move upstream in the supply chain from retail to manufacturing. There may be a lack of coordination if each stage of the supply chain only optimizes its local objective without considering the impact on the complete chain. It also results in information distortion between the different stages of the supply chain.

A variation in information demands leads to increased production expenses and supply chain expenses in an effort to deliver the ordered quantity in time. Manufacturers accomplish demanded capacity and production but when the orders come to a downstream level, they end up with surplus capacity and inventory. The bullwhip effect affects the costs related to manufacturing, inventory, replenishment lead time, transportation, labour, product availability, and relationships across the supply chain.

Manufacturing cost   The bullwhip effect increases manufacturing cost in the supply chain.

Inventory cost   To handle the increased variability of demand, a company has to carry an increased level of inventory than what is required in the absence of bullwhip effect. Accordingly, the warehouse space is more occupied, all of which leads to an increase in holding or carrying costs of storage services.

Replenishment lead time   Prolongs the lead time—the time period from the moment of purchasing to the moment of receiving the order—because of scheduling difficulty.

Transportation cost   The bullwhip effect increases transportation costs within a supply chain. This is due to disorders in the orders being met, which results in fluctuations in transportation requirements over time where a situation arises that requires the maintenance of a surplus transportation capacity to cover the higher demand periods.

Labour cost　The bullwhip effect increases labour costs associated with shipping and receiving in the supply chain.

Product availability　The bullwhip effect decreases the level of product availability, which can lead to deficiency of retail inventory when the retailers run out of stock. This results in lost sales for the supply chain and is due to the large fluctuation of orders, which makes it harder to supply all distributors' and retailers' orders on time.

Relationships across the supply chain　The bullwhip effect negatively impacts performance at every stage and, thus, hurts the relationships between different stages of the supply chain. It also leads to loss of trust between different stages and makes any potential coordination efforts difficult.

Thus, the bullwhip effect makes a supply chain inefficient by increasing costs and decreasing responsiveness. It reduces the profitability of a supply chain by making it more expensive to provide a given level of product availability.

Coordination obstacles

Any factor that leads to either local optimization by different stages of the supply chain or an increase in information distortion and variability within the supply chain is an obstacle to coordination. The major obstacles relate to incentives, information processing, operational issues, pricing, and behavioural issues.

Incentive obstacles　A situation in which incentives are offered at different stages or to participants in a supply chain leading to actions that increase variability and reduce total supply chain profits. These focus only on the local impact of an action and result in decisions that do not maximize total supply chain profits.

Information processing obstacles　Situations in which demand information is distorted due to movement across different stages of the supply chain and lack of coordination. It leads to increased variability in orders within the supply chain. Demand forecasting based on the stream of orders received from the downstream stage results in a magnification of fluctuations in demand as we move up the supply chain from the retailer to the manufacturer. Lack of information sharing between stages of the supply chain magnifies the bullwhip effect.

Operational obstacles　Actions taken in the course of placing and filling orders that lead to an increase in variability.

Pricing obstacles　Situations in which the pricing policies for a product (lot-size-based quantity discounts and price fluctuations) leads to an increase in variability of orders placed. This is due to lot-size-based discounts which increase the size of orders being placed. This magnifies the bullwhip effect.

Behavioural obstacles　It refers to learning problems within organizations that contribute to the bullwhip effect. These problems are related to the structure of the supply chain and the communication between different stages. This is due to the local optimization by different stages of the supply chain. Lack of trust between different partners and different stages of the supply chain lead to fluctuations and the successive stages becomes enemies rather than partners.

Triple 'A' supply chain

Companies focus on building supply chains to deliver the goods and services to consumers as quickly and inexpensively as possible. They also create teams, streamline processes, lay down the technologies, and invest in shared infrastructure. All those companies and initiatives are persistently aimed at greater speed and cost-effectiveness. The aims of the companies change when business is booming. Managers concentrate on maximizing speed during boom time. Firms desperately try to minimize the supply costs during recession. Top-performing supply chains possess three very different qualities.

1. Great supply chains are *agile*. They react speedily to sudden changes in demand or supply.
2. They *adapt* over time as market structures and strategies evolve.
3. They *align* the interests of all the firms in supply network so that companies optimize the chain's performance when they maximize their interests.

Only supply chains that are agile, adaptable, and aligned provide companies with sustainable competitive advantage. The agility and alignment factors emphasize the relationships' importance in the supply chain.

SUMMARY

A supply chain is a business process that links manufacturers, retailers, customers, and suppliers in the form of a chain to develop and deliver products as a single virtual organization of pooled skills and resources. Supply chain management (SCM) is an extension of the concept of logistics management. Logistics management is primarily concerned with optimizing flows within the organization while SCM recognizes that internal integration itself is not sufficient. Supply chains encompass the companies and the business activities needed to design, make, deliver, and use a product or service.

Supply chain management basically consists of a systemic, strategic coordination of the traditional business functions and the tactics across these business functions within a particular company and across businesses within the supply chain for the purposes of improving the long-term performance of the individual companies and the supply chain as a whole. SCM views the supply chain and the organizations in it as a single entity. Taken individually, different supply chain requirements often have conflicting needs.

Effective supply chain management requires simultaneous improvements in both customer service levels and the internal operating efficiencies of the companies in the supply chain. Supply chain management is the coordination of production, inventory, location, and transportation among the participants in a supply chain to achieve the best mix of responsiveness and efficiency for the market being served. Bullwhip effect results from information disorder or the fluctuations in orders that increases within a supply chain from retailers to wholesalers to manufacturers to suppliers. Only supply chains that are agile, adaptable, and aligned provide companies with a sustainable competitive advantage.

KEYWORDS

Bullwhip effect It is the result of information disorder or the fluctuations in orders that increases as they move up within a supply chain from retailers to wholesalers to manufacturers to suppliers.

Logistics management It is primarily concerned with optimizing flows within the organization.

Supply chain It is a business process that links manufacturers, retailers, customers, and suppliers in the form of a chain to develop and deliver products as a single virtual organization of pooled skills and resources.

Supply chain management (SCM) It consists of a systemic, strategic coordination of the traditional business functions and the tactics across these business functions within a particular company and across businesses within the supply chain.

EXERCISES

Concept Review Questions

1. Effective supply chain management requires simultaneous improvements in both customer service levels and the internal operating efficiencies of the companies in the supply chain. Explain.
2. Is supply chain management (SCM) an extension of the concept of logistics management? Elaborate.

Critical Thinking Question

Do you think supply chain management is too nebulous a concept to be followed by small and medium enterprises (SMEs) in India who understand logistics management well?

Project Assignment

Conduct a research about the metrics that are increasingly used to evaluate the performance of a supply chain. Do you think that Robert Kaplan's 'balanced score card' approach can be integrated with these metrics for evolving a better performance measurement system since an effective supply chain management system requires simultaneous improvements in both customer service levels and internal operating efficiency?

REFERENCES

Bowersox, Donald J., David J. Closs, and M.B. Cooper (2002), *Supply Chain and Logistics Management*, Irwin McGraw-Hill, New York.

Braithwaite, Alan and Richard Wilding (2004), 'The Laws of Logistics and Supply Chain Management' in *Financial Times Handbook of Management*, 3rd edition, Pearson Power, pp. 249–59.

Lambert, Douglas M., James R. Stock, and Lisa M. Ellrain (1998), *Fundamentals of Logistics Management*, Irwin McGraw-Hill, New York.

43

Kaizen

INTRODUCTION

Japan attained the status of a world economic power after about four decades following World War II. Large-scale absorption of technology imported from USA and a countrywide adoption of productivity and quality improvement programmes inspired by American experts, such as Dr Deming and Dr Juran, coupled with some indigenous innovative production practices saw a growing demand for Japanese goods worldwide. Japanese manufacturing excellence has seen introduction of automation, robots, and flexible manufacturing technologies to take advantage of the changing market and customer requirements. All Japanese companies were following a common philosophy of *kaizen*, which meant never-ending improvement and maintaining standards of produced goods that involves gradual, unending improvements, doing 'little things' better, and setting and achieving higher standards. Kaizen as a philosophy is practised not only in Japanese economic life but also its social life.

Kaizen (*kai*—change, *zen*—to become good) means continuous slow improvement involving everyone from top managers to workers. It is a policy that is followed by leading Japanese companies. Kaizen is an overriding concept, the unifying thread running through the philosophy, the systems, and the problem-solving tools developed in Japan over the last half-century. In an organization that follows Kaizen, every employee is encouraged to come up with innovative ideas. The philosophy of Kaizen has enabled the Japanese management to take a systematic and

Learning Objectives

After studying this chapter, you will be able to:
- Understand the philosophy of kaizen
- Examine the link between innovation and kaizen
- Learn about quality control and kaizen
- Understand the different tools of kaizen

a collaborative approach to cross-functional problem solving. On the contrary, in the West cross-functional problems are often seen in terms of conflict resolution. In fact, engineers in Japan are often warned that there will be no progress if they keep on doing things exactly the same way all the time.

Kaizen and Management

Management has two major components—maintenance and improvement. Maintenance refers to activities directed towards maintaining current standards of operation, while improvements refer to those activities that improve current standards. Under the maintenance function the management first establishes policies, rules, directives, and standard operating procedures (SOP). The management uses discipline to get conformance if people are able to follow the standard but do not do so. It uses training or reviews the standards if employees are willing but are unable to follow the standards.

The higher up the manager is, the more he is concerned with improvement. In Japanese companies the top management is always pressing for improvement. Once this is done, it becomes the management's job to see that the new standards are implemented and maintained. Maintenance and improvement have, thus, become inseparable for most Japanese managers. Improvement may be referred to as the stage between kaizen and innovation.

Process-oriented vs result-oriented management The concept of kaizen epitomizes the process-oriented thinking in Japanese companies, in contrast to the result-oriented thinking that characterizes most of the Western companies. Kaizen believes in introducing continuous improvements in the process of production, manufacture, delivery, and communication related to the product or service. In a typical North American company, an individual's contribution may be valued only for its concrete results, irrespective of the efforts that person has put in.

It is suggested that result-oriented criteria for evaluating people's performance are probably a legacy of the 'mass-production society' and that the process-oriented criteria is gaining momentum in the post-industrial, high-tech society. The kaizen concept stresses upon the management's supportive and simulative role in the people's efforts to improve the processes. On one hand, the management needs to develop a process-oriented criteria and on the other, the controlling aspect of management looks only at the performance or the results of the effort. A manager by definition may have to bother about results but most of the successful managers are also process-oriented with a genuine concern for:

- discipline;
- time management;
- skill development;
- participation and involvement;
- morale; and
- communication.

In short, such managers are people-oriented. The message of kaizen is that not a single day should go by without some kind of improvement being made somewhere in the company.

Kaizen and Innovation

There are two components of improvement—innovation and kaizen. Innovation has a more dramatic and short-term effect. Kaizen, which strives for continuous improvement, will have a subtle but a more long-lasting effect. Innovation affects mostly the science and technology part of the manufacturing chain, while the most visible gains of kaizen have been observed in the areas of production and marketing. Ideally, innovation will give rise to a step ladder improvement curve while the kaizen approach will lead to positively sloped steps as it not only arrests the deterioration of the new technology (innovation) once it has been established, but improves it by incremental steps till the next level of innovation comes through.

Between the two contrasting approaches to improvement—the gradualist approach and the great-leap forward approach—Japanese companies favour the first approach. Western management worships innovation, which is often dramatic. Kaizen, however, is often non-dramatic and subtle, and its results are seldom immediately visible.

Kaizen and Quality Control

The terms quality and productivity may mean different things to different people; however, the same becomes meaningless when we talk about improvements. Any improvement is eventually going to lead to improvements in quality and productivity. The starting point for improvements is recognizing the problem and the need to improve. Kaizen emphasizes on being aware of the problem and provides clues for identifying them. The problem-solving process and standardization of the new process is also related to kaizen. In short, anything; from equipment for production to human behaviour that needs improvement effort comes under the ambit of kaizen. As is the case with many western companies, quality control was initially applied to the manufacturing processes but in Japan, the realization soon set in that inspection alone cannot improve the quality of the product; the quality had to be built into the process. Hence, quality control (QC) was positioned as a vital management tool, that is, it was perceived as a tool for overall improvement in managerial performance.

Kaizen Tools

The various tools of kaizen have been explained in this section. The 3-Mu checklist of kaizen activities involves *muda* (waste), *muri* (strain), and *mura* (discrepancy). As per Imai (1986), a number of check points in the aforementioned areas are helpful in the areas of improvements. These are manpower, techniques, time, facilities, materials, jigs and fixtures, inventory, etc. For example, if an organization underutilizes manpower, if its workers are under stress, or if it does not have the right manpower in certain areas of production, the 3-Mu check is a good way to identify areas where kaizen interventions may be very productive.

The five step kaizen movement includes *seiri* (straighten up), *seiton* (put things in order), *seiso* (clean up), *seiketsu* (personal cleanliness), and *shitsuke* (discipline).

The five Ws are who, what, where, when, why, and the one H is 'how'. The 4-M checklist includes man (operator), machine (facilities), material, and the method of operation.

Pareto diagrams, cause–effect diagrams, histograms, control charts, scatter diagrams, graphs, and check sheets are some of the kaizen problem-solving tools. Pareto diagrams classify problems according to the priority, whereas cause–effect diagrams, also known as fishbone graphs, are used to analyse the characteristics of a problem situation and the factors that cause them. Histograms, control charts, scatter diagrams, graphs, and check sheets are other graphical tools that indicate the strength and direction of the relationship between variables for the purpose of detection and correction.

The new seven tools of kaizen are relations diagram, affinity diagram, tree diagram, matrix diagram, matrix data-analysis diagram, process decision programme chart (PDPC), and arrow diagram. Imai (1986) advocates the use of these new seven tools to go beyond the analytical approach and to use them for a design approach towards problem solving. Relations diagram serves to clarify the cause–effect relations among many interrelated factors, whereas the affinity diagram is essentially a brain-storming method to generate ideas that are then grouped as per the subject matter. A tree diagram is used to show the relationship between goals and measures. Matrix diagrams are used to clarify the relationship between two different factors. It is based on data analysis and provides numerical results. A process decision programme chart is a concept taken from the field of operations research. It is used to take care of unexpected developments that have a potential for serious consequences. An arrow diagram is used in critical path method (CPM) and programme evaluation and review technique (PERT) of project management and shows the necessary steps to implement a plan. Kaizen plays a prominent part in the following areas:

- profit planning;
- customer satisfaction;
- total quality control (TQC) programmes;
- suggestion system;
- small-group activities;
- Just-In-Time (JIT) production;
- systems improvement;
- cross-functional management;
- policy implementation or deployment;
- quality deployment;
- total productivity maintenance;
- supplier relations;
- top management commitment;
- corporate culture; and
- problem solving

SUMMARY

Kaizen is a Japanese concept that seeks continuous to ongoing improvement involving top managers, managers, and workers. The kaizen strategy has enabled the Japanese management to take a systematic and collaborative approach to cross-functional problem solving. The management has two major components—maintenance and improvement. Maintenance refers to activities directed towards maintaining current standards of operation, whereas improvements refer to those activities that improve current standards. In Japanese companies the top management is always pressing for improvement—a stage between kaizen and innovation. Any improvement eventually leads to improvements in the areas of quality and productivity.

Kaizen emphasizes on being aware about the problem and provides clues for identifying them. The problem-solving process and standardization of the new process is also related to kaizen. The philosophy of kaizen epitomizes the process-oriented thinking in Japanese companies as compared to the result-oriented thinking that characterizes most of the Western companies. The kaizen concept stresses the management's support and the people's efforts to improve the processes. The various tools of kaizen are relations diagram, affinity diagram, tree diagram, matrix diagram, matrix data-analysis diagram, process decision programme chart, and arrow diagram. Kaizen plays a prominent part in the areas of systems improvement, cross-functional management, quality control, total productivity maintenance, top-management commitment, and problem solving.

KEYWORDS

Kaizen   It refers to ongoing improvement involving everyone.

Kaizen problem-solving tools   These are Pareto diagrams, cause–effect diagrams, histograms, control charts, scatter diagrams, graphs, and check sheets.

Kaizen tools   These are relations diagram, affinity diagram, tree diagram, matrix diagram, matrix data-analysis diagram, process decision programme chart, and arrow diagram.

Kaizen vs innovation   Continuous improvement as compared to breakthrough next level change.

EXERCISES

Concept Review Questions

1. Compare kaizen with the concepts of innovation and quality circles.
2. Describe the new and the classical problem-solving tools of kaizen.

Critical Thinking Question

Is kaizen a process intervention or a result-driven intervention?

Project Assignment

Form a team and look for areas around your institution (e.g., student mess, hostel, library, canteen, classroom, computer lab, etc.) where you can analyse some chronic problems and use kaizen tools for continuous improvement. To understand the processes involved, you should involve one or two persons working in those areas. Prepare a report and present it to the managers responsible for these areas.

REFERENCE

Imai, M. (1986), *Kaizen*, Random House, New York.

44

Six Sigma

Learning Objectives

After studying this chapter, you will be able to:

- Understand the origins of Six Sigma approach
- Comprehend the roadmap for implementing Six Sigma
- Understand different components of Six Sigma
- Elaborate the five-step process (process power) of implementing Six Sigma

INTRODUCTION

The concept of Six Sigma originated in the manufacturing division of Motorola where millions of parts were made using repeated processes. Eventually it evolved and is now applied to non-manufacturing processes too. The Six Sigma methodology improves the existing business processes by constantly reviewing and retuning the processes. It relies heavily on statistical techniques to reduce defects and measure quality. It also incorporates the basic principles and techniques used in business and engineering. Business process management initiatives such as call centres, customer support, supply chain management, and project management have seen its prolific application.

SIX SIGMA

Six Sigma method is a 'measure of goodness' involving the application of statistical methods to business processes to improve operating efficiency, reduce variation, avoid defects, and reduce waste. More specifically, it is a methodology and set of tools used to reduce quality problems to less than 3.4 defects per million opportunities (DPMO) or better (Table 44.1). Six Sigma is a management philosophy focused on business process improvements. It seeks to eliminate waste, rework, mistakes; increase customer satisfaction; and, finally, increase profitability and competitiveness. Six Sigma is a management philosophy aimed at customer satisfaction. If a corporation is producing a product or service, which does not meet the customer's needs, then it will not be competitive or profitable. Reworking a product or service as a result of inefficient processes not only results in increased cost of material, labour, and time but also in lost customers and poor reputation. It is the key to customer involvement. It is not only important to gain a customer but also to retain one. From here, the corporation should go backwards and look at their processes to improve the product based on customers' requirements. Once these processes are identified, then there must be a numerical, objective approach to evaluate current practices and future goals.

The Greek symbol σ (sigma) refers to the amount of variation in a process around its mean value. Statistics is a primary tool used in Six Sigma. In fact, the name Six Sigma is derived from statistics. Sigma is a Greek symbol, which denotes standard deviation, in other words, variation around the mean value, typically on a bell curve. Processes have acceptable upper and lower limits. An organization following the Six Sigma method makes only 3.4 DPMO. Six Sigma is concerned with reducing the variations to get more output within those limits. Generally, anything outside these limits is considered to be a defect—an unacceptable outcome. Six Sigma is about defining the best measures of a process, implementing them, tracking them, and making adjustments so that more of the outcomes fall in the acceptable range by reducing the number of defects.

The five steps to implementing Six Sigma are as follows:

1. Identify core processes and key customers: The business seeks to identify the core or value-added processes that deliver products and service to customers, that is, the 'value-delivering' processes are identified.
2. Define customer requirements: In this step, the 'output requirements' and 'service requirements' of the customers are identified. This keeps the firm in touch with the customer and provides the basis for measuring performance in customer satisfaction.
3. Measure current performance: Measuring customer satisfaction as well as operational efficiency helps keep the firm doing the 'right things right'.
4. Prioritize, analyse, and implement improvements: A project-based approach for identifying 'high-potential improvement opportunities' and a fact-based approach using risk and ROI analysis is used at this stage.
5. Expand and integrate the Six Sigma system: In this step, the processes, controls, measures, and infrastructure are established till Six Sigma becomes embedded in the company's culture.

TABLE 44.1 Sigma level vs DPMO

Sigma level	Defects per million opportunities (DPMO)
1 sigma	690,000
2 sigma	308,537
3 sigma	66,807
4 sigma	6,210
5 sigma	233
6 sigma	3.4

Six Sigma Professionals

There are five levels of professionals who coordinate their activities to successfully implement the Six Sigma method. Individuals at various levels of the organization have to be selected and trained according to the level they are expected to fulfil—(1) executive leader; (2) champion; (3) master black belt; (4) black belt; and (5) green belt.

Executive leader   The executive leader is a high-level executive who is committed to the success of Six Sigma. He should be knowledgeable about the Six Sigma process and should assign key individuals in the champion–sponsor position. The key to a successful Six Sigma programme is breaking down the boundaries within the organization. The executive leader must be committed to this programme and provide leadership both to promote teamwork and collaboration among all the players in the programme.

Champion   The champion also needs to be a high-level executive. He should oversee the individuals in the black belt positions. They should provide resources to complete the job and assist the black belts to select projects. Benchmarking with other organizations is another high-level executive position that ensures the management's commitment to this programme. This position decides what needs to be done and provides assistance to the black belts, both with monetary resources as well as a dedicated staff. In addition, this position benchmarks with other organizations in order to gain key information in processes they may need to improve.

Master black belt   The master black belt provides resources for the black belt experts on statistical methods and expertise on the Six Sigma process. He also works with the champion–sponsor to select the projects. The master black belt has technical expertise in the Six Sigma process as well as statistical methods. Initially, the master black belt is an individual from a Six Sigma consulting firm who instructs the black belts on the Six Sigma process. Eventually, a black belt in the organization who has become an expert replaces this individual. They are responsible for the training of the black belts and green belts. In addition, they play a key role in overseeing the statistical calculations of the processes as well as assisting with project selection.

Black belt   The black belts are the leaders of the Six Sigma process and possess management and technical skills. They are responsible for bringing the project vision to reality. They are completely dedicated to the Six Sigma programme and oversee the green belts. The black belts of the Six Sigma process are the true leaders of process change. The executive level may decide what needs to be done, the black belts decide how to do it. They must have both management skills and technical skills to work with the green belts and others to bring the projects to fruition. Due to the importance of this position and the details involved, Six Sigma is their only responsibility.

Green belt   The green belts are considered to be the project leaders. They support the black belts in completing the project. The green belt position works closely with the black belts to decide how to complete the project. They are individuals who are trained in Six Sigma but are also 'close to the action' so they can provide the necessary constructive input to improve the process.

The Six Sigma process

Six Sigma aims at improving processes and producing goods with zero defects. There are two methods to achieve this goal. The first is define, measure, analyse, improve, control (DMAIC) and the second is to define, measure, analyse, design, and verify (DMADV).

DMAIC It involves defining the problem, measuring where you stand, analysing where the problem starts, improving the situation, and controlling the new process to confirm that it is fixed. The black belts attend four training sessions taught by the master black belts to clearly understand these steps. These sessions are broken up so that the black belts can take what they learned and apply it to their initial projects. The theory behind this is that they are not overwhelmed with too much information all at once. Another good way to remember DMAIC is 'dumb managers always ignore customers'.

The various steps are explained in this section.

1. Define: A numerical parameter must be used to define the problem. There must be an objective way to measure the problem. In addition, the goal is not to manage the problem but to solve it. Therefore, there must be a focus on the problem, not on the outcome.
2. Measure: Again, a numerical measurement of the current process is necessary in order to change the process. What are the results of the current process? What are the competitor's processes? The focus must be on the critical quality issues that the customer finds important.
3. Analyse: Once the measurements are available, it is necessary to analyse this data. This will eliminate the gap between the current practice and the desired goal—achieving 3.4 defects in one million opportunities.
4. Implement: After analysis, changes need to be implemented to achieve this goal. Everyone should be involved in suggesting ways to improve the processes, especially those that work directly with the process. The green belts and black belts in an organization act on these suggestions.
5. Control: Once changes have been made to the process to achieve new operating limits, then the black belt must oversee measures to keep these operating limits in place and then on to the next project in order to achieve the Six Sigma goal. This project is only one in several to incrementally achieve the Six Sigma.

DMADV As explained earlier, the various aspects of DMADV are define, measure, analyse, design, and verify.

1. Define: It involves the definition of internal and external goals of the customers and the project.
2. Measure: Quantification of the customer needs as well as the goals of the management.
3. Analyse: It involves the analysis of the options as well as the existing process to determine the cause of error origination and evaluate corrective measures.
4. Design: It involves the design of a new process to the existing one in order to eliminate the error origination that meets the target specification.
5. Verify: This step involves verification, by simulation or otherwise, of the performance of the developed design and its ability to meet the target needs.

The difference between DMADV and DMAIC exists only in the way the last two steps are handled. In DMADV, instead of the 'improve' and 'control' steps, which focus on re-adjusting and controlling by one way or other, the 'design' and 'verification' steps deal with redesigning the process to fit customer needs.

At the crux of the Six Sigma programme, advanced by GE's Jack Welch and instituted at many other major corporations such as Motorola, is a renewed focus on eliminating errors, waste, and rework. Six Sigma is based on designated teams (people power) that focus solely on solving specific problems (process power), which may lead to efficiencies that delight customers and, by saving the company money, enhance the bottom line. What distinguishes Six Sigma from other popular quality management techniques, such as TQM and ISO 9000, is that each team has a clear goal; moreover, employees benefit because companies usually link financial incentives to a team's goal.

Chowdhury (2001) has created a fictional story that exemplifies the benefits of Six Sigma. In this book, Joe, a middle-aged manager is unexpectedly laid off from his position at a fast-food franchise company. He is worried and anxious about his next move. He calls Larry, his old friend and former co-worker, whose career is thriving. Over lunch, Larry explains how he has practised Six Sigma, both to advance his career and to increase profits for his employer. He teaches the programme's basics to an initially sceptical, then wildly excited and enthusiastic Joe.

SUMMARY

The Six Sigma methodology improves the existing business processes by constantly reviewing and retuning the processes of production. It is a management philosophy aimed at customer satisfaction by improving the quality of products. The goal is to improve processes to achieve only 3.4 defects per million opportunities (DPMO). The Greek symbol σ (sigma) refers to the amount of variation in a process around the mean value for that process. Processes have acceptable upper and lower limits. The Six Sigma roadmap consists of five steps to implementing Six Sigma. They are:

1. Identify core processes and key customers.
2. Define customer requirements.
3. Measure current performance.
4. Prioritize, analyse, and implement improvements.
5. Expand and integrate the Six Sigma system.

The five professionals involved in the Six Sigma method are the executive leader, champion, master black belt, black belt, and green belt. The executive leader is a high-level executive who is committed to the success of Six Sigma and should be knowledgeable about the Six Sigma process. The champion should oversee individuals in the black belt positions and assist black belts to select projects. The master black belt provides expertise on the Six Sigma process and has technical expertise in the Six Sigma process as well as statistical methods. Initially, the master black belt is an individual from a Six Sigma consulting firm who instructs the black belts on the Six Sigma process. The black belts in the Six Sigma process are the true leaders of process change. The green belts work closely with the black belts to decide how to complete the project. The five-step process the black belts follow when overseeing a project is define, measure, analyse, improve, and control (DMAIC), and define, measure, analyse, design, and verify (DMADV).

KEYWORDS

Champion A champion oversees individuals in the black belt positions.

DMADV It refers to these steps—define, measure, analyse, design, and verify.

DMAIC   It refers to these steps—define, measure, analyse, improve, and control.

Executive head   The executive leader is a high-level executive who is committed to the success of Six Sigma and is knowledgeable about the Six Sigma process.

Green belt   They work closely with the black belts to decide how to complete the project.

Master black belt   A master black belt is an individual from a Six Sigma consulting firm who instructs the black belts on the Six Sigma process.

Six Sigma   It is a management philosophy aimed at customer satisfaction by improving the quality of its products.

EXERCISES

Concept Review Questions

1. How is Six Sigma different from other quality interventions?
2. Describe the five-step road map for implementing Six Sigma.
3. Elaborate on the five-step DMAIC process followed by black belts.

Critical Thinking Question

Why do you think that Six Sigma programmes have not become a feature of public services delivery systems in India?

Project Assignment

Use the Internet to do some research and locate numerous case studies of successful implementation of Six Sigma to improve processes. Pay special attention to the pioneers of Six Sigma approach namely Motorola and GE. How are Indian companies faring in the implementation of Six Sigma, especially in the BPO industry? Discuss.

REFERENCE

Chowdhury, Subir (2001), *The Power of Six Sigma*, Kaplan Business, New York, http://www.isixsigma. com/books/default.asp?tab= directory, accessed on 22 October 2007.

45

The Japanese 5S Practice

INTRODUCTION

The 5S approach to management originated in Japan, a country where factories are not only clean but also function in a disciplined and organized manner. The logic behind the 5S approach is that organization, neatness, cleanliness, standardization, and discipline at the workplace are the basic requirements for producing high-quality products and services, with little or no waste, and with high levels of productivity. Surprisingly, this powerful tool has been unknown outside Japan. However, companies worldwide now recognize the significance of the 5S approach as an effective means of increasing efficiency and productivity. The 5S stands for five Japanese words—*seiri, seiton, seiso, seiketsu,* and *shitsuke* (Osada 1991). Table 45.1 shows the meaning and typical examples for each of these words and the related concepts. Hiroyuki Hirano's book titled *Five Pillars of the Visual Workplace* calls them alternatively as sort, systematize, arrange, shine, standardize, and sustain.

Seiri or sorting out Put things in order. Remove what is not needed and keep what is needed.

Seiton or systematic arrangement Place things in such a way that they can be easily reached whenever they are needed.

Seiso or shine and clean Keep things clean and polished. Remove trash or dirt from the workplace.

Seiketsu or standardization Maintain cleanliness after cleaning.

Shitsuke or sustained discipline Maintaining the habit and developing an attitude towards earlier 4Ss and to inspire pride and adherence to standards thus established.

TABLE 45.1   The 5S terminology

Japanese	English	Meaning	Typical example
Seiri	Structurize	Organization	Throw away rubbish
Seiton	Systematize	Neatness	30-second retrieval of a document
Seiso	Sanitize	Cleaning	Individual cleaning responsibility
Seiketsu	Standardize	Standardization	Transparency of storage
Shitsuke	Self-discipline	Discipline	Practice 5S daily

The 5S approach is a series of steps for individuals and teams to arrange their work areas for optimum safety, comfort, and productivity. It is a management technique for achieving workplace excellence, leading to organizational excellence. It is an approach for organizing, cleaning, developing, and sustaining a productive work environment. It is a set of workplace organization rules designed to increase efficiency and help enable lean manufacturing. The intent of 5S is to have only what you need available in the workplace, a designated place for everything, a standard way of doing things, and the discipline to maintain it. The 5S approach focuses on effective workplace organization and standardized work procedures. It was first implemented in manufacturing and subsequently introduced in other departments of organizations. 5S can be implemented in any type of business, from manufacturing to service sector organizations, such as fast-food restaurants, supermarkets, and libraries.

Seiri or sorting out

We tend to accumulate things, a legacy from those times when resources were scarce, supply of goods was naturally restricted, and people would hold on to things lest they need it someday. Today, in most of the industrial economies of the world there is an abundance of goods, services, and information so much so that sorting through these things to find the relevant has become an art and a skill.

One thumb rule for sorting out things is to keep only the things that are needed. Find out what you have, and determine what is necessary in each work area. This requires distinguishing between what is needed and what is not. A team goes through all items (tools, equipment, material, etc.) and questions their use on a regular basis. Items that are used very infrequently or not used should be red-tagged. Sorting makes it easier to find the things you need and makes additional space. The mantra is 'when in doubt, throw it out'. Organization is about separating the things which are necessary for the job from those that are not, and keeping the number of necessary ones as low as possible and at a convenient location. Most important of all is to know what to discard, what to save, and how to save things so that they can be accessed later.

The art of organization lies in stratification management. It involves deciding how important something is and then reducing the unnecessary inventory. At the same time one has to ensure that important things are close at hand and can be reached with great efficiency. A plan for stratification is suggested in Table 45.2.

TABLE 45.2   Stratification plan

Usage	Frequency of use	Storage method
Low	Things not used in the past year	Throw them or store them at a distance
Average	Things used only once in two to six months	Store in a central place in the workplace
High	Things used every day to once a week	Store near the workplace or carry by person

Most of the people cannot differentiate between what they need and what they want and, thus, err on the conservative side of saving things 'just in case'. It is worth emphasizing the importance of organizing called 'one-is-best'. Some of the guiding principles for practising *seiri* are:

1. Separate needed items from the unwanted ones.
2. Remove unwanted items from working areas. Items never used must be totally discarded, while items that are not needed at present must be stored somewhere else.
3. All items in excess must be removed from working areas. This includes work-pieces, supplies, personal items, tools, instruments, and equipment.
4. Store items needed by the members of the group in a common storage area and assign a person to organize and manage the common storage area.
5. Store items that are only needed by an individual in his own working area.
6. Organize working as well as storage area.

Seiton or systematic arrangement

Seiton refers to arranging the needed items so that they are easy to use and labelling them so that anyone can find them and put them away. It is a question of how quickly you can get the things you need and how quickly you can put them away. You have to analyse why getting things out and putting them away takes so long. The keyword in this definition is 'anyone'. Labelling is mostly for other people who need what is in the area, when the area 'owner' is away. In the work area, commonly used tools should be readily available. For this we need to organize them in such a way that everything has a place where it belongs. Items used often are placed closer to employee. There are four steps in achieving systematic arrangement.

1. Analyse the status quo: Typical problems that are encountered here are—not knowing what things are called, not being sure where things are kept, storage sites are far away and scattered, things are not labelled, no ledger is maintained to indicate whether it is finished or somebody is using it, too big or heavy to carry, etc.
2. Decide where things belong: The second step is to decide where things belong and there needs to be a criteria for deciding this. An object can have two names or two different things have the same name. These problems have to be rectified as soon as possible.

3. Decide how things should be put away: The third step is to decide how things should be put away. Storage has to be done with retrieval in mind. Everything should have a name. There should be a place for every object and everything should be kept in its place. There should be quick identification and safe storage; for example, heavy things should be stacked at the bottom.

4. Obey the put-away rules: This means putting things back to where they belong and obeying the rules.

For systematizing you must ask yourself these questions: What do I need to do my job? Where should I locate this item? How many of this item do I need? Some of the main principles for practising *seiton* are:

1. Place tools and instructional manual close to the work area.
2. Design the storage areas such that the entrance is wide and the depth shallow
3. Lay out the storage area with the wall to conserve space.
4. Store similar items together and different items in separate rows.
5. Use smaller bins to organize small items.
6. Use colour codes for quickly identifying items.
7. Clearly label each item and its storage areas (as it leads to visibility).
8. Use see-through cover for visibility.

Seiso or shining and cleaning

Cleaning should be done by everyone in the organization. It is believed that while cleaning, one is cleaning his mind too. This involves bringing the workspace back to proper order by the end of each day. At the end of the day if you just let it go back to being disorganized, you have accomplished nothing. So regular cleaning is required—that is why this step is called 'shine'. Cleaning is making sure everything is clean, functioning, and ready to go. It also includes inspection. This will help you stop problems, and wear and maintenance needs, before they become serious. It requires periodic (at least once a day) cleanup, responsible person(s) identified for cleanup, establishment of cleanup–restocking methods (tools, checklists, etc.), and periodic supervisor inspection.

The phrase 'the best cleaning is to not need cleaning', sums up this practice. Some of the guiding principles for practising *seiso* are:

1. Use covers or devices to prevent and reduce the possible amount of dirt.
2. Investigating the sources of dirtiness and implementing a plan to eliminate these causes.
3. Cover cords, legs of machines, and tables so that dirt can be easily and quickly removed.
4. Operators must clean their own equipment and working area, and perform basic preventive maintenance.
5. An orderly progression of cleaning in the factory environment by equipment and location will often identify causes of various problems in production processes.

Seiketsu or standardization

Standardization refers to continually and repeatedly maintaining the first three Ss. It embraces both personal organization and cleanliness of the environment. Visual management is an effective means for continuous improvement in production processes, quality, safety, and customer services. One effective method of visual management is to put up appropriate labels. Colour coding and the use of appropriate colour schemes can create a pleasant work environment. Transparency by making covers of lockers and closed shelves reveal the disorder and chaos within makes defunct the practice of 'out of sight, out of mind' by organizing such places. Put systems in place to ensure that what have been accomplished remains in effect. Establish standardized procedures (may be written standards) and practices, and make them into habits. Avoid backsliding into old work habits. An excellent way to make people aware of, and remind them about the standards is to use labels, signs, posters, and banners. The phrase 'see and recognize best people and methods', sums up the guiding principle of this practice.

Shitsuke or sustained discipline

Discipline means instilling the ability of doing things the way they are supposed to be done. Self-discipline is important because it reaches beyond discipline. Discipline is a process of repetition and practice till it becomes a habit. Once the 5S system is set up, it should not be assumed that nothing will change. One needs to establish a formal system for monitoring and evaluating the results of the 5S system. Maintaining correct procedures should become a habit. The phrase, 'the less self-discipline you need, the better', sums up this practice.

Thus, following the 5S approach ensures effective and quality production. It improves efficiency and productivity, quality, safety, reduces break-downs, makes the plant customer-ready at all times, reduces inventory and supply costs, and finally, spreads a positive and healthy attitude by creating a clean and organized work environment.

SUMMARY

The 5S practice is an approach for organizing, cleaning, developing, and sustaining a productive work environment. It is a set of workplace organization rules designed to increase efficiency and help enable lean manufacturing. The 5S philosophy focuses on effective workplace organization and standardized work procedures. It consists of *seiri* or sorting out things, *seiton* or systematic and proper arrangement, *seiso* or shine–clean, *seiketsu* or standardizing purity, and *shitsuke* or discipline.

Practising *seiri* in an organization entails keeping only those things that are needed. The art of organization lies in stratification management. Some of the guiding principles for practising *seiri* are—separate needed items from the useless ones and remove the latter from working areas. Items never used must be discarded while items not needed now must be stored. Store items only needed by each individual in his own working area. Organize the working or storage area.

Seiton refers to arranging the needed items so that they are easy to use and labelling them so that anyone can find and put them away. The points to be noted in *seiton* are—analyse the status quo; decide where and how things should be put away; create a place for everything; keep everything in its place; and obey the put away rules. The phrase 'A place for everything and everything in its place' summarizes this aspect of 5S. Different items should be placed in separate rows. Use small bins to organize small items. Use colour coding for quickly identifying items. Clearly label each item and its storage areas (leads to visibility).

Seiso or shining and cleaning means that regular cleaning is required within the workplace to keep things in a working condition. It is believed that the workplace should be brought back to the proper order at the end of the day.

Seiketsu or standardization refers to continual and repeatedly maintaining the first three Ss. It embraces both personal organization and cleanliness of the environment.

Shitsuke or sustained discipline indicates that self-discipline is important because it reaches beyond discipline. 'The less self-discipline you need,

the better' sums up this practice. Visual management is an effective means for continuous improvement in production processes, quality, safety, and customer services. Establish standardized procedures (may be written standards) and practices, and make them into habits. Finally, avoid back-sliding into old work habits. Following the 5S practice ensures effective production with quality management.

KEYWORDS

5S approach   It stands for five Japanese words, *seiri*, *seiton*, *seiso*, *seiketsu*, and *shitsuke*.

Seiketsu   Standardizing purity and maintaining cleanliness after cleaning.

Seiri   Sorting out, putting things in order, removing what is not needed, and keeping what is needed.

Seiso   Keep things clean and polished. There should be no trash or dirt in the workplace.

Seiton   Systematic and proper arrangement. Place things in such a way that they can be easily reached whenever they are needed.

Shitsuke   Sustain or discipline indicates that self-discipline is important because it reaches beyond discipline.

EXERCISES

Concept Review Questions

1. How does the dictum 'a place for everything and everything in its place' translate into workplace efficiency?
2. How is visual management used as an effective tool for continuous improvement in many areas of a company? Discuss by giving examples.
3. Why is commitment and self-discipline such an important element in the 5S framework?

Critical Thinking Questions

1. How does implementation of 5S lead to such dramatic improvements in workplace productivity?

2. Is 5S, like the quality circles concept, a Japanese tool that is difficult to implement in India?

Project Assignment

Discuss the validity of application of 5S to such commonplace processes such as in your study place. Do you think it is worthwhile to apply the 5S procedure to your study place? How? Plan and present your observations or views before the class to persuade them to do likewise.

REFERENCE

Osada, T. (1991), *The 5S's—Five Keys to a Total Quality Environment*, Asian Productivity Organization, Tokyo.

46

Total Quality Management

Learning Objectives

After studying this chapter, you will be able to:
- Understand the concept of total quality management (TQM)
- Learn the concepts forwarded by quality gurus
- Examine quality assurance, quality control, and quality planning
- Examine quality management systems and quality initiatives in Indian companies

INTRODUCTION

Total quality management (TQM) is a concept that originated in the 1950s. It is practised by companies to improve organizational effectiveness to meet and even exceed customer satisfaction levels. The strategic implementation of TQM involves continuous improvement of the quality, reducion of the costs, and delivery of goods in time as well as pushing for innovation thus strengthening the competitive edge in the process. It encompasses all aspects of the organizational and production processes. From choosing the right production equipment, to the right personnel, and the right strategy of marketing and customer service, the principles of TQM were developed over the past few years by management gurus such as Deming, Juran, Crosby, and Japanese pioneers such as Ishikawa, Shigeo Shingo, and Yoshio Kondo.

The quality concepts involved in TQM have worked so well in the manufacturing sector that these can well be applied to services such as banking, transportation, retailing, etc. Total quality management provides the overall concept that fosters continuous improvement in an organization. It emphasizes upon a systematic, integrated, consistent, and organization-wide perspective that involves everything and everyone. In other words, TQM is an important element of corporate culture that represents a vision as well as some behavioural patterns shared by all the members of the organization. Let us now understand the different elements of TQM.

Total It refers to everything, including human resources and equipment, associated with the company that is involved in continuous improvement.

Quality   It refers to the 'expressed and implied requirements' of the customers that are met fully, that is, based on the customers' perceptions of a product's design and how well the design matches the original specifications as well as the stated or implied needs of the consumers. This is the fundamental definition that meets 'the totality of features and characteristics of a product or service that bears on its ability to meet a stated or implied need' (ISO 1994); 'fitness for use' (Juran 1988); and 'conformance to requirement' (Crosby 1979).

Management   It means that top management and executives are fully committed to the philosophy of TQM. Satisfying the consumer's needs and expectations implies that a company needs to define accurately, early in its product/service development cycle, various attributes related to design, performance, price, safety, and delivery specifications from the consumer's perspective. Crosby (1992) broadened the definition further, defining it as 'quality means getting everyone to do what they have agreed to do and to do it right the first time'. The modern trend in quality management is to exceed expectations of the consumers and delight them.

QUALITY GURUS

Three Western management gurus—Edwards Deming, Joseph M. Juran, and Philip Crosby have been credited with developing the concept of TQM to a totally new level. This section also elaborates on the work of Japanese gurus of quality management namely Kaoru Ishikawa, Shigeo Shingo, and Yoshio Kondo.

Edwards Deming   Born in 1900, Dr W. Edwards Deming completed his doctorate in mathematical physics before working in US Government service where he applied statistical process control concepts in his work at National Bureau of Census that led to almost six-fold productivity improvement in some processes. After World War II, Deming was sent to Japan by General MacArthur as an advisor to the Japanese Census Board. There he gained eminence by giving lectures to the executives of Japanese companies by emphasizing on a systematic approach to problem-solving for quality improvement programmes. The captains of Japanese industry adopted and implemented his concepts with an enthusiasm beyond his expectations making Deming probably the most famous quality guru. His systematic approach to problem-solving later came to be known as plan-do-check-act (PDCA) cycle or the Shewart Cycle. Deming pushed senior managers to become actively involved in their company's quality improvement programmes. His idea helped revive the post-war Japanese economy. His thinking in the late 1980s can be best expressed as management by positive cooperation, which creates a new climate consisting of three elements—(1) joy in work; (2) innovation; and (3) cooperation.

Joseph M. Juran   Dr Joseph Juran was born in 1904 and started out as an engineer in 1924. He published the *Quality Control Handbook* in 1951, which led to his international eminence. Juran, like Deming, was also invited to Japan by Japan Union of Scientists and Engineers (JUSE) in early 1950s and conducted seminars for top and middle-level executives. Juran emphasized that quality control should

Exhibit 46.1　Juran's quality trilogy

Quality planning
- Identify the customers.
- Determine the needs and requirement of those customers.
- Translate those needs into specifications.
- Develop a product that can fit the requirements of customers.
- Optimize the product features considering the trade-off between the company's objectives and customer needs.

Quality improvement
- Develop a process capable of producing the product.
- Optimize the process.

Quality control
- Prove that the process can produce the product under operating conditions through process capability studies.
- Finally transfer the process to operations.

be conducted as an integral part of management control. He is best known for the quality trilogy which includes quality planning, quality improvement, and quality control (Exhibit 46.1).

Philip Crosby　Philip Crosby was born in 1926 and began his career as a reliability engineer. He worked his way up in IT&T and became its Director of Quality with worldwide responsibilities for quality. In 1979 he published a bestseller, *Quality is Free*. Crosby's name is best known in relation to the concepts of 'do it right first time' and 'zero defects'. He does not believe that workers should take prime responsibility for poor quality. According to Crosby, management should set the tone on quality and workers follow their example. Crosby's quality improvement process is based upon:

1. Quality is defined as 'conformance to requirements', not as goodness or elegance
2. The system for creating quality is prevention not appraisal
3. The performance standard must be 'zero defects' and not 'that is close enough'

Kaoru Ishikawa　Professor Ishikawa was born in 1915 and graduated in engineering from Tokyo University. He is best known as a pioneer of the quality circle movement in Japan. Through his writings, he simplified statistical techniques for workers to understand and practice quality control. He emphasized good data collection and presentation. The Ishikawa diagram (cause and effect diagram) and Pareto diagrams were some of the tools advocated by him for sorting and documenting the causes of variation in production quality. Ishikawa developed simple quality control tools for company-wide quality effort and believed that quality does not mean the quality of the product alone, but also of after-sales service, quality of management, the company, and ultimately, the human being.

Shigeo Shingo　Shigeo Shingo was born in 1909 and graduated as a mechanical engineer before being employed by Taipei Railway Factory in Taiwan in the area of quality management. During his varied career at Toyota Motor Company, Mitsubishi Heavy Industries, and Matsushita Electric Industrial Company he gained eminence in training workers for quality and productivity improvement.

Shingo introduced the concept of mistake-proofing poke-yoke, which prevented the worker from making errors and avoiding defects. Shingo introduced simple mechanical devices into assembly operations which prevented incorrect assembling or missed parts, thus fool-proofing the process against the defects. These devices are known as poke-yoke devices. The approach was successfully applied at various plants for defect-free operations. Shingo also contributed to the development of Just-In-Time (JIT) whereby inputs are delivered to the production process just as they are needed.

Yoshio Kondo Professor Kondo was born in 1924 and graduated from Kyoto University. He believed that quality is more compatible with human nature than other productivity parameters. He advocated that human work should have the component of creativity, physical activity, and social interaction. Kondo sees no basic contradiction between creativity, leadership, and humanity, and proposes effective ways to develop both creativity and leadership.

QUALITY

Quality assurance and quality control are often used interchangeably to refer to the actions performed for ensuring the quality of a product or service. However, both terms have multiple interpretations.

Quality assurance refers to all the planned and systematic activities implemented within the quality system that evoke confidence that a product or service will fulfil requirements for quality, in terms of fitness for use, and conformance to legal and environmental standards. *Quality control* refers to the measures that ensure that all the equipment, processes, and personnel within an organization adhere to rules that maintain the required level of quality from the first to the final stage of production. *Quality planning* constitutes all those processes connected with determining the needs of customers and optimizing the product features so as to meet the customer's needs.

Quality Improvement

The seven tools of quality improvement listed here help organizations generate ideas; analyse, develop, and evaluate processes; and collect data.

1. Flowchart/process map: A graphical tool for process understanding, a flowchart creates a graphical representation of the steps in a process. A process map adds lists of inputs and outputs for each step.
2. Check sheet: A simple data-recording device, a check sheet is custom designed by the user, which allows him/her to interpret the results easily. It organizes data by category and shows how many times each particular data occurs. This information is helpful as more data is collected.

3. Cause and effect diagram: A tool for analysing process dispersion. It is also referred to as the 'Ishikawa diagram', after Kaoru Ishikawa who developed it, and the 'fishbone diagram', because the complete diagram resembles a fish skeleton. The diagram illustrates the main causes adding to an effect (symptom).

4. Pareto chart: A graphical tool for ranking causes according to its significance. It is based on the Pareto principle, which was first defined by Juran in 1950. The principle, named after nineteenth century Italian economist Vilfredo Pareto, suggests that most effects come from relatively few causes, that is, 80 per cent of the effects come from 20 per cent of the possible causes.

5. Histogram: A graphic summary of variation in a set of data. The pictorial nature of the histogram displays patterns that are difficult to detect in a simple table of numbers.

6. Control chart: A chart with upper and lower control limits on which values of some statistical measure for a series of samples or sub-groups are plotted. The chart frequently shows a central line to help detect a trend of plotted values towards either control limit.

7. Scatter diagrams: A graphical technique used to analyse the relationship between two variables. Two sets of data are plotted on a graph, with the y-axis being used for the variable to be predicted and the x-axis being used for the variable to make the prediction. The graph displays possible relationships among variables. The variables must be evaluated to check if they are actually related or only appear to be related.

TQM Implementation Strategy

Although the indicators of business results differ from industry to industry and from company to company, the following seven business performance areas that are related to both short-term and long-term results need to be considered while implementing TQM:

1. Customer satisfaction
2. Employee motivation
3. Market share and growth rate
4. Return on total assets
5. Revenue growth
6. Total asset turnover rate
7. Cash flow

To ensure that short-term business results do not suffer when TQM is initiated, a well-planned strategy that encourages short-term business success to give momentum to TQM process is required. Juran advised 'Do not swallow the whole elephant at one time, eat it bit by bit'. Companies can run out of steam after attempting to implement TQM for a few years, partly because the annual results do not meet the expectations. Therefore, strategies should be devised at the start so that the TQM process is limited only by imagination, enthusiasm, and motivation (Wang 1999).

Wang (1999) goes on to recommend the integration of strategic planning with TQM. The main aim of TQM is to 'do things right the first time', whereas strategic planning aims mainly to 'do right things'. In combination, they are expected to allow organizations to 'do the right things right the first time'.

The experiences of successful TQM-oriented companies show that the integration of key business requirements is achieved by following a set of core values and concepts.

- customer-driven quality in products and services;
- corporate responsibility and citizenship;
- continuous individual and organizational learning;
- management leadership in quality initiatives;
- system's thinking;
- focus on results;
- supply chain quality;
- employee participation and development;
- built-in prevention and reliability;
- long-term vision, planning, and commitment; and
- fast response to markets and customers.

Quality Management Systems

Globally, there are quality management systems that provide a structured approach to the development and implementation of quality management systems.

Many quality-conscious companies require their suppliers to have ISO 9000 certification provided by the International Standard Organization (ISO). The ISO 9000 series was developed by a technical committee working under ISO in Geneva. The series took several years in the making and was an outcome of previous work of military standards in World War II and the British Standards Institution's BS5750 series. In 1987, ISO published the ISO 9000 series. This series is a family of quality management and quality assurance standards. This family consists of 17 different standards out of which only ISO 9001, ISO 9002, and ISO 9003 are quotable standards (i.e., can be audited against) while the rest are only guidelines. ISO 9000 series sets out implementable methods in an organization that assure that the customer's requirements are fully met. It comprises of documented system, invokes total company involvement, and also acts as a basis for effective management control. ISO 9000 is significantly different from normal engineering standards, such as units of measure, product specification, test methods, etc. set by agencies such as the Bureau of Indian Standards (BIS). ISO 9000 standard requirements are complementary and not an alternative to these engineering standards. Companies should, however, consider implementing ISO 9000 as the first milestone along the path of TQM and quality excellence.

Quality Initiatives in Indian Companies

The boom in the Indian economy has seen a proliferation of goods. Whether it is automobile components, machines, or textiles, the costs are lower and quality is comparable to the best worldwide. The examples are Infosys, Wipro, TCS, and Satyam in software; Sundaram Fasteners and Bharat Forge in manufacturing;

and a plethora of companies in textiles. According to Natrajan (1999) the quality evolution in post-independent India followed the following stages:

1. Inspection of products in factories and receiving departments
2. Statistical quality control and sampling plans
3. Process quality control in manufacturing industries
4. The ISI mark was recognized as a quality standard for products
5. ISO 9000 certification for manufacturing
6. ISI 9000 certification for service industries
7. Kaizen for continuous quality improvement
8. Quality circles for management of quality
9. Juran and Crosby methods for TQM
10. Adoption of Malcolm Baldrige award criteria

SUMMARY

Total quality management (TQM) is concept that fosters continuous improvement in all aspects of an organization, including human resources and equipment. Deming, Juran, and Crosby are the pioneers of quality management who have developed the concept of TQM wholly to a new level. Deming with his famous 14 points pushed senior managers to become active in their company's quality improvement programmes. Juran emphasized that quality control should be conducted as an integral part of management control and developed the quality trilogy comprising quality planning, quality improvement, and quality control. Crosby developed the concepts of 'zero defects' and 'do it right the first time'.

The terms quality assurance and quality control are used interchangeably. Quality assurance refers to all the planned and systematic activities implemented within the quality system. It evokes confidence that a product or service will fulfil requirements for quality. Quality control refers to all measures that ensure that all the equipment, processes, and personnel within an organization adhere to rules that maintain the required level of quality from the first to the final stage of production.

Quality planning constitutes determining the needs of those customers and optimizing the product features so as to meet the customer's needs. The seven tools of quality improvement help organizations generate ideas; analyse, develop, evaluate processes; and collect data. They are flowchart/process map, check sheet, cause and effect diagram, Pareto chart, histogram, control chart, and scatter diagram. Quality offers organizations significant opportunities for improvement, including reduced costs, increased sales, better performance schedule, and more satisfied customers. A successful quality system does more than ensure the quality of products and services; it drives vigorous operations and leads to a healthy bottom line.

Customer satisfaction, employee motivation, market share and growth rate, return on total assets, revenue growth, total asset turnover rate, and cash flow are some elements to be considered while implementing TQM. Organizations such as the International Standard Organization (ISO) and Bureau of Indian Standards (BIS) set standards of quality for products and organizations.

KEYWORDS

Fishbone diagram Also known as the cause and effect diagram, it describes the relationship between variables.

Quality assurance It ensures that quality planning activities give the confidence that a product or service will fulfil requirements of quality.

Quality control   It refers to the actions performed to ensure that the required level of quality of a product, service, or process is maintained.

Quality planning   All the planned and systematic activities implemented within the quality system.

Total quality management (TQM)   It is the overall concept that fosters continuous improvement in human resources and equipment of an organization.

Zero defects   The standard forwarded by Crosby for quality conformance.

EXERCISES

Concept Review Questions

1. Define total quality management (TQM). Why should it be integrated with strategic management?
2. Compare and contrast the work of the three Western gurus of TQM with their Japanese counterparts.
3. What factors should be kept in mind while implementing TQM in an organization?
4. Describe the evolution of quality management practices in India in the new millennium.

Critical Thinking Questions

1. Quality guru Philip Crosby advocates 'quality is free' which seems to run counter to popular perception that quality costs money'. How do you reconcile the apparent contradiction?

2. Price acts as a surrogate cue for quality, true or false? Does it apply to all categories of products and services? Discuss.
3. Why has the quality circles concept not been such a success in India in comparison to Japan? Give your reasons.

Project Assignment

According to Deming, 'Quality is not something you install like a new carpet or a set of book shelves. You implant it. Quality is something you work at. It is a learning process'. What did he mean by it? If Deming's theories are exemplified by Japan's Toyota, mention any three Indian companies who have excelled by following the TQM philosophy and practices.

REFERENCES

Crosby, P.B. (1979), *Quality is Free: The Art of Making Quality Certain*, McGraw-Hill, New York.

Deming, W.E. (1982), *Out of Crisis*, Cambridge University Press, Cambridge.

Ishikawa, Kaoru (1986), *Guide to Quality Control*, Asian Productivity Organization, Tokyo.

ISO 9002:1994, 'Quality Systems [Model for Quality Assurance in Production, Installation and Servicing], International Organization for Standardization, Geneva, Switzerland.

Juran, J.M. (1988), *Juran on Planning for Quality*, Free Press.

Juran, J.M. and Frank M. Gryana Jr. (1973), *Quality Planning and Analysis*, Tata McGraw-Hill, New Delhi.

Kondo Y. (1993), *Companywide Quality Control*, 3A Corporation, Tokyo.

Natrajan, Ganesh (1999), *India (1) in TQM: Concepts and Practice*, Asian Productivity Organization, Tokyo, pp. 36–46.

Shingo, Shigeo (2007), *The Sayings of Shingo Shigeo*, Productivity Press, Tokyo.

Wang, Chih-Han (1999), *The 21st Century Quality Perspectives in TQM: Concepts and Practice*, Asian Productivity Organization, Tokyo, pp. 7–17.

47

Technology Management

INTRODUCTION

Technology is a composite of techniques, comprising craft skills requiring the dexterity of hand and eye, and conceptual skills such as operating data, design engineering, construction, production, and maintenance. It is generally accepted that the systematic application of technology led to the gradual sophistication of economic activities that in turn caused a great improvement in the standard of living in developed countries over the past 200 years. Thus, technology is the engine of growth for the national economy. Technology is a 'means' for transforming the natural world into a man-made world. The production system of a country is the key factor in transforming natural resources into produced resources. Natural resources may be geophysical (hydrological and oceanographic), geographic (land, water, and air), living creatures (fisheries and cattle), plants (vegetation and forests), raw materials (minerals, ores, and rocks), and energy (coal, oil, and gas). The produced resources in a country may include goods (food, medicine, and apparel), materials (chemicals and hardware components), machinery (machine tools, vehicles, and instruments), infrastructure (buildings, roads, dams, and ports), and energy (electricity).

Technology in production systems

Any transformation of natural resources (Fig. 47.1) into produced resources may be schematically described in terms of inputs, outputs, production activity, and technology.

The production activity involved in the conversion of natural resources into produced resources may be viewed as

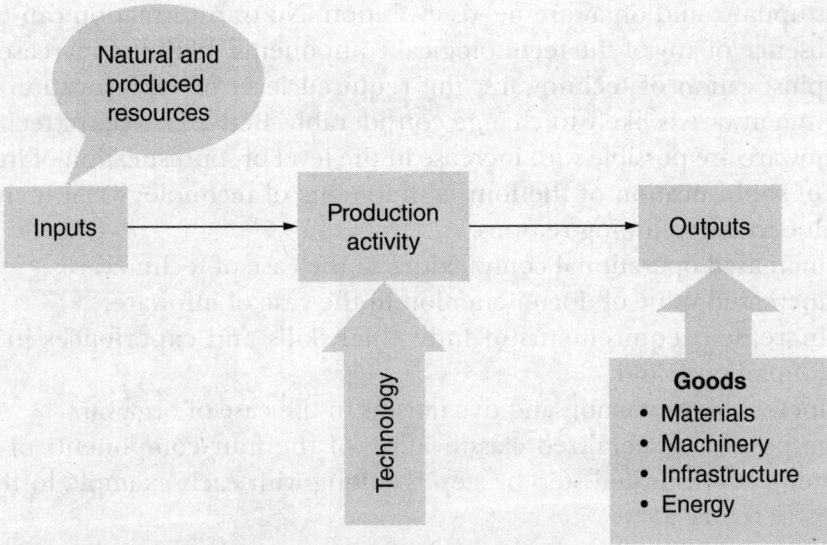

FIGURE 47.1   Transformation process

comprising of transformation stages, which can be broadly classified as—cultivating, gathering, pre-processing, processing, manufacturing, constructing, assembling, packaging, distributing, and supporting. For example, petroleum refining involves processing, agriculture involves cultivating, soft drink bottling involves packaging, appliance repairing involves supporting, etc.

COMPONENTS OF TECHNOLOGY

Technology is generally understood to be merely a physical tool for transformation. Very often it is not clearly recognized that technology is a combination of both physical tools and the related know-how either to make or to use those tools. Without the know-how or practical knowledge, a tool is not a useful technology. When one looks at the complex processes for the transformation of resources, one can discern four basic components of technology as follows:

Technoware   It is the object-embodied technology that consists of tools, equipment, machines, vehicles, and physical facilities.

Humanware   It is the person-embodied technology that refers to experiences, skills, knowledge, wisdom, and creativity.

Infoware   It is the document-embodied technology that includes all kinds of documentation pertaining to process specifications, procedures, theories, and observations.

Orgaware   It is the institution-embodied technology that is required to facilitate the effective integration of technoware, humanware, and infoware, and consists of management practices and linkages.

The effective use of these four components requires that certain conditions be satisfied; technoware needs operators, humanware needs motivation, infoware needs update, and orgaware needs evolution. No transformation can take place in the absence of any of the technological components. With the increase in the level of sophistication of technoware, the required level of sophistication of infoware and humanware is likely to change considerably. Better choices of technoware and humanware are possible with increase in the level of sophistication of infoware. The level of sophistication of the four components of technology can increase step by step due to the following reasons:

- increased operational complexities in the case of technoware;
- increased value of documentation in the case of infoware;
- increased requirements of individual skills and experiences in the case of humanware; and
- increased interaction and dynamisms in the case of orgaware.

One possible generalized classification of the four components of technology, becoming sophisticated step by step is (along with each example in the brackets) may be as follows:

Technoware   Manual tools (hand drill) → powered equipment (power drill) → general purpose machines (centre lathe) → special purpose machines (air jet weaving loom) → automatic machines (soft drink bottling plant) → computerized machines (bar code sensing register) → integrated facilities (computer chip manufacturing).

Infoware   Familiarizing facts (brochure) → describing facts (technical booklet) → specifying facts (performance and usage specifications) → utilizing facts (operating and maintenance manuals) → comprehending facts (design data and calculations) → generalizing facts (comparative techno-economic performance data) → assessing facts (state-of-the-art information).

Humanware   Operating ability (semi-skilled operator) → setting ability (skilled operator) → repairing ability (maintenance technician) → reproducing ability (production engineer) → adapting ability (design engineer) → improving ability (improvement engineer) → innovating ability (development engineer).

Orgaware   Individual linkages (garage shop) → collective linkages (cottage industry) → departmental linkages (small-scale industry) → enterprise linkages (medium-scale industry) → industrial linkages (large-scale industry) → national linkages (multi-location industry) → global linkages (transnational corporations).

TECHNOLOGY ACQUISITION, TRANSFER, AND PROTECTION

Specialized technical information and services are used for manufacturing competitive products. Such services may be needed not only in the areas of production but also in distribution (e.g., container technology) and sales. Operating companies rather than engineering companies are usually chosen as suppliers of such services, since their experience in both manufacturing and marketing becomes available to the client. However, many operating companies may not have all the expertise necessary to install a manufacturing plant. In these cases, the operating companies may employ engineering companies as subcontractors, or directly subcontract for the necessary services.

In developed countries, the *patent* system plays the important role of protecting the inventions of an industrial utility. In exchange for public disclosure of the full informational content of an invention, which gives the interested public the possibility of further improving it or seeking substitutes, the State, through the patent law, confers on the patent owner (patentee) certain exclusive rights for a limited period. These principally concern rights of—excluding others from making, using and selling the invented product, and the technique or process in the national territory where the patent has been issued. Under the patent statutes, the patentee has property rights over the invention, which can be exercised or conferred in full or part to others (sell or license) by them. This means that although the information of the patent stands published, the patentee obtains the right to prohibit unauthorized persons from using the patented information for commercial gain. The State provides for the enforceability of the patentee's rights. The 'make, use, and sell' rights are separate rights, and the patentee has the discretion over the extent of the rights he/she confers to the licensees. Under the use and sale rights, a patent system can operate to prevent the importation of a patented product or, in some countries, prevent importation of a product made by a patented process. When the patent lapses, its information enters the public domain and, thus, can be freely employed by anyone without reference to the patentee.

For developing countries, the know-how agreement is by far the most important means of acquiring technology. *Know-how* is a phase between technical assistance and patents. Like technical assistance, know-how is a package of technical information; however, unlike it, a substantial portion of the information is confidential, which gives its possessor some technical and/or marketing advantage over those using information that is not confidential. Like the patent, ownership can be ascribed to know-how; however, the owner of know-how, unlike the owner of a patent has no legal recourse to prevent third parties from developing and employing the substance of the unpatented know-how. Know-how is a body of information that emerges from the practical experience of working the patent—from the testing of raw materials, operational sequences, machines, products, and markets.

A *trademark* is any 'thing' that helps a consumer to distinguish between one company's products from another. It may be a word or a phrase, logo, sound, or package design; as long as it is used as a way of identifying that one brand is different from another. Trademarks are essentially limited monopolies over the use of symbols in business. The government grants trademark owners the right to exclude all other businesses from using a similar mark on related goods or services. Since the government can enforce this exclusivity, trademarks are considered assets of a business, and thus can be licensed or even mortgaged as collateral.

The words trademark, copyright, and patent, are often used interchangeably but incorrectly by most people. They are all intangible property that can be bought, sold, or licensed; however, each protects completely different interests. Patents protect new inventions, discoveries, and designs, while copyrights protect original works of authorship such as literary works, paintings, computer programs, sculpture, and architectural designs.

An organization may, however, opt to develop the information itself if it has the necessary skills and can bear the costs and risks of development, or it can seek sources of this knowledge. In developed countries, where skills and entrepreneurship are abundant, know-how is often purchased after the decision is taken on whether to develop it or license it. It is also known as the 'make or buy decision'. In developing countries, the decision to license is usually more expedient, and the source is often the patent owner.

For a developing country, the technology transfer is not only the immediate access to advanced techniques of production but also a means of educating and training its citizens in the use of technological information and working techniques. Also, it is recognized that the use of technology carries with it an element of risk, which should be borne almost solely by the entrepreneur. Risk is not always associated with the inadequacies or unsuitability of technology—it could lie in the insufficiency of the demand, underestimation of investment, court restraints, such as, for patent infringements, etc. Political and social factors also influence the choice of technology. Financial considerations may favour a particular technology, since the firm intending to use it may be able to obtain high foreign capital inputs which the economy needs, or at the opposite end of the spectrum, a technology may be welcome if it is not tied to capital participation.

Technology, markets, and investment share a triangular relationship. The entrepreneur's task is to choose a technology that will minimize the risks in investment and markets. Market factors influence the choice of technology, primarily, in terms of its viability with respect to product volume, product mix, and product quality. The selected technology should give an adequate financial return on a given base load, that is, the entrepreneur's share of market under the conditions of mature markets. At the minimum load, the selected technology should yield a return of investment at, or above, the discounted rate. The maximum load, of course, depends upon the design capacity of the plant. In terms of product mix, a selected product of the mix should be capable of economic runs. A change of mix should not lead to a sharp rise in the average cost of production or rate of consumption of raw materials. In other words, the technology should be flexible enough and readily adaptable. The choice of technology is again influenced by the quality of the product desired. Stringent product specifications can indeed require the use of sophisticated technologies. Investment costs and operating costs can, thus, rise sharply and threaten investment returns. The choice of technology profoundly affects investment and operating costs. An entrepreneur may select a particular technology because of limited funds or lack of foreign exchange, while accepting the disadvantage of high operating costs. However, tax concessions may also make a project requiring a large investment attractive, provided that its operation costs are low.

The most efficient method of comparing projects is that of discounted cash flow (DCF) method. These evaluations are based on the principle that money has a time value, whereas net present value (NPV) takes into account the net discounted income over the life of the asset. Any project will be profitable if its NPV is positive at an assumed discount rate. NPV analysis permits choice between project alternatives, with higher NPV projects preferred. According to DCF analysis, everything that has a NPV of zero or more is taken at a discount rate of X per cent. Knowing the NPV of a project gives no indication of whether the project is close to the margin of acceptability. For this another measure of profitability, known as the internal rate of return (IRR) is calculated by setting NPV equal to zero and calculating the yield. Thus, in assessing technology alternatives, project returns should be the guiding financial criterion. Both NPV and IRR need to be compared, and the combined technology–project arrangement should be used to maximize NPV in the alternative selected.

Technology and technique

Technology, in licensing terminology, is different from technique, that is, it is composed of proprietary and non-proprietary (specialized) information and skills, use of which gives its owner a competitive or superior technical position. Eventually, technology becomes obsolete or is incorporated into a set of techniques, readily available from numerous professionals who compete in rendering technical services. Transfer of technology permits both immediate access to advanced means of production and control over the means of production, that is, control over the supply. Such control, however, is not always accompanied by control over technology. This is achieved only when the skills, information, and the technical excellence that make up technology are transferred to the managers and workers of the enterprise where it can eventually diffuse into the economy. Control over the supply is usually the direct objective of industrialization; control over technology on the other hand is the objective of development. Thus, the overall industrial objective of a country is to gain both types of control. Subsequent growth would manifest itself in the diffusion of technology among different industries. Technology transfer should attempt to bring about this growth.

JAPANESE INNOVATION IN HIGH-TECHNOLOGY AREAS

Japanese firms made a transition from 'imitators' to 'innovators' during 1980s. This was achieved through the use of variety of strategies and integration of technologies with managerial functions. Bowonder and Miyake (1993) list some of the generic characteristics of Japanese innovations as given in this section.

Emphasis on commercial utilization This has become possible due to the interaction between marketing, manufacturing, design, and engineering functions. For example, while the concept of fuzzy logic was developed in USA, 80 per cent of its applications have been by Japanese firms.

Intense diffusion of technologies Large trading houses and international sales networks along with continuous product modification and functional coordination make Japanese firms the masters of rapid diffusion. For example, as soon as the concept of intelligent buildings emerged, many Japanese firms started using the concept.

Kaizen or incremental innovation Japanese firms follow a philosophy of continuous improvement (Imai 1986), rather than wait for a major breakthrough innovation.

For example, Citizen watches had imported horological technology from USA and France but improved it sufficiently to export the same to other countries such as India when it transferred the same to HMT Ltd.

Multiple competencies technology   Much of Japanese innovation has been achieved through the integration of advanced technologies and multidisciplinary and multifunctional coordination known as technology fusion (Kodama 1990). For example, Toyota and Fujitsu jointly developed automotive electronics technology and Nippon Steel developed the CNC factory technology with Hitachi.

Integrated marketing   Japanese firms such as Mitsubishi, Toshiba, and Hitachi use marketing networks in the form of trading houses, intermediaries, and direct marketing to achieve integrated marketing as the information flow in every direction is greatly facilitated for achieving excellence in innovation.

Organization learning   Japanese companies have exhibited creative learning. Nonaka (1990) has shown that organizational learning has been a very important element of the Japanese innovation system. For instance, Nippon Steel Corporation used its core competency in networking in its eight plants to diversify into information technology.

Bowonder and Miyake (1993) schematically represent the configuration of various interacting elements of organizational innovation as given in Fig. 47.2.

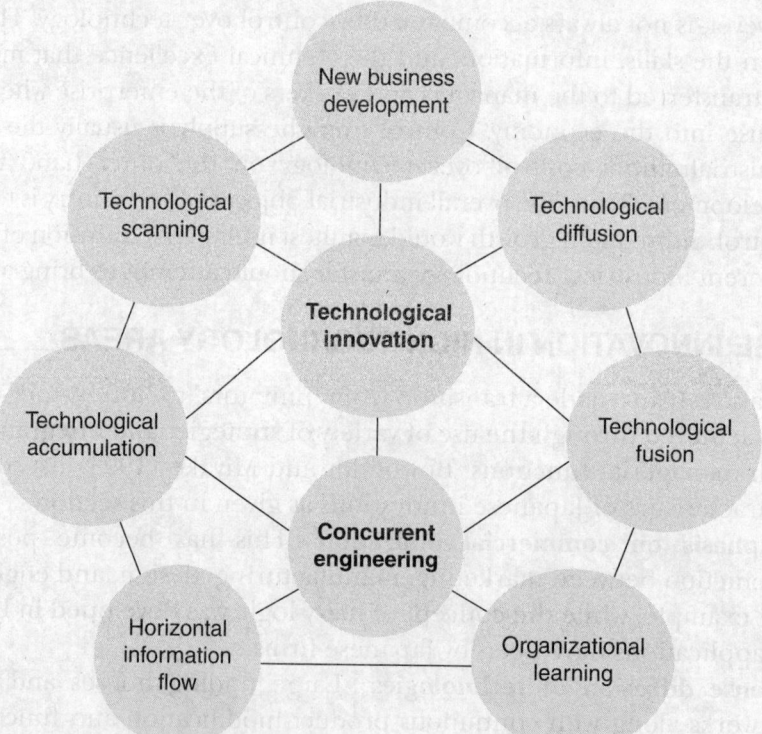

FIGURE 47.2   Organizational innovation configuration

Source: Republished with permission of Inderscience Enterprises Limited (UK), from 'Japanese Innovation in Advanced Technologies: An Analysis of Functional Integration', Bowonder, B. and T. Miyake (1993); International Journal of Technology Management, vol. 8, no. 1/2, pp. 135–156.

SUMMARY

Technology is a composite of techniques, comprising craft skills. Technology is a means for transforming the natural world into a man-made world. There are four components of technology—technoware, the object-embodied technology that consists of tools, equipment, machines, vehicles, physical facilities, etc.; humanware, the person-embodied technology that refers to experiences, skills, knowledge, wisdom, creativity, etc.; infoware, the document-embodied technology that includes all kinds of documentation pertaining to process specifications, procedures, theories, observations, etc; and orgaware, the institution-embodied technology that is required to facilitate the effective integration of technoware, humanware, and infoware and consists of management practices, linkages, etc. However, it is essential to have know-how or knowledge of the practical use of technology before putting it into use.

In any resource transformation process, all components of technology are required simultaneously. Transfer of technology permits both immediate access to the advanced means of production and control over the means of production, that is, control over the supply. Such control, however, is not always accompanied by control over technology. Technology transfer should attempt to bring about this growth. In developed countries, the patent system plays the important role of protecting the inventions of industrial utility. In exchange for public disclosure of the full informational content of an invention, it confers on the patent owner (patentee) certain exclusive rights for a limited period. For developing countries, by far the most important means of acquiring technology is the know-how agreement.

Political and social factors also influence the choice of technology. Technology, markets, and investment share a triangular relationship. The choice of technology is influenced by the quality of the product desired. The entrepreneur's task is to choose a technology that will minimize his/her risks in investment and markets. Choice of technology profoundly affects investment and operating costs. Net present value (NPV) analysis permits choice between project alternatives, with higher NPV projects preferred. Both NPV and internal rate of return (IRR) need to be compared, and the combined technology–project arrangement should be used to maximize NPV in the alternative selected.

KEYWORDS

Discounted cash flow (DCF) method   The evaluations of the DCF method are based on the premise that money has a time value.

Humanware   It is the person-embodied technology that refers to experiences, skills, knowledge, wisdom, and creativity.

Infoware   It is the document-embodied technology that includes all kinds of documentation pertaining to process specifications, procedures, theories, and observations.

Internal rate of return (IRR)   It is a measure of profitability, which is calculated by setting the NPV equal to zero and calculating the yield.

Know-how agreement   Applicable in developing countries, in a know-how licence agreement the owner of know-how, unlike the owner of a patent has no legal recourse to prevent third parties from developing and employing the substance of the unpatented know-how.

Net present value (NPV)   It takes into account the net discounted income over the life of the asset. Any project will be profitable if its NPV is positive at an assumed discounted rate.

Orgaware   It is the institution-embodied technology that is required to facilitate the effective integration of technoware, humanware, and infoware and consists of management practices and linkages.

Patent   Rights conferred exclusively to the inventor excluding others from making, using, and selling the invented product, technique, or process in the national territory where the patent has been issued.

Technology   It is tool for transformation consisting of technoware, humanware, infoware, and orgaware elements.

Technology transfer   It permits both immediate access to advanced means of production and control over the means of production.

Technoware   It is the object-embodied technology that consists of tools, equipment, machines, vehicles, and physical facilities.

EXERCISES

Concept Review Questions

1. Explain how the choice of a particular technology affects investment and operating costs.
2. Describe Japanese companies' path to innovation in advanced technology area.
3. What is the difference between technology and science?

Critical Thinking Questions

1. Despite a massive investment of $45 billion in automation by GM under CEO Roger Smith in 1980s, the company's market share fell from 48 per cent to 36 per cent. What could have gone wrong in this exercise of cutting labour costs and trying to meet the competition of Japanese carmakers? Toyota, and not GM, turned out to be the largest car manufacturer of the world as per statistics released in year 2007.
2. Palm, the world's first successful PDA product has been steadily losing ground to Microsoft and Compaq. Was Palm slow in incorporating changes in technology? Discuss.

Project Assignment

Find out the process and various formalities involved in filing a patent in India. Take a few commonplace products such as water tap, compact fluorescent lamp (CFL) lighting fixtures, spark plugs, etc., and conduct a patent search to analyse how extensively technology has been protected in these products.

REFERENCES

Bowonder, B. and T. Miyake (1993), 'Japanese Innovation in Advanced Technologies: An Analysis of Functional Integration', *International Journal of Technology Management*, vol. 8, no. 1/2, pp. 135–156.

Imai, M. (1986), *Kaizen*, Random House, New York.

Kodama, F. (1990), 'Japanese Innovations in Mechatronics Technology', in J. Sigurdson (ed.), *Measuring the Dynamics of Technological Change*, Frances Pinter, London, pp. 47–53.

Nonaka, I. (1990), 'Redundant Overlapping Organization', *California Management Review*, vol. 26, pp. 27–38.

48

Management Information Systems and IT

INTRODUCTION

We are living in the age of information as is evident from the boom in the media and new ways of communicating. The whole complexion of tools, techniques, relationships, and decision-making has been undergoing a total change. Hence, the question 'why study information systems and information technology?' may seem awkward in the present scenario. The study of information technology (IT) has become as essential as studying marketing, customer relationship management (CRM), accounting, finance, human resource management, operations management, or any other major business function for successful management of any organization. As such one cannot visualize management activities in isolation to information management.

One of the early civilian applications of information systems was the forecasting of the US presidential election in 1952 by the Columbia Broadcasting System (CBS). At that time, information systems were used mainly to automate the routine clerical work of large administrative departments. It was mainly the economies of scale that justified cost of computers and made any other application economically unviable. The typical computer systems developed in the early era were payroll and general ledger systems, that is, they were mainly used for data processing. In the mid-1960s, the advent of mainframe computers gave rise to the idea of developing corporate databases in order to

Learning Objectives

After studying this chapter, you will be able to:
- Understand the need and importance of information systems in the present business environment
- Examine emerging business trends and the role of technology
- Know about information technology and its relevance
- Learn about computer-based information systems and their use
- Understand the concept of management information systems (MIS)
- Learn how to organize information systems

supply senior management with accurate up-to-date information about the business for decision-making. These information systems were referred to as management information systems (MIS) and included reports on monthly production, financial information, inventory, account receivables, accounts payable, etc. It was naïve to believe that the shortcomings in management, planning, organization, and control could be overcome by information systems.

In late 1970s and early 1980s, it became fashionable to talk about 'expert systems' which would mimic procedures followed by some experts in the area of decision-making. It was also during this time that the use of computers to assist senior management in decision-making in their functional areas gave birth to decision support systems (DSS). It tends to focus on less structured decisions for which information requirements are not always clear, especially 'what-if' questions. Parallel to this development, a significant development in 1970s was the growth of microprocessors and minicomputers, which gave rise to the potential of enhancing office productivity through computers. Further, it became clear that dispersed microcomputers were unlikely to be powerful without connecting them, thus, giving rise to the importance of telecommunications. The era of convergence and rise of strategic information systems (SIS) had begun.

The corporate sector has been the most affected by the IT revolution. The difference between performing, less-performing, and non-performing organizations in the fast-changing environment lies in their effective and efficient decision-making capability. In fact, the success of an organization in today's business environment largely depends upon their ability to have relevant data and its information processing that can enable them to respond to different problem situations. The focus of organizations has shifted to a more customer-friendly approach these days. The greatest tool that enables them in this process is the use of IT-supported innovative methods such as e-commerce, mass customization, CRM, and business alliances.

The world is moving towards a digital economy, which can be viewed as a major economic, societal, and organizational change, affecting all organizations and corporate entities. This change has led to the automation of business processes by using the Internet, intranets, extranet, and wide area networks (WANs) to connect organizations and various stakeholders within and outside the organization. The digital economy is characterized by the extensive use of IT methods and tools, in general, and the Internet in particular. Thus, IT has become a driving force for organizational growth. Today, new business models are emerging that are dramatically reducing cost, while increasing quality, improving customer service, and speed. Companies are trying to transform themselves by imbibing and incorporating e-businesses and converting their information systems to web-based systems by automating as many business processes as possible. An accelerated rate of technological change, complexity, and turbulence and a move toward a global economy characterize the present day business environment. Further, there is an ever increasing competitive pressure on business entities. Organizational responses to changing business environment include strategic information systems, continuous improvements, business process restructuring, business process re-engineering, electronic commerce, and business alliances. Information technology has been playing the most crucial role in these developments.

INFORMATION TECHNOLOGY

Information technology (IT) refers to the network of all information systems in an organization. It has become a major agent of change, supporting critical response activities in all functional areas of management—human resource, operations, marketing, finance, etc. in all organizations in both the private and the public sector. Therefore, learning or knowing about IT is essential because of its important role in the management of organizations. We are getting more and more dependent on IT as time passes. Also, IT-related jobs ensure a higher salary.

Business entities use a wide variety of information systems, constituting different technologies. It is important to understand that information systems and information technology are two distinct concepts. As against the term, information systems, IT relates to various kinds of hardware that are required for the system to operate. In simple context, the hardware used could be pen, paper, files, journals, and books. However, hardware, in the context of IT, relates to computer-based information systems and use of the following technologies:

- Computer hardware technologies: Input–output and storage devices that support information systems.
- Computer software technologies: Operating systems, web browsers such as Google, Yahoo!, MSN, and others, business application software, etc.
- Telecommunications network technologies: Telecommunication technologies that enable wire-based and wireless access and support for Internet and intranet networks.
- Data resource management technologies: Database and data processing management systems software for development, access, and maintenance of the databases in an organization.

The major generic technological advancements and developments in the field of information technology are—increasing cost or performance, proliferation of object technology, and introduction of component-based development. The major developments in the field of business since the advent of IT are the increasing use of the Internet and intranets, mobile commerce, portals, optical networks, storage networks, and web services.

Information Technology and Business

In the emerging business environment the major trends that have emerged since the early 1990s are specialization, decentralization, and globalization, unprecedented growth in the services sector, and entrepreneurship, especially in the form of start-ups that are technology driven. These changes have added a new dimension in their management. Technology has been playing a very important role in business decisions in the backdrop of these changes.

Specialization The concept of specialization and its relevance to creation of wealth was discussed by the father of economics, Adam Smith (1723–1790), in the *Wealth of Nations.* He highlighted the concept of specialization and trade as the major source of wealth. Smith emphasized on the need for laissez-faire (free) policy in trade, taxation, and regulation to enable economic entities to benefit from specialization. Smith's book focuses on the concept of economic growth; growth that could be achieved through specialization, that is, by increasing division of labour. This essentially means the breaking down of large jobs into many tiny components that are carried out by a labour force that becomes expert in performing a particular task in the chain of activities, leading to increased efficiency. In the present day industrial scenario, the concept of specialization have improved productivity and efficiency leading to competitive advantage, and technology has had a great role to play in this improvement. It has resulted in a greater need for specialized technical skills, specialized, and sophisticated MIS tools and, above all, increased, improved, and efficient communication.

Decentralization It is the policy that delegates decision-making authority through-out an organization, relatively away from a central authority. Decentralization has become imperative for large companies which have many branches in the same location or at different locations within and outside the country. Some features of a decentralized organization are fewer tiers to the organizational structure, wider span of control, and a bottom-to-top flow of ideas that impact decision-making. This has also resulted in lesser requirement of manpower, as certain tiers may not be required for effective and efficient delivery of customer service. Decentraliza-tion has led to implications for technology in terms of efficient communication needs, lower cost of performing management activities, and low-maintenance tech-nology.

Globalization The opening up of economies worldwide by different countries has led to the increased flow of goods and services amongst countries. This increasing interdependency is leading to a greater flow of technology, businesses, people, and raw materials across countries. As a result, more and more global and multinational corporations are emerging. This has posed a great challenge to corporate entities. Today, it is normal for managers of almost every company to deal with international transactions on a routine basis. Even small businesses, having created their own niches, have links in other nations. This trend of globalization has been mainly facilitated by technology—from communication, quality control, and managements to transportation. Communication technology, coupled mainly in terms of Internet and intranet, has revolutionized the speed and pace with which businesses are crossing natural boundaries. Communication technology is especially important for businesses in the service sector such as retail, banking, hotel, tourism, air travel, consulting, programming, design, and marketing. Due to the availability of sophisticated communication technologies, the concept of an organization as a physical entity is becoming blurred. Information technology is the key to successfully manage business entities in the global set-up.

Growth in the service sector   The service sector has been growing at an unprecedented pace in different developing economies of the world. In the Indian economy too, the service sector has grown fast and now accounts for more than 53 per cent of India's gross national product (GNP), at factor cost in 2004–05 as against 36.58 per cent in 1980–81. The share of primary sector has fallen from 41.8 per cent in 1980–81 to 22.9 per cent in 2004–05. The increase in the service sector's share in the GDP indicates the structural transformation that has been taking place in the Indian economy. This change has also brought Indian economy closer to the fundamentals of a developed economy.

The tertiary sector of the economy covers a wide gamut of activities such as trading, banking and finance, entertainment, real estate, transportation, security, management and technical consultancy, among several others. In all the aforesaid services areas, IT plays a crucial role in information processing, storage, and access with a view to take decisions so as to provide improved services to the consumers. Application of information technology in these areas is enabling business entities to develop a competitive edge.

Entrepreneurship   The understanding of entrepreneurship owes much to the work of economist Joseph Schumpeter and the Austrian School of Economics. According to Schumpeter (1962), an entrepreneur is a person who is willing and able to convert a new idea or invention into a successful innovation. Entrepreneurship forces 'creative destruction' across the markets and industries, simultaneously creating new products and business models. In this way, creative destruction is largely responsible for the dynamism of industries and long-run economic growth. The start-up ventures in a variety of product and service lines in general and technology-driven ventures in particular are increasing at a fast pace. The new generation is far more creative and innovative. They would like to exercise their own independent initiative by venturing into their own ventures. One of the key opportunities that has emerged for start-up ventures is in the area of IT itself. However, to manage any business in today's turbulent environment requires a great deal of input from IT.

Thus, the five aforementioned trends—specialization, decentralization, globalization, growth in service sector, and entrepreneurship are leading to great implications for technology. Further growth in these sectors has necessitated a need for continuous innovations in the IT industry to avail emerging opportunities.

INFORMATION SYSTEMS

An information system (IS) collects, processes, stores, and disseminates information for a specific and well-defined purpose. A computer-based information system uses computers to perform some or all of these activities. Thus, an IS can be defined as an organized combination of people, hardware, software, communication networks, data resources which involve collection, storage and retrieval, and the supply of information throughout the organization. 'People have relied on information systems to communicate with each other using a variety of physical devices (hardware), information processing instructions and procedures (software), communication channels (networks), and stored data (data resources) since the dawn of civilization' (O'Brien and Marakas 2006). The recent change in information system over the years has mainly taken place on account of technological developments in hardware, software, networks, and data resources.

Management Information Systems

The first step towards an understanding of the application of information technology to solve business problems is to learn and know about management information systems (MIS). All of us might have an experience of using computer and software for something or the other. However, use of computers is just one small component of MIS.

Management information systems or computer information systems (CIS) consists of five related components—hardware, software, people, procedures, and collection of data (Post and Anderson 1997). It is a general name for the academic discipline that deals with the application of people, technologies, and procedures, collectively known as information systems, to solve business problems. MIS is different from regular information systems as it is used to analyse other information systems applied in operational activities in the organization (O'Brien 1999). However, before going into further details, it is essential to understand the meaning of management, information, and system. Management is the act of setting, coordinating, conducting, and supervising the various processes of production. Information is the collection of facts on the basis of which decisions and conclusions may be made. System is a group of independent but interrelated elements comprising a unified whole.

Thus, MIS may be defined as an organized and holistic system of processing data by using suitable hardware and software. It enables managers to take decisions to achieve well-defined goals and objectives.

It broadly refers to a computer-based system that provides managers with the tools and techniques for collecting, organizing, and evaluating information and using the same for efficient and effective running of their departments. To provide past, present, and future information, an MIS can include software that helps in decision-making, relevant databases with regard to the particular problem in hand, the hardware resources pertaining to the system, decision support systems, people and project management applications, and other computerized processes that help the department to run efficiently.

Academically, the term MIS is also commonly used to refer to the various information management methods linked to the automation or support of human decision-making such as decision support systems, expert systems, and executive information systems. It is a computer system that uses a mainframe or minicomputer, designed to provide management personnel with timely and up-to-date information on different aspects of organization's performance such as territory-wise sales, profit or product, inventory of finished goods and raw materials vis-à-vis sales, and in comparison to competitors. The system's output information should be in a format that can be used by managers at all levels of the organization—strategic, tactical, and operational. A good example of an MIS report brought out by a mutual fund is a monthly magazine giving details on various mutual fund schemes for existing and prospective investors.

Organization of information systems

Information systems can be organized in different ways according to the organizational hierarchy—function, line, and staff. The organizational hierarchy-based information systems focuses on the level of management vis-à-vis information needs. Such an information system can target its output to the board level, top management level, middle management level, and officer level. The focus of organizational hierarchy-based system could be on department, enterprise-wide, and inter-organizational. As against hierarchy-based systems, the focus of functional information system is on various managerial functions such as human resources, operations, marketing, and finance. Inter-organizational information systems (IOS) connect two or more organizations and play a major role in e-business. Transaction processing system (TPS) covers the core repetitive organizational transactions. The data collected in a TPS is used for purchasing, billing, payrolls, etc. to build other support systems. The major functional information systems in an organization are accounting, finance, manufacturing (operations), human resources, and marketing.

Information systems and business professionals

Having understood the basics of information technology, information systems, and MIS, we need to know the information requirements of business professionals in managing business issues and problems. Although business professionals may not be able to understand the deeper aspects of information systems, it is important for them to have a broad knowledge of the system to better appreciate the whole framework. This awareness along with knowledge about basics can help them a lot in applying information systems and technologies in their specific context.

The five areas of information system about which business professionals need to have basic knowledge are—foundation concepts, information technologies, business applications, development processes, and management challenges (O'Brien 1999). Foundation concepts refer to the knowledge and understanding about behavioural, technical, business, and managerial concepts related to various components and roles of information systems. Information technology, as described earlier, refers to knowledge about hardware, software, networks, database management, data processing, and Internet technologies. Business applications knowledge pertains to the uses of information systems in functional and other areas of operations so as to develop a competitive advantage in business. The knowledge about development processes refers to understanding how information professionals plan, develop, and implement information systems to avail business opportunities and safeguard the organization against business threats. Above all, business professionals should be clear about the challenge of ethically managing information technology at organizational, competitive, and global levels.

Enterprise resource planning systems

Enterprise resource planning (ERP) systems is a packaged business software system that integrates business processes to share common data and practices across the enterprise to produce information for use in real time. This system is different from other legacy systems in that it enables all business transactions to be entered, processed, monitored, and reported. An ERP system also introduces 'best practices'. In fact, the successful implementation of an ERP system requires that business processes be aligned with ERP software by re-engineering. SAP, Oracle, and PeopleSoft are some of major vendors of ERP software. Before ERP systems, material requirement planning (MRP) systems and manufacturing resource planning (MRPII) had taken off from reorder point systems, which mainly had the function of inventory management. While MRP took care of demand-based production planning, MRPII focused on process control and cost reporting. ERP systems provide seamless integration of financial accounting, supply chain management, human resource functions, etc. Acquisition of an ERP system is a business decision. The company must weigh both the tangible and intangible benefits. The most important tangible benefits are inventory reduction and productivity improvement, whereas information visibility and customer response are important intangible benefits. The important ERP cost elements are software, hardware, consulting, and training or implementation team costs. As ERP projects involve considerable time and cost, it may take four to five years before the benefits are realized.

SUMMARY

The study of management information and information technology has become essential vital components for successful management of any organization. Organizational responses to changing business environment include strategic information systems, continuous improvements, business process restructuring, business process re-engineering, electronic commerce, and business alliances.

An information system collects, processes, stores, and disseminates information for a specific and well-defined purpose. Information technology refers to the network of all information systems in an organization. Business entities depend and use a wide variety of information systems that use forms of different information technology (IT). It is important to understand that information system and information technology are two distinct concepts. However, in the present technological society, information technology relates to computer-based information systems and their use of computer hardware, computer software technologies, telecommunications network technologies, and data resource management technologies.

Management information systems (MIS) or computer information systems (CIS) consists of five related components—hardware, software, people, procedures, and collection of data. MIS refers to the department that manages information systems in organizations. Information systems can be organized in different ways such as organizational hierarchy-, functional-, line- and staff-based, etc. The five areas of information system about which business professionals need to have basic knowledge are—foundation concepts, information technology, business applications, development processes, and management challenges (O'Brien 1999). ERP systems is a packaged business software system that integrates business processes to share common data and practices across the enterprise to produce information for use in real time.

KEYWORDS

Decentralization It is the policy to delegate decision-making authority throughout an organization, relatively away from a central authority.

Enterprise resource planning (ERP) systems It is a packaged business software system that integrates business processes to share common data and practices across the enterprise to produce information for use in real time.

Globalization Opening up of economies worldwide by different countries has led to increased flow of goods and services amongst countries.

Information systems It collects, processes, stores, and disseminates information for a specific and well-defined purpose.

Information technology It refers to the network of all information systems in an organization.

Inter-organizational information systems (IOS) It connects two or more organizations and plays a major role in e-business.

Management information systems (MIS) It deals with the application of people, technologies, and procedures to solve business problems.

Specialization It refers to the breaking down of large jobs into many tiny components that are carried out by a labour force that becomes expert in performing a particular task in the chain of activities, leading to increased efficiency.

Transaction processing system It covers the core repetitive organizational transactions.

EXERCISES

Concept Review Questions

1. What is the relevance and need for studying information systems and information technology?
2. What is meant by digital economy? How has it affected organizational change?
3. What are the four major trends that emerged from early 1990s? In what way have these trends affected business operations and relevance of role of technology? Define computer-based information technology.
4. Define management information systems (MIS) and its relevance in managing businesses.
5. What is meant by information systems?

6. What are the different ways in which information systems can be organized?

Project Assignments

1. Identify one company from the manufacturing industry and another from the service industry. Collect details on their information technology and MIS. Compare and contrast these details to highlight typical differences. What changes would you suggest to improve their information system?
2. Schematically design an MIS for your institute's library.

REFERENCES

Cannan, Edwin and Max Lerner (1937), *An Inquiry into Nature and Causes of the Wealth of Nations* (Adam Smith), Modern Library, New York.

O'Brien, J. (1999), *Management Information Systems: Managing Information Technology in the Internetworked Enterprise* (in English), Irwin McGraw-Hill, Boston, pp. 6–7.

O'Brien, James A. and George M. Marakas (2006), *Management Information Systems*, 7th edition, McGraw-Hill International, New York, p. 6.

Post, Gerald V. and David L. Anderson (1997), *Management Information Systems: Solving Business Problems with Information Technology*, Tata McGraw-Hill Publishing Company Limited, New Delhi.

Schumpeter, Joseph A. (1962), *Capitalism, Socialism and Democracy*, 3rd edition, Harper Torchbooks, New York.

49

International Management

MANAGEMENT INFORMATION SYSTEMS AND IT 535

Learning Objectives

After studying this chapter, you will be able to:
- Understand the effect of globalization
- Comprehend the importance of managing across cultures
- Understand cross-cultural approach to international management
- Appreciate project GLOBE
- Understand the factors associated with designing global strategies
- Comprehend different theories of multinational corporation

INTRODUCTION

Globalization is becoming an increasingly pervasive phenomenon. The growth in international trade, foreign direct investment, and technology transfer have diminished many barriers that had isolated the economies of various countries. International business now comprises a large portion of the world's total business. Some global companies have their annual revenues greater than the gross domestic product (GDP) of many countries. For many companies, globalization is no more an option but only a strategic imperative. The worldwide ideological shift to market-based economy along with the creation and acceptance of the World Trade Organization (WTO) by virtually every important country has further increased the pace of globalization. Tremendous technological advances in the domain of communication and transportation have transformed the world into a global village.

The emergence of regional free-trade zones such as the European Union, the North American Free Trade Association (NAFTA), the Latin American South Common Market (MERCOSUR), and the Association of South East Asian Nations (ASEAN) have also increased the rate of international investment and trade between the countries that are geographically close to each other. For companies to be successful in the global arena, it is not enough to replicate their domestic strategies on a bigger scale since the global landscape is replete with uncertainty, complexity, and diversity in its sociocultural, politico-legal and economic environments. International management deals with the application of management concepts, techniques, and practices in a multinational, multicultural environment.

The year 2007 would probably go down as the year when corporate India acquired companies abroad. The setting was provided in 2006 when everyone watched in disbelief as Laxmi Mittal acquired Arcelor, a European company. It was followed by Tata's acquisition of Corus in 2007. Both these acquisitions generated a lot of misunderstandings, initially, on account of their different cultural mindsets. However, finally, business logic prevailed.

MANAGING ACROSS DIFFERENT CULTURES

Margaret Mead (1955), the internationally well-known anthropologist defines culture as 'a body of learned behaviour which a group of people who share the same tradition transmit entire to their children … it covers not only the arts and sciences, religions, and philosophies … but also the system of technology, the political practices…'. Hence, culture is a learnt, shared, and trans-generational knowledge that forms the basis of our values, attitudes, and behaviour. Considering the existence of different cultures in the world, cultural differences must be accounted for into the practices of international management by global companies. Decision-making styles, risk-taking ability, group-behaviour, achievement orientation, resistance to change, etc., are some of the factors that are related to dimensions of a culture and influence organizational practices. It is important for international managers to be sensitized to these differences in cultures, the lack of which can otherwise hinder progress. Cultural diversity as well as cultural similarities have been studied by different researchers through cultural dimensions.

Hofstede (1991), a Dutch researcher conducted an intensive organization-based study of IBM's cultural dimensions by conducting two surveys (through questionnaires) of more than 100,000 respondents from 70 different countries. These cultural dimensions are explained in this section.

Power distance   It is defined as the extent to which less powerful members of institutions accept that power is distributed unequally. This has consequences for an organization. The organizations in high power-distance countries will exhibit centralized decision-making and organization structures, which will be relatively tall with lower levels occupied by jobs entailing lesser qualifications. In contrast, countries which are low on this dimension will exhibit flatter organization structures and decentralized decision-making.

Uncertainty avoidance   It is defined as the extent to which people feel threatened by ambiguous situations and avoid uncertainty. The cultures that are high on this dimension have a high need for security. The implications for organizations is that it leads to a high degree of formalization, less risk-taking by managers, less ambitious employees, and lower labour turnover.

Individualism vs collectivism   It refers the extent to which people look after themselves and their immediate family (individualism) vs the extent they belong to the groups and look after one another in the group (collectivism). Cultures high on individualism are also, generally, wealthy with a high per capita income. The implication for organizations is that there is individual initiative and people are rewarded based on their market value, while in cultures high on collectivism, there is less individual initiative and people are promoted based on seniority.

Masculinity vs femininity   It refers to a culture in which important values in the society are money, things, and success (masculinity) in contrast to a culture in which important things in the society are quality of life and caring for others (femininity). Cultures high on the masculinity dimension value wealth and success and the implication for organizations is that because of fierce competition there is high job stress and higher degree of control. On the other hand, cultures, which are low on this dimension have workplaces that promote cooperation, give responsibility to employees, and have concern for the environment.

GLOBAL LEADERSHIP AND ORGANIZATIONAL BEHAVIOUR EFFECTIVENESS (GLOBE) RESEARCH PROGRAMME

Project GLOBE uses a network of social scientists and management academicians from different countries of the world to examine different dimensions of organizational and country culture. The idea of a global research programme was conceived by Robert J. House in 1991. Project GLOBE has identified nine dimensions of culture. There is a high agreement within-organization and within-culture and high differentiation between-organizations and between-culture with respect to these dimensions. The GLOBE research programme is based conceptually on motivation theory, leadership theory, Hofstede's theory of culture, and contingency theory.

As discussed earlier, values and beliefs held by members of different cultures influence the behaviour of individuals, groups, and institutions. Hofstede uses four cultural dimensions—power distance, uncertainty avoidance, individualism vs collectivism, and masculinity vs femininity. To these, the GLOBE project adds three more dimensions—humanistic, performance, and future orientation. It also measures collectivism on two scales. It splits Hofstede's masculinity dimension into two cultural dimensions namely gender egalitarianism and assertiveness. GLOBE research programme, thus, uses nine operationalized attributes of cultures. These are explained in this section.

Uncertainty avoidance   It is defined as the extent to which members of an organization or society make an effort to avoid uncertainty by the formalization of activities in order to control or reduce ambiguity about the future; most of the people, hence, prefer to live structured lives and do not like surprises.

Power distance   It is defined as the degree to which members acquiesce willingly to inequity in the distribution of power at different hierarchical levels of an organization or society. In these cultures, followers will be expected to follow their leaders unquestioningly.

Collectivism I   It is defined as the degree to which institutions, both organizational and societal, reward group loyalty at the cost of individual goals. In these cultures, collective actions and collective resource allocations are encouraged and rewarded.

Collectivism II   It is defined as the degree to which individuals express cohesiveness in their organizations or families. In these cultures, for example, aged parents live with their children in a joint family structure.

Gender egalitarianism   It is the extent to which an organization or a society reduces the differences between the roles of men and women. In some cultures, in contrast, boys rather that girls may be encouraged to pursue higher education.

Assertiveness   It is the degree to which individuals in organizations or societies are demanding, dominant, and assertive in social relationships.

Future orientation   It is the degree to which individuals in organizations or societies are concerned with future and emphasize activities such as scenario building, planning, investing for future, etc. In contrast, in certain cultures, people prefer to live in the present rather in future and, hence, they do not believe in delaying gratification.

Performance orientation   It refers to the extent to which group members of an organization or society are rewarded for excellence and continuous improvement.

Humane orientation   It is the degree to which human values, such as, being upright, just, selfless, caring, and kind to others, are rewarded by organizations and societies.

Finally, the cross-cultural approach to international management is a contingency approach that holds that effective managerial practices in different cultures is a function of cultural dimensions and multinational companies should be sensitive to this fact.

GLOBAL STRATEGIES

Kogut (1985) writes that the design of international strategies is dependent on the dynamics between the comparative advantage of countries and the competitive advantage of firms. Comparative advantage is a location-specific advantage that influences the decisions such as where to market and where to source, whereas the competitive advantage is firm-specific advantage such as brand equity, proprietary technology, managerial resources, etc., that cannot be imitated by competitors without taking substantial risk and incurring huge costs. Hence, the three modes of international competition are based on—(1) comparative advantage among countries; for example, outsourcing of business processes from USA to countries such as India that have a comparative advantage in terms of lower wages; (2) competitive advantage among firms; for example, Nissan imports cars made by Suzuki India in Europe and sells them under the Nissan brand; and (3) the interplay of competitive and comparative advantage, which generates a complex pattern and firms compete on the basis of relative superior configurations of outsourcing, intellectual property, and product–market decisions. As per Kogut (1985), the key operating dimensions of a global strategy are:

- recognition of potential profit opportunities; and
- creation of organizational flexibility that responds to the changes in the environment.

Bartlett and Ghoshal (1987) contend that the most successful multinational companies in late 1980s were operating and competing in different industries with a particular set of rules; for example, in consumer electronics industry the firms were seeking global economies of scale; in packaged goods industry it was local responsiveness; and in the telecommunications equipment industry it was worldwide knowledge sharing (mainly in technology). Their research that consisted of interacting with 250 managers from nine of the world's largest multinational companies revealed that managers of multinational companies (MNCs) are now faced with the task of optimizing efficiency, responsiveness, and learning in their global operations.

Consumer electronics industry, assumed the attributes of a classic global industry after the invention of transistor at Bell Labs in 1947 and other technological developments such as integrated circuits and automation of the manufacturing processes along with falling transportation and communication costs, etc. Firms such as Matsushita were ideally placed to exploit the economies of scale better than companies such as Philips and GE who were entrenched in the country by country approach developed during an earlier, less conducive environment.

On the contrary, in consumer packaged goods industry, national responsiveness, rather than global integration, is the key strategic requirement to achieve economies of scale. Unilever understood this and its multinational strategy led it to build strong national companies such as the erstwhile Hindustan Lever Limited in India, which was sensitive to local needs and was allowed to operate and exploit local opportunities without any interference from the headquarters. Procter and Gamble (P&G), instead, took time to adapt and learn that the parent company's practices and products cannot be simply transplanted in different markets.

In the telecom switching equipment manufacturing industry, the key strategic requirements were still different from those required in consumer electronics industry and branded packaged industry. In this industry, the ability to learn in different markets and develop new technologies for their worldwide application became factors of strategic importance. LM Ericsson, through its approach of adaptation of its innovative products and processes technologies in international markets, scored over other companies following either global economies of scale strategy or responsiveness strategy.

Bartlett and Ghoshal (1987) give a nomenclature to these three strategic approaches of multinational companies as global strategy, multinational strategy, and international strategy (Fig. 49.1). The global strategy has global economies of scale, multinational strategy focuses on national responsiveness, and international

Source: Reprinted by permission of Harvard Business Review. From book title by authors Bartlett, C.A. and S. Ghoshal, Boston, MA, 1998. Copyright © 1998 by Harvard Business Publishing; all rights reserved.

FIGURE 49.1   Strategic approaches of multinational companies

strategy has knowledge transfer and learning as its focus. The authors go on to add that from the late 1980s the international environment underwent a major transformation and as such it was difficult for a multinational firm to succeed with a uni-dimensional strategic capability that might incorporate only efficiency, responsiveness, or learning. Companies must, instead, focus on all the three goals simultaneously since emerging international environment demands transnational capabilities.

Bartlett and Ghoshal (1987) further discuss the organizational complexity that results when a company decides to go international, whereby, an area dimension is now added to the structures based on product and function. They contend that strong geographic management is essential for dispersed responsiveness capability, strong product/business management for global efficiency, and strong functional management for worldwide learning capability. So the challenge for a multinational company is to possess a differentiated influence structure in which different groups have different roles for different activities. For example, Unilever has a strategy that is high on national responsiveness in India and its marketing function is high on differentiation, whereas the R&D function is high on globalization (Fig. 49.2). The ability to manage this multidimensional organizational capability in a flexible and in a balanced manner is the distinguishing characteristic of a transnational company.

THEORIES OF MULTINATIONAL CORPORATION

The product life cycle (PLC) theory formulated by Vernon (1966), and the learning model developed by Johanson and Vahlne (1977) have been used to explain how a company becomes multinational. Vernon reasoned that a company, after developing its local market, may start getting export orders due to a demand from a segment of high-end customers from other countries. As the volume of export orders shows

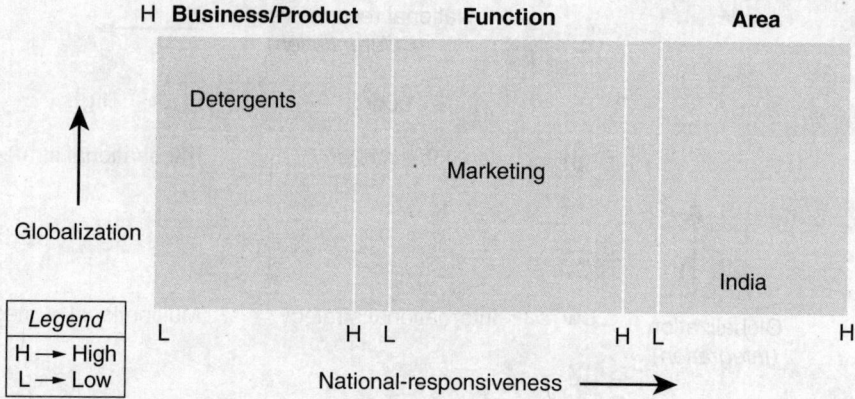

Source: © 1987 from MIT Sloan Management Review/Massachusetts Institute of Technology. All rights reserved. Distributed by Tribune Content Agency.

FIGURE 49.2   Unilever's differentiated structure

a reasonable growth, the company may consider setting up local manufacturing facilities in the importing country to meet local competition and avoid adverse regulatory environment. The overseas manufacturing facilities would in time serve local markets with local production, substituting exports. As the price of the product continues to decrease on account of lower factor costs in the new market, the new market may itself start exporting to the less-developed markets, which in turn, will replicate the process and so on. Finally, as the product becomes standardized and is available at much lower prices, the home country itself may start importing it from less-developed countries. This process may be likened to the global strategy based on global economies of scale factor as discussed by Bartlett and Ghoshal (1998).

Vernon (1979) states that in the late 1970s, American MNCs were more likely to introduce new products simultaneously in several markets by establishing production networks globally, primarily because of closing of the income gaps between USA and Europe, and secondly, because of speed of product emulation. This process may be likened to the multinational strategy based on national responsiveness factor as detailed by Bartlett and Ghoshal (1998).

Johanson and Vahlne found with respect to the internationalization process of companies that 'they often develop their international operations in small steps, rather than by making large foreign production investments at single points in time'. The process begins by first exporting through an agent, progressing to a sales subsidiary, and finally through a manufacturing subsidiary. For example, Swedish firms would first establish a subsidiary in some neighbouring Nordic country, and then expand into Europe before going global. Similarly, USA-based firms tended to set up their first subsidiary in Canada. However, British firms were more likely to set up a subsidiary in Australia than in France. Thus, it was found that the 'psychic distance' in terms of culture, stage of industrial development, and business practices was more important than physical contiguity. This process of internationalization happens due to an increase in knowledge and learning in the new environment.

This process is similar to the international strategy based on learning and technology as described by Bartlett and Ghoshal (1998).

The environment has become much more complex and uncertain in the new millennium and the internationalization process of multinational companies has become greatly varied. The companies operate as global networks of value chains that use different strategies in different markets and partner with other networks of value chains to exploit value before changing their form and adapting to exploit the next wave of opportunities. To paraphrase Bartlett and Ghoshal (1998), such companies become transnational companies. They try to derive global economies of scale and use national responsiveness and lessons from different markets.

SUMMARY

International management deals with applying management concepts, techniques, and practices in a multinational, multicultural environment. Cultural diversity and cultural similarities have been studied by different researchers through the concept of cultural dimensions. Hofstede's IBM survey used four dimensions—individualism vs collectivism, masculinity vs femininity, tolerance vs intolerance of uncertainty, and power distance. Global leadership and organizational behaviour effectiveness research programme (GLOBE) also examined the interrelationships between dimensions of societal culture, organizational culture and practices, and organizational leadership.

Nine dimensions of cultures have been identified that differentiate societies and organizations. With respect to these dimensions, there is a high within-culture and within-organization agreement and high between-culture and between-organization differentiation.

The design of international strategies is dependent on the dynamics between the comparative advantage of countries and the competitive advantage of firms. The three strategic approaches of multinational companies are global strategy, multinational strategy, and international strategy. Global strategy has global economies of scale, multinational strategy focuses on national responsiveness, and international strategy has knowledge transfer and learning as its focus. The current complex global environment requires a transnational strategy that focuses on all factors simultaneously.

KEYWORDS

Comparative advantage These are the location-specific advantages that are the basis for competing with rivals.
Competitive advantage These are the firm-specific advantages that are the basis for competing with rivals.
Cultural dimensions The attributes of culture that are used to differentiate one culture from another.
Globalization The production and distribution of products and services of a standard type on a worldwide basis.
National responsiveness The need to understand different needs of customers in different markets and responding to those needs and regulatory environments to produce products and services that are tailor-made for those regional markets.
Project GLOBE The GLOBE entity is a network of social scientists and management scholars from different cultures throughout the world, working to examine the interrelationships between societal culture, organizational culture and practices, and organizational leadership.
Transnational corporation A multinational firm with a multidimensional strategic capability that focuses on efficiency, responsiveness, and learning simultaneously so as to succeed in the current complex global environment.

EXERCISES

Concept Review Questions

1. How are GLOBE dimensions of culture different from those used by Hofstede in his IBM study?
2. Differentiate between global, international, multinational, and transnational strategies.
3. Compare Vernon's PLC theory with the learning model developed by Johanson and Vahlne.

Critical Thinking Questions

1. Critically analyse Arcelor–Mittal and Tata–Corus deals from a cross-cultural perspective.

2. What does it take to be a successful transnational company? How does organizational complexity imposed by geographical dispersion on top of functional and product structure gets taken care of in a transnational company?

Project Assignment

Prepare a list of dos/don'ts for the senior executives of an Indian company who would be involved in intense negotiations with their counterparts for establishing joint ventures for their company in an Arabic country, in Japan, and in USA.

REFERENCES

Bartlett, C.A. and S. Ghoshal (1987), 'Managing Across Borders: The New Strategic Requirements', *MIT Sloan Management Review*, Summer Issue.

Bartlett, C.A. and S. Ghoshal (1987), 'Managing Across Borders: The New Organizational Responses', *MIT Sloan Management Review*, Fall Issue.

Bartlett, C.A. and S. Ghoshal (1998), *Managing Across Borders: The Transnational Solution*, 2nd edn, Harvard Business School Press, Boston.

Hofstede, Geert (1991), *Cultures and Organizations: Software of the Mind*, McGraw-Hill U.K. Ltd, London.

Johanson, J. and J.E. Vahlne (1977), 'The Internationalization Process of the Firm—A Model of Knowledge Development and Increasing Foreign Market Commitments', *Journal of International Business Studies*, vol. 8, pp. 23–32.

Kogut, Bruce (1985), 'Designing Global Strategies: Comparative and Competitive Value-Added Chains', *MIT Sloan Management Review*, Summer Issue.

Mead, Margaret (ed) (1955), *Cultural Patterns and Technical Change Series*, UNESCO, New York.

Vernon, R. (1966), 'International Investment and International Trade in the Product Cycle', *Quarterly Journal of Economics*, vol. 80, pp. 190–207.

Vernon, R. (1979), 'The Product Cycle Hypothesis in a New International Environment', *Oxford Bulletin of Economics and Statistics*, vol. 41, pp. 255–267.

www.thunderbird.edu/wwwfiles/ms/globe, accessed on 15 January 2008.

50

Online Social Media

It's a people driven economy, stupid!

ERIK QUALMAN, SOCIALNOMICS

INTRODUCTION

Over the past decade social media has become a strong tool of communication all over the world. Fast penetration of Internet, decreased cost of browsing, more educated and tech-savvy population as well as sophisticated mobile technology have transformed this medium to one of the most popular and effective ways of communication not only in the developed world, but also in developing countries, like India. Online social media has created a complimentary universe for people around the globe, satisfying their instinct to connect and communicate with others in real time through a virtual world. It has given people the freedom to communicate with the outside world while sitting in the comfort of their homes. The common man has been empowered with the advent of this latest form of communication. Organizations can no longer afford to ignore the voice of their customers who are active on online social media.

There was a time when social media was thought to be meant only for teenagers. But the scenario has changed dramatically, now people in the age group of 35–45 rank among the most prolific users of social media. Several people in the age group of 65 and above are on various social media sites, sharing information with their family, friends, and also gathering news. Globally people spend approximately 10 per cent of their online time in social media of some form or other (Ganley and Lampe 2009).

Learning Objectives

After studying this chapter, you will be able to:

- Learn about the evolution of social media
- Understand the characteristics of social media
- Gain an insight into the classification of different types of social medias
- Investigate the reasons why people want to share personal information on social media
- Gain a broad understanding of classification of a social media user
- Understand the power of social media in transforming businesses
- Learn how to craft social media strategy, set goals, and identify target audience
- Understand how it is imperative to engage customers for the success of a social media strategy
- Become aware of the issues related to calculation of returns of social media spending

HISTORY OF SOCIAL MEDIA

Although social media is not very old, still there have been hundreds of social media sites around the world. Usenet, created in 1979 by Tom Truscott and Jim Ellis from Duke University, allowed individuals to post public messages online. This is considered to be the earliest form of online social media. Six Degrees, launched in 1997, was considered to be the first social network site. It allowed its users to create a profile and become friends with other users. The era of the modern age social media started with the foundation of Open Diary, created by Bruce Ableson and Susan Ableson, in 1998. It brought online diary writers together into a community through its website and permitted readers to comment on another person's post.

Live Journal became another popular social network during the end of the twentieth century. It was built for users who kept a blog, and would constantly update them. It encouraged its users to follow one another and also interact amongst themselves. Blogger, developed by Pyra Labs and, later bought by Google in 2003, allowed private or multi-user blogs with time-stamped entries.

The launch of Wikipedia, in 2001, is an important event in the history of social media. It is considered as the largest and most popular general reference website in the Internet. This collaboratively provided multilingual free online encyclopedia, with more than 30 million articles in 287 languages.

Founded in 2002, Friendster is recognized as the first modern general social network. But social media started to get more attention with the arrival of MySpace in 2003. In the next three years, it went onto to become the most popular social network in the world. It allowed users to completely customize the look of their profiles, post music from various artists, and even embed videos. LinkedIn launched in the same year is the first mainstream social network, devoted to business and career. With the introduction of Photo bucket and Delicious, people around the world for the first time got the taste of major photo sharing and book marking sites respectively.

The Google owned social networking site Orkut, launched in 2004, enjoyed huge popularity for some time, while YouTube emerged as the first major video sharing site soon after. But the world of social media was revolutionized with the advent of Facebook and Twitter. Mark Zuckerberg founded Facebook in 2004, in the beginning the membership was restricted to Harvard students only, but by 2006 they gradually opened the membership to anyone above 13 years. With more than 1 billion registered users, Facebook now has more people in it than any nation on earth, except for China and India. Twitter, the most popular micro-blogging site, also has over 200 million active users. Google+, the latest social networking site, is also rapidly gaining popularity among businesses and common people alike.

---

[1]Online Social Media (OSM) is popularly known as Social Media. Henceforth, both will be used interchangeably.

WHAT IS SOCIAL MEDIA?

Social media (also known as online social media or OSM)[1] is characterized by the democratization of information, transforms people from passive readers to content creators, and empowers them to disseminate knowledge in a many-to-many communication platform. Internet-based applications, platforms, and media, that employ Web 2.0 technology to facilitate interaction, collaboration, and content sharing constitute social media. Blogs, social network sites (SNS), video sharing sites, photo sharing sites, and bookmarking tools are some examples of social media.

Web 2.0 technology and user-generated content (UGC) are the two important pillars of social media. Web 2.0 is an advanced technology which utilizes RSS Feed, Adobe Flash, and AJAX to facilitate software developers and end-users in their attempt to utilize World Wide Web (WWW) for creating, publishing, and modifying contents in a participative and collaborative fashion (Kaplan and Haenlein 2010). It has given common people the freedom to create their online presence and opened the doors of the virtual world to people from all spheres of life.

Creative contents from individuals, working outside their professional routines and practices, published on a publicly accessible website or on a social networking site that makes it available to a select group of people qualify as UGC (OECD 2007). Therefore, a website of a company cannot be termed as a product of UGC, although it is available to general public, for it is created by professionals working as per their routine work.

Types of Social Media

Social media includes different forms of communication tools like Internet forums, blogs, micro-blogs, wiki, photo/video/link sharing, bookmarking, rating, to name a few.

Following are the nine different social media sites as identified by Evans (2011) based on their prominent characteristics.

   (i) Social news sites (e.g., Digg, Reddit, NewsVine, Kirtsy, etc.)
  (ii) Social networking (e.g., MySpace, Facebook, Orkut, etc.)
 (iii) Social bookmarking (e.g., Delicious, Magnolia, etc.)
 (iv) Social sharing (e.g., YouTube, Flickr, etc.)
  (v) Social events (e.g., Eventful, Meetup, etc.)
 (vi) Blogs (e.g., Blogger, etc)
(vii) Micro-blogging (e.g., Twitter, Plurk, etc.)
(viii) Wikis (e.g., Wikipedia, etc.)
 (ix) Forums and message boards

However, with rapid change in the technology prevailing in social media world the basis of this classification loses its significance. For example, with more than 250 billion photos uploaded and an average of 350 million photos being uploaded daily, Facebook has emerged as the largest photo sharing site in the world.

Kaplan and Haenlein (2010) classified social media based on insights from two research streams namely media research (social presence and media richness) and social processes (self-presentation and self-disclosure) as shown in Table 50.1.

TABLE 50.1 Classification of social media

Insights from social processes research		Insights from media research Social presence/media richness		
		Low	Medium	High
Insights from social processes research	**High**	Blogs	Social networking sites (e.g., Facebook)	Virtual social world (e.g., Second Life)
Self-presentation/ self-disclosure	**Low**	Collaborative projects (e.g., Wikipedia)	Content communities (e.g., YouTube)	Virtual game worlds (e.g., World of Warcraft)

Source: Republished with permission of Elsevier, from 'Users of the world, unite! The challenges and opportunities of Social Media'; Business Horizons, 59–68; Kaplan, A. M. and M. Haenlein (2010)

Insights from media research

Intimacy (closeness of relationship signifying relationship strength) and immediacy of the medium (synchronous vs. asynchronous) are two factors that influence social presence. Varying degree of media richness leads to different amounts of information being transmitted at a given time period, leading to different levels of disambiguation, which is one of the main purpose of any type of media.

Insights from social processes research

There are certain variations in the way self-presentation is handled by different social media. Self-presentation allows one to project oneself consistently to others in a desired manner. In the absence of a verification process, it may give a different impression of one than his/her real self. On the other hand, in self-disclosure, conscious or unconscious revelation of oneself is required to develop a close relationship. Because of this theoretical foundation, the classification proposed by Kaplan and Haenlein (2010) gains importance.

WHY PEOPLE WANT TO SHARE?

Social media is not devoid of having various possible adverse effects on people. As people disclose more information, reduced privacy makes them more vulnerable leading to security issues online as well as in the real world. There have been cases where children have been subjected to abuse/exploitation on the social media; employees have been sacked from their jobs for making posts which portrayed their employer or boss's in a negative light. In some instances, people have been jailed for making comments against influential people in the society or raising their voice against the government (Exhibit 50.1).

Although it is quite natural for people to share their personal information with others, but it is still not clear why anyone would want to share a lot of personal information with others. And spend so much time and energy, even when one is unsure whether others are actually interested in hearing their voices or not, is an enigma worth researching. Researchers have tried to investigate from the perspectives of motivational drivers of media usage, philosophical writings on group action, and socio-psychological research on social identity. Broadly, there may be two

Exhibit 50.1 Examples of adverse effect of social media

A self-made prank video featuring two Domino's employees in USA showing them contaminating pizzas and sandwiches created a huge rage in the social media and a loss of reputation of the global brand. The employees were later arrested as per the prevailing government rules and both of them lost their jobs. After this, Dominos revised their recruitment policy.

Prominent Egyptian blogger Alaa Abdel Fattah was jailed twice, first in 2006 by the Mubarak regime, and then in 2011 for allegedly inciting violence through his revolutionary blog. His arrest led to a widespread call for his release from different corners of the world. Another blogger Ahmed Douma also suffered the same fate in December 2013 for describing the government to be like criminals and predicting its fall.

Ambikesh Mohapatra, a professor of Jadavpur University in Kolkata, India, was arrested in 2012 for circulating a cartoon of the Chief Minister of West Bengal, Mamata Banerjee, and the then railway minister, Mukul Roy. A small scale industrialist in Puducherry was arrested on charges of posting 'offensive' messages on Twitter targeting Union Finance Minister P. Chidambaram's son Karti's finances. These arrests led to a wide scale protest from people who feared that their freedom of expression was being curbed. This finally led to some rethinking regarding the government machinery about the rules and regulations governing the social media.

determinants for willingness to share or communicate, one as an individual and the other as a member of a group.

People may exchange free information as they find it hedonic and having a utilitarian value in it. Entertainment, feeling of being social, of being accepted among a peer group, to get emotional support, and for building a social identity, etc., constitute as having hedonic value. On the other hand utilitarian value can be characterized as functional, task-related, rational, cognitive, or instrumental, that leads to tangible and objective benefits.

It is interesting to note that Darwinian models imply self-centeredness to such an extent that altruistic acts are undertaken only when they are calculated to improve one's chances of survival. Putting this into exchange of information in social media context, we may say that someone exchanges information with the expectation that the act would be reciprocated by other online members in the community.

Research suggests that people may perceive five different kinds of values (Dholakia, Bagozzi, and Pearo 2007): (1) purposive, (2) self-discovery, (3) maintaining interpersonal connectivity, (4) social enhancement, and (5) entertainment. Purposive value is derived by accomplishing some predetermined activity, while self-discovery involves gaining deeper understanding about oneself through social interaction. These values are moderated by one's personal and group norms, leading to a desire to participate in a virtual community and exchange information. Since the values perceived by people are different and the moderating values also vary widely, level of participation between people may also differ.

TYPES OF SOCIAL MEDIA USER

A manager should have broad understanding of social media user classification in order to be able to effectively communicate with the target users. Different types of users need different types of stimuli to get activated in social media.

Based on the intensity of use, IP and Wagner (2008) classified users of blogs into four different categories: habitual users, active users, personal users, and blogging lurkers. Habitual users are users with the highest intensity, who feel a compulsion to write blog entries, comment on other people's blogs, and thus spend a lot of time for this activity; while active users visit their blogs less frequently, during their leisure time, comment on their own and their friend's blogs. Personal users meanwhile use blogs as their personal diaries, sharing it with only a select few. They have the tendency to restrict user comments in their blogs. The least involved are the blogging lurkers, who share very little information but maintain blogs primarily to get access to blogs of other people. Although this classification was based on blog usage intensity, it may be generalized for other types of social media as well.

Foster et al. classified social media users on the basis of the levels of interactive participation and information needs as shown in Table 50.2. Social media technology (SMT) mavens are the most interactive in nature, and look for information and satisfaction of socialization needs in different kinds of networks. On the other hand, minimally involved are the ones who are the least likely to participate in any kind of online activity. Socializers primarily attempt to socialize through use of the social media (SM), while info seekers use SM primarily in search of the required information.

APPREHENSIONS ABOUT SOCIAL MEDIA USAGE

Although social media has been recognized as a powerful tool in the modern management world, still there is skepticism in a lot of people about the efficiency of its use for productive purposes. Many people would simply ignore social media as a passing fad for youth and teenagers. Others are apprehensive about finding their target audience through social media. Then there are people who are wary of using social media for their businesses, along with the fear of divulging too much personal information, and losing privacy in the process. The severest challenge is posed by people who would simply stick to their old and proven strategy of using conventional media for business purposes and complain that social media destroys the beauty of communication. Some others do not see the need for having social media because they have websites for their businesses.

TABLE 50.2   Social media user classification

Interactive participation	High	Socializers	SMT maven
	Low	Minimally involved	Info seeker
		Low	High
		Information needs	

POWER OF SOCIAL MEDIA

All the above apprehensions may seem quite natural, although they may lack logic. When telephone was first used for business purposes while some companies continued to use letters to communicate with their clients, usage of letters for communication was simply perceived to be slow. Social media gives its users the power to connect with a lot of people in less time and increases efficiency. The world of management, especially marketing, has transformed from selling to relationship building. Social media aids in this transformation process. More business can be generated through proper relationship building which helps one to be at the top of mind of customers.

Social media cannot be considered to be a passing fad, as its foundation lies in the basic instincts of people to communicate with others and share information with their near and dear ones. It is true that social media started as a personal communication medium, but it is up to the businesses to efficiently use it for their own benefit. A study done in 2013 showed that 34 per cent of Fortune 500 companies actively blog, 77 per cent maintains Twitter accounts, 70 per cent have Facebook pages, and 69 per cent have YouTube accounts. This data is testimony to the fact that social media cannot be ruled out from business strategies any more.

Although in its early days, the young generation was the forerunners in embracing social media, the demographics of people using various social media sites are changing quite rapidly. The fastest growing segment of social media users is 45–55 years of age (Pick 2013). As of January 2013, the five largest social networks based on active monthly users were: Facebook (1 billion), YouTube (800 million), and Google+ (343 million), followed by Twitter and LinkedIn with 200 million active monthly users each (Baur 2013).

With the advent of online news, there is a lot of debate about the future of newspapers and magazines. The advertisements in the print media and television advertisements are losing their effectiveness in many an instance. As Internet has penetrated deep into most of the countries and the users have matured with their experience, they have begun ignoring advertising banners and pop-ups. In these circumstances, social media may be the right alternative for the business owners and managers alike. Engaging customers by creating interesting conversations businesses can reach their desired goals through proper use of this comparatively new media.

As people are swarming to social media, it is highly unlikely not to find one's prospective customer on social media. For example, Facebook users outnumber the population of the USA by three times. About 23 per cent of Facebook users check their accounts five or more times every day, and 80 per cent of Facebook users prefer to connect with brands on Facebook. In the USA, more people watch videos on YouTube than they do on television. As technology divide is waning rapidly, this trend would not take long to catch up in other countries. Twitter has established itself as a great marketing tool with 34 per cent of marketers claiming to have generated leads using Twitter (Pick 2013). About 52 per cent

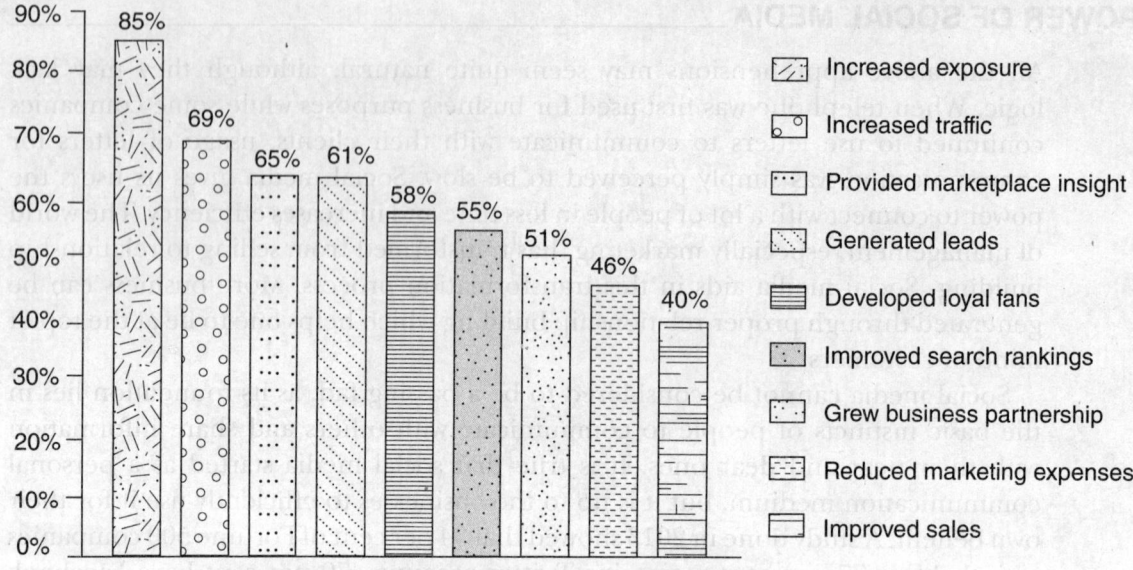

Source: Based on *Social Media Marketing Industry Report 2012*

FIGURE 50.1   Why companies use social media

of consumers revealed that blogs had impacted their purchasing decisions, while 57 per cent of marketers acquired customers via their blogs (B2B-Infographics-Admin 2013).

Figure 50.1 shows why different companies use social media.

Being a relatively new tool of communication, social media definitely poses difficulty in terms of calculation of its ROI. But many companies have worked around that issue as well, that will be discussed later in this chapter. Finally, the business owners and managers should realize that the risk of making mistakes in their use of social media should not be a hindrance in accepting it, as mistakes are unavoidable in other business strategies too.

SOCIAL MEDIA MARKETING IN MODERN AGE

Social media marketing is a special form of online marketing with the objective of using social media platforms to pursue a customer-oriented marketing campaign. This form of marketing allows for the well-directed address of particular customer groups and helps in building trust on a brand. Figure 50.2 shows some commonly used social media tools.

A report made in 2013 by Universal Maccann International suggested that 36 per cent of active Internet users were more positive about companies that have blogs and 32 per cent trusted bloggers' opinion on products and services. Another report found that 43 per cent of social networkers in Europe had visited a personal space of a brand and 16 per cent had already had a dialogue or sent a message to a brand (Microsoft Digital Advertising Solutions 2007). People generally visit a brand or a

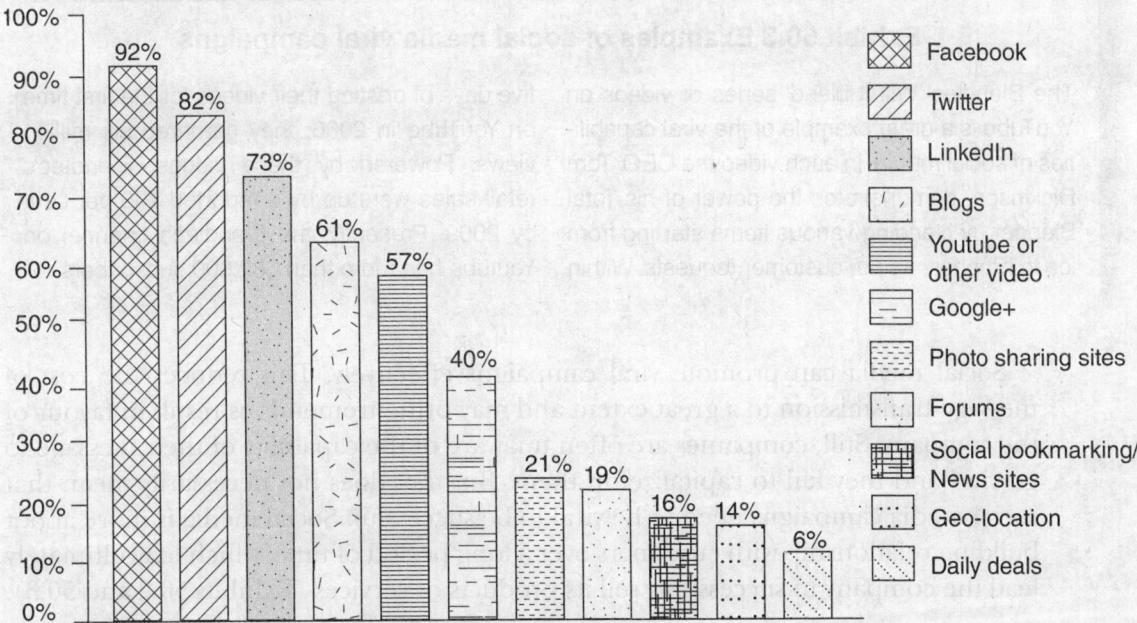

Legend:
- Facebook
- Twitter
- LinkedIn
- Blogs
- Youtube or other video
- Google+
- Photo sharing sites
- Forums
- Social bookmarking/News sites
- Geo-location
- Daily deals

Values: 92%, 82%, 73%, 61%, 57%, 40%, 21%, 19%, 16%, 14%, 6%

Source: Based on *Social Media Marketing Industry Report 2012*

FIGURE 50.2 Commonly used social media tools

fan page on a social network to get news/product updates, view promotions, view/download music and video, for posting their opinions, or to connect with other users.

Social media marketing is somewhat different from traditional marketing, as marketers are not in control of their content or image in a social media. They have to give more freedom to customers, listen to their voices, and reciprocate almost in real time to see their social media strategy being a success. Some companies have used social media for crowdsourcing, that is, to generate ideas from people. There are other companies which have changed their business decisions as a result of their social media communication with the customers.

Exhibit 50.2 Examples of social media campaigns

In 2006, Dell created a blog to be able to interact with its customers better and to effectively address customer service issues, which was a main cause of concern at that time. Later on, in February 2007, Dell launched IdeaStorm for the purpose of crowdsourcing. In the next four and a half years, the company fetched approximately 16,000 ideas and implemented close to 500 of them (Wasserman 2011).

Domino's launched a campaign titled 'Oh Yes We Did'. During this campaign they encouraged customers to share their opinion and effectively turned the negative opinions into positive ones by changing some of their recipes and pleasing customers in the process.

Exhibit 50.3 Examples of social media viral campaigns

The Blendtec 'Will it blend' series of videos on YouTube is a great example of the viral capabilities of social media. In each video the CEO, Tom Dickinson, demonstrates the power of his Total Blender by blending various items starting from ice to iPhones, as per customer requests. Within five days of posting their videos for the first time on YouTube in 2006, they garnered six million views. Powered by these videos, Blendtec's retail sales were up by a reported 700 per cent by 2009. Presently, the Blendtech channel on Youtube has more than 682,000 subscribers.

Social media can promote viral campaigns effectively. This reduces the cost of message transmission to a great extent and may bring tremendous result in favour of the company. Still, companies are often unaware of the capability of their message to go viral and they fail to capitalize on them. But that does not necessarily mean that social media campaigns need to be viral to be successful. Social media is more about building relationship with customers over a long period of time, which may ultimately lead the company to successfully sell its products or services (Exhibits 50.2 and 50.3).

CRAFTING SOCIAL MEDIA STRATEGY, SETTING GOALS, AND IDENTIFYING TARGET AUDIENCE

The efficiency of social media usage depends on a proper fit between the desired goal and the nature of social media adopted for achieving it. Goals will also differ in accordance with the specific social media being used. Identifying target audience is a step forward in attaining social media goals. As a general trend, Twitter is more popular among executives and busy professionals, while Pinterest boasts of huge user base among women. Facebook is more popular among teenagers and youth. But having said that, the managers of the modern organization should remember that users generally have a tendency to cross-pollinate among various social media sites and thus it would be logical to use multiple such sites to achieve optimum success.

Although specifying general goals without any mention of the type of social media is vague, still this may give a broad idea about how one can proceed to specify goals. The following can be some specific general goals.

- Number of times the message is viewed
- Number of fans/likes acquired
- Number of shares
- Number of positive/negative comments
- Number of clicks on the link
- Duration of time a user had spent on the message
- Number of people who proceeded to purchase after coming directly from the social media message
- Duration of time the message enjoyed conversation among its users
- Number of discussions that started from the message

Companies should identify all departments that should be part of the social media strategy. This would again depend on the size of the company. A multinational company may have departments looking after marketing, sales, finance, Internet marketing, content marketing, public relations, and legal aspects as part of its social media strategy team, whereas a small entrepreneurial venture may have to do with one or two individuals. In order to maximize efficiency, even the frequency of updates, tone of conversation, time of update, etc., needs to be properly discussed in the strategy.

Companies need to sensitize their employees regarding their use of social media. Although it may seem to be the personal choice of employees to engage in social media as per their wish outside their duty hours, still they need to understand that their actions or comments have a deep impact on the image of the company. Giving access to social media sites at the workplace also constitutes a topic for debate. Although many companies have taken active measures to converse with their customers through various social media sites, with 90 per cent of Inc. 500 companies using at least one major social media platform (Cohen 2013), still 26 per cent of the companies block access to social media sites in their workplaces, and 31 per cent have no social media policy in place.

SOCIAL MEDIA ENGAGEMENT TECHNIQUE

Social media is more about the consumers and less about the brand. Here consumer has the ultimate power to control the brand. But that does not necessarily mean that managers have nothing to do to control their brand image. In fact, it is the duty of the managers to connect with users through interesting conversation with the help of proper content creation and thus collaborating with the users in real time through this virtual media. They need to understand that consumers are more interested to talk to a face and less to a brand logo. Therefore, giving a human touch to the online community is of vital importance.

Social media is not just a place to share discount coupons or flood its users with advertisements. The rising popularity of social media is because of its ability to add value to its users in the way they want. It is rather a platform for permission-marketing, where users can voluntarily opt for a solution to their problems at hand. Therefore, a direct marketing strategy may not be welcome in most of the social media sites. In fact, for a marketer it would be wise to find different ways to add value to the users. This may be in the form of giving proper suggestion to resolve a problem, or spending time to understand the problems of a user.

To be accepted by the community of social media users, a company should search for the proper communities of its interest, listen to the community members and respond to their queries. It should also create interesting content and build conversations around them. Successful social media strategy generally meets one or more of the PARC principles, that is, it should be participatory, authentic, resourceful, and credible (Barker, Barker, Bormann, and Neher 2013). Apart

Exhibit 50.4 An example of pretentions exposed

In November 2006, a marketing company employed by Sony's American division created a website entitled 'All I want for Xmas is a PSP', in order to create a viral campaign. The site featured a blog purportedly written by one person called 'Charlie', a teenage boy who attempted to get his friend Jeremy's parents to buy him a PSP. It provided a 'music video' of either Charlie or Jeremy 'rapping' about the PSP. It did not take long for the visitors of the website to recognize that the website was registered with a marketing company. The campaign was thus exposed on sites such as YouTube and Digg. Sony had to confess that the site was created as a part of a marketing campaign, which was 'poorly executed'.

from these, a marketer should also remember that the virtual communities are an extension of the real world, and hence basic courtesy should be maintained just as in the real world. Pretentions are more easily exposed in the online world than can be imagined. Hence, companies and people representing those companies should stick to the real self to be accepted in social media (Exhibit 50.4).

MONITORING SOCIAL MEDIA STRATEGY

Once implemented, companies should actively monitor their social media strategy and the campaigns. Delay in responding to negative comments made by users may be catastrophic for organizations. But monitoring this vast world of social media is not an easy job, it demands patience, data analysis, and problem-solving skills among others. As a first step towards monitoring, the strategy should identify keywords that need to be tracked in their targeted platforms.

Fortunately for marketers, there are some monitoring tools available in the market, some that are available free of charge, while others are chargeable. Once keywords are selected, Google Alerts provides free information about the mention of any of the keywords. Radian6 is a buzz-tracking software at the enterprise-level that allows to observe the previous 90 days activity around the keywords. Techrigy is another paid software that monitors keywords and can perform some basic sentiment analysis, providing insight about whether the users talk about the brand in a positive manner or negative way.

Monitoring may also provide information about the influencers in a community. Monitoring also helps to identify the demographics of the users, and thus help in making the strategy successful. Monitoring also helps to compare the result of social media strategy with the actual plan and therefore helps in taking proper corrective action.

MEASURING RETURNS OF SOCIAL MEDIA SPENDING

Like any other form of marketing, in social media too, marketers are responsible for the money spent. But it is not easy to calculate the return on investment of this media and is perhaps one of the most daunting tasks faced by marketers today, as is evident from the fact that less than one in seven companies measured their return on investment for social media marketing during the first two years of implementation. But if the goals are set right and the objectives of the strategy were quantifiable, then it may not be an impossible task to accomplish. Success or failure in social media should be weighed in terms of 4I's: (1) Involvement, (2) Interaction, (3) Intimacy, and (4) Influence (Haven 2007).

Social media measurement may be determined with a combination of qualitative and quantitative aspects. The objective is to determine the volume of content and the sentiments towards a brand or topic on the social web. This is a direct result of the goal set by the organization for its social media implementation. Companies are shifting focus from traditional financial measurement of return on investment to softer qualitative aspects, such as number of followers gained, number of visits to the webpage, text analysis, etc., against the marketing budget for achieving these goals. It would be wise to benchmark to get a feel about where the company stands and thus find out ways for improvements. Over a longer term, the company should compare its key performance indicators and attempt to assess the degree of progress.

Measuring qualitative aspects is of equal importance, as quantitative measurements may fail to provide a clear picture of the customers' attitude towards a brand. For example, a brand name may be mentioned in both positive and negative ways. While a quantitative measurement will simply count the number of times the brand name is mentioned, it will not reveal what the customers are thinking about the brand. Sentiment analysis or opinion mining is a way to detect basic mood, attitude or emotion of the people talking about a brand in the online space. However, automatic sentiment analysis using software still lacks maturity. Hence, a manager dealing with measuring return on investment of social media efforts should be particularly careful during analysis and while coming to any conclusion. While some companies have adopted methods for measuring various qualitative KPIs (key performance indicators), still there is no wide consensus among industries regarding this issue and it should be best left to the management of an organization to decide ways to measure as per their strategic goals.

SUMMARY

Social media (also known as online social media or OSM) is characterized by the democratization of information. It transforms people from passive readers to content creators, and empowers them to disseminate knowledge in a many-to-many communication platform. Internet based applications, platforms, and media that employ Web 2.0 technology to facilitate interaction, collaboration, and content sharing constitute social media. Blogs, social network sites (SNS), video sharing sites, photo sharing sites, and bookmarking tools are some examples of social media. Social media includes different forms of communication tools like Internet forums, blogs, micro-blogs, wiki, photo/video/link sharing, bookmarking, rating, to name a few.

Foster et al. classified social media users on the basis of the levels of interactive participation and information needs. SMT mavens are the most interactive in nature, and look for information and satisfaction of socialization needs in different kinds of networks. On the other hand, minimally involved are the ones who are the least likely to participate in any kind of online activity. Socializers primarily attempt to socialize through use of the social media (SM), while info seekers use SM primarily in search of the required information.

Social media cannot be considered to be a passing fad, as its foundation lies in the basic instincts of people to communicate with others and share information with their near and dear ones. It is true that social media started as a personal communication medium, but it is up to the businesses to efficiently use it for their own benefit. Social media marketing is somewhat different from traditional marketing, as marketers are not in control of their content or image in a social media. Some companies have used social media for crowd sourcing, that is, to generate ideas from people. There are other companies which have changed their business decisions as a result of their social media communication with the customers. The efficiency of social media usage depends on a proper fit between the desired goal and the nature of social media adopted for achieving it. Goals will also differ in accordance with the specific social media being used. Identifying target audience is a step forward in attaining social media goals.

Once implemented, companies should actively monitor their social media strategy and the campaigns. Delay in responding to negative comments made by users may be catastrophic for organizations. But monitoring this vast world of social media is not an easy job; it demands patience, data analysis, and problem-solving skills among others. Success or failure in social media should be weighed in terms of 4I's: (1) involvement, (2) interaction, (3) intimacy, and (4) influence.

KEYWORDS

Blogs   A type of social media.
Crowd sourcing   The marketing strategy used by some companies for generating ideas from people.
SMT mavens   Social media technology users who are the most interactive in nature, and look for information and satisfaction of socialization needs in different kinds of networks.
Social media   The Internet based applications, platforms, and media that employ Web 2.0 technology to facilitate interaction, collaboration, and content sharing.
Social media marketing   A special form of online marketing with the objective of using social media

platforms to pursue a customer-oriented marketing campaign.
Social media strategy   A proper fit between the desired goal and the nature of social media adopted for achieving it.
Social network site (SNS)   A type of social media.
Web 2.0   An important pillar of social media that uses RSS Feed, Adobe Flash, and AJAX to help software developers and end-users use WWW for creating, publishing, and modifying contents in a participative and collaborative manner.

EXERCISES

Concept Review Questions

1. How has social media evolved?
2. What can be the basis of categorization of different types of social media?
3. Define what is meant by social-presence, media-richness, self-presentation, and self-disclosure.
4. What are the important parameters for crafting a successful social media strategy?

5. Discuss the power of social media on the common man as well as on businesses in recent times. Give specific instances if this power is for good or for worse.
6. What are the key issues involved in the measurement of returns on social media spending?

Critical Thinking Questions

1. What in your opinion should be an optimal mix of traditional and social media while designing a marketing campaign for a new product launch by an FMCG company in India?
2. Identify categories that have substantial presence on social media and product categories that have limited presence. Critically examine the reasons for such a difference.
3. Evaluate from the ethical standpoint the correctness of the action of some large social media players to sell data of visitors thus compromising their privacy.
4. Critically suggest how government websites can more meaningfully engage visitors and inspire conversations.

REFERENCES

Barker, M., D. Barker, N. Bormann, and K. Neher (2013), *Social Media Marketing: A Strategic Approach*, Cengage Learning, Delhi.

Baur, L. (2013), '5 Reasons that Social Media may Never Die', http://www.techi.com/2013/02/5-reasons-that-social-media-may-never-die/, accessed on 19 February 2013.

Bagozzi, R.P., U.M. Dholakia, and L.R.K.Pearo(2007), 'Antecedents and Consequences of Online Social Interactions',*Media Psychology*,vol. 9, no. 1, pp. 77–114.

Briggs, C. (2009), 'BlendTec will It Blend? Viral Video Case Study', http://www.socialens.com/wp-content/uploads/2009/04/20090127_case_blendtec11.pdf, accessed on 19 February 2013.

Bullas, J. (2013), '12 Awesome Social Media Facts and Statistics for 2013', http://www.jeffbullas.com/2013/09/20/12-awesome-social-media-facts-and-statistics-for-2013/, accessed on 14 July 2014.

Cohen, Heidi (2013), 'Social Media & Small Business: 16 Facts You Need', http://heidicohen.com/social-media-small-business-facts-you-need-now/, accessed on 20 February 2013.

'Cool Infographics in B2B Marketing', http://infographicb2b.com/2013/07/15/seo-content-marketing-what-you-need-to-know-and-do-infographic/, accessed on 15 July 2013.

Evans, L. (2011), *Social Media Marketing: Strategies for Engaging in Facebook, Twitter and Other Social Media*, 1st edition, New Delhi, Dorling Kindersley (India) Pvt. Ltd.

Foster, M., B.West, and A. Francescucci (2011),'Exploring Social Media User Segmentation and Online Brand Profiles',*Journal of Brand Management*, vol. 19, no. 1, pp. 4–17.

Ganley, D. and C. Lampe (2009), 'The Ties That Bind: Social Network Principles in Online communities', *Decision Support Systems*, vol. 47, issue 3, pp. 266–274.

Haven, B. (2007), *Marketing's New Key Metric: Engagement*, Forrester.

IP, R.K. and C. Wagner (2008), 'Weblogging: A Study of Social Computing and Its Impact on Organizations', *Decision Support Systems*, vol. 45, pp. 242–250.

Kaplan, A.M. and M. Haenlein (2010), 'Users of the World, Unite! The Challenges and Opportunities of Social Media', *Business Horizons*, vol. 53, pp. 59–68.

Loughnane, E. (2005), 'Net Success Interviews', lulu.com, accessed on 14 July 2014.

Luna, N. (2009), 'Burger King: Unfriend 10 Facebook Friends, Get a Free Whopper', Orange County Register, http://fastfood.ocregister.com/2009/01/08/burger-king-unfriend-10-facebook-friends-get-a-free-whopper/10980/, accessed on 14 July 2014.

McGrail, M. (2013), 'Infographic—Social Media Statistics for 2013', http://www.velocitydigital.co.uk/infographic-social-media-statistics-for-2013/, accessed on 14 July 2014.

Microsoft Digital Advertising Solutions (2007), 'Word of the Web Guidelines for Advertisers: Understanding Trends and Monetising social Networks', http://advertising.microsoft.com/uk/WWDocs/User/en-uk/Advertise/Partner%20Properties/Piczo/Word%20of%20the%20Web%20Social%20Networking%20Report%20Ad5.pdf, accessed on 14 July 2014.

OECD (2007), 'Participative Web and End-User Content: Web 2.0, Wikis and Social Networking',

Organization for Economic Cooperation and Development, Paris.

Pick, T., (2013), '101 Vital Social Media and Digital Marketing Statistics', http://socialmediatoday.com/tompick/1647801/101-vital-social-media-and-digital-marketing-statistics-rest-2013, accessed on 14 July 2014.

Stelzner, Michael A. (2012), *Social Media Marketing Industry Report2012*,'How Marketers are Using Social Media to Grow Their Businesses, Copyright of Social Media Examiner.

Smith, J. (2009), 'Whopper Sacrifice Forced to Disable Behavior by Facebook', http://www.insidefacebook.com/2009/01/14/whopper-sacrifice-shut-down-by-facebook/, accessed on 14 July 2014.

Universal Maccann International (2008), 'Power to the People—Social Media Tracker Wave 3, www.slideshare.net/mickstravellin/universal-mccann-international-social-media-research-wave-3, accessed on 14 November 2014.

Wall, A. (2013), 'Top 10 Social Media Disasters of All Time', http://blog.processindustryforum.com/digitalmarketing/top-10-social-media-disasters/, accessed on 14 November 2014.

Wasserman, T. (2011), 'How Dell's Social Suggestion Box Empowered Fans and Improved the Company', http://mashable.com/2011/08/25/dell-brand-suggestion-box/, accessed on 25 August 2012.

51

Project Management

INTRODUCTION

Projects are ubiquitous all around us and its management has become very critical whether for public or personal ends. So what is the difference between project management and management of any other business or enterprise? Running a business is about managing a perpetual entity while managing a project is about managing change. Usually it is not about managing a business. Hence, managing a project calls for a different set of skills and competencies in comparison to a line manager. While a project manager thrives on change, the line manager tries hard to maintain status quo and has an aversion to change and disruption.

Technically a project is defined as a 'unique set of coordinated activities, with definite starting and finishing points, undertaken by an individual or organization to meet specific objectives within defined schedule, cost, and performance parameters' (BS 6079).

As stated in the above definition, a project must meet certain objectives. Generically, these objectives must meet four fundamental criteria (see Fig. 51.1)

1. The project must be completed on time.
2. The project must be completed within the budgeted cost.
3. The project must meet the specified requirements in terms of quality.
4. Certain projects must also meet the safety standards.

The order of priority given to any of these objectives is dependent both on the industry as well as on the nature of the individual project. For example, in designing a manned vehicle for sending in space, safety may be of

Learning Objectives

After studying this chapter, you will be able to:
- Understand the essential difference between project management and any business enterprise management
- Comprehend the generic objectives that a project must achieve
- Gain an insight into the various stages of a project life cycle
- Gain a broad understanding of nine knowledge areas that contain the processes needed to achieve an effective project management program
- Understand the project initiation phase, project planning phase, project execution phase, project monitoring and control phase, and finally project closure phase
- Learn about project network analysis and what is meant by a critical path
- Learn about two important network analysis tools, namely PERT and CPM

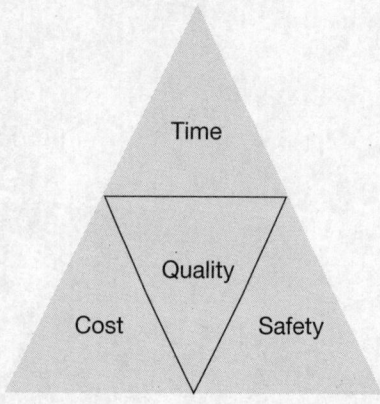

FIGURE 51.1   Generic objectives for a project

paramount importance, even though the final product may cost more than what was budgeted, or may get delayed, or some criteria in terms of deliverables may be compromised.

THE GENERIC PROJECT LIFE CYCLE PROCESS CATEGORIES

The following are five generic process categories that are typical of almost all projects (see Fig. 51.2).

1. Initiating—scope and authorization of the project
2. Planning—management of the project
3. Executing—execution of project groups to complete the work
4. Monitoring and controlling—monitoring and taking corrective actions to control the progress of the project
5. Closure—formal closing of the project

A Guide to the Project Management Body of Knowledge (2013) explains that there are nine knowledge areas that contain the processes needed to achieve an effective project management program. Each of these processes may fall into one of the five basic process categories. The matrix structure of the processes are shown in the following table (Table 51.1) such that every activity can be related to one knowledge area and one process category.

Phase I: Initiation of the project   During this phase (see Fig. 51.3) a business scenario for a particular alternative to a business problem or a business

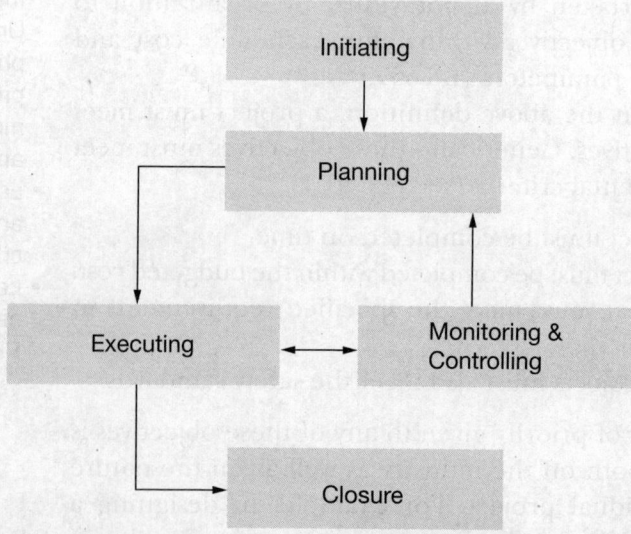

FIGURE 51.2   Five generic process categories typical of almost all projects

TABLE 51.1   Knowledge area and process category matrix

Process category / Knowledge area	Initiating Planning Executing Monitoring and controlling Closure
Project integration management	[Coordination with other areas to work together throughout the project]
Project scope management	[Ensuring that the project includes the requirements and nothing more]
Time management	[Ensure that the project is completed on schedule]
Cost management	[Ensure that the project is completed as per budget]
Quality management	[Ensure that the project meets its quality requirements and specifications]
Human resource management	[Organize/staff and lead the project team together]
Communication management	[Management of information]
Risk management	[Identification, assessment, and management of risk of a project]
Procurement management	[Acquisition of the materials and services needed to complete the project]

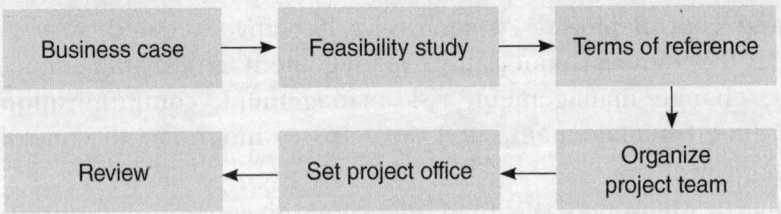

FIGURE 51.3   Six stages of phase I: Initiation of the project

opportunity is identified through a feasibility study that is conducted to investigate, which alternatively is most feasible and viable. Next, the terms of reference comprising the vision, objectives, scope, and deliverables for the new project are put down. The project team is selected and organized, and a project office established. Finally a review of phase I is conducted.

Phase II: Project planning   After the initiation phase, the next phase of the project planning is estimating time, cost, and adequate resources for the work needed, and to effectively manage risks during the project execution. Following are the various plans generated at this stage (see Fig. 51.4).

The first step in the project planning phase is to create a *project plan* through a 'work breakdown structure' (WBS) that includes a hierarchical set of activities and tasks required to complete the project. These are then sequenced along with an assessment of the level of effort required to undertake these so that the appropriate resources are allocated. A detailed project schedule is then formed that is used by the project manager to assess the progress of the project throughout the project life cycle. A *resource plan* then lists the type and specification of the resources (men, materials, equipment, etc.) required. A *financial plan* (i.e., budget) is then created that enables the

Project plan

Resource plan

Financial plan

Quality plan

Risk plan

Acceptance plan

Communication plan

Procurement plan

FIGURE 51.4   Eight plans generated at the project planning phase

project manager to measure, monitor, and control the forecast expenses versus the actual expenses throughout the project life cycle.

A *quality plan* is a set of criteria and standards that needs to be achieved to meet the expectations of the customer is documented in the next step. While developing a *risk plan* it is necessary to assess, manage, and mitigate all forecasted critical project risks through different strategies prior to the execution of the project. An *acceptance plan* is then created to help clarify the completion criteria for each project deliverable that provide formal acceptance from the customer that it meets the requirements as originally stated. A *communication plan* then identifies how and how often each of the stakeholders will be kept informed about the progress of the project. The last planning activity within the planning phase, namely, a *procurement plan*, provides a detailed description of the process of the selection of a supplier (i.e., the tender process), as well as the ordering and delivery of the products (i.e., the procurement process).

Phase III: Project execution phase   At this stage of the project phase the plans created during the project planning phase are executed and implemented.

Phase IV: Monitor and control phase   As each plan is being executed, various management tools and techniques (namely, time management, cost management, quality management, change management, risk management, communication management, procurement management, etc.) are used to monitor and control the deliverables of the project.

Phase V: Project closure phase   At the final stage a project closure report is documented and handed over to the project sponsor (customer) for his approval. As the project manager is responsible for undertaking various activities identified in the project closure report, the project is closed only when all the activities listed in the report have been completed. A post-implementation review may be undertaken to identify learning's from the present project before undertaking future projects.

PROJECT NETWORK ANALYSIS

Network analysis is the generic name given to certain specific techniques which can be used for the planning, management, and control of projects. A network shows the sequential relationship among activities using nodes and arrows. An arrow leading from tail to head indicates an *activity*, a time consuming effort that is required to perform a part of the work, whereas a node is represented by a circle ⬤ and indicates an *event*, a point in time where one or more activities start and/ or finish.

Based on an example given in the activity and its predecessor's table (see Table 51.2), the corresponding network is illustrated in Fig. 51.5.

The major use of networks is to schedule the projects. Various network tools help in determining how long the project will take for completion and also when each activity should be scheduled. The expected project duration is determined

TABLE 51.2 Activity and its predecessor/s table

Activity	A	B	C	D	E	F	G	H	I	J	K
Predecessor	-	-	B	A	B	B	C	D	E	H, I	F, G

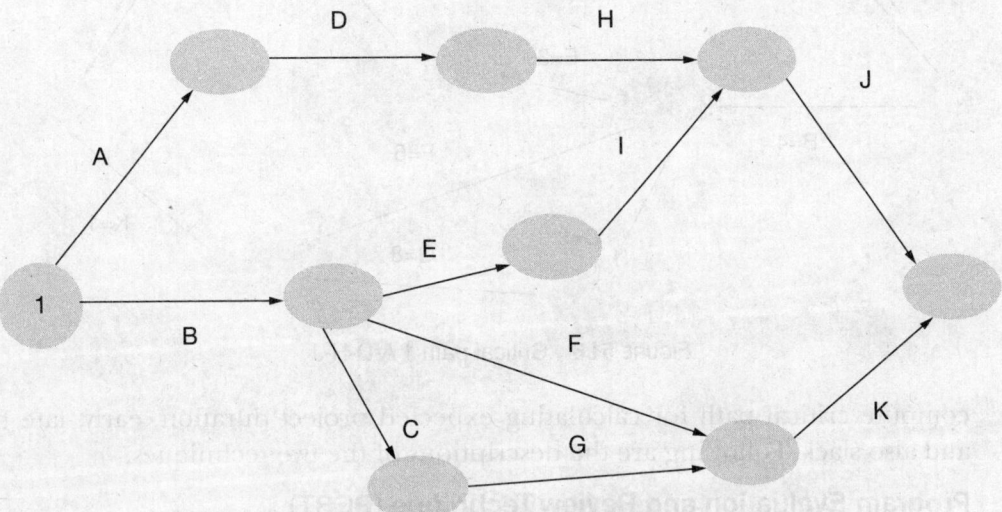

FIGURE 51.5 Network diagram

by finding the longest 'path' (i.e., any route comprising one or more activities connected in sequence) through the network.

Let us assume the activities indicated in the network diagram (see Fig. 51.5) take the number of days as indicated against these for completion, namely., A=2, B=4, C=9, D=10, E=3, F=6, G=8, H=5, I=7, J=11, and K=1. This network has the following four paths leading from the origin to termination.

Path 1 is **A-D-H-J** ; Path 2 is **B-E-I-J**; Path 3 is **B-F-K**; and Path 4 is **B-C-G-K**.

The four paths take 28, 25, 11, and 22 days respectively to complete. The *critical path* (see Fig. 51.6) is path 1 **A-D-H-J**, the longest and is of duration of 28 days. Shortening the activities on the critical path will shorten the project duration while as the non-critical activities can be delayed somewhat without delaying the project duration. Conversely, any delay in any activities along the critical path will result in delay in the completion of the project, hence the importance of determining the critical path in a network diagram.

The planning methods assume that whenever an activity is scheduled, the requisite resources will be at hand but that is not always the case in the real world. Further, project cost and project duration are interdependent variables. The network methods, namely, program evaluation and review techniques (PERT) and critical path method (CPM) are the two techniques that enable the project managers to incorporate uncertainty and cost implication into project schedule estimates respectively. Both PERT and CPM are termed as critical path methods because both

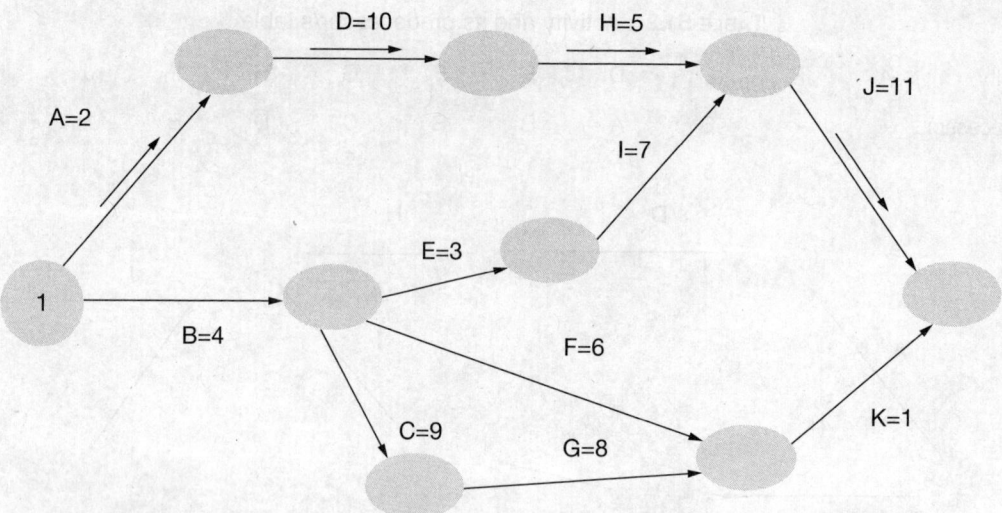

FIGURE 51.6 Critical path 1 A-D-H-J

compute critical path for calculating expected project duration, early, late times, and also slack. Following are the descriptions of the two techniques.

Program Evaluation and Review Technique (PERT)

PERT evolved for application in projects (e.g., R&D) where there is an uncertainty associated with the nature and duration of activities. It uses three time estimates namely optimistic, most likely, and pessimistic.

Let us assume the time taken for various activities in the network diagram shown in Fig. 51.5, namely, A=2, B=4, C=9, D=10, E=3, F=6, G=8, H=5, I=7, J=11, and K=1are the most likely estimates (represented by 'm'). Let us also assume that the pessimistic estimates (represented by 'b') of the activities along the critical path **A-D-H-J** are 3, 11, 6 and 12 respectively while as the optimistic estimates (represented by 'a') for the same activities are 1, 9, 4 and 10 respectively.

The three estimates are related in the form of β distribution with parameters 'a' and 'b' as end points and the 'm' as modal point. Based on β distribution, the variance $v=\Sigma[(b-a)/6]2$ and Mean expected time $te=[(a+4m+b)/6]$.

Calculating variance for the critical path A-D-H-J activities we have $v=\Sigma[(b-a)/6]^2=2.67$

Assuming distribution of project durations to be approximated by normal distribution, the project manager as a decision-maker can now ask the question about the likelihood of the project getting finished before or after the expected date. For example, if his query is about what is the probability of this project finishing in 27.5 days?

The Z value is given by $Z=[(27.5-28)/\sqrt{2.67}]=0.305$

Looking at the Z tables reveals that the Z value of 0.305 corresponds to a probability of 60 per cent approximately, which is the likelihood the project will finish in 27.5 days.

The project manager can also ask the question in terms of what is the likely duration of completion for a confidence level of 99 per cent.

In that case $[(T-28)/\sqrt{2.67}]=2.58$ (As Z value at 99 per cent confidence level $=2.58$)

Which gives with T = 32.2 days

The project manager's query is thus answered. The likely duration of completion of the project with a confidence level of 99 per cent is 32.2 days.

Critical Path Method (CPM)

In contrast to PERT, CPM is a deterministic method as only one point estimate of the activities is used. However, project managers instead try to estimate the trade-off between project duration and project cost by using CPM. The idea is to try to reduce the duration of the project at the least possible cost (by deploying additional resources). When maximum effort is applied, say by having additional workforce or overtime, so that the activity can be completed in the shortest possible time, the activity is said to be 'crashed'. It is going to cost more nevertheless. Different activities would have different time–cost relationships while these are being crashed. This can be captured by marginal trade-off analysis, which is the science and art of organizing the components of a project, through cost-to-time namely cost slope.

For example, for the critical path **A-D-H-J** if the A, D, H, and J activities can be crashed to 1, 9, 4, and 10 from say the normal time of 2, 10, 5, and 11 respectively. If

Research Insight

- For more than two decades, K.A. Brown, R. Ettenson and N.L. Hyer worked with many teams from a wide variety of industries, including aerospace, health care, the military, education, entertainment, consumer electronics, and financial services. Through research they found out that project teams are fairly good at articulating some of the obvious factors that lead to less-than-successful project performance but often overlook more subtle root causes. Often an ill-defined problem will doom a project from the start. Many projects fail because they are launched without a clearly articulated reason why they are being pursued

  Source: Based on Brown et al. (2011).

- Research has also shown that teams whose members bring conflict to the surface early on in a project tend to be more successful than those who allow conflicts to simmer.

  Source: Based on Brown et al. (1990).

- Big projects fail at an astonishing rate. Complicated long-term projects are usually executed by a series of teams working in parallel tracks. If managers fail to anticipate what can go wrong, those tracks will not converge successfully at the end to attain the objectives of the project. Project managers should avoid the trap of focusing on time and cost while ignoring performance.

  Source: Based on Matta and Ashkenas (2003).

the costs of the A, D, H, and J activities increase from ₹20, 30, 40, and 50 for normal time to 25, 36, 49, and 56 after crashing respectively, their cost slopes would then be [(25–20)/(2–1),(36–30)/(10–9),(49–40)/(5–4),(56–50)/(11–10)] or 5, 6, 9, and 6 respectively. If we crash all the activities on the critical path, then the project cost will additionally increase by ₹24 and the duration will reduce to 24 days. It is no more the critical path as its duration is lesser than the duration of Path B-E-I-J which now emerges as the critical path. The project manager can look at it in a path-by-path approach or crash all activities simultaneously. Since reducing the duration of an activity increases its cost, delaying from the crash time also reduces the cost. Non-critical activities can thus be stretched to increase savings. The project manager needs to take call in order to achieve the objectives of the project in an optimal manner.

PROJECT COST CONTROL

Variances are deviations from any schedule or cost from the plan of a project. These need to be calculated in order to measure cost performance in relation to work accomplished for a project.

Suppose a project is scheduled to spend ₹1 lakh for each of the first eight weeks of the project but the actual expenditure at the end of week eight is six lakhs.

Therefore, budgeted cost of work schedule (BCWS) = 8 lakhs and the actual cost of work performed (ACWP) = 6 lakhs. If we also know the budgeted cost for the work performed (BCWP) which is the budgeted amount of cost for the completed work, let us assume is 5 lakhs. Then following is the way we can calculate the cost and schedule variances for the project.

Cost variance % (CVP)=CV/BCWP=[BCWP–ACWP]/BCWP=[5–6]/5=(– 20%)

Schedule variance % (SVP)=SV/BCWS=[BCWP–BCWS]/BCWS=[5–8]/8=(–37.5%)

Hence, we can conclude that the above project is overrunning costs along with being behind schedule. Variances may be integrated into a cost/schedule reporting system that are reported then to all organizational levels for necessary action if these exceed the critical values. The critical values are established in accordance with objectives and policies. Following are the questions that need to be asked.

- What is the impact on time, cost, and performance of the project?
- What are the corrective actions required to eliminate or reduce the problems causing the variance?

SUMMARY

Project management is the science and art of organizing the components of a project and application of knowledge, skills, and techniques to execute these productively.

Project management is essentially about managing change. Network analysis is the general name given to certain specific techniques which can be used for the planning, management, and control of projects. A network shows the sequential relationships among activities using nodes and arrows. The expected project duration is determined by finding the longest 'path' (i.e., any route comprising of one or more activities connected in sequence) through the network called the critical path. The network methods, namely, *program evaluation and review techniques* (PERT) and *critical path method* (CPM) are the two techniques that enable the project managers to incorporate uncertainty and cost implication into project schedule estimates respectively.

KEYWORDS

Critical path method (CPM) A deterministic method as only one point estimate of the activities is used; and project managers try to estimate the trade-off between project duration and project cost by using it.

Generic objectives for a project The four fundamental objectives that a project must meet.

Network diagram Shows the sequential relationships among activities using nodes and arrows.

Program evaluation and review technique (PERT) A network method that enables project managers to incorporate uncertainty and cost implication into project schedule estimates.

Project closure The fifth and last phase of the project life cycle that refers to formal closing of the project.

Project cost control Any deviation from any schedule or cost from the plan of a project needs to be calculated in order to measure cost performance in relation to work accomplished for a project.

Project execution The third phase of the project life cycle that refers to execution of project groups to complete the work.

Project network analysis The generic name given to certain specific techniques which can be used for the planning, management, and control of projects.

Project planning The second phase of the project life cycle that refers to management of the project.

EXERCISES

Concept Review Questions

1. What is the difference between project management and management of any business enterprise?
2. What are the nine knowledge areas that contain the processes needed to achieve an effective project management program?
3. What are the different components of project initiation phase and project planning phase?
4. Define critical path and explain how it is computed in a network.
5. What is the essential difference between PERT and CPM?

Critical Thinking Questions

1. In your opinion what is the one skill that a project manager needs to be successful?
2. What methods from network analysis will you use to deliver the results for your class group project?

3. Critically analyse the statement 'A successful manager does not have to be good at everything but instead should know how to assemble a team with diverse competencies'.

Project Assignments

1. Consider a course project given to your group. List down the activities and estimated time required for each of the activities. Next create a network diagram. Identify the critical path and total network slack time.
2. Volunteer yourself for project cost control of a student led event organized in your institute. Generate cost and schedule variances for different programs of the project for effective management of the event.

REFERENCES

A Guide to the Project Management Body of Knowledge (PMBOK Guide) (2013), Newtown Square, Pennsylvania, Project Management Institute, Inc., January 1.

Archibald, Russel D. (2013), *Managing High Technology Programs and Projects*, John Wiley, New York.

Brown, K.A., R. Ettenson, and N.L. Hyer (2011), 'Why Every Project Needs a Brand (and How to Create One)', *MIT Sloan Management Review*, vol. 52, no. 4, Summer, pp. 61–68.

Brown, K.A., T.D. Klastorin, and J.L. Valluzzi (1990), 'Project Performance and the Liability

of Group Harmony', *IEEE Transactions on Engineering Management*, vol. 37, issue no. 2, May, pp. 117–125.

BS6079-1:2010 (BS6079 / BS 6079), *Project Management: Principles and Guidelines for the Management of Projects,British Standards Institute, UK.*

Matta, N.F. and R.N. Ashkenas (2003), 'Why Good Projects Fail Anyway', *Harvard Business Review*, vol. 81, no. 9, September, pp. 109–114.

Index

About the Authors

Anil Bhat is presently Professor and Head, Department of Management, BITS, Pilani. He graduated with a degree in Mechanical Engineering in 1982 from REC (now NIT), Srinagar and obtained his doctorate (fellowship) from Indian Institute of Management (IIM) Bangalore. He is a member of the Academy of Management and a fellow of the Institution of Engineers, India. He is a certified Entrepreneur Educator from Stanford Technology Ventures Program (STVP), Stanford, National Entrepreneurship Network (NEN), and IIMB. He is also a member of the Research Board and a faculty advisor of the Center for Entrepreneurial Leadership (CEL) at BITS, Pilani. He has to his credit more than 80 publications and has guided many PhD research scholars.

With 25 years of distinguished academic, administrative, and managerial experience, Dr Bhat believes that business is a force for good and his management philosophy is anchored around the goal of maximizing the impact of individual actions for the good of society.

Arya Kumar is presently, Dean-Alumni Relations and Professor-Economics and Finance at BITS Pilani. Previously, he worked as Director at Lal Bahadur Shastri Institute of Management (LBSIM), New Delhi. Prior to joining LBSIM, he served as Professor of Economics and Finance; Dean, Student Welfare Division; and Chief, Entrepreneurship Development and IPR Unit, at BITS, Pilani. He was also coordinating the activities of Alumni Affairs Division, Technology Business Incubator, and CEL at BITS, Pilani. With more than four decades of diversified experience in educational institutions, research organizations, banks, and other financial institutions, his basic interests lie in the areas of entrepreneurship, strategic management, values in management, and financial management. He has contributed many research articles to reputed publications.

Dr Kumar has been honoured with Distinguished Faculty Award in recognition and appreciation of his dedication, interest, enthusiasm, and attitude in accomplishing his assigned mission of teaching by BITSAA International in its Global Meet 2011; Global Excellence Award for Outstanding Contribution to Management Education 2012 by Management Teachers Consortium (MTC); and Entrepreneurship Educator and Mentor Special Jury Award for promotion of Entrepreneurship Education in the Entrepreneurship Education Conclave organized by NEN in collaboration with the Ministry of Skill Development and Entrepreneurship, New Delhi, in 2015.

Related Titles

PERSONALITY DEVELOPMENT AND SOFT SKILLS, 2E [9780199459742]

Barun K. Mitra, *IIT Kharagpur*

The book aims to provide crucial insights into various facets of developing one's personality, as well as to improve written, verbal, and non-verbal communication skills. Special attention has been paid to the specific needs of a job aspirant, such as writing of effective CVs, participation in group discussions, tackling job interviews, and to hone one's public speaking and speed-reading skills. The book provides an overview of the growing importance of modern learning mechanisms such as the Language Laboratory.

Key Features

- Provides inputs on avoiding common mistakes in speaking English
- Provides several case studies, examples, and illustrations to elucidate the concepts discussed
- Contains several classroom-based activities for students to develop their personalities and enhance their soft skills

COMMUNICATION SKILLS, 2E [9780199457069]

Sanjay Kumar, *Consultant* & **Pushp Lata**, *BITS Pilani*

The second edition of this bestselling textbook, *Communication Skills*, aims to enrich the content with new sections and examples which cover the core components of professional communication. All six sections, including basics of communication, English language, listening, speaking, reading, and writing skills, have been thoroughly revised and made as concise as possible. Due to its exhaustive coverage and practical approach, this textbook is suitable not only for students, but also for professionals.

Key Features

- Covers English grammar in detail with plenty of examples, practice tests, and exercises
- Provides numerous samples of business letters, reports, proposals, paragraphs, essays, and email correspondence
- Includes interesting illustrations in the text and Wisewell Quips series at the end of the chapters that emphasize the nuances of English language

FUNDAMENTALS OF TECHNICAL COMMUNICATION [9780199457472]

Meenakshi Raman, *BITS Pilani, Goa* & **Sangeeta Sharma**, *BITS Pilani*

Adopting a functional and practical approach, the book discusses the basics of technical communication—listening, speaking, reading, and writing (LSRW). In addition to numerous examples and practice exercises, it provides support for laboratory sessions through a companion CD.

Key Features

- User-friendly approach with simple and easy-to-understand language
- Numerous examples and practice exercises
- Model test papers at the end of the book
- A number of useful videos and audio exercises, as well as text supplements in the companion CD
- Videos on professional presentations and group discussion
- Listening and speaking practice exercises on telephonic conversation, phonetics, and more